Flexible Rails

Flexible Rails

FLEX 3 ON RAILS 2

PETER ARMSTRONG

MANNING

Greenwich
(74° w. long.)

For online information and ordering of this and other Manning books, please visit www.manning.com. The publisher offers discounts on this book when ordered in quantity. For more information, please contact:

> Special Sales Department
> Manning Publications Co.
> Sound View Court 3B   fax: (609) 877-8256
> Greenwich, CT 06830   email: orders@manning.com

Rails, Ruby on Rails, and the Rails logo are trademarks of David Heinemeier Hansson. Flash, Flex, and Flex Builder are trademarks of Adobe Systems Incorporated. Furthermore, many of the designations used by manufacturers and sellers to distinguish their products are claimed as trademarks. Where those designations appear in this book, and Peter Armstrong was aware of a trademark claim, the designations have been printed in initial capital letters or in all capitals.

Much effort went into the preparation of this book. However, the publisher and author assume no responsibility for errors or omissions, or for damages that may result from the use of information (including program listings) contained herein. The opinions expressed within are solely the personal opinions of Peter Armstrong.

♾ Recognizing the importance of preserving what has been written, it is Manning's policy to have the books we publish printed on acid-free paper, and we exert our best efforts to that end. Recognizing also our responsibility to conserve the resources of our planet, Manning books are printed on paper that is at least 15% recycled and processed without the use of elemental chlorine.

Manning Publications Co.	Copyeditor:	Tiffany Taylor
Sound View Court 3B	Typesetter:	Gordan Salinovic
Greenwich, CT 06830	Cover designer:	Leslie Haimes

ISBN 1-933988-50-9
Printed in the United States of America
1 2 3 4 5 6 7 8 9 10 – MAL – 13 12 11 10 09 08

For Caroline and Evan

brief contents

contents

foreword

It was early in 2006 when I was discussing my fanaticism for the emerging framework Ruby On Rails down at the pub with friends. I mentioned to Mike Jones, a career Flash developer, that I thought Ruby On Rails would be great for integrating with his new favorite plaything, the Adobe Flex 2 beta. Here were two technologies born of the desire to make cool things easier to build. It was a match made in heaven, and I knew someone would do it soon.

In April and May of that year, I wrote a two-part tutorial on my blog liverail.net and also delivered a presentation at the London Flash Platform User Group, developing a RIA CRUD interface in Flex with a Ruby On Rails backend.

This was only the start of a wave of people marrying the two technologies that were gaining traction in the development community, from Flash/Flex developers with their first forays into backend development to seasoned Ruby programmers who would never have dreamed of developing anything on Flash, scared off by "The Timeline." Since my initial blog posts, several people have taken to Flex and Rails with a lot of passion, developing integration software, launching startups, and posting blogs—none more so than Peter, who was dedicated/passionate/foolish enough to believe there was a whole book on the subject waiting to be written.

Time has proven him right, and Peter has run with the concept and seen it grow in strength, with new start-ups in Flex and Rails launched every month. Peter has continually delivered Flexible Rails, keeping up to date with Flex 3 and Rails 2 and working with Cairngorm (the Flex MVC framework), and he's at the cutting edge with RubyAMF. Peter's book delivers tutorial after tutorial, leading us through the complete lifecycle of his phantom RIA startup pomodo from database to desktop with Adobe AIR.

If you are looking to develop your next RIA startup, internal data-warehousing client, or just something a bit different, this book will be your cup of tea.

STUART ECCLES
TECHNICAL DIRECTOR AND CO-FOUNDER
MADE BY MANY LTD., U.K.

preface

On January 31, 2006, after over a year and a half of working with Flex and more than six months of playing with Rails (building toy apps, reading *Agile Web Development with Rails,* and so on), I finally realized that for many applications Rails was the perfect server-side technology to complement Flex—and on the flip side, that Flex offered capabilities that were either difficult, impossible, buggy, or merely annoying to do with JavaScript/AJAX/DHTML on the client side (especially if, like me, you're not a JavaScript guru like Thomas Fuchs). Despite the productivity of Rails, at the end of the day we're still dealing with the joys of HTML, JavaScript, CSS, and browser compatibility issues.

So, I did what I always do whenever I have a Really Great Idea: I registered a domain name. I wanted a name that would be good for promoting a possible book about using Flex and Rails together, so the natural choice was flexiblerails.com. I also got flexiblerails.net and .org because I was so sure how good an idea this was. By January 2006, the massive success of *Agile Web Development with Rails* had put dollar signs in the heads not only of publishers but also of many in the Rails community who had blogs. After all, writing a book couldn't be much harder than writing a few blog posts, right?

I then did what I typically do whenever I have a Really Great Idea: *nothing.*

Between the demands of my job and my two-year-old son, I was too busy, too tired, and so forth. Besides, I had a lot of Really Great Ideas (and domain names to go with them), and I wasn't acting on any of them.

So, time passed.

Then, it was announced that the Flex 2 SDK would be free (as in beer), and I thought again: Yep, Flex and Rails will be perfect together, especially because Flex 2 will be so much better than Flex 1.5.

Again: *nothing*. I'm too busy; I'm too tired; I'd rather play Civ 4; the list went on.

Then, Flex 2 went through its beta cycles and was released, with Flex Builder costing only $499, half of what had been expected.

Again: *nothing*.

Then, in July 2006, I stumbled upon an excellent tutorial by Stuart Eccles on liverail.net which had been written on April 16, 2006, about using Flex and Rails together, and then upon another one (written on the same day!) on Christophe Coenraets' blog, and I realized that I wasn't alone in thinking this really was a Really Great Idea—and that if I was ever going to write anything about it, I'd better get off my butt and do it *now*.

> **NOTE** The ironic thing was that the liverail.net tutorial rails application was called (you guessed it) *flexiblerails*. For me, this was truly the "get off your butt and do something, you moron" moment: *The first really good tutorial about Flex and Rails together used the same name for its example application that I had registered as a domain name months earlier!* (If anyone cares: I registered flexiblerails.com on January 31, 2006. Stuart Eccles published part 1 of his excellent tutorial on April 16, 2006, and I had missed seeing it until July 2006!) If I hadn't loved my domain name so much, I would have named this book something else, so as not to cause confusion between this book and the tutorial on his blog. I hope that this chronology is a sufficient acknowledgment of—and even an homage to—his tutorial: This book would not exist if his tutorial hadn't motivated me to finally do what I had already thought of doing.

I released the first Alpha Version of this book in self-published form in September 2006. It was buggy and had terrible formatting for the code samples. Despite this, I got amazing feedback from many readers, which led to a much better book as a result. Over the year that followed, I released numerous revised Alpha and then Beta versions, adding iterations, updating Rails versions, rewriting the entire book, and so on. Throughout this process, my readers were remarkably helpful and patient, even though the roadmap for the book kept changing almost monthly.

As the book got better and more popular, publishers became interested. Manning approached me and we worked out a contract that ensured I could keep all of my promises to my existing readers while working with Manning to revise the book. During this time, Flex 3 went to Beta 2, and Rails 2 went to pre-release status. So, I rewrote the book *again*, this time using Flex 3 and Rails 2. The book doesn't use all the new features, but it does use some of them, the RESTful URLs are correct, and so on. During the author review process, I did yet another pass through the code, re-creating all the code samples by following along with my own book, using Release Candidate 1 of Rails 2 (1.99.0). Then, just after the book went into typesetting, Rails 2 final (2.0.1) was released. So, during typesetting, I did yet another pass through the book, following along again using Rails 2.0.1. So, while the text of the book refers to Rails 1.99.0, rest assured that it has been tested with both Rails 1.99.0 and Rails 2.0.1.

This book has been part of my life for almost two years, consuming countless evenings and weekends. My sincere hope is that it will be an enjoyable read for you, and that you can build something great using the code written in it as the foundation.

acknowledgments

First and foremost, I never would have finished this book without the infinite patience and support of my wife Caroline. Thank you.

I have had very supportive friends as well. Thomas Yip gave me much appreciated early encouragement and very insightful, extensive feedback on the first version. Steven Baker introduced me to many people within the Rails community who saw the potential when my toy Flex + Rails app was little more than Hello World. Len and Mike Epp have been great friends throughout; thanks especially to Len for his hospitality when I was working on this book from his flat in London. Finally, an enormous thank you to Dima Berastau for convincing me that my book was done, when I still thought that I should delay it for another 3–6 months to add 200–300 more pages to it.

Next, thanks to my father: In late summer 2006, he took time during a visit to read the first 200-page version and contributed numerous helpful grammar suggestions. Most interestingly, I think he finally really understood what I do for a living.

I won't thank any readers by name, because I would need to name the hundreds of readers who helped me with feedback and encouragement when this book existed in self-published form.

An enormous thank-you to Christopher Bailey for jumping in at the last minute to do the technical proofreading for the book—and to not only do it, but to do it extremely well. Chris runs Cobalt Edge LLC (cobaltedge.com), a software development and consulting company. He is V.P. of Engineering at Bring Light (bringlight.com), an online social network inspiring a new generation of philanthropy. Chris also contributes to Building Web Apps (buildingwebapps.com), a great resource for increasing your web development knowledge. Chris lives with his wife, and two children, in Eugene, OR.

Thanks to Adam Springer, Tim Steele, Matt Wyman, and Steve Byrne. Thanks also to Ross Ladell, Cary Newfeldt, Brad Sokol, Justin Damer, Hao Vuong, Joel Greensite, and Darrell Snow.

Thanks to the following people at Adobe: Mike Potter, Ryan Stewart, Duane Nickull and Suzanne Nguyen.

Thanks to the peer reviewers, who provided invaluable feedback on the book shortly before it went into production: Erik Hatcher, Arne Pfeilsticker, Louis F. Springer, Brent Schooley, Christopher Bailey, Mike Tian-Jian Jiang, Robert Dempsey, Christophe Bun, Paul Fernando Larini, and Jeremy Anderson

Thanks to the many people at Manning:

First, thanks to Mike Stephens for approaching me in the first place, and for enabling me to meet my commitments to my existing readers. Also, thanks for his patience with me: Shortly after he acquired what he thought was a "finished" book, I decided that I needed to miss the deadline in order to rewrite the book to use Flex 3 and Rails 2 and to add a RubyAMF chapter. The book is much better for it, so thanks for taking the gamble.

Next, thanks to my editor Douglas Pundick, who got the pleasure of working with me when I was at my most clueless about how "real" books are put together, and for dealing with me cheerfully as I attempted to rewrite the book from half the Starbucks locations in London and various hotels in Italy.

Thanks to publisher Marjan Bace for his support of an unorthodox book that had a very unorthodox origin. Thanks very much to project editor Mary Piergies, who handled the schedule changes and the production effort that spanned the Christmas holiday season with grace. Next, an enormous thank-you to my copyeditor Tiffany Taylor: You're Manning's secret weapon! (I could go on and on, but that would be verbose, so I'll edit out for you.) Another enormous thank-you to my proofreader, Maureen Spencer—this quote from one of her emails sums up her dedication: "I finished my read of Chapter 11 during the Caroling." Thank you so much for your efforts in the proofreading and your cheerfulness as this book impacted your Christmas and New Year holidays.

Finally, an apology to my son Evan: Daddy *finally* finished his book! I'm sorry it took so long.

about this book

Many technical books I've bought are like Disneyland: They seem promising, but they're expensive, the examples are Mickey Mouse, they take forever, and I end up disappointed.

This is not one of those books.

In *Flexible Rails*, we'll build a real application—well, as close to a real application as you can get in a book. As we go, I'll explain the concepts introduced by the code, as well as explain the code itself. The code is all MIT-licensed, so you can take whatever you want from it and use it as the basis of whatever Web 2.0 startup you're dreaming of, without owing me (or Manning) a penny. (If you *do* make millions, I won't say no to unsolicited gifts, of course!)

Roadmap

Like many applications developed iteratively, this book contains four parts:

1 Getting started

2 Building the application

3 Refactoring

4 Finishing up

In part 1, "Getting started," we'll do the necessary setup work that will let us get to the fun stuff in the rest of the book. We'll install everything, do a Flex and Rails version of "Hello World," and then get user creation and login working in Rails and hook up the Flex UI to it. This part contains three iterations:

- *Iteration 1 "Why are we here? Where are we going?"*—This iteration provides the motivation for the book, an understanding of the history of Flex and Rails and how they fit together, and an overview of the book.

- *Iteration 2 "Hello World"*—This iteration contains three separate sets of instructions (Windows or Mac OS X + Flex Builder 3, Windows + Flex SDK, and Mac OS X + Flex SDK) for installing everything we need and getting "Hello World" running.

- *Iteration 3 "Getting started"*—In this iteration, we'll set up MySQL and then add account-creation and login functionality to our Rails application, using the restful_authentication plugin. We then hook up the Flex UI to use the Rails account creation and login functionality.

In part 2, "Building the application," we'll do a deep dive using Flex with Rails. By the end of it, we'll have mastered the basics of using Flex with Rails. This part contains four iterations:

- *Iteration 4 "Creating the main Flex UI"*—In this iteration, we'll build a stubbed-out UI for the main part of the Flex application.

- *Iteration 5 "Expanding the Rails code, RESTfully"*—Next, we'll add new Rails models and controllers for the tasks, projects, and locations—as well as the migrations needed to create their database tables. We also introduce REST in this iteration. Finally, we'll address some basic security concerns that need to be considered at the outset.

- *Iteration 6 "Flex on Rails"*—In this iteration, we'll hook up most of the main Flex UI we'll build in iteration 4 to the Rails controllers we'll build in iteration 5.

- *Iteration 7 "Validation"*—We'll add full validation support on the Rails side and the Flex side to the account-creation process.

At this point, we'll be ready to think about higher-level topics, which we'll do in part 3, "Refactoring." This part includes two iterations:

- *Iteration 8 "Refactoring to Cairngorm"*—We'll refactor the code we wrote in part 2 to use Cairngorm, an application framework for Flex.

- *Iteration 9 "Holding state on the client properly"*—We'll refactor the code again, this time to add a proper object model instead of just using XML on the client.

At the end of this part, we'll have a much better understanding of design in Flex and of the options available to us for data exchange between Flex and Rails. Doing the refactoring to decouple the object model from its method of transport (currently XML) will enable us to consider using an alternate method of transport.

In the final part, "Finishing up," we'll finish the application, refactor it to use RubyAMF, and extend it to run on the Adobe Integrated Runtime (AIR).

This part contains three iterations:

- *Iteration 10 "Finishing the application"*—In this iteration, we'll build the remaining features in pomodo.
- *Iteration 11 "Refactoring to RubyAMF"*—We'll refactor pomodo to use RubyAMF instead of XML for sending data between Flex and Rails. Because AMF is a binary protocol and XML is text (and verbose text at that), this has the potential to lead to substantial performance improvements.
- *Iteration 12 "Rails on AIR (Adobe Integrated Runtime)"*—In this last iteration of the book, we'll convert the code to run on AIR and modify the Notely feature that we'll build in this iteration to take advantage of AIR-specific features. This won't be a complete tutorial introduction to AIR; instead, it will give you a taste of one of the exciting ways to take your Flex + Rails applications beyond the traditional web application model.

The overall approach of this book is "Flex and Rails Immersion"—instead of getting bogged down in theory and boring you with contrived examples, we'll build a real application together and learn everything as we go. Also, I don't pretend that the book exists in isolation: I reference many excellent resources, including not only the relevant books but also numerous blog posts. One of the hallmarks of the Rails community in particular is the number of prolific bloggers—most people in the Rails community learn from these blogs, so the honest thing to do is to provide a brief explanation in the book and reference them for the full explanation, instead of paraphrasing them.

What the book doesn't compete with

This book is intended to be an informative, interesting, useful, and occasionally mildly entertaining tutorial for software developers, regardless of how much Flex, Ruby, or Rails experience they have. This book is not attempting to provide a full Ruby, Rails, Flex, or ActionScript 3 tutorial—each of those topics needs an entire book. Luckily, they already have excellent books:

- *Ruby*—*Programming Ruby,* 2nd ed.; *The Ruby Way,* 2nd ed.
- *Rails*—*Agile Web Development with Rails,* 2nd ed.
- *Ruby and Rails*—*Ruby for Rails,* 1st ed.
- *Flex 3*—*Flex 3 Developer's Guide* (a free 1,435-page PDF from Adobe)
- *ActionScript 3*—*Programming ActionScript 3.0* (a free 576-page PDF from Adobe)

This book does *not* compete with any of these books—it assumes that you either have them (or the knowledge contained in them) or are willing to buy them. (The Flex and ActionScript 3 PDFs are free.) If you're going to do any serious work with Rails, you should buy the second edition of *Programming Ruby* (the first edition is free but outdated), the second edition of *Agile Web Development with Rails (AWDwR)*, and/or the first edition of *Ruby for Rails*.

What this book *will* try to do is provide enough information and external references that someone with no Flex, Ruby, or Rails experience can follow along and find help when necessary, but not so much that it would become annoying to someone who already understands all the basics of either Rails or Flex. My assumption is that most readers are coming from one camp (a Rails developer wanting to learn Flex as an alternative to AJAX or a Flex developer looking for a server-side technology other than Java). That said, if you have no Flex or Rails experience, but you have web or desktop UI software-development experience, you should be able to follow along with this book: Many readers have done exactly this.

A note about the iterations

All the code in the book is available for download from http://www.flexiblerails.com/code-samples as well as from the publisher's website at http://www.manning.com/armstrong or http://www.manning.com/FlexibleRails. The download is one big zip file that contains a separate folder for each completed iteration in the book, except iteration 1, for which there is no code. This way, you can start at any iteration and follow along by using the directory from the previous iteration. Or, if you don't like typing, you can load each completed iteration as you read.

Because I'm lazy (in the good programmer way), they aren't all separate projects—they're copies of the same project at various stages. I recommend creating a staging-area folder called current and having Flex Builder point at it. This way, if you want to start at the end of any given iteration, you can delete your current folder and copy that iteration in place of the current one. When you relaunch Flex Builder, all it sees is that a bunch of files have changed—the project is the same. If you're using the Flex Framework SDK, this doesn't apply to you.

Finally, note that this procedure has no correspondence to anything you would do when actually coding. For real development, use Subversion (or Git) and have it ignore the public\bin directory you'll be creating for the Flex output. See appendix A for details on using Subversion with Flex and Rails. If you're using Git, you don't need a tutorial.

Which Flex?

The short answer is: Flex 3.

The longer answer is that much of the book was originally written using Flex 2, and that the code was updated to Flex 3 Beta 2 before the most recent rewrite. So, the code in the book was all produced using Flex 3 Beta 2. During the typesetting process, the Flex code was tested with Flex 3 Beta 3. This had no effect except in iteration 12 ("Rails on AIR"): Flex 3 Beta 3 renamed `Shell.shell` to `NativeApplication.nativeApplication`, so the iteration 12 code was updated accordingly. All the Flex code—except for iteration 12, which uses AIR—will work in Flex 2 and Flex 3.

Which Rails?

The short answer is: Rails 2.

The slightly longer answer is that the *most recent rewrite* of this book was done using the first release candidate of Rails 2, whose gem version is 1.99.0. Rails 2 final, whose gem version is 2.0.1, was released when the book was already in typesetting. So, during typesetting, I updated my Rails to 2.0.1 and did another full pass through the book, following along using Rails 2.0.1. So, while the text of the book refers to Rails 1.99.0, rest assured that it has been tested with both Rails 1.99.0 and Rails 2.0.1. The code that is available for download from http://www.flexiblerails.com/code-samples, as well as from the publisher's website, uses Rails 1.99.0. (Because I followed along with Rails 2.0.1, I could have released this code as well. However, its format wouldn't have matched—copying and pasting from a PDF removes the formatting—so I didn't do this.)

The *really long answer* is that I have rewritten this book more than twice: I started writing the early iterations when Rails was at version 1.1. The iterations were originally shorter, and there were more than 20 of them. (It turns out that this is an unmaintainable nightmare for this style of book, since bugfixes must be ported forward.) So, in May 2007 I *completely rewrote the book,* dramatically reducing the number of iterations and updating the code to Rails 1.2. In summer 2007, I made an agreement to publish the book with Manning. However, Rails 2 went to preview release shortly afterward, so the book would have been outdated before it was off the press. So, in October 2007 I *completely rewrote the book again,* updating the version of Rails to the preview release of Rails 2 (gem version 1.2.3.7707). Then, in November and December 2007 during the Author Review phase of the book I updated the book to be based on the first release candidate of Rails (gem version 1.99.0), by following along from the beginning. Finally, during typesetting I ensured that the code worked with Rails 2 final (gem version 2.0.1), by following along *again* from the beginning.

Writing is indeed rewriting, especially when the topic is as fast-moving as the combination of Flex and Rails.

Understanding the code examples

For readability, I'll show the source code of a file with **new or modified lines of code in bold italics** and ~~lines of code that should be deleted shown in strikethrough~~. I'll often omit unchanged portions of a file, using an ellipsis (...) to take the place of the unchanged code. If a large section of code is being deleted, I'll often use an ellipsis inside the code being deleted (because showing tons of strikethrough code is a waste of paper). If you're pasting code from the code samples into your code, make sure you omit or delete any lines shown in strikethrough. Furthermore, note that the book uses 64-column code. This results in some purely format-related modifications to generated Rails code in order to make it fit nicely within 64 columns. These changes may not be shown as modified or explained, because that would be tedious. Finally, note that sometimes it isn't possible to get code to fit nicely in 64 columns—Rails code is often written in a way that favors long lines, and inline event-handling in MXML code lends itself to longer lines too. In these cases, the code will just auto-wrap, and a continuation symbol will be shown.

A complete code zip file is available for download from http://www.flexiblerails.com/code-samples, as well as from the publisher's website.

Author Online

Purchase of *Flexible Rails* includes free access to a private web forum run by Manning Publications where you can make comments about the book, ask technical questions, and receive help from the authors and from other users. To access the forum and subscribe to it, point your web browser to http://www.manning.com/FlexibleRails or http://www.manning.com/armstrong. This page provides information on how to get on the forum once you are registered, what kind of help is available, and the rules of conduct on the forum.

Manning's commitment to our readers is to provide a venue where a meaningful dialogue between individual readers and between readers and the author can take place. It is not a commitment to any specific amount of participation on the part of the authors, whose contribution to the book's forum remains voluntary (and unpaid). We suggest you try asking the author some challenging questions, lest his interest stray!

The Author Online forum and the archives of previous discussions will be accessible from the publisher's website as long as the book is in print.

About the author

Peter Armstrong has been a Flex developer since July 2004 (since Flex 1.0) and he has been tracking Ruby on Rails since mid-2005 (since before Rails 1.0). Before switching to Flex, he spent five years as a Java Swing developer, with a brief stint as a PHP developer during the dotcom bubble in 2000. As someone with a heavy Swing background, Peter initially found Flex appealing because it felt very familiar—more like Swing development than web development. After more than five years of working with Java, Ruby and Ruby on Rails felt like a breath of fresh air.

Peter is the organizer of The Vancouver Ruby/Rails Meetup Group (http://ruby.meetup.com/112/). He has spoken about using Flex with Rails at the Vancouver Flash/Flex Meetup Group, at a RailsConf 2007 BOF, at the Vancouver RIA Developer Camp, at Rails to Italy 2007 and at VanDev.

The author's website for this book is at http://www.flexiblerails.com. The blog for this book is at http://www.flexiblerails.com/blog. Peter's personal blog is at http://www.peterarmstrong.com. Peter's consulting company, focused on Flex and Rails development, training, and workshops, is http://www.ruboss.com.

Peter lives with his wife Caroline and his son Evan in the Vancouver, British Columbia area. When he's not coding, writing, reading, or being a husband and dad, Peter likes to snowboard and play computer games. If it wasn't for Desktop Tower Defense, Slashdot, and reddit, this book would have been done a month earlier—if not more!

about the cover illustration

The figure on the cover of *Flexible Rails* is called "Jeune Bourbonnaise" or a young woman from Bourbonnais, a historical region and former province of central France in the Massif Central. The illustration is taken from a French travel book, *Encyclopedie des Voyages* by J. G. St. Saveur, published in 1796. Travel for pleasure was a relatively new phenomenon at the time and travel guides such as this one were popular, introducing both the tourist as well as the armchair traveler to the inhabitants of other regions of the world, as well as to the uniforms and costumes of French soldiers, civil servants, tradesmen, merchants, and peasants.

The diversity of the drawings in the *Encyclopedie des Voyages* speaks vividly of the uniqueness and individuality of the world's towns and provinces just 200 years ago. This was a time when the dress codes of two regions separated by a few dozen miles identified people uniquely as belonging to one or the other. The travel guide brings to life a sense of isolation and distance of that period and of every other historic period except our own hyperkinetic present.

Dress codes have changed since then and the diversity by region, so rich at the time, has faded away. It is now often hard to tell the inhabitant of one continent from another. Perhaps, trying to view it optimistically, we have traded a cultural and visual diversity for a more varied personal life. Or a more varied and interesting intellectual and technical life.

We at Manning celebrate the inventiveness, the initiative, and the fun of the computer business with book covers based on the rich diversity of regional life two centuries ago brought back to life by the pictures from this travel guide.

Part 1

Getting started

In this part, we'll do the necessary setup work to get to the fun stuff in the rest of the book. We'll install everything, do a Flex and Rails version of "Hello World," and then get user creation and login working in Rails and hook up the Flex UI to it.

This part contains three iterations:

- *Iteration 1: "Why are we here? Where are we going?"*—This iteration provides the motivation for the book, an understanding of the history of Flex and Rails and how they fit together, and an overview of the book.

- *Iteration 2: "Hello World"*—This iteration contains three separate sets of instructions (Windows or Mac OS X + Flex Builder 3, Windows + Flex SDK, and Mac OS X + Flex SDK) for installing everything we need and getting "Hello World" running. You only need to read the section that applies to you.

- *Iteration 3: "Getting started"*—In this iteration, we'll set up MySQL and add account creation and login functionality to our Rails application, using the restful_authentication plugin. We'll then hook up the Flex UI to use the Rails account creation and login functionality. Finally, we'll set up the most minimal of tests. At the end of this iteration, we'll have a good starting point for any Flex + Rails application.

Why are we here?
Where are we going?

HTML sucks all the joy out of programming for me
HTML+CSS, that is
I'm so glad I don't have to do the design work for our apps
I'm trying to design a simple form
and I'm hating life
It's seriously making me want to not work on this anymore
…
html makes it so easy to write forms that look like crap
and SO HARD to write forms that look nice
that's so backwards

—Jamis Buck,
Signal vs. Noise [Fly on the Wall], July 17, 2007[1]

---

[1] http://www.37signals.com/svn/posts/495-fly-on-the-wall-paying-attention-to-users-mow-the-lawn-vs-cut-the-grass-chowder-html-forms.

There is a *lot* of hype these days around Flex and Rails. I'll try my hand at it for a few paragraphs, too.

Ruby on Rails, or just Rails for short, has been revolutionizing web application development since its introduction in 2004. Nowadays, it seems that a new "Web 2.0" company that uses Rails is spawned every 10 seconds.

Flex is a sexy framework that lets us write code that feels more like coding a desktop application—except it runs inside the Flash player! Because it targets the Flash player, we can build new Rich Internet Applications (RIAs) without worrying about browser compatibility nonsense, JavaScript, CSS, and so on.

> **NOTE**   The preferred term now seems to be *rich Internet applications*. I don't pre-fer it, though, because rIa isn't a good-looking acronym. As a curmudg-eonly form of protest (I'm an old-school Flex developer—I used to code Flex 1.0 while walking uphill both ways in the snow…), I'm going to call them Rich Internet Applications in the book. Also, the full capitalization of Rich Internet Applications may be coming back into fashion, in response to a Microsoft evangelist having attempted to make RIA stand for "Rich Interactive Applications"—so I'm shouting "get off my lawn" in an avant-garde way, I guess.

Because Flex 3 targets one platform (Flash 9), we don't have to worry about plat-form compatibility issues. The Write Once, Run Anywhere (WORA) dream that client-side Java programmers had—before it turned into "write once, debug everywhere"—can finally be realized, but with Flex. Flex achieves what previous technologies such as Java applets failed miserably in attempting: applications that feel like desktop applications, but which run inside any modern web browser on Windows and Mac.

> **NOTE**   Write Once, Run Anywhere was essentially realized on the server side but not on the client side. On the client side, AWT was terrible, and Swing doesn't look like any of the platforms it runs on. SWT is an excellent alter-native to Swing, because it gives us native widgets. However, SWT can't be used in an applet yet, so we can't run it in a web browser. It's just useful for building applications like Eclipse—and like Flex Builder 3, which is built on top of the Eclipse Rich Client Platform (RCP).

But here's a little-known secret, which this book is the first book to cover: *Flex and Rails work amazingly well together!*

We can use Flex 3 and Rails 2 to build RIAs today that look and feel more like Web 3.0 than many of the "me too [point oh]" Web 2.0 sites we see copying each other today. This book will show you how to get started doing exactly this.

In this iteration, we'll get an overview of Flex and Rails, their history, and how they can be used together.

Iterations

In this book, the chapters are called *iterations*. I've done this because we'll develop an application iteratively throughout the book—it has nothing specific to do with Flex or Rails. (That said, both Flex and Rails lend themselves to an iterative style of development.) Each iteration advances the state of the application further. You can start following along with the book at the beginning of any iteration, using the code from the end of the previous iteration.

This chapter has no code—it's just an introduction. I'm calling it "iteration 1" instead of "introduction" as a cunning way of getting you to read it, because many people skip introductions and dive right into chapter 1. *I love it when a plan comes together!*

1.1 Overview of the features and strengths of Flex 3 and Rails 2

Now that you're all excited, let's take a deep breath and get an overview of both platforms. This section will present a high-level overview of both and then show how they can be combined. Don't worry if you don't understand a particular point here; it will be explained later.

1.1.1 Overview of Flex 3

In Flex 3, we write code in MXML (XML files with a .mxml extension; *M* for Macromedia) and ActionScript (text files with a .as extension) files and compile them into a SWF file, which runs in the Flash player. This SWF is referenced by an HTML file, so that when a user with a modern web browser loads the HTML file, it plays the Flash movie (prompting the user to download Flash 9 if it's not present). The SWF contained in the web page can interact with the web page it's contained in and with the server it was sent from.

Even if you've never created a Flash movie in your life, don't consider yourself a designer, and wouldn't recognize the Timeline if you tripped over it, you can use Flex to create attractive applications that run in the Flash player. Flex development is easily learned by any intermediate-level developer with either web or desktop UI (such as Windows Forms or Java Swing) programming experience.

1.1.2 Overview of Rails 2

Figure 1.1 shows how Rails provides a standard three-tier architecture (presentation tier, model tier, persistence tier) as well as a Model-View-Controller (MVC) architecture. As the diagram shows, Rails takes care of everything between the web server and the database.

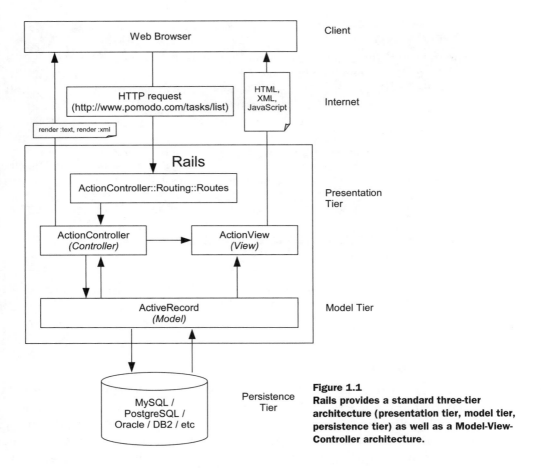

Figure 1.1
Rails provides a standard three-tier architecture (presentation tier, model tier, persistence tier) as well as a Model-View-Controller architecture.

The typical sequence is as follows:

1   A user visits a particular URL in their web browser (makes an HTTP request).

2   This request goes over the Internet to the web server in which Rails is running (such as WEBrick, lighttpd, Mongrel, or Apache).

3   That web server passes the request to the routing code in Rails, specifically `ActionController::Routing::Routes`. These routes are defined in config\routes.rb. The default route turns HTTP requests into method calls on controllers.

4   The controller (such as `TasksController`) method (such as `index`) is called. It communicates with various ActiveRecord models (which are persisted to and retrieved from a database of our choosing). The controller method then can do one of the following things:

- Set some instance variables and allow a view template (a specially named .html.erb file, for example) to be used to produce HTML, XML, or JavaScript, which is sent to the browser. This is the job of Action View. Together, Action View and Action Controller form Action Pack.
- Bypass the view mechanism and do rendering directly via a call to the render method. This method can produce plain text (render :text => "foo"), XML (render :xml => @task), and so on.

1.1.3   *Overview of using Flex 3 and Rails 2 together*

Figure 1.2[2] shows how Flex and Rails can be used together.

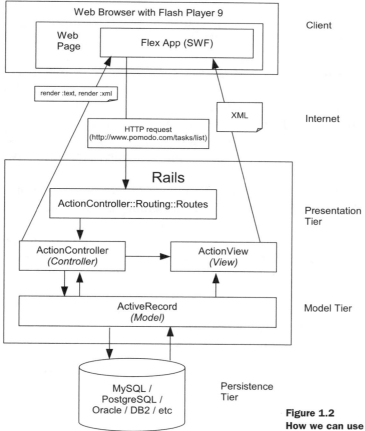

Figure 1.2
How we can use Flex and Rails together

---

[2] The diagram "Fig 7. The complete MVC Architecture for a Thin-Client Web Application" at http://www.uidesign.net/Articles/Papers/UsingMVCPatterninWebInter.html inspired the design of my block diagrams.

1.2   *Flash 9? Are you kidding me?*

The reference to Flash 9 earlier may have set off alarm bells in your head: "Isn't Flash 9 somewhat new? How many people will be able to run my app?" Table 1.1 should put this concern in perspective[3].

Table 1.1   **Worldwide ubiquity of Adobe Flash Player by version—June 2007**

	Flash Player 7 (released September 2003)	**Flash Player 8 (released August 2005)**	**Flash Player 9 (released June 2006)**
Mature markets	99.3%	98.5%	90.3%
US/Canada	99.4%	98.7%	90.5%
Europe	99.1%	98.2%	90.5%

As of June 2007, Flash 9 has over 90% market penetration in "mature markets" (US, Canada, UK, Germany, France, and Japan). Furthermore, note that Flash 8 has achieved 98% market penetration in less than two years—which is extremely good.

Despite how productive Flex 3 and Rails 2 are for development, it will still take you *some* time to build your killer app. And in that time, our target market is getting larger by the day. (If you haven't accomplished much in a given day, you can still feel good that you grew your target market.)

Finally, note that most of your early adopters will be, well, early adopter types. These are the TechCrunch reading, Digg/del.icio.us/reddit using types. These people will have Flash 9 or won't mind getting it.

One more thing: If you work in an enterprise environment, the adoption percentages for different Flash versions among consumers today are much less of a concern than if you're trying to develop a consumer-facing product. As long as your IT department allows the Flash player to be installed, you can mandate that users upgrade their Flash Player versions when they first use your app. The installation and upgrade process is extremely smooth, which is a major reason why you see Flash used everywhere today, whereas Java applets are little more than a historical curiosity.

---

[3] This is taken from a much more complete set of tables at http://www.adobe.com/products/player_census/flashplayer/version_penetration.html.

NOTE You might think this is a significant hurdle (and it may be one in your case), but note that AJAX apps have their own security issues because of cross-site scripting, and so on—IT departments sometimes have issues with JavaScript as well. At least with Flex 3, it's a binary decision: If our user has or can get Flash 9, you're good to go. With AJAX, it's a question of IE 6, IE 7, Firefox 1.0, Firefox 1.5, Safari, Opera, JavaScript enabling, ad infinitum (definitely doable, but by no means as simple).

Speaking of history, it's nice to know a bit of the history of Flex and Rails, to see how they have evolved over the last few years. This is useful because it helps us understand why no one was thinking about using Flex with Rails in 2004, why a few people started thinking about it in 2006, and why many people are thinking of the combination now.

1.3 *History*

In 2004, two frameworks were released that have gone on to dominate web and RIA development: Macromedia Flex in March 2004 and Ruby on Rails in July 2004. The two frameworks initially couldn't have seemed more different.

Ruby on Rails was a free, Open Source, web application framework that strongly appealed to web developers who were frustrated either with PHP or with J2EE. IDEs were spurned, and a fairly obscure Macintosh-only text editor called TextMate was hailed as the greatest achievement of Western civilization. (Emacs and vi were for old people, presumably.) In many blog postings, the enterprise was portrayed as something evil to be ignored, changed, or destroyed. XML was to be avoided at all costs: In *Agile Web Development with Rails* (Dave Thomas et al, Pragmatic Bookshelf, 2006), reason #10 of "Dave's Top 10 Reasons To Like Rails" is "No XML!" The claim was often made that we could write an entire web application in Rails in fewer lines of code (LOC) than the amount of code just in the XML configuration files of a web application built with EJBs.

NOTE For an example of an article highlighting the reduced LOC, see http://rewrite.rickbradley.com/pages/moving_to_rails/.

Regarding XML, Ruby 1.8 (which Rails runs on) does have support for XML, but Rails prefers to use YAML for its configuration files. (YAML, which stands for YAML Ain't Markup Language, is a "straightforward machine parsable data serialization format designed for human readability and interaction with scripting languages": www.yaml.org.) The phrase "No XML!" can be rephrased more accurately but less catchily as "No XML configuration files everywhere, and no XML needed to define our database schema."

Macromedia Flex 1.0 and 1.5 (which both used ActionScript 2.0) were server products that ran in a J2EE application server that compiled MXML files and ActionScript files into Flash applications (SWFs). Typically, MXML files were used to lay out GUI components, which were developed in either MXML or Action-Script. Flex 1.0 and 1.5 were priced at enterprise levels: about $15,000 USD *per CPU* for the server product.[4] Because the server side of a Flex application was typically J2EE, a lot of XML configuration files were typically needed along with XML for the database mapping.

MXML files can, and typically do, contain ActionScript in inline `<mx:Script>` blocks. MXML files are transformed into ActionScript before being compiled into a SWF along with the ActionScript files, so the "what should be done in Action-Script and what should be done in MXML" line was always blurry. A large project typically has lots of both kinds of files. To summarize, table 1.2 shows what the two frameworks looked like in their early days.

Table 1.2   Flex 1.0 and Rails 1.0 compared

	Flex 1.0	**Rails 1.0**
Cost	Expensive!	Free
Code is	Proprietary	Open source
XML is	Everywhere	Considered evil
IDE	Flex Builder (based on Dreamweaver)	None

In the more than three years since Rails' release, a lot has changed. Rails has become one of the most influential frameworks in web application development. It seems that every day, some new Web 2.0 app is released that is built on it. This is partly due to the marketing prowess of David Heinemeier Hansson (DHH to his followers) and 37signals, but also to a large extent due to the productivity advantages in faster development time and reduced lines of code to maintain that Rails provides. Rails has also vastly improved its support for XML: ActiveRecord now has a `to_xml` method that we'll use a lot in this book.

In the past three years, Flex has also progressed rapidly for an enterprise-class product, as shown in table 1.3.

Flex 3 has better performance and download sizes (due to the framework cache) than Flex 2. Furthermore, Flex 2 has *vastly* better performance (in some

---

[4] This wasn't competing with PHP; it was competing with Laszlo, which also was a very expensive product that let you write GUI code in XML that got compiled to a SWF.

Table 1.3 **Flex version history**

Date	Flex version	ActionScript version
March 2004	1.0	2.0
October 2004	1.5	2.0
June 2006	2.0	3.0
October 2007	3.0 Beta 2	3.0

case, up to *ten times* faster) than Flex 1.0 and 1.5, as well as better XML handling and an updated version of ActionScript. Another advantage of Flex 2 over Flex 1.0 and 1.5 is cost savings: Whereas Flex 1.0 and 1.5 are expensive server products, Flex 2 and Flex 3 can be used in their Flex Framework SDK versions with a command-line compiler without paying Adobe a penny. Flex 3 also features a further cost savings for IDE users: Flex Builder 3 Standard Edition is half the price of Flex Builder 2. (Of course, if you want the new profiler, you're still paying a nontrivial sum to get the Professional Edition.)

In April 2007, Adobe announced the open sourcing of the Flex 3 framework under the Mozilla Public License (MPL). This is huge news in the world of RIA development.

> **NOTE** Although the Flex framework has been open sourced, the Flash player is not open source. This, of course, prompts the typical reaction among the more vocal free software advocates. My position is that the open sourcing of Flex *is* big news and that the choice of the MPL (as opposed to, say, the GPL) is a huge step by Adobe in ensuring the commercial adoption of Flex.

That said, even though the Flex framework is free and is being open sourced, if you're using Windows or Mac you may want to buy Flex Builder 3. It will sell[5] for $249 USD (Standard Edition) or $699 USD (Professional Edition, which will include the charting components, profiler, and so on).

> **NOTE** Adobe also sells a server-side product called Live Cycle Data Services (formerly Flex Data Services), which has a restricted free version for smaller deployments. It won't be covered in this book.

---

[5] http://www.onflex.org/ted/2007/10/flex-3-beta-2-lower-price-flex-builder.php.

Table 1.4 shows what the two frameworks look like now.

Table 1.4   Flex 3 and Rails 2 compared

	Flex 3.0	**Rails 2.0**
Cost	Free	Free
Code is	Open Source	Open Source
XML is	Everywhere	Ambivalent; it's still avoided in configuration files, but XML output is included by default in RESTful controllers
IDE	Flex Builder 3 ($249 Standard Edition, $699 Professional Edition)	Free (Aptana RadRails, Eclipse with the RDT plug-in, NetBeans) and commercial offerings

Flex 3 is much more similar to Flex 2 than Flex 2 is to Flex 1.5. If it wasn't for the addition of the Adobe Integrated Runtime (AIR) which we'll introduce in iteration 12, Flex 3 probably should have been called Flex 2.5. (The code in this book was originally written in Flex 2; it compiled and ran in Flex 3 unchanged.)

Now that we understand how Flex and Rails have evolved and where they are today, let's look at what we'll accomplish in this book.

1.4   A preview of the book

The project we'll create throughout this book is called *pomodo*. Why pomodo? Because it's a stupid, meaningless name, and a prominent feature of Web 2.0 is meaningless names, often with missing vowls. (It also features rounded corners and gradient fills,[6] which we will use, too.) Pomodo will be a variation on a To Do list application.

What will be different about pomodo? For one, its UI will be in Flex, so we can create a cool-looking To Do list with little effort. Second, it will be a *Getting Things Done* (GTD) style To Do list, meaning that tasks will be organized into projects and will have locations. In addition, pomodo will use the concept of a Next Action, which is essentially the next task in each project that has nothing blocking it.

Why a To Do list application? There are two reasons. First, because of 37signals' Ta-da List, Basecamp, and Backpack products, the Rails community used to seem a bit obsessed with To Do lists: In the early days of Rails, they were often the "one step beyond Hello World" application built in many fine tutorials

---

[6] It turns out that Stuart Eccles makes this same joke in his presentation to the London Flash Platform User Group: http://www.lfpug.com/ruby-on-rails-for-the-flex-developer-22062006-stuart-eccles/#more-11.

GTD

David Allen's *Getting Things Done* (Penguin, 2002) is a great book about time management. If you haven't read it already, buy it and read it. Briefly, it involves going to Staples and spending $500 on office supplies and a big filing cabinet (I did this), writing down everything in your brain (a la the main character in the film *Memento*, who had to always remind himself, "Remember Sammy Jenkins"), and using lots of folders (43 of them—hence the name of the popular website www.43folders.com) to run your life. The elegance and efficacy of the approach, combined with the paper cuts and environmental devastation caused by using so much paper, has inspired countless programmers (myself included) to write their own GTD-style application or to abuse an existing tool (such as a wiki, outlining tool, Outlook, or Gmail) to make it work in a GTD style. The problem with GTD as presented in David Allen's book is that it assumes our world revolves around paper (and, quaintly, that we have a secretary). This may be true for the executives who go to his seminars, but it's *not* true for software developers.

online. Second, and more seriously, since the application is a GTD-style To Do list application, it will have enough features to demonstrate a significant subset of Flex and Rails features, but still be small enough and with a simple enough domain to be fully understood while learning the frameworks and how they interact. I could have created something (say, a cool-looking chess game) that better showed off the eye-candy features of Flex. However, I decided this wouldn't have been as useful: Most of us are (unfortunately) building applications that look more like To Do lists than games. Also, since this is a book about how Flex and Rails can be used together, the pure eye-candy features are superfluous.

1.5 Summary

Flex and Rails fit together well and have evolved to be a better fit because of Flex going Open Source. We can develop with Flex Builder using either Windows or OS X, or with the Flex SDK using Windows, OS X, or Linux.

Hello World

Hello World
— Brian Kernighan

Let's get coding! Until I get "Hello World" running in a language, I can't start learning much. Because we're focusing on using Flex with Rails, we have three "Hello World" versions to do: Flex only, Rails only, and the combination in which Flex talks to Rails.

First you need to install the software you'll need to follow along with the rest of the book. The goal of this book is to save you time in getting up to speed using Flex and Rails together. As such, I don't want to say "install everything" and leave you to your own devices figuring out what to install. But I don't know whether you're using Windows, OS X, or Linux, and whether you want to use Flex Builder (on Windows or OS X only) or the Flex SDK. So that you get a book that is as tailored to your needs as possible, this iteration has four sections—but you only need to read two of them:

- Everyone should read section *2.1:* "Installing Everything."
- If you have a Windows PC or a Mac and want to use Flex Builder 3, read section *2.2:* "Windows or Mac OS X + Flex Builder 3."
- If you have a Windows PC and want to use the Flex 3 SDK, read section 2.3: "Windows + Flex SDK."
- If you have a Mac or a Linux PC and want to use the Flex 3 SDK, read section *2.4:* "Mac OS X (or Linux) + Flex SDK."

The rest of the book from iteration 3 onward is written as though you're using Flex Builder 3 on Windows. I have to assume something, because I don't want to write three books.

NOTE Most people prefer IDEs; whether that is a good or bad thing is irrelevant—it's just a fact. (In the typical corporate environment, how many typical Java developers use Eclipse or IDEA versus how many use Emacs or vi exclusively?) Also, I took a reader poll, and Windows users slightly outnumbered Mac users.

Q. Should I use Flex Builder 3 or the Flex 3 Framework SDK?

A. The SDK is free, and using it is fairly straightforward. However, using it isn't as easy as using Flex Builder 3. Flex Builder 3 is built on top of Eclipse and is available in standalone form or as an Eclipse plug-in. The standalone version will cost $249 for the Standard Edition (and $699 for the Professional Edition).There will presumably be a 30-day trial version for Windows and Mac, so you can determine if it's worth it without spending any money. (I bought Flex Builder 2 for $499 of my own money, so you're getting a deal on Flex Builder 3 Standard.) As I write this, Flex Builder 3 is in Beta 2, so you can download the time-limited Beta for free.

Although most of the book is written as though you're following along using Flex Builder, compiling on the command line is straightforward.

2.1   Installing everything

In this section, we'll install the software required to follow along with the rest of the book. You need a Windows PC to which you have administrator access or a Mac running OS X, because you must install MySQL, Ruby, Rails, and either Flex Builder 3 or the Flex SDK on it. To use all that happily, at least 512 MB of RAM is required, with 1 GB or higher preferred. (I started writing this book on an old desktop PC with 512 MB of RAM, so it can be done.)

2.1.1   Installing Ruby

The first thing we'll do is install Ruby.

Installing Ruby on Windows

Install Ruby by downloading the latest one-click Ruby installer from http://rubyforge.org/frs/?group_id=167. This book uses Ruby 1.8.5. Make sure you find the `Path` variable in System Variables and add c:\ruby\bin; (or wherever_you_put_ruby\bin;) to the beginning of the `Path`. More detailed instructions are available in many fine tutorials online, such as http://allaboutruby.wordpress.com/2006/01/09/installing-rails-on-windows-step-by-step-tutorial/.

Installing Ruby on Mac OS X

You need a PowerPC or Intel Mac running a recent version of OS X (Tiger or Leopard). The best explanations about how to install Ruby (as well as Rails, MySQL, and Mongrel or lighttpd) are found at the following tutorials:

- http://hivelogic.com/articles/2005/12/01/ruby_rails_lighttpd_mysql_tiger
- http://hivelogic.com/narrative/articles/ruby-rails-mongrel-mysql-osx

I've followed both of these tutorials on different Macs running OS X Tiger, and they both work. I'd normally be embarrassed to say "Go to this blog; it will tell you," but there is nothing I can say here that isn't said better there. Even *Agile Web Development with Rails (AWDwR)*, the bible of Rails development, delegates its explanation of how to install Ruby and Rails on Mac OS X to this blog post.

OS X Leopard has recently been released and is easier to work with for Ruby: Ruby is included by default (and is not broken, unlike on Tiger), and Mongrel and Rails are also included. (You will still need to update your Rails to Rails 2, however, as shown in the next step.)

If you have no success using the instructions at the Hivelogic site, another approach is James Duncan Davidson's approach (http://duncandavidson.com/archives/164). Yet another approach is to use Locomotive (http://locomotive.raaum.org/), which bundles everything you need together into one easy-to-install package. You can also see the fine tutorial at http://developer.apple.com/tools/rubyonrails.html.

2.1.2 Installing Rails

The final version of Rails 2 has recently been released. You can follow along using the most recently released version of Rails 2 by typing `gem install rails` in a Windows Command Prompt or `sudo gem install rails` in an OS X Terminal window. Note that running gem install rails may fail with the following error: "OpenURI::HTTPError: 404 Not Found reading http://gems.rubyforge.org/gems/actionpack-2.0.1.gem". If this happens, just run it again (a few times if necessary) until it works.

While this book has been tested with Rails 2.0.1, if you want to follow along with the version of Rails 2 that was used during the copy-edit process, use the first Release Candidate (gem version 1.99.0).

To install the first Release Candidate version (1.99.0) of Rails 2.0, run the following command at a Command Prompt:

```
C:\peter\flexiblerails>
  gem install rails -v 1.99.0 -source
  http://gems.rubyonrails.org --include-dependencies
Successfully installed rails-1.99.0
Successfully installed activesupport-1.99.0
...
Installing RDoc documentation for activeresource-1.99.0...
```

WARNING Under no circumstances should you try to follow along using Rails 1.2.x: It won't work.

To confirm that you have the correct version of Rails 2, run `gem list` at a Command Prompt/Terminal window. The rails gem should list version 2.0.1 or 1.99.0 and any other earlier versions you have installed. For example, here's a slightly reformatted version of what gem list tells me for the rails gem:

```
...
rails (2.0.1, 1.99.0, 1.2.5, 1.2.3.7707, 1.2.3, 1.2.2, 1.2.1)
...
```

Note about Rails versions

I began writing this book when Rails was at version 1.1. I revised it to update it to Rails 1.2, and then I rewrote it to use Rails 2. When I was rewriting the book to use Rails 2, I used the first Preview Release of Rails 2 (rails gem version 1.2.3.7707). I then updated my Rails version to the first Release Candidate of Rails 2 (gem version 1.99.0) during the copy-editing phase of the book. Then, during typesetting, I updated my Rails version to 2.0.1. Following along with either Rails 1.99.0 or 2.0.1 will work.

2.1.3 Installing MySQL

Install MySQL 5 by going to http://mysql.com/downloads/mysql/5.0.html and downloading and running the appropriate installer.

Q. But I don't want to use MySQL! I want to use PostgreSQL/Oracle/DB2/SQLite!

A. That's fine. One of the main components of Rails is ActiveRecord, which supports many databases. For this book, we'll assume MySQL. Any other supported database should work, but you may have to deal with subtle differences. Note that Rails 2 has moved some database adapters (everything other than MySQL, PostgreSQL, and SQLite) out of the core Rails distribution. To install adapters for Oracle, SQL Server, and so on, see http://ryandaigle.com/articles/2007/9/30/what-s-new-in-edge-rails-your-db-adapter-may-have-left-the-building for the appropriate command.

If you're on Windows, you may choose to install the latest version of SQLyog, a GUI client for MySQL that has a free version, from http://www.webyog.com/sqlyog/download_sqlyogfree.html. On OS X, you may choose to install CocoaMySQL from http://cocoamysql.sourceforge.net/. This is an optional step—if you prefer the command-line MySQL tools or some other MySQL GUI tool, feel free to skip it.

2.1.4 Installing Flex

In this step, we'll install either Flex Builder 3 (which includes the Flex SDK) or the standalone Flex SDK. Depending on whether you're using Flex Builder 3 or the Flex SDK, please follow along with the appropriate subsection.

Installing Flex Builder 3 on Windows or OS X

Download and install Flex Builder 3 standalone. As I write this, Flex Builder 3 is in Beta 2 and can be downloaded from http://labs.adobe.com/technologies/flex/ flexbuilder3/. In Q1 2008, it should be out of Beta and probably available for download from http://www.adobe.com/products/flex/downloads/. When running the Flex Builder 3 installer, choose to install Flash 9 for Firefox (if you have it, which you should) and either IE or Safari depending on your platform. Install JSEclipse, but don't install the Cold Fusion extensions, because Rails will be used instead of Cold Fusion or a Java application server.

At this point, it's tempting to try to install the Ruby Development Tools (RDT) or RadRails inside Flex Builder 3. After all, Flex Builder 3 is built on top of Eclipse Rich Client Platform (RCP), which is a subset of the Eclipse Platform. I have done this in the past: I got a version of RDT (0.8.1.609062100PRD) working inside of Flex Builder 2. With Flex Builder 3, this was a bit trickier: I could not get any version of RDT working inside Flex Builder 3 Beta 2. However, when Flex Builder 3 Beta 3 was released I got RDT version 0.9.1.200711131528NGT installed in it and working. Briefly, the instructions to do this are as follows: In Flex Builder 3 Beta 3, go to Help > Software Updates > Find and Install... Then, choose "Search for new features to install" and click Next. Click the "New Remote Site..." button to add a new remote site to download updates from. Set its name to RDT and its URL to http://updatesite.rubypeople.org/release. Click Finish. In the "Select the features to install" dialog, ensure you expand the RDT feature and deselect the "Ruby Mylyn Connector Feature"—this feature does not install correctly, which causes the install to fail if you leave it selected. Only the core RDT feature is required. Finally, click Finish to install RDT. When the install is done, you will be prompted to restart Flex Builder; click yes to do so.

If you *really* want syntax highlighting for Ruby and if you can't get RDT installed into your version of Flex Builder 3, you can download and install an IDE such as Aptana (with RadRails), Code Gear's 3rdRail, NetBeans or IDEA. Also, if you're using a Mac, you can configure TextMate to edit your Ruby code and set it up as an external editor from within Flex Builder (by leaving the *.rb file association unset). If you download the Aptana IDE, then be sure you install RadRails according to the instructions at http://www.aptana.com/download_rails_rdt.php. Having done this, you can then run both Aptana and Flex Builder 3 at the same time. (Note that if you do this, you may have issues with overlapping projects.)

Skip ahead to section 2.1.6: "Creating the Rails project."

Installing the Flex SDK on Windows, OS X, or Linux

Before we install the Flex SDK, we need to install Flash 9 by going to http://www.adobe.com/shockwave/download/download.cgi?P1_Prod_Version=ShockwaveFlash. (If you're using Linux, you can download a Beta of Flash Player 9 from http://labs.adobe.com/technologies/flashplayer9/.) After following the instructions, go to http://www.macromedia.com/software/flash/about/ to confirm that you have version 9 of the Flash Player installed.

Next, install the Flex 3 SDK. As I write this, Flex 3 is in Beta 2, which is available for download from http://labs.adobe.com/technologies/flex/sdk/flex3sdk.html. Select the license agreement check box about halfway down the page, and then click the Download Flex 3 SDK 3 Beta 2 for All Platforms (ZIP, 68.6 MB) link under Latest Milestone: Flex 3 SDK Beta 2. We'll download a file named flex3sdk_b2_100107.zip.

Windows instructions:

Move the file to c:\, and (assuming you have WinZip installed) unzip it by right-clicking it and choosing WinZip > Extract to Folder C:\flex3sdk_b2_100107. Open a Command Prompt in the samples directory, and run the build-samples script. This takes forever, so go grab a coffee when it's running:

```
C:\flex3sdk_b2_100107\samples\explorer>build.bat
Loading configuration file C:\flex3sdk_b2_100107\frameworks\flex-config.xml
This beta will expire on Thu Jan 31 00:00:00 PST 2008.
(...lots of output skipped...)
```

To play around with the Flex samples, open the samples explorer HTML file. For me, this is file:///C:/flex3sdk_b2_100107/samples/explorer/explorer.html.

Skip ahead to section 2.1.5: "Installing a text editor or IDE (SDK users only)."

OS X (or Linux) instructions:

Move the file to the home directory. Create a directory called flex3sdk, move the flex3sdk_b2_100107.zip file into it, and then unzip it using the unzip command:

```
/Users/peterarmstrong > mkdir flex3sdk
/Users/peterarmstrong > mv flex3sdk_b2_100107.zip flex3sdk
/Users/peterarmstrong > cd flex3sdk
/Users/peterarmstrong/flex3sdk > unzip flex3sdk_b2_100107.zip
     (...lots of output skipped...)
```

We need to add the flex3sdk/bin directory to our path so mxmlc will work. To do so, we add lines similar to the following to the .bash_profile file in our home directory:

```
export FLEX_HOME=/Users/peterarmstrong/flex3sdk
export PATH=$PATH:/$FLEX_HOME/bin
```

TIP The .bash_profile file doesn't appear in Finder, but it appears in Text-Mate's File > Open dialog (or in Dired mode in Emacs, and so on). To see the hidden files in a directory, do `ls -lag` in a Terminal window.

Close the Terminal, open a new one (a low-tech way to refresh the path), and run the following commands to check that `mxmlc` is present and correct:

```
/Users/peterarmstrong > mxmlc -version
Version 3.0 build 183453
/Users/peterarmstrong > mxmlc -help
Adobe Flex Compiler (mxmlc)
Version 3.0 build 183453
Copyright (c) 2004-2006 Adobe Systems, Inc. All rights reserved.
...
```

To make the samples and bin directories executable, `cd` to the samples directory, and run the `build-samples` script. The `build-samples` script takes forever (on my G4 Mac Mini anyway), so go grab a coffee when it's running:

```
/Users/peterarmstrong/flex3sdk > chmod -R 755 samples
/Users/peterarmstrong/flex3sdk > chmod -R 755 bin
/Users/peterarmstrong/flex3sdk > cd samples/explorer
/Users/peterarmstrong/flex3sdk/samples/explorer >
./build.sh
(...lots of output skipped...)
```

To play around, open the samples explorer HTML file. For me, this is file:///Users/peterarmstrong/flex3sdk/samples/explorer/explorer.html.

2.1.5 *Installing a text editor or IDE (SDK users only)*

If we installed the Flex SDK, we don't have Flex Builder—so we need to pick some other text editor or IDE to use. Chances are you already have a favorite IDE or text editor. There are many good text editors (Emacs, TextMate, vi) and IDEs (Code Gear's 3rdRail, NetBeans, IDEA, and Aptana + RadRails) to choose from. In this iteration, we'll install Aptana with RadRails for Windows users and TextMate for OS X users.

Windows users: installing Aptana with RadRails

This section uses Aptana (with RadRails) because it's free. RadRails includes Ruby syntax highlighting via the RDT plug-in and many other features, such as AIR support. You can download Aptana RadRails from http://www.aptana.com/download_rails_rdt.php. Download the standalone version by choosing Download Aptana IDE (Win).

Install Aptana by running the installer, choosing Custom Install, and choosing to install Sun JRE 1.6.0 as well. I chose to not use any file associations, because any Eclipse-based product takes a while to start and I don't like doing that accidentally.

When the install is done, launch Aptana. When we first launch Aptana, we're prompted for a workspace. I chose C:\peter\aptana_workspace (creating a new folder there). This doesn't really matter, because we'll ignore the default for pomodo, but be sure to select the Use This as the Default and Do Not Ask Again check box so Aptana doesn't ask you on startup every time. We'll install the Rad-Rails plug-in into Aptana later in this iteration, so don't try to figure it out now.

OS X users: installing TextMate

If you wish to go the text-editor route, and you don't already have a favorite text editor, I recommend TextMate. If you haven't installed TextMate and wish to try it, you can download a trial from http://macromates.com/. If you're a die-hard Emacs user, I recommend Aquamacs (http://aquamacs.org/) on OS X. If you're a vi user (or a Linux user), you don't need my advice.

Because many Mac-using Rails developers use TextMate, I will too for this iteration. If you want the screenshots to look like what you're doing, then install TextMate.

2.1.6 *Creating the Rails project*

Now it's time to have some fun: We'll create a Rails project. Regardless of whether we're using Flex Builder 3 or the Flex SDK, this step is the same; there are separate instructions for Windows and OS X / Linux.

IMPORTANT In Rails 2.0.2 and above the default database is SQLite; in Rails 2.0.1 and below it is MySQL. If you are using Rails 2.0.2 or above, you will need to say "rails -d mysql pomodo" in the following commands; if you are using Rails 2.0.1 or below you can just say "rails pomodo". Since this book is using MySQL, I have modified the commands below to say "rails -d mysql pomodo" (since chances are you are following along using Rails 2.0.2 or above)—even though when I last ran these commands I was using Rails 2.0.1 and it was not necessary to do so.

Windows version

Without further ado, let's create the project. (By now you should have a shortcut to Command Prompt in your Quick Launch bar, because you'll be using lots of Command Prompts when doing Rails development.) Open a Command Prompt in the directory you'll be creating the project in (I used c:\peter\flexiblerails), and enter the following commands:

```
C:\peter\flexiblerails>mkdir current
C:\peter\flexiblerails>cd current
C:\peter\flexiblerails\current>rails -d mysql pomodo
 (...lots of output skipped...)
C:\peter\flexiblerails\current>cd pomodo
C:\peter\flexiblerails\current\pomodo>ruby script\server
=> Booting WEBrick...
=> Rails application started on http://0.0.0.0:3000
=> Ctrl-C to shutdown server; call with --help for options
```

TIP   I recommend setting your shortcut to Command Prompt to start in your equivalent of c:\peter\flexiblerails\current\pomodo. Right-click the shortcut, choose Properties, and modify the Start In directory in the Shortcut tab. This will save you a lot of time.

Check to see if we're up and running. Point the web browser at http://localhost:3000/. We should see the screen shown in figure 2.1.

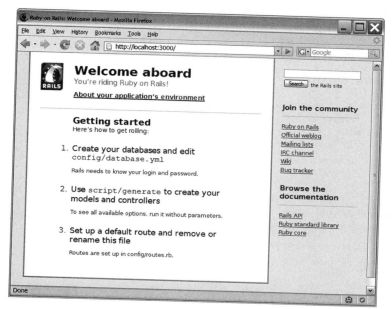

Figure 2.1
We're on Rails!

Congratulations: We're on Rails! Leave this Command Prompt window open with WEBrick running.

OS X version

Without further ado, let's create the project. (By now you should have the Terminal application on your Dock, because you'll be using lots of Terminal windows when doing Rails development.) Open a Terminal window, and enter the following commands. You create a flexiblerails directory and inside that a current directory. You then run the `rails pomodo` command to create our application, and start WEBrick with `ruby script/server`:

```
/Users/peterarmstrong > mkdir flexiblerails
/Users/peterarmstrong > cd flexiblerails
/Users/peterarmstrong/flexiblerails > mkdir current
/Users/peterarmstrong/flexiblerails > cd current
/Users/peterarmstrong/flexiblerails/current > rails -d mysql pomodo
(...lots of output skipped...)
/Users/peterarmstrong/flexiblerails/current > cd pomodo
/Users/peterarmstrong/flexiblerails/current/pomodo >
ruby script/server
=> Booting WEBrick...
=> Rails application started on http://0.0.0.0:3000
=> Ctrl-C to shutdown server; call with --help for options
```

To check that we're up and running, point the web browser to http://localhost:3000/. We should see the screen shown in figure 2.2.

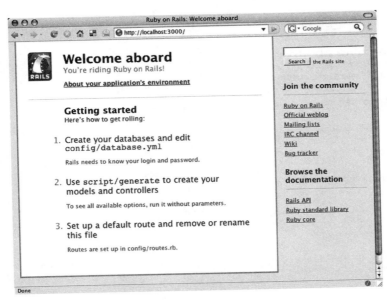

Figure 2.2
We're on Rails!

Congratulations: We're on Rails! Leave this Terminal window open with WEBrick (or Mongrel if you followed the Hivelogic instructions) running.

2.1.7 *How to read the rest of this iteration*

Please follow along with the rest of this iteration reading only the section that applies to you:

- If you're using Flex Builder 3 with either a Windows PC or a Mac, read section 2.2: "Windows or Mac OS X + Flex Builder 3."
- If you're using the Flex Framework SDK with a Windows PC, read section 2.3: "Windows + Flex SDK."
- If you're using the Flex Framework SDK with a Mac or a Linux PC, read section 2.4: "Mac OS X (or Linux) + Flex SDK."

2.2 *Windows or Mac OS X + Flex Builder 3*

Welcome, fellow Flex Builder 3 users! You get to follow along with the entire book written specifically for you.

2.2.1 *Creating the Flex project*

Now, let's do some preparation and then get our project into Flex Builder 3 and create a proper "Hello World." Open a new Command Prompt (aren't you glad you made that shortcut?) in the pomodo directory, and enter the following commands:

```
C:\peter\flexiblerails\current\pomodo>mkdir app\flex
```

```
C:\peter\flexiblerails\current\pomodo>mkdir public\bin
```

Next, in Flex Builder, choose File > New > Flex Project. Give the project the name pomodo, uncheck the Use Default Location check box, and click Browse to browse to the location where you ran the rails pomodo command and then into the pomodo directory that was created by the rails pomodo command (for me, this is C:\peter\flexiblerails\current\pomodo). Leave Application Type set to Web Application (Runs in Flash Player), and leave Application Server Type set to None. The dialog now looks like the one shown in figure 2.3.

Click Next. We're taken to the dialog where we set the compiled Flex application location (the output folder). For me, this is public\bin, as shown in figure 2.4. The bin

Figure 2.3 New Flex Project Wizard, step 1

folder is arbitrarily named, but it's essential that it be underneath the public folder because that is what Rails makes publicly available to visitors to our site.

Figure 2.4
New Flex Project Wizard, step 2

Click Next. We're taken to the dialog panel where we set build paths. Set Main Source Folder to app\flex. This app\flex location is also arbitrary, but I like it because Rails keeps folders under app private—and we don't want our Flex code public, just as we don't want our Rails code public. Finally, rename pomodo.mxml to Pomodo.mxml.

> **NOTE**   We rename pomodo.mxml to Pomodo.mxml in the New Flex Project dialog to conform to ActionScript class-naming conventions, which include using `TitleCase` for classes. (An MXML file is a class—specifically, a subclass of its root node.)

With these changes made, the dialog should look like figure 2.5.

Click Finish. The new pomodo project is loaded, and a file called Pomodo. mxml is created in the app\flex folder and opened. Before we add to it, go to the Project menu and uncheck the Build Automatically menu item. We don't want to have Flex Builder doing a rebuild every time we save—this gets annoying in a hurry.

Figure 2.5   New Flex Project Wizard, step 3

2.2.2 *"Hello World" from Flex*

Next, to add a button ❶ with a "hello world!" label, modify the Pomodo. mxml file so it looks like listing 2.1.

Listing 2.1   app\flex\Pomodo.mxml

```
<?xml version="1.0" encoding="utf-8"?>
<mx:Application
    xmlns:mx="http://www.adobe.com/2006/mxml"
```

```
        layout="absolute">
        <mx:Button label="hello world!"/>        
      </mx:Application>
```

Code width

I'm modifying much of the Rails-generated code to be 64-column code, because I need to fit the code and the cueball annotations within 68 columns. Because these diffs would be extremely distracting, I'm not using the bold italic font for them.

Instead, I'll modify the code first and pretend the 64-column code is what the generator produced. Then, we'll make changes and show those changes with the bold italic font for additions and strikethrough font for deletions. If you're following along running all the commands yourself, you can either make your code match the book by making the appropriate changes or just be grateful that you have more than 64 columns to work with. ("[64 columns] should be enough for anybody," anyone? At least it's proof that you don't need 200 column lines to write Ruby code: The Rails source code seems to have been written by people determined to use every pixel of their 30-inch monitors—it's *very* wide.)

Save the Pomodo.mxml file, and then choose the Project > Build All menu item or click the Build All toolbar button (this button only shows up if we've unchecked Project > Build Automatically):

The project is built. Switch back to our web browser, and go to http://localhost:3000/bin/Pomodo.html. We see the screen shown in figure 2.6.

Figure 2.6
"Hello World" from Flex

We now have our first running Flex 3 application!

NOTE If you don't see a running application, chances are you didn't save Pomodo.mxml. We *need* to save our files before doing a build—Flex Builder 3 doesn't do this for us by default. Note that we can choose File > Save All to save all modified files. This command is Ctrl+Shift+S with the Default key bindings (or Ctrl+X, S with the Emacs key bindings enabled).

You may have noticed that I pulled a fast one: Where did the Pomodo.html file come from? The short answer is that Flex Builder created it for us. We'll look into it later; for now, just know that it's a wrapper that loads the Pomodo.swf file that our Pomodo.mxml file gets compiled into. Note also that although we picked public\bin as our output folder, the URL starts with *bin*; this is because public is the root.

2.2.3   *"Hello World" from Rails*

Now, let's switch gears and do a "Hello World" in Rails before we move on to having Flex talk to Rails. First we need to set the *.rb, *.bat, and *.log file associations in Flex Builder to use the built-in Text Editor. Choose Window > Preferences, and expand the General / Editors / File Associations node of the tree on the left. Add a new content type of *.rb, and add an associated editor called Text Editor. Once we've done this, the associated editors pane will show "Text Editor (default)" when the *.rb file type is selected in the file types list. This is shown in figure 2.7.

Follow the same process to associate *.bat and *.log with the Text Editor.

Now, even though we aren't going to be using the database, we need to configure it. This wasn't true in Rails 1.x, but it's true in Rails 2. We'll start by creating a tiny batch file and a small SQL script to create a new database. In Flex Builder,

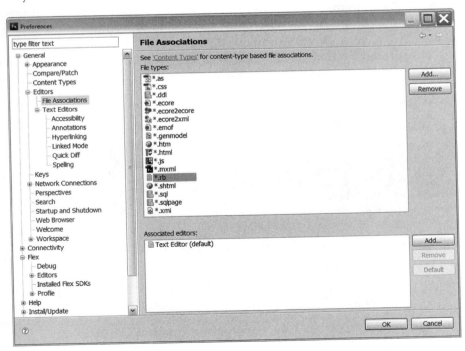

Figure 2.7   Setting the *.rb file association

right-click the root pomodo folder in the Navigator, and choose New > File. Name the new file newdb.bat, and set its contents as shown in listing 2.2.

TIP   If you're on OS X, create a similar shell script—but don't include `call`: This is Windows-only. (Just say `rake db:migrate`.)

Listing 2.2   newdb.bat

```
mysql -h localhost -u root -p <db\create.sql
call rake db:migrate
```

This batch file connects to MySQL, prompting for the root password, and runs the `db\create.sql` SQL script we'll create next. Then, it calls `rake db:migrate` to run the migrations we'll create.

(Don't run this batch file yet; we haven't defined any migrations or created the create.sql script.) Now, create a file called create.sql in the db folder with the contents shown in listing 2.3 (change `YourPasswordHere` to some top-secret password).

Listing 2.3   db\create.sql

```
drop database if exists pomodo_development;
create database pomodo_development;
drop database if exists pomodo_test;
create database pomodo_test;
drop database if exists pomodo_production;
create database pomodo_production;
GRANT ALL PRIVILEGES ON pomodo_development.* TO 'pomodo'@'localhost'
  IDENTIFIED BY 'YourPasswordHere' WITH GRANT OPTION;
GRANT ALL PRIVILEGES ON pomodo_test.* TO 'pomodo'@'localhost'
  IDENTIFIED BY 'YourPasswordHere' WITH GRANT OPTION;
GRANT ALL PRIVILEGES ON pomodo_production.* TO 'pomodo'@'localhost'
  IDENTIFIED BY 'YourPasswordHere' WITH GRANT OPTION;
```

NOTE   In Rails 2 there is an improved way to do this: use the new rake db:drop and rake db:create targets. (I learned about these targets after the book was already in typesetting.)

Next, edit the config\database.yml file to use the connection information for the pomodo user (see listing 2.4).

Listing 2.4   config\database.yml

```
# MySQL (default setup).  Versions 4.1 and 5.0 are recommended.
#
# Install the MySQL driver:
#   gem install mysql
# On MacOS X:
```

```
#   sudo gem install mysql -- --with-mysql-dir=/usr/local/mysql
# On Windows:
#   gem install mysql
#       Choose the win32 build.
#       Install MySQL and put its /bin directory on your path.
#
# And be sure to use new-style password hashing:
#   http://dev.mysql.com/doc/refman/5.0/en/old-client.html
development:
  adapter: mysql
  encoding: utf8
  database: pomodo_development
  username: pomodo         ❶
  password: YourPasswordHere
  host: localhost

# Warning: The database defined as 'test' will be erased and
# re-generated from your development database when you run 'rake'.
# Do not set this db to the same as development or production.
test:
  adapter: mysql
  encoding: utf8
  database: pomodo_test
  username: pomodo         ❷
  password: YourPasswordHere
  host: localhost

production:
  adapter: mysql
  encoding: utf8
  database: pomodo_production
  username: pomodo         ❸
  password: YourPasswordHere
  host: localhost
```

We replace the username of root with pomodo and set the password (change
YourPasswordHere to your password) for the development ❶, test ❷, and production ❸ databases.

Now, we'll run the create script, even though we haven't defined any database
migrations yet. Stop your server, and run newdb.bat:

```
c:\peter\flexiblerails\current\pomodo>newdb.bat

c:\peter\flexiblerails\current\pomodo>
mysql -h localhost -u root -p  0<db\create.sql
Enter password: *******

c:\peter\flexiblerails\current\pomodo>call rake db:migrate
c:0:Warning: require_gem is obsolete. Use gem instead.
```

```
(in c:/peter/flexiblerails/current/pomodo)

c:\peter\flexiblerails\current\pomodo>
```

Note that we didn't enter the MySQL root user's password in the newdb.bat file, so we were prompted for it because we specified the -p option.

Next, create a file called hello_controller.rb in app\controllers, and set its contents as shown in listing 2.5.

Listing 2.5 app\controllers\hello_controller.rb

```
class HelloController < ApplicationController
  def sayhello
    render :text => "hello world!"
  end
end
```

This code creates a class called `HelloController` that extends `ApplicationController`. It has one method, `sayhello`, which renders the string "hello world!" to the browser as text with the `render :text => "hello world!"` call.

Start the server again:

```
c:\peter\flexiblerails\current\pomodo>ruby script\server
```

Back in our web browser, go to the following URL: http://localhost:3000/hello/sayhello. We see something like figure 2.8.

A typical Rails tutorial would now explain how views work with controllers, we'd add a view .html.erb, and so on. But we're not interested in normal Rails views, except for occasional debugging purposes, so we'll skip all that—it's covered better in *AWDwR*.

Figure 2.8 "Hello World" from Rails

2.2.4 *"Hello World" from Flex and Rails*

Now, let's do something interesting. (Finally!) Go back to Pomodo.mxml, and modify it to look like listing 2.6.

Listing 2.6 app\flex\Pomodo.mxml

```
<?xml version="1.0" encoding="utf-8"?>
<mx:Application
    xmlns:mx="http://www.adobe.com/2006/mxml"
    layout="vertical"
    backgroundGradientColors="[#ffffff, #c0c0c0]"
    width="100%"
    height="100%">
```

```
<mx:HTTPService
    id="helloSvc"
    url="/hello/sayhello"
    method="POST"/>
<mx:Button label="call hello service"
    click="helloSvc.send()"/>
<mx:TextInput text="{helloSvc.lastResult}"/>
</mx:Application>
```

Let's see what this does. Build the project (by choosing Project > Build All or clicking the toolbar button), and reload http://localhost:3000/bin/Pomodo.html in the browser. We see something like figure 2.9.

Figure 2.9   Pomodo, the one-button version

Admire the gradient fill: The venture capitalists should come knocking any minute! Let's see if it works. Click the Call Hello Service button, and the result should be something like figure 2.10.

We did it! *Business Week* will make us a paper millionaire in no time. We can close our Series A or Angel round, have a drink, and then start the next iteration. Don't worry: Soon we'll start talking about *why* the code does

Figure 2.10   Hello Web 2.0 millions!

what it does. If I started explaining it now, it wouldn't be "Hello World."

Proceed to Iteration 3.

2.3   *Windows + Flex SDK*

This is the Way of the Frugal Developer—we didn't pay for Flex Builder, and our laptop or desktop probably costs much less than a shiny Mac Book Pro would have.

2.3.1   *Creating the Aptana RadRails project*

Let's do some preparation and then get our project into Aptana RadRails and create a proper "Hello World." It's a good idea to modify the Command Prompt shortcut to start in the pomodo directory by right-clicking it and choosing Properties. This will save us a few seconds many times as we work through this book.

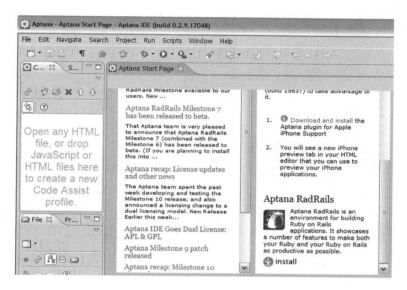

**Figure 2.11
The Aptana
IDE, showing the
Aptana Start Page**

First, however, we need to configure Aptana to install RadRails. (Yes, as of 12 December 2007, even though we downloaded the RadRails version of Aptana, it isn't installed out of the box.) When we launch Aptana, the Aptana Start Page is shown. Scroll down the Plug-ins panel, and click the Install button for Aptana RadRails, as shown in figure 2.11.

We're prompted with a dialog where we can choose the features to install. Select the Aptana RadRails feature, and click Next. Accept the terms of the license agreements for Aptana RadRails and Ruby Development Tools, and click Next. Finally, click Finish to install RadRails and RDT. When we're warned about installing an unsigned feature, choose Install All. When the install finishes, click Yes to restart the Aptana IDE. (Aptana is built on Eclipse, and Eclipse likes to restart itself after it adds a feature.) Close the Aptana Start Page.

Now, choose File > New > Rails Project. We're taken to the New Rails Project Wizard page. Deselect the Generate Rails Application Skeleton and Create a WEBrick Server options.

NOTE   Yes, we could leave these options selected and skip the command-line stuff to create the project, but I wanted this iteration to be useful to people using text editors instead of RadRails. I certainly didn't want to have to write four versions of iteration 2!

Set the Project Name to pomodo. Next, deselect the Use Default Location check box, and click Browse. Navigate to the pomodo project directory, which for me is

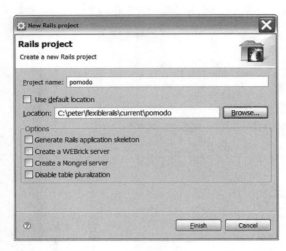

Figure 2.12
RadRails project options

C:\peter\flexiblerails\current\pomodo. When we're finished, the dialog should look like figure 2.12.

Click Finish, and our project will be created.

2.3.2 *"Hello World" from Flex*

Open a Command Prompt in the pomodo directory, and enter the following commands shown in **boldface**:

```
C:\peter\flexiblerails\current\pomodo>mkdir app\flex

C:\peter\flexiblerails\current\pomodo>mkdir public\bin
```

The app\flex location is where we're putting all our Flex code, and the public\bin location is where the compiled output goes. The app\flex location is somewhat arbitrary, but I like it because Rails keeps folders under app private (and we don't want our Flex code public, just as we don't want our Rails code public). The public\bin folder is also arbitrarily named, but it's essential that the bin folder be underneath the public folder because that is what Rails makes publicly available to visitors to our site.

Next, switch back to Aptana and show the Rails Navigator, choosing Window > Show View > Rails Navigator if it's not shown. Right-click the pomodo folder at the top, or click in the Rails Navigator and press F5 to refresh the view. Expand the app directory, right-click the flex directory, and choose New > File. Enter the File Name Pomodo.mxml, and click Finish. Set the file's contents to be as shown in listing 2.7.

Listing 2.7   app\flex\Pomodo.mxml

```
<?xml version="1.0" encoding="utf-8"?>
<mx:Application xmlns:mx="http://www.adobe.com/2006/mxml"
    layout="absolute">
    <mx:Button label="hello world!"/>
</mx:Application>
```

This creates a new `mx:Application` (the top-level component of a Flex app is always `mx:Application`) containing a button that displays the text "hello world!" Choose File > Save.

Now, let's set about compiling the Flex application.

TIP   The best resource for how to use the compilers is *Building and Deploying Flex Applications*, a 260-page (as of Flex 3, Beta 2) PDF (flex3_buildanddeploy.pdf). You can download it from http://www.adobe.com/support/documentation/en/flex/. Pay close attention to the chapter "Using the Flex Compilers."

First, we need to configure our environment variables to have the `FLEX_HOME` variable set. Also, I like to put that in my `PATH` (so that I can run `mxmlc` without specifying its full path).

Choose Start > Settings > Control Panel > System. Choose the Advanced tab, and click the Environment Variables button. In the System Variables section, click the New button. Add a new system variable with the path to the Flex SDK, as shown in figure 2.13.

Click OK. Next, we add `%FLEX_HOME%\bin` to the beginning of our path (see figure 2.14).

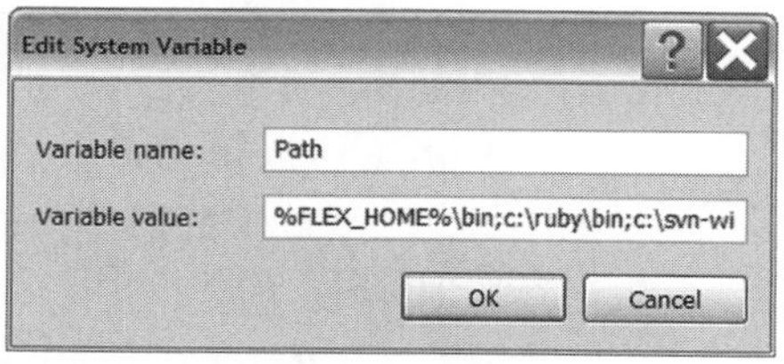

Click OK, click OK to close the Environment Variables dialog, and click OK to close the System Properties.

Now that we've done this, launch a new Command Prompt (because our environment variables aren't refreshed in the already-opened ones), and run the following commands to check that `mxmlc` is present and correct:

Figure 2.13   Setting `FLEX_HOME`

Figure 2.14   Adding `FLEX_HOME` to the path

```
c:\peter\flexiblerails\current\pomodo>mxmlc -version
Version 3.0 build 183453

c:\peter\flexiblerails\current\pomodo>mxmlc -help
Adobe Flex Compiler (mxmlc)
Version 3.0 build 183453
Copyright (c) 2004-2006 Adobe Systems, Inc. All rights reserved.
...
```

Next, we'll compile Pomodo.mxml:

```
C:\peter\flexiblerails\current\pomodo >cd app\flex
C:\peter\flexiblerails\current\pomodo\app\flex>mxmlc Pomodo.mxml
Loading configuration file C:\flex3sdk_b2_100107\frameworks\flex-config.xml
This beta will expire on Thu Jan 31 00:00:00 PST 2008.
C:\peter\flexiblerails\current\pomodo\app\flex\Pomodo.swf (142854 bytes)

C:\peter\flexiblerails\current\pomodo\app\flex>
```

We now have a Pomodo.swf file, which contains our compiled Flex application. Move the Pomodo.swf file into pomodo\public\bin, and see if we can load it directly:

```
C:\peter\flexiblerails\current\pomodo\app\flex>
move Pomodo.swf ..\..\public\bin
```

Now, load http://localhost:3000/bin/ Pomodo.swf in a browser. Depending on our browser configuration, it may work and load the Pomodo application, or we may get something like figure 2.15.

That's not what we wanted!

It turns out that we need an HTML wrapper file. (Even if Pomodo.swf did load in our browser, many of our users may get the dialog in figure 2.15. So, we need a wrapper anyway.) The HTML wrapper file is best described in the

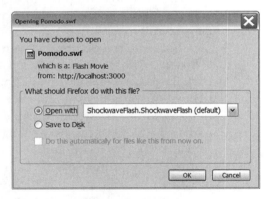

Figure 2.15 Um, that's not a Flex app...

"Creating a simple wrapper" section of *Building and Deploying Flex Applications*. We'll just do *what* we're supposed to do and leave the *why* for that PDF. Create a file called Pomodo.html inside app\flex, and put in it the code[1] shown in listing 2.8.

NOTE   Don't add line breaks inside the codebase and pluginspage attribute values.

---

[1] This code is a simplified copy-paste-modify of the code from *Building and Deploying Flex Applications*.

Listing 2.8   app\flex\Pomodo.html

```html
<html>
<body>
<script src="mysource.js"></script>
<noscript>
<object id='pomodo'
  classid='clsid:D27CDB6E-AE6D-11cf-96B8-444553540000'
  codebase='http://download.macromedia.com/pub/shockwave/cabs/
  ➥flash/swflash.cab#version=9,0,0,0'
  height='100%' width='100%'>
<param name='src' value='Pomodo.swf'/>
<embed name='Pomodo'
  pluginspage='http://www.macromedia.com/shockwave/download/
  ➥index.cgi?P1_Prod_Version=ShockwaveFlash'
  src='Pomodo.swf' height='100%' width='100%'/>
</object>
</noscript>
</body>
</html>
```

Similarly, create a new file called mysource.js in app\flex. Set its contents as shown in listing 2.9.

Listing 2.9   app\flex\mysource.js

```javascript
document.write("<object id='Pomodo' classid='clsid:D27CDB6E-AE6D-11c
  ➥f-96B8-444553540000' codebase='http://download.macromedia.com/pu
  ➥b/shockwave/cabs/flash/swflash.cab#version=9,0,0,0' height='100%
  ➥' width='100%'>");
document.write("<param name='src' value='Pomodo.swf'/>");
document.write("<embed name='pomodo' src='Pomodo.swf' pluginspage='h
  ➥ttp://www.macromedia.com/shockwave/download/index.cgi?P1_Prod_Ve
  ➥rsion=ShockwaveFlash' height='100%' width='100%'/>");
document.write("</object>");
```

NOTE   Each of these document.write calls is *one line only*—this file is *four* lines long, *not nine*, and each line begins with document.write.

Next, *copy* both these files to pomodo\public\bin:

```
C:\peter\flexiblerails\current\pomodo\app\flex>
copy Pomodo.html ..\..\public\bin
        1 file(s) copied.

C:\peter\flexiblerails\current\pomodo\app\flex>
```

```
copy mysource.js ..\..\public\bin
        1 file(s) copied.
```

```
C:\peter\flexiblerails\current\pomodo\app\flex>
```

Try loading http://localhost:3000/bin/Pomodo.html. Note that although we picked public\bin as our output folder, the URL starts with *bin*; this is because public is the root.

NOTE   If you get a blank screen, chances are you messed up the copy-paste of the document.write calls.

We should see the screen shown in figure 2.16.

We now have a running Flex 3 application built using the Flex 3 SDK!

Figure 2.16   **"Hello World" from Flex**

2.3.3   *"Hello World" from Rails*

Now, let's switch gears and do a "Hello World" in Rails before we move on to having Flex talk to Rails. First, however, we need to set the *.bat and *.log file associations in Aptana to use the built-in text editor. Choose Window > Preferences, and expand the General / Editors / File Associations node of the tree on the left. Add a new content type called *.bat, and add an Associated Editor called Text Editor. After we do this, the Associated Editors pane shows Text Editor (Default) when the *.bat file type is selected in the File Types list. Next, do the same for *.log.

Even though we won't be using the database, we need to configure it. This wasn't true in Rails 1.x, but it's true in Rails 2. We'll start by creating a tiny batch file and a small SQL script to create a new database. In Aptana, right-click the root pomodo folder in the Navigator, and choose New > File. Name the batch file newdb.bat, and set its contents as shown in listing 2.10.

Listing 2.10   newdb.bat

```
mysql -h localhost -u root -p <db\create.sql
call rake db:migrate
```

This connects to MySQL, prompting for the root password, and then runs the db\create.sql SQL script we'll create next. Then, it calls rake db:migrate to run the migrations we'll create.

(Don't run this batch file yet; we haven't defined any migrations or created the create.sql script.) Now, create a file called create.sql in the db folder with the contents shown in listing 2.11 (change YourPasswordHere to some top-secret password).

Listing 2.11 db\create.sql

```
drop database if exists pomodo_development;
create database pomodo_development;
drop database if exists pomodo_test;
create database pomodo_test;
drop database if exists pomodo_production;
create database pomodo_production;
GRANT ALL PRIVILEGES ON pomodo_development.* TO 'pomodo'@'localhost'
  IDENTIFIED BY 'YourPasswordHere' WITH GRANT OPTION;
GRANT ALL PRIVILEGES ON pomodo_test.* TO 'pomodo'@'localhost'
  IDENTIFIED BY 'YourPasswordHere' WITH GRANT OPTION;
GRANT ALL PRIVILEGES ON pomodo_production.* TO 'pomodo'@'localhost'
  IDENTIFIED BY 'YourPasswordHere' WITH GRANT OPTION;
```

NOTE   In Rails 2 there is an improved way to do this: use the new rake db:drop and rake db:create targets. (I learned about these targets after the book was already in typesetting.)

Next, edit the config\database.yml file to use the connection information for the pomodo user (see listing 2.12).

Listing 2.12 config\database.yml

```
# MySQL (default setup).  Versions 4.1 and 5.0 are recommended.
#
# Install the MySQL driver:
#   gem install mysql
# On MacOS X:
#   sudo gem install mysql -- --with-mysql-dir=/usr/local/mysql
# On Windows:
#   gem install mysql
#       Choose the win32 build.
#       Install MySQL and put its /bin directory on your path.
#
# And be sure to use new-style password hashing:
#   http://dev.mysql.com/doc/refman/5.0/en/old-client.html
development:
  adapter: mysql
  encoding: utf8
  database: pomodo_development
  username: pomodo        ❶
  password: YourPasswordHere
  host: localhost

# Warning: The database defined as 'test' will be erased and
# re-generated from your development database when you run 'rake'.
```

```
# Do not set this db to the same as development or production.
test:
  adapter: mysql
  encoding: utf8
  database: pomodo_test
  username: pomodo        ❷
  password: YourPasswordHere
  host: localhost

production:
  adapter: mysql
  encoding: utf8
  database: pomodo_production
  username: pomodo        ❸
  password: YourPasswordHere
  host: localhost
```

We replace the username of root with pomodo and set the password (change YourPasswordHere to your password) for the development ❶, test ❷, and production ❸ databases.

Now we'll run the create script, even though we haven't defined any database migrations yet. Stop the server, and run newdb.bat:

```
c:\peter\flexiblerails\current\pomodo>newdb.bat

c:\peter\flexiblerails\current\pomodo>
mysql -h localhost -u root -p  0<db\create.sql
Enter password: *******

c:\peter\flexiblerails\current\pomodo>call rake db:migrate
c:0:Warning: require_gem is obsolete. Use gem instead.
(in c:/peter/flexiblerails/current/pomodo)

c:\peter\flexiblerails\current\pomodo>
```

Note that we didn't enter the root password in the newdb.bat file, so we're prompted for it because we specified the -p option.

Next, create a file called hello_controller.rb in app\controllers, and set its contents as shown in listing 2.13.

Listing 2.13   app\controllers\hello_controller.rb

```
class HelloController < ApplicationController
  def sayhello
    render :text => "hello world!"
  end
end
```

Figure 2.17
"Hello World" from Rails

This creates a class called `HelloController` that extends `ApplicationControl-ler`. It has one method, `sayhello`, which renders the string "hello world!" to the browser as text with the `render :text => "hello world!"` call.

Start the server again:

```
c:\peter\flexiblerails\current\pomodo>ruby script\server
```

Next, in our web browser, we go to the following URL: http://localhost:3000/hello/sayhello. We see something like figure 2.17.

The typical Rails tutorial would now explain how views work with controllers, and we would go about adding a view .html.erb file, and so on. However, we're not that interested in normal Rails views, except for occasional debugging purposes. So, we'll skip all that—it's covered better in *AWDwR*.

2.3.4 *"Hello World" from Flex and Rails*

Now, let's do something interesting. (Finally!) Go back to Pomodo.mxml, and modify it to look like listing 2.14.

Listing 2.14 app\flex\Pomodo.mxml

```
<?xml version="1.0" encoding="utf-8"?>
<mx:Application
    xmlns:mx="http://www.adobe.com/2006/mxml"
    layout="vertical"
    backgroundGradientColors="[#ffffff, #c0c0c0]"
    width="100%"
    height="100%">
    <mx:HTTPService
        id="helloSvc"
        url="/hello/sayhello"
        method="POST"/>
    <mx:Button label="call hello service"
        click="helloSvc.send()"/>
    <mx:TextInput text="{helloSvc.lastResult}"/>
</mx:Application>
```

Let's see what this does. Save the file, open a new Command Prompt in app\flex, recompile, and move the SWF:

```
C:\peter\flexiblerails\current\pomodo\app\flex>mxmlc Pomodo.mxml
Loading configuration file C:\flex3sdk_b2_100107\frameworks\
flex-config.xml
This beta will expire on Thu Jan 31 00:00:00 PST 2008.
C:\peter\flexiblerails\current\pomodo\app\flex\Pomodo.swf
(217919 bytes)

C:\peter\flexiblerails\current\pomodo\app\flex>
move Pomodo.swf ..\..\public\bin
Overwrite C:\peter\flexiblerails\current\pomodo\public\bin\
Pomodo.swf? (Yes/No/All): y

C:\peter\flexiblerails\current\pomodo\app\flex>
```

Go to http;//localhost:3000/bin/Pomodo.html. You should see what is shown in figure 2.18; if you don't, hold down the Ctrl key and click reload.

Figure 2.18
Pomodo: the one-button version

Admire the gradient fill: The venture capitalists should come knocking any minute! Let's see if it works. Click the Call Hello Service button (see figure 2.19).

We did it! *Business Week* will make us paper millionaires in no time. We can close our Series A or Angel round, have a drink, and then start the next iteration.

Figure 2.19
Hello Web 2.0 millions!

Don't worry: Soon we'll start talking about *why* the code does what it does. If I started explaining it now, it wouldn't be "Hello World."

You should now be able to follow along with the iterations in the book, because the `mxmlc Pomodo.mxml` command will automatically bring in dependent files.

> Proceed to Iteration 3.

2.4 *Mac OS X (or Linux) + Flex SDK*

Welcome, fellow Mac users! We don't just have shiny computers, we also have TextMate: the Preferred Text Editor of the Leaders of the Rails Community. (People who think *really* different and don't like TextMate can use Aquamacs, vi, or whatever text editor they wish. Linux users, this includes you: you can follow along with this iteration, adapting it for your configuration as necessary.)

2.4.1 *Creating the TextMate project (or launch Emacs or vi)*

If you're using Emacs or vi, launch that now, and navigate to the flexiblerails/current directory. These instructions assume TextMate—I have to assume something.

Launch TextMate, and choose File > New Project. Drag the flexiblerails/current/pomodo folder from the Finder onto the Drag Files And Folders Here section. (Or just drag it onto the TextMate icon in the dock instead of doing all that.) Choose File > Save Project to save the pomodo project. (Save it in the flexiblerails/current/pomodo folder.) Name the project file pomodo (the extension will automatically be .tmproj).

2.4.2 *"Hello World" from Flex*

Open a new Terminal window, and create the following directories:

```
/Users/peterarmstrong/flexiblerails/current/pomodo > mkdir app/flex
/Users/peterarmstrong/flexiblerails/current/pomodo >
mkdir public/bin
```

This app/flex location is somewhat arbitrary, but I like it because Rails keeps folders under app private (and we don't want our Flex code public, just as we don't want our Rails code public). The public/bin folder is also arbitrarily named, but it's essential that the bin folder be underneath the public folder because that is what Rails makes publicly available to visitors to our site.

In the app/flex directory, create a file called Pomodo.mxml, and set its contents as shown in listing 2.15.

Listing 2.15   app/flex/Pomodo.mxml

```
<?xml version="1.0" encoding="utf-8"?>
<mx:Application xmlns:mx="http://www.adobe.com/2006/mxml"
    layout="absolute">
    <mx:Button label="hello world!"/>
</mx:Application>
```

This creates a new `mx:Application` (the top-level component of a Flex app is always `mx:Application`) containing a button that displays the text "hello world!"

Now, let's set about compiling the Pomodo.mxml Flex application.

> **TIP**   The best resource for how to use the compilers is *Building and Deploying Flex Applications,* a 260-page (as of Flex 3, Beta 2) PDF (flex3_buildanddeploy.pdf). You can download it from http://www.adobe.com/support/documentation/en/flex/. Pay close attention to the chapter "Using the Flex Compilers."

Compile Pomodo.mxml:

```
/Users/peterarmstrong/flexiblerails/current/pomodo > cd app/flex
/Users/peterarmstrong/flexiblerails/current/pomodo/app/flex >
mxmlc Pomodo.mxml
Loading configuration file /Users/peterarmstrong/flex3sdk/
    ➥frameworks/flex-config.xml
This beta will expire on Thu Jan 31 00:00:00 PST 2008.
/Users/peterarmstrong/flexiblerails/current/pomodo/app/flex/
    ➥Pomodo.swf (142697 bytes)
/Users/peterarmstrong/flexiblerails/current/pomodo/app/flex > ls
Pomodo.mxml      Pomodo.swf
```

Hooray! We now have a Pomodo.swf file, which contains our compiled Flex application. Let's move the Pomodo.swf file into pomodo/public/bin and see if we can load it directly:

```
/Users/peterarmstrong/flexiblerails/current/pomodo/app/flex >
mv Pomodo.swf ../../public/bin/
```

Load http://localhost:3000/bin/Pomodo.swf in a browser. Depending on our browser configuration, it may work and load the pomodo application, or we may get something like figure 2.20.

That's not what we wanted!

It turns out that we need an HTML wrapper file. (Even if Pomodo.swf loaded in our browser,

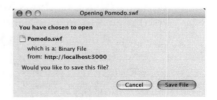

Figure 2.20   Um, that's not a Flex app...

many of our users may get the dialog in figure 2.22, on page 49. So, we need a wrapper anyway.) The HTML wrapper file is best described in the "Creating a simple wrapper" section of *Building and Deploying Flex Applications*. We'll just do *what* we're supposed to do and leave the *why* for that PDF. Create a file called Pomodo.html inside app/flex, and put in it the code[2] from listing 2.16.

NOTE Don't add line breaks inside the codebase and pluginspage attribute values.

Listing 2.16   app\flex\Pomodo.html

```
<html>
<body>
<script src="mysource.js"></script>
<noscript>
<object id='pomodo'
  classid='clsid:D27CDB6E-AE6D-11cf-96B8-444553540000'
  codebase='http://download.macromedia.com/pub/shockwave/cabs/
  ➥flash/swflash.cab#version=9,0,0,0'
  height='100%' width='100%'>
<param name='src' value='Pomodo.swf'/>
<embed name='Pomodo'
  pluginspage='http://www.macromedia.com/shockwave/download/
  ➥index.cgi?P1_Prod_Version=ShockwaveFlash'
  src='Pomodo.swf' height='100%' width='100%'/>
</object>
</noscript>
</body>
</html>
```

Similarly, create a new file called mysource.js in pomodo/app/flex. Set its contents as shown in listing 2.17.

Listing 2.17   app\flex\mysource.js

```
document.write("<object id='Pomodo' classid='clsid:D27CDB6E-AE6D-11c
  ➥f-96B8-444553540000' codebase='http://download.macromedia.com/pu
  ➥b/shockwave/cabs/flash/swflash.cab#version=9,0,0,0' height='100%
  ➥' width='100%'>");
document.write("<param name='src' value='Pomodo.swf'/>");
document.write("<embed name='pomodo' src='Pomodo.swf' pluginspage='h
  ➥ttp://www.macromedia.com/shockwave/download/index.cgi?P1_Prod_Ve
  ➥rsion=ShockwaveFlash' height='100%' width='100%'/>");
document.write("</object>");
```

---

[2] This code is a simplified copy-paste-modify of the code from *Building and Deploying Flex Applications*.

NOTE   Each of these `document.write` calls is *one line only*—this file is *four* lines long, *not nine*, and each line begins with `document.write`.

Next, *copy* both these files to pomodo\public\bin:

```
/Users/peterarmstrong/flexiblerails/current/pomodo/app/flex >
cp Pomodo.html ../../public/bin/
/Users/peterarmstrong/flexiblerails/current/pomodo/app/flex >
cp mysource.js ../../public/bin/
```

Try loading http://localhost:3000/bin/Pomodo.html. Note that although we picked public/bin as our output folder, the URL starts with *bin*. This is because public is the root.

NOTE   If you get a blank screen, chances are you messed up the copy-paste of the `document.write` calls.

We see the screen shown in figure 2.21.

We now have a running Flex 3 application on OS X!

Figure 2.21
"Hello World" from Flex

2.4.3   *"Hello World" from Rails*

Now, let's switch gears and do a "Hello World" in Rails, before we move on to having Flex talk to Rails.

Even though we aren't going to use the database, we need to configure it. This wasn't true in Rails 1.x, but it's true in Rails 2. We'll start by creating a tiny shell script and a small SQL script to create a new database. Create a file called newdb.sh in the current/pomodo directory, and set its contents as shown in listing 2.18.

Listing 2.18   newdb.sh

```
#!/bin/sh
mysql -h localhost -u root -p <db/create.sql
rake db:migrate
```

This shell script connects to MySQL, prompting for the root password, and runs the db\create.sql SQL script we'll create next. Then, it calls `rake db:migrate` to run the migrations we'll create. Save the file, and make it executable (`chmod 755 newdb.sh`).

(Don't run this script yet; we haven't defined any migrations or created the create.sql script.) Now, create a file called create.sql in the db folder, with the contents shown in listing 2.19 (change `YourPasswordHere` to some top-secret password).

Listing 2.19   db/create.sql

```
drop database if exists pomodo_development;
create database pomodo_development;
drop database if exists pomodo_test;
create database pomodo_test;
drop database if exists pomodo_production;
create database pomodo_production;
GRANT ALL PRIVILEGES ON pomodo_development.* TO 'pomodo'@'localhost'
  IDENTIFIED BY 'YourPasswordHere' WITH GRANT OPTION;
GRANT ALL PRIVILEGES ON pomodo_test.* TO 'pomodo'@'localhost'
  IDENTIFIED BY 'YourPasswordHere' WITH GRANT OPTION;
GRANT ALL PRIVILEGES ON pomodo_production.* TO 'pomodo'@'localhost'
  IDENTIFIED BY 'YourPasswordHere' WITH GRANT OPTION;
```

NOTE   In Rails 2 there is an improved way to do this: use the new rake db:drop and rake db:create targets. (I learned about these targets after the book was already in typesetting.)

Next, edit the config\database.yml file to use the connection information for the pomodo user (see listing 2.20).

Listing 2.20   config\database.yml

```
# MySQL (default setup).  Versions 4.1 and 5.0 are recommended.
#
# Install the MySQL driver:
#   gem install mysql
# On MacOS X:
#   sudo gem install mysql -- --with-mysql-dir=/usr/local/mysql
# On Windows:
#   gem install mysql
#       Choose the win32 build.
#       Install MySQL and put its /bin directory on your path.
#
# And be sure to use new-style password hashing:
#   http://dev.mysql.com/doc/refman/5.0/en/old-client.html
development:
  adapter: mysql
  encoding: utf8
  database: pomodo_development
  username: pomodo         ❶
  password: YourPasswordHere
```

```
    host: localhost

# Warning: The database defined as 'test' will be erased and
# re-generated from your development database when you run 'rake'.
# Do not set this db to the same as development or production.
test:
  adapter: mysql
  encoding: utf8
  database: pomodo_test
  username: pomodo        ➋
  password: YourPasswordHere
  host: localhost

production:
  adapter: mysql
  encoding: utf8
  database: pomodo_production
  username: pomodo        ➌
  password: YourPasswordHere
  host: localhost
```

We replace the username of root with pomodo and set the password (change
YourPasswordHere to your password) for the development ➊, test ➋, and production ➌ databases.

Now we'll run the create script, even though we haven't defined any database
migrations yet. Stop the server, and run newdb.sh:

```
/Users/peterarmstrong/flexiblerails/current/pomodo > ./newdb.sh
Enter password:
/usr/bin/rake:17:Warning: require_gem is obsolete.  Use gem instead.
(in /Users/peterarmstrong/flexiblerails/current/pomodo)
/Users/peterarmstrong/flexiblerails/current/pomodo >
```

Note that we didn't enter the root password in the newdb.sh file, so we're
prompted for it because we specified the -p option.

Next, create a file called hello_controller.rb in app/controllers, and set its contents as shown in listing 2.21.

Listing 2.21   app/controllers/hello_controller.rb

```
class HelloController < ApplicationController
  def sayhello
    render :text => "hello world!"
  end
end
```

Figure 2.22   **"Hello World" from Rails**

This creates a class called `HelloController` that extends `ApplicationController`. It has one method, `sayhello`, which renders the string "hello world!" to the browser as text with the `render :text => "hello world!"` call.

Start the server again:

```
/Users/peterarmstrong/flexiblerails/current/pomodo > ruby script/server
```

In our web browser, we go to the following URL: http://localhost:3000/hello/sayhello. We see something like figure 2.22.

The typical Rails tutorial would now explain how views work with controllers, and we would go about adding a view .html.erb file, and so on. However, we're not that interested in normal Rails views, except for occasional debugging purposes. So, we'll skip all that—it's covered better in *AWDwR*.

2.4.4   *"Hello World" from Flex and Rails*

Now, let's do something interesting. (Finally!) Go back to Pomodo.mxml, and modify it to look like listing 2.22.

Listing 2.22   app/flex/Pomodo.mxml

```xml
<?xml version="1.0" encoding="utf-8"?>
<mx:Application
    xmlns:mx="http://www.adobe.com/2006/mxml"
    layout="vertical"
    backgroundGradientColors="[#ffffff, #c0c0c0]"
    width="100%"
    height="100%">
    <mx:HTTPService
        id="helloSvc"
        url="/hello/sayhello"
        method="POST"/>
    <mx:Button label="call hello service"
        click="helloSvc.send()"/>
    <mx:TextInput text="{helloSvc.lastResult}"/>
</mx:Application>
```

Save the file, then recompile and move the swf:

```
/Users/peterarmstrong/flexiblerails/current/pomodo/app/flex >
mxmlc Pomodo.mxml
Loading configuration file /Users/peterarmstrong/flex3sdk/
  ➥frameworks/flex-config.xml
This beta will expire on Thu Jan 31 00:00:00 PST 2008.
/Users/peterarmstrong/flexiblerails/current/pomodo/app/
  ➥flex/Pomodo.swf (217912 bytes)
/Users/peterarmstrong/flexiblerails/current/pomodo/app/flex >
mv Pomodo.swf ../../public/bin/
```

Next, we reload http://localhost:3000/bin/Pomodo.html in our browser (see figure 2.23).

Figure 2.23   Pomodo: the one-button version

Admire the gradient fill: The venture capitalists should come knocking any minute! Let's see if it works. Click the Call Hello Service button (see figure 2.24).

Figure 2.24   Hello Web 2.0 millions!

We did it! *Business Week* will make us paper millionaires in no time. We can close our Series A or Angel round, have a drink, and then start the next iteration. Don't worry: Soon we'll start talking about *why* the code does what it does. If I started explaining now, it wouldn't be "Hello World."

We should now be able to follow along with the iterations in the book, because the `mxmlc Pomodo.mxml` command will automatically bring in dependent files.

2.5 *Summary*

It's easy to get up and running creating Flex and Rails applications, and almost as easy to start having Flex talking to Rails. Although sending text back and forth doesn't seem that interesting, it's the foundation for the many interesting things we'll do later. We'll soon switch to sending XML, but XML is just specially format-ted text—so understanding the basics is important.

In the next iteration, in addition to sending XML, we'll set up MySQL, and add account create and login functionality to our pomodo Rails application using the restful_authentication plug-in. We'll then hook up the Flex UI to use the Rails account create and login functionality. At the end of the next iteration, we'll have an excellent starting point for any Flex + Rails application—especially the one we're building in this book.

Getting started 3

Perhaps one day this too will be pleasant to remember.

—Virgil

In this iteration, we'll start making some real headway in our application. By the end of it, we'll have a good starting point for any Flex + Rails application, and the pomodo application in particular. We'll start by freezing Rails and then installing and running `restful_authentication`, and then creating and running the migration to create users. Next, we'll switch to the Flex side and get user creation and login functional. Finally, we'll ensure that the minimal test suite passes.

This iteration is a bit of a long, hard slog—hence the opening quote. Please rest assured that the book gets a lot more fun after this iteration is over.

Note

The folders in the code zip file show the code at the *end* of each iteration. You can start at any iteration from 3–12 in this book by beginning with the code in the folder from the *previous* iteration; if you aren't interested in following along with the early stuff but want to follow along starting with iteration 9, you should read iterations 1–8 and then start iteration 9 with the code from the `iteration08` folder. You would rename the project from iteration08 to pomodo and import it using the same procedure as is shown next.

3.1 *If you're starting here*

If you've been following along, skip to section 3.2.

If you're starting here and wish to follow along, copy the appropriate folder of source code for iteration 2 (either iteration02_flexbuilder_windows, iteration02_sdk_mac or iteration02_sdk_windows) from the code zip file, paste it where you want to work, and rename it to `current`. If you're using Flex Builder, edit the .project file with a text editor to rename the project from `iteration02` to `pomodo`, as shown in listing 3.1.

Listing 3.1 .project file

```
<?xml version="1.0" encoding="UTF-8"?>
<projectDescription>
        <name>pomodo</name>
        <comment></comment>
...
</projectDescription>
```

Figure 3.1
**Importing an existing project (not a
zipped export) into Flex Builder (step 1)**

Next, choose File > Import > Other, and select General / Existing Projects into
Workspace (see figure 3.1).

> **Note**
> We aren't choosing File > Import > Flex Project because in FlexBuilder 3 Beta 2
> and below that assumes there is an exported projectzip file to import. In Flex
> Builder 3 Beta 3 (and presumably above) it works: you can specify a project folder
> to import from.

Click Next. We see the Import Projects dialog shown in figure 3.2. Click Browse,
browse to the location of the new current\pomodo directory, and click OK. The

Figure 3.2
Importing pomodo into Flex Builder

root directory will be set and the `pomodo` project selected. Don't choose "Copy projects into workspace"—we're happy with the project where it is. The dialog should look like figure 3.2.

Click Finish.

Q. Why do I need to rename the project in the .project file if I'm starting with a project from the code zip file I downloaded from http://www.flexiblerails.com/code-samples? Shouldn't the project be called `pomodo`?

A. When I was writing this book, I needed to maintain all the iterations in order to fix bugs in them (yes, my code sometimes has bugs too). So, when I finished an iteration, I copied the current folder to a folder named after the iteration (such as iteration03) and then edited the .project file to rename the project from `pomodo` to the name of the iteration (again, such as iteration03). This allowed me to have all the iterations open in Flex Builder at once as separate projects. It did mean, however, that the code in the zip file has these projects named iteration03, iteration04, and so on instead of pomodo. That is why if you want to start at a given iteration and have your project still be called `pomodo` you need to rename the project in the .project file. Finally, note that for iteration 2 only, I created three folders of source code: iteration02_flexbuilder_windows, iteration02_sdk_mac and iteration02_sdk_windows. (The rest of the iteration folders are taken from the Flex Builder and Windows combination.)

Before we plow ahead adding new features, we're going to do two small things: freeze the Rails version and disable browser navigation integration.

3.2 *Freezing the Rails version*

NOTE This section is optional. You can follow along with the book (except for the part where I tell you to read source code in vendor\rails) just fine even if you skip this section. So, if you have problems following along, please skip ahead to section 3.3. This section also requires that you have Subversion installed and working from the command line. To check, type svn –version at a command prompt: you should see a version of svn listed, something like "svn, version 1.4.2". If you need help installing Subversion see appendix A.

Freezing the Rails version will ensure that if we want to load any of iterations 3–12 at a later date (and if Rails has substantially changed in the meantime), the Rails code will still work. Also, it's a good thing to do because it will let us look through the Rails source code. Recall that in section 2.1.2 you chose to install either the latest and greatest version of Rails 2 or to install the release candidate version (1.99.0, also known as RC1) of Rails 2 that was used during the copy edit of the book. In this section, you are choosing to freeze to a specific version of Rails. To freeze to the release candidate version RC1, run the following command from inside the pomodo directory:

```
c:\peter\flexiblerails\current\pomodo>
rake rails:freeze:edge TAG=rel_2-0-0_RC1
...tons of output omitted...
```

To freeze to the 2.0 release of Rails, run the following command from inside the pomodo directory:

```
c:\peter\flexiblerails\current\pomodo>
rake rails:freeze:edge TAG=rel_2-0-1
...tons of output omitted...
```

This creates a rails directory containing all the Rails source code in the vendor directory. Our application will use the version of Rails 2 in this directory instead of whatever versions are installed as gems.

Note that it's also a good idea to freeze your Rails version if you'll be deploying in an environment (such as shared hosting) where you can't control the Rails version installed. *Actually, it's a good idea before deploying, period.*

3.3 *Disabling browser navigation integration*

We'll do one other thing to ensure that the experience of following along with the code is as pleasant as possible: disabling the browser navigation integration. Flex 3 has the ability to integrate with the browser navigation so that actions like the user clicking the Back button have an effect in your application. Although this is promising, it makes following along a pain—reloading the application when there is a bunch of extra stuff in the URL can cause annoying side effects. We'll turn off this feature for the purposes of this book.

> **NOTE** SDK users, you can skip this section—this only affects Flex Builder users. (You can use this feature, but you need to add it yourself instead of needing to turn it off.)

Right-click the pomodo project in the Flex Navigator, and choose the Flex Compiler option. Deselect the Enable Integration with Browser Navigation check box in the HTML Wrapper section, as shown in figure 3.3.

Figure 3.3   Disabling browser navigation integration in the HTML wrapper

Click OK. We're prompted with the warning shown in figure 3.4.

Click OK.

Now that we *finally* have everything set up correctly, let's start building something.

Figure 3.4   HTML wrapper overwriting files warning

3.4   *Adding login functionality to Rails*

Because we're building a multi-user GTD-style To-Do list application in the book, we'll need to add login functionality at some point. So, we're going to cheat a bit. Later in the book, in iteration 5, we'll refactor all the Rails code we're about to write to a more RESTful style. Because we know this, we'll use the RESTful style of authentication now, without me explaining REST. That way, when it's time to explain REST, I'll explain the login code that we've already been using and then refactor the existing Rails code to the RESTful style. If we used a different login generator, we would have wanted to either refactor its output or throw it away and do what we're about to do.

> ### Rails Engines and reusability
>
> The inability to reuse generator output is one of the motivations behind Rails Engines (http://rails-engines.org/). Unfortunately, Rails Engines are controversial in the Rails community and as such are beyond the scope of this book. However, it would be dishonest to talk about reuse and not mention them. My recommendation is that once you understand Rails well enough to think about design in it, go to the Rails Engines link and think for yourself.

In addition to installing and running the restful_authentication generator, we'll also edit our Rails code to get the generated code working with the HTML views. Yes, even though this is a book about using Flex with Rails, HTML still has its place for scaffolding and ad-hoc testing of controllers.

3.4.1 *Installing and running restful_authentication*

We'll begin by installing Rick Olson's restful_authentication plugin.

TIP This plugin is also used by Geoffrey Grosenbach (Mr. "Topfunky") in his "PeepCode RESTful Rails" screencast (http://peepcode.com/ articles/2006/10/08/restful-rails). I found this screencast to be a useful companion to the discussions of REST in *Agile Web Development with Rails* (*AWDwR*) and in DHH's "Discovering a world of Resources on Rails" RailsConf 2006 keynote (http://media.rubyonrails.org/ presentations/worldofresources.pdf). The "PeepCode RESTful Rails" screencast is an hour and a half long, but it's much more enjoyable than many movies. I recommend buying and watching it before reading iteration 5.

Let's install the restful_authentication plugin.[1] Run the following command, and note all the files that are created (and read the usage message):

```
c:\peter\flexiblerails\current\pomodo>
ruby script\plugin install -r 3072 http://svn.techno-
  ➡weenie.net/projects/plugins/restful_authentication/
+ ./README
+ ./Rakefile
+ ./generators/authenticated/USAGE
...output omitted...
c:\peter\flexiblerails\current\pomodo>
```

Make sure you read the usage message, which is output by the installer to the command line. This command installs the 2007-12-12 version of the restful_ authentication generator into pomodo\vendor\plugins\restful_authentication. (We're using a specific version of the generator to ensure that the code it generates matches the book.)

Next, let's use the restful_authentication generator. We aren't going to specify --include-activation, because email confirmation of account creation is— along with all of ActionMailer—beyond the scope of the book. Note that because I am assuming Windows, I will say ruby instead of ./ to run the scripts:

NOTE Mac OS X and Linux users: from here on, the book is written assuming Windows—I have to assume something. Make sure you use / instead of \, and on OS X if a command doesn't work then try sudo in front of it. (In reality, if you're following along using Flex Builder, not much is different.)

---

[1] http://peepcode.com/articles/2006/10/08/restful-rails at 04:54 in the screencast (peepcode-003-rest.mov).

```
c:\peter\flexiblerails\current\pomodo>
ruby script\generate authenticated user sessions
...output omitted...
```

Running this generator creates a bunch of new files and directories, as well as a migration[2] (db\migrate\001_create_users.rb). It's always a good idea to read all the code that a generator creates for you, as we'll soon see.

3.4.2 *Editing and running the CreateUsers migration, and checking the result*

We'll edit the migration now to add first and last names; see listing 3.2.

Listing 3.2 db\migrate\001_create_users.rb

```
class CreateUsers < ActiveRecord::Migration
  def self.up
    create_table "users", :force => true do |t|
      t.column :login,                      :string
      t.column :email,                      :string
      t.column :first_name,                 :string, :limit => 80    ❶
      t.column :last_name,                  :string, :limit => 80    ❷
      t.column :crypted_password,           :string, :limit => 40
      t.column :salt,                       :string, :limit => 40
      t.column :created_at,                 :datetime
      t.column :updated_at,                 :datetime
      t.column :remember_token,             :string
      t.column :remember_token_expires_at,  :datetime
    end
  end

  def self.down
    drop_table "users"
  end
end
```

The restful_authentication generator creates an `ActiveRecord::Migration` subclass called `CreateUsers`, whose up method creates the users table in a database-agnostic way and whose down method drops the users table in a database-agnostic way. All this code is added for us by running the generator; all we need to do is to add columns for the first ❶ and last ❷ names. We limit the length in both cases to 80 characters.

---

[2] Migrations are explained extremely well at the following blog post: http://glu.ttono.us/articles/2005/10/27/the-joy-of-migrations.

Switch to the Command Prompt where your WEBrick server is running, and kill it using Ctrl-C. Because we recently changed the database configuration in config\database.yml, we'll need to stop and start our server. For now, we stop it; we'll start it again later.

Next, now that we've edited the migration that creates a users table, let's run the newdb.bat script to re-create the databases and run the migration:

```
c:\peter\flexiblerails\current\pomodo>newdb.bat

c:\peter\flexiblerails\current\pomodo>
mysql -h localhost -u root -p  0<db\create.sql
Enter password: *******

c:\peter\flexiblerails\current\pomodo>call rake db:migrate
c:0:Warning: require_gem is obsolete.  Use gem instead.
(in c:/peter/flexiblerails/current/pomodo)
== 1 CreateUsers: migrating
 =====================================================
-- create_table("users", {:force=>true})
   -> 0.2500s
== 1 CreateUsers: migrated (0.2500s)
 =====================================================


c:\peter\flexiblerails\current\pomodo>
```

Confirm that the databases were created and the users table was created:

```
c:\peter\flexiblerails\current\pomodo>mysql -u root -p
Enter password: *******
Welcome to the MySQL monitor.  Commands end with ; or \g.
Your MySQL connection id is 6 to server version: 5.0.24-community-nt

Type 'help;' or '\h' for help. Type '\c' to clear the buffer.

mysql> show databases;
+--------------------+
| Database           |
+--------------------+
| information_schema |
| mysql              |
| pomodo_development |
| pomodo_production  |
| pomodo_test        |
| test               |
+--------------------+
6 rows in set (0.00 sec)

mysql>
```

So far, so good. Let's check that the pomodo_development database looks good:

```
mysql> use pomodo_development;
Database changed
mysql> show tables;
+-----------------------------+
| Tables_in_pomodo_development |
+-----------------------------+
| schema_info                 |
| users                       |
+-----------------------------+
2 rows in set (0.00 sec)

mysql> describe users;
+---------------------------+--------------+------+-----+---------+
| Field                     | Type         | Null | Key | Default |
+---------------------------+--------------+------+-----+---------+
| id                        | int(11)      | NO   | PRI | NULL    |
| login                     | varchar(255) | YES  |     | NULL    |
| email                     | varchar(255) | YES  |     | NULL    |
| first_name                | varchar(80)  | YES  |     | NULL    |
| last_name                 | varchar(80)  | YES  |     | NULL    |
| crypted_password          | varchar(40)  | YES  |     | NULL    |
| salt                      | varchar(40)  | YES  |     | NULL    |
| created_at                | datetime     | YES  |     | NULL    |
| updated_at                | datetime     | YES  |     | NULL    |
| remember_token            | varchar(255) | YES  |     | NULL    |
| remember_token_expires_at | datetime     | YES  |     | NULL    |
+---------------------------+--------------+------+-----+---------+
11 rows in set (0.01 sec)

mysql> select * from users;
Empty set (0.00 sec)
```

Looks good. Note that the "Extra" column isn't shown here for space considerations; all it shows is that the id column is auto_increment. Also note the first_name and last_name fields that we added. Furthermore, note that running the migration added an id field, which is the primary key—even though we didn't specify one in the migration. This was done because one of the principles of Rails is *convention over configuration*—and one of its conventions (which makes your life easier in Rails if you follow it) is to have a primary key called id.

But what is that schema_info table?

The short answer is that it was created by running the migration, and it has one field called version that stores the version of the database schema we're using:

```
mysql> describe schema_info;
+----------+----------+------+-----+----------+-------+
| Field    | Type     | Null | Key | Default  | Extra |
+----------+----------+------+-----+----------+-------+
| version  | int(11)  | YES  |     | NULL     |       |
+----------+----------+------+-----+----------+-------+
1 row in set (0.01 sec)

mysql> select * from schema_info;
+----------+
| version  |
+----------+
|        1 |
+----------+
1 row in set (0.00 sec)

mysql>
```

Currently, the version is 1. This lets the migration script know what version the database schema is currently at when you migrate to a different version.

Before we proceed, we should edit the User model to make the new `first_name` and `last_name` attributes mass-assignable from the `params` hash. (If that didn't make sense, don't worry—we'll cover it later.) Edit the `User` model as shown in listing 3.3.

Listing 3.3   app\models\user.rb

```
...
  # prevents a user from submitting a crafted form that bypasses
  # activation
  # anything else you want your user to change should be added
  # here.
  attr_accessible :login, :email, :password,
    :password_confirmation, :first_name, :last_name        ❶
...
```

We add the new `first_name` and `last_name` attributes ❶ to the same magic-sounding `attr_accessible` call as the other attributes. (The attribute names start with colons at the front because they're `Symbol`s; this too will be explained later.)

Next, we'll edit config\routes.rb to add the RESTful routes, as we were instructed to do by the generator.

3.4.3   Adding RESTful routes

Grab the code from the instructions that were output to the command line by the generator, and paste it in as shown in listing 3.4.

Listing 3.4   config\routes.rb

```
ActionController::Routing::Routes.draw do |map|
  # The priority is based upon order of creation:
  # first created -> highest priority.
...
  # Sample resource route (maps HTTP verbs to controller actions
  # automatically):
  #   map.resources :products              ① User
  map.resources :users        <            resource
  map.resource  :session      <        ② Session resource

  map.signup '/signup', :controller => 'users',    <  ③ Special signup URL
    :action => 'new'
  map.login  '/login', :controller => 'sessions',  <  ④ Special login URL
    :action => 'new'
  map.logout '/logout', :controller => 'sessions', <  ⑤ Special logout URL
    :action => 'destroy'

  # Sample resource route with options:
  #   map.resources :products,
  #     :member => { :short => :get, :toggle => :post },
  #     :collection => { :sold => :get }
...
end
```

The brief explanation of this is as follows: We're setting up RESTful resources for users ① and the session ② and adding some special routes to give pretty URLs for signup ③, login ④, and logout ⑤. Routing is complicated, and not something you learn in chapter 3 of a book—well, not this book, anyway!

Save the file. That's it for the routes for now. When looking through the files the generator produced for us *(always do this!)*, we saw some instructions in the Users-Controller and SessionsController that we need to follow. We'll do that now.

3.4.4   Modifying the includes and before_filter as instructed by the comments

First, we edit the SessionsController, as shown in listing 3.5.

Listing 3.5   app\controllers\sessions_controller.rb

```
  # This controller handles the login/logout function of the site.
  class SessionsController < ApplicationController
    # Be sure to include AuthenticationSystem in
    # Application Controller instead
    include AuthenticatedSystem     <  ① Deleted include
```

```
  # render new.rhtml
  def new
  end
...unchanged code omitted...
end
```

We delete ❶ the AuthenticatedSystem include.

Next, we edit the UsersController, as shown in listing 3.6.

Listing 3.6 app\controllers\users_controller.rb

```
class UsersController < ApplicationController
  # Be sure to include AuthenticationSystem in Application
  # Controller instead
  include AuthenticatedSystem      ⊲──❶ Deleted include

  # render new.rhtml
  def new
  end

  def create
    @user = User.new(params[:user])
    @user.save!
    self.current_user = @user
    redirect_back_or_default('/')
    flash[:notice] = "Thanks for signing up!"
  rescue ActiveRecord::RecordInvalid
    render :action => 'new'
  end

end
```

We delete ❶ the AuthenticatedSystem include here also.

Next, we add the include which we just deleted to the ApplicationController, as shown in listing 3.7.

Listing 3.7 app\controllers\application.rb

```
# Filters added to this controller apply to all controllers in
# the application. Likewise, all the methods added will be
# available for all controllers.

class ApplicationController < ActionController::Base
  helper :all # include all helpers, all the time
  include AuthenticatedSystem      ❶
```

```
# See ActionController::RequestForgeryProtection for details
# Uncomment the :secret if you're not using the cookie session
# store
# TODO - this will be uncommented once we explain sessions
# in iteration 5.
# protect_from_forgery          ❷
# :secret => 'dd92c128b5358a710545b5e755694d57'
end
```

By adding the include `AuthenticatedSystem` here ❶, we ensure that all controllers will include it by default (because they all extend `ApplicationController`). Furthermore, we *temporarily* comment out the `protect_from_forgery` call ❷ until iteration 5, because I don't want to talk about CSRF attacks before having explained what a session is. Also note that your :secret will be different than this one—otherwise it wouldn't be much of a :secret.

Continuing, we need to do as we're told by our test code (and per Geoffrey Grosenbach's screencast[3]) and add the include `AuthenticatedTestHelper` line to test\test_helper.rb (see listing 3.8 ❶) and remove it from `UserTest` (listing 3.9 ❷), `SessionsControllerTest` (listing 3.10 ❸), and `UsersController-Test` (listing 3.11 ❹).

Listing 3.8   test\test_helper.rb

```
ENV["RAILS_ENV"] = "test"
require File.expand_path(File.dirname(__FILE__) +
   "/../config/environment")
require 'test_help'

class Test::Unit::TestCase
   include AuthenticatedTestHelper          ❶
...
```

Listing 3.9   test\unit\user_test.rb

```
require File.dirname(__FILE__) + '/../test_helper'

class UserTest < Test::Unit::TestCase
   # Be sure to include AuthenticatedTestHelper in
   # test/test_helper.rb instead.
```

---

[3] http://peepcode.com/articles/2006/10/08/restful-rails, at 07:05 in the screencast (peepcode-003-rest.mov).

```
   # Then, you can remove it from this and the functional test.
   include AuthenticatedTestHelper          ❷
   fixtures :users

   def test_should_create_user
...
```

Listing 3.10   test\functional\sessions_controller_test.rb

```
require File.dirname(__FILE__) + '/../test_helper'
require 'sessions_controller'

# Re-raise errors caught by the controller.
class SessionsController; def rescue_action(e) raise e end; end

class SessionsControllerTest < Test::Unit::TestCase
   # Be sure to include AuthenticatedTestHelper in
   # test/test_helper.rb instead
   # Then, you can remove it from this and the units test.
   include AuthenticatedTestHelper          ❸

   fixtures :users
...
```

Listing 3.11   test\functional\users_controller_test.rb

```
require File.dirname(__FILE__) + '/../test_helper'
require 'users_controller'

# Re-raise errors caught by the controller.
class UsersController; def rescue_action(e) raise e end; end

class UsersControllerTest < Test::Unit::TestCase
   # Be sure to include AuthenticatedTestHelper in
   # test/test_helper.rb instead
   # Then, you can remove it from this and the units test.
   include AuthenticatedTestHelper          ❹

   fixtures :users
...
```

I won't talk much about testing in the book. However, we'll ensure that our tests all pass at the end of this iteration so we can *pretend* we're testing.

NOTE Testing is very important. The fact that I'm relegating it to a brief section in appendix B doesn't reflect my opinion on the importance of testing. Instead, it reflects my desire to make this book *enjoyable to read*. This isn't a book about testing; there are other books for that.

That's it for following along modifying generated code. Next, we'll test account creation using the HTML views.

3.4.5 *Testing account creation from HTML*

Even though this is a book about Flex and Rails together, it's useful to test Rails from HTML occasionally. (It's especially useful with tools like Firebug, in order to fake form values, and so on.) Now, we'll ensure that account creation and login work.

NOTE If you've left your server running since iteration 2, kill it with Ctrl-C. We modified config files, so we need to restart the server.

Start your server:

```
c:\peter\flexiblerails\current\pomodo>ruby script\server
=> Booting WEBrick...
=> Rails application started on http://0.0.0.0:3000
=> Ctrl-C to shutdown server; call with --help for options
```

Next, open a browser window, and go to http://localhost:3000/signup. Because we defined the following route in config\routes.rb

```
map.signup '/signup', :controller => 'users',
  :action => 'new'
```

this will trigger the new action of the UsersController (see listing 3.12).

Listing 3.12 app\controllers\users_controller.rb

```
class UsersController < ApplicationController
  # render new.rhtml            ❶
  def new
  end
...
```

This action is empty, so as the comment ❶ says, the new.rhtml file (shown in listing 3.13) is rendered.

Listing 3.13 app\views\users\new.rhtml

```
<%= error_messages_for :user %>
<% form_for :user, :url => users_path do |f| -%>
<p><label for="login">Login</label><br/>
<%= f.text_field :login %></p>
```

```
<p><label for="email">Email</label><br/>
<%= f.text_field :email %></p>

<p><label for="password">Password</label><br/>
<%= f.password_field :password %></p>

<p><label for="password_confirmation">Confirm Password</label><br/>
<%= f.password_field :password_confirmation %></p>

<p><%= submit_tag 'Sign up' %></p>
<% end -%>
```

We see the screen shown in figure 3.5.

Enter ludwig for the login, lvb@pomodo.com for the email, and foooo for the password and password confirmation.

Click Sign Up. We're taken to the Rails Welcome Aboard screen. This seems strange; the reason is that we haven't defined a default route, so the index.html file in the public directory (the Rails Welcome Aboard screen) is shown.

Let's check to see if our user was created:

```
mysql> select id, login, email, first_name, last_name from users;
+----+--------+----------------+------------+-----------+
| id | login  | email          | first_name | last_name |
+----+--------+----------------+------------+-----------+
|  1 | ludwig | lvb@pomodo.com | NULL       | NULL      |
+----+--------+----------------+------------+-----------+
1 row in set (0.00 sec)

mysql>
```

Hooray!

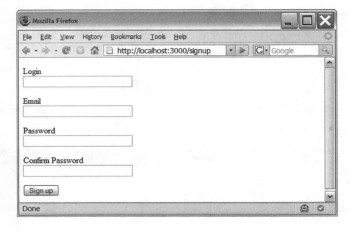

Figure 3.5
HTML signup screen

3.4.6 *Testing login from HTML*

Let's try logging in. Go to http://localhost:3000/login; we see the screen shown in figure 3.6.

Next, let's test that a bad login fails correctly. If we enter bogus data (either a wrong password for ludwig or a nonexistent user) and click Log In, the login screen is shown again, but the URL changes to http://localhost:3000/session for reasons I'll explain later (look in the `SessionsController` create method if you're curious); see figure 3.7.

If we log in as ludwig with the correct password, we're taken to the Welcome Aboard screen again. This gives us enough confidence in our login system to proceed with trying to log in from Flex.

We'll do this next.

Figure 3.6 HTML login screen

Figure 3.7 Failed HTML login

3.5 *Adding login functionality to Flex*

In this section, we'll add login functionality to Flex. Before we get ahead of ourselves, however, we should take some time to understand what exactly we did in our "Hello World" example earlier.

3.5.1 *"Hello World," this time with meaning!*

Let's revisit Pomodo.mxml and actually understand what is going on in the code this time. Recall that the running application currently looks as shown in figure 3.8.

**Figure 3.8
Pomodo, revisited**

The code currently looks like listing 3.14.

Listing 3.14   app\flex\Pomodo.mxml

```
<?xml version="1.0" encoding="utf-8"?>
<mx:Application          ❶
    xmlns:mx="http://www.adobe.com/2006/mxml"
    layout="vertical"          ❷
    backgroundGradientColors="[#ffffff, #c0c0c0]"          ❸
    width="100%"          ❹
    height="100%">          ❺
    <mx:HTTPService          ❻
        id="helloSvc"          ❼
        url="/hello/sayhello"          ❽
        method="POST"/>          ❾
    <mx:Button label="call hello service"
        click="helloSvc.send()"/>          ❿
    <mx:TextInput text="{helloSvc.lastResult}"/>          ⓫
</mx:Application>
```

Let's understand what this code is doing. First, look at the top-level tag: `mx:Application` ❶. The root of a Flex application is always an `Application`. The `mx:` part identifies the XML namespace[4] that the `Application` component is from. We use a vertical layout ❷ to make the components flow vertically. Other choices are horizontal (for horizontal flow) and absolute (where you specify the x,y of each top-level container). The `backgroundGradientColors` ❸ specify the start and end of the gradient fill for the background—and what Web 2.0 era application would be complete without a gradient fill?

The `HTTPService` ❻ makes a call to the `sayhello` method of the `HelloController`, due to the way Rails does routing. Simplistically, in the default routing, URLs are mapped /controller_name/action_name. The controller name is capitalized, and the Controller part is assumed, so /hello maps to `HelloController`, and sayhello maps to the sayhello action (which is a method); url="/hello/sayhello" ❽ maps to the sayhello method of the `HelloController` class. We aren't passing any parameters right now; you'll do this soon when you try to log in.

The id of the `HTTPService` is helloSvc ❼. In MXML, the id property of a component becomes its variable name (the MXML file is a class, and the id is the name of a global variable inside that class). If we don't provide an id for a component, Flex provides one for us—but then we don't know what it is, so we can't refer to

---

[4] We could have said `<foo:Application xmlns:foo="http://www.adobe.com/2006/mxml"` ..., but that would confuse every Flex coder on the planet, because `mx:` is the convention.

Figure 3.9
**Using absolute width and
height values** (`width="300"
height="100"`) **to set the
size of a Flex application**

the component in your code. Sometimes this is fine: We don't need to refer to the
`TextInput`, so we don't bother giving it an id. We need to give the `helloSvc`
`HTTPService` an id, though, so we can call its `send` method when the button's
`click` event is broadcast ❿ and so we can refer to the last result from this `HTTPS-`
`ervice` in the binding to the `text` property of the `TextInput` ⓫. Note that we
have to specify an HTTP method of `POST` ❾ because the default value of the
`method` property of `HTTPService` is `GET`. We'll talk a *lot* more about HTTP methods
in iteration 8.

Finally, the width ❹ and height ❺ of 100% specify the size of the Flex application relative to the size of the browser window. We can also use absolute values of
pixels; for example, `width="300" height="100"` looks like figure 3.9 below (note
the white background of the web page that the Flex application is in).

3.5.2 Binding? What the...?

Binding is a complicated topic that can be explained simplistically in one phrase:
"It automagically copies the value of variable `x` into variable `y` whenever `x`
changes." However, binding needs a much more detailed treatment to be fully
understood. See the *Flex 3 Developer's Guide* in the Flex 3 Beta 2 documentation zip
file for the full treatment; here we'll summarize it. The curly braces in
`text="{helloSvc.lastResult}"` (⓫ in listing 3.14) code indicate a binding—
that is, the value of `helloSvc.lastResult` should be copied into `resultTI.text`
whenever it changes.

> **NOTE** Not all variables can be used as a source of a binding: To be the source,
> the variable must be `Bindable`. This was new in Flex 2 (and is still true in
> Flex 3)—in Flex 1.5 and below you could essentially use anything as the
> source of a binding, but some things wouldn't work. (Yes, I'm oversimpli-
> fying—trust me, you don't want the details. Ever.)

Anyway, binding can be done with an `<mx:Binding>` element as well as with the
shorter curly-brace syntax. The code in listing 3.15 is equivalent to the original
Pomodo.mxml. (Don't make this change, though—or, if you do, revert it after testing it.)

Listing 3.15 app\flex\Pomodo.mxml

```
<?xml version="1.0" encoding="utf-8"?>
<mx:Application
    xmlns:mx="http://www.adobe.com/2006/mxml"
    layout="vertical"
    backgroundGradientColors="[#ffffff, #c0c0c0]"
    width="100%"
    height="100%">
    <mx:HTTPService
        id="helloSvc"
        url="/hello/sayhello"
        method="POST"/>
    <mx:Button label="call hello service"
        click="helloSvc.send()"/>
    <mx:Button label="call hello service" click="helloSvc.send()"/>
    <mx:TextInput id="resultTI"/>            ❶
    <mx:Binding source="String(helloSvc.lastResult)"
        destination="resultTI.text"/>        ❷
</mx:Application>
```

Note that we had to give the `TextInput` ❶ an id so we could refer to it in the `destination` property of the binding ❷. Also, note that we have to cast the source to a `String`, whereas we don't have to do that with the curly brace syntax.

3.5.3 *This MXML looks strange*

Yes, MXML looks different the first time you see it—even if you're used to XML. One thing to keep in mind is that setting an attribute can mean different things. For example, consider the following `Button` (this is legal MXML if the other functions and variables exist):

```
<mx:Button id="bar" label="foo"
    enabled="{someFunctionThatReturnsBoolean(someArg, someOtherArg)}"
    color="#CCDDEE" click="doSomething()"/>
```

A lot is going on here:

- The `Button` is being created with an `id` of `bar`, instead of an automatically assigned `id`.

- The `label` property of the `Button` is being set to `"foo"`.

- The `enabled` property of the `Button` is being bound to the result of the function `someFunctionThatReturnsBoolean` that will automatically be called whenever either of `someArg` or `someOtherArg` changes. (This assumes that `someArg` and `someOtherArg` are `Bindable`.)

- The `color` style of the `Button` is being set to #CCDDEE.

- An event handler is being created to handle the `click` event. When that event is dispatched, the `doSomething()` method will be called.

A simple attribute assignment in MXML can be a static (for example, a `String`) or dynamic (such as a `Binding`) property setting, a style setting, or an event-handler assignment. What is amazing is that this quickly begins to feel natural. (I'm not sure if this is a testament to Flex, to the human mind in general, or to the mind of the programmer in particular. Trust me: It becomes second nature.) Furthermore, the Flex API docs are good about identifying what something is (properties, styles, and so on are grouped together).

3.5.4 *Flex 3 documentation? Where?*

The Flex 3 Beta 2 documentation zip file is currently available for download at http://download.macromedia.com/pub/labs/air/air_b2_docs_flex_100107.zip. Note that when Flex 3 is out of beta, the documentation will presumably be moved to http://www.adobe.com/support/documentation/en/flex/. Currently (in November 2007) this URL still has Flex 2 documentation, because that is the most current production release of Flex.

Download and unzip the file. It contains a wealth of well-written information about Flex, in the form of both PDF (of course) manuals and API docs that are like the Java API docs.

The PDFs listing in table 3.1 are contained in the documentation zip file.

Table 3.1 Flex documentation

File name	Number of pages	Document name
flex3_buildanddeploy.pdf	260	Building and Deploying Flex Applications
flex3_createextendcomponents.pdf	177	Creating and Extending Flex Components
flex3_devguide.pdf	1435	Flex 3 Developer's Guide
flex3_usingflexbuilder.pdf	219	Using Flex Builder
programmingas3.pdf	576	Programming ActionScript 3.0
air_devappsflex.pdf	304	Developing AIR Applications with Adobe Flex

This is a total of 2,971 pages! Luckily, the documentation is also searchable from within Flex Builder 3 via Help > Help Contents.

The API docs are in the langref folder. Open the index.html file, and bookmark it or set it as your homepage. (I find it helpful to have this and the Rails API docs in tabs that automatically open when I start Firefox.)

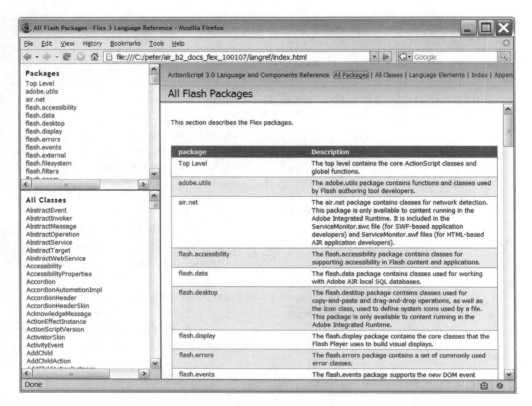

Figure 3.10   The Flex 3 API documentation

Figure 3.10 shows the API docs, so you know you're looking at what I'm referring to.

Knowing what you know now, let's try to create accounts and log in from Flex. We'll start by properly stubbing out a UI. This is going to get interesting.

3.5.5   *Stubbing out an account-creation and login UI in Flex*

Although it's possible to create an entire Flex application in one MXML file, this works only for the most trivial of applications (that is, toy examples such as the one-button pomodo above). We're not building a toy example in this book, however, so there's no reason for us to start as though we are—all this leads to is a pile of tedious refactoring, sooner rather than later.

So, we'll start building components from the outset. We'll put these components in a package called com.pomodo.components. ActionScript 3 uses the same "backwards domain name" convention as Java, so we'll create a com\pomodo\components directory inside app\flex. The app\flex\com\pomodo\components folder is where we'll store our reusable MXML and ActionScript components.

NOTE ActionScript 3 supports packages with fewer restrictions than it did in ActionScript 2. It also supports namespaces. There are many details about what you can and can't do with classes, packages, and namespaces; we'll keep things simple and use the "one class per file" and "package in its folder" approach because it's the most straightforward and familiar to Java programmers.)

We'll also create an assets directory in com\pomodo\assets to store images, and so on. Create the directories in app\flex as follows:

```
c:\peter\flexiblerails\current\pomodo>cd app\flex

C:\peter\flexiblerails\current\pomodo\app\flex>mkdir com

C:\peter\flexiblerails\current\pomodo\app\flex>mkdir com\pomodo

C:\peter\flexiblerails\current\pomodo\app\flex>mkdir com\pomodo\assets

C:\peter\flexiblerails\current\pomodo\app\flex>mkdir com\pomodo\components
```

We'll create two components: AccountCreateBox (where users create new accounts) and LoginBox (where users log in). We'll start with AccountCreateBox (see listing 3.16).

Listing 3.16   app\flex\com\pomodo\components\AccountCreateBox.mxml

```xml
<?xml version="1.0" encoding="utf-8"?>
<mx:VBox xmlns:mx="http://www.adobe.com/2006/mxml" width="100%"         ❶
    height="100%" label="Create Account">
    <mx:Form labelWidth="150">              ❷  mx:Form: a layout tool
        <mx:FormItem required="true" label="Username">
            <mx:TextInput id="loginTI"/>        ❹              ❸  Displays
        </mx:FormItem>                                              red asterisk
        <mx:FormItem required="true" label="Email Address">
            <mx:TextInput id="emailTI"/>
        </mx:FormItem>
        <mx:FormItem label="First Name">
            <mx:TextInput id="firstNameTI"/>
        </mx:FormItem>
        <mx:FormItem label="Last Name">
            <mx:TextInput id="lastNameTI"/>
        </mx:FormItem>
        <mx:FormItem required="true" label="Password">        ❺
            <mx:TextInput id="passwordTI"
                displayAsPassword="true"/>
        </mx:FormItem>                            ❻  Shows asterisks,
                                                    not text
```

```
            <mx:FormItem required="true" label="Confirm Password">
                <mx:TextInput id="confirmPasswordTI"
                    displayAsPassword="true"/>
            </mx:FormItem>
            <mx:FormItem>
                <mx:Button id="createAccountButton"        ❼
                    label="Create Account"/>
            </mx:FormItem>
        </mx:Form>
    </mx:VBox>
```

The root of `AccountCreateBox` is a `VBox` ❶, so that's what we're subclassing. A `VBox` lays out its children vertically; hence the *V*. We then create a `Form` ❷, which contains various `FormItems` (for example, ❸). Note that unlike forms in HTML, the `<mx:Form>` (and `<mx:FormItem>`) tags are *purely layout tools*.

NOTE   Let me emphasize this, because this is one of the most common misconceptions for developers coming to Flex from HTML: *Nothing* special happens because the fields are in an `mx:Form`. A `Form` is just a layout container—it's 100% about appearance, 0% about functionality.

These `FormItems` (for example, ❺) contain various controls, mostly `mx:Text-Inputs` for login ❹, email, first and last name, password ❻, and password confirmation. The `createAccountButton` ❼ is also inside a `FormItem`. This `FormItem` specifies no label property, though, so it defaults to the empty string. Note that many of the `FormItems` have `required="true"` (for example, ❸). This has no effect other than to add a red asterisk (*) beside the form field.

NOTE   This red asterisk is *just a visual cue* to the user. To make a `FormItem` behave as required, you need to use validation. We'll look at validation soon. For now, note that the value of required has *no effect* on its child components.

Finally, note the use of `displayAsPassword="true"` on `passwordTI` ❻ and `confirmPasswordTI`. This makes the `TextInput` display asterisks (*) instead of showing the letters typed.

Next, create the `LoginBox` (listing 3.17).

Listing 3.17   app\flex\com\pomodo\components\LoginBox.mxml

```
<?xml version="1.0" encoding="utf-8"?>
<mx:VBox xmlns:mx="http://www.adobe.com/2006/mxml" width="100%"   ❶
    height="100%" label="Login">          ❷
    <mx:Form labelWidth="150">
        <mx:FormItem required="true" label="Username">       ❸
            <mx:TextInput id="loginTI"/>
```

```
        </mx:FormItem>
        <mx:FormItem required="true" label="Password">          ❹
            <mx:TextInput id="passwordTI"
                displayAsPassword="true"/>
        </mx:FormItem>
        <mx:FormItem>              ❺
            <mx:Button id="loginButton" label="Login"/>
        </mx:FormItem>
    </mx:Form>
</mx:VBox>
```

This is another `VBox` ❶ containing a `Form` ❷, with `FormItems` containing a `Text-Input` for login ❸, password ❹, and a login button ❺.

Next, get the logo_md.png image from http://www.flexiblerails.com/files/logo_md.png (right-click the image, and choose Save Image As), and save it to the app\flex\com\pomodo\assets directory.

Also, delete the hello_controller—we're getting beyond "Hello World" now. Finally, modify Pomodo.mxml (see listing 3.18).

Listing 3.18   app\flex\Pomodo.mxml

```
<?xml version="1.0" encoding="utf-8"?>
<mx:Application
    xmlns:mx="http://www.adobe.com/2006/mxml"
    xmlns:pom="com.pomodo.components.*"              ❶
    layout="vertical"
    backgroundGradientColors="[#ffffff, #c0c0c0]"
    horizontalAlign="center"              ❷
    verticalAlign="top"              ❸
    width="100%"
    height="100%">
<mx:Script>              ❹
<![CDATA[              ❺
    [Bindable]              ❻
    private var _reviews:String =              ❼
        '"pomodo, the hot new RIA by 38noises, is taking ' +
        'over Web 2.0." --Michael Arrington*\n"I wish I\'d ' +
        'invested in 38noises instead of that other company."' +
        ' --Jeff Bezos*\n"38noises closed angel funding at a ' +
        'party in my bathroom last night." --Om Malik*';
    ]]>
</mx:Script>
    <mx:Image source="com/pomodo/assets/logo_md.png" />              ❽
    <mx:Label              ❾
        text="The simple, GTD-style TODO list application."/>
    <mx:Spacer height="10"/>              ❿
    <mx:Text width="500" text="{_reviews}"/>              ⓫
```

```
    <mx:Spacer height="10"/>         ⑫
    <mx:Accordion width="400" height="300">        ⑬
        <pom:AccountCreateBox/>       ⑭
        <pom:LoginBox/>     ⑮
    </mx:Accordion>
    <mx:Label text="*did not say this, but might someday!"/>      ⑯
    <mx:HTTPService          ⑰
        id="helloSvc"
        url="/hello/sayhello"
        method="POST"/>
    <mx:Button label="call hello service"
        click="helloSvc.send()"/>       ⑱
    <mx:TextInput text="{helloSvc.lastResult}"/>        ⑲
</mx:Application>
```

We start by adding a new XML namespace pom for our custom components in com.pomodo.components ❶. We then set the horizontal and vertical alignment to center ❷ and top ❸ respectively. This affects the alignment of all the components that are directly contained in the Application.

Next, we're inlining ❹ ActionScript 3 code for the first time. The <![CDATA[❺ and]]> is essential inside the <mx:Script> tag (so you can type code instead of XML), so Flex Builder adds it for you after you type <mx:Script>. Currently, there is just a variable (var) called _reviews ❼ which holds some static reviews as a stub for a service call that would show reviews. This variable is the source of a data binding ⑪, so we need to mark it with the [Bindable] annotation ❻. (If this was a real constant instead of a stub, we would use const rather than var, and not use [Bindable] because constants don't change.)

Now, we add an mx:Image ❽ for our spiffy logo, an mx:Label ❾ containing our slogan, and a couple mx:Spacers ❿ ⑫ around an mx:Text whose text attribute ⑪ is bound to the _reviews variable containing our fake reviews ❼. It's nice to see some fake quotes from various industry luminaries, to motivate ourselves to ship the app and as placeholders for the *real* (obviously gushing) quotes that will surely start pouring in once we launch. Furthermore, in keeping with the Web 2.0 spirit, we need a name for our fake company, as well as for our fake product. In honor of the "me too" aspect of what we're doing, the name we'll use for our company is 38noises. (Yep, always one for the cheap laugh.)

Next, we create an Accordion ⑬ (always good for style points) that holds the two custom components: pom:AccountCreateBox ⑭ and pom:LoginBox ⑮. Note that in the components (❶ in each of the earlier listings), we set the label properties to Create Account and Login—the label property is used by the Accordion to determine the label to show on the navigator buttons (accordion headers). Finally, we add our disclaimer ⓰ Label, and delete the old code ⓱⓲⓳.

To build, select the pomodo project in the navigator, and choose Project > Clean from the menu bar (see figure 3.11).

Leave Start a Build Immediately selected, and click OK.

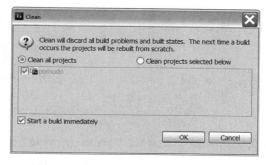

Figure 3.11   Doing a clean build in Flex Builder

TIP We need to do a clean build here to ensure that Flex Builder detects the logo image we added to the source tree, so that Flex Builder will copy it (and the com\pomodo\assets path) to the public\bin directory as part of the build. If you don't do this, you may see a missing image instead of the logo.

Command-line users: Create the com\pomodo\assets directory tree under public\bin, and copy the logo_md.png file there.

Now that our build is done, go to http://localhost:3000/bin/Pomodo.html (see figure 3.12).

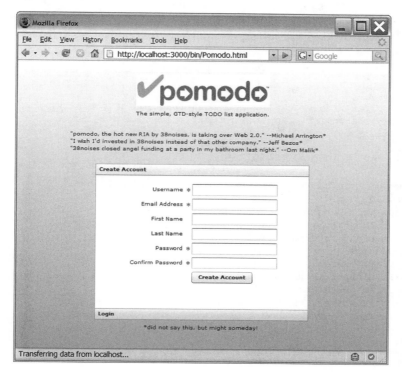

Figure 3.12
The splash screen

Not bad as far as book code goes. We have a Web 2.0–style logo with the obligatory pastel green, a sexy Accordion for account creation and login (click the Login accordion button to see the login form smoothly scroll into view), a gradient fill, fake quotes, the works. Note that the Forms in the AccountCreateBox and Login-Box both set their labelWidth properties to 150. This is done so they line up nicely, which looks better when switching views in the Accordion. It's the little things like that which will get us acquired.

3.5.6 *Making account create and login functional*

If we *are* going to get acquired, I suppose we had better at least implement account create and login from Flex. We'd like to do it RESTfully, because we're using the restful_authentication generator. Also, that's what the cool kids are doing, and we figure it should add another million or so to our valuation. Problem is, *we don't understand what the heck REST is yet.* So, we'll pass for now and refactor the code later once we do know.

We'll start by adding methods that talk to Flex to SessionsController and UsersController. First, SessionsController; see listing 3.19.

NOTE Listing 3.19 shows code written in a way that we would never write in Rails: It creates a second method called create_xml instead of using respond_to. I'm doing this because I haven't explained REST yet; once I do explain REST, I'll obviously refactor this. Advanced Rails users, just hold your nose and follow along.

Listing 3.19 app\controllers\sessions_controller.rb

```
# This controller handles the login/logout function of the site.
class SessionsController < ApplicationController
  # render new.rhtml
  def new
  end

  # Once we explain REST in the book this will obviously be
  # refactored.
  def create_xml          ❶
    self.current_user =
      User.authenticate(params[:login], params[:password])
    if logged_in?
      if params[:remember_me] == "1"
        self.current_user.remember_me
        cookies[:auth_token] = {
          :value => self.current_user.remember_token,
          :expires => self.current_user.remember_token_expires_at
        }
      end
```

```
        render :xml => self.current_user.to_xml      ❷
      else
        render :text => "badlogin"      ❸
      end
    end

  def create      ❹
...
```

We create a new method called `create_xml` ❶ in the `SessionsController`. It's a copy-paste-modify of the `create` method ❹ which was created for us. (We don't worry about refactoring the duplicated code out into a method, because we know we'll be refactoring this later when we convert to REST.) Upon successful login, we render XML of the `current_user` ❷. If the login fails, we render the text "badlogin" ❸.

Next, we edit `UsersController` as shown in listing 3.20.

Listing 3.20   app\controllers\users_controller.rb

```
class UsersController < ApplicationController
  # render new.rhtml
  def new
  end

  # Once we explain REST in the book this will obviously be
  # refactored.
  def create_xml      ❶
    @user = User.new(params[:user])
    @user.save!
    self.current_user = @user
    render :xml => @user.to_xml      ❷
  rescue ActiveRecord::RecordInvalid      ❸
    render :text => "error"
  end

  def create      ❹
...
```

We create a new method called `create_xml` ❶ in the `UsersController`. Again, it's a copy-paste-modify of the `create` method ❹ that was created for us. (Similarly, this duplication will be refactored away when we convert to REST.) Upon successful creation of a new user, we render the XML of the `current_user` ❷. If the user creation fails, we render the text "error" ❸.

Having added these `create_xml` methods, let's use them from Flex. We need to modify `AccountCreateBox` and `LoginBox`. First, `AccountCreateBox`; see listing 3.21.

Listing 3.21 app\flex\com\pomodo\components\AccountCreateBox.mxml

```
<?xml version="1.0" encoding="utf-8"?>
<mx:VBox xmlns:mx="http://www.adobe.com/2006/mxml" width="100%"
    height="100%" label="Create Account">
<mx:Metadata>                              ①  Declare Metadata for custom event
    [Event(name="accountCreate",
           type="com.pomodo.events.AccountCreateEvent")]
</mx:Metadata>
<mx:Script>
<![CDATA[                                   ②  Import works
    import mx.controls.Alert;                  as in Java
    import mx.rpc.events.ResultEvent;
    import com.pomodo.events.AccountCreateEvent;

    private function createAccount():void {    ③
        svcAccountCreate.send();
    }

    private function handleAccountCreateResult(  ④
    event:ResultEvent):void {
        var result:Object = event.result;
        if (result == "error") {
            Alert.show("Your account was not created.",
                "Error");
        } else {
            dispatchEvent(new AccountCreateEvent(XML(result)));
        }
    }
]]>
</mx:Script>
    <mx:HTTPService          ⑤
        id="svcAccountCreate"
        url="/users/create_xml"
        contentType="application/xml"
        resultFormat="e4x"
        method="POST"
        result="handleAccountCreateResult(event)">
        <mx:request>
            <user>
                <login>{loginTI.text}</login>
                <email>{emailTI.text}</email>
                <first_name>{firstNameTI.text}</first_name>
                <last_name>{lastNameTI.text}</last_name>
                <password>{passwordTI.text}</password>
                <password_confirmation>
                    {confirmPasswordTI.text}
                </password_confirmation>
            </user>
        </mx:request>
    </mx:HTTPService>
    <mx:Form labelWidth="150">
```

```
        <mx:FormItem required="true" label="Username">
            <mx:TextInput id="loginTI"/>
        </mx:FormItem>
        <mx:FormItem required="true" label="Email Address">
            <mx:TextInput id="emailTI"/>
        </mx:FormItem>
        <mx:FormItem label="First Name">
            <mx:TextInput id="firstNameTI"/>
        </mx:FormItem>
        <mx:FormItem label="Last Name">
            <mx:TextInput id="lastNameTI"/>
        </mx:FormItem>
        <mx:FormItem required="true" label="Password">
            <mx:TextInput id="passwordTI"
                displayAsPassword="true"/>
        </mx:FormItem>
        <mx:FormItem required="true" label="Confirm Password">
            <mx:TextInput id="confirmPasswordTI"
                displayAsPassword="true"/>
        </mx:FormItem>
        <mx:FormItem>
            <mx:Button id="createAccountButton"
                label="Create Account"
                click="createAccount()"/>          ❻
        </mx:FormItem>
    </mx:Form>
</mx:VBox>
```

We start at the end, modifying the `createAccountButton` to call a function called `createAccount` ❻ when it's clicked. (See, we're adding an inline event handler for a `click` event and hardly thinking twice—I told you MXML becomes second nature!) Next, we add this `createAccount` function ❸ inside an `<mx:Script>` block. It calls the `send` function of an `HTTPService` called `svcAccountCreate` ❺. Doing this invokes the service with the properties that have been set on it, both statically and via bindings.

Let's look at the properties of `svcAccountCreate`. We set its `url` property to `/users/create_xml`, which means that calling this service invokes the newly created `create_xml` method of the `UsersController`. We set the `contentType` property to `application/xml`, meaning that we're sending the request as XML. We set the `resultFormat` property to `e4x`, meaning that the "value returned is XML and is returned as literal XML in an ActionScript XML object, which can be accessed using ECMAScript for XML (E4X) expressions."[5] (Basically, you use E4X[6]

---

[5] http://livedocs.adobe.com/flex/2/langref/mx/rpc/http/HTTPService.html#resultFormat.

[6] See the Flex documentation and also http://life.neophi.com/danielr/2006/04/flex_2_beta_2_actionscript_3_a.html for a good introduction to E4X.

to access the result.) We specify the HTTP method to be POST, and we specify that the result event is handled by the handleAccountCreateResult method. Finally, we set the request property of svcAccountCreate to an XML document whose root is user and whose child nodes are bound from the various controls in the form.

What's going on is subtle: When we call the service, we set the request property. Because the request property is XML, we define the value of the XML as the child of the request element. If we didn't like that approach, we could have also said request="{someXMLVar}" to bind the value of someXMLVar into the request.

Once the service returns, the result triggers the handleAccountCreateResult event handler. Inside it, we access the event.result. If it's the text *error*, we show an Alert dialog displaying a terse error message. Otherwise, we assume success, so we dispatch a new event called AccountCreateEvent with the result, cast to XML. The XML(result) cast is necessary because the user variable is typed in the Event.

NOTE   In ActionScript 3, XML is a native type like Number and doesn't need to be imported.

At the top of the file, we declare some custom mx:Metadata ❶ that declares that we're broadcasting an event whose name is accountCreate and whose type is com.pomodo.events.AccountCreateEvent. Doing this lets us handle the event nicely from the component that uses the AccountCreateBox (we'll see this momentarily).

Finally, note the import statements ❷: These work just as they do in Java. The asterisk (*) syntax is supported to import a package, but it isn't recommended because it may lead to unnecessary classes being imported, which leads to larger SWF file sizes and slower load times. (Use it only if you're sure you want to use every class from a package, now and in the future.)

Speaking of the AccountCreateEvent, let's create it now. Create an events directory in app\flex\com\pomodo (if you're using Flex Builder, you can right-click the com\pomodo folder and choose New > Folder), and add the new AccountCreateEvent as shown in listing 3.22.

Listing 3.22   app\flex\com\pomodo\events\AccountCreateEvent.as

```
package com.pomodo.events {
    import flash.events.Event;

    public class AccountCreateEvent extends Event {        ❶
        public static const ACCOUNT_CREATE:String =
            "accountCreate";        ❷
```

```
        public var user:XML;          ❸

        public function AccountCreateEvent(user:XML) {     ❹
            super(ACCOUNT_CREATE);      ❺
            this.user = user;        ❻
        }
    }
}
```

This is our first ActionScript 3 class. (Well, not really: MXML is actually turned into ActionScript. However, it's the first one we have created *ourselves*.) It's a lot simpler, too: AccountCreateEvent extends flash.events.Event ❶, which is the base class for all events. It defines an ACCOUNT_CREATE constant ❷ for the name of the Event. Note that this is the same name we declared we were broadcasting in the Metadata in AccountCreateBox—this isn't an accident. Next, we declare a public var for the user and set its type to be XML ❸. In the constructor ❹, we take the XML for the user as a parameter. We first call the superclass constructor with the name of the Event ❺, and then we use the XML we received to set ❻ the user instance variable we defined ❸.

Next, we modify the LoginBox (see listing 3.23).

Listing 3.23   app\flex\com\pomodo\components\LoginBox.mxml

```
<?xml version="1.0" encoding="utf-8"?>
<mx:VBox xmlns:mx="http://www.adobe.com/2006/mxml" width="100%"
    height="100%" label="Login">
<mx:Metadata>    ❶
    [Event(name="login", type="com.pomodo.events.LoginEvent")]     ❷
</mx:Metadata>
<mx:Script>
<![CDATA[
    import mx.controls.Alert;
    import mx.rpc.events.ResultEvent;
    import com.pomodo.events.LoginEvent;

    private function login():void {     ❸
        svcAccountLogin.send(      ❹
            {login: loginTI.text, password: passwordTI.text});
    }

    private function handleAccountLoginResult(     ❺
    event:ResultEvent):void {
        var result:Object = event.result;     ❻
        if (result == "badlogin") {     ❼
            Alert.show("The username or password is wrong.",     ❽
                "Login Error");
```

```
            } else {
                dispatchEvent(new LoginEvent(XML(result)));      ⑨
            }
        }
    ]]>
    </mx:Script>
        <mx:HTTPService
            id="svcAccountLogin"          ⑩
            url="/sessions/create_xml"         ⑪
            resultFormat="e4x"          ⑫
            method="POST"          ⑬
            result="handleAccountLoginResult(event)"/>       ⑭
        <mx:Form labelWidth="150">
            <mx:FormItem required="true" label="Username">
                <mx:TextInput id="loginTI"/>
            </mx:FormItem>
            <mx:FormItem required="true" label="Password">
                <mx:TextInput id="passwordTI"
                    displayAsPassword="true"/>
            </mx:FormItem>
            <mx:FormItem>
                <mx:Button id="loginButton" label="Login"
                    click="login()"/>          ⑮
            </mx:FormItem>
        </mx:Form>
    </mx:VBox>
```

These changes are similar to what we just did with AccountCreateBox. First, we declare some Metadata ❶, which declares a custom Event ❷ of type LoginEvent (which we'll create momentarily). Next, we create a login ❸ function that invokes a svcAccountLogin HTTPService by calling its send method ❹. Note that we're passing the parameters to svcAccountLogin as an anonymous object (essentially a hash) ❹, whose fields are defined inside the {}. This anonymous object functions as a dictionary, like a hash in Ruby or a HashMap in Java. In Action-Script 3, you can create anonymous objects like this. This practice was more common in ActionScript 2; in ActionScript 3, it's recommended that you type your objects. (The fact that curly braces are also used for bindings can be confusing to newcomers—especially if you put anonymous objects inside bindings!)

TIP   The ActionScript 3 syntax for an anonymous object is {key1: value1, key2: value2, ...}, whereas the Ruby syntax for a hash is {key1 => value1, key2 => value2, ...}. Don't forget what language you're coding in—because I learned ActionScript before Ruby, I tend to want to use colons in my Ruby hashes!

Note that when you do svcAccountLogin.send() ❹, Flex translates the anonymous object into proper HTTP POST data (you can look at what Rails receives in log\development.log). Next, we define a function handleAccountLoginResult ❺ that takes a ResultEvent, gets its result property ❻, and shows an Alert ❽ if it's "badlogin" ❼ or dispatches a custom LoginEvent ❾ containing the result otherwise. We define the svcAccountLogin ❿, setting its URL ⓫ to "/sessions/ create_xml", which means that the create_xml action of the SessionsController will be invoked. We specify the resultFormat of "e4x" ⓬ and an HTTPMethod of POST ⓭, and we hook up the result handler ⓮. Note that because we don't specify the contentType, it defaults to "application/x-www-form-urlencoded". This is a normal HTTP POST: key-value pairs. This is why we pass an anonymous object in the send call ❹.

Next, we create the LoginEvent (see listing 3.24).

Listing 3.24   app\flex\com\pomodo\events\LoginEvent.as

```
package com.pomodo.events {
    import flash.events.Event;

    public class LoginEvent extends Event {          ❶
        public static const LOGIN:String = "login";      ❷

        public var user:XML;          ❸

        public function LoginEvent(user:XML) {          ❹
            super(LOGIN);          ❺
            this.user = user;          ❻
        }
    }
}
```

This is a copy-paste-modify of the AccountCreateEvent. The numbers match the previous explanation, so there's no need to go over this again. All we're doing is specifying a different event name (login).

Now that we have defined our custom events and built the custom components to call HTTPServices that talk to the Rails controllers, all we have left to do is to modify Pomodo.mxml. Let's do that now; see listing 3.25.

Listing 3.25   app\flex\Pomodo.mxml

```
<?xml version="1.0" encoding="utf-8"?>
<mx:Application
    xmlns:mx="http://www.adobe.com/2006/mxml"
    xmlns:pom="com.pomodo.components.*"
    layout="vertical"
```

```
        backgroundGradientColors="[#ffffff, #c0c0c0]"
        horizontalAlign="center"
        verticalAlign="top"
        width="100%"
        height="100%">
<mx:Script>
<![CDATA[
    import com.pomodo.events.AccountCreateEvent;          ❶
    import com.pomodo.events.LoginEvent;

    [Bindable]
    private var _reviews:String =
        '"pomodo, the hot new RIA by 38noises, is taking ' +
        'over Web 2.0." --Michael Arrington*\n"I wish I\'d ' +
        'invested in 38noises instead of that other company."' +
        ' --Jeff Bezos*\n"38noises closed angel funding at a ' +
        'party in my bathroom last night." --Om Malik*';
    ]]>

    private function handleAccountCreate(e:AccountCreateEvent):    ❷
    void {
        showMain();
    }

    private function handleLogin(e:LoginEvent):void {     ❸
        showMain();
    }

    private function showMain():void {     ❹
        mainStack.selectedChild = mainBox;
    }
]]>
</mx:Script>
    <mx:ViewStack id="mainStack" width="100%" height="100%">     ❺
        <mx:VBox id="splashBox" horizontalAlign="center"     ❻
            verticalAlign="middle" width="100%" height="100%">
            <mx:Image source="com/pomodo/assets/logo_md.png"/>
<mx:Label text="The simple, GTD-style TODO list application."/>
            <mx:Spacer height="10"/>
            <mx:Text width="500" text="{_reviews}"/>
            <mx:Spacer height="10"/>
            <mx:Accordion width="400" height="300">
                <pom:AccountCreateBox
                    accountCreate="handleAccountCreate(event)"/>     ❼
                <pom:LoginBox login="handleLogin(event)"/>     ❽
            </mx:Accordion>
<mx:Label text="*did not say this, but might someday!"/>
        </mx:VBox>
        <pom:MainBox id="mainBox"/>     ❾
    </mx:ViewStack>
</mx:Application>
```

We start by importing our new events ❶. Next, we create functions to handle the
accountCreate ❼ and login ❽ events: handleAccountCreate ❷ and handle-
Login ❸.

TIP   If you define your events first and add the mx:Metadata annotations,
      Flex Builder will autosuggest your events along with the standard Flex
      events. This is a good sanity check that you're doing things correctly.

Both of these functions call the showMain ❹ function, which sets the selected-
Child of the new ViewStack we're creating called mainStack ❺ to be the main-
Box ❾. (We'll create the MainBox class momentarily.) Note that we move the
various other items inside a new VBox called splashBox ❻. This way, when the
mainStack selectedChild switches, everything is hidden.

Create the MainBox, which for now is a stub; see listing 3.26.

Listing 3.26   app\flex\com\pomodo\components\MainBox.mxml

```xml
<?xml version="1.0" encoding="utf-8"?>
<mx:VBox xmlns:mx="http://www.adobe.com/2006/mxml"
    width="100%" height="100%" backgroundColor="#FFFFFF">
    <mx:Label text="TODO"/>
</mx:VBox>
```

Let's see if it works. Rebuild and reload. We see the same screen as before, as
shown in figure 3.13—so far, so good. Click the Login accordion button, and
enter a Username of ludwig and a Password of foooo.

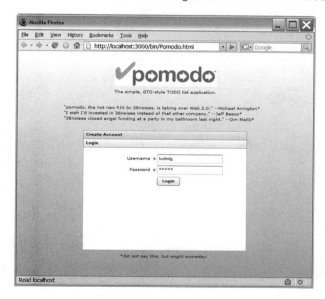

Figure 3.13
Filling in the login form

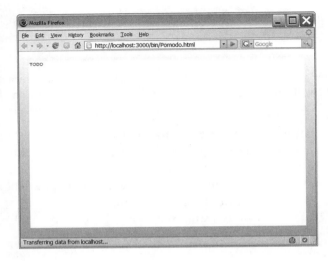

Figure 3.14
Logged in

Click the Login button. You see the screen shown in figure 3.14.

Hooray!

Now, let's test account creation. Go to http://localhost:3000/bin/Pomodo.html again, and create a new user with Username `peter`, Email Address `peter@pomodo.com`, First Name `Peter`, Last Name `Armstrong`, and Password `foooo` (see figure 3.15).

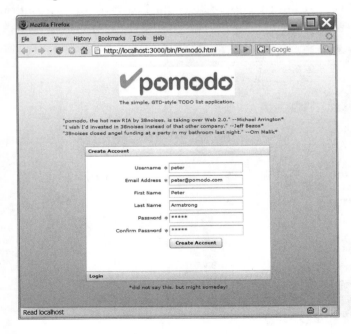

Figure 3.15
Creating an account

Click Create Account. We see the same TODO screen shown in figure 3.12, on page 79, as we did when logging in.

Before we get too excited, however, there are a couple loose ends to tidy up. First, the screen as shown in figure 3.12 shows the MainBox not extending the full size of the browser—we still see about 10 pixels of our gradient fill. Now, I like gradient fills as much as the next Web 2.0 developer, but before we declare this a feature, we have to admit that this isn't what we had intended. Let's fix this bug. Also, while we're at it, we should do a small refactoring and extract the splashBox stuff into its own custom component, and make a couple of minor layout tweaks. We'll do this first, as shown in listing 3.27.

Listing 3.27 app\flex\com\pomodo\components\SplashBox.mxml

```
<?xml version="1.0" encoding="utf-8"?>
<mx:VBox xmlns:mx="http://www.adobe.com/2006/mxml"
    xmlns:pom="com.pomodo.components.*"
    horizontalAlign="center" verticalAlign="top"
    width="100%" height="100%">
<mx:Metadata>                          ❶
    [Event(name="accountCreate",          ❷
        type="com.pomodo.events.AccountCreateEvent")]
    [Event(name="login", type="com.pomodo.events.LoginEvent")]    ❸
</mx:Metadata>
<mx:Script>
<![CDATA[
    import com.pomodo.events.AccountCreateEvent;
    import com.pomodo.events.LoginEvent;

    [Bindable]
    private var _reviews:String =
        '"pomodo, the hot new RIA by 38noises, is taking ' +
        'over Web 2.0." --Michael Arrington*\n"I wish I\'d ' +
        'invested in 38noises instead of that other company."' +
        ' --Jeff Bezos*\n"38noises closed angel funding at a ' +
        'party in my bathroom last night." --Om Malik*';
]]>
</mx:Script>
    <mx:VBox width="500" horizontalAlign="center">
        <mx:Image source="com/pomodo/assets/logo_md.png" />
        <mx:Label
            text="The simple, GTD-style TODO list application."/>
        <mx:Spacer height="10"/>
        <mx:Text width="100%" text="{_reviews}"/>
        <mx:Spacer height="10"/>
        <mx:Accordion width="400" height="300">
            <pom:AccountCreateBox/>        ❹
            <pom:LoginBox/>        ❺
```

```
        </mx:Accordion>
        <mx:Label text="*did not say this, but might someday!"/>
    </mx:VBox>
</mx:VBox>
```

■

The whole file is new, but it's basically a cut and paste from Pomodo.mxml. Note that we also declare with `Metadata` ❶ that we're broadcasting the `accountCreate` ❷ and `login` ❸ events. Also, note that we aren't handling these on `pom:AccountCreateBox` ❹ and `pom:LoginBox` ❺. We could handle them there, but then we'd have to dispatch some other event to be handled by Pomodo.mxml. If we created an event such as `showMain`, we would lose information (what happened: a new account or a login). This would limit our ability to do custom things in response to these specific events.

Next, we'll modify Pomodo.mxml again. A little searching of the API docs indicates that the spacing is probably caused by the values of `paddingLeft`, and so on. We'll modify those as well as deleting the code we moved to the `SplashBox` (see listing 3.28).

Listing 3.28   app\flex\Pomodo.mxml

```
<?xml version="1.0" encoding="utf-8"?>
<mx:Application
    xmlns:mx="http://www.adobe.com/2006/mxml"
    xmlns:pom="com.pomodo.components.*"
    layout="vertical"
    backgroundGradientColors="[#ffffff, #c0c0c0]"
    horizontalAlign="center"
    verticalAlign="top"
    paddingLeft="0"        ❶
    paddingRight="0"
    paddingTop="0"
    paddingBottom="0"
    width="100%"
    height="100%">
<mx:Script>
<![CDATA[
    import com.pomodo.events.AccountCreateEvent;
    import com.pomodo.events.LoginEvent;

    [Bindable]               ❷
    private var _reviews:String =
        '"pomodo, the hot new RIA by 38noises, is taking ' +
        'over Web 2.0." --Michael Arrington*\n"I wish I\'d ' +
        'invested in 38noises instead of that other company."' +
        ' --Jeff Bezos*\n"38noises closed angel funding at a ' +
        'party in my bathroom last night." --Om Malik*';
```

```
        private function handleAccountCreate(e:AccountCreateEvent):
        void {
            showMain();
        }

        private function handleLogin(e:LoginEvent):void {
            showMain();
        }

        private function showMain():void {
            mainStack.selectedChild = mainBox;
        }
    ]]>
    </mx:Script>
        <mx:ViewStack id="mainStack" width="100%" height="100%">
            <mx:VBox id="splashBox" horizontalAlign="center"     ❸
                verticalAlign="middle" width="100%" height="100%">
    ...
                </mx:Accordion>
    <mx:Label text="*did not say this, but might someday!"/>
                </mx:VBox>
            <pom:SplashBox id="splashBox"        ❹
                accountCreate="handleAccountCreate(event)"
                login="handleLogin(event)"/>
            <pom:MainBox id="mainBox"/>
        </mx:ViewStack>
    </mx:Application>
```

We start by setting the padding attributes ❶. We then delete the _reviews ❷ and all the code in the splashBox ❸, replacing it with our new SplashBox ❹. Note that we handle the accountCreate and login events from the SplashBox, calling the same methods that used to be called by handling events from the Account-CreateBox and LoginBox.

Rebuild and reload. Go to the login form, and enter a Username of ludwig and a password of foooo.

Nothing happens.

The reason is simple: We had hoped the events from the AccountCreateBox or LoginBox would somehow magically pass through the SplashBox. It turns out that this can be done, but you need to turn it on by modifying the events. (Swing developers: Guess what the property is called.)

It turns out we need to set the bubbles property of the Event to true for it to "bubble" through the component hierarchy. As an ex-Java UI developer, I assume this is a performance optimization. The bubbles property is the second argument to the Event constructor. Set it now (see listing 3.29 ❶ and listing 3.30 ❷).

Listing 3.29   app\flex\com\pomodo\events\AccountCreateEvent.as

```
package com.pomodo.events {
    import flash.events.Event;

    public class AccountCreateEvent extends Event {
        public static const ACCOUNT_CREATE:String =
            "accountCreate";

        public var user:XML;

        public function AccountCreateEvent(user:XML) {
            super(ACCOUNT_CREATE, true);        ❶
            this.user = user;
        }
    }
}
```

Listing 3.30   app\flex\com\pomodo\events\LoginEvent.as

```
package com.pomodo.events {
    import flash.events.Event;

    public class LoginEvent extends Event {
        public static const LOGIN:String = "login";

        public var user:XML;

        public function LoginEvent(user:XML) {
            super(LOGIN, true);        ❷
            this.user = user;
        }
    }
}
```

Having done this, rebuild, reload, and log in as ludwig. We see the screen shown
in figure 3.16.

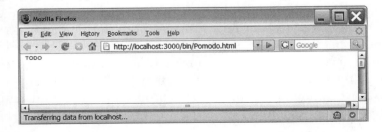

Figure 3.16
The MainBox stub

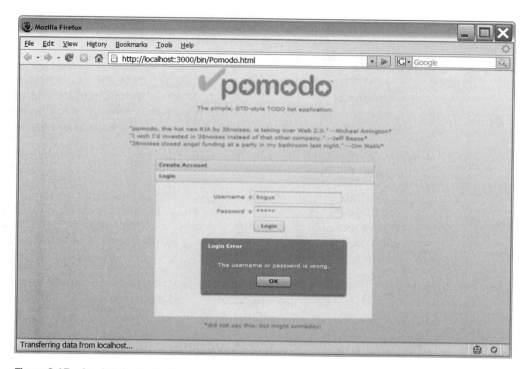

Figure 3.17 An alert for bad login

The login event was heard, and the MainBox is shown. There is no more gradient fill border, so the padding attribute changes worked.

Next, reload the app and try to log in with bogus information. We see something like figure 3.17.

Notice how the app is grayed out and disabled behind the modal, somewhat transparent Alert dialog. Who knew a login error could be sexy?

Because we have just added the ability to create users and log in, we should now add some sample data that is automatically created for us when we run newdb.bat. This way, we won't have to re-create the ludwig user if we decide to start from scratch. (Also, as we add more data to the fixtures later, it will let us start from any iteration and have a running database nicely populated, instead of trying to figure out what data to put in it.)

3.6   *Adding data to the test fixtures*

We could use an SQL script to load sample data (and earlier versions of this book did so), but we should be as database-agnostic as possible. This motivation naturally

leads us to consider using data-only migrations (see *AWDwR*, p. 274, for more information) to load test data. However, it's considered bad practice to load anything
other than reference data this way.

NOTE See the "Data Migrations" section (p. 276) in *AWDwR* for an example of this
admonition: "Be warned: the only data you should load in migrations is
data that you'll also want to see in production: lookup tables, predefined
users, and the like. Don't load test data into your application this way."

What to do? Are we stuck using an SQL script?
Fortunately not. Fixtures to the rescue!

NOTE To be honest, I'm not sure if the following approach is considered a fine
way to do things in normal development. For the purposes of developing
a book example (specifically, *this* book example) iteratively, however, it
works well. So, this is what I'm using for this book. I'm not claiming it
constitutes "best practice."

Running the authenticated generator created a users.yml test fixture in test/fix-
tures. It has two users (quentin and aaron), and we're going to add two more
(ludwig and wolfgang); see listing 3.31.

Listing 3.31   test\fixtures\users.yml

```
quentin:
  id: 1
  login: quentin
  email: quentin@example.com
  salt: 7e3041ebc2fc05a40c60028e2c4901a81035d3cd
  crypted_password: 00742970dc9e6319f8019fd54864d3ea740f04b1 # test
  created_at: <%= 5.days.ago.to_s :db %>


aaron:
  id: 2
  login: aaron
  email: aaron@example.com
  salt: 7e3041ebc2fc05a40c60028e2c4901a81035d3cd
  crypted_password: 00742970dc9e6319f8019fd54864d3ea740f04b1 # test
  created_at: <%= 1.days.ago.to_s :db %>


ludwig:        ❶
  id: 3
  login: ludwig
  email: lvb@pomodo.com
  first_name: Ludwig
  last_name: van Beethoven
```

```
salt: cf1bc466e9dedd7d687e967ba37947971d44ab6e
crypted_password: fc3f2237b0edbeab2c08eecbc7bd6ef9b2124080 # foooo
created_at: <%= 5.days.ago.to_s :db %>


wolfgang:         ❷
  id: 4
  login: wolfgang
  email: wam@pomodo.com
  first_name: Wolfgang
  last_name: Mozart
  salt: 945da846ec9a4f29c10e21789bfb213d62f8fee5
  crypted_password: 2f6ffa90ee8a87c2121b813eb68265130f9b1410 # barrr
  created_at: <%= 1.days.ago.to_s :db %>
```

We base the ludwig ❶ and wolfgang ❷ users on the quentin and aaron users, adding `first_name` and `last_name`, making their ids 3 and 4 (because those are the next in the sequence), and setting `salt` and `crypted_password` to what we got from `mysql` when we created the ludwig and wolfgang users manually. (Well, *you* didn't create a wolfgang user, but *I* did before doing this step.)

Next, modify the newdb.bat file to load the test fixtures ❶ after running the migrations, as shown in listing 3.32.

Listing 3.32   newdb.bat

```
mysql -h localhost -u root -p <db\create.sql
call rake db:migrate
call rake db:fixtures:load         ❶
```

Stop your server, run newdb.bat, and start your server again:

```
C:\peter\flexiblerails\current\pomodo>newdb.bat

C:\peter\flexiblerails\current\pomodo>
mysql -h localhost -u root -p  0<db\create.sql
Enter password: *******

C:\peter\flexiblerails\current\pomodo>call rake db:migrate
c:0:Warning: require_gem is obsolete.  Use gem instead.
(in C:/peter/flexiblerails/current/pomodo)
== 1 CreateUsers: migrating
   =====================================================
-- create_table("users", {:force=>true})
   -> 0.1090s
== 1 CreateUsers: migrated (0.1090s)
   =====================================================
```

```
c:0:Warning: require_gem is obsolete.  Use gem instead.
(in C:/peter/flexiblerails/current/pomodo)

C:\peter\flexiblerails\current\pomodo>ruby script\server
=> Booting WEBrick...
=> Rails application started on http://0.0.0.0:3000
=> Ctrl-C to shutdown server; call with --help for options
```

Next, check mysql:

```
mysql> select id, login, email, first_name, last_name from users;
+----+----------+--------------------+------------+---------------+
| id | login    | email              | first_name | last_name     |
+----+----------+--------------------+------------+---------------+
|  1 | quentin  | quentin@example.com | NULL       | NULL          |
|  2 | aaron    | aaron@example.com  | NULL       | NULL          |
|  3 | ludwig   | lvb@pomodo.com     | Ludwig     | van Beethoven |
|  4 | wolfgang | wam@pomodo.com     | Wolfgang   | Mozart        |
+----+----------+--------------------+------------+---------------+
4 rows in set (0.00 sec)

mysql>
```

Finally, log in as ludwig (or wolfgang, quentin, or aaron) to confirm that everything still works.

If you think that loading test data from the fixtures into the development database is unseemly, note that when we're playing with the app during development, we're really doing ad hoc testing. So, this isn't too out of place.

Before we stop this iteration, we'll run the tests to ensure that we haven't horribly broken things.

3.7   Checking the tests

We need to check our tests. For example, if a test counted the number of users created by the fixtures, we would have broken that test because we added new users. (The restful_authentication plugin's generator produced some tests for us; see test\functional and test\unit for details.) Let's run these now by running the rake command (the default target is to run the tests, which is the same as running rake test; run rake --tasks to see all the different tasks we can choose from):

```
c:\peter\flexiblerails\current\pomodo>rake
12345678901234567890123456789012345678901234567890123456789012345678901234
c:0:Warning: require_gem is obsolete. Use gem instead.
(in c:/peter/flexiblerails/current/pomodo)
c:/ruby/bin/ruby -Ilib;test "c:/ruby/lib/ruby/gems/1.8/gems/
  ➡rake-0.7.3/lib/rake/rake_test_loader.rb"
  ➡"test/unit/user_test.rb"
```

```
Loaded suite c:/ruby/lib/ruby/gems/1.8/gems/rake-0.7.3/lib/rake/
    rake_test_loader
Started
. . . . . . . . . . . .
Finished in 0.953 seconds.

13 tests, 26 assertions, 0 failures, 0 errors
c:/ruby/bin/ruby -Ilib;test "c:/ruby/lib/ruby/gems/1.8/gems/
    ➥rake-0.7.3/lib/rake/rake_test_loader.rb"
    ➥"test/functional/sessions_controller_test.rb"
    ➥"test/functional/users_controller_test.rb"
Loaded suite
    ➥c:/ruby/lib/ruby/gems/1.8/gems/rake-0.7.3/lib/rake/rake_test_loader
Started
. . . . . . . . . . . .
Finished in 0.875 seconds.

14 tests, 26 assertions, 0 failures, 0 errors
c:/ruby/bin/ruby -Ilib;test "c:/ruby/lib/ruby/gems/1.8/gems/
    ➥rake-0.7.3/lib/rake/rake_test_loader.rb"

c:\peter\flexiblerails\current\pomodo>
```

The 13 tests in unit\user_test.rb all pass, as do the 14 functional tests in test\functional. This gives us confidence that we haven't broken everything and that we can use this completed iteration as the basis for bigger and better things.

Before we end this iteration, two more things are useful to consider at this point: configuring Flex Builder and setting up Subversion and Subclipse. Subversion is covered in appendix A; how to configure Flex Builder to run and debug pomodo is covered in the next subsection. If you aren't using Flex Builder, feel free to skip the next subsection.

Subversion and Subclipse

For real development, there is a strong chance you'll be using Subversion—unless you're one of the cool kids who has switched to Git (http://git.or.cz/). How should you set up Subversion to work with Flex and Rails? I could just say "have it ignore the public\bin directory" and be done with it, but this is a fairly common question. I provide a bit of guidance in appendix A; it should be helpful if you plan to use Subversion with Flex and Rails and want a quick introduction on what to do.

3.8 *Configuring Flex Builder to run and debug pomodo*

It would be nice to be able to click the little green circle with the "play" triangle in it to run pomodo. Much more important, Flex Builder 3 ships with a proper debugger, and we should learn to use it. We'll accomplish both of these tasks now.

First, let's click the green play button shown in figure 3.18.

The application will run, but the URL will be your equivalent of file:///C:/peter/flexiblerails/current/pomodo/public/bin/Pomodo.html. This isn't what we want: We want http://localhost:3000/bin/Pomodo.html so that Rails serves up the page containing our Flex application. So, we need to configure the run target. Click the drop-down arrow beside the Run button, and choose Other, as shown in figure 3.19.

Figure 3.18   The run button under the Navigate menu

Figure 3.19   Configuring the run targets by choosing Other

We see the Run dialog. Because we just ran the Pomodo project from the Run button, there is already a launch configuration called Pomodo in the Flex Application folder: It's what has the wrong URLs. All we need to do is edit the URLs to be http://localhost:3000/bin/Pomodo.html, and we're set. As shown in figure 3.20, deselect Use Defaults, and edit the URLs.

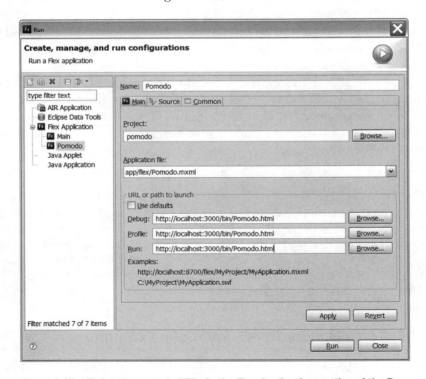

Figure 3.20   Fixing the pomodo URLs in the Flex Application section of the Run configuration dialog

NOTE   Flex SDK users: There is a command-line debugger called fdb. See http://www.adobe.com/devnet/flex/articles/client_debug_08.html for details.

Click the Apply button to save, and then click Close to close the dialog. We can now click the Run toolbar button to run the pomodo app and the Debug toolbar button to debug the pomodo app.

3.9   *Summary*

We've accomplished a *lot* in this iteration. We got login working in Rails and hooked up the Flex UI to it. In so doing, we learned some of the basics of Rails routing and of Flex. Furthermore, we now have a good starting point for any Flex + Rails application, and the pomodo application in particular. (It has flaws, however, as you'll discover in iteration 5.)

The next iteration, besides being a lot shorter, is really fun. In it, we'll gather requirements and design and build almost the entire Flex UI—in a lot less code than you'd expect.

The code at this point is saved as the iteration03 folder.

Part 2

Building the application

In part 1, we were introduced to Flex and Rails and to using them together. We've made account creation and login look nice (and work too), but the app itself is just a big TODO. On the upside, most of what we've done so far is applicable to any application we could create, so it's nice to have iteration03 as a starting point. Starting there is further ahead than just `rails pomodo`, that's for sure.

In part 2, we do a deep dive using Flex with Rails. By the end of it, you'll have mastered the basics of using Flex with Rails. You'll then be ready to think about higher-level topics, which we'll do in part 3 where we refactor the work we're doing in part 2 to use RESTful design and then Cairngorm.

This part contains four iterations:

- *Iteration 4*—"Creating the main Flex UI," in which we'll build a stubbed-out UI for the main part of the Flex application.

- *Iteration 5*—"Expanding the Rails code, RESTfully," in which we'll add new Rails models and controllers for the tasks, projects, and locations resources—as well as the migrations needed to create their database tables. We'll also introduce REST in this iteration, because we're using the now-RESTful scaffold command in Rails 2 to create these resources. Finally, we'll address some basic security concerns that need to be considered at the outset.

- *Iteration 6*—"Flex on Rails," in which we'll hook up most of the main Flex UI we'll build in iteration 4 to the Rails controllers we'll build in iteration 5.

- *Iteration 7*—"Validation," in which we'll add full validation support on the Rails side and the Flex side to the account-creation process. This is a nice place to cover validation because it's a fairly self-contained section.

Creating the main Flex UI

First: **every great system has a command shell.** *It is always an integral part of the system. It's been there since the system was born. The designer of the system couldn't imagine life without a command shell. The command shell is a full interface to the system: anything you can do with the system in some other way can also be done in the command shell.*

—Steve Yegge,
http://steve-yegge.blogspot.com/2007/01/pinocchio-problem.html

In this iteration, we'll create a completely stubbed-out GUI for our application, in order to clarify our requirements. After such a long previous iteration, it will be nice to have some fun in this one.

4.1   Requirements

We're creating a *Getting Things Done* (GTD) style To Do list application. As such, we'll need tasks, projects to put them in, and locations where tasks will be done. We'll want the UI to be focused on easy entry of tasks, because GTD focuses on entering tons of tasks. We'll also want a place to store random notes, because GTD is all about a Zen-like clearing of your mind of all the stuff that distracts you. Finally, it would be nice to have a handy calendar available. For the moment, we won't worry about putting anything *in* the calendar—we'd only worry about that if we were trying to sell our app on eBay. Although it would be fairly straightforward (if time-consuming and painful) to build the full Outlook mess of features into pomodo, we're going to "Get Real" and ship something now. (The full Outlook killer app will have to wait until the second edition of this book!) Finally, one more requirement: a command shell. Why? I'll defer to the earlier Steve Yegge quote.

With these high-level requirements, we can sit down in Flex Builder and start experimenting. Flex Builder has a Design mode for MXML files (the tab to the right of the Source tab), which lets us drag and drop a GUI together. If you've ever used a GUI builder such as the one in Visual Basic, Visual C#, or JBuilder, you should feel right at home. You can go there now and start experimenting with what you think the ideal design for this application would be. This book isn't going to teach Flex Builder, so this is left as an exercise for you. (A PDF entitled *Using Flex Builder* is in the documentation zip file that I hope you downloaded in iteration 3 in the "Flex 3 documentation? Where?" section,[1] and it covers this topic more than adequately.)

When you're done experimenting, move on to the next section to see what I came up with.

4.2   Design

Figure 4.1 shows the design I chose. Chances are, you could have easily outdone me.

This UI includes many of the typically used Flex controls. It has a `TabNavigator` for the Tasks, Projects, Locations, and Notely (haha) tabs. It uses an `Accordion` for

---

[1] This file is currently at http://download.macromedia.com/pub/labs/air/air_b2_docs_flex_100107.zip, but this will change when Flex 3 is out of Beta. See iteration 3 for details.

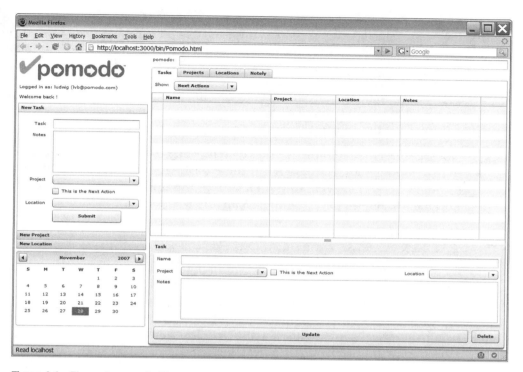

Figure 4.1   The main pomodo UI

the New Task, New Project, and New Location boxes. It has a `DataGrid` for the Tasks (and for the Projects and Locations) and a `Panel` for the Task details (and the Project and Location details). It even includes the typically overstuffed Web 2.0 buttons. Also, note that if we widen our browser window, the UI expands accordingly.

> **NOTE** One of the common criticisms of Flash UIs is that they're a fixed size. This example shows that this doesn't have to be true. It's obviously easier to make a fixed-size UI than to make a UI that resizes appropriately, but it's not Flex's fault that many developers are lazy. It's certainly as easy to build a UI that resizes nicely in Flex as it is in, say, Swing.

The UI also incorporates the notion of a *Next Action*, allowing a task to be the Next Action of a project. (I'm capitalizing *Next Action* because it's a GTD idea and deserves to be capitalized.) Furthermore, we add a simple `ComboBox` for filtering tasks. Next Actions is the default, because that's what we should be focused on, but we'll also provide options to show all tasks or tasks in a given project or at a given location.

NOTE Other common and useful controls that aren't covered in the book include AdvancedDataGrid and Tree. There are a lot of controls, and this isn't a Flex "complete reference" book. Note that the AdvancedDataGrid could have been used with great effect for the tasks data grid—for example, grouping the tasks by project or location. However, we can't do everything in this book, and it's important to show the basics (such as DataGrid) before the advanced stuff. (Also, while Tree is part of the Flex SDK, AdvancedDataGrid costs money.)

Not bad for a first attempt, if I do say so myself. It's fairly clean and simple, which, thanks to 37signals, is where it's at these days. (In fact, because at 38noises we're so totally about Less Features, the fact that this app *doesn't do anything at all* right now means that we have a winner! *Ship it!*)

4.3 Code

As you've probably guessed, the design in the previous section is the running code we'll have at the end of this iteration, not something I mocked up in Photoshop or Fireworks. Flex is so great that it's almost as fast, if not faster,[2] to code the visual appearance of something than it is to draw it. (Note that this is true even *without* using the visual design functionality in Flex Builder, once you know Flex well enough.) Without further ado, let's look at the new Flex code (the Rails code is unchanged). We'll start with the MainBox; see listing 4.1.

Listing 4.1   app\flex\com\pomodo\components\MainBox.mxml

```
<?xml version="1.0" encoding="utf-8"?>
<mx:VBox xmlns:mx="http://www.adobe.com/2006/mxml"        ❶
    width="100%" height="100%" backgroundColor="#FFFFFF">
    <mx:Label text="TODO"/>
</mx:VBox>
<mx:HBox xmlns:mx="http://www.adobe.com/2006/mxml"        ❷
    xmlns:pom="com.pomodo.components.*"                   ❸
    minWidth="1000"        ❹
    minHeight="680"
    paddingLeft="5"        ❺
    paddingRight="5"
    paddingTop="5"
    paddingBottom="5"
    width="100%"
    height="100%"
```

---

[2] This is true especially for me because I can't draw—my drawings in Brain Age look like my 3 year old did them!

```
        backgroundColor="#FFFFFF">
<mx:Script>
<![CDATA[
    [Bindable]
    public var user : XML;        ❻
]]>
</mx:Script>
    <mx:HBox width="100%" height="100%">           ❼
        <mx:VBox width="300" height="100%">           ❽
            <mx:Image source="com/pomodo/assets/logo_md.png"/>    ❾
            <mx:Label text="{'Logged in as: ' + user.login +   ❿
                ' (' + user.email + ')'}"/>       ⓫
            <mx:Label text="{'Welcome back ' + user.first_name +   ⓬
                '!'}"/>
            <mx:Accordion width="100%" height="350">      ⓭
                <pom:TaskCreateBox id="taskCreateBox"/>   ⓮
                <pom:ProjectCreateBox id="projectCreateBox"/>   ⓯
                <pom:LocationCreateBox id="locationCreateBox"/>   ⓰
            </mx:Accordion>
            <mx:DateChooser id="dateChooser" width="100%"/>   ⓱
        </mx:VBox>
        <mx:VBox width="100%" height="100%">      ⓲
            <pom:CommandShell/>      ⓳
            <mx:TabNavigator width="100%" height="100%">   ⓴
                <pom:TasksListBox id="tasksTab"/>    ㉑
                <pom:ProjectsListBox id="projectsTab"/>    ㉒
                <pom:LocationsListBox id="locationsTab"/>   ㉓
                <pom:Notely id="notelyTab"/>    ㉔
            </mx:TabNavigator>
        </mx:VBox>
    </mx:HBox>
</mx:HBox>
```

We begin by deleting the old VBox code ❶ and creating an HBox ❷. (Actually, I renamed it, but it's easier to show it being deleted.) We then add the XML namespace for our components ❸ and set the minimum width and height ❹. If the control that contains the MainBox gets smaller than this, the MainBox will add scrollbars instead of shrinking further. Next, we set some padding ❺ because we got rid of it in Pomodo.mxml. We add a Bindable variable for the current user ❻; it's typed as XML, because that's what we get back from Rails.

Next, we create an HBox ❼ to hold a two-column layout. (There is no limit to the number of things in an HBox or VBox—I'm calling it a two-column layout because that's what it is. We could have made a six-column layout.) The left column is a VBox ❽ containing our logo ❾ and a couple of labels welcoming the user ❿⓫. We also try to welcome the user by their first_name ⓬. However, as we'll soon see, this doesn't work well. Don't worry—we'll fix this problem soon.

Now, we add an Accordion ⑬ with our custom TaskCreateBox ⑭, Project-
CreateBox ⑮, LocationCreateBox ⑯, and DateChooser ⑰. (That's quite the column.) The right column is a VBox ⑱ containing our custom CommandShell ⑲ and
a TabNavigator ⑳ containing tabs for each of the TasksListBox ㉑,
ProjectsListBox ㉒, LocationsListBox ㉓, and Notely ㉔.

From this code, you can tell we have a *lot* of custom components to create!
Before we do that, however, let's modify Pomodo.mxml to pass the user in; see listing 4.2.

Listing 4.2   app\flex\Pomodo.mxml

```
<?xml version="1.0" encoding="utf-8"?>
<mx:Application
    xmlns:mx="http://www.adobe.com/2006/mxml"
    xmlns:pom="com.pomodo.components.*"
    layout="vertical"
    backgroundGradientColors="[#ffffff, #c0c0c0]"
    horizontalAlign="center"
    verticalAlign="top"
    paddingLeft="0"
    paddingRight="0"
    paddingTop="0"
    paddingBottom="0"
    width="100%"
    height="100%">
<mx:Script>
<![CDATA[
    import com.pomodo.events.AccountCreateEvent;
    import com.pomodo.events.LoginEvent;

    [Bindable]
    private var _user : XML;            ❶

    private function handleAccountCreate(e:AccountCreateEvent):
    void {
        showMain();
        login(e.user);                  ❷
    }

    private function handleLogin(e:LoginEvent):void {
        showMain();
        login(e.user);                  ❸
    }

    private function showMain():void {
    private function login(user:XML):void {   ❹
        _user = user;                   ❺
        mainStack.selectedChild = mainBox;
```

```
        }
    ]]>
    </mx:Script>
        <mx:ViewStack id="mainStack" width="100%" height="100%">
            <pom:SplashBox id="splashBox"
                accountCreate="handleAccountCreate(event)"
                login="handleLogin(event)"/>
            <pom:MainBox id="mainBox" user="{_user}"/>        ❻
        </mx:ViewStack>
    </mx:Application>
```

We begin by creating a `Bindable` variable called `_user` ❶. We then rename the `showMain` function to `login` ❹ and make it take the user XML as a parameter that we use to set ❺ the `_user` variable. We modify the call from `handleAccountCreate` ❷ and `handleLogin` ❸ to call `login` with the user property of the given event. Finally, we add the `user="{_user}"` ❻ binding to actually pass the `_user` into the `mainBox`.

That was easy. Now, let's create the components.

First, the `CommandShell`; see listing 4.3.

Listing 4.3   app\flex\com\pomodo\components\CommandShell.mxml

```
<?xml version="1.0" encoding="utf-8"?>
<mx:HBox xmlns:mx="http://www.adobe.com/2006/mxml" width="100%">
    <mx:Label text="pomodo:"/>
    <mx:TextInput id="cmdTI" width="100%"/>
</mx:HBox>
```

There's not much to say about that. Next, the `TaskCreateBox`; see listing 4.4.

Listing 4.4   app\flex\com\pomodo\components\TaskCreateBox.mxml

```
<?xml version="1.0" encoding="utf-8"?>
<mx:VBox xmlns:mx="http://www.adobe.com/2006/mxml"
    width="100%" height="100%" label="New Task">
    <mx:Form width="100%" height="100%">
        <mx:FormItem label="Task">
            <mx:TextInput id="nameTI" width="200"/>
        </mx:FormItem>
        <mx:FormItem label="Notes">
            <mx:TextArea id="notesTI" width="200" height="100"/>
        </mx:FormItem>
        <mx:FormItem label="Project">
            <mx:ComboBox id="projectsCB" width="200"/>        ❶
```

```
        </mx:FormItem>
        <mx:FormItem label="">
            <mx:CheckBox id="nextActionCheckbox"          ❷
                label="This is the Next Action"/>
        </mx:FormItem>
        <mx:FormItem label="Location">
            <mx:ComboBox id="locationsCB" width="200"/>          ❸
        </mx:FormItem>
        <mx:FormItem>
            <mx:Button label="Submit" width="160" height="30"/>
        </mx:FormItem>
    </mx:Form>
</mx:VBox>
```

By now, these mx:Forms are pretty boring. Note that this one contains a couple of ComboBoxes ❶❸. A ComboBox is similar to an HTML select tag; it's not interesting at the moment because it has no dataProvider set. There is also a CheckBox ❷ to specify whether the task is the Next Action in a Project.

Next, the ProjectCreateBox; see listing 4.5.

Listing 4.5   app\flex\com\pomodo\components\ProjectCreateBox.mxml

```
<?xml version="1.0" encoding="utf-8"?>
<mx:VBox xmlns:mx="http://www.adobe.com/2006/mxml"
    width="100%" height="100%" label="New Project">
    <mx:Form width="100%" height="100%">
        <mx:FormItem label="Name">
            <mx:TextInput id="nameTI" width="200"/>
        </mx:FormItem>
        <mx:FormItem label="Notes">
            <mx:TextArea id="notesTI" width="200" height="100"/>
        </mx:FormItem>
        <mx:FormItem>
            <mx:Button label="Submit" width="160" height="30"/>
        </mx:FormItem>
    </mx:Form>
</mx:VBox>
```

Having just looked at the TaskCreateBox, there is nothing interesting to say about this one.

Now, the LocationCreateBox; see listing 4.6.

Listing 4.6   app\flex\com\pomodo\components\LocationCreateBox.mxml

```
<?xml version="1.0" encoding="utf-8"?>
<mx:VBox xmlns:mx="http://www.adobe.com/2006/mxml"
    width="100%" height="100%" label="New Location">
```

```
    <mx:Form width="100%" height="100%">
        <mx:FormItem label="Name">
            <mx:TextInput id="nameTI" width="200"/>
        </mx:FormItem>
        <mx:FormItem label="Notes">
            <mx:TextInput id="notesTI" width="200"/>
        </mx:FormItem>
        <mx:FormItem>
            <mx:Button label="Submit" width="160" height="30"/>
        </mx:FormItem>
    </mx:Form>
</mx:VBox>
```

By now you've probably realized that copy-paste-modify is the standard way of developing MXML. You can do complex things purely in ActionScript to try to reduce the amount of this, but we're trying to keep the code simple.

Next, the `TasksListBox`; see listing 4.7.

Listing 4.7   app\flex\com\pomodo\components\TasksListBox.mxml

```
<?xml version="1.0" encoding="utf-8"?>
<mx:VDividedBox xmlns:mx="http://www.adobe.com/2006/mxml"        ❶
    width="100%" height="100%" label="Tasks">                    ❷
<mx:Script>
<![CDATA[
    public const NEXT_ACTIONS:int = 0;          ❸
    public const ALL_TASKS:int = 1;
    public const TASKS_IN_PROJECT:int = 2;
    public const TASKS_AT_LOCATION:int = 3;

    private const SHOW_CHOICES:Array = [        ❹
        {label:"Next Actions", data:NEXT_ACTIONS,
            hasSubChoice:false},
        {label:"All Tasks", data:ALL_TASKS,
            hasSubChoice:false},
        {label:"Tasks in Project:", data:TASKS_IN_PROJECT,
            hasSubChoice:true},
        {label:"Tasks at Location:", data:TASKS_AT_LOCATION,
            hasSubChoice:true}];

    [Bindable]
    private var _subChoices:Array;              ❺
]]>
</mx:Script>
    <mx:VBox width="100%" height="60%">         ❻
        <mx:HBox width="100%" paddingLeft="5" paddingRight="5">      ❼
            <mx:Label text="Show:"/>
            <mx:ComboBox id="mainChoiceCB"      ❽
                dataProvider="{SHOW_CHOICES}"/>
```

```
                    <mx:ComboBox id="subChoiceCB" width="100%"        ❾
                        dataProvider="{_subChoices}"
                    visible="{mainChoiceCB.selectedItem.hasSubChoice}"/>   ❿
            </mx:HBox>
            <mx:DataGrid id="tasksGrid" width="100%" height="100%">   ⓫
                <mx:columns>    ⓬
                    <mx:DataGridColumn headerText="" width="25"/>    ⓭
                    <mx:DataGridColumn headerText="Name"    ⓮
                        width="250"/>
                    <mx:DataGridColumn headerText="Project"
                        width="150"/>
                    <mx:DataGridColumn headerText="Location"
                        width="150"/>
                    <mx:DataGridColumn headerText="Notes"/>
                    <mx:DataGridColumn headerText="" width="60"/>    ⓯
                </mx:columns>
            </mx:DataGrid>
        </mx:VBox>
        <mx:Panel id="summaryPanel" title="Task" width="100%"      ⓰
            height="40%" paddingLeft="5" paddingRight="5"
            paddingTop="5" paddingBottom="5">
            <mx:HBox width="100%">
                <mx:Label text="Name" width="50"/>
                <mx:TextInput id="nameTI" width="100%"/>
            </mx:HBox>
            <mx:HBox width="100%" verticalAlign="middle">
                <mx:Label text="Project" width="50"/>
                <mx:ComboBox id="projectCB" width="200"/>
                <mx:CheckBox label="This is the Next Action"/>
                <mx:Spacer width="100%"/>
                <mx:Label text="Location"/>
                <mx:ComboBox id="locationCB"/>
            </mx:HBox>
            <mx:HBox width="100%" height="100%">
                <mx:Label text="Notes" width="50"/>
                <mx:TextArea id="notesTI" width="100%"       ⓱
                    height="100%"/>
            </mx:HBox>
            <mx:ControlBar width="100%" horizontalAlign="center">   ⓲
                <mx:Button id="updateButton" label="Update"
                    width="100%" height="30"/>
                <mx:Button id="deleteButton" label="Delete"
                    height="30"/>
            </mx:ControlBar>
        </mx:Panel>
    </mx:VDividedBox>
```

This is more interesting. We're creating an `mx:VDividedBox` ❶, which as a VBox with adjustable dividers in between each child. (This is the two-child JSplitPane in Swing generalized to *n* children—hooray for Flex!) It has a Tasks label ❷, which is used by the `TabNavigator` (in `MainBox`) as the tab name. It contains two children: a `VBox` ❻ and a `Panel` ⓰.

The `VBox` ❻ contains an `HBox` ❼, which contains a label and a couple of `ComboBoxes` ❽❾. The `mainChoiceCB` ❽ has its `dataProvider` set to the `SHOW_CHOICES` Array ❹ which is built out of anonymous `Objects` containing `label`, `data`, and `hasSubChoice` properties. Similarly, the `subChoiceCB` ❾ has its `dataProvider` bound to the array of `_subChoices` ❺. The `data` property is set to one of the constants we're defining ❸. (Note that constants are usually `static`, and these probably should be too.)

The interesting bit of code is the binding to the `visible` property ⓰ of the second `ComboBox` based on the `selectedItem` of the first. This lets us show the second `ComboBox` only if the first `ComboBox` has a choice that has subchoices, as specified by a flag.

The `VBox` ❻ also contains a `DataGrid` ⓫, which specifies its columns ⓬ as an Array of `mx:DataGridColumn`. Note that we have two columns with blank headers—the first one will be used for a check box ⓭, and the second will be used for a Delete button ⓯. Finally, note that the typical column's name is set in the `headerText` ⓮.

Other than this, it's more of the same, with the exception of two small new things: a `TextArea` ⓱, which is a multiline text-input control (`TextInput` is single line); and a `ControlBar` ⓲, which is essentially a funky-looking `HBox`.

Next, the `ProjectsListBox`, which is a copy-paste-modify of the `TasksListBox`; see listing 4.8.

Listing 4.8   app\flex\com\pomodo\components\ProjectsListBox.mxml

```
<?xml version="1.0" encoding="utf-8"?>
<mx:VDividedBox xmlns:mx="http://www.adobe.com/2006/mxml"
    width="100%" height="100%" label="Projects">
    <mx:DataGrid id="projectsGrid" width="100%" height="60%">
        <mx:columns>
            <mx:DataGridColumn headerText="" width="25"/>
            <mx:DataGridColumn headerText="Name" width="400"/>
            <mx:DataGridColumn headerText="Notes"/>
            <mx:DataGridColumn headerText="" width="60"/>
        </mx:columns>
    </mx:DataGrid>
    <mx:Panel id="summaryPanel"
        title="Project" width="100%" height="40%"
        paddingLeft="5" paddingRight="5" paddingTop="5"
        paddingBottom="5">
        <mx:HBox width="100%">
            <mx:Label text="Name" width="50"/>
            <mx:TextInput id="nameTI" width="100%"/>
        </mx:HBox>
```

```
        <mx:HBox width="100%" height="100%">
            <mx:Label text="Notes" width="50"/>
            <mx:TextArea id="notesTI" width="100%"
                height="100%"/>
        </mx:HBox>
        <mx:ControlBar width="100%" horizontalAlign="center">
            <mx:Button id="updateButton" label="Update"
                width="100%" height="30"/>
            <mx:Button id="deleteButton" label="Delete"
                height="30"/>
        </mx:ControlBar>
    </mx:Panel>
</mx:VDividedBox>
```

Finally, the LocationsListBox, which is another copy-paste-modify; see listing 4.9.

Listing 4.9   app\flex\com\pomodo\components\LocationsListBox.mxml

```
<?xml version="1.0" encoding="utf-8"?>
<mx:VDividedBox xmlns:mx="http://www.adobe.com/2006/mxml"
    width="100%" height="100%" label="Locations">
    <mx:DataGrid id="locationsGrid" width="100%" height="60%">
        <mx:columns>
            <mx:DataGridColumn headerText="Name" width="400"/>
            <mx:DataGridColumn headerText="Notes"/>
            <mx:DataGridColumn headerText="" width="60"/>
        </mx:columns>
    </mx:DataGrid>
    <mx:Panel id="summaryPanel" title="Location" width="100%"
        height="40%" paddingLeft="5" paddingRight="5"
        paddingTop="5" paddingBottom="5">
        <mx:HBox width="100%">
            <mx:Label text="Name" width="50"/>
            <mx:TextInput id="nameTI" width="100%"/>
        </mx:HBox>
        <mx:HBox width="100%" height="100%">
            <mx:Label text="Notes" width="50"/>
            <mx:TextArea id="notesTI" width="100%"
                height="100%"/>
        </mx:HBox>
        <mx:ControlBar width="100%" horizontalAlign="center">
            <mx:Button id="updateButton" label="Update"
                width="100%" height="30"/>
            <mx:Button id="deleteButton" label="Delete"
                height="30"/>
        </mx:ControlBar>
    </mx:Panel>
</mx:VDividedBox>
```

NOTE These three files are so similar that we could be tempted to create a component that handles tasks, projects, and locations. We'll resist this temptation for now, because at the beginning of a project it's a good idea to keep the MXML simple—stupid, even—until the design begins to emerge.

Finally, `Notely`; see listing 4.10.

Listing 4.10 app\flex\com\pomodo\components\Notely.mxml

```
<?xml version="1.0" encoding="utf-8"?>
<mx:VBox xmlns:mx="http://www.adobe.com/2006/mxml"
    width="100%" height="100%" label="Notely" paddingLeft="5"
    paddingRight="5" paddingTop="5" paddingBottom="5">
    <mx:TextArea width="100%" height="100%"/>
    <mx:ControlBar width="100%" horizontalAlign="center">
        <mx:Button id="saveButton" label="Save" width="100%"
            height="30"/>
        <mx:Button id="revertButton" label="Revert"
            height="30"/>
    </mx:ControlBar>
</mx:VBox>
```

Although there is no interesting code here, we've made an interesting design decision: We're only including Save and Revert buttons. This means the user only ever has one document, not multiple documents. I told you we were going to keep things simple!

Rebuild, reload, and log in as ludwig. We see the running app that showed earlier in figure 4.1.

4.4 Summary

That's it for this iteration! If you were on the fence about Flex, I hope this short iteration has given you a taste of how quickly you can build elegant UIs. Note that real Flex development isn't all this easy; but what we just did isn't a lie, either. This is fine code to build on, not something that needs to be thrown away—unlike wizard-generated code in other languages I have used. In the next iteration, we'll make this UI fully functional.

The code at this point is saved as the iteration04 folder.

5

Expanding the
Rails code, RESTfully

WS-Death Star

—David Heinemeier Hansson

In this iteration, we'll finally learn about this RESTful stuff we've been talking about, as we add new models and controllers for the tasks, projects, and locations, along with the migrations needed to create their database tables. We'll also address some basic security concerns that need to be considered at the outset.

5.1   A brief note about REST

Before we dive in and create the model classes and migrations for tasks, projects, and locations, I want to give enough background about REST and how we're using it in this book. I'll start with a disclaimer.

5.1.1   Disclaimer: doing REST wrong

Readers who are REST experts and/or went to Scott Raymond's excellent "Doing REST Right" RailsConf 2007 presentation[1] may, at various points in this iteration, be tempted to scream "What about idempotence?" "You should be returning status codes, not just sending XML responses," or "REST isn't about CRUD and `respond_to`, but you're making it seem like it is!" I ask those readers to please bear with me: Explaining REST properly would take a full book. Thankfully, an excellent one is already available: *RESTful Web Services,* by Leonard Richardson and Sam Ruby (O'Reilly Media, 2007). If you care about REST, buy that book[2] and read it. You can also read one of many good articles[3] about REST online. Then, as you read this iteration, you can shake your head knowingly when I oversimplify things.

> **Status codes**
>
> *(This note is for advanced Rails developers.)* Although I'll leave alone the scaffold-generated code that produces the various abnormal (that is, everything other than 200 OK) HTTP status codes (for example, `:status => :unprocessable_ entity`), the HTTP status codes don't reliably show up inside Flash in many browsers. There is hope for the future (especially with AIR), so I won't delete the code that produces the non-200 status codes from the Rails controllers. (Also, if you're using format.xml as an API for non-Flash player based clients, the status codes may be useful.) That said, I'll basically ignore this issue in the book and use the body of what is produced by `render :xml` and `render :text` instead of trying to use the status codes.

---

[1] Download the slides from http://conferences.oreillynet.com/presentations/rails2007/raymond_scott. pdf.

[2] http://www.crummy.com/writing/RESTful-Web-Services/.

[3] For example, http://www.pluralsight.com/blogs/tewald/archive/2007/04/26/46984.aspx.

> **Status codes** *(continued)*
>
> This isn't as "pure" as returning status codes only, but it works. We can hope this situation improves with future browser and Flash player releases, but until then this is the pragmatic thing to do. (The situation should currently be better with AIR, but because this isn't a book about AIR I'm not going to get into that— even in the final iteration that ports pomodo to AIR.) If you're interested in an advanced discussion, see http://www.atnan.com/2007/6/11/can-as3-do-rest-or-not for details. An in-depth discussion of browser compatibility issues doesn't belong here, because this information is always in flux and is of interest only if you're a REST purist determined to use status codes. If this is you, you're already a pretty advanced developer, so see the aforementioned link and follow your nose from there.

With that out of the way, let's consider what REST is and why we should use a RESTful approach in the first place.

5.1.2 *What is REST?*

Before we begin the process of converting pomodo to be RESTful, let's take an extremely brief look at what REST is.

REST (Representational State Transfer) is a way of building web services that focuses on simplicity and an architecture style that is "of the web." This can be described as a Resource Oriented Architecture (ROA); see *RESTful Web Services* for details. As you can probably infer from its $20-word full title, REST grew out of a PhD thesis—Roy Fielding's, to be precise. However, unlike most PhD theses, it has grown into something revolutionary. DHH puts it like this, in typical DHH style,[4] in the foreword to *RESTful Web Services*:

> *A renaissance of HTTP appreciation is building and, under the banner of REST,*
> *shows a credible alternative to what the merchants of complexity are trying to ram*
> *down everyone's throats; a simple set of principles that every day [sic] developers*
> *can use to connect applications in a style native to the Web.*

In sum, REST is the anointed good-guy side of the eternal struggle pitting good versus evil, us against them, Apple versus Microsoft, the rebels versus the evil empire. Put on your jeans and turtleneck and meet me at the barricades—after you finish reading this iteration, of course.

---

[4] Visualize DHH ordering a sandwich: "This panini is a revolution of simplicity in the complexity of baguettes and croissants that the merchants of pastry are trying to ram down everyone's throats."

On a more serious note, table 5.1 explains everything you could possibly need to know about REST.

Table 5.1 The seven standard RESTful controller methods[a]

#	Method	Sample URL paths	Pretend HTTP method	Actual HTTP method	Corresponding CRUD method	Corresponding SQL method
1	index	/tasks /tasks.xml	GET	GET	READ	SELECT
2	show	/tasks/1 /tasks/1.xml	GET	GET	READ	SELECT
3	new	/tasks/new /tasks/new.xml	GET	GET	-	-
4	edit	/tasks/1/edit	GET	GET	READ	SELECT
5	create	/tasks /tasks.xml	POST	POST	CREATE	INSERT
6	update	/tasks/1 /tasks/1.xml	PUT	POST	UPDATE	UPDATE
7	destroy	/tasks/1 /tasks/1.xml	DELETE	POST	DELETE	DELETE

a. This table is inspired by DHH's "Discovering a world of Resources on Rails" (slide 7), as well as the table on p. 410 of *AWDwR 2nd ed.* and the tables in Geoffrey Grosenbach's REST cheat sheet.

Fine, so it doesn't explain *everything*. Also, as REST gurus such as Scott Raymond will remind you, this table isn't about REST at all, but about the way that Rails *implements* REST. Heck, even that sentence is wrong: Rails doesn't implement REST—it provides some conventions that you can use along with HTTP to build an app in the RESTful style. *(Argh, if I continue like this I'm never going to write anything.)*

Although it doesn't explain everything, the table *does* show the seven standard controller methods, some sample URL paths, and so on. The purpose of what these methods all do and the pretend and actual HTTP methods that trigger them will become clear as we start using them.

Before we dive in to the tasks, projects, and locations, let's think back to the UsersController and the SessionsController and why we have two of them (as opposed to, say, a controller called Accountcontroller that handled account creation and login). Think about what those controllers do: The act of creating a user is done by the create method in the UsersController, whereas the act of logging in is done by the create method in the SessionsController. The create method is one of the standard seven methods used in a RESTful design, as shown in row 5 of table 5.1. This is one consequence of RESTful design: We end up with more controllers (nouns) and fewer actions (verbs) in each of them.

The best way to start learning RESTful design in Rails is to look at one of the outputs of the scaffold generator—it will have all seven of the methods for us to examine. We'll do that momentarily. First, let's consider why we should use a RESTful approach.

5.1.3   *Why use a RESTful approach?*

This seems like a simple enough question, but it's fairly deep.

The short answer is, "because DHH says so"—this is how you're supposed to design things in Rails 2. This is reinforced by the fact that the scaffolding works this way now, and if the Rails core team is pushing REST all the way into the scaffolding, then even newbies are supposed to use it. The reason is that using a RESTful design helps us organize our controllers better, forces us to think harder about our domain, and gives us a nice API for free.

The long answer to the question was provided by DHH in his RailsConf 2006 keynote presentation "Discovering a world of Resources on Rails." The slides for the presentation are at http://media.rubyonrails.org/presentations/worldofresources.pdf, and a video of the presentation is at http://www.scribemedia.org/2006/07/09/dhh/. If you haven't seen that presentation, I strongly urge you to stop reading right now and watch the video while following along with the slides. This will take about an hour, but it's time well spent.

REST is also discussed extensively in Chapter 20 of *Agile Web Development with Rails, 2nd ed.* (*AWDwR*). Unless you're already a RESTful Rails guru who is just reading this book for the Flex stuff, I strongly encourage you to read that section of *AWDwR* right now, buying the book if you haven't already. This book will be a lot more understandable if you do so.

Finally, I recommend that you buy and watch the "PeepCode RESTful Rails" screencast from http://peepcode.com/articles/2006/10/08/restful-rails. This screencast greatly helped me learn how REST was used in Rails. Also note that Geoffrey Grosenbach has a *free* REST cheat sheet available at http://topfunky.com/clients/peepcode/REST-cheatsheet.pdf. Doing all this will take a while; I'll wait. When you're well RESTed (sorry, I'll try to stop now), we'll dive in and use the now-RESTful `scaffold` command to create the new resources.

Now that I've spent a couple of pages talking about/around REST, we're about ready to create some RESTful resources. Before we do that, however, we have one small mystery to solve.

5.2   *Calling the user by name*

We're trying to be polite in MainBox.mxml and say

```
<mx:Label text="{'Welcome back ' + user.first_name +
'!'}"/>
```

However, this produced "Welcome back !" in figure 4.1 in the previous iteration—the first_name isn't showing up! We're confident this isn't due to bad data, because we created the ludwig user in a test fixture that is run by newdb.bat. As a sanity check, let's run newdb.bat, check in MySQL to confirm that the data is all present and correct, and then start the server and look at the UI again.

Stop the server, and run the newdb.bat script:

```
c:\peter\flexiblerails\current\pomodo>newdb.bat

c:\peter\flexiblerails\current\pomodo>
mysql -h localhost -u root -p  0<db\create.sql
Enter password: ******

c:\peter\flexiblerails\current\pomodo>call rake db:migrate
c:0:Warning: require_gem is obsolete.  Use gem instead.
(in c:/peter/flexiblerails/current/pomodo)
== 1 CreateUsers: migrating
   ====================================================
-- create_table("users", {:force=>true})
   -> 0.1250s
== 1 CreateUsers: migrated (0.1250s)
   ========================================

c:0:Warning: require_gem is obsolete.  Use gem instead.
(in c:/peter/flexiblerails/current/pomodo)
```

Let's see if the user info made it into the database. Connect to MySQL, and check:

```
mysql> select id, login, email, first_name, last_name from users;
+----+----------+---------------------+------------+---------------+
| id | login    | email               | first_name | last_name     |
+----+----------+---------------------+------------+---------------+
|  1 | quentin  | quentin@example.com | NULL       | NULL          |
|  2 | aaron    | aaron@example.com   | NULL       | NULL          |
|  3 | ludwig   | lvb@pomodo.com      | Ludwig     | van Beethoven |
|  4 | wolfgang | wam@pomodo.com      | Wolfgang   | Mozart        |
+----+----------+---------------------+------------+---------------+
4 rows in set (0.00 sec)
```

The good news is that the first_name made it into the database from the fixture that is run by newdb.bat.

Next, start the server:

```
c:\peter\flexiblerails\current\pomodo>ruby script\server
=> Booting WEBrick...
=> Rails application started on http://0.0.0.0:3000
=> Ctrl-C to shutdown server; call with
   --help for options
```

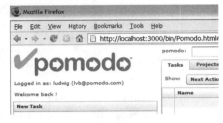

Finally, log in as ludwig. The MainBox appears, but as shown in figure 5.1, we're still not greeting Ludwig by his first name.

There's a bug somewhere—we're just not sure if it's on the Flex side or the Rails side.

Figure 5.1   Our not-so-polite application

5.2.1   Adding a primitive debug console to Flex

It would help us understand what was going on is if we had a quick and dirty way of debugging from within our running Flex application. On the Rails side, we have script\console and also the log file in log\development.log, but it would be nice to have something to help us from within Flex. (We have the Flex Builder debugger [or fdb for SDK users], but something simpler may be handy.) Lots of the data is XML, so it would be useful to have a `TextArea` we could dump it to. Let's build that now. We'll put a bit of effort into building a good debug console (or at least a good API to it), because this will end up saving us a ton of time in the long run.

> **NOTE**   The Flex Builder debugger is good enough that the debug console approach is a lot less necessary than it would have been with previous Flex versions. But it's still useful, especially if you're using the SDK and don't want to use fdb. It's also a security blanket for me, after having spent so much time writing Flex 1.0 and 1.5 code.

We'd like the ability to call a static utility function somewhere and have a debug message added to an `Array` of debug messages. These debug messages should be timestamped so we can see when they happened, and so on.

We'll start by defining a class for debug messages. Create the folder app\flex\com\pomodo\util, and create a new file called DebugMessage.as in it. Set its contents as shown in listing 5.1.

Listing 5.1   app\flex\com\pomodo\util\DebugMessage.as

```
package com.pomodo.util {
    public class DebugMessage {
        [Bindable]
        public var time:Date;      ❶
```

```
    [Bindable]
    public var message:String;          ❷

    public function DebugMessage(message:String) {
        time = new Date();          ❸
        this.message = message;          ❹
    }

    public function toString():String {          ❺
        return "[" + time + "] " + message;          ❻
    }
    }
}
```

This class has public `Bindable` properties for the time ❶ and message ❷. The time is set to a new `Date` ❸ in the constructor, which has the effect of creating a time-stamp because the default constructor for `Date` sets its time to the system time. The message that is passed in to the constructor is also stored ❹. The `toString()` function ❺ works the same way as it does in Java and as `to_s` does in Ruby, returning a `String` to display for the object. We display the time (which uses the `toString()` of `Date` to do this) in square brackets ❻, followed by the message.

Next, we'll create the `DebugPanel`; see listing 5.2.

Listing 5.2   app\flex\com\pomodo\components\DebugPanel.mxml

```
<?xml version="1.0" encoding="utf-8"?>
<mx:Panel xmlns:mx="http://www.adobe.com/2006/mxml"
    title="Debug Console" width="100%" height="200">
<mx:Script>
<![CDATA[
    import mx.collections.ArrayCollection;
    import com.pomodo.util.DebugMessage;

    [Bindable]
    private var _messages:ArrayCollection;          ❶

    public function addMessage(msg:DebugMessage):void {          ❷
        if (_messages == null) {
            _messages = new ArrayCollection();
        }
        _messages.addItem(msg);          ❸
        updateMessages();          ❹
    }

    private function clearMessages():void {          ❺
        _messages.source.splice(0);
        updateMessages();          ❻
    }
```

```
        private function updateMessages():void {
            //(This is somewhat inefficient since we're processing
            //the entire Array every time.)
            debugTA.text = _messages.source.join("\n");
        }
    ]]>
    </mx:Script>
        <mx:TextArea id="debugTA" width="100%" height="100%"/>
        <mx:Button label="clear" click="clearMessages()"/>
    </mx:Panel>
```

The addMessage function ❷ adds ❸ a DebugMessage to the _messages Array-
Collection ❶, creating it if necessary. It then calls ❹ updateMessages(). The
clearMessages function ❺ clears the Array inside the _messages Array-
Collection (splice(0) starts at the beginning and deletes all elements of the
Array). As the comment says, the way that updateMessages ❻ works is inefficient.
However, we don't care at the moment because it's just debug code. If it becomes
a problem, we can deal with it later.

Finally, we'll modify Pomodo.mxml; see listing 5.3.

Listing 5.3   app\flex\Pomodo.mxml

```
<?xml version="1.0" encoding="utf-8"?>
<mx:Application
    xmlns:mx="http://www.adobe.com/2006/mxml"
    xmlns:pom="com.pomodo.components.*"
    layout="vertical"
    backgroundGradientColors="[#ffffff, #c0c0c0]"
    horizontalAlign="center"
    verticalAlign="top"
    paddingLeft="0"
    paddingRight="0"
    paddingTop="0"
    paddingBottom="0"
    width="100%"
    height="100%">
<mx:Script>
<![CDATA[
    import com.pomodo.components.DebugPanel;      ◁─┐
    import com.pomodo.events.AccountCreateEvent;     ├── Add import
    import com.pomodo.events.LoginEvent;             │
    import com.pomodo.util.DebugMessage;          ◁─┘

    [Bindable]
    private var _user : XML;

    public static function debug(str:String):void {    ❶
        application.debugPanel.addMessage(
```

```
            new DebugMessage(str));        ❷
    }

    private function handleAccountCreate(e:AccountCreateEvent):
    void {
        login(e.user);
    }

    private function handleLogin(e:LoginEvent):void {
        login(e.user);
    }

    private function login(user:XML):void {
        _user = user;
        debug("user = " + user);          ❸
        mainStack.selectedChild = mainBox;
    }
]]>
</mx:Script>
    <mx:VDividedBox width="100%" height="100%">     ❹
        <mx:ViewStack id="mainStack" width="100%" height="100%">
            <pom:SplashBox id="splashBox"
                accountCreate="handleAccountCreate(event)"
                login="handleLogin(event)"/>
            <pom:MainBox id="mainBox" user="{_user}"/>
        </mx:ViewStack>
        <pom:DebugPanel id="debugPanel" width="100%"     ❺
            height="0%"/>
    </mx:VDividedBox>
</mx:Application>
```

We create a public static debug function ❶ that gets the debugPanel via the application static variable that Pomodo inherits from its Application base class. We then call the addMessage() function ❷ of the DebugPanel, passing it a new DebugMessage that we've constructed with the string we were provided. We call this new debug function in the login function ❸. (Outside of Pomodo, we'll call this function with Pomodo.debug(); here, we can just call debug().) Next, we wrap a VDividedBox ❹ around our existing mainStack. We add the DebugPanel to it ❺ and set its height to 0%. This means it will start off hidden at the bottom, until we drag the divider up to see it.

NOTE   Having a debug console permanently available is cheesy. However, it's simple to explain, so that's what I'm doing. Before we deploy the application in production, we'll obviously need to comment out the DebugPanel and the body of the debug function, as well as remove the VDividedBox that wraps the ViewStack.

5.2.2 *The case of the missing first name*

Now that we've built our debug console, let's see it in action. Rebuild and reload the app, and log in as ludwig. Next, drag the divider up from the bottom of the window to show the debug console (see figure 5.2).

Hmmm. The debug console shows the <user> as having a child of <first-name> (with the correct name, Ludwig). However, we were expecting <first_name>!

Clearly this is a bug, but is the bug in Flex or Rails? More specifically: The XML is wrong, but is Flex or Rails mangling it?

NOTE We *could* say user.child('first-name') in the MainBox, and it would work. (Try it.) But we can't say user.first-name, because Flex will think we're subtracting some variable called name from user.first. We're stubborn, and we like the sexy E4X (ECMAScript for XML) syntax (such as user.first_name), so we're *not* going to give in and use user.child('first-name'). Besides, not knowing where the hyphen came from is unsettling. (Another workaround would be to not have underscores in our table column names. However, this smells like accepting defeat too easily—and by this point, this is making us mad.) Also, trying to figure this out should be instructive.

Figure 5.2   The debug console showing the user XML

Let's fire up script\console and do some investigating on the Rails side. Running script\console runs the interactive Ruby debugger, irb, but in the environment of our running Rails app. We know that the id of ludwig is 3, so we can use that to do a find:

```
c:\peter\flexiblerails\current\pomodo>ruby script\console    Tested with
Loading development environment (Rails 2.0.1)    ◁───────    Rails 2.0.1
>> ludwig = User.find(3)
=> #<User id: 3, login: "ludwig", email: "lvb@pomodo.com",    ❶ first_name
first_name: "Ludwig", last_name: "van Beethoven",    ◁────────    is Ludwig
crypted_password: "fc3f2237b0edbeab2c08eecbc7bd6ef9b2124080",
salt: "cf1bc466e9dedd7d687e967ba37947971d44ab6e",
created_at: "2007-10-11 05:11:32", updated_at: nil,
remember_token: nil, remember_token_expires_at: nil>
>>
```

(Leave script\console open.) All the attributes look present and correct. Specifically, first_name is correctly set to "Ludwig" ❶. We also know that the act of logging in is the act of creating a new session and that the SessionsController# create_xml method is used; see listing 5.4.

Listing 5.4   app\controllers\sessions_controller.rb

```
# This controller handles the login/logout function of the site.
class SessionsController < ApplicationController
...
  def create_xml
    self.current_user =
      User.authenticate(params[:login], params[:password])
    if logged_in?
      if params[:remember_me] == "1"
        self.current_user.remember_me
        cookies[:auth_token] = {
          :value => self.current_user.remember_token,
          :expires => self.current_user.remember_token_expires_at
        }
      end
      render :xml => self.current_user.to_xml        ❶
    else
      render :text => "badlogin"
    end
  end
...
```

After a successful login, we send self.current_user.to_xml ❶ to the client.

Because we're logging in as ludwig, let's see what calling to_xml looks like for him. Back to script\console we go:

```
>> ludwig.to_xml
=> "<?xml version=\"1.0\" encoding=\"UTF-8\"?>\n<user>\n
  ➡<created-at type=\"datetime\">2007-10-11T05:11:32+01:00
  ➡</created-at>\n
  ➡<crypted-password>fc3f2237b0edbeab2c08eecbc7bd6ef9b2124080
  ➡</crypted-password>\n  <email>lvb@pomodo.com</email>\n
  ➡<first-name>Ludwig</first-name>\n  <id type=\"integer\">3      ❶
  ➡</id>\n  <last-name>van Beethoven</last-name>\n  <login>
  ➡ludwig</login>\n  <remember-token></remember-token>\n
  ➡<remember-token-expires-at type=\"datetime\">
  ➡</remember-token-expire\s-at>\n
    ➡<salt>cf1bc466e9dedd7d687e967ba37947971d44ab6e</salt>\n
  ➡<updated-at type=\"datetime\"></updated-at>\n</user>\n"
>>
```

Looking at the output, we see (❶) the following:

```
<first-name>Ludwig</first-name>
```

Aha! It's Rails' fault after all! The attribute (as we saw earlier) is first_name, but to_xml is giving us first-name. Where did first-name come from?

The answer turns out to be: from the *really*[5] *stupid* default behavior of the to_xml method. By default, it calls a method called dasherize to convert underscores to hyphens. This is an egregious violation of the Principle of Least Astonishment:

> *The* Principle of Least Astonishment *states that the result of performing some operation should be obvious, consistent, and predictable, based upon the name of the operation and other clues.*
>
> —http://c2.com/cgi/wiki?PrincipleOfLeastAstonishment

5.2.3 *Fixing to_xml temporarily*

Fortunately, Rails 1.2 added the ability to turn off this "feature" for an individual method call by passing :dasherize => false to the to_xml method. Let's see what happens for ludwig if we call to_xml with :dasherize => false. Back to script\console we go:

```
>> ludwig.to_xml(:dasherize => false)
=> "<?xml version=\"1.0\" encoding=\"UTF-8\"?>\n<user>\n
  ➡<created_at type=\"datetime\">2007-10-11T05:11:32+01:00
  ➡</created_at>\n
    ➡<crypted_password>fc3f2237b0edbeab2c08eecbc7bd6ef9b2124080
  ➡</crypted_password>\n  <email>lvb@pomodo.com</email>\n
    ➡<first_name>Ludwig</first_name>\n  <id type=\"integer\">3     ❶
  ➡</id>\n  <last_name>van Beethoven</last_name>\n  <login>
  ➡ludwig</login>\n  <remember_token></remember_token>\n
    ➡<remember_token_expires_at type=\"datetime\">
```

---

[5] Really, really, *really, really, REALLY.*

```
⇒</remember_token_expires_at>\n
   ⇒<salt>cf1bc466e9dedd7d687e967ba37947971d44ab6e</salt>\n
⇒<updated_at type=\"datetime\"></updated_at>\n</user>\n"
>>
```

Looking at the output, we see that this produces the following ❶:

```
<first_name>Ludwig</first_name>
```

Good. Let's check whether applying this fix to our `create_xml` method fixes login. Modify the `SessionsController` as shown in listing 5.5.

Listing 5.5   app\controllers\sessions_controller.rb

```ruby
# This controller handles the login/logout function of the site.
class SessionsController < ApplicationController
...
  # Once we explain REST in the book this will obviously be
  # refactored.
  def create_xml
    self.current_user =
      User.authenticate(params[:login], params[:password])
    if logged_in?
      if params[:remember_me] == "1"
        self.current_user.remember_me
        cookies[:auth_token] = {
         :value => self.current_user.remember_token,
         :expires => self.current_user.remember_token_expires_at
        }
      end
      render :xml => self.current_user.to_xml(          ⟵──────┐  Using :dasherize
        :dasherize => false)                                   └─ => false
    else
      render :text => "badlogin"
    end
  end
...
end
```

Reload (we don't need to rebuild, because we only changed Rails code), and log in as ludwig. We see the screen shown in figure 5.3.

It worked!

We could fix the `create_xml` method in the `UsersController` too. However, this is really infuriating. We'll be using `to_xml` all the time from

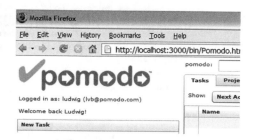

Figure 5.3   Welcome back, not broken by dasherize

Rails, and there is no good reason for `dasherize` to be on by default. We want a more permanent solution.

5.2.4   *Fixing to_xml permanently*

In Ruby, if we don't like something, we can always change it. That's what we'll do here.

> **NOTE**   One great thing about Ruby that is slightly unsettling if you have a Java background is that you can open a class or module definition anywhere and add or override methods. This sounds like it would create absolute chaos, but the upside is that because you aren't treated like a child, you can do things you need to do without having to beg the all-powerful library author to please make a change for you. ("Dear DHH, please change your framework to make it play better with Flex....") As someone with years of Java experience, there have been a few times when I've cursed the author of a given class for making a certain method say package private or making a certain class final. In Ruby, you're not treated like an idiot.

Open the `ApplicationController`. We're going to override some of Rails' default behavior. Specifically, we'll override a few methods to force[6] the value of `:dasherize` to be false, instead of the default value of true or any value explicitly passed in; see listing 5.6.

Listing 5.6   app\controllers\application.rb

```
module ActiveSupport #:nodoc:
  module CoreExtensions #:nodoc:
    module Hash #:nodoc:
      module Conversions          ❶
        # We force :dasherize to be false, since we never want
        # it true.  Thanks very much to the reader on the
        # flexiblerails Google Group who suggested this better
        # approach.
        unless method_defined? :old_to_xml        ❷
          alias_method :old_to_xml, :to_xml        ❸
          def to_xml(options = {})          ❹
            options.merge!(:dasherize => false)          ❺
            old_to_xml(options)          ❻
          end
        end
      end
    end
  end
end
```

---

[6] Thanks *very* much to the reader on the flexiblerails Google Group who suggested this approach.

```
    module Array #:nodoc:
      module Conversions      ❼
        # We force :dasherize to be false, since we never want
        # it to be true.
        unless method_defined? :old_to_xml
          alias_method :old_to_xml, :to_xml
          def to_xml(options = {})
            options.merge!(:dasherize => false)
            old_to_xml(options)
          end
        end
      end
    end
  end
end
module ActiveRecord #:nodoc:
  module Serialization      ❽
    # We force :dasherize to be false, since we never want it to
    # be true.
    unless method_defined? :old_to_xml
      alias_method :old_to_xml, :to_xml
      def to_xml(options = {})
        options.merge!(:dasherize => false)
        old_to_xml(options)
      end
    end
  end
end


# Filters added to this controller apply to all controllers in
# the application. Likewise, all the methods added will be
# available for all controllers.

class ApplicationController < ActionController::Base
  helper :all # include all helpers, all the time
  include AuthenticatedSystem

  # See ActionController::RequestForgeryProtection for details
  # Uncomment the :secret if you're not using the cookie session
  # store
  # TODO - this will be uncommented once we explain sessions
  # in iteration 5.
  # protect_from_forgery
  # :secret => 'dd92c128b5358a710545b5e755694d57'
end
```

We start by overriding to_xml for the ActiveSupport::CoreExtensions::Hash::Conversions module ❶. We don't want to alias the method twice (or we'll get stack overflows—try it without this guard to see), so we proceed `unless method_defined?` `:old_to_xml` ❷.[7] (I like code that reads like English.) If we haven't already defined `:old_to_xml`, we first call `alias_method` ❸ to make a copy of the `to_xml` method called `old_to_xml`. We then override `to_xml` ❹, taking the same options `Hash` as `to_xml`. We don't bother changing the default of `:dasherize` in the options `Hash`, because this wouldn't have the desired effect if a caller explicitly set `:dasherize => true`. Next, we call `options.merge!` to force `:dasherize` to be false ❺. This works because the `Hash merge!` method causes entries in the `Hash` parameter to clobber entries with the same key in the `Hash` whose `merge!` method is being called. Finally, with `:dasherize` properly forced to be false (and any other options preserved intact), we call `old_to_xml` ❻ to invoke the original `to_xml` method we overrode.

We do the same steps for the `ActiveSupport::CoreExtensions::Array::Conversions` module ❼ and the `ActiveRecord::Serialization` module ❽.

NOTE If you're using Rails 1.2.x or below in some other project, you need to replace `ActiveRecord::Serialization` with `ActiveRecord::XmlSerialization`.

With this done, we can go back to `SessionsController` and remove `:dasherize => false` (see listing 5.7, ❶ and ❷).

Listing 5.7   app\controllers\sessions_controller.rb

```
# This controller handles the login/logout function of the site.
class SessionsController < ApplicationController
...
  # Once we explain REST in the book this will obviously be
  # refactored.
  def create_xml
    self.current_user =
      User.authenticate(params[:login], params[:password])
    if logged_in?
      if params[:remember_me] == "1"
        self.current_user.remember_me
        cookies[:auth_token] = {
          :value => self.current_user.remember_token,
          :expires => self.current_user.remember_token_expires_at
        }
      end
      render :xml => self.current_user.to_xml(          ❶
```

[7] The `unless method_defined?` guard approach is taken from a thread from 2006-01-13 on rails@lists.rubyonrails.org. Thanks very much to the person who posted a helpful explanation. (I had tried things like `unless ((defined? :old_to_xml) == "method")` with no success.)

```
        :dasherize => false)
      render :xml => self.current_user.to_xml        ❷
    else
      render :text => "badlogin"
    end
  end
...
end
```

Reload (we don't need to rebuild, because we only changed Rails code), and log in as ludwig. We see the "Welcome back Ludwig!" greeting, and looking at the XML shows the first_name, last_name, and so on, unmangled. We can also reload and create a new user to see that the XML is unmangled for new users too.

Now that we've fixed the to_xml methods, we can go ahead and create our data model for tasks, projects, and locations. This is typically done by using something called *scaffolding*. Note that as of Rails 2, the non-RESTful scaffold command has been replaced by what used to be called scaffold_resource: What we used to invoke with scaffold_resource is now invoked with scaffold. So, as of Rails 2, there is no escaping REST, because there is no non-RESTful scaffold.

5.3 Creating the new resources (including migrations, models, and controllers)

Now that we've done some thinking about what we want pomodo to be, we've arrived at the beginnings of a data model. We've said "We'll need tasks, projects to put them in, and locations where tasks will be performed."

5.3.1 Creating the Task, Project, and Location resources

Let's do some code generation. Note that we don't need to create a user model, because we already have one. We do, however, need to create new Task, Project, and Location resources. We'll use the now-RESTful scaffold command (formerly known as scaffold_resource) to generate new RESTful models, controllers, and so on for the tasks, projects, and locations. To see a description of the scaffold command's usage, stop your server and run the following command:

```
c:\peter\flexiblerails\current\pomodo>
ruby script\generate scaffold
Usage: script/generate scaffold ModelName [field:type,
    ↪field:type]
...read the full description on the command line...
Examples:
    `./script/generate scaffold post` # no attributes, view will
```

```
➥be anemic
   `./script/generate scaffold post title:string body:text
➥published:boolean`
   `./script/generate scaffold purchase order_id:integer
➥amount:decimal`
```

```
c:\peter\flexiblerails\current\pomodo>
```

Run the commands shown in listing 5.8, noting that we're including every field in the model so that we get nice scaffolded views.

Listing 5.8 Commands

```
c:\peter\flexiblerails\current\pomodo>
ruby script\generate scaffold Task user_id:integer
  ➥project_id:integer location_id:integer name:string
  ➥notes:text next_action:boolean completed:boolean
      exists  app/models/
...
      create     db/migrate/002_create_tasks.rb
      create  app/controllers/tasks_controller.rb
      create  test/functional/tasks_controller_test.rb
      create  app/helpers/tasks_helper.rb
       route  map.resources :tasks

c:\peter\flexiblerails\current\pomodo>
ruby script\generate scaffold Project user_id:integer
  ➥name:string notes:text completed:boolean
      exists  app/models/
...
      create     db/migrate/003_create_projects.rb
      create  app/controllers/projects_controller.rb
      create  test/functional/projects_controller_test.rb
      create  app/helpers/projects_helper.rb
       route  map.resources :projects

c:\peter\flexiblerails\current\pomodo>
ruby script\generate scaffold Location user_id:integer
  ➥name:string notes:text
      exists  app/models/
...
      create     db/migrate/004_create_locations.rb
      create  app/controllers/locations_controller.rb
      create  test/functional/locations_controller_test.rb
      create  app/helpers/locations_helper.rb
       route  map.resources :locations

c:\peter\flexiblerails\current\pomodo>
```

Running these commands creates a ton of new files in the controllers, helpers, and models directories, as well as new subdirectories in the views directory. Let's see what the new models look like; see listing 5.9.

Listing 5.9   `app\models\task.rb, app\models\project.rb, app\models\location.rb`

```
class Task < ActiveRecord::Base
end      ❶

class Project < ActiveRecord::Base
end

class Location < ActiveRecord::Base
end
```

Not much there right now (❶, ha ha) is there? Because these models extend (with `<`) `ActiveRecord::Base`, they can be mapped to the equivalent database tables. Because we also created the controllers and views with the `script\generate scaffold` command and ensured that we specified all the fields, we can use a prebuilt web interface to Create, Read, Update, and Delete (CRUD) them.

> **What's Active Record?**
>
> Active Record is an object-relational mapping (ORM) pattern described by Martin Fowler as follows: "An object that wraps a row in a database table or view, encapsulates the database access, and adds domain logic on that data."[8] If you're new to Rails and Active Record, I strongly recommend taking a break and reading chapters 17–19 of *AWDwR*.

5.3.2 Adding the associations to the model

Recall that we said "we'll need tasks, projects to put them in, and locations where tasks will be performed." We could restate these requirements artificially as follows: A user has many tasks. A user has many projects. A task belongs to a user. A task belongs to a project. A task belongs to a location. A project belongs to a user. A project has many tasks.

These requirements can be expressed as the following Rails code, which we'll edit now. We start by editing the `Task` class (listing 5.10), `Project` class (listing 5.11), and `Location` class (listing 5.12).

---
[8] http://api.rubyonrails.com/files/vendor/rails/activerecord/README.html.

Listing 5.10 app\models\task.rb

```
class Task < ActiveRecord::Base
  belongs_to :user       ❶
  belongs_to :location     ❷
  belongs_to :project      ❸
end
```

Users ❶, locations ❷, and projects ❸ all have many tasks, so the task "belongs to" each of them.

Listing 5.11 app\models\project.rb

```
class Project < ActiveRecord::Base
  belongs_to :user       ❶
  has_many :tasks        ❷
end
```

A project has many tasks ❷ and a user has many projects, so the project "belongs to" a user ❶.

Listing 5.12 app\models\location.rb

```
class Location < ActiveRecord::Base
  belongs_to :user       ❶
  has_many :tasks        ❷
end
```

A location has many tasks ❷ and a user has many locations, so the location "belongs to" a user ❶.

Next, we add three associations to the User class, as shown in listing 5.13. We'll take a brief tour of the rest of the code to learn some Ruby and Rails basics as we go.

Listing 5.13 app\models\user.rb

```
require 'digest/sha1'
class User < ActiveRecord::Base
  has_many :tasks        ❶
  has_many :projects      ❷
  has_many :locations     ❸

  # Virtual attribute for the unencrypted password
  attr_accessor :password
```

```
validates_presence_of :login, :email
validates_presence_of :password, :if => :password_required?
validates_presence_of :password_confirmation,
  :if => :password_required?
validates_length_of :password, :within => 4..40,
  :if => :password_required?
validates_confirmation_of :password,
  :if => :password_required?
validates_length_of :login, :within => 3..40
validates_length_of :email, :within => 3..100
validates_uniqueness_of :login, :email,
  :case_sensitive => false
before_save :encrypt_password

# prevents a user from submitting a crafted form that bypasses
# activation
# anything else you want your user to change should be added
# here.
attr_accessible :login, :email, :password,
  :password_confirmation

# Authenticates a user by their login name and unencrypted
# password.  Returns the user or nil.
def self.authenticate(login, password)
  u = find_by_login(login) # need to get the salt
  u && u.authenticated?(password) ? u : nil
end
```

4 **Class method**

```
# Encrypts some data with the salt.
def self.encrypt(password, salt)
  Digest::SHA1.hexdigest("--#{salt}--#{password}--")
end
```

5 **Class method**

```
# Encrypts the password with the user salt
def encrypt(password)
  self.class.encrypt(password, salt)
end
```

6 **Instance method**

```
def authenticated?(password)
  crypted_password == encrypt(password)
end
```

7

```
def remember_token?
  remember_token_expires_at &&
    Time.now.utc < remember_token_expires_at
end

# These create and unset the fields required for remembering
# users between browser closes
```

```
def remember_me
  remember_me_for 2.weeks        ❽
end

def remember_me_for(time)
  remember_me_until time.from_now.utc
end

def remember_me_until(time)
  self.remember_token_expires_at = time
  self.remember_token =
    encrypt("#{email}--#{remember_token_expires_at}")
  save(false)
end

def forget_me
  self.remember_token_expires_at = nil
  self.remember_token = nil
  save(false)
end

protected        ❾
  # before filter
  def encrypt_password         ❿
    return if password.blank?
    self.salt = Digest::SHA1.hexdigest(
➥ "--#{Time.now.to_s}--#{login}--") if new_record?
    self.crypted_password = encrypt(password)
  end

  def password_required?
    crypted_password.blank? || !password.blank?
  end

end
```

We start by adding has_many :tasks ❶, has_many :projects ❷, and has_many :locations ❸ method calls to add the associations. These calls add a ton of methods to the User class—see section 18.3 of *AWDwR* for details. These methods reflect the association between the tables. For example, the User has_many :tasks, and the Task belongs_to the :user. So, the tables are named users and tasks (plural), and the model classes are named User and Task. In the tables, the tasks table has a column called user_id, which points at the row of the users table for the user whom this task "belongs to." (See the explanation and diagrams in section 18.2 of *AWDwR* for details.) Note that although the user_id column in the tasks table is a foreign key that references the users table, Rails doesn't require us to define the foreign key constraint in our database. Even though we're not bothering to do so, you should. (Do as I say, not as I do.)

The `authenticate` method ❹ is defined with `self.`, meaning that it's a class method. A class method is similar to a static method in Java and other languages: It isn't associated with a specific instance of the given class. (In Ruby, it's a method of the class object.) We call it by saying `User.authenticate(somelogin, some-password)` rather than creating a specific `User` (say someuser) and calling `someuser.authenticate(somelogin, somepassword)`.

Note that although we can't overload methods in Ruby by a different number of arguments, we can create a `class` method ❺ and an `instance` method ❻ that have the same name. This is possible because they're methods of different objects. (This is explained well in *Ruby for Rails*—I'm not just plugging that because it's also a Manning book; I mean it.)

The `authenticated?` ❼ method ends with a question mark, which is part of the name. (It has no effect other than to make the code more readable: "Call this method to ask a question and get the answer.") The `remember_me_for 2.weeks` ❽ line is beautiful. It uses the `weeks` method, which was added to the Ruby `Fixnum` class by Active Support. If you try this in irb, it won't work (because irb uses just Ruby, not Ruby as enhanced by Rails); you need to use ruby script\console for it to work:

```
c:\peter\flexiblerails\current\pomodo>irb
irb(main):001:0> 2.class
=> Fixnum
irb(main):002:0> 2.weeks
NoMethodError: undefined method `weeks' for 2:Fixnum
        from (irb):2
irb(main):003:0> exit

c:\peter\flexiblerails\current\pomodo>ruby script\console
Loading development environment.
>> 2.weeks
=> 1209600
>>
```

There are 1209600 (60*60*24*14) seconds in two weeks. Now you know.

The `protected` statement ❾ changes the access control for subsequent methods to `protected` (callable by instances of the class and its subclasses only). Note that the `protected` statement is a method call, because in Ruby class definitions are executable code. The `encrypt_password` method ❿ is a protected instance method that is used to encrypt a given password. It's specified as a `before_save` filter. We'll discuss filters and validation methods later.

Although we're considering what is added by Active Support, note that it also adds `dasherize`:

```
c:\peter\flexiblerails\current\pomodo>irb
irb(main):001:0> "bad_idea".dasherize
NoMethodError: undefined method `dasherize' for "bad_idea":String
        from (irb):1
irb(main):002:0> exit

c:\peter\flexiblerails\current\pomodo>ruby script\console
Loading development environment (Rails 1.2.3)
>> "bad_idea".dasherize
=> "bad-idea"
>> exit

c:\peter\flexiblerails\current\pomodo>
```

Specifically, it's added by the `Inflector::Inflections` class, as shown in listing 5.14.

NOTE See chapter 15 of *AWDwR* for the various extensions to the core Ruby classes made by Active Support.

Listing 5.14 vendor\rails\activesupport\lib\active_support\inflector.rb

```
require 'singleton'
...
module Inflector
...
  class Inflections
    include Singleton
...
  # Replaces underscores with dashes in the string.
  #
  # Example
  #   "puni_puni" #=> "puni-puni"
  def dasherize(underscored_word)
    underscored_word.gsub(/_/, '-')
  end
...
end

require File.dirname(__FILE__) + '/inflections'
```

5.3.3 *A tour of the TasksController*

The `script\generate scaffold` command created more code in the controllers and views than in the models. In order to demystify it, we'll look at the code that was created for the `TasksController` (the code for the `ProjectsController` and

LocationsController is essentially the same). This code, shown in listing 5.15, is the basis for table 5.1; after you've read this code, that table will make more sense.

Listing 5.15   app\controllers\tasks_controller.rb

```
class TasksController < ApplicationController            ◄───┐    ❶ All controllers extend
  # GET /tasks                                                      ApplicationController
  # GET /tasks.xml         ❷ Render HTML or XML
  def index     ◄─┘          based on format
    @tasks = Task.find(:all)

    respond_to do |format|
      format.html # index.html.erb
      format.xml  { render :xml => @tasks }
    end
  end

  # GET /tasks/1
  # GET /tasks/1.xml
  def show       ❸
    @task = Task.find(params[:id])

    respond_to do |format|
      format.html # show.html.erb
      format.xml  { render :xml => @task }
    end
  end

  # GET /tasks/new
  # GET /tasks/new.xml
  def new        ❹
    @task = Task.new

    respond_to do |format|
      format.html # new.html.erb
      format.xml  { render :xml => @task }
    end
  end

  # GET /tasks/1/edit
  def edit       ❺
    @task = Task.find(params[:id])
  end

  # POST /tasks
  # POST /tasks.xml
  def create     ❻
    @task = Task.new(params[:task])

    respond_to do |format|
```

```
        if @task.save
          flash[:notice] = 'Task was successfully created.'
          format.html { redirect_to(@task) }
          format.xml  { render :xml => @task, :status => :created,
            :location => @task }
        else
          format.html { render :action => "new" }
          format.xml  { render :xml => @task.errors,
            :status => :unprocessable_entity }
        end
    end
  end

  # PUT /tasks/1
  # PUT /tasks/1.xml
  def update          ❼
    @task = Task.find(params[:id])

    respond_to do |format|
      if @task.update_attributes(params[:task])
        flash[:notice] = 'Task was successfully updated.'
        format.html { redirect_to(@task) }
        format.xml  { head :ok }
      else
        format.html { render :action => "edit" }
        format.xml  { render :xml => @task.errors,
          :status => :unprocessable_entity }
      end
    end
  end

  # DELETE /tasks/1
  # DELETE /tasks/1.xml
  def destroy         ❽
    @task = Task.find(params[:id])
    @task.destroy

    respond_to do |format|
      format.html { redirect_to(tasks_url) }
      format.xml  { head :ok }
    end
  end
end
```

First, note that all controllers extend `ApplicationController` ❶. Next, we see that `scaffold` gives us a lot, creating the seven standard Rails methods—index ❷, show ❸, new ❹, edit ❺, create ❻, update ❼, and destroy ❽—that are used by

RESTful controllers. These are *the only methods* we should have in a RESTful controller: If you think you're special and need more, well, as Scott Raymond[9] quoted *Fight Club,* "You are not a special or unique snowflake." If you think you're unique, try adding a noun—if we had rolled our own `UsersController` with `create` and `login` methods, the refactoring would have been to add a noun (session), thus having a `SessionsController` and a `UsersController`, both with the standard `create` method. The `restful_authentication` generator skipped this step for us.

Note that each method has a comment showing the URL + fake HTTP request combination that triggers it. For example, the `index` method ❷ (which is triggered by a GET to /tasks or /tasks.xml) finds all the tasks and stores them in `@tasks`. Then, inside the `respond_to` block, it checks if the requested format was html (and renders index.html.erb if it was) or xml (and renders `@tasks`, which is syntactic sugar for `@tasks.to_xml`).

Keep in mind that the automatically generated code in the controller and views that is created by the `scaffold` command is just that: scaffolding to help us get going. There's nothing magical about it. The first thing we typically do is start modifying and deleting methods generated by the `scaffold` command. Developers who have had bad experiences with tools such as Visual Blub++[10] generating hundreds of lines of unintelligible code that had to be left alone or everything would explode may be predisposed to think of scaffolding as something suspicious. Once you realize it's just a way to get past the programming equivalent of writer's block, you'll be a lot happier. (If only there was a script\generate `scaffold` for books!)

At this point, if you want to scan through the .html.erb templates (so named because they're processed by ERb, Embedded Ruby) in app\views\tasks, feel free to do so. These scaffolded views (and the similar ones in app\views\projects and app\views\locations) are useful for testing. Because we're using Flex instead of Action View, we'll leave explanations of how Action View works to other books (such as *AWDwR*). If you have to output HTML, Rails has you covered, with Action View for HTML and RJS templates for JavaScript.

Looking back at our running UI, we realize we've forgotten the poor Notely tab. We'll continue to ignore it for now, because it would be boring and because we want to minimize the amount of code that is dragged through the refactorings we'll do. We'll revisit it later.

---

[9] http://conferences.oreillynet.com/presentations/rails2007/raymond_scott.pdf, slide 30.

[10] If you haven't read http://www.cabochon.com/~stevey/blog-rants/bob-paradox.html and http://www.cabochon.com/~stevey/blog-rants/tour-de-babel.html yet, do it as a reward at the end of this iteration. Steve Yegge's blog is one of the highlights of the Ruby community.

5.3.4 *Understanding how routing works to set the requested format*

Earlier, I glossed over something that is fairly deep: I said the respond_to block is used to check if the requested format was html (and renders index.html.erb if it was) or xml (and renders @tasks, which is syntactic sugar for @tasks.to_xml). But how does the client set the requested format, and how is this configured in Rails? To answer that, we need to look at routing. I've been ignoring routing up to now; it's time to change that. Before we proceed, let's get rid of the Welcome Aboard screen: *delete the public\index.html file now.* **(It overrides the default route, and I've been welcomed aboard enough.)**

Next, we'll examine and modify the routes.rb file, adding the default route. When you log in from HTML, the best thing to see would be a list of tasks. We'll modify config\routes.rb; see listing 5.16.

Listing 5.16   config\routes.rb

```
ActionController::Routing::Routes.draw do |map|        ❶ Keep new resource-
  map.resources :locations          ◄──────────────────   based routes together

  map.resources :projects

  map.resources :tasks

  # The priority is based upon order of creation:
  # first created -> highest priority.

  # Sample of regular route:
  #   map.connect 'products/:id', :controller => 'catalog',
  #     :action => 'view'
  # Keep in mind you can assign values other than :controller
  # and :action

  # Sample of named route:
  #   map.purchase 'products/:id/purchase',
  #     :controller => 'catalog', :action => 'purchase'
  # This route can be invoked with
  # purchase_url(:id => product.id)

  # Sample resource route (maps HTTP verbs to controller actions
  # automatically):
  #   map.resources :products      ❷ Keep new resource-
  map.resources :tasks        ◄──────   based routes together
  map.resources :projects
  map.resources :locations
  map.resources :users        ❸
  map.resource  :session      ❹

  map.signup '/signup', :controller => 'users',
    :action => 'new'
```

```
map.login '/login', :controller => 'sessions',
  :action => 'new'
map.logout '/logout', :controller => 'sessions',
  :action => 'destroy'

# Sample resource route with options:
#   map.resources :products,
#     :member => { :short => :get, :toggle => :post },
#     :collection => { :sold => :get }

# Sample resource route with sub-resources:
#   map.resources :products,
#     :has_many => [ :comments, :sales ],
#     :has_one => :seller

# Sample resource route within a namespace:
#   map.namespace :admin do |admin|
#     # Directs /admin/products/* to Admin::ProductsController
#     # (app/controllers/admin/products_controller.rb)
#     admin.resources :products
#   end

# You can have the root of your site routed with map.root --
# just remember to delete public/index.html.
# map.root :controller => "welcome"        ❺              ❻ index action of Tasks-
map.root :controller => "tasks"            ◁──────           Controller is default

# See how all your routes lay out with "rake routes"        ❼

# Install the default routes as the lowest priority.
map.connect ':controller/:action/:id'
map.connect ':controller/:action/:id.:format'    ❽
end
```

Note that we've set up (well, the restful_authentication generator did) a special set of routes for the users and sessions resources with the map.resources :users ❸ (note the plural form) and map.resource :session ❹ (note the singular form) calls.

NOTE   For an explanation of plural vs. singular resources, see http://api. rubyonrails.org/classes/ActionController/Resources.html. Note that the new Rails 2.0 convention is to use plural resources by default; see http:// weblog.rubyonrails.org/2007/9/30/rails-2-0-0-preview-release for more information. Also, note that if you use restful_authentication with Rails 1.2.x in some other project, you will need to specify the controller name with map.resource :session, :controller => 'sessions'. See the restful_authentication README file in vendor\plugins\restful_ authentication for details.

So that we can keep track of the routes when looking at routes.rb, we move ❶ the new resource-based routes down to be with the other ones ❷. (I reordered them, but that is just because I think of them in that order—the priority change doesn't matter to us.)

We also uncomment the default route (map.root) ❺ to make the root of the site be the index action of the TasksController ❻—the index action is the default action, so we don't need to specify it. (Part of the learning curve of Rails is getting to know all the defaults.)

Next, we see that the lowest-priority route ❽ is :controller/:action/ :id.:format, which will extract the format (after the .) into something (the :format) the respond_to block processes. (The respond_to block's parameter is also a variable named format, because that makes it clear what it's responding to.)

Finally, we're advised by a helpful comment ❼ that as of Rails 2 we can do rake routes to see how the routes are laid out. Let's do that now, in listing 5.17.

NOTE   The rake routes command produces extremely wide output, nicely lined up in columns. It looks great on the command line, but doesn't translate well to 64-column book code. Please see at the output on the command line before reading the explanation.

Listing 5.17   Commands

```
c:\peter\flexiblerails\current\pomodo>rake routes
c:0:Warning: require_gem is obsolete.  Use gem instead.
(in c:/peter/flexiblerails/current/pomodo)
tasks GET    /tasks {:action=>"index", :controller=>"tasks"}        ❶
formatted_tasks GET    /tasks.:format {:action=>"index",
      ➥:controller=>"tasks"}
POST   /tasks {:action=>"create", :controller=>"tasks"}        ❷
POST   /tasks.:format {:action=>"create", :controller=>"tasks"}
...
POST   /users {:action=>"create", :controller=>"users"}        ❸
POST   /users.:format {:action=>"create", :controller=>"users"}       ❹
...
POST   /session {:action=>"create", :controller=>"sessions"}       ❺
POST   /session.:format {:action=>"create",         ❻
  ➥:controller=>"sessions"}
...
/:controller/:action/:id
/:controller/:action/:id.:format        ❼

c:\peter\flexiblerails\current\pomodo>
```

The `Task`, `Project`, and `Location` resources that we created with the `scaffold` command are all displayed ❶. (Note that I omitted most of them in the output.) Note that they all use the plural form. The routes are in highest-to-lowest priority, so you see that the `:controller/:action/:id.:format` route ❼ is the lowest priority. Above that, other routes match URLs that look like `/users.:format` ❹ and `/session.:format` ❻. There are also routes that match URLs with no format specified after an extension, such as `/users` ❸ and `/session` ❺; these routes ensure that the appropriate default actions are called. Also, note that the lines show different (pretend) HTTP methods that are paired with the URL format to produce what is used to determine the match: a `GET` to `/tasks` ❶ matches the `index` action, whereas a `POST` to `/tasks` matches the `create` action❷.

> **NOTE** You can also use HTTP headers to set the requested format; but using the file extension is easier to do from Flex, so I'll focus on it and ignore the HTTP headers approach. Just know that the HTTP headers approach exists.

5.3.5 *Making the UsersController and SessionsController RESTful*

Now that we've seen how the `TasksController` generated by the `scaffold` command uses the same methods to handle requests that want HTML and XML responses, and now that we understand how routing works to specify the desired `:format`, we can go back and modify the `UsersController` and `Sessions-Controller` to use this technique and then modify our Flex code to use the updated controllers.

First, we modify the `UsersController`, as shown in listing 5.18.

Listing 5.18   app\controllers\users_controller.rb

```
class UsersController < ApplicationController
  # GET /users/new
  # GET /users/new.xml        ⊲── Add URL + HTTP method
  # render new.rhtml              comment for documentation
  def new
  end


  # Once we explain REST in the book this will obviously be      ❶
  # refactored.
  def create_xml
    @user = User.new(params[:user])
    @user.save!
    self.current_user = @user
    render :xml => @user.to_xml
  rescue ActiveRecord::RecordInvalid
    render :text => "error"
  end
```

```
# POST /users          ◁──┐  Add URL + HTTP method
# POST /users.xml         │  comment for documentation
def create      ❷
  cookies.delete :auth_token
  # protects against session fixation attacks, wreaks havoc
  # wreaks request forgery protection.
  # uncomment at your own risk
  # reset_session
  @user = User.new(params[:user])
  @user.save!
  self.current_user = @user
  redirect_back_or_default('/')
  flash[:notice] = "Thanks for signing up!"
  respond_to do |format|      ❸
    format.html do
      redirect_back_or_default('/')
      flash[:notice] = "Thanks for signing up!"
    end
    format.xml  { render :xml => @user.to_xml }
  end
rescue ActiveRecord::RecordInvalid
  render :action => 'new'
  respond_to do |format|      ❹
    format.html { render :action => 'new' }
    format.xml { render :text => "error" }
  end
end

end
```

Inside the create ❷ method, we create respond_to blocks for the normal ❸ and exceptional ❹ conditions. We move code that was in the create method into the format.html blocks, and we move the code from the old create_xml method ❶ into the format.xml blocks. We then delete the create_xml method. Note the two types of block syntax: the multiline do ... end and the single-line { ... }.

Next, we make essentially the same changes to the SessionsController, as shown in listing 5.19.

Listing 5.19   app\controllers\sessions_controller.rb

```
# This controller handles the login/logout function of the site.
class SessionsController < ApplicationController
  # GET /session/new       ◁──┐  Add URL + HTTP method
  # GET /session/new.xml      │  comment for documentation
  # render new.rhtml
  def new
  end
```

```
# Once we explain REST in the book this will obviously be          1
# refactored.
def create_xml
  self.current_user =
    User.authenticate(params[:login], params[:password])
  if logged_in?
    if params[:remember_me] == "1"
      self.current_user.remember_me
      cookies[:auth_token] = {
        :value => self.current_user.remember_token,
        :expires => self.current_user.remember_token_expires_at
      }
    end
    render :xml => self.current_user.to_xml
  else
    render :text => "badlogin"
  end
end

# POST /session        ◁─┐   Add URL + HTTP method
# POST /session.xml       │   comment for documentation
def create
  self.current_user =
    User.authenticate(params[:login], params[:password])
  if logged_in?
    if params[:remember_me] == "1"
      self.current_user.remember_me
      cookies[:auth_token] = {
        :value => self.current_user.remember_token ,
        :expires =>
          self.current_user.remember_token_expires_at }
    end
    redirect_back_or_default('/')
    flash[:notice] = "Logged in successfully"
    respond_to do |format|        2
      format.html do
        redirect_back_or_default('/')
        flash[:notice] = "Logged in successfully"
      end
      format.xml  { render :xml => self.current_user.to_xml }
    end
  else
    render :action => 'new'
    respond_to do |format|        3
      format.html { render :action => 'new' }
      format.xml { render :text => "badlogin" }
    end
  end
end
```

```
# DELETE /session        ◁──┐   Add URL + HTTP method
# DELETE /session.xml        │   comment for documentation
def destroy
  self.current_user.forget_me if logged_in?
  cookies.delete :auth_token
  reset_session
  flash[:notice] = "You have been logged out."
  redirect_back_or_default('/')
end
end
```

Again, we create two respond_to blocks ❷❸ inside create, move the old code from create inside the format.html sections, and move the code from create_xml inside the format.xml sections. We then delete the create_xml method ❶. Note that we haven't bothered to implement logout from Flex yet, so we haven't modified destroy. We'll add logout functionality later.

Having made these changes, we need to update the Flex code to point at the create methods instead of the create_xml methods. Looking back at the rake routes command, we see that the client code is simple: To get back XML, all we need to do is set the format that the client wants to be XML by specifying a .xml extension when doing a POST to /users.xml (❹ in Listing 5.17) or to /session.xml (❻ in Listing 5.17). (Now you see why I showed the routes when I did rake routes earlier.)

We start by modifying the AccountCreateBox, as shown in Listing 5.20.

Listing 5.20   app\flex\com\pomodo\components\AccountCreateBox.mxml

```
<?xml version="1.0" encoding="utf-8"?>
<mx:VBox xmlns:mx="http://www.adobe.com/2006/mxml" width="100%"
    height="100%" label="Create Account">
...
    <mx:HTTPService
        id="svcAccountCreate"
        url="/users/create_xml"          ❶
        url="/users.xml"                 ❷
        contentType="application/xml"
        resultFormat="e4x"
        method="POST"
        result="handleAccountCreateResult(event)">
...
    </mx:HTTPService>
...
</mx:VBox>
```

We change the URL from /users/create_xml ❶ to just /users.xml ❷.
Next, we modify the LoginBox, as shown in Listing 5.21.

Listing 5.21   app\flex\com\pomodo\components\LoginBox.mxml

```
<?xml version="1.0" encoding="utf-8"?>
<mx:VBox xmlns:mx="http://www.adobe.com/2006/mxml" width="100%"
    height="100%" label="Login">
...
    <mx:HTTPService
        id="svcAccountLogin"
        url="/sessions/create_xml"          ❶
        url="/session.xml"        ❷
        resultFormat="e4x"
        method="POST"
        result="handleAccountLoginResult(event)"/>
...
</mx:VBox>
```

We change the URL from /sessions/create_xml ❶ to just /session.xml ❷.

IMPORTANT   The URL is /session.xml, *not* /sessions.xml, since the routes.rb defines
the route for them as the singular map.resource :session, not the plural map.resources :sessions.

Rebuild, reload, and log in as ludwig. It still works!

5.3.6   *Editing and running the migrations*

Now, let's edit and then run the new migrations we've created by running the
scaffold command. It does an excellent job, but it's not psychic. Specifically, we
need to manually add restrictions like :default => 0, :null => false, and
:limit => 100. We'll edit the CreateTasks migration first, as shown in listing 5.22.

Listing 5.22   db\migrate\002_create_tasks.rb

```
class CreateTasks < ActiveRecord::Migration    ◁──────────┐ Extend
    def self.up                    ◁───── ❷ Create tasks table    ❶ ActiveRecord::Migration
      create_table :tasks do |t|         ❸
        t.integer :user_id, :default => 0, :null => false       ❹
        t.integer :project_id    ❺
        t.integer :location_id
        t.string :name, :limit => 100, :default => "",       ❻
          :null => false
        t.text :notes       ❼
        t.boolean :next_action, :null => false, :default => false    ❽
        t.boolean :completed, :null => false, :default => false
```

```
        t.timestamps      ⑨
      end
    end
                        ⑩  Drop tasks
                            table
    def self.down    ←
      drop_table :tasks    ⑪
    end
  end
```

The `CreateTasks` class extends `ActiveRecord::Migration` ❶, as all migrations do. The up method ❷ creates a new tasks table with the `create_table` method call ❸, which takes a block that does the work; the `down` method ⑩ deletes it with the `drop_table` ⑪ call. In the up method, we specify the data types of each new column, such as `integer` ❹, `string` ❻, `text` ❼, and `boolean` ❽. These are then mapped to the equivalent database data types: for example, `boolean` becomes a `tinyint(1)` in MySQL. Also note that the `:project_id` ❺ and `:location_id` columns serve the purpose of foreign keys to the projects and locations tables—but to have foreign keys, we need to add them ourselves. The `timestamps` ❾ call adds two columns: created_at and updated_at, which Rails treats specially, ensuring that they're automatically set. This is often a good thing to have, so we'll leave them there even though they won't be needed in this book.

Next, we make similar modifications to the `CreateProjects` and `Create-Locations` migrations (see listings 5.23 and 5.24).

Listing 5.23   db\migrate\003_create_projects.rb

```
class CreateProjects < ActiveRecord::Migration
  def self.up
    create_table :projects do |t|
      t.integer :user_id, :default => 0, :null => false
      t.string :name, :limit => 100, :default => "",
        :null => false
      t.text :notes
      t.boolean :completed, :null => false, :default => false

      t.timestamps
    end
  end

  def self.down
    drop_table :projects
  end
end
```

Listing 5.24 db\migrate\004_create_locations.rb

```
class CreateLocations < ActiveRecord::Migration
  def self.up
    create_table :locations do |t|
      t.integer :user_id, :default => 0, :null => false
      t.string :name, :limit => 100, :default => "",
        :null => false
      t.text :notes

      t.timestamps
    end
  end

  def self.down
    drop_table :locations
  end
end
```

At this point, we'd normally run the new migrations with rake db:migrate, and you're welcome to do this if you choose. For the purposes of this book, however, we'll run the newdb.bat script, which starts over, deletes the database, creates a new one, and then runs rake db:migrate and rake db:fixtures:load. This way, I hope to reduce the number of issues that occur if you're reading the book but only following along with some iterations—the newdb.bat script ensures we're on the same page. (If you want to follow along later in the iterations, please run newdb.bat.)

```
c:\peter\flexiblerails\current\pomodo>newdb.bat

c:\peter\flexiblerails\current\pomodo>
mysql -h localhost -u root -p  0<db\create.sql
Enter password: *******
c:\peter\flexiblerails\current\pomodo>call rake db:migrate
c:0:Warning: require_gem is obsolete.  Use gem instead.
(in c:/peter/flexiblerails/current/pomodo)
== 1 CreateUsers: migrating =====================================
-- create_table("users", {:force=>true})
   -> 0.1250s
== 1 CreateUsers: migrated (0.1250s)
   =========================================

== 2 CreateTasks: migrating =====================================
-- create_table(:tasks)
   -> 0.1250s
== 2 CreateTasks: migrated (0.1250s)
   =========================================

== 3 CreateProjects: migrating =====================================
```

Create tasks table

Create projects table

```
-- create_table(:projects)
   -> 0.1870s
== 3 CreateProjects: migrated (0.1870s)
   ========================================

== 4 CreateLocations: migrating =================================   <────┐
-- create_table(:locations)
   -> 0.1250s
== 4 CreateLocations: migrated (0.1250s)
   ===================================

c:0:Warning: require_gem is obsolete.  Use gem instead.
(in c:/peter/flexiblerails/current/pomodo)


c:\peter\flexiblerails\current\pomodo>
```

**Create
locations table**

Next, open a Command Prompt, run the mysql client, and connect to
pomodo_development. We'll confirm that the migrations had the desired effect.
Note that for space considerations, I'm omitting the Extra column; all it shows is
that the id field is auto_increment:

```
mysql> describe tasks;
+-------------+--------------+------+-----+---------+
| Field       | Type         | Null | Key | Default |
+-------------+--------------+------+-----+---------+
| id          | int(11)      | NO   | PRI | NULL    |
| user_id     | int(11)      | NO   |     | 0       |
| project_id  | int(11)      | YES  |     | NULL    |
| location_id | int(11)      | YES  |     | NULL    |
| name        | varchar(100) | NO   |     |         |
| notes       | text         | YES  |     | NULL    |
| next_action | tinyint(1)   | NO   |     | 0       |
| completed   | tinyint(1)   | NO   |     | 0       |
| created_at  | datetime     | YES  |     | NULL    |
| updated_at  | datetime     | YES  |     | NULL    |
+-------------+--------------+------+-----+---------+
10 rows in set (0.13 sec)

mysql> describe projects;
+-------------+--------------+------+-----+---------+
| Field       | Type         | Null | Key | Default |
+-------------+--------------+------+-----+---------+
| id          | int(11)      | NO   | PRI | NULL    |
| user_id     | int(11)      | NO   |     | 0       |
| name        | varchar(100) | NO   |     |         |
| notes       | text         | YES  |     | NULL    |
| completed   | tinyint(1)   | NO   |     | 0       |
| created_at  | datetime     | YES  |     | NULL    |
| updated_at  | datetime     | YES  |     | NULL    |
+-------------+--------------+------+-----+---------+
```

```
7 rows in set (0.02 sec)

mysql> describe locations;
+------------+--------------+------+-----+---------+
| Field      | Type         | Null | Key | Default |
+------------+--------------+------+-----+---------+
| id         | int(11)      | NO   | PRI | NULL    |
| user_id    | int(11)      | NO   |     | 0       |
| name       | varchar(100) | NO   |     |         |
| notes      | text         | YES  |     | NULL    |
| created_at | datetime     | YES  |     | NULL    |
| updated_at | datetime     | YES  |     | NULL    |
+------------+--------------+------+-----+---------+
6 rows in set (0.02 sec)
```

5.3.7 Ad hoc testing with the HTML views

Next, let's quickly play with the HTML views that were created by the scaffold command, to do some ad hoc testing. Start your server, and go to http://localhost:3000/tasks to trigger the index action; we see the screen shown in figure 5.4.

Hey, wait a second, where did these tasks come from?

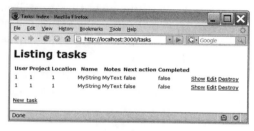

Figure 5.4 Listing tasks with the scaffold-created HTML views

Oh yeah, that's right: newdb.bat runs rake db:fixtures:load. It's a good guess that creating the new Task, Project, and Location resources created new fixtures. Looking in test\fixtures, we see that yes, that's what happened. For example, the tasks fixture is shown in listing 5.25.

Listing 5.25 test\fixtures\tasks.yml

```
# Read about fixtures at http://ar.rubyonrails.org/classes/Fixtures.html
one:               ◄────  First task,
  id: 1                   called one
  user_id: 1
  project_id: 1
  location_id: 1
  name: MyString
  notes: MyText
  next_action: false                      created_at and
  completed: false                        updated_at
  created_at: 2007-10-19 12:26:25  ◄──── timestamps set
  updated_at: 2007-10-19 12:26:25         automatically
two:
```

```
id: 2
user_id: 1
project_id: 1
location_id: 1
name: MyString
notes: MyText
next_action: false
completed: false
created_at: 2007-10-19 12:26:25
updated_at: 2007-10-19 12:26:25
```

Let's add a new location and a new task. Go to http://localhost:3000/locations; we see the screen shown in figure 5.5.

Click the New Location link to be taken to http://localhost:3000/locations/new, and fill out the form as shown in figure 5.6.

Click the Create button to create the new location; we see the screen shown in figure 5.7.

Figure 5.5 Listing locations with the `scaffold`-created HTML views

Figure 5.6 Listing locations with the `scaffold`-created HTML views

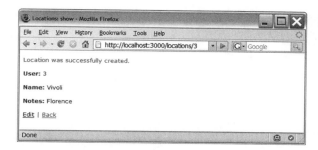

Figure 5.7 Showing the new location with the `scaffold`-created HTML views

Checking in MySQL, we see it was created and has an id of 3:

```
mysql> select id, user_id, name, notes, created_at from locations;
+----+---------+----------+----------+---------------------+
| id | user_id | name     | notes    | created_at          |
+----+---------+----------+----------+---------------------+
|  1 |       1 | MyString | MyText   | 2007-10-19 12:27:11 |
|  2 |       1 | MyString | MyText   | 2007-10-19 12:27:11 |
|  3 |       3 | Vivoli   | Florence | 2007-10-20 20:25:50 |
+----+---------+----------+----------+---------------------+
3 rows in set (0.00 sec)

mysql>
```

Next, go to http://localhost:3000/tasks/new, and fill in the New Task form as shown in figure 5.8.

Figure 5.8
Creating a new task with the `scaffold`**-created HTML views**

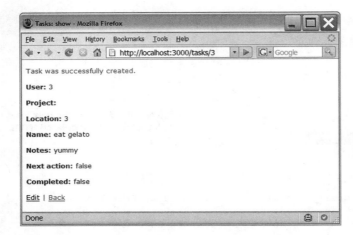

Figure 5.9
Newly created task with the
`scaffold`-created HTML views

After we click the Create button, we see the screen shown in figure 5.9.

Checking in the database shows the new `Task` is stored, along with the tasks created by the fixtures:

```
mysql> select * from tasks\G
*************************** 1. row ***************************
        id: 1
   user_id: 1
project_id: 1
location_id: 1
      name: MyString
     notes: MyText
next_action: 0
 completed: 0
created_at: 2007-10-19 12:26:25
updated_at: 2007-10-19 12:26:25
*************************** 2. row ***************************
        id: 2
   user_id: 1
project_id: 1
location_id: 1
      name: MyString
     notes: MyText
next_action: 0
 completed: 0
created_at: 2007-10-19 12:26:25
updated_at: 2007-10-19 12:26:25
*************************** 3. row ***************************
        id: 3
   user_id: 3
project_id: NULL           ❶
location_id: 3             ❷
```

```
      name: eat gelato
     notes: yummy
next_action: 0
  completed: 0
 created_at: 2007-10-20 20:29:28      ❸
 updated_at: 2007-10-20 20:29:28
3 rows in set (0.00 sec)
```

Note that the project_id ❶ is NULL because we didn't set it, whereas the location_id ❷ is 3. Also, note that the created_at and updated_at timestamps ❸ are set to the time the task was created.

NOTE   Don't worry that you see all the tasks, and so on, when you play with the UI. We'll fix this later in this iteration.

That's enough playing with the HTML views. We won't see them much more in the book—after all, this is a book about using Flex and Rails together, not about using or modifying the scaffold-created HTML views. We've seen enough to expect that they should work and to have a vague sense of how the RESTful routing works. We also have a strong motivation to read the resources—it *is* a world of resources after all—listed earlier in the iteration.

5.4 *Security*

Now that we've created the models, controllers, and some scaffolded views, we're almost ready to hook up the new controllers to our Flex GUI. Before we do this, however, we need to examine the security of the controllers. Because controller actions are just public methods, we need to protect them somehow so that people can't maliciously view, edit, or delete each other's tasks, projects, locations, or user accounts by messing with the predictable Rails URLs. Security through obscurity doesn't work.

In short, we need to do four things:

- Ensure destructive actions are done by POST
- Ensure everything (except creating a new account and logging in) can only be done by a logged-in user
- Ensure that logged-in users can only modify things (tasks, projects, locations) that belong to them
- Protect against Cross-Site Request Forgery (CSRF) attacks

All of these are necessary for our app to be secure. Implementing them is what we'll do next.

> **NOTE** I'm not claiming these things (A) are *sufficient* for the app to be secure, just that (B) they're *necessary*. (B implies A; A doesn't imply B.) Security is a complex topic that I can't cover fully in this book.

5.4.1 *Ensuring destructive actions are done by POST*

The good news is that because we're using 100% RESTful resources, we get this for free! The reason why is that the routing does its matching based on the pretend HTTP method + URL combination, and all the destructive actions with the RESTful routing scheme use a pretend HTTP method of POST, PUT, or DELETE. (As you'll see later, these all are POST, hence the "pretend HTTP method.") For non-RESTful controllers (which used to be all there was), we have to do stuff like this:

```
verify :method => :post, :only => [ :destroy, :create, :update ],
       :redirect_to => { :action => :list }
```

This restricts the destroy, create, and update methods to using POST. We allow the index, list, show, new, and edit methods to use GET. (Note that edit doesn't really edit, it just gets something in a format suitable for editing. Think of it as similar to the show action.)

Note that there are two choices for restricting access: :only and :except. The :only approach is risky, because if we add new methods that are destructive, we need to remember to add them to the :only Array.

5.4.2 *Requiring login*

Besides creating the new models, we've created new controllers for tasks (TasksController), projects (ProjectsController), and locations (LocationsController). Because they all extend the ApplicationController, they all include AuthenticatedSystem. However, we currently don't *use* this in any way—which means there is no security, and all the actions are exposed. For example, we can go to http://localhost:3000/logout to log out and then to http://localhost:3000/tasks/list (or http://localhost:3000, now that we've set up the default route) to get a task list without being logged in. (Because we got rid of the index.html file, we're taken to the default route after logout, so this vulnerability is blatantly obvious.) We can then edit and delete these tasks, and so on. Not cool.

The solution is to add before_filter :login_required to the controllers. The login_required method is part of the AuthenticatedSystem module, which is mixed into the Application (more on the notion of a mixin soon); see listing 5.26.

Listing 5.26 lib\authenticated_system.rb

```
module AuthenticatedSystem
  protected
```

```
. . .
      # Filter method to enforce a login requirement.
      #
      # To require logins for all actions, use this in your       ❶
      # controllers:
      #
      #   before_filter :login_required
      #
      # To require logins for specific actions, use this in your
      # controllers:
      #
      # before_filter :login_required, :only => [ :edit, :update ]
      #
      # To skip this in a subclassed controller:
      #
      #   skip_before_filter :login_required       ❷
      #
      def login_required
        authorized? || access_denied
      end
. . .
  end
```

As the comment says, we specify `before_filter :login_required` ❶ in our controllers to require login for all actions, and we can say `skip_before_filter :login_required` ❷ to turn this off. Because it's so important not to get this wrong, we'll add `before_filter :login_required` (❶ in listing 5.27) to the `ApplicationController` (which all controllers extend) instead of to individual subclasses. Then, if we're forgetful and create a new controller without specifying the `before_filter`, it will be secure by default. This is shown in listing 5.27.

Listing 5.27   app\controllers\application.rb

```
. . .
# Filters added to this controller apply to all controllers in
# the application. Likewise, all the methods added will be
# available for all controllers.

class ApplicationController < ActionController::Base
  helper :all # include all helpers, all the time
  include AuthenticatedSystem
  before_filter :login_required       ❶

  # See ActionController::RequestForgeryProtection for details
  # Uncomment the :secret if you're not using the cookie session
  # store
  # TODO - this will be uncommented once we explain sessions
  # in iteration 5.
```

```
# protect_from_forgery
# :secret => 'dd92c128b5358a710545b5e755694d57'
end
```

That was easy.

Next, we need to turn this off in the `UsersController` and `SessionsController`, or we won't be able to log in: the login action requires a login, so we'll be redirected to the login—repeatedly! See figure 5.10.

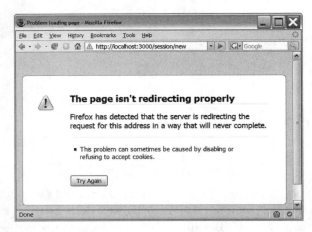

Figure 5.10
Luckily for our poor server, Firefox is smart enough to catch infinite redirection.

Start with the `SessionsController`; see listing 5.28.

Listing 5.28 app\controllers\sessions_controller.rb

```
# This controller handles the login/logout function of the site.
class SessionsController < ApplicationController
  skip_before_filter :login_required          ❶

  # GET /session/new
  # GET /session/new.xml
  def new
...
```

We skip the `login_required before_filter` ❶ for all actions. If we wanted to skip it only for some particular action `foo`, we'd say `skip_before_filter :login_required, :only => :foo`.

Next, the `UsersController`; see listing 5.29.

Listing 5.29 app\controllers\users_controller.rb

```
class UsersController < ApplicationController
  skip_before_filter :login_required
```

```
# GET /users/new
# GET /users/new.xml
def new
...
```

Same skip, different controller. We can confirm that this works by going to http://localhost:3000/login and logging in.

5.4.3 Access control

Next on our security checklist is ensuring that logged-in users can only modify things (such as tasks, projects, and locations) that belong to them. Just ensuring a user is logged in is *not* good enough—we don't want users viewing, modifying, and deleting each other's stuff.

To see the problem, all we need to do is log in as ludwig. The task list shows the tasks of all the users—the User column has ids of 1 and 3, as shown in figure 5.11.

Click the New Task link, and enter a new task with the Name "drink espresso" (a much needed task this far into the iteration!), as shown in figure 5.12.

Click Create. We see figure 5.13.

Note that we didn't set the user, letting it default to 0, and the task was still created! This is obviously something we need to prevent. We shouldn't let the user set the id in the first place—we should only create tasks belonging to the current user. For example, we can currently create the task shown in figure 5.14.

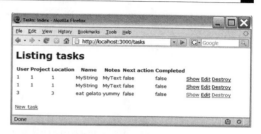

Figure 5.11   Tasks list showing tasks of all users

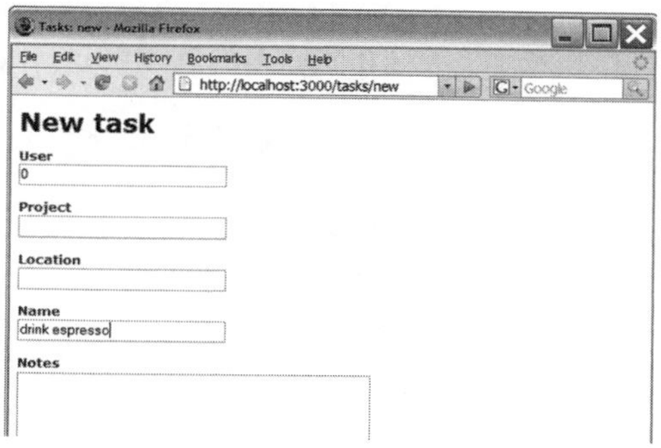

Figure 5.12   A new task for Ludwig (HTML)

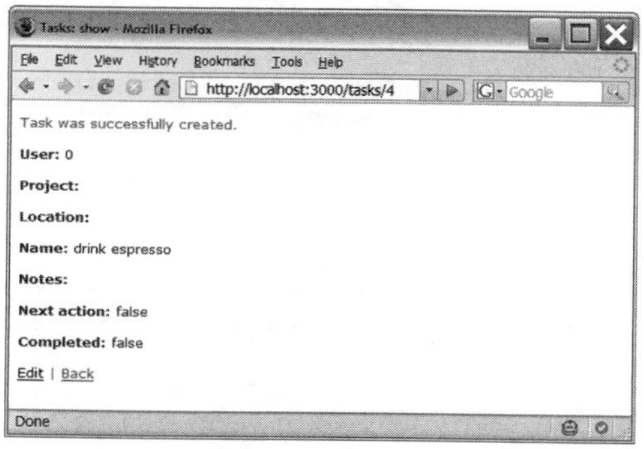

Figure 5.13   Tasks list showing task belonging to no user

Click Create, and the task is created. Next, go to http://localhost:3000/tasks again; the result appears in figure 5.15.

Observe how the task list shows the new task not belonging to ludwig as well as the new task belonging to nobody, neither of which we should have been able to create.

Note that the solution isn't "remove the id field from the form": We'd still need to be wary of the user maliciously modifiying the form submission (for example, using Firebug). We need to fix this issue properly—and right now, as part of the security fixes. This vulnerability exists in the `Tasks-Controller` as well as in the `ProjectsController` and `LocationsController` (try it).

Figure 5.14   Creating a task that doesn't belong to the current user

We'll start by modifying the `TasksController`; see listing 5.30.

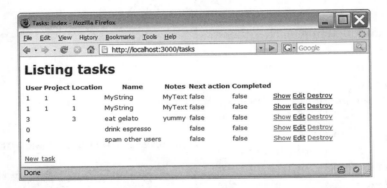

**Figure 5.15
Task list showing all tasks**

Listing 5.30   app\controllers\tasks_controller.rb

```ruby
class TasksController < ApplicationController        ❶
  # GET /tasks
  # GET /tasks.xml
  def index
    @tasks = Task.find(:all)                          ❷
    @tasks = current_user.tasks                       ❸

    respond_to do |format|
      format.html # index.html.erb
      format.xml  { render :xml => @tasks }
    end
  end
...We are doing more modifications, continued below...
```

We start by replacing the `Task.find(:all)` ❷ with `current_user.tasks` ❸. But right now this looks like magic: Where did `current_user.tasks` come from? Heck, where did `current_user` come from? Before we can proceed to fix the `TasksController`, we should figure this out.

Understanding current_user, current_user.tasks, and sessions

As we know, the `TasksController` (along with all the controllers) extends `ApplicationController` (❶ in listing 5.30). The `ApplicationController` class extends `ActionController::Base` and also includes the `AuthenticatedSystem` module (this include is how we added the login functionality), as shown in listing 5.31.

Listing 5.31 app\controllers\application.rb

```
...
class ApplicationController < ActionController::Base
  helper :all # include all helpers, all the time
  include AuthenticatedSystem          ❶
...
```

Including a module is Ruby's way of using the mixin approach to get the benefits of multiple inheritance without the gotchas of multiple inheritance. The methods in the module become "mixed in" to the class. Because `ApplicationController` includes `AuthenticatedSystem` ❶, it gets all of its methods. And because all our controllers extend `ApplicationController`, they all inherit those methods. We should look at the `AuthenticatedSystem` module, shown in listing 5.32, to see what they're getting.

Listing 5.32 lib\authenticated_system.rb

```
module AuthenticatedSystem
  protected
...
    def logged_in?
      current_user != :false
    end

    # Accesses the current user from the session.  Set it to
    # :false if login fails so that future calls do not hit the
    # database.
    def current_user        ❶
      @current_user ||= (login_from_session ||          ❷
  login_from_basic_auth || login_from_cookie || :false)
    end

    # Store the given user in the session.
```

```
    def current_user=(new_user)        ❸
      session[:user] = (new_user.nil? || new_user.is_a?(Symbol))        ❹
➡   ? nil : new_user.id
      @current_user = new_user
    end
...
```

The `AuthenticatedSystem` module has a `current_user` method ❶ that returns the
`@current_user` ❷ from the session and a `current_user=` method ❸ that stores the
current user in the session. (The `method_name=` syntax in Ruby is how setter methods are written.) This method uses something called `session[:user]` ❹, which is
the session.

We haven't encountered the session until now—what is it? Rails, being a web
application framework, includes session management, which it manages for us
when we're working with Rails normally. It does so by automatically populating
the session (which is retrieved with the `session` method call—we can often[11] omit
parentheses from method calls in Ruby) with various properties that we can set in
it. The `session` is essentially a dictionary, mapping keys to values. We can add new
key/value pairs to it, and they will be there for us[12] on the next requests when
Rails loads the session.

Calling `current_user` gets us the `@current_user`, which turns out to be an
instance of the `User` class. But where did the `tasks` in `current_user.tasks` come
from? Looking at the code for the `User` model, no `tasks` method is visible;
instead, we see listing 5.33.

Listing 5.33   app\models\user.rb

```
require 'digest/sha1'
class User < ActiveRecord::Base
  has_many :tasks        ❶
  has_many :projects
  has_many :locations
...
```

Where did `tasks` come from? The answer is that the `has_many :tasks` method
call ❶ in the `User` model creates a bunch of methods in the `User` class.

NOTE   For the complete list of methods added, see p. 335–336 of *AWDwR*.

---

[11] To learn the details, see *Programming Ruby* or *Ruby for Rails*.

[12] The values we put in the session are subject to restrictions; see section 21.2 of *AWDwR* for details.

One of these methods is `tasks`, which returns the tasks associated with this user.

TIP This is explained well in the article "Association Proxies," which is the basis for the approach I'm taking: http://www.therailsway.com/2007/3/26/ association-proxies-are-your-friend. Go read it now; I'll wait. (It's also explained on p. 336 of *AWDwR*. Read that, too.)

Essentially, `current_user.tasks` does a `find`, which is constrained by the association proxies to return only tasks that belong to the `current_user`.

Now that we understand better what is going on, where were we? Oh yes: We were modifying the TasksController.

Modifying the TasksController to use association proxies

Let's examine the whole file now, with all the changes we're making. Listing 5.34 shows the code.

Listing 5.34 app\controllers\tasks_controller.rb

```ruby
class TasksController < ApplicationController            ❶
  # GET /tasks
  # GET /tasks.xml
  def index
    @tasks = Task.find(:all)          ❷
    @tasks = current_user.tasks            ❸

    respond_to do |format|
      format.html # index.html.erb
      format.xml  { render :xml => @tasks }
    end
  end

  # GET /tasks/1
  # GET /tasks/1.xml
  def show
    @task = Task.find(params[:id])         ❹
    @task = current_user.tasks.find(params[:id])
    respond_to do |format|
      format.html # show.html.erb
      format.xml  { render :xml => @task }
    end
  rescue ActiveRecord::RecordNotFound => e         ❺
    prevent_access(e)
  end

  # GET /tasks/new
  # GET /tasks/new.xml
  def new
    @task = Task.new
```

```
    respond_to do |format|
      format.html # new.html.erb
      format.xml  { render :xml => @task }
    end
end

# GET /tasks/1/edit
def edit
  @task = Task.find(params[:id])                    ❻
  @task = current_user.tasks.find(params[:id])
rescue ActiveRecord::RecordNotFound => e            ❼
  prevent_access(e)
end

# POST /tasks
# POST /tasks.xml
def create
  @task = Task.new(params[:task])

  respond_to do |format|
    if @task.save
      flash[:notice] = 'Task was successfully created.'
      format.html { redirect_to(@task) }
      format.xml  { render :xml => @task, :status => :created,
        :location => @task }
    else
      format.html { render :action => "new" }
      format.xml  { render :xml => @task.errors,
        :status => :unprocessable_entity }
    end
  end
  @task = current_user.tasks.build(params[:task])    ❽
  respond_to do |format|
    if @task.save
      format.html do
        flash[:notice] = 'Task was successfully created.'   ❾
        redirect_to(@task)
      end
      format.xml  { render :xml => @task, :status => :created,
        :location => @task }
    else
      format.html { render :action => "new" }
      format.xml  { render :xml => @task.errors,
        :status => :unprocessable_entity }
    end
  end
end

# PUT /tasks/1
# PUT /tasks/1.xml
def update
```

```
@task = Task.find(params[:id])          ⑩
@task = current_user.tasks.find(params[:id])

respond_to do |format|
  if @task.update_attributes(params[:task])
    flash[:notice] = 'Task was successfully updated.'
    format.html { redirect_to(@task) }
    format.xml  { head :ok }
  else
    format.html { render :action => "edit" }
    format.xml  { render :xml => @task.errors,
      :status => :unprocessable_entity }
  end
end
rescue ActiveRecord::RecordNotFound => e          ⑪
  prevent_access(e)
end

# DELETE /tasks/1
# DELETE /tasks/1.xml
def destroy
  @task = Task.find(params[:id])          ⑫
  @task = current_user.tasks.find(params[:id])
  @task.destroy

  respond_to do |format|
    format.html { redirect_to(tasks_url) }
    format.xml  { head :ok }
  end
rescue ActiveRecord::RecordNotFound => e          ⑬
  prevent_access(e)
end

private
  def prevent_access(e)          ⑭
    logger.info "TasksController#prevent_access: #{e}"
    respond_to do |format|
      format.html { redirect_to(tasks_url) }
      format.xml  { render :text => "error" }
    end
  end
end
```

We explained ❶–❸ earlier. Continuing with show, we replace the Task.find ❹ with current_user.tasks.find, which uses the association proxies to return only tasks that belong to the current_user, as I've explained. Although this seems complex, it makes our life simpler: If we do our find() calls on the association of the thing that has many of them (in our case, the current_user) instead of calling the static method of the class (such as `Task.find(...)`), we can't screw up and let users have access to stuff they shouldn't have.

Suppose a malicious user is hacking, and they've modified the `id` (say, with Firebug). What will happen? Simple: an `ActiveRecord::RecordNotFound` exception will be raised, which we handle with a `rescue` ❺ statement (the Ruby version of `catch` in ActionScript 3 and Java).

> **NOTE**   Active Record throws an exception when a `find` with a specific `id` matches nothing, because it considers that to be exceptional. Finding by other criteria returns an empty result. (See the "To Raise, or Not to Raise?" sidebar on p. 298 of *AWDwR* to learn why.)

After we ~~catch~~ rescue the exception, we call a new private method called `prevent_access` ⓮. This method logs the exception with the `logger.info` call (because we're presumably interested if a user is hacking) and does a `respond_to` block that does a redirect if the requested format is HTML and renders "error" if the requested format is XML. (No, "error" is *not* XML. But it works, and if the user is hacking, then there is no reasonable error to show. Besides, creating nice XML error messages is boring reading.) This rescue-and-call-`prevent_access` approach is so useful, we use it throughout ❼⓫⓭. Note that redirecting the user with no indication that we know what they're up to is a good approach. If someone is hacking, we don't want to help them.

Continuing, we use the identical `current_user.tasks` approach in the `edit` ❻, `create` ❽, `update` ❿, and `destroy` ⓬ methods.

Note that we move the `flash[:notice]` (this "flash" has nothing to do with Flash; it's essentially a hash for passing state between requests) inside the `format.html` ❾—this is a hack that is needed when dealing with HTML; we don't need it when sending responses to Flex, so there's no reason to build it.

Having made these changes, let's reload http://localhost:3000/tasks (if you've been following along, you're already logged in as ludwig; if not, log in as ludwig first). We see figure 5.16.

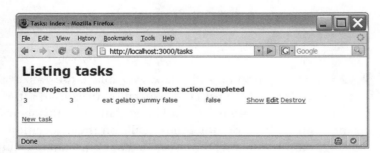

Figure 5.16
Ludwig's task list

That's better! The only task that belongs to ludwig is to eat gelato, so that's all that shows up. (If anyone deserves some gelato right now, we do.) You can play with the tasks, creating new ones, logging in as different users, and so on. When you're satisfied that it works, we'll move on and make the same changes to projects and locations.

Fixing the ProjectsController and LocationsController

We'll make changes that are essentially identical to those we made to the Tasks-Controller, so no explanation is needed. Because all the changes have been explained and shown in diff form when discussing TasksController, I'll just show the resulting files for the ProjectsController and LocationsController. (It's easier to appreciate the code without the deleted code cluttering up the listing, and it's also easier for you to copy and paste from this way.)

> **TIP** Literally, the way I made these changes, and the way I recommend you make these changes, is to copy the content of the tasks_controller.rb file, paste it into projects_controller.rb, and then do a case-sensitive Edit > Find/Replace, replacing Task with Project and task with project. When you're done, make the equivalent changes in locations_controller.rb. If you're cautious, save copies of the files beforehand and use a diff tool like WinMerge to compare the code to the previous code to ensure that you didn't make any mistakes.

First, the ProjectsController; see listing 5.35.

Listing 5.35   app\controllers\projects_controller.rb

```
class ProjectsController < ApplicationController
  # GET /projects
  # GET /projects.xml
  def index
    @projects = current_user.projects

    respond_to do |format|
      format.html # index.html.erb
      format.xml  { render :xml => @projects }
    end
  end

  # GET /projects/1
  # GET /projects/1.xml
  def show
    @project = current_user.projects.find(params[:id])

    respond_to do |format|
      format.html # show.html.erb
```

```ruby
      format.xml  { render :xml => @project }
    end
  rescue ActiveRecord::RecordNotFound => e
    prevent_access(e)
  end

  # GET /projects/new
  # GET /projects/new.xml
  def new
    @project = Project.new

    respond_to do |format|
      format.html # new.html.erb
      format.xml  { render :xml => @project }
    end
  end

  # GET /projects/1/edit
  def edit
    @project = current_user.projects.find(params[:id])
  rescue ActiveRecord::RecordNotFound => e
    prevent_access(e)
  end

  # POST /projects
  # POST /projects.xml
  def create
    @project = current_user.projects.build(params[:project])
    respond_to do |format|
      if @project.save
        format.html do
          flash[:notice] = 'Project was successfully created.'
          redirect_to(@project)
        end
        format.xml  { render :xml => @project,
          :status => :created, :location => @project }
      else
        format.html { render :action => "new" }
        format.xml  { render :xml => @project.errors,
          :status => :unprocessable_entity }
      end
    end
  end

  # PUT /projects/1
  # PUT /projects/1.xml
  def update
    @project = current_user.projects.find(params[:id])

    respond_to do |format|
      if @project.update_attributes(params[:project])
```

```
        flash[:notice] = 'Project was successfully updated.'
        format.html { redirect_to(@project) }
        format.xml  { head :ok }
      else
        format.html { render :action => "edit" }
        format.xml  { render :xml => @project.errors,
          :status => :unprocessable_entity }
      end
    end
  rescue ActiveRecord::RecordNotFound => e
    prevent_access(e)
  end

  # DELETE /projects/1
  # DELETE /projects/1.xml
  def destroy
    @project = current_user.projects.find(params[:id])
    @project.destroy

    respond_to do |format|
      format.html { redirect_to(projects_url) }
      format.xml  { head :ok }
    end
  rescue ActiveRecord::RecordNotFound => e
    prevent_access(e)
  end

  private
    def prevent_access(e)
      logger.info "ProjectsController#prevent_access: #{e}"
      respond_to do |format|
        format.html { redirect_to(projects_url) }
        format.xml  { render :text => "error" }
      end
    end
  end
end
```

Next, the LocationsController; see listing 5.36.

Listing 5.36   app\controllers\locations_controller.rb

```
class LocationsController < ApplicationController
  # GET /locations
  # GET /locations.xml
  def index
    @locations = current_user.locations

    respond_to do |format|
      format.html # index.html.erb
```

```ruby
        format.xml  { render :xml => @locations }
    end
  end

  # GET /locations/1
  # GET /locations/1.xml
  def show
    @location = current_user.locations.find(params[:id])

    respond_to do |format|
      format.html # show.html.erb
      format.xml  { render :xml => @location }
    end
  rescue ActiveRecord::RecordNotFound => e
    prevent_access(e)
  end

  # GET /locations/new
  # GET /locations/new.xml
  def new
    @location = Location.new

    respond_to do |format|
      format.html # new.html.erb
      format.xml  { render :xml => @location }
    end
  end

  # GET /locations/1/edit
  def edit
    @location = current_user.locations.find(params[:id])
  rescue ActiveRecord::RecordNotFound => e
    prevent_access(e)
  end

  # POST /locations
  # POST /locations.xml
  def create
    @location = current_user.locations.build(params[:location])
    respond_to do |format|
      if @location.save
        format.html do
          flash[:notice] = 'Location was successfully created.'
          redirect_to(@location)
        end
        format.xml  { render :xml => @location,
          :status => :created, :location => @location }
      else
        format.html { render :action => "new" }
        format.xml  { render :xml => @location.errors,
          :status => :unprocessable_entity }
```

```
        end
      end
  end

  # PUT /locations/1
  # PUT /locations/1.xml
  def update
    @location = current_user.locations.find(params[:id])

    respond_to do |format|
      if @location.update_attributes(params[:location])
        flash[:notice] = 'Location was successfully updated.'
        format.html { redirect_to(@location) }
        format.xml  { head :ok }
      else
        format.html { render :action => "edit" }
        format.xml  { render :xml => @location.errors,
          :status => :unprocessable_entity }
      end
    end
  rescue ActiveRecord::RecordNotFound => e
    prevent_access(e)
  end

  # DELETE /locations/1
  # DELETE /locations/1.xml
  def destroy
    @location = current_user.locations.find(params[:id])
    @location.destroy

    respond_to do |format|
      format.html { redirect_to(locations_url) }
      format.xml  { head :ok }
    end
  rescue ActiveRecord::RecordNotFound => e
    prevent_access(e)
  end

  private
    def prevent_access(e)
      logger.info "LocationsController#prevent_access: #{e}"
      respond_to do |format|
        format.html { redirect_to(locations_url) }
        format.xml  { render :text => "error" }
      end
    end
end
```

There is no change in either of these two controllers that we didn't do to the `TasksController`. This works the same way for both the `ProjectsController` and `LocationsController` because the `User` model has `has_many` calls for `:tasks`, `:projects`, and `:locations`. and LocationsController.

Protecting against CSRF attacks

Thankfully, this is done for us in `ApplicationController`; all we need to do now is uncomment it, as shown in listing 5.37.

Listing 5.37 app\controllers\application.rb

```
...
class ApplicationController < ActionController::Base
  helper :all # include all helpers, all the time
  include AuthenticatedSystem
  before_filter :login_required

  # See ActionController::RequestForgeryProtection for details
  # Uncomment the :secret if you're not using the cookie session
  # store
  # TODO - this will be uncommented once we explain sessions
  # in iteration 5.
  protect_from_forgery           ❶
  # :secret => 'dd92c128b5358a710545b5e755694d57'
end
```

We delete the obsolete comment and uncomment the `protect_from_forgery` ❶ call. Perhaps surprisingly, we don't need to do anything special here for use by Flex. Please consult the Rails online documentation about CSRF attacks (especially http://weblog.rubyonrails.org/2007/9/30/rails-2-0-0-preview-release and http://ryandaigle.com/articles/2007/9/24/what-s-new-in-edge-rails-better-cross-site-request-forging-prevention).

Before we declare this iteration a success, we need to expand our fixtures and make the new tests pass. (We should also add tests, but we won't because testing isn't the focus of the book.)

5.5   Expanding our fixtures and keeping our tests passing

We want to add some decent test data to the tasks, projects, and locations fixtures. This way, we'll be able to load it in when we run newdb.bat at the beginning of a given iteration. That will give us a consistent starting point so it's easy to follow along with the book.

We'll start with locations.yml; see listing 5.38.

Listing 5.38   test\fixtures\locations.yml

```
# Read about fixtures at http://ar.rubyonrails.org/
  ➥classes/Fixtures.html
one:
  id: 1
  user_id: 1
  name: MyString
  notes: MyText
  created_at: 2007-10-19 12:27:11
  updated_at: 2007-10-19 12:27:11
two:
  id: 2
  user_id: 1
  name: MyString
  notes: MyText
  created_at: 2007-10-19 12:27:11
  updated_at: 2007-10-19 12:27:11

#ludwig's locations

ludwig_home:
  id: 1
  user_id: 3
  name: Home

ludwig_opera_house:
  id: 2
  user_id: 3
  name: Opera House

#wolfgang's locations

wolfgang_home:
  id: 3
  user_id: 4
  name: Home

wolfgang_opera_house:
  id: 4
  user_id: 4
  name: Opera House
```

We remove the scaffold-created locations (because we'll be testing with ludwig) and add new locations for ludwig and wolfgang. (As defined in users.yml, 3 is ludwig's id and 4 is wolfgang's id.)

Next, projects.yml; see listing 5.39.

Listing 5.39   test\fixtures\projects.yml

```
# Read about fixtures at http://ar.rubyonrails.org/
  ➥classes/Fixtures.html
one:
  id: 1
  user_id: 1
  name: MyString
  notes: MyText
  completed: false
  created_at: 2007-10-19 12:26:51
  updated_at: 2007-10-19 12:26:51
two:
  id: 2
  user_id: 1
  name: MyString
  notes: MyText
  completed: false
  created_at: 2007-10-19 12:26:51
  updated_at: 2007-10-19 12:26:51

#ludwig's projects

ludwig_project_one:
  id: 1
  user_id: 3
  name: Music
  notes: I don't need any notes; I'm Beethoven!

ludwig_project_two:
  id: 2
  user_id: 3
  name: Health
  notes: Figure out what's wrong with mine!

#wolfgang's projects

wolfgang_project_one:
  id: 3
  user_id: 4
  name: Music
  notes: All my music is good copy; I don't take notes either!!

wolfgang_project_two:
  id: 4
  user_id: 4
  name: Fashion
  notes: Set the wig trend...
```

Similarly, we remove the `scaffold`-created projects (because we'll be testing with ludwig) and add new projects for ludwig and wolfgang.

Finally, having defined the projects and locations in YAML, we know what their ids will be. Now we can define the tasks and have them belong to appropriate projects and locations; see listing 5.40.

Listing 5.40   test\fixtures\tasks.yml

```
# Read about fixtures at http://ar.rubyonrails.org/
  ➥classes/Fixtures.html
one:
  id: 1
  user_id: 1
  project_id: 1
  location_id: 1
  name: MyString
  notes: MyText
  next_action: false
  completed: false
  created_at: 2007-10-19 12:26:25
  updated_at: 2007-10-19 12:26:25
two:
  id: 2
  user_id: 1
  project_id: 1
  location_id: 1
  name: MyString
  notes: MyText
  next_action: false
  completed: false
  created_at: 2007-10-19 12:26:25
  updated_at: 2007-10-19 12:26:25

#ludwig's tasks

ludwig_task_one:
  id: 1
  user_id: 3
  project_id: 1
  location_id: 1
  name: Finish eighth symphony
  notes: Done.  Yay!
  next_action: false
  completed: true

ludwig_task_two:
  id: 2
  user_id: 3
  project_id: 1
  location_id: 1
  name: Finish ninth symphony
```

```
notes: Ode to beer maybe?  Ode to cheese?
next_action: true
completed: false

ludwig_task_three:
  id: 3
  user_id: 3
  project_id: 2
  name: Buy a new hearing aid
  notes: This is driving me crazy
  next_action: false
  completed: false

ludwig_task_four:
  id: 4
  user_id: 3
  name: Go to Bed, Bad and Beyond for some new dishes
  notes: These lead steins are so 1700s
  next_action: false
  completed: false

#wolfgang's tasks

wolfgang_task_one:
  id: 5
  user_id: 4
  project_id: 4
  name: Get a wig
  notes: Every composer needs a wig
  next_action: false
  completed: true

wolfgang_task_two:
  id: 6
  user_id: 4
  project_id: 3
  location_id: 3
  name: Finish Opera
  notes: The Engagement of Figaro?  The Divorce of Figaro?
  next_action: true
  completed: false

wolfgang_task_three:
  id: 7
  user_id: 4
  project_id: 4
  name: Get a new wig
  notes: This one makes me look silly
  next_action: false
  completed: false
```

We create tasks for ludwig and wolfgang.

Having done all this, we have a consistent basis from which to start subsequent iterations by running newdb.bat, because this drops our database, re-creates it, runs all our migrations, and then loads all our fixtures including these new ones.

Run newdb.bat to ensure this works, and then run the tests with `rake`. The result is shown in listing 5.41.

Listing 5.41   Output

```
c:\peter\flexiblerails\current\pomodo>newdb.bat
...
c:\peter\flexiblerails\current\pomodo>rake
...
Started
..............
Finished in 1.047 seconds.

16 tests, 29 assertions, 0 failures, 0 errors
...
Started
FFFFFFFFFFFFFF........FFFFFFF.....
Finished in 2.062 seconds.
...
35 tests, 50 assertions, 21 failures, 0 errors       ❶
...
Errors running test:functionals!

c:\peter\flexiblerails\current\pomodo>
```

Ruh roh! ❶

Looking at the trace in the Command Prompt window, we see a ton of errors. Thankfully, it's pretty clear what happened: We updated our fixtures and didn't update the tests. And because we've added the `before_filter :login_required`, our tests need to simulate logging in. We'll fix both of these issues now, and that should make our tests pass.

We'll start with the `LocationsControllerTest`; see listing 5.42.

Listing 5.42   test\functional\locations_controller_test.rb

```
...
class LocationsControllerTest < Test::Unit::TestCase
  fixtures :users       ❶

  def setup
    @controller = LocationsController.new
```

```
    @request    = ActionController::TestRequest.new
    @response   = ActionController::TestResponse.new
    login_as :ludwig        ❷
  end
  . . .
```

We load the :users fixtures ❶ so we can login_as :ludwig ❷. That's it. Next, we make identical changes to the ProjectsControllerTest and TasksController-Test (see listings 5.43 and 5.44).

Note that in Rails 2 RC1 (gem version 1.99.0) these tests extend Test::Unit::TestCase by default; in Rails 2 final (2.0.1) they extend Action-Controller::TestCase by default. If you are using Rails 2.0.1 or higher you need to replace ActionController::TestCase with Test::Unit::TestCase and to you need to add the entire setup method—not just the login_as :ludwig line–for all three classes. As such, I'm formatting all this code in bold italic, even though with Rails 1.99.0 much of it will be generated for you.

Listing 5.43   test\functional\projects_controller_test.rb

```
. . .
class ProjectsControllerTest < Test::Unit::TestCase
  fixtures :users

  def setup
    @controller = ProjectsController.new
    @request    = ActionController::TestRequest.new
    @response   = ActionController::TestResponse.new
    login_as :ludwig
  end
. . .
```

Listing 5.44   test\functional\tasks_controller_test.rb

```
. . .
class TasksControllerTest < Test::Unit::TestCase
  fixtures :users

  def setup
    @controller = TasksController.new
    @request    = ActionController::TestRequest.new
    @response   = ActionController::TestResponse.new
    login as :ludwig
  end
. . .
```

With these changes made, let's run our tests again:

```
c:\peter\flexiblerails\current\pomodo>rake
Started
. . . . . . . . . . . . . . .
Finished in 0.953 seconds.

16 tests, 29 assertions, 0 failures, 0 errors
Started
. . . . . . . . . . . . . . . . . . . . . . . . . . . . . . .
Finished in 2.016 seconds.

35 tests, 65 assertions, 0 failures, 0 errors
. . .
c:\peter\flexiblerails\current\pomodo>
```

That was easy!

5.6   *Summary*

We now have a decent, reasonably secure foundation to build on. We can call the user by name; we have a debug console; heck, we've even fixed to_xml. Beyond that, we dove fairly deep into Rails, learning about REST, creating RESTful Task, Project, and Location resources; and we learned routing. We even got a handle on security, which is made easier by using the RESTful approach and the association proxies. Finally, we expanded fixtures so we don't have to manually enter test data for ad hoc testing.

In the next iteration, we'll hook up our Flex UI to our new tasks, projects, and locations controllers. This will be fun. Take a break, grab an espresso (and some gelato, if you wish) and start fresh in the next iteration.

> The code at this point is saved as the iteration05 folder.

Flex on Rails

6

Web 2.0, proper noun
  The name given to the social and technical sophistication and
  maturity that mark the—Oh, screw it. Money! Money money money!
  Money! The money's back! Ha ha! Money!

—Greg Knauss, "The Devil's Dictionary" (2.0),[1]
http://www.eod.com/devil/archive/web_20.html

---

[1] This is a reference to The Devil's Dictionary by Ambrose Bierce, which is great reading too.

In this fairly substantial iteration, we'll finally hook up most of the main Flex UI to the Rails controllers, including the new `TasksController`, `ProjectsController`, and `LocationsController`. Given the work we've done on the account creation and login panels, you may think it's just going to be a matter of defining a bunch of `HTTPServices` and hooking them up. If so, you're essentially right. But the details matter, of course.

Let's dive in.

6.1   *Setup*

If you didn't run newdb.bat at the end of the last iteration, run it now. Doing so ensures that the tasks, projects, and locations we defined in the fixtures at the end of the previous iteration are loaded:

```
c:\peter\flexiblerails\current\pomodo>newdb.bat
...
```

Next, we start our server with `ruby script\server`, go to http://localhost:3000, and log in as ludwig (his password is *foooo*, as specified in users.yml). We see the screen shown in figure 6.1.

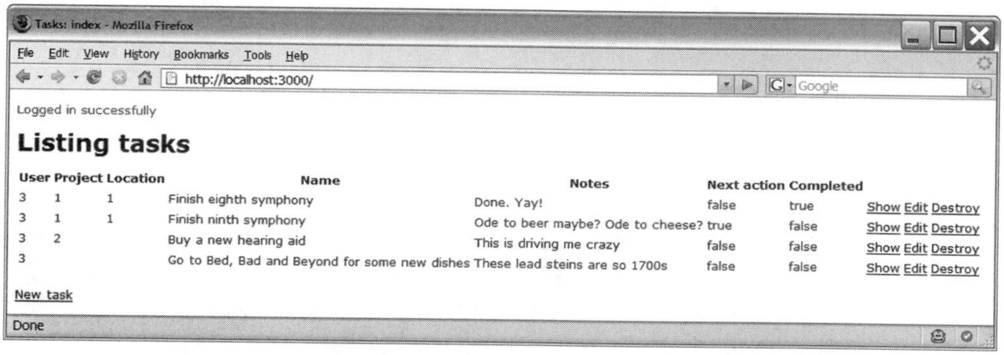

Figure 6.1   Ludwig's tasks, created in fixtures (HTML)

6.2   *Listing tasks in Flex*

If we then go to http://localhost:3000/bin/Pomodo.html and log in as ludwig, the tasks list looks like figure 6.2.

Our first task will be to get ludwig's tasks to show up in the Tasks `DataGrid`. To begin with, we won't worry about making the `ComboBox` that filters them have any effect—we'll just show the user's tasks. We'll also only display the `project_id` and `location_id` of the tasks for now.

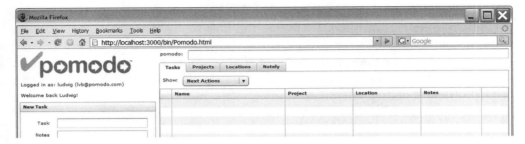

Figure 6.2   No tasks yet in Flex

I have some great news: The RESTful `scaffold` command has already done a *lot* of the work for us, as shown in listing 6.1.

Listing 6.1   app\controllers\tasks_controller.rb

```
class TasksController < ApplicationController
  # GET /tasks
  # GET /tasks.xml        ❶
  def index
    @tasks = current_user.tasks

    respond_to do |format|
      format.html # index.html.erb
      format.xml  { render :xml => @tasks }        ❷
    end
  end
...
```

To get a list of tasks nicely formatted in XML for use by Flex, all we need to do is send a GET to /tasks.xml ❶. The render :xml => @tasks syntax ❷ is syntactic sugar for render :xml => @tasks.to_xml. (Rails has come a long way regarding XML, from hatred of it to syntactic sugar for it.) There is prebuilt support for XML in the other actions in the TasksController as well, which we can use with some or no modification. (Who knew DHH loved Flex so much?)

Who knew?

I sure didn't! See http://www.37signals.com/svn/posts/487-what-if-i-actually-like-html-css-and-javascript for the background, and scroll down in the comments to see your humble author attempt to persuade DHH he is mistaken. (I like challenges.)

Who knew? *(continued)*

The ironic thing about this is that even though DHH isn't a fan of Flex, one of the most significant effects of the improved—and now standard—support of REST in Rails is to make support for Rich Internet[2] Applications almost work right out of the box! (Maybe Rails 3 will fix to_xml and come with scaffolded Flex views?)

Note one subtlety here: Because we're rendering XML, we don't need to set instance variables like `@tasks` in the Rails controllers. We only need to set instance variables if we're having rendering done by a view template that depends on them. Having less code is a good thing, so I often leave the instance variables where they are instead of moving them inside the format.html block and creating local variables for use in the format.xml block. Also note that if we use Builder to produce XML (more on that later), we need instance variables.

Next, we modify the `TasksListBox`, as shown in listing 6.2.

Listing 6.2   app\flex\com\pomodo\components\TasksListBox.mxml

```
<?xml version="1.0" encoding="utf-8"?>
<mx:VDividedBox xmlns:mx="http://www.adobe.com/2006/mxml"      ❶ Add creation-
    width="100%" height="100%" label="Tasks"                     Complete
    creationComplete="listTasks()">                              handler
<mx:Script>
<![CDATA[
    import mx.rpc.events.ResultEvent;        ⬅── Add import

    public const NEXT_ACTIONS:int = 0;
    public const ALL_TASKS:int = 1;
    public const TASKS_IN_PROJECT:int = 2;
    public const TASKS_AT_LOCATION:int = 3;

    private const SHOW_CHOICES:Array = [
        {label:"Next Actions", data:NEXT_ACTIONS,
            hasSubChoice:false},
        {label:"All Tasks", data:ALL_TASKS,
            hasSubChoice:false},
```

---

[2] Speaking of wars of words: Sorry, Scott Barnes, it's *Rich Internet Application*, not *Rich Interactive Application*. (If you're bored, see http://blog.digitalbackcountry.com/?p=1080 vs. http://blogs.msdn.com/msmossyblog/archive/2007/10/10/why-i-choose-to-use-interactive-not-internet-in-ria.aspx for details, and http://www.25hoursaday.com/weblog/2007/10/20/IfYouFightTheWebYouWillLose.aspx for Dare Obsanjo's amusing follow-up.)

```
            {label:"Tasks in Project:", data:TASKS_IN_PROJECT,
                hasSubChoice:true},
            {label:"Tasks at Location:", data:TASKS_AT_LOCATION,
                hasSubChoice:true}];

    [Bindable]
    private var _subChoices:Array;                      ② Call HTTPService
                                                            send method
    public function listTasks():void {
        svcTasksList.send();
    }                                                         Handle HTTPService ③
                                                                         result

    private function handleTasksListResult(event:ResultEvent):
    void {
        var resultXML: XML = XML(event.result);
        Pomodo.debug("TasksListBox#handleTasksListResult:\n" +
            resultXML.toString());
    }                                       svcTasksList HTTPService ④
]]>                                          to invoke /tasks.xml
</mx:Script>
    <mx:HTTPService id="svcTasksList" url="/tasks.xml"
        resultFormat="e4x"                       ⑤ Set tasksXLC source
        result="handleTasksListResult(event)"/>     using lastResult of
    <mx:XMLListCollection id="tasksXLC"             svcTasksList
        source="{XMLList(svcTasksList.lastResult.children())}"/>
    <mx:VBox width="100%" height="60%">
        <mx:HBox width="100%" paddingLeft="5" paddingRight="5">
            <mx:Label text="Show:"/>
            <mx:ComboBox id="mainChoiceCB"                    tasksGrid ⑥
                dataProvider="{SHOW_CHOICES}"/>             dataProvider
            <mx:ComboBox id="subChoiceCB" width="100%"        is tasksXLC
                dataProvider="{_subChoices}"
                visible="{mainChoiceCB.selectedItem.hasSubChoice}"/>
        </mx:HBox>
        <mx:DataGrid id="tasksGrid" width="100%" height="100%"
            dataProvider="{tasksXLC}">
            <mx:columns>
                <mx:DataGridColumn headerText="" width="25"
                    dataField="completed"/>
                <mx:DataGridColumn headerText="Name" width="300"
                    dataField="name"/>
                <mx:DataGridColumn headerText="Project"             Set
                    width="150" dataField="project_id"/>        dataField
                <mx:DataGridColumn headerText="Location"        properties ⑦
                    width="150" dataField="location_id"/>
                <mx:DataGridColumn headerText="Notes"
                    dataField="notes"/>
                <mx:DataGridColumn headerText="" width="60"/>
            </mx:columns>
```

```
        </mx:DataGrid>
    </mx:VBox>
  ...
  </mx:VDividedBox>
```

We start by defining an `HTTPService` `svcTasksList` ❹, which does a `GET` to `/tasks.xml` (thus triggering the index action of the `TasksController`) and specifies a `resultFormat` of `e4x` so the result of the service can be handled with the new E4X XML API. We then take the `lastResult` ❺ of this service, which is an XML document, get its children (which is an `XMLList` of the tasks), and make this be the source of an `XMLListCollection` called `tasksXLC` ❺. We do this with a binding to the `source` attribute.

We have to call this `listTasks` function ❷ from somewhere, in order to have it call the service and get the results. The logical place to do so *for now* is in a `creationComplete` event handler ❶, because that event gets broadcast when the `TasksListBox` is created.

We set the `dataProvider` of the `tasksGrid` to be the `tasksXLC` ❻ `XMLListCollection` we just finished populating. We also modify the `DataGridColumns` ❼ to have their `dataField` properties set to the data field in the XML they're for.

Finally, we add a `result` handler to the `svcTasksList` ❻, which calls a `handleTasksListResult` ❸ function. We do this so that we can extract the `event.result` XML and output it to our debug console. Note that we didn't need to import `Pomodo` in order to call `Pomodo.debug` ❸—it's our `Application`, so we get it for free.

Let's see what this does. Rebuild, reload, and log in as ludwig. We see a nice tasks list, as shown in figure 6.3.

Furthermore, we can open the debug console to see the XML we got back for the tasks (scroll past the XML for the ludwig user); see listing 6.3.

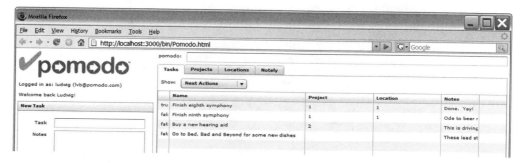

Figure 6.3 Task list in Flex!

Listing 6.3   Output

```
[Sun Oct 21 11:47:16 GMT+0200 2007]
  ➥TasksListBox#handleTasksListResult:
<tasks type="array">
  <task>
    <completed type="boolean">true</completed>
    <created_at type="datetime"/>
    <id type="integer">1</id>
    <location_id type="integer">1</location_id>
    <name>Finish eighth symphony</name>
    <next_action type="boolean">false</next_action>
    <notes>Done.  Yay!</notes>
    <project_id type="integer">1</project_id>
    <updated_at type="datetime"/>
    <user_id type="integer">3</user_id>
  </task>
...
```

We're currently just displaying the project_id and location_id, but we'll soon do more.

6.2.1 Should we use to_xml with :include?

If you have experience with to_xml, you may be wondering why we didn't do the following[3] (shown in listing 6.4) in the previous section, to list the projects and locations.

Listing 6.4   app\controllers\tasks_controller.rb

```
class TasksController < ApplicationController
  # GET /tasks
  # GET /tasks.xml
  def index
    @tasks = current_user.tasks

    respond_to do |format|
      format.html # index.html.erb
      format.xml  { render :xml => @tasks }              ❶
      format.xml  { render :xml => @tasks.to_xml(        ❷
        :include => [:project, :location]) }
    end
  end
...
```

---

[3] Thanks to Jason Tuttle of Studio 1H (http://www.studio1h.com) for help with this section.

Making this change ❶❷ would make the to_xml bring the Project and the Location that the Task belongs_to come along in the XML as child elements of the tasks. If you try it (make this change, reload, and log in as ludwig), you'll get something like the output shown in listing 6.5 in your debug console.

Listing 6.5   Output

```
[Mon Oct 22 00:03:51 GMT+0200 2007]
TasksListBox#handleTasksListResult:
<tasks type="array">
  <task>
    <completed type="boolean">true</completed>
    <created_at type="datetime"/>
    <id type="integer">1</id>
    <location_id type="integer">1</location_id>
    <name>Finish eighth symphony</name>
    <next_action type="boolean">false</next_action>
    <notes>Done.  Yay!</notes>
    <project_id type="integer">1</project_id>
    <updated_at type="datetime"/>
    <user_id type="integer">3</user_id>
    <project>          ❶
      <completed type="boolean">false</completed>
      <created_at type="datetime"/>
      <id type="integer">1</id>
      <name>Music</name>
      <notes>I don't need any notes; I'm Beethoven!</notes>
      <updated_at type="datetime"/>
      <user_id type="integer">3</user_id>
    </project>
    <location>        ❷
      <created_at type="datetime"/>
      <id type="integer">1</id>
      <name>Home</name>
      <notes/>
      <updated_at type="datetime"/>
      <user_id type="integer">3</user_id>
    </location>
  </task>
...the rest of ludwig's tasks are also shown with children here...
</tasks>
```

You can see the projects ❶ and locations ❷ that the tasks belong to coming along as child elements.

This *would* let us easily display the names of the projects and locations that the tasks belong to. Should we do this?

Not in this case: Because we're also going to display projects and locations in their own `DataGrids`, we need to have the full lists of projects and locations anyway. It makes sense to do as much work as possible in Flex as opposed to in Rails. This isn't because we prefer writing Flex code—coding in Ruby is lots of fun—but because it makes sense to put as much burden as possible on the *client* instead of on the server.

Also, there would be another potential drawback: Not only would we be making the server do more work (making the response time slower), we would also potentially be sending a *lot* more data back from the server (making the response time slower still). (Say the user had 8 projects, 4 locations, and 400 tasks—do you want to send the project and location 400 times as child elements of the 400 tasks?)

As the author of this book, I have another advantage: *I can see the future!* (Well, the future of the book, anyway.) I plan to use `ComboBoxes` in the `taskGrid` to change the projects and locations. We'll need to have all the projects and locations at our disposal before we display the `taskGrid` in the future (because the projects and locations will be used as the `dataProviders` for those `ComboBoxes`).

In this case, it's in our best interest to keep the XML coming back from Rails via `to_xml` as small and simple as possible. This way of thinking is much more like that of someone writing a Java Swing application (or an AJAX app that is JavaScript-heavy) that talks to a server rather than that of someone writing a traditional web app, where the client is fairly stupid and the server does many tasks that should be done on the client.

The important lesson here is: Don't port your thinking about how to build traditional Rails views to Flex. Flex is different and can do more for you.

> **TIP**   Don't think of MXML files as .html.erb templates—MXML is just a convenient way of writing ActionScript 3 code.

Because we're not going to use this approach, please revert the code as shown in listing 6.6.

Listing 6.6   app\controllers\tasks_controller.rb

```ruby
class TasksController < ApplicationController
  # GET /tasks
  # GET /tasks.xml
  def index
    @tasks = current_user.tasks

    respond_to do |format|
      format.html # index.html.erb
      format.xml  { render :xml => @tasks }
      format.xml  { render :xml => @tasks.to_xml(
```

~~:include => [:project, :location]) }~~
        end
      end
    ...

6.3   *Creating tasks in Flex*

Let's now start making real headway on the app by creating tasks from the Flex UI. For our first attempt, we won't set the location or project of a Task yet; we'll just try to get the name and notes saved.

We already have a create method, shown in listing 6.7; let's try to use it as-is.

Listing 6.7   app\controllers\tasks_controller.rb

```ruby
class TasksController < ApplicationController
...
  # POST /tasks
  # POST /tasks.xml
  def create
    @task = current_user.tasks.build(params[:task])         ❶
    respond_to do |format|
      if @task.save         ❷
        format.html do
          flash[:notice] = 'Task was successfully created.'
          redirect_to(@task)
        end
        format.xml  { render :xml => @task, :status => :created,         ❸
          :location => @task }
      else
        format.html { render :action => "new" }
        format.xml  { render :xml => @task.errors,         ❹
          :status => :unprocessable_entity }
      end
    end
  end
...
end
```

We're already using the association proxies[4] in the create method to call the build method ❹ of the current_user's tasks association (which was created by the has_many :tasks method call in the User class) to create an instance ❶ of

---

[4] This is based on http://www.therailsway.com/2007/3/26/association-proxies-are-your-friend. See that article as well as *AWDwR* (p. 312) for more information about save! vs. save and build! vs. build.

the `Task` class, which has the `user_id` properly set to the `id` of the `current_user`. We then attempt to save the new `Task` ❷. If we succeed, we render the XML ❸ of the new `@task` (implicitly calling `to_xml`), setting the `:status` and `:location` (more about those soon) as well. If we failed, we render the XML ❹ of the new `@task`'s errors, setting the `:status` also.

We need to modify the Flex code to trigger the `create` action. We'll start by creating a new event to dispatch when the `Task` is created. Because we've created an `AccountCreateEvent` for new user accounts, you're probably thinking that we'll create a `TaskCreateEvent`. We could do this. However, we'll be doing a lot of things with tasks (as well as projects, locations, and so on). If we continue with this approach, we'll have an explosion of `Events`. This feels like it violates the Don't Repeat Yourself (DRY) principle championed in *The Pragmatic Programmer* and adhered to closely in Rails.

What do we do? Two approaches come to mind:

- Have events for each action (such as `index` and `create`), and add a parameter that specifies what the object attached to the event is (such as `Task` and `Project`)

- Have events for each type (such as `Task` and `Project`), and add a parameter that explains the action (such as `index` and `create`)

Somewhat arbitrarily, we'll go with the second option. Why? Primarily because it lets us have variables named `task` instead of `thing` on the event. This is arbitrary, but it seems straightforward and promising, so that's what we'll do.

Right-click the LoginEvent.as file in the events folder, and choose Copy. Next, right-click the events folder and choose paste. Name the file TaskEvent.as, and set its contents to be as shown in listing 6.8.

Listing 6.8   app\flex\com\pomodo\events\TaskEvent.as

```
package com.pomodo.events {
    import flash.events.Event;

    public class TaskEvent extends Event {              ❶
        public static const TASK_CREATE:String = "taskCreate";     ❷

        public var task:XML;        ❸

        public function TaskEvent(type:String, task:XML) {      ❹
            super(type);
            this.task = task;
        }
    }
}
```

We're creating a `TaskEvent` class ❶ for all `Task` events. This constant
`TASK_CREATE` ❷ is used by classes that use the `TaskEvent`. It exists to catch typos at
compile time. The `task` XML variable ❸ stores whatever task is associated with the
event. The constructor ❹ for the new `TaskEvent` assigns the passed-in `task` to the
`task` property. It also sets the `type` property to the passed-in `type` by passing it to
the superclass constructor in the `super(type)` call.

Next, modify the `TaskCreateBox` as shown in listing 6.9.

Listing 6.9 app\flex\com\pomodo\components\TaskCreateBox.mxml

```
<?xml version="1.0" encoding="utf-8"?>
<mx:VBox xmlns:mx="http://www.adobe.com/2006/mxml"
    width="100%" height="100%" label="New Task">
<mx:Metadata>                                                        ❶
  [Event(name="taskCreate", type="com.pomodo.events.TaskEvent")]     ❷
</mx:Metadata>
<mx:Script>
<![CDATA[
    import mx.rpc.events.ResultEvent;                                 ❸
    import com.pomodo.events.TaskEvent;

    private function handleTaskCreateResult(event:ResultEvent):       ❹
    void {
        var resultXML: XML = XML(event.result);                      ❺
        Pomodo.debug("TaskCreateBox#handleTaskCreateResult:\n" +      ❻
            resultXML.toString());
        dispatchEvent(new TaskEvent(TaskEvent.TASK_CREATE,            ❼
            resultXML));
    }

    private function doTaskCreate():void {                           ❽
        svcTasksCreate.send();                                       ❾
    }
]]>
</mx:Script>
    <mx:HTTPService
        id="svcTasksCreate"                                          ❿
        url="/tasks.xml"                                             ⓫
        contentType="application/xml"                               ⓬
        resultFormat="e4x"                                          ⓭
        method="POST"
        result="handleTaskCreateResult(event)">
        <mx:request>                                                ⓮
            <task>                                                  ⓯
                <name>{nameTI.text}</name>                          ⓰
                <notes>{notesTI.text}</notes>                       ⓱
            </task>
        </mx:request>
    </mx:HTTPService>
```

```
<mx:Form width="100%" height="100%">
    <mx:FormItem label="Task">
        <mx:TextInput id="nameTI" width="200"/>
    </mx:FormItem>
    <mx:FormItem label="Notes">
        <mx:TextArea id="notesTI" width="200" height="100"/>
    </mx:FormItem>
    <mx:FormItem label="Project">
        <mx:ComboBox id="projectsCB" width="200"/>
    </mx:FormItem>
    <mx:FormItem label="">
        <mx:CheckBox id="nextActionCheckbox"
            label="This is the Next Action"/>
    </mx:FormItem>
    <mx:FormItem label="Location">
        <mx:ComboBox id="locationsCB" width="200"/>
    </mx:FormItem>
    <mx:FormItem>
        <mx:Button label="Submit" width="160" height="30"
            click="doTaskCreate()"/>          ⓲
    </mx:FormItem>
    </mx:Form>
</mx:VBox>
```

We start by defining an `HTTPService svcTasksCreate` ⓾ that does a `POST` to the /tasks.xml ⓫ URL (thus triggering the `create` method and ensuring the `respond_to` format is xml) with a `contentType` of application/xml ⓬ so it can send XML data. It specifies a `resultFormat` of e4x ⓭ so the result of the service can be handled with the new E4X XML API. The XML data we're sending is constructed dynamically when the `send()` function is called. We set the value of the `request` property ⓮ by specifying the XML for the `task` ⓯ and binding to the `name` ⓰ and `notes` ⓱ properties.

We modify the Submit button to call a new `doTaskCreate` function ❽, which calls the `send` function ❾ of the `svcTasksCreate` service when the `click` event of the Submit button is handled ⓲.

The `handleTaskCreateResult` function ❹ casts the `event.result` to XML (because that's what it is) and stores it in the `resultXML` ❺ local variable. We then call `Pomodo.debug` ❻ to output the XML text to the debug console, and we dispatch ❼ the new `TaskEvent` whose type is `TaskEvent.TASK_CREATE` and whose task is the `resultXML`.

Finally, we add the imports ❸ of `ResultEvent` and our new `TaskEvent` and also declare some `Metadata` ❶ for the new `TaskEvent` we're broadcasting, whose name is `taskCreate` ❷. This `Event` metadata declares that the component broadcasts this event, so that other components can handle it by name in MXML.

We have one more thing to do to tie this all together. We need to handle the `taskCreate` event in the `MainBox` and act accordingly in order to refresh the task list. Thankfully this is trivial, as shown in listing 6.10.

Listing 6.10 app\flex\com\pomodo\components\MainBox.mxml

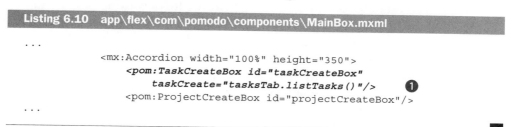

```
. . .
        <mx:Accordion width="100%" height="350">
            <pom:TaskCreateBox id="taskCreateBox"
                taskCreate="tasksTab.listTasks()"/>        ❶
            <pom:ProjectCreateBox id="projectCreateBox"/>
. . .
```

We modify the `taskCreateBox` to handle the `taskCreate` event and call `tasksTab.listTasks()` ❶. This triggers a call to `svcTasksList.send()` in the `TasksListBox`, which gets us the updated list of tasks.

Q. Isn't this less efficient than maintaining an Array on the client and adding the new task to it?

A. Yes. However, it's simpler. Also, if we end up having multiple users adding and removing from the same task list at a later date, we would have to deal with that on the client. Although this book hopes to provide code that's as useful as possible, this still is book code—and this isn't a book about caching. We'll just sidestep the problem for now by calling the service every time.

With this last change made, rebuild, reload, and log in as ludwig. We can now create a new task (the name and notes). Add `eat dinner` for the task and `yummy` for the notes (see figure 6.4), and click Submit.

The new task is created and shows up in the tasks `DataGrid`.

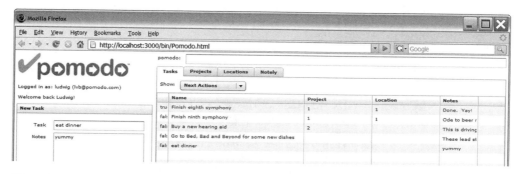

Figure 6.4 Creating a task from Flex

6.4 *Creating and listing projects and locations in Flex*

Now that we can add tasks with a name and notes, we'll add the ability to list and to create projects and locations. This will involve a lot of copying-pasting-modifying of code we've already seen for tasks, so we'll keep the explanations brief.

On the Rails side, the `ProjectsController` and `LocationsController` already have `create` methods that can send XML when that is the requested format, so there is nothing to do there. We'll start by modifying the `ProjectsListBox` and the `LocationsListBox` to display the projects and locations. First the `ProjectsList-Box`; see listing 6.11.

Listing 6.11   app\flex\com\pomodo\components\ProjectsListBox.mxml

```
<?xml version="1.0" encoding="utf-8"?>
<mx:VDividedBox xmlns:mx="http://www.adobe.com/2006/mxml"
    width="100%" height="100%" label="Projects"
    creationComplete="listProjects()">        ❶
<mx:Script>
<![CDATA[
    import mx.rpc.events.ResultEvent;

    public function listProjects():void {       ❷
        svcProjectsList.send();
    }

    private function handleProjectsListResult(   ❸
    event:ResultEvent):void {
        var resultXML:XML = XML(event.result);
        Pomodo.debug(
            "ProjectsListBox#handleProjectsListResult:\n" +
            resultXML.toString());
    }
]]>
</mx:Script>
    <mx:HTTPService         ❹
        id="svcProjectsList"
        url="/projects.xml"
        resultFormat="e4x"
        result="handleProjectsListResult(event)"/>
    <mx:XMLListCollection id="projectsXLC"      ❺
    source="{XMLList(svcProjectsList.lastResult.children())}"/>

    <mx:DataGrid id="projectsGrid" width="100%" height="60%"
        dataProvider="{projectsXLC}">        ❻
        <mx:columns>
            <mx:DataGridColumn headerText="" width="25"      ❼
                dataField="completed"/>
            <mx:DataGridColumn headerText="Name" width="400"
```

```
                    dataField="name"/>
                <mx:DataGridColumn headerText="Notes"
                    dataField="notes"/>
                <mx:DataGridColumn headerText="" width="60"/>
            </mx:columns>
        </mx:DataGrid>
    ...
    </mx:VDividedBox>
```

We start by creating a `svcProjectsList` ❹ HTTPService whose `url` is `/projects.xml`, meaning that it invokes the action in the `ProjectsController` with a desired format of `xml`. This `svcProjectsList` has its `send` function called by the `listProjects` function ❷, which is called in response to the `creationComplete` event ❶ being dispatched by the `ProjectsListBox`. When the service returns, the `result` event is dispatched and the `handleProjectsListResult` ❸ function is invoked. This function outputs debug information. We create a `projectsXLC XMLListCollection` ❺ whose source is the last result from the `svcProjectsList` service. We then bind the `dataProvider` of the `projectsGrid` ❻ to this `XMLListCollection`. Finally, we modify the columns to set the `dataField` property ❼.

Next, we make the equivalent changes to the `LocationsListBox`; see listing 6.12.

Listing 6.12   app\flex\com\pomodo\components\LocationsListBox.mxml

```xml
<?xml version="1.0" encoding="utf-8"?>
<mx:VDividedBox xmlns:mx="http://www.adobe.com/2006/mxml"
    width="100%" height="100%" label="Locations"
    creationComplete="listLocations()">
<mx:Script>
<![CDATA[
    import mx.rpc.events.ResultEvent;

    public function listLocations():void {
        svcLocationsList.send();
    }

    private function handleLocationsListResult(
    event:ResultEvent):void {
        var resultXML: XML = XML(event.result);
        Pomodo.debug(
            "LocationsListBox#handleLocationsListResult:\n"
            + resultXML.toString());
    }
]]>
</mx:Script>
    <mx:HTTPService
        id="svcLocationsList"
```

```
        url="/locations.xml"
        resultFormat="e4x"
        result="handleLocationsListResult(event)"/>
  <mx:XMLListCollection id="locationsXLC"
  source="{XMLList(svcLocationsList.lastResult.children())}"/>

  <mx:DataGrid id="locationsGrid" width="100%" height="60%"
      dataProvider="{locationsXLC}">
      <mx:columns>
          <mx:DataGridColumn headerText="" width="25"
              dataField="completed"/>
          <mx:DataGridColumn headerText="Name" width="400"
              dataField="name"/>
          <mx:DataGridColumn headerText="Notes"
              dataField="notes"/>
          <mx:DataGridColumn headerText="" width="60"/>
      </mx:columns>
  </mx:DataGrid>
...
</mx:VDividedBox>
```

At this point, we can optionally rebuild, reload, and log in as ludwig to check that the list functionality works.

Having made these changes, we press on and add the create functionality for projects and locations. We know that once we create projects and locations, we'll want to dispatch the appropriate events. Just as we created a TaskEvent, we'll create a ProjectEvent and a LocationEvent. These events will literally be a copy-paste-modify of the TaskEvent. First the ProjectEvent; see listing 6.13.

Listing 6.13   app\flex\com\pomodo\events\ProjectEvent.as

```
package com.pomodo.events {
    import flash.events.Event;

    public class ProjectEvent extends Event {
        public static const PROJECT_CREATE:String =
            "projectCreate";

        public var project:XML;

        public function ProjectEvent(type:String, project:XML) {
            super(type);
            this.project = project;
        }
    }
}
```

Next, the `LocationEvent`; see listing 6.14.

Listing 6.14   app\flex\com\pomodo\events\LocationEvent.as

```
package com.pomodo.events {
    import flash.events.Event;

    public class LocationEvent extends Event {
        public static const LOCATION_CREATE:String =
            "locationCreate";

        public var location:XML;

        public function LocationEvent(type:String,
        location:XML) {
            super(type);
            this.location = location;
        }
    }
}
```

Having created these events, we'll now modify the `ProjectCreateBox` and `LocationCreateBox` to make the appropriate service calls and dispatch them when successful. This is a copy-paste-modify of what we did in the `TaskCreateBox`, so the explanation will be shorter. First, the `ProjectCreateBox`; see listing 6.15.

Listing 6.15   app\flex\com\pomodo\components\ProjectCreateBox.mxml

```
<?xml version="1.0" encoding="utf-8"?>
<mx:VBox xmlns:mx="http://www.adobe.com/2006/mxml"
    width="100%" height="100%" label="New Project">
<mx:Metadata>
    [Event(name="projectCreate",            ❶
            type="com.pomodo.events.ProjectEvent")]
</mx:Metadata>
<mx:Script>
<![CDATA[
    import mx.rpc.events.ResultEvent;
    import com.pomodo.events.ProjectEvent;

    private function handleProjectCreateResult(      ❷
    event:ResultEvent):void {
        var resultXML: XML = XML(event.result);
        Pomodo.debug(
            "ProjectCreateBox#handleProjectCreateResult:\n" +
            resultXML.toString());
        dispatchEvent(new ProjectEvent(
```

```
                     ProjectEvent.PROJECT_CREATE, resultXML));
        }

        private function doProjectCreate():void {        ❸
            svcProjectsCreate.send();
        }
    ]]>
    </mx:Script>
        <mx:HTTPService        ❹
            id="svcProjectsCreate"
            url="/projects.xml"
            contentType="application/xml"
            resultFormat="e4x"
            method="POST"
            result="handleProjectCreateResult(event)">
            <mx:request>
                <project>
                    <name>{nameTI.text}</name>
                    <notes>{notesTI.text}</notes>
                </project>
            </mx:request>
        </mx:HTTPService>

        <mx:Form width="100%" height="100%">
            <mx:FormItem label="Name">
                <mx:TextInput id="nameTI" width="200"/>
            </mx:FormItem>
            <mx:FormItem label="Notes">
                <mx:TextArea id="notesTI" width="200" height="100"/>
            </mx:FormItem>
            <mx:FormItem>
                <mx:Button label="Submit" width="160" height="30"
                    click="doProjectCreate()"/>        ❺
            </mx:FormItem>
        </mx:Form>
    </mx:VBox>
```

We start by defining an HTTPService svcProjectsCreate ❹, which sends XML
to the create method (and requests XML from it with the .xml extension) in the
ProjectsController. This service is called when the doProjectCreate function
is called ❸, which includes when the Submit button is clicked ❺. When this service returns, the handleProjectCreateResult function ❷ is called, which outputs some debug information and then dispatches a new ProjectEvent of type
ProjectEvent.PROJECT_CREATE. Finally, we add some Metadata ❶ declaring
this, so we can handle it.

Next, we make the equivalent changes to the LocationCreateBox; see listing 6.16.

Listing 6.16   app\flex\com\pomodo\components\LocationCreateBox.mxml

```
<?xml version="1.0" encoding="utf-8"?>
<mx:VBox xmlns:mx="http://www.adobe.com/2006/mxml"
    width="100%" height="100%" label="New Location">
<mx:Metadata>
    [Event(name="locationCreate",
           type="com.pomodo.events.LocationEvent")]
</mx:Metadata>
<mx:Script>
<![CDATA[
    import mx.rpc.events.ResultEvent;
    import com.pomodo.events.LocationEvent;

    private function handleLocationCreateResult(
    event:ResultEvent):void {
        var resultXML: XML = XML(event.result);
        Pomodo.debug(
            "LocationCreateBox#handleLocationCreateResult:\n" +
            resultXML.toString());
        dispatchEvent(new LocationEvent(
            LocationEvent.LOCATION_CREATE, resultXML));
    }

    private function doLocationCreate():void {
        svcLocationsCreate.send();
    }
]]>
</mx:Script>
    <mx:HTTPService
        id="svcLocationsCreate"
        url="/locations.xml"
        contentType="application/xml"
        resultFormat="e4x"
        method="POST"
        result="handleLocationCreateResult(event)">
        <mx:request>
            <location>
                <name>{nameTI.text}</name>
                <notes>{notesTI.text}</notes>
            </location>
        </mx:request>
    </mx:HTTPService>

    <mx:Form width="100%" height="100%">
        <mx:FormItem label="Name">
```

```
            <mx:TextInput id="nameTI" width="200"/>
        </mx:FormItem>
        <mx:FormItem label="Notes">
            <mx:TextInput id="notesTI" width="200"/>
        </mx:FormItem>
        <mx:FormItem>
            <mx:Button label="Submit" width="160" height="30"
                click="doLocationCreate()"/>
        </mx:FormItem>
    </mx:Form>
</mx:VBox>
```

Similar to what we did with tasks, we need to handle the `projectCreate` and `locationCreate` events in the `MainBox` and act accordingly to refresh the project and location lists, respectively. This is similarly easy, as shown in listing 6.17.

Listing 6.17   app\flex\com\pomodo\components\MainBox.mxml

```
. . .
            <mx:Accordion width="100%" height="350">
                <pom:TaskCreateBox id="taskCreateBox"
                    taskCreate="tasksTab.listTasks()"/>
                <pom:ProjectCreateBox id="projectCreateBox"        ❶
                    projectCreate="projectsTab.listProjects()"/>
                <pom:LocationCreateBox id="locationCreateBox"      ❷
                    locationCreate="locationsTab.listLocations()"/>
            </mx:Accordion>
. . .
```

We modify the `projectCreateBox` and the `locationCreateBox` to handle the `projectCreate` ❶ and `locationCreate` ❷ events, and we call the `projects-Tab.listProjects` ❶ and `locationsTab.listLocations` ❷ functions respectively to trigger the update.

That's it! Rebuild, reload, and log in as ludwig. We see the Projects grid, as shown in figure 6.5.

Figure 6.5
The populated
Projects grid in Flex

We also see the Locations grid; see figure 6.6.

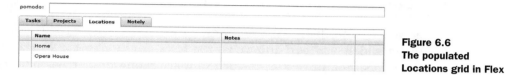

**Figure 6.6
The populated
Locations grid in Flex**

We can create new projects; see figure 6.7.

Figure 6.7   New project updating the Projects grid

We can also create new locations; see figure 6.8.

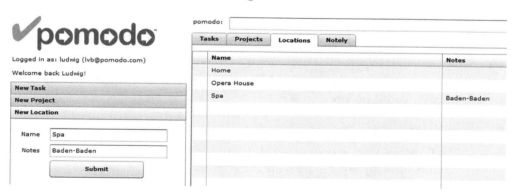

Figure 6.8   New location updating the Locations grid

Hooray! (It sure would be nice to be in Baden-Baden right now. Instead, we'll keep pressing forward, hooking up our Flex UI, with Baden-Baden as step 4 after "3. Profit!!!").

6.5 *Making the Projects and Locations ComboBoxes work in the TaskCreateBox*

Now that we have the ability to create projects and locations, we'll finally add the ability to set which Project and Location a Task belongs_to. Not all Tasks belong to a Location or Project—for example, eating dinner has neither. It's definitely legal for a Task to have no Project or Location.

First we'll get the existing projects and locations to show up in the ComboBoxes in the new task form. As usual, we won't worry about making the UI work until it looks like we want it to.

Examining the code, we realize we've gotten ourselves into a pickle: The TasksListBox knows the list of Tasks, the ProjectsListBox knows the list of Projects, and the LocationsListBox knows the list of Locations. However, there is currently no (clean) way for the TaskCreateBox to get at the list of Projects and Locations—and it needs these, so it can show them in the ComboBoxes.

What should we do?

We could create public properties on the various ___ListBox classes, so that other components could bind to their data. However, this seems like it would be a mess, with little bits of data everywhere. We'll do a little refactoring, where we pull the data from the ___ListBox classes into the MainBox and pass it into the various ___CreateBox and ___ListBox classes that need it.

> **NOTE**   We'll refactor the code to use Cairngorm later, which uses an even more centralized approach.

Let's do the refactoring quickly and then proceed with getting the projects and locations to show up.

6.5.1 *Refactoring the list data location*

We'll cut and paste code from the three ListBox classes into the MainBox. Somewhat arbitrarily, we'll start with the MainBox. If you're following along, copy and paste this from the other classes; see listing 6.18.

Listing 6.18   app\flex\com\pomodo\components\MainBox.mxml

```
<?xml version="1.0" encoding="utf-8"?>
<mx:HBox xmlns:mx="http://www.adobe.com/2006/mxml"
    xmlns:pom="com.pomodo.components.*"
    minWidth="1000"
    minHeight="680"
    paddingLeft="5"
    paddingRight="5"
```

```
        paddingTop="5"
        paddingBottom="5"
        width="100%"
        height="100%"
        backgroundColor="#FFFFFF"
        creationComplete="handleCreationComplete()">      ①
<mx:Script>
<![CDATA[
        import mx.rpc.events.ResultEvent;       ②

        [Bindable]
        public var user : XML;

        public function listTasks():void {        ③
            svcTasksList.send();
        }

        private function handleTasksListResult(event:ResultEvent):      ④
        void {
            var resultXML: XML = XML(event.result);
            Pomodo.debug("MainBox#handleTasksListResult:\n" +
                resultXML.toString());
        }

        public function listProjects():void {        ⑤
            svcProjectsList.send();
        }

        private function handleProjectsListResult(        ⑥
        event:ResultEvent):void {
            var resultXML: XML = XML(event.result);
            Pomodo.debug("MainBox#handleProjectsListResult:\n" +
                resultXML.toString());
        }

        public function listLocations():void {        ⑦
            svcLocationsList.send();
        }

        private function handleLocationsListResult(        ⑧
        event:ResultEvent):void {
            var resultXML: XML = XML(event.result);
            Pomodo.debug("MainBox#handleLocationsListResult:\n" +
                resultXML.toString());
        }

        private function handleCreationComplete():void {        ⑨
            listTasks();
            listProjects();
            listLocations();
        }
```

```
    ]]>
    </mx:Script>
    <mx:HTTPService                    ⑩
        id="svcTasksList"
        url="/tasks.xml"
        resultFormat="e4x"
        result="handleTasksListResult(event)"/>
    <mx:XMLListCollection id="tasksXLC"        ⑪
        source="{XMLList(svcTasksList.lastResult.children())}"/>


    <mx:HTTPService                    ⑫
        id="svcProjectsList"
        url="/projects.xml"
        resultFormat="e4x"
        result="handleProjectsListResult(event)"/>
    <mx:XMLListCollection id="projectsXLC"        ⑬
    source="{XMLList(svcProjectsList.lastResult.children())}"/>


    <mx:HTTPService                    ⑭
        id="svcLocationsList"
        url="/locations.xml"
        resultFormat="e4x"
        result="handleLocationsListResult(event)"/>
    <mx:XMLListCollection id="locationsXLC"        ⑮
    source="{XMLList(svcLocationsList.lastResult.children())}"/>


    <mx:HBox width="100%" height="100%">
        <mx:VBox width="300" height="100%">
            <mx:Image source="com/pomodo/assets/logo_md.png"/>
            <mx:Label text="{'Logged in as: ' + user.login +
                ' (' + user.email + ')'}"/>
            <mx:Label text="{'Welcome back ' + user.first_name +
                '!'}"/>
            <mx:Accordion width="100%" height="350">
                <pom:TaskCreateBox id="taskCreateBox"
                    taskCreate="listTasks()"/>        ⑯
                <pom:ProjectCreateBox id="projectCreateBox"
                    projectCreate="listProjects()"/>        ⑰
                <pom:LocationCreateBox id="locationCreateBox"
                    locationCreate="listLocations()"/>        ⑱
            </mx:Accordion>
            <mx:DateChooser id="dateChooser" width="100%"/>
        </mx:VBox>
        <mx:VBox width="100%" height="100%">
            <pom:CommandShell/>
            <mx:TabNavigator width="100%" height="100%">
                <pom:TasksListBox id="tasksTab"
                    tasksXLC="{tasksXLC}"/>        ⑲
                <pom:ProjectsListBox id="projectsTab"
                    projectsXLC="{projectsXLC}"/>        ⑳
                <pom:LocationsListBox id="locationsTab"
```

```
            locationsXLC="{locationsXLC}"/>        ㉑
                <pom:Notely id="notelyTab"/>
            </mx:TabNavigator>
        </mx:VBox>
    </mx:HBox>
</mx:HBox>
```

We start by cutting and pasting the various HTTPServices ⑩⑫⑭ and the
XMLListCollections ⑪⑬⑮ from the TasksListBox, ProjectsListBox, and
LocationsListBox. We pass these XMLListCollections via data binding into the
TasksListBox ⑲, ProjectsListBox ⑳, and LocationsListBox ㉑. (We'll create
Bindable public variables with the same name in these classes momentarily.) We
also modify the taskCreate ⑯, projectCreate ⑰, and locationCreate ⑱ event
handlers to call the listTasks ❸, listProjects ❺, and listLocations ❼ functions that have been moved to this component. These functions call the send
function of the various HTTPServices. The result handlers ❹❻❽ have also been
moved to the MainBox. We also add a creationComplete handler ❶ that calls the
handleCreationComplete function ❾, which has been newly created to call all
three of the list functions when the MainBox is created. (This is cleaner: We're
handling one creationComplete event, not three.) Finally, we add an import ❷.

Next, we modify the three ListBox classes. We'll start with the TasksListBox;
see listing 6.19.

Listing 6.19   app\flex\com\pomodo\components\TasksListBox.mxml

```
<?xml version="1.0" encoding="utf-8"?>
<mx:VDividedBox xmlns:mx="http://www.adobe.com/2006/mxml"
    width="100%" height="100%" label="Tasks">        ❶
    creationComplete="listTasks()">
<mx:Script>
<![CDATA[
    import mx.rpc.events.ResultEvent;        ❷
    import mx.collections.XMLListCollection;        ❸

    public const NEXT_ACTIONS:int = 0;
...
    [Bindable]
    private var _subChoices:Array;

    public function listTasks():void {        ❹
        svcTasksList.send();
    }

    private function handleTasksListResult(event:ResultEvent):        ❺
    void {
```

```
    var resultXML: XML = XML(event.result);
    Pomodo.debug("TasksListBox#handleTasksListResult:\n" +
        resultXML.toString());
}
[Bindable]
public var tasksXLC:XMLListCollection;                     6
]]>
</mx:Script>
    <mx:HTTPService id="svcTasksList" url="/tasks.xml"      7
        resultFormat="e4x"
        result="handleTasksListResult(event)"/>
    <mx:XMLListCollection id="tasksXLC"                      8
        source="{XMLList(svcTasksList.lastResult.children())}"/>
    <mx:VBox width="100%" height="60%">
        <mx:HBox width="100%" paddingLeft="5" paddingRight="5">
...
</mx:VDividedBox>
```

We add an import ❸ and add a public `Bindable` property ❻ for the `tasksXLC` that is being passed in from the `MainBox`. (We choose this name because it's the same name as the `tasksXLC` that we used to create in MXML; thus, we don't need to modify the `dataProvider` binding.) We then delete the `creationComplete` handler ❶, the `ResultEvent` import ❷, the `listTasks` ❹ and `handleTasksListResult` ❺ functions, the `svcTasksList` HTTPService ❼, and the `tasksXLC` ❽ XMLListCollection. (The use of the public var instead of the mx:XMLList-Collection is a style preference—we could have left the `mx:XMLListCollection` and gotten rid of its source property setting.)

Next, we'll make essentially the same changes to the `ProjectsListBox`; see listing 6.20.

Listing 6.20   app\flex\com\pomodo\components\ProjectsListBox.mxml

```
<?xml version="1.0" encoding="utf-8"?>
<mx:VDividedBox xmlns:mx="http://www.adobe.com/2006/mxml"
    width="100%" height="100%" label="Projects">
    creationComplete="listProjects()">                      1
<mx:Script>
<![CDATA[
    import mx.rpc.events.ResultEvent;                        2
    import mx.collections.XMLListCollection;                 3

    [Bindable]
    public var projectsXLC:XMLListCollection;                4
    public function listProjects():void {                    5
        svcProjectsList.send();
```

```
        }

        private function handleProjectsListResult(        ❻
        event:ResultEvent):void {
            var resultXML:XML = XML(event.result);
            Pomodo.debug(
                "ProjectsListBox#handleProjectsListResult:\n" +
                resultXML.toString());
        }
    ]]>
    </mx:Script>
    <mx:HTTPService                    ❼
        id="svcProjectsList"
        url="/projects.xml"
        resultFormat="e4x"
        result="handleProjectsListResult(event)"/>
    <mx:XMLListCollection id="projectsXLC"              ❽
    source="{XMLList(svcProjectsList.lastResult.children())}"/>
    <mx:DataGrid id="projectsGrid" width="100%" height="60%"
        dataProvider="{projectsXLC}">
        <mx:columns>
...
        </mx:columns>
    </mx:DataGrid>
...
</mx:VDividedBox>
```

We add an `import` ❸ and add a public `Bindable` property ❹ for the `projectsXLC`
that is being passed in from the `MainBox`. We then delete the `creationComplete`
handler ❶, the `ResultEvent` import ❷, the `listProjects` ❺ and `handle-
ProjectsListResult` ❻ functions, the `svcProjectsList` HTTPService ❼, and
the `projectsXLC` ❽ XMLListCollection.

Finally, we make essentially the same changes to the `LocationsListBox`; see
listing 6.21.

Listing 6.21   app\flex\com\pomodo\components\LocationsListBox.mxml

```
<?xml version="1.0" encoding="utf-8"?>
<mx:VDividedBox xmlns:mx="http://www.adobe.com/2006/mxml"
    width="100%" height="100%" label="Locations">
    creationComplete="listLocations()">
<mx:Script>
<![CDATA[
    import mx.rpc.events.ResultEvent;
    import mx.collections.XMLListCollection;

    [Bindable]
```

```
    public var locationsXLC:XMLListCollection;
    public function listLocations():void {
        svcLocationsList.send();
    }

    private function handleLocationsListResult(
    event:ResultEvent):void {
        var resultXML: XML = XML(event.result);
        Pomodo.debug(
            "LocationsListBox#handleLocationsListResult:\n"
            + resultXML.toString());
    }
]]>
</mx:Script>
    <mx:HTTPService
        id="svcLocationsList"
        url="/locations.xml"
        resultFormat="e4x"
        result="handleLocationsListResult(event)"/>
    <mx:XMLListCollection id="locationsXLC"
    source="{XMLList(svcLocationsList.lastResult.children())}"/>
    <mx:DataGrid id="locationsGrid" width="100%" height="60%"
        dataProvider="{locationsXLC}">
        <mx:columns>
...
        </mx:columns>
    </mx:DataGrid>
...
</mx:VDividedBox>
```

Having made these changes, rebuild, reload, and log in as ludwig. Nothing appears to have changed, which is always good in a refactoring. (The debug messages will say MainBox, but that doesn't count.)

6.5.2 *Making the projects and locations show up*

Let's get the projects and locations to show up in the ComboBoxes. This is easier than the refactoring we just did. Essentially, all we need to do is to copy and paste the projectsXLC and locationsXLC from the ProjectsListBox and Locations-ListBox into the TaskCreateBox and then hook up the bindings. Let's start with the TaskCreateBox; see listing 6.22.

> **Listing 6.22 app\flex\com\pomodo\components\TaskCreateBox.mxml**

```
<?xml version="1.0" encoding="utf-8"?>
<mx:VBox xmlns:mx="http://www.adobe.com/2006/mxml"
    width="100%" height="100%" label="New Task">
```

```
<mx:Metadata>
  [Event(name="taskCreate", type="com.pomodo.events.TaskEvent")]
</mx:Metadata>
<mx:Script>
<![CDATA[
    import mx.collections.XMLListCollection;        ❶
    import mx.rpc.events.ResultEvent;
    import com.pomodo.events.TaskEvent;

    [Bindable]
    public var projectsXLC:XMLListCollection;        ❷

    [Bindable]
    public var locationsXLC:XMLListCollection;       ❸

    private function handleTaskCreateResult(event:ResultEvent):
    void {
        var resultXML: XML = XML(event.result);
        Pomodo.debug("TaskCreateBox#handleTaskCreateResult:\n" +
            resultXML.toString());
        dispatchEvent(new TaskEvent(TaskEvent.TASK_CREATE,
            resultXML));
    }

    private function doTaskCreate():void {
        svcTasksCreate.send();
    }
]]>
</mx:Script>
    <mx:HTTPService
        id="svcTasksCreate"
        url="/tasks.xml"
        contentType="application/xml"
        resultFormat="e4x"
        method="POST"
        result="handleTaskCreateResult(event)">
        <mx:request>
            <task>
                <name>{nameTI.text}</name>
                <notes>{notesTI.text}</notes>
            </task>
        </mx:request>
    </mx:HTTPService>

    <mx:Form width="100%" height="100%">
        <mx:FormItem label="Task">
            <mx:TextInput id="nameTI" width="200"/>
        </mx:FormItem>
        <mx:FormItem label="Notes">
            <mx:TextArea id="notesTI" width="200" height="100"/>
```

```
            </mx:FormItem>
            <mx:FormItem label="Project">
                <mx:ComboBox id="projectsCB" width="200"
                    labelField="name" dataProvider="{projectsXLC}"/>          ❹
            </mx:FormItem>
            <mx:FormItem label="">
                <mx:CheckBox id="nextActionCheckbox"
                    label="This is the Next Action"/>
            </mx:FormItem>
            <mx:FormItem label="Location">
                <mx:ComboBox id="locationsCB" width="200"
                    labelField="name"
                    dataProvider="{locationsXLC}"/>          ❺
            </mx:FormItem>
            <mx:FormItem>
                <mx:Button label="Submit" width="160" height="30"
                    click="doTaskCreate()"/>
            </mx:FormItem>
        </mx:Form>
    </mx:VBox>
```

We start by importing XMLListCollection ❶ and pasting the projectsXLC ❷ and locationsXLC ❸ variable definitions into the TaskCreateBox. We then set the dataProvider of the projectsCB ❹ and locationsCB ❺ accordingly, ensuring in both cases that we set the labelField to the name property. (If we don't do this, we get the full XML shown in the ComboBox drop-down—try it to see.)

Next, we need to set these variables in bindings (❶ and ❷ in listing 6.23) from MainBox; see listing 6.23.

Listing 6.23 app\flex\com\pomodo\components\MainBox.mxml

```
. . .
            <mx:Accordion width="100%" height="350">
                <pom:TaskCreateBox id="taskCreateBox"
                    taskCreate="listTasks()"
                    projectsXLC="{projectsXLC}"          ❶
                    locationsXLC="{locationsXLC}"/>          ❷
                <pom:ProjectCreateBox id="projectCreateBox"
. . .
```

That's it! Rebuild, reload, and log in as ludwig. We see the screen shown in figure 6.9.

We have our projects and locations ComboBoxes populated with the projects and locations in their respective DataGrids. Let's see if they update live: Switch to

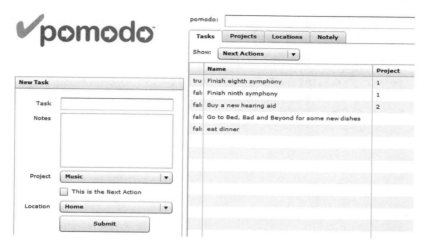

Figure 6.9   The populated project and location `ComboBoxes`

the New Project view, and add a project whose name is `Take a Vacation` and whose notes are `Snowboarding!` (I'm sure Beethoven would have loved snowboarding.) Click Submit, and click the Projects tab to see the new Take a Vacation project added. Next, switch back to the New Task VBox in the `Accordion`, and confirm that the new Take a Vacation project appears in the Project `ComboBox` dropdown. (We can confirm that adding a new location shows up right away in both places also.)

6.5.3   *Using a ComboBox prompt*

Before we get too full of ourselves, we have to remember that these `ComboBoxes` don't currently *do* anything. Also, note that there is no way to select "no project" or "no location." Let's fix this problem. Our first idea is to use the `prompt` property, which was added to `ComboBox` in Flex 2 and remains in Flex 3. According to the API docs for `ComboBox`:

> *A prompt is a String that is displayed in the TextInput portion of the ComboBox when selectedIndex = -1. It's usually a String like "Select one...". If there is no prompt, the ComboBox control sets selectedIndex to 0 and displays the first item in the dataProvider.*

Modify the `projectsCB` in the `TaskCreateBox` as follows to add a prompt (❶ in listing 6.24).

```
        . . .
                <mx:FormItem label="Project">
                    <mx:ComboBox id="projectsCB" width="200"
                        labelField="name" dataProvider="{projectsXLC}"
                        prompt="- None -"/>           ❶
                </mx:FormItem>
        . . .
```

Logged in as: ludwig (lvb@pomodo.com)

Welcome back Ludwig!

Figure 6.10
The None prompt

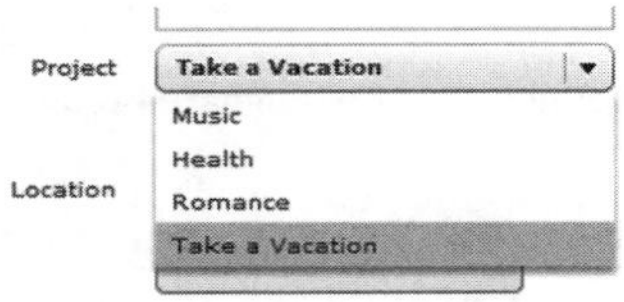

Figure 6.11   The missing None prompt

Rebuild, reload, and log in as ludwig. We see the result shown in figure 6.10.

This looks like a winner. But let's test it to see if there are any issues. Choose Take a Vacation from the Project ComboBox. Next, we change our mind and decide that we have too much work to take a vacation (typical). Try to change back to None by selecting it from the drop-down list. As shown in figure 6.11, *it's not there!*

Once the prompt disappears when we choose an item in the ComboBox, we can't get the prompt back.

The prompt isn't going to work. Modify the projectsCB in the TaskCreateBox to remove the prompt (see listing 6.25 ❶).

```
        . . .
                <mx:FormItem label="Project">
                    <mx:ComboBox id="projectsCB" width="200"
                        labelField="name" dataProvider="{projectsXLC}"/>      ❶
                </mx:FormItem>
        . . .
```

With this done, we can turn our attention to adding a None object to the `Combo-Box` `dataProvider`.

6.5.4 *Adding a None object to the ComboBox dataProvider*

What we need is a placeholder in the beginning of the list of projects for None. This isn't currently in the XML data coming from Rails, but it's a UI need. We need to modify the `dataProvider` of the `ComboBox` to have a None object at the front. However, we don't want this None object to show up in the Projects `Data-Grid`—we can't add it to the `projectsXLC` itself, or it would show up in both places. Also note that we need to also create a None object for locations.

Let's do this now for both projects and locations, by modifying what the `Main-Box` passes in to the `TaskCreateBox`; see listing 6.26.

Listing 6.26   app\flex\com\pomodo\components\MainBox.mxml

```
<?xml version="1.0" encoding="utf-8"?>
<mx:HBox xmlns:mx="http://www.adobe.com/2006/mxml"
...
<mx:Script>
<![CDATA[
    import mx.rpc.events.ResultEvent;
    import mx.collections.XMLListCollection;          ❶

    [Bindable]
    public var user : XML;

    [Bindable]
    private var _projectsAndNoneXLC:XMLListCollection;   ❷

    [Bindable]
    private var _locationsAndNoneXLC:XMLListCollection;  ❸

    public static const NO_PROJECT_XML:XML =    ❹
        <project>
            <name>- None -</name>
            <id type="integer">0</id>
        </project>

    public static const NO_LOCATION_XML:XML =    ❺
        <location>
            <name>- None -</name>
            <id type="integer">0</id>
        </location>

    public function listTasks():void {
        svcTasksList.send();
    }
```

```
    ...
    private function handleCreationComplete():void {
        listTasks();
        listProjects();
        listLocations();
    }

    private function getProjectsAndNone(projectsXL:XMLList):        ❻
    XMLListCollection {
        var retval:XMLListCollection =
            new XMLListCollection(projectsXL.copy());
        retval.addItemAt(NO_PROJECT_XML, 0);
        return retval;
    }

    private function getLocationsAndNone(locationsXL:XMLList):      ❼
    XMLListCollection {
        var retval:XMLListCollection =
            new XMLListCollection(locationsXL.copy());
        retval.addItemAt(NO_LOCATION_XML, 0);
        return retval;
    }
    ]]>
</mx:Script>
...
    <mx:HTTPService
        id="svcProjectsList"
        url="/projects.xml"
        resultFormat="e4x"
        result="handleProjectsListResult(event)"/>
    <mx:XMLListCollection id="projectsXLC"
    source="{XMLList(svcProjectsList.lastResult.children())}"/>
    <mx:Binding
        source="{getProjectsAndNone(projectsXLC.source)}"      ❽
        destination="_projectsAndNoneXLC"/>

    <mx:HTTPService
        id="svcLocationsList"
        url="/locations.xml"
        resultFormat="e4x"
        result="handleLocationsListResult(event)"/>
    <mx:XMLListCollection id="locationsXLC"
    source="{XMLList(svcLocationsList.lastResult.children())}"/>
    <mx:Binding
        source="{getLocationsAndNone(locationsXLC.source)}"      ❾
        destination="_locationsAndNoneXLC"/>

    <mx:HBox width="100%" height="100%">
        <mx:VBox width="300" height="100%">
            <mx:Image source="com/pomodo/assets/logo_md.png"/>
            <mx:Label text="{'Logged in as: ' + user.login +
```

```
                    ' (' + user.email + ')'}"/>
        <mx:Label text="{'Welcome back ' + user.first_name +
            '!'}"/>
        <mx:Accordion width="100%" height="350">
            <pom:TaskCreateBox id="taskCreateBox"
                taskCreate="listTasks()"
                projectsXLC="{projectsXLC}"
                locationsXLC="{locationsXLC}"/>
                projectsXLC="{_projectsAndNoneXLC}"        ❿
                locationsXLC="{_locationsAndNoneXLC}"/>        ⓫
            <pom:ProjectCreateBox id="projectCreateBox"
                projectCreate="listProjects()"/>
            <pom:LocationCreateBox id="locationCreateBox"
            locationCreate="listLocations()"/>
        </mx:Accordion>
        <mx:DateChooser id="dateChooser" width="100%"/>
    </mx:VBox>
    <mx:VBox width="100%" height="100%">
  ...
        </mx:VBox>
    </mx:HBox>
</mx:HBox>
```

We import XMLListCollection ❶ and then create two XMLListCollections:
_projectsAndNoneXLC to hold the user's projects and the None object ❷ and
_locationsAndNoneXLC ❸ to do the same for locations. Next, we create two
XML constants that represent what None looks like for a Project ❹ and for a
Location ❺. Because the projectsCB ComboBox has labelField="name", this
attribute is provided because it will be displayed. An id of 0 is provided, because
that is obviously illegal (ids of legitimate projects start at 1). This same logic applies
to the None Location ❺. We also create a method getProjectsAndNone ❻ that
takes an XMLList and return an XMLListCollection that contains the
noProjectXML at the beginning, followed by a copy of the projectsXL XMLList
that was passed in. We add a similar method called getLocationsAndNone ❼ for
Locations. Next, we create an mx:Binding ❽ to populate our new
_projectsAndNoneXLC with the result of calling getProjectsAndNone on the
source property of the projectsXLC XMLListCollection, which is an XMLList.
This is why getProjectsAndNone takes an XMLList as its parameter, not an
XMLListCollection. Now, we create an equivalent mx:Binding to populate the
new _locationsAndNoneXLC ❾ XMLListCollection. Finally, we bind these new
XMLListCollections into the projectsXLC ❿ and locationsXLC ⓫ properties of
the taskCreateBox.

Let's see if that works. Rebuild, reload, and log in as ludwig. Note that, as before, the `projectsCB` ComboBox starts out as None. However, this time None is in the drop-down list. We can select a different project such as Take a Vacation in the drop-down list and then select None again. This also works for the `locations-CB` ComboBox.

6.5.5 *Saving the project and location choices*

Before we get too smug, we should keep in mind that the project and location combo boxes still don't *have any effect:* Regardless of what we choose in them, a new task is saved with no project and location. We need to make the choice get saved and loaded. This is what we'll accomplish here.

First, let's look in the database to clarify exactly what we mean by "no project and location." We recently created an "eat dinner" task; let's see what it looks like, in listing 6.27.

Listing 6.27   Commands

```
mysql> select * from tasks where name = "eat dinner"\G
*************************** 1. row ***************************
         id: 8
    user_id: 3
 project_id: NULL        ❶
location_id: NULL        ❷
       name: eat dinner
      notes: yummy
next_action: 0
  completed: 0
 created_at: 2007-10-22 01:06:10
 updated_at: 2007-10-22 01:06:10
1 row in set (0.01 sec)
```

The `project_id` ❶ and `location_id` ❷ are NULL (unlike those of the tasks such as "Finish ninth symphony" that we created in the fixtures). Let's try modifying the `TaskCreateBox` in the simplest way we can imagine; see listing 6.28.

Listing 6.28   app\flex\com\pomodo\components\TaskCreateBox.mxml

```
...
    <mx:HTTPService
        id="svcTasksCreate"
        url="/tasks.xml"
        contentType="application/xml"
        resultFormat="e4x"
        method="POST"
```

```
                result="handleTaskCreateResult(event)">
            <mx:request>
                <task>
                    <name>{nameTI.text}</name>
                    <notes>{notesTI.text}</notes>
        <project_id>{XML(projectsCB.selectedItem).id}</project_id>      ❶
        <location_id>{XML(locationsCB.selectedItem).id}</location_id>    ❷
                </task>
            </mx:request>
        </mx:HTTPService>
    ...
```

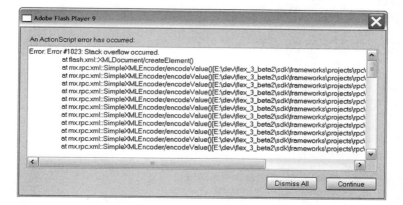

**Figure 6.12
Well, Flex didn't
like that binding.**

We bind the project_id ❶ and location_id ❷ to the id of the selectedItem of
the projectsCB ❶ and locationsCB ❷. Rebuild, reload, and log in as ludwig.
Enter the Task have a coffee with Notes this iteration is taking forever
in the Take a Vacation project at the Spa location. Click Submit (see figure 6.12).

Maybe in some future version of Flex it will work; in Flex 3 Beta 2, however, it
doesn't. Let's work around that by setting instance variables and binding to them
in the XML; see listing 6.29.

Listing 6.29   app\flex\com\pomodo\components\TaskCreateBox.mxml

```
    ...
    [Bindable]
    public var locationsXLC:XMLListCollection;

    [Bindable]
    private var _selectedProjectId:int;      ❶

    [Bindable]
    private var _selectedLocationId:int;      ❷
```

```
        private function handleTaskCreateResult(event:ResultEvent):
        void {
            var resultXML: XML = XML(event.result);
            Pomodo.debug("TaskCreateBox#handleTaskCreateResult:\n" +
                resultXML.toString());
            dispatchEvent(new TaskEvent(TaskEvent.TASK_CREATE,
                resultXML));
        }

        private function doTaskCreate():void {
            _selectedProjectId = XML(projectsCB.selectedItem).id;      ❸
            _selectedLocationId = XML(locationsCB.selectedItem).id;     ❹
            svcTasksCreate.send();
        }
    ]]>
</mx:Script>
    <mx:HTTPService
        id="svcTasksCreate"
        url="/tasks.xml"
        contentType="application/xml"
        resultFormat="e4x"
        method="POST"
        result="handleTaskCreateResult(event)">
        <mx:request>
            <task>
                <name>{nameTI.text}</name>
                <notes>{notesTI.text}</notes>
                <project_id>{_selectedProjectId}</project_id>       ❺
                <location_id>{_selectedLocationId}</location_id>     ❻
            </task>
        </mx:request>
    </mx:HTTPService>

    <mx:Form width="100%" height="100%">
...
    </mx:Form>
</mx:VBox>
```

We create two variables for the selected project ❶ and location ❷ ids and set their values ❸❹ based on the id attribute of the selectedItem of the ComboBoxes right before calling svcTasksCreate.send(). This way, the id of the selected-Item is bound to the project_id ❺ and location_id ❻ properties of the task in the request. Once again, rebuild, reload, and log in as ludwig. Enter the Task have a coffee with Notes this iteration is taking forever in the Take a Vacation project at the Spa location. Click Submit; see figure 6.13.

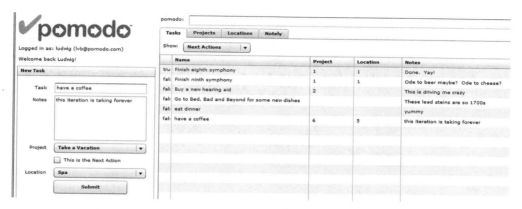

Figure 6.13   A Much Deserved Vacation Indeed!

The "have a coffee" task is created, with the `Project` and `Location` ids set to the ids of the Take a Vacation project and the Spa location, respectively.

6.6   *About that None project and location*

If you were paying close attention, you may have noticed that I pulled a fast one in the last section: We submit the new tasks without doing anything special (in Flex or in Rails) if the task has a None project or location. To see the result of this more clearly, log in as ludwig and add a new Task "drink another coffee" with Notes "very necessary", and leave the Project and Location with None selected.

You'll see the screen shown in figure 6.14.

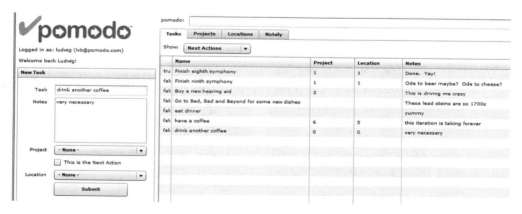

Figure 6.14   Drinking coffee with a project and location of 0

Looking in MySQL, we see the the results shown in listing 6.30.

Listing 6.30   Commands

```
mysql> select * from tasks where name = "drink another coffee"\G
*************************** 1. row ***************************
        id: 10
   user_id: 3
project_id: 0          ❶
location_id: 0
      name: drink another coffee
     notes: very necessary
next_action: 0
 completed: 0
created_at: 2007-10-22 05:52:03
updated_at: 2007-10-22 05:52:03
1 row in set (0.00 sec)

mysql> select * from tasks where id=4\G
*************************** 1. row ***************************
        id: 4
   user_id: 3
project_id: NULL       ❷
location_id: NULL
      name: Go to Bed, Bad and Beyond for some new dishes
     notes: These lead steins are so 1700s
next_action: 0
 completed: 0
created_at: NULL
updated_at: NULL
1 row in set (0.00 sec)

mysql>
```

The new task "drink another coffee" has 0 for its project_id ❶ and location_id, whereas the "Go to Bed, Bad and Beyond for some new dishes" (yeah, I thought that was funny when I wrote it, but I'm sick of it now too) task has a project_id ❷ and location_id of NULL.

Although we don't want to have to write special-case code to handle "no project" or "no location," it means that currently there can be two separate versions of "no project" for a task: NULL or 0 in the project_id column. This is Very Bad (and Beyond).

> **NOTE**   It's Even Worse if you care about things like foreign keys: It won't work. (No project has an id of 0.) We can't let the project_id be set to 0 in the database.

What to do?

We could try sending `null` from Flex. However, this path leads to madness: How do you differentiate between the `null` of "not updating" and the `null` of "no project" when using `update_attributes` in Rails?

Another thing we could do is to use the Null Object pattern and create a project and a location for None. Each user would have their own None project and location. In effect, all tasks would have a project and location, but some would have the None ones. This would solve some problems but create others: We'd have to filter them out of the list of projects and locations, prevent them from being deleted, and so on.

We do want to be able to pass 0 instead of `null`/`nil` from Flex to Rails as the `project_id` and `location_id` of a task with no project and location. (It's debatable whether Rails should pass `nil` or `0`; we'll stick with nil for now.) We also know that we should be saving `NULL` in the database instead of `0`.

We could solve this lots of ways. I'll choose to use the `before_save` callback in the Task model; see listing 6.31.

Listing 6.31   app\models\task.rb

```
class Task < ActiveRecord::Base
  belongs_to :user
  belongs_to :location
  belongs_to :project

  def before_save                                    ❶
    self.project_id = nil if self.project_id == 0    ❷
    self.location_id = nil if self.location_id == 0  ❸
  end
end
```

We define the `before_save` ❶ method, which is a callback[5] method that Active Record ensures gets called before saving. In it, we set the `project_id` ❷ and `location_id` ❸ to nil if either of them are 0.

With this change made, create a new Task called `drink espresso` with Notes `very necessary`, leaving Project and Location as None. The Project and Location columns will be correctly blank, instead of 0. Checking in MySQL, we see that our `before_save` method worked (see listing 6.32).

---

[5] See section 19.2, "Callbacks," in *AWDwR* for details.

Listing 6.32   Commands

```
mysql> select * from tasks where name = "drink espresso"\G
*************************** 1. row ***************************
          id: 11
     user_id: 3
  project_id: NULL     ❶
 location_id: NULL     ❷
        name: drink espresso
       notes: very necessary
 next_action: 0
   completed: 0
  created_at: 2007-10-22 06:08:38
  updated_at: 2007-10-22 06:08:38
1 row in set (0.00 sec)
```

The project_id ❶ and location_id ❷ are NULL. Now we're getting somewhere.

6.7   Updating and deleting tasks, projects, and locations

Now that we've gotten New Task, New Project, and New Location working; it's time to take a big step and get update and delete working.

Q. What about the Next Action check box? Are you going to ignore it?

A. For now, yes. We'll implement it later. (I'm also ignoring the "pomodo:" command shell at the top of the screen, but that will be ignored for a lot longer. The grand ambition I had earlier is starting to be tempered by the reality of implementing [and explaining] everything.)

We'll start by modifying the Rails controllers.

6.7.1   Adding update_xml and destroy_xml methods to the Rails controllers

The first thing we'll do is modify the update and destroy methods in the Rails controllers. Although the new RESTful scaffold command created methods for us, what they return when XML format is requested is too idealistic for use with Flex. (Translation: Status codes don't work in Flash 9, so we send XML for everything.)

We'll start with the TasksController; see listing 6.33.

Listing 6.33 app\controllers\tasks_controller.rb

```
...
  # PUT /tasks/1
  # PUT /tasks/1.xml
  def update
    @task = current_user.tasks.find(params[:id])

    respond_to do |format|
      if @task.update_attributes(params[:task])
        flash[:notice] = 'Task was successfully updated.'
        format.html { redirect_to(@task) }
        format.xml  { head :ok }              ❶
        format.xml  { render :xml => @task }  ❷
      else
        format.html { render :action => "edit" }
        format.xml  { render :xml => @task.errors,
          :status => :unprocessable_entity }
      end
    end
  rescue ActiveRecord::RecordNotFound => e
    prevent_access(e)
  end

  # DELETE /tasks/1
  # DELETE /tasks/1.xml
  def destroy
    @task = current_user.tasks.find(params[:id])
    @task.destroy

    respond_to do |format|
      format.html { redirect_to(tasks_url) }
      format.xml  { head :ok }               ❸
      format.xml  { render :xml => @task }   ❹
    end
  rescue ActiveRecord::RecordNotFound => e
    prevent_access(e)
  end
...
```

We're updating the create ❷ and destroy ❹ methods to render :xml => @task instead of call head :ok ❶❸ to send an OK HTTP header.

Next, we'll make the same changes to the ProjectsController; see listing 6.34.

Listing 6.34 app\controllers\projects_controller.rb

```
...
  # PUT /projects/1
  # PUT /projects/1.xml
```

```
def update
  @project = current_user.projects.find(params[:id])

  respond_to do |format|
    if @project.update_attributes(params[:project])
      flash[:notice] = 'Project was successfully updated.'
      format.html { redirect_to(@project) }
      format.xml  { head :ok }
      format.xml  { render :xml => @project }
    else
      format.html { render :action => "edit" }
      format.xml  { render :xml => @project.errors,
         :status => :unprocessable_entity }
    end
  end
rescue ActiveRecord::RecordNotFound => e
  prevent_access(e)
end

# DELETE /projects/1
# DELETE /projects/1.xml
def destroy
  @project = current_user.projects.find(params[:id])
  @project.destroy

  respond_to do |format|
    format.html { redirect_to(projects_url) }
    format.xml  { head :ok }
    format.xml  { render :xml => @project }
  end
rescue ActiveRecord::RecordNotFound => e
  prevent_access(e)
end
...
```

Finally, make the same changes to the LocationsController; see listing 6.35.

Listing 6.35 app\controllers\locations_controller.rb

```
...
# PUT /locations/1
# PUT /locations/1.xml
def update
  @location = current_user.locations.find(params[:id])

  respond_to do |format|
    if @location.update_attributes(params[:location])
      flash[:notice] = 'Location was successfully updated.'
      format.html { redirect_to(@location) }
      format.xml  { head :ok }
```

```
    format.xml  { render :xml => @location }
  else
    format.html { render :action => "edit" }
    format.xml  { render :xml => @location.errors,
      :status => :unprocessable_entity }
  end
end
rescue ActiveRecord::RecordNotFound => e
  prevent_access(e)
end

# DELETE /locations/1
# DELETE /locations/1.xml
def destroy
  @location = current_user.locations.find(params[:id])
  @location.destroy

  respond_to do |format|
    format.html { redirect_to(locations_url) }
    format.xml  { head :ok }
    format.xml  { render :xml => @location }
  end
rescue ActiveRecord::RecordNotFound => e
  prevent_access(e)
end
...
```

So far, so good.

6.7.2 *Getting ComboBox itemRenderers to work in the TasksListBox*

Next, we'll add the necessary code to the MainBox and the TasksListBox to implement ComboBox itemRenderers[6] in the TasksListBox. (Using a custom item-Renderer lets you customize what is shown in a DataGrid cell, beyond just changing the text with a function.)

> **WARNING** This section contains much trickier Flex code than you've seen before. Ensure you're well-caffeinated, and then proceed. (If this code seems opaque, don't despair: The rest of the Flex code in the book is easier than this.)

---

[6] See http://www.visualconcepts.ca/blog/index.cfm/2006/6/22/ComoboBox-RendererEditor-for-20 for a useful article about ComboBox renderers and editors in Flex 2. (It helped me understand them better.)

We'll start with the MainBox, because we need to do some setup work there; see listing 6.36.

Listing 6.36   app\flex\com\pomodo\components\MainBox.mxml

```
...
<?xml version="1.0" encoding="utf-8"?>
<mx:HBox xmlns:mx="http://www.adobe.com/2006/mxml"
    xmlns:pom="com.pomodo.components.*"
    minWidth="1000"
    minHeight="680"
    paddingLeft="5"
    paddingRight="5"
    paddingTop="5"
    paddingBottom="5"
    width="100%"
    height="100%"
    backgroundColor="#FFFFFF"
    creationComplete="handleCreationComplete()">
<mx:Script>
<![CDATA[
    import mx.rpc.events.ResultEvent;                    ❶ Add
    import mx.collections.ArrayCollection;     ◁————┘     imports
    import mx.collections.IViewCursor;
    import mx.collections.XMLListCollection;

    [Bindable]
    public var user : XML;

    [Bindable]                                    ❷ Flag to check
    private var _gotProjects : Boolean;    ◁————┘   for projects

    [Bindable]                                    ❸ Flag to check
    private var _gotLocations : Boolean;   ◁————┘   for locations

    [Bindable]
    private var _projectsAndNoneXLC:XMLListCollection;

    [Bindable]
    private var _locationsAndNoneXLC:XMLListCollection;

    [Bindable]                                    ❹ Map project id (key)
    private var _projectIdMap:Object;      ◁————┘   to project (value)

    [Bindable]                                    ❺ Map location id (key)
    private var _locationIdMap:Object;     ◁————┘   to project (value)
...
    public function listProjects():void {
        svcProjectsList.send();
    }
```

```
private function handleProjectsListResult(
event:ResultEvent):void {
    _gotProjects = true;
    var resultXML: XML = XML(event.result);
    Pomodo.debug("MainBox#handleProjectsListResult:\n" +
        resultXML.toString());
    updateProjectIdMap();
}

public function listLocations():void {
    svcLocationsList.send();
}

private function handleLocationsListResult(
event:ResultEvent):void {
    _gotLocations = true;
    var resultXML: XML = XML(event.result);
    Pomodo.debug("MainBox#handleLocationsListResult:\n" +
        resultXML.toString());
    updateLocationIdMap();
}

private function handleCreationComplete():void {
    listTasks();
    _gotProjects = false;
    _gotLocations = false;
    listProjects();
    listLocations();
}

private function getProjectsAndNone(projectsXL:XMLList):
XMLListCollection {
    var retval:XMLListCollection =
        new XMLListCollection(projectsXL.copy());
    retval.addItemAt(NO_PROJECT_XML, 0);
    return retval;
}

private function getLocationsAndNone(locationsXL:XMLList):
XMLListCollection {
    var retval:XMLListCollection =
        new XMLListCollection(locationsXL.copy());
    retval.addItemAt(NO_LOCATION_XML, 0);
    return retval;
}

private function updateProjectIdMap():void {
    _projectIdMap = {};
    _projectIdMap[0] = NO_PROJECT_XML;
    var projectsCursor:IViewCursor =
```

6 Set project flag

7 Rebuild _projectIdMap

8 Set location flag

9 Rebuild _locationIdMap

10 Delete manual listTasks call and...

11 ...initialize flags to false.

12

13 Rebuild _projectIdMap

14

15

```
            projectsXLC.createCursor();              ⑯
        while (!projectsCursor.afterLast) {          ⑰
            var project:XML = XML(projectsCursor.current);    ⑱
            _projectIdMap[project.id] = project;     ⑲
            projectsCursor.moveNext();               ⑳
        }
        listTasksIfMapsPresent();                    ㉑
    }

    private function updateLocationIdMap():void {    ㉒  ──►  Rebuild
        _locationIdMap = {};                                  _locationIdMap
        _locationIdMap[0] = NO_LOCATION_XML;
        var locationsCursor:IViewCursor =
            locationsXLC.createCursor();
        while (!locationsCursor.afterLast) {
            var location:XML = XML(locationsCursor.current);
            _locationIdMap[location.id] = location;
            locationsCursor.moveNext();
        }
        listTasksIfMapsPresent();
    }

    private function listTasksIfMapsPresent():void {    ㉓
        if (_gotProjects && _gotLocations) {            ㉔
            listTasks();    ◄───────         Call listTasks()
        }                            ㉕       only if both
    }                                        maps populated
]]>
</mx:Script>
...
    <mx:HBox width="100%" height="100%">
...
        <mx:VBox width="100%" height="100%">
            <pom:CommandShell/>
            <mx:TabNavigator width="100%" height="100%">
                <pom:TasksListBox id="tasksTab"              ㉖
                    tasksXLC="{tasksXLC}"
                    projectIdMap="{_projectIdMap}"           ㉗
                    locationIdMap="{_locationIdMap}"         ㉘
                    projectsAndNone="{_projectsAndNoneXLC}"  ㉙
                    locationsAndNone="{_locationsAndNoneXLC}"/>  ㉚
                <pom:ProjectsListBox id="projectsTab"
                    projectsXLC="{projectsXLC}"/>
                <pom:LocationsListBox id="locationsTab"
                    locationsXLC="{locationsXLC}"/>
                <pom:Notely id="notelyTab"/>
            </mx:TabNavigator>
        </mx:VBox>
    </mx:HBox>
</mx:HBox>
```

We start by adding a couple of imports ❶. Next, we add two flags that we'll use to check whether we've retrieved the projects ❷ and locations ❸. We add two Objects that function as associative arrays (hashes): _projectIdMap ❹ and _locationIdMap ❺. These will map the id of a project to its project and the id of a location to its location. This will be useful, as we'll soon see.

Next, in the handleProjectsListResult function, we set _gotProjects to true ❻ and call the updateProjectIdMap ❼ function. Similarly, in the handle-LocationsListResult function, we set _gotLocations to true ❽ and call the updateLocationIdMap ❾ function.

In the handleCreationComplete function ❿, we delete the call to listTasks and set the _gotProjects ⓫ and _gotLocations ⓬ flags to false. We don't call listTasks until we have the projects and locations returned and the maps populated. (This is because we'll be using these maps in the ComboBox itemRenderers we'll create shortly—if the tasks come back too soon, the ComboBox rendering won't happen correctly, and we'd need to call listTasks again anyway.)

Q. Why create two flags? Why not just check whether _projectIdMap and _locationIdMap are empty?

A. The reason is that they may well *be empty*. A new user may conceivably have no projects or locations. (We may have default ones, but we may not. Regardless, we shouldn't write code that brittle.) I thought it was cleaner to use flags.

Next, we create the updateProjectIdMap ⓭ function. It creates a new Object ⓮ (the {} syntax is equivalent to saying new Object();). It then adds the NO_PROJECT_XML to the Object ⓯ with a key of 0.

NOTE   Remember: This is a hash, not an array. Just because we're using numbers as keys doesn't make them array indices.

Now, we loop over the elements of the projectsXLC. This is done by getting an IViewCursor on the projectsXLC ⓰ and iterating over it ⓱. Each current ⓲ element is retrieved and cast to XML, and an entry in the _projectIdMap is created for it ⓳. The cursor is then advanced ⓴. After the loop is done, we call list-TasksIfMapsPresent ㉑.

The updateLocationIdMap function ㉒ is essentially the same as the updateProjectIdMap function, but for locations.

The listTasksIfMapsPresent ㉓ function checks whether we have _gotProjects and _gotLocations ㉔. If so, it calls listTasks ㉕.

Finally, we modify the tasksTab ㉖ to set its projectIdMap ㉗, location-IdMap ㉘, projectsAndNone ㉙, and locationsAndNone ㉚ properties (which we'll create momentarily) via bindings.

Phew.

Now for the TasksListBox. It's long, so we'll break the code into two parts with explanation in the middle; see listing 6.37.

Listing 6.37   app\flex\com\pomodo\components\TasksListBox.mxml

```
<?xml version="1.0" encoding="utf-8"?>
<mx:VDividedBox xmlns:mx="http://www.adobe.com/2006/mxml"
    width="100%" height="100%" label="Tasks">
<mx:Script>
<![CDATA[
    import mx.collections.XMLListCollection;
    import mx.controls.Alert;
    import mx.rpc.events.ResultEvent;
    import com.pomodo.components.MainBox;
    import com.pomodo.events.TaskEvent;

    public const NEXT_ACTIONS:int = 0;
    public const ALL_TASKS:int = 1;
    public const TASKS_IN_PROJECT:int = 2;
    public const TASKS_AT_LOCATION:int = 3;

    private const SHOW_CHOICES:Array = [
        {label:"Next Actions", data:NEXT_ACTIONS,
            hasSubChoice:false},
        {label:"All Tasks", data:ALL_TASKS,
            hasSubChoice:false},
        {label:"Tasks in Project:", data:TASKS_IN_PROJECT,
            hasSubChoice:true},
        {label:"Tasks at Location:", data:TASKS_AT_LOCATION,
            hasSubChoice:true}];

    [Bindable]
    private var _subChoices:Array;

    [Bindable]
    public var tasksXLC:XMLListCollection;

    [Bindable]
    public var projectIdMap:Object;          ❶

    [Bindable]
    public var locationIdMap:Object;         ❷

    [Bindable]
    public var projectsAndNone:XMLListCollection;    ❸
```

Add imports, including importing MainBox to use its constants ← (pointing to `import mx.controls.Alert;`)

```
[Bindable]
public var locationsAndNone:XMLListCollection;          ④

public function getProject(project_id:int):XML {        ⑤
    if (projectIdMap == null) {
        return MainBox.NO_PROJECT_XML;
    }
    return projectIdMap[project_id];
}

public function getLocation(location_id:int):XML {      ⑥
    if (locationIdMap == null) {
        return MainBox.NO_LOCATION_XML;
    }
    return locationIdMap[location_id];
}

public function updateTaskProject(task:XML, project:XML):  ⑦
void {
    if (task.project_id != project.id) {                ⑧
        var params:Object = new Object();               ⑨
        params['task[project_id]'] = project.id;        ⑩
        params['_method'] = "PUT";                      ⑪
        svcTasksUpdate.url = "/tasks/" + task.id + ".xml";  ⑫
        svcTasksUpdate.send(params);                    ⑬
    }
}

public function updateTaskLocation(task:XML, location:XML):  ⑭
void {
    if (task.location_id != location.id) {
        var params:Object = new Object();
        params['task[location_id]'] = location.id;
        params['_method'] = "PUT";
        svcTasksUpdate.url = "/tasks/" + task.id + ".xml";
        svcTasksUpdate.send(params);
    }
}

private function handleTasksUpdateResult(event:ResultEvent):  ⑮
void {
    var newTask:XML = XML(event.result);
    for (var i:int = 0; i < tasksXLC.length; i++) {     ⑯
        var ithTask:XML = XML(tasksXLC.getItemAt(i));
        if (ithTask.id == newTask.id) {
            tasksXLC.setItemAt(newTask, i);
            break;
        }
    }
}
```

```
]]>
</mx:Script>
...continues below...
```

We start by adding some `imports`. Note that we need to import `MainBox` to use its constants. This is a bit cheesy, because `TasksListBox` shouldn't know about `MainBox`. (This will be addressed when we refactor to Cairngorm.) Next, we add `Bindable` variables for `projectIdMap` ❶, `locationIdMap` ❷, `projectsAndNone` ❸ and `locationsAndNone` ❹, all of which are passed in from `MainBox`. (Yes, this is also cheesy and will be addressed when we refactor to Cairngorm.)

We then create a `getProject` ❺ function that takes a `project_id` and returns the XML for the project. It ensures that the `projectIdMap` is non-null and returns `projectIdMap[project_id]`. (It also exists to help us get around warnings in binding expressions. The same [] syntax is used for `Array` access and map access, so the compiler is trying to be nice and can get confused sometimes.) Similarly, we create a `getLocation` ❻ function that takes a `location_id` and returns the XML for the location.

Next, we create an `updateTaskProject` ❼ method to update the project that a task is in. It ensures that the project is in fact different ❽ by comparing the `project_id`. If so, it creates a `params Object` to use as an associative array ❾ and then sets two keys in it:

- `task[project_id]` ❿—This is the project id attribute we're updating.
- `_method` ⓫ to `"PUT"`—this is necessary because we can't send a `PUT` but instead send a `POST` and provide the `_method` parameter as a hack that Rails is wired to look for, as explained in the previous iteration.

It also sets the `url` of the `svcTasksUpdate` ⓬ to a dynamically set URL that will be formed by doing a String concatenation of `"/tasks/"` + `task.id` + `".xml"` ⓬, thus triggering the update action (requesting a `:format` of xml) in the `TasksController` for the task with the `id` specified in the URL. The `updateTaskProject` method then calls `svcTasksUpdate` ⓭.

Setting the `task[project_id]` may seem weird, but realize that we're going to end up triggering `update_attributes` with `params[:task]` in the `update` method of the `TasksController`. The update method created by `scaffold` generically updates any attributes of the task it's given, so we might as well use it from Flex. (Thanks again to Stuart Eccles, who took this approach before REST support in Rails existed.)

Next, we take the same approach in `updateTaskLocation` ⓮.

We then create the `handleTasksUpdateResult` function ⓯, which is invoked when the `svcTasksUpdate` service (in listing 6.38) returns. When a `Task` is updated, we want to replace the element of the `tasksXLC` `XMLListCollection` with the new XML for the `Task`. It casts the `newTask` to XML and then does a stupid for loop ⓰, checking the `id` of each task to find the one that matches. (I tried to use an `IViewCursor`, but doing that doesn't give us a nice way to get the index, because we're abstracted from that—because I needed the index to set the item, I used a `for` loop. Oh well.) When a match is found, we replace it and break.

Continuing, we encounter the Flex equivalent of the red pill, as shown in listing 6.38.

Listing 6.38   app\flex\com\pomodo\components\TasksListBox.mxml

```
...continued from above...
]]>
</mx:Script>
    <mx:HTTPService                            ⓱
        id="svcTasksUpdate"                    ⓲
        resultFormat="e4x"
        method="POST"                          ⓳
        result="handleTasksUpdateResult(event)"/>
    <mx:VBox width="100%" height="60%">
        <mx:HBox width="100%" paddingLeft="5" paddingRight="5">
            <mx:Label text="Show:"/>
            <mx:ComboBox id="mainChoiceCB"
                dataProvider="{SHOW_CHOICES}"/>
            <mx:ComboBox id="subChoiceCB" width="100%"
                dataProvider="{_subChoices}"
            visible="{mainChoiceCB.selectedItem.hasSubChoice}"/>
        </mx:HBox>
        <mx:DataGrid id="tasksGrid" width="100%" height="100%"
            dataProvider="{tasksXLC}">
            <mx:columns>
                <mx:DataGridColumn headerText="" width="25"
                    dataField="completed"/>
                <mx:DataGridColumn headerText="Name" width="300"
                    dataField="name"/>
                <mx:DataGridColumn headerText="Project" width="150"    ⓴
                    dataField="project_id"/>
                    <mx:DataGridColumn                      ㉑
                        headerText="Project"
                        dataField="project_id"
                        width="150"
                        editable="false"
                        sortable="false">
                        <mx:itemRenderer>                   ㉒
                            <mx:Component>                  ㉓
```

```
<mx:ComboBox                                                 (24)
    width="150"                          (25)
    labelField="name"                       (26)
    dataProvider="{outerDocument.projectsAndNone}"                (27)
    selectedItem="{outerDocument.getProject(data.project_id)}"          (28)
    dataChange="handleDataChange(XML(data))"              (29)
    change="outerDocument.updateTaskProject(XML(data),        (30)
    XML(selectedItem))">
    <mx:Script>                 (31)
    <![CDATA[             (32)
        private function handleDataChange(data:XML):void {        (33)
            if (data != null) {           (34)
                selectedItem =
                    outerDocument.getProject(data.project_id);      (35)
            } else {
                selectedItem = MainBox.NO_PROJECT_XML;      (36)
            }
        }
    ]]>
    </mx:Script>
</mx:ComboBox>
                        </mx:Component>
                    </mx:itemRenderer>
                </mx:DataGridColumn>
                <mx:DataGridColumn headerText="Location"
                    width="150"
                    dataField="location_id"/>
                <mx:DataGridColumn                (37)
                    headerText="Location"
                    dataField="location_id"
                    width="150"
                    editable="false"
                    sortable="false">
                    <mx:itemRenderer>
                        <mx:Component>
<mx:ComboBox
    width="150"
    labelField="name"
    dataProvider="{outerDocument.locationsAndNone}"
    selectedItem="{outerDocument.getLocation(data.location_id)}"
    dataChange="handleDataChange(XML(data))"
    change="outerDocument.updateTaskLocation(XML(data),
    XML(selectedItem))">
    <mx:Script>
    <![CDATA[
        private function handleDataChange(data:XML):void {
            if (data != null) {
                selectedItem =
                    outerDocument.getLocation(data.location_id);
            } else {
                selectedItem = MainBox.NO_LOCATION_XML;
```

```
                }
            }
        ]]>
      </mx:Script>
  </mx:ComboBox>
                        </mx:Component>
                    </mx:itemRenderer>
                </mx:DataGridColumn>
                <mx:DataGridColumn headerText="Notes"
                    dataField="notes"/>
                <mx:DataGridColumn headerText="" width="60"/>
            </mx:columns>
          </mx:DataGrid>
      </mx:VBox>
      <mx:Panel id="summaryPanel" title="Task" width="100%"
          height="40%" paddingLeft="5" paddingRight="5"
          paddingTop="5" paddingBottom="5">
  ...
      </mx:Panel>
  </mx:VDividedBox>
```

We start innocently enough, declaring an mx:HTTPService ⓱ with an id of svcTasksUpdate ⓲. It will do a POST ⓳ that will, as we saw earlier, masquerade as a PUT to the dynamically set URL that will look like "/tasks/{id}.xml", thus triggering the update action (requesting a :format of xml) in the TasksController for the task with the id in the URL.

Next, we have some fun. We delete the old definition of the Project column ⓴ and replace it with a new one ㉑. (Hey hey you you I don't like your Project column!) Inside it, we declare an mx:itemRenderer ㉒ that contains an interesting bit of MXML syntax that was introduced in Flex 2: <mx:Component> ㉓. The mx:Component *defines a new scope* in the MXML file. (It's like an MXML document inside an MXML document.) Inside the mx:Component, we create an mx:ComboBox ㉔: This is in effect the root element of our nested MXML component.

> **NOTE** Just so this point doesn't get glossed over: An MXML file defines a subclass of its root element. The root element of the TasksListBox is a VDividedBox, so that is what we're subclassing. Inside this subclass, we use (by composition) various classes such as mx:DataGrid, and so on. Inside one of the DataGridColumns of the DataGrid, we needed a custom itemRenderer that was a ComboBox. So, we created a subclass of mx:ComboBox inline in our MXML inside the mx:Component element. This custom MXML component is like a normal MXML component: It can have an mx:Script block, local variables and functions, even import statements.

Continuing, we set the `width` ㉕ and `labelField` ㉖. Next, we bind the `data-Provider` ㉗ of our nested `ComboBox` to `outerDocument.projectsAndNone`.

> **TIP** The `outerDocument` variable is the reference that the nested MXML component has to its parent MXML component. Through this reference, we can access public properties, call public functions, and so forth.

Now, we bind the `selectedItem` to the `outerDocument.getProject (data.project_id)` ㉘, which shows us calling a function of the `outerDocument` and binding to the result. Whenever the `data.project_id` changes, we'll call this function. This is how we respond to changes in data to select the appropriate element. Next, we hook up the `dataChange` event to a `handleDataChange` ㉝ function. This has a purpose similar to that of the `selectedItem` binding ㉙: It keeps the `ComboBox` current. We then handle the change event, which is broadcast when the user clicks the `ComboBox` and makes a selection. We call the `outerDocument.updateTaskProject(XML(data), XML(selectedItem))` ㉚ in order to update the project of the selected task to the `selectedItem` of the `ComboBox`.

> **NOTE** This is what the somewhat magical `data` property is: the row that is being rendered. (We're defining an `itemRenderer`, remember.) Because our rows are `Tasks`, that's what the `data` is: the XML of a `Task`.

Next, we create a nested `<mx:Script>` ㉛ block, complete with its own `<![CDATA[` ㉜ block (trippy, isn't it?). We define the `handleDataChange` ㉝ function, which takes the XML data (which is a task) and sets the `selectedItem` to the `project_id` of the task ㉟ if it's non-null ㉞ and to `MainBox.NO_PROJECT_XML` if it's null ㊱. This is how we respond appropriately to the null projects coming from Rails.

Finally, we do the same thing ㊲ for `Locations`. (You didn't think I was going to add cueball numbers for all those lines, did you?)

Phew.

Rebuild, reload, and log in as ludwig. The Tasks grid looks like figure 6.15.

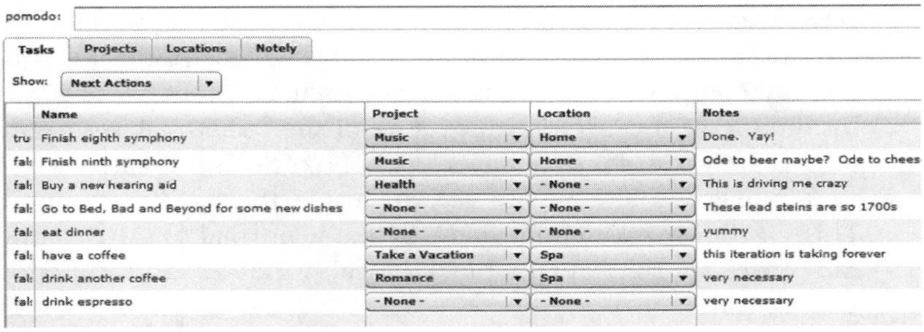

Figure 6.15 The most beautiful ComboBoxes we've ever seen

We can select them, and the changes take effect with immediate service calls, and so on. Hooray!

Thankfully, that was the trickiest Flex code we'll write in the book.

6.7.3 *Adding Delete buttons*

With that out of the way, we'll add Delete buttons for the tasks next. This will be extremely easy in comparison—but the fact that it will be easy shows how far we've come; see listing 6.39.

Listing 6.39 app\flex\com\pomodo\components\TasksListBox.mxml

```
...
    private function handleTasksUpdateResult(event:ResultEvent):
    void {
        var newTask:XML = XML(event.result);
        for (var i:int = 0; i < tasksXLC.length; i++) {
            var ithTask:XML = XML(tasksXLC.getItemAt(i));
            if (ithTask.id == newTask.id) {
                tasksXLC.setItemAt(newTask, i);
                break;
            }
        }
    }

    public function deleteTask(task:XML):void {                    ❶
        svcTasksDestroy.url = "/tasks/" + task.id + ".xml";        ❷
        svcTasksDestroy.send({_method:"DELETE"});                  ❸
    }

    private function handleTasksDestroyResult(                     ❹
    event:ResultEvent):void {
        if (event.result == "error") {
            Alert.show("The task was not successfully deleted.",   ❺
                "Error");
        } else {
            var deleteTask:XML = XML(event.result);               ❻
            var deleteId:int = deleteTask.id;                     ❼
            for (var i:int = 0; i < tasksXLC.length; i++) {       ❽
                var ithTask:XML = XML(tasksXLC.getItemAt(i));     ❾
                if (ithTask.id == deleteId) {
                    tasksXLC.removeItemAt(i);
                    break;
                }
            }
        }
    }
]]>
</mx:Script>
    <mx:HTTPService
```

```
        id="svcTasksUpdate"
        resultFormat="e4x"
        method="POST"
        result="handleTasksUpdateResult(event)"/>
<mx:HTTPService
    id="svcTasksDestroy"          ❿
    resultFormat="e4x"
    method="POST"
    result="handleTasksDestroyResult(event)"/>
<mx:VBox width="100%" height="60%">
...
            <mx:DataGridColumn headerText="Notes"
                dataField="notes"/>
            <mx:DataGridColumn headerText="" width="70"    ⓫
                editable="false">
            <mx:itemRenderer>              ⓬
                <mx:Component>            ⓭
                    <mx:Button label="delete"       ⓮
        click="outerDocument.deleteTask(XML(data))"/>
                </mx:Component>
            </mx:itemRenderer>
        </mx:DataGridColumn>
        </mx:columns>
    </mx:DataGrid>
</mx:VBox>
<mx:Panel id="summaryPanel" title="Task" width="100%"
...
```

We start by creating the deleteTask function, which invokes ❶ the send function ❸ of svcTasksDestroy ❿ to delete the given task. Note that to do this we need to fake an HTTP DELETE by sending a POST and setting a _method: "DELETE" parameter ❷ (for variety, I used the anonymous object syntax). Also note that we specify which task we're deleting by including its id in the URL ❷.

Next, we create the handleTasksDestroyResult ❹ function, which displays an Alert ❺ in case of an error and which deletes the task from the XMLList-Collection on success. To do this, we cast the event.result to XML (because it's the Task XML) ❻ and extract its id ❼ to search for. Now, we loop through the tasksXLC ❽, getting each task ❾ and comparing its id with the id we're searching for. If we find a match, we remove that task and break, because there can be only one task with that id. This causes the tasksGrid to automatically update, because its dataProvider is bound to the tasksXLC.

Next, we create the svcTasksDestroy ❿. Note that its method is POST and that we don't specify a URL because we'll be setting it dynamically.

Figure 6.16   Task delete buttons

Finally, we modify the dataGridColumn with the empty headerText ⓫ to contain an itemRenderer ⓬. The itemRenderer defines an inline mx:Component ⓭, which is a Button ⓮ with the label "delete" and a click handler that calls the deleteTask function of the outerDocument. We also modify the column width to 70 pixels ⓫ from 60, to be wide enough to show the "delete" label of the button.
    Trivial!
    With that done, rebuild, reload, and log in as ludwig. We see the screen shown in figure 6.16.
    Click the Delete buttons for any tasks you want to delete. They all work as expected.

6.7.4   Adding Completed CheckBoxes to the TasksListBox

Next, we'll add a custom itemRenderer to the TasksListBox to create a CheckBox that indicates whether a task is completed. This is basically more of the same, except we'll need to add a utility function first.
    Create a new file called XMLUtils.as in app\flex\com\pomodo\util, and set its content as shown in listing 6.40.

Listing 6.40   app\flex\com\pomodo\util\XMLUtils.as

```
package com.pomodo.util {
    public class XMLUtils {
        public static function xmlListToBoolean(         ❶
        xmlList:XMLList):Boolean {
            return xmlList.toString() == "true";
        }
    }
}
```

The xmlListToBoolean function ❶ converts an XMLList into a Boolean. It does this by checking whether its toString is "true". As the comment says, this is necessary because Boolean("false") is true.

Next, we modify the TasksListBox yet again; see listing 6.41.

Listing 6.41   app\flex\com\pomodo\components\TasksListBox.mxml

```
...
    public function getLocation(location_id:int):XML {
        if (locationIdMap == null) {
            return MainBox.NO_LOCATION_XML;
        }
        return locationIdMap[location_id];
    }

    public function updateTaskCompleted(task:XML,          ❶
    completed:Boolean):void {
        var params:Object = new Object();
        params['task[completed]'] = completed;
        params['_method'] = "PUT";
        svcTasksUpdate.url = "/tasks/" + task.id + ".xml";
        svcTasksUpdate.send(params);
    }
...
]]>
</mx:Script>
    <mx:HTTPService
        id="svcTasksUpdate"
        resultFormat="e4x"
        method="POST"
        result="handleTasksUpdateResult(event)"/>
...
    <mx:VBox width="100%" height="60%">
...
        <mx:DataGrid id="tasksGrid" width="100%" height="100%"
            dataProvider="{tasksXLC}">
            <mx:columns>
                <mx:DataGridColumn headerText="" width="25"      ❷
                    dataField="completed"/>
                <mx:DataGridColumn                      ❸
                    headerText=""
                    width="25"
                    dataField="completed"
                    editable="false">
                    <mx:itemRenderer>                 ❹
                        <mx:Component>              ❺
<mx:HBox width="25" paddingLeft="5">
    <mx:Script>
        <![CDATA[
            import com.pomodo.util.XMLUtils;            ❻

            private function updateCompleted():void {      ❼
```

```
            outerDocument.updateTaskCompleted(          ⑧
                XML(data),          ⑨
                !XMLUtils.xmlListToBoolean(data.completed));          ⑩
        }
    ]]>
</mx:Script>
<mx:CheckBox          ⑪
    selected="{XMLUtils.xmlListToBoolean(data.completed)}"
    click="updateCompleted()"/>
</mx:HBox>
                </mx:Component>
            </mx:itemRenderer>
        </mx:DataGridColumn>
        <mx:DataGridColumn headerText="Name" width="300"
            dataField="name"/>
    . . .
```

We start by creating the updateTaskCompleted function ❶, which calls svcTasksUpdate just like the ComboBox itemRenderers do. Next, we delete the old DataGridColumn definition ❷ and replace it with a new one ❸. It contains yet another itemRenderer ❹, which defines yet another Component ❺. This time, we import our new XMLUtils class ❻ and create an updateCompleted ❼ function that calls outerDocument.updateTaskCompleted ❽ with the XML(data) ❾ of the task and the toggled Boolean value of the completed property ❿. Finally, we create the CheckBox ⑪, bind its selected property to the result of XMLUtils. xmlListToBoolean(data.completed), and add the updateCompleted function as a click event hander.

Positively *boring* by now, isn't it?

Rebuild, reload, and (say it with me) log in as ludwig. We see check boxes beside the task names. Uncheck "Finish eighth symphony," and check "Buy a new hearing aid."[7] The Tasks grid will look like figure 6.17.

Figure 6.17 Check boxes in the `TasksListBox`

---

[7] If any Beethoven fans think I'm being cruel: I love Beethoven. I've had his nine symphonies on repeat in iTunes for much of the writing of this book. That is a *long* time.

6.7.5 *Editing the task name and notes in the TasksListBox*

The `TasksListBox` contains a `tasksGrid` `mx:DataGrid` and also a `summaryPanel` `mx:Panel`. Where should we edit the task name and notes? Both places? It turns out that the `tasksGrid` isn't a good place to edit the name and notes of a task. We could do it, but there would be some controversial decisions to make that would seem like bugs to some users, regardless of which option we chose. For example, should tabbing out of a field be an edit? How about pressing the Enter key? What about the Escape key? How about clicking somewhere else in the application?

We could implement all this and make decisions about each of these choices, but we wouldn't learn anything more about using Flex with Rails. (I did it: Trust me, it wasn't worthwhile.) All we'd do is kill a few trees, real or virtual. So we won't. Instead, we'll implement editing of the task name and notes (as well as everything else in a task, minus the Next Action concept we'll continue ignoring for now) in the `summaryPanel` at the bottom.

Once again, we modify the `TasksListBox`; see listing 6.42.

Listing 6.42   app\flex\com\pomodo\components\TasksListBox.mxml

```
<?xml version="1.0" encoding="utf-8"?>
<mx:VDividedBox xmlns:mx="http://www.adobe.com/2006/mxml"
    width="100%" height="100%" label="Tasks">
<mx:Script>
<![CDATA[
    import mx.collections.XMLListCollection;
    import mx.controls.Alert;
    import mx.rpc.events.ResultEvent;
    import com.pomodo.components.MainBox;
    import com.pomodo.events.TaskEvent;
    import com.pomodo.util.XMLUtils;          ❶

    public const NEXT_ACTIONS:int = 0;
...
    public function getLocation(location_id:int):XML {
        if (locationIdMap == null) {
            return MainBox.NO_LOCATION_XML;
        }
        return locationIdMap[location_id];
    }

    public function updateSelectedTaskFromSummaryPanel():void {      ❷
        var selectedTask:XML = XML(tasksGrid.selectedItem);
        var params:Object = new Object();
        params['task[name]'] = nameTI.text;
        params['task[project_id]'] = projectCB.selectedItem.id;
        params['task[location_id]'] =
            locationCB.selectedItem.id;
```

```
            params['task[completed]'] = completedCB.selected;
            params['task[notes]'] = notesTI.text;
            params['_method'] = "PUT";
            svcTasksUpdate.url = "/tasks/"+ selectedTask.id +".xml";
            svcTasksUpdate.send(params);
        }
    ...
    ]]>
    </mx:Script>
    ...
        <mx:Panel id="summaryPanel" title="Task" width="100%"
            height="40%" paddingLeft="5" paddingRight="5"
            paddingTop="5" paddingBottom="5">
            <mx:HBox width="100%">
                <mx:Label text="Name" width="50"/>
                <mx:TextInput id="nameTI" width="100%"
                    text="{tasksGrid.selectedItem.name}"/>           ❸
                <mx:CheckBox id="completedCB" label="Completed"      ❹
                    selected="{XMLUtils.xmlListToBoolean(
⇒ tasksGrid.selectedItem.completed)}"
                    />
            </mx:HBox>
            <mx:HBox width="100%" verticalAlign="middle">
                <mx:Label text="Project" width="50"/>
                <mx:ComboBox id="projectCB" width="200"              ❺
                    labelField="name"
                    dataProvider="{projectsAndNone}"
selectedItem="{getProject(tasksGrid.selectedItem.project_id)}"
                    />
                <mx:CheckBox label="This is the Next Action"/>
                <mx:Spacer width="100%"/>
                <mx:Label text="Location"/>
                <mx:ComboBox id="locationCB" width="200"             ❻
                    labelField="name"
                    dataProvider="{locationsAndNone}"
selectedItem="{getLocation(tasksGrid.selectedItem.location_id)}"
                    />
            </mx:HBox>
            <mx:HBox width="100%" height="100%">
                <mx:Label text="Notes" width="50"/>
                <mx:TextArea id="notesTI" width="100%" height="100%"  ❼
                    text="{tasksGrid.selectedItem.notes}"/>
            </mx:HBox>
            <mx:ControlBar width="100%" horizontalAlign="center">
                <mx:Button id="updateButton" label="Update"
                    width="100%" height="30"
                    click="updateSelectedTaskFromSummaryPanel()"      ❽
                    enabled="{tasksGrid.selectedItem != null}"/>
                <mx:Button id="deleteButton" label="Delete"
                    height="30"
                    click="deleteTask(XML(tasksGrid.selectedItem))"   ❾
```

```
            enabled="{tasksGrid.selectedItem != null}"/>
        </mx:ControlBar>
      </mx:Panel>
  </mx:VDividedBox>
```

We start by importing XMLUtils ❶. This is interesting, for once: We already imported XMLUtils in a nested mx:Component, but we still need to import it if we want to use it in the outer MXML component. Next, we create an updateSelected-TaskFromSummaryPanel ❷ function, which updates all the properties of the selected task in the tasksGrid (using the same RESTful approach) with the values of the controls in the summaryPanel.

Now, we hook up all the controls in the summary panel. We bind the text property of the nameTI to tasksGrid.selectedItem.name ❸. And we add a CheckBox control called completedCB and bind it to the result of calling XMLUtils.xmlList-ToBoolean(tasksGrid.selectedItem.completed) ❹.

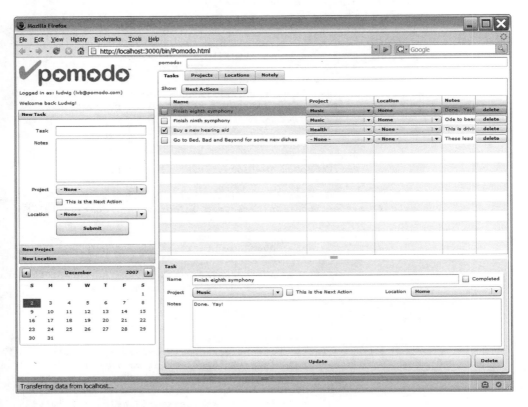

Figure 6.18 The summaryPanel, **implemented**

Next, we bind the `dataProvider` and `selectedItem` properties of the `projectCB` ❺ and `locationCB` ❻ to the correct properties. (These are found by looking at how we did the `ComboBox itemRenderers`—yet another thing that is easy after I threw you into the deep end with them.)

We bind the `text` property of the `notesTI` to `tasksGrid.selected-Item.notes` ❼. Finally, we implement click handlers and enabled bindings for the Update ❽ and Delete ❾ buttons. The enabled bindings ensure that the buttons aren't enabled if we have no `selectedItem`; the click handlers call the appropriate functions, which trigger service calls.

Rebuild, reload, and log in as ludwig. We see the screen shown in figure 6.18.

Experiment with the `summaryPanel`. Note that nothing takes effect until we click Update. This is by design.

This is starting to look cool!

6.7.6 Adding Delete buttons and Completed check boxes to the ProjectsListBox and LocationsListBox

We have one more thing to do before we call this iteration finished: We need to implement the Delete buttons, Completed check boxes, and `summaryPanels` of the `ProjectsListBox` and `LocationsListBox`.

First, we add support for update and delete to the `ProjectEvent` and `LocationEvent`. (We didn't need to add these for tasks because we handled them internally in the `TasksListBox`—with projects and locations, however, we need to notify the outside world of what is happening, so we must add these to the events.) This is *really* easy; all we need to do is add new type codes for update and delete.

First, the `ProjectEvent`; see listing 6.43.

Listing 6.43   app\flex\com\pomodo\events\ProjectEvent.as

```
  . . .
      public class ProjectEvent extends Event {
          public static const PROJECT_CREATE:String = "projectCreate";

          public static const PROJECT_UPDATE:String =
              "projectUpdate";

          public static const PROJECT_DELETE:String =
              "projectDelete";
  . . .
```

Next, the `LocationEvent`; see listing 6.44.

Listing 6.44   app\flex\com\pomodo\events\LocationEvent.as

```
. . .
    public class LocationEvent extends Event {
        public static const LOCATION_CREATE:String =
            "locationCreate";

        public static const LOCATION_UPDATE:String =
            "locationUpdate";

        public static const LOCATION_DELETE:String =
            "locationDelete";
. . .
```

Next, we'll modify the ProjectsListBox; see listing 6.45.

Listing 6.45   app\flex\com\pomodo\components\ProjectsListBox.mxml

```
<?xml version="1.0" encoding="utf-8"?>
<mx:VDividedBox xmlns:mx="http://www.adobe.com/2006/mxml"
    width="100%" height="100%" label="Projects">
<mx:Metadata>                                                     ❶
    [Event(name="projectUpdate",
            type="com.pomodo.events.ProjectEvent")]
    [Event(name="projectDelete",
            type="com.pomodo.events.ProjectEvent")]
</mx:Metadata>
<mx:Script>
<![CDATA[
    import mx.controls.Alert;                    ❷
    import mx.collections.XMLListCollection;
    import mx.rpc.events.ResultEvent;            ❸
    import com.pomodo.events.ProjectEvent;
    import com.pomodo.util.XMLUtils;

    [Bindable]
    public var projectsXLC:XMLListCollection;

    public function updateSelectedProjectFromSummaryPanel():     ❹
    void {
        var selectedProject:XML =
            XML(projectsGrid.selectedItem);
        var params:Object = new Object();
        params['project[name]'] = nameTI.text;
        params['project[completed]'] = completedCB.selected;
        params['project[notes]'] = notesTI.text;
        params['_method'] = "PUT";
        svcProjectsUpdate.url =
            "/projects/" + selectedProject.id + ".xml";
```

```
        svcProjectsUpdate.send(params);
    }

    public function updateProjectCompleted(project:XML,        ❺
    completed:Boolean):void {
        var params:Object = new Object();
        params['project[completed]'] = completed;
        params['_method'] = "PUT";
        svcProjectsUpdate.url =
            "/projects/" + project.id + ".xml";
        svcProjectsUpdate.send(params);
    }

    public function deleteProject(data:Object):void {        ❻
        svcProjectsDestroy.url =
            "/projects/" + data.id + ".xml";
        svcProjectsDestroy.send({_method:"DELETE"});
    }

    private function handleProjectsUpdateResult(        ❼
    event:ResultEvent):void {
        dispatchEvent(new ProjectEvent(
            ProjectEvent.PROJECT_UPDATE, XML(event.result)));
    }

    private function handleProjectsDestroyResult(        ❽
    event:ResultEvent):void {
        if (event.result == "error") {
            Alert.show(
                "The project was not successfully deleted.",
                "Error");
        } else {
            dispatchEvent(new ProjectEvent(
                ProjectEvent.PROJECT_DELETE,
                XML(event.result)));
        }
    }
}
]]>
</mx:Script>
    <mx:HTTPService        ❾
        id="svcProjectsUpdate"
        resultFormat="e4x"
        method="POST"
        result="handleProjectsUpdateResult(event)"/>
    <mx:HTTPService        ❿
        id="svcProjectsDestroy"
        resultFormat="e4x"
        method="POST"
        result="handleProjectsDestroyResult(event)"/>
    <mx:DataGrid id="projectsGrid" width="100%" height="60%"
        dataProvider="{projectsXLC}">
```

```
        <mx:columns>
            <mx:DataGridColumn                      ⑪
                headerText=""
                width="25"
                dataField="completed"
                editable="false">
                <mx:itemRenderer>
                    <mx:Component>                  ⑫
<mx:HBox width="25" paddingLeft="5">                ⑬
    <mx:Script>
        <![CDATA[
            import com.pomodo.util.XMLUtils;

            private function updateCompleted():void {    ⑭
                outerDocument.updateProjectCompleted(
                    XML(data),
                    !XMLUtils.xmlListToBoolean(data.completed));
            }
        ]]>
    </mx:Script>
    <mx:CheckBox
        selected="{XMLUtils.xmlListToBoolean(data.completed)}"    ⑮
        click="updateCompleted()"/>
</mx:HBox>
                    </mx:Component>
                </mx:itemRenderer>
            </mx:DataGridColumn>
            <mx:DataGridColumn headerText="Name" width="400"
                dataField="name"/>
            <mx:DataGridColumn headerText="Notes"
                dataField="notes"/>
            <mx:DataGridColumn headerText="" width="70"            ⑯
                editable="false">
                <mx:itemRenderer>
                    <mx:Component>
                        <mx:Button label="delete"
            click="outerDocument.deleteProject(XML(data))"/>       ⑰
                    </mx:Component>
                </mx:itemRenderer>
            </mx:DataGridColumn>
        </mx:columns>
    </mx:DataGrid>
    <mx:Panel id="summaryPanel"
        title="Project" width="100%" height="40%"
        paddingLeft="5" paddingRight="5" paddingTop="5"
        paddingBottom="5">
        <mx:HBox width="100%">
            <mx:Label text="Name" width="50"/>
            <mx:TextInput id="nameTI" width="100%"                 ⑱
                text="{projectsGrid.selectedItem.name}"/>
            <mx:CheckBox id="completedCB" label="Completed"        ⑲
selected="{XMLUtils.xmlListToBoolean(
```

```
➥projectsGrid.selectedItem.completed)}"/>
        </mx:HBox>
        <mx:HBox width="100%" height="100%">
            <mx:Label text="Notes" width="50"/>
            <mx:TextArea id="notesTI" width="100%" height="100%"     ⑳
                text="{projectsGrid.selectedItem.notes}"/>
        </mx:HBox>
        <mx:ControlBar width="100%" horizontalAlign="center">
            <mx:Button id="updateButton" label="Update"
                width="100%" height="30"
                click="updateSelectedProjectFromSummaryPanel()"      ㉑
                enabled="{projectsGrid.selectedItem != null}"/>
            <mx:Button id="deleteButton" label="Delete"
                height="30"
            click="deleteProject(XML(projectsGrid.selectedItem))"     ㉒
                enabled="{projectsGrid.selectedItem != null}"/>
        </mx:ControlBar>
    </mx:Panel>
</mx:VDividedBox>
```

First, we add `Metadata` ❶ for the `projectUpdate` and `projectDelete` events. Next, we add some `imports` ❷❸. We add the `updateSelectedProjectFrom-SummaryPanel` ❹ function, which updates the project based on the values of the controls in the `summaryPanel`. Now, we add functions to update ❺ and delete ❻ a project, by calling the appropriate services ❾❿. We also add handlers ❼❽ for their results, both of which dispatch `ProjectEvents` indicating what happened (`PROJECT_UPDATE`, `PROJECT_DELETE`). We modify the `DataGridColumn` with no title ⓫ to contain an `itemRenderer` ⓬ that has a `Component` ⓭ that is an `HBox` containing a `CheckBox` ⓯ whose selected property is bound the same way it is in the `TasksListBox`. (We use the `HBox` to align the `CheckBox` nicely. Yes, this is cheesy.) This `Component` contains an `updateCompleted` function ⓮, which is called when the `CheckBox` is clicked.

Next, we modify the other `DataGridColumn` with no header text ⓰ to contain an `itemRenderer` containing a `Component` that is a `Button`, specifically a Delete button ⓱.

Finally, we hook up the `summaryPanel` ⓲–㉒), just as we did with the `Tasks-ListBox`.

Now we'll modify the `LocationsListBox`; see listing 6.46. This is so similar that I won't explain it, except to note that we're deleting a column (❶ below) that was created accidentally. (I regret having decided that `Locations` would exist, to be honest! For the rest of the book, we'll skimp on the explanations about the `Loca-tion` code—all the concepts that apply to `Locations` apply equally to `Projects`.)

Listing 6.46   app\flex\com\pomodo\components\LocationsListBox.mxml

```
<?xml version="1.0" encoding="utf-8"?>
<mx:VDividedBox xmlns:mx="http://www.adobe.com/2006/mxml"
    width="100%" height="100%" label="Locations">
<mx:Metadata>
    [Event(name="locationUpdate",
           type="com.pomodo.events.LocationEvent")]
    [Event(name="locationDelete",
           type="com.pomodo.events.LocationEvent")]
</mx:Metadata>
<mx:Script>
<![CDATA[
    import mx.controls.Alert;
    import mx.collections.XMLListCollection;
    import mx.rpc.events.ResultEvent;
    import com.pomodo.events.LocationEvent;
    import com.pomodo.util.XMLUtils;

    [Bindable]
    public var locationsXLC:XMLListCollection;

    public function updateSelectedLocationFromSummaryPanel():
    void {
        var selectedLocation:XML =
            XML(locationsGrid.selectedItem);
        var params:Object = new Object();
        params['location[name]'] = nameTI.text;
        params['location[notes]'] = notesTI.text;
        params['_method'] = "PUT";
        svcLocationsUpdate.url =
            "/locations/" + selectedLocation.id + ".xml";
        svcLocationsUpdate.send(params);
    }

    public function deleteLocation(data:Object):void {
        svcLocationsDestroy.url =
            "/locations/" + data.id + ".xml";
        svcLocationsDestroy.send({_method:"DELETE"});
    }

    private function handleLocationsUpdateResult(
    event:ResultEvent):void {
        dispatchEvent(new LocationEvent(
            LocationEvent.LOCATION_UPDATE, XML(event.result)));
    }

    private function handleLocationsDestroyResult(
    event:ResultEvent):void {
        if (event.result == "error") {
            Alert.show(
```

```
                            "The location was not successfully deleted.",
                            "Error");
                } else {
                    dispatchEvent(new LocationEvent(
                        LocationEvent.LOCATION_DELETE,
                        XML(event.result)));
                }
            }
        }
    ]]>
    </mx:Script>
        <mx:HTTPService
            id="svcLocationsUpdate"
            resultFormat="e4x"
            method="POST"
            result="handleLocationsUpdateResult(event)"/>
        <mx:HTTPService
            id="svcLocationsDestroy"
            resultFormat="e4x"
            method="POST"
            result="handleLocationsDestroyResult(event)"/>
        <mx:DataGrid id="locationsGrid" width="100%" height="60%"
            dataProvider="{locationsXLC}">
            <mx:columns>
                <mx:DataGridColumn headerText="" width="25"          ❶
                    dataField="completed"/>
                <mx:DataGridColumn headerText="Name" width="400"
                    dataField="name"/>
                <mx:DataGridColumn headerText="Notes"
                    dataField="notes"/>
                <mx:DataGridColumn headerText="" width="70"
                    editable="false">
                    <mx:itemRenderer>
                        <mx:Component>
                            <mx:Button label="delete"
                    click="outerDocument.deleteLocation(XML(data))"/>
                        </mx:Component>
                    </mx:itemRenderer>
                </mx:DataGridColumn>
            </mx:columns>
        </mx:DataGrid>
        <mx:Panel id="summaryPanel" title="Location" width="100%"
            height="40%" paddingLeft="5" paddingRight="5"
            paddingTop="5" paddingBottom="5">
            <mx:HBox width="100%">
                <mx:Label text="Name" width="50"/>
                <mx:TextInput id="nameTI" width="100%"
                    text="{locationsGrid.selectedItem.name}"/>
            </mx:HBox>
            <mx:HBox width="100%" height="100%">
                <mx:Label text="Notes" width="50"/>
```

```
        <mx:TextArea id="notesTI" width="100%" height="100%"
            text="{locationsGrid.selectedItem.notes}"/>
    </mx:HBox>
    <mx:ControlBar width="100%" horizontalAlign="center">
        <mx:Button id="updateButton" label="Update"
            width="100%" height="30"
            click="updateSelectedLocationFromSummaryPanel()"
            enabled="{locationsGrid.selectedItem != null}"/>
        <mx:Button id="deleteButton" label="Delete"
            height="30"
      click="deleteLocation(XML(locationsGrid.selectedItem))"
            enabled="{locationsGrid.selectedItem != null}"/>
    </mx:ControlBar>
</mx:Panel>
</mx:VDividedBox>
```

Finally, we modify the MainBox to handle the new events that are being broadcast; see listing 6.47.

Listing 6.47   app\flex\com\pomodo\components\MainBox.mxml

```
. . .
        <mx:TabNavigator width="100%" height="100%">
            <pom:TasksListBox id="tasksTab"
                tasksXLC="{tasksXLC}"
                projectIdMap="{_projectIdMap}"
                locationIdMap="{_locationIdMap}"
                projectsAndNone="{_projectsAndNoneXLC}"
                locationsAndNone="{_locationsAndNoneXLC}"/>
            <pom:ProjectsListBox id="projectsTab"
                projectsXLC="{projectsXLC}"
                projectUpdate="listProjects()"     ❶
                projectDelete="listProjects()"/>    ❷
            <pom:LocationsListBox id="locationsTab"
                locationsXLC="{locationsXLC}"
                locationUpdate="listLocations()"   ❸
                locationDelete="listLocations()"/>  ❹
            <pom:Notely id="notelyTab"/>
        </mx:TabNavigator>
. . .
```

We handle the various update ❶❸ and delete ❷❹ events and call the list-Projects ❶❷ and listLocations ❸❹ functions in response. This triggers the projectsXLC and/or locationsXLC to be re-created, which will refresh the appropriate DataGrid. This works, but it causes a minor annoyance (see the exercises at the end of the iteration).

That's it! Really. Rebuild, reload, and log in as ludwig. We can now update and delete projects and locations as well as tasks.

6.8 Keeping our tests passing

Finally, let's run the tests again; see listing 6.48.

Listing 6.1   Output

```
c:\peter\flexiblerails\current\pomodo>rake
...
Started
...............
Finished in 2.203 seconds.

16 tests, 29 assertions, 0 failures, 0 errors
...
Started
.....................................
Finished in 2.344 seconds.

35 tests, 65 assertions, 0 failures, 0 errors

c:\peter\flexiblerails\current\pomodo>
```

Everything still works. We're *finally* done with this iteration!

The code at this point is saved as the iteration06 folder.

6.9 Summary

In hooking up most of the main Flex UI to the TasksController, Projects-Controller, and LocationsController, you've seen a substantial example of how Flex and Rails can be used together using HTTPService. Next, in the final iteration of this part of the book, we'll cover everybody's favorite topic: Validation.

6.10 Exercises for the reader

1 Refactor the various summaryPanel components out into their own components, passing the selectedItem into them. What are the tradeoffs of doing this?

2 Make the summaryPanel trigger service calls "live," as opposed to using an Update button.

3 Updating the completed state of project in the `projectsGrid` has an unfortunate consequence for the `summaryPanel`. Why? How would you fix it?

4 Implement the Next Action concept, Notely, the pomodo command shell, and filtering tasks with the Show `ComboBox`. (My version of this is done in iteration 10.)

Validation 7

Make it idiot-proof, and someone will make a better idiot.

—Unknown

Adding error-checking and -handling to a GUI application (desktop or web) is something that is usually an afterthought and a horribly tedious chore. Most programmers hate the task, but we have to do it: We can't just pop up a dialog saying "O NOES!!"—much as we'd like to—if the user does anything wrong. And no matter how simple and elegant we make our applications, two forces are against us:

- In the Real World, services go down (server crashes, database issues, and so on).
- The world is full of, um, less sophisticated users.

Worse yet, even advanced UI frameworks have historically provided basically nothing as far as a standard validation framework. Like it or not, "has great error messages" hasn't been considered a major selling point of an app. So, we were left cobbling together our own, usually as an afterthought.

Fortunately, both Flex and Rails are different than the norm in this respect: For both Flex and Rails, validation is an integral part of the framework. This is good, because doing something wrong is an *integral* part of how users will use our applications.

The built-in Flex validation support is nice looking. When I first saw validation in action in Flex 1.0, my reaction was essentially "ooh, shiny." The controls have red borders, and red error callouts (tooltips) appear by the fields. However, there are some major deficiencies with validators in Flex 1.x: We can't assign ids to them, and we can't bind to their properties. This can be the source of much frustration, because it greatly limits their reusability. The good news is that Flex 2 fixed these problems (and they are still fixed in Flex 3): Validators can have ids, and we can bind to their properties.

The bottom line is this: We can use the built-in validation support in Flex and Rails to create user-friendly applications that deal with error conditions in a much better way than is the norm today.

In this iteration, we'll add full validation support on the Rails side and the Flex side to the account-creation process. This is a good place to do this because it's a fairly self-contained section, and because the current error-handling there is terrible. (Also, I don't know about you, but I'm sick of looking at the Tasks grid!)

7.1 *Revisiting the HTML account signup screen*

We'll start by revisiting the account signup screen. First, stop the server, run newdb.bat, and start the server. Next, go to http://localhost:3000/signup and try to add a new user with a Login of ludwig, an Email of blah, a Password of foo, and a Confirm Password of bar (see figure 7.1).

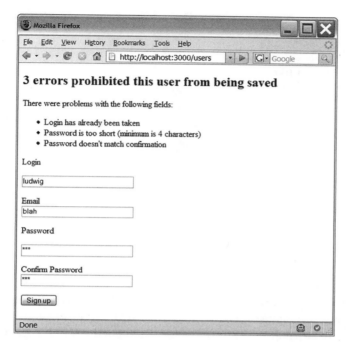

Figure 7.1
Validation errors in Rails

Let's take a quick look at the code that accomplishes all this, starting with the create action of the UsersController, which is what is invoked when the form in app\views\users\new.rhtml is submitted; see listing 7.1.

Listing 7.1   app\controllers\users_controller.rb

```
class UsersController < ApplicationController
  skip_before_filter :login_required

  # GET /users/new
  # GET /users/new.xml
  # render new.rhtml     ❶
  def new
  end

  # POST /users
  # POST /users.xml
  def create    ❷
    cookies.delete :auth_token
    # protects against session fixation attacks, wreaks havoc
    # wreaks request forgery protection.
    # uncomment at your own risk
    # reset_session
```

```
    @user = User.new(params[:user])        ❸
    @user.save!        ❹
    self.current_user = @user
    respond_to do |format|        ❺
      format.html do
        redirect_back_or_default('/')
        flash[:notice] = "Thanks for signing up!"
      end
      format.xml  { render :xml => @user.to_xml }
    end
  rescue ActiveRecord::RecordInvalid        ❻
    respond_to do |format|        ❼
      format.html { render :action => 'new' }        ❽
      format.xml { render :text => "error" }        ❾
    end
  end

end
```

The create method ❷ constructs a new User out of the params ❸ and stores it in @user. It then calls @user.save! ❹, which will throw a RecordInvalid exception ❻ if the save fails (because the save! method was called instead of the save method, which returns false). In normal operation, we use a respond_to block ❺; we also use a respond_to block in the rescue ❼. In that respond_to block, when HTML is the requested format, we render :action => 'new' ❽ to render the new.rhtml file ❶; when XML is the requested format, we render the text "error" ❾.

We still don't know how those error messages got produced or displayed. Let's look at the new.rhtml file, because that's what is being rendered. (The new convention in Rails 2 is to name .rhtml files .html.erb; I assume this will be done inside the restful_authentication generator at some point. When this is done, the file to look at will presumably be new.html.erb.) Anyway, look at new.rhtml; see listing 7.2.

Listing 7.2   app\views\users\new.rhtml

```
<%= error_messages_for :user %>        ❶
<% form_for :user, :url => users_path do |f| -%>
<p><label for="login">Login</label><br/>
<%= f.text_field :login %></p>

<p><label for="email">Email</label><br/>
<%= f.text_field :email %></p>

<p><label for="password">Password</label><br/>
<%= f.password_field :password %></p>
```

```
<p><label for="password_confirmation">Confirm Password</label><br/>
<%= f.password_field :password_confirmation %></p>

<p><%= submit_tag 'Sign up' %></p>
<% end -%>
```

The `<%= error_messages_for :user %>` function call ❶ inserts the error messages for the user (wherever they came from) into the output of the new.rhtml file. Note that this new.rhtml file is the same view that is used to render the normal non-error state of the new user form—in that case, there are no errors to show.

But where did the error messages for the user come from? Let's look at the User model; see listing 7.3.

Listing 7.3 app\models\user.rb

```
require 'digest/sha1'
class User < ActiveRecord::Base
  has_many :tasks
  has_many :projects
  has_many :locations

  # Virtual attribute for the unencrypted password
  attr_accessor :password

  validates_presence_of :login, :email          ❶
  validates_presence_of :password, :if => :password_required?          ❷
  validates_presence_of :password_confirmation,          ❸
    :if => :password_required?
  validates_length_of :password, :within => 4..40,          ❹
    :if => :password_required?
  validates_confirmation_of :password,          ❺
    :if => :password_required?
  validates_length_of :login, :within => 3..40          ❻
  validates_length_of :email, :within => 3..100          ❼
  validates_uniqueness_of :login, :email,          ❽
    :case_sensitive => false
  before_save :encrypt_password
  ...
end
```

Eight validation method calls (❶–❽) are used in the User class. These methods (`validates_length_of`, `validates_presence_of`, and so on) are class methods known as *validation helpers*. Calling them configures the Active Record model class to do specific validations before saving.

> **NOTE** There are methods called `validate`, `validate_on_create`, and `validate_on_update` that we can implement in a class that extends `ActiveRecord::Base`; however, the helpers are so, well, helpful that we can develop productively using validations in Rails for a while without knowing they exist. Now that you *do* know, see the "Validation" section (19.1) of *AWDwR* for complete details of all the Rails validation helpers and the `validate`, `validate_on_create`, and `validate_on_update` methods.

When we tried to sign up with a Login of ludwig, a Password of foo, and a Confirm Password of bar, we failed the `validates_length_of` `:password` ❹ validation, the `validates_uniqueness_of` `:login` ❽ validation, and the `validates_` `confirmation_of` `:password` ❺ validation.

We've failed the validation; what happens next?

First, all the errors from the validations are added to the errors (`ActiveRecord::Errors`) associated with the `User` model. Then, as we mentioned earlier, because we've failed the validation, the `@user.save!` call (❸ in `UsersController`) won't throw a `RecordInvalid` error. We end up in the `rescue` clause (❺ in `UsersController`), and the new.rhtml template is rendered because of the `render :action => 'new'` in the `UsersController`.

That's the quick tour of normal Rails validation. For the lengthy tour, see section 19.1 of *AWDwR*.

7.2 *Rails and Flex validation—should you stay DRY?*

We're interested in how Rails validation integrates with Flex validation. So, we'll build the mechanism to hook up the Rails errors with Flex. We're also interested in purely client-side Flex validation, but even though this is easier, we'll consider it after we've done the harder task of integrating Rails validation.

The reason for this ordering is instructive: If we do our job in the purely client-side Flex validations, we can prevent many errors from happening on the server side (because we won't submit the erroneous data). However, because on the server we can *never* trust the client, we need to do the same validations on the server anyway. We hope they will all be redundant, but we do need to do them.

If you're coming from the Rails side, you may be wondering: Does this violate the Don't Repeat Yourself (DRY) principle that's so important in Rails? Yes, it does. Sorry about that.

If you want to stay totally DRY, you can do no validation on the client other than reporting the Rails validation errors. This is less work, but it's less user-friendly because you aren't detecting errors as early as possible. It's probably better to let users know as soon as possible about bad form inputs, so they can be spared the dreaded "fill out form > submit > fix errors > submit > fix more errors > submit > oh, more errors, forget it, I give up!" process.

If you're trying to detect and indicate errors as early as possible, some of the validations you can do are purely client side (for example, your email address has no @ sign), and some can involve calls to the server.

We'll use both of these. Let's get coding.

7.3 *Understanding Rails validation, and building custom XML for errors*

Let's start by going to http://local-host:3000/bin/Pomodo.html and trying to create a user with Username `ludwig`, Email `foo`, Password `foo`, and Confirm Password `bar` (see figure 7.2).

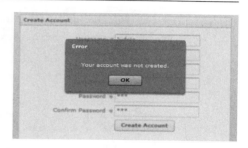

Figure 7.2   Not the most meaningful error in the world

That's unfortunate. We don't indicate the errors with the password being too short or not matching its confirmation. Also, we don't highlight the errors coming back from Rails. Worse yet, we don't even *have* any errors coming back from Rails— the `rescue ActiveRecord::RecordInvalid` in the `create` method of the `Users-Controller` currently does `render :text => "error"` in its `format.xml` block.

Let's see if we can fix that. We think about it for a minute and decide that we want to do is send XML of the errors over to Flex. It worked well for users, tasks, projects, and so on—it should work for errors too. Let's look at what the `to_xml` of the errors looks like; see listing 7.4.

Listing 7.4   app\controllers\users_controller.rb

```
.
class UsersController < ApplicationController
...
  def create
    @user = User.new(params[:user])
    @user.save!
...
  rescue ActiveRecord::RecordInvalid
    logger.info "user errors: #{@user.errors.to_xml}"      ❶
    respond_to do |format|
      format.html { render :action => 'new' }
```

```
        format.xml { render :text => "error" }
      end
    end
end
```

We add a debug message ❶ before the respond_to block. Next, click Create Account in Flex to once again attempt to create a user with Username ludwig, Email foo, Password foo, and Confirm Password bar (we don't need to rebuild, because this is just a Rails change). Looking at development.log, we see the result shown in listing 7.5.

Listing 7.5   Output (log\development.log)

```
Processing UsersController#create (for 127.0.0.1
  ➥at 2007-10-23 07:03:21) [POST]
...
user errors: <?xml version="1.0" encoding="UTF-8"?>
<errors>
  <error>Login has already been taken</error>
  <error>Password is too short (minimum is 4 characters)</error>
  <error>Password doesn't match confirmation</error>
</errors>
Completed in 0.06300 (15 reqs/sec) | Rendering: 0.00000 (0%) |
  ➥DB: 0.01500 (23%) | 200 OK [http://localhost/users.xml]
```

We see the user errors, which are listed in an XML document with a root of <errors> and three <error> elements. Surely we're all set.

Wait a minute—this is bad. Looking at the contents of each <error> element, we realize something unfortunate: There is *no way* to associate the error with the field (such as login or password) that it's for. Even if we sent the errors to the Flex client using @user.errors.to_xml, we wouldn't be able to attach them to the correct fields. That's pretty useless. It looks like we need to write our own method to get the XML we want for the errors.

Let's call this method to_xml_full.

Before we proceed, let's define what we want the XML to look like—requirements are a good thing. Our goal is to produce XML that looks like this if we try to create a duplicate ludwig user with a password of foo and a password confirmation of bar:

```
<?xml version="1.0" encoding="UTF-8"?>
<errors>
  <error message="Password doesn't match confirmation"
    field="password"/>
```

```
<error
  message="Password is too short (minimum is 4 characters)"
  field="password"/>
<error message="Login has already been taken" field="login"/>
</errors>
```

Each `<error>` will have a `field` attribute that defines the field the error is for.

In thinking about how to build `to_xml_full`, we decide to use one of the handiest approaches in writing slightly more advanced Rails code: looking at the source code of Rails. We'll do that now.

NOTE   The best way to start figuring out *what* to look for is to look at the API docs at http://api.rubyonrails.com. Once you've done that, reading through the source code is a good thing to do. Having the source code for Rails in vendor\rails makes this a lot easier—and ensures that you're looking at the code you're actually using!

We'll start by looking at the `ActiveRecord::Errors` class; see listing 7.6.

Listing 7.6   vendor\rails\activerecord\lib\active_record\validations.rb

```
module ActiveRecord
...
  # Active Record validation is reported to and from this
  ➡object, which is used by Base#save to
  # determine whether the object in a valid state to be saved.
  ➡See usage example in Validations.
  class Errors
    include Enumerable

    def initialize(base) # :nodoc:
      @base, @errors = base, {}         ❶
    end
...
    # Returns all the full error messages in an array.
...
    def full_messages                   ❷
      full_messages = []

      @errors.each_key do |attr|        ❸
        @errors[attr].each do |msg|     ❹
          next if msg.nil?              ❺

          if attr == "base"            ❻
            full_messages << msg
          else
            full_messages << @base.class.human_attribute_name(   ❼
      ➡attr) + " " + msg
```

```
          end
        end
      end
      full_messages
    end
...
    def to_xml(options={})
      options[:root] ||= "errors"
      options[:indent] ||= 2
      options[:builder] ||= Builder::XmlMarkup.new(        ❽
  ➡:indent => options[:indent])

      options[:builder].instruct! unless options.delete(
  ➡:skip_instruct)
      options[:builder].errors do |e|
        full_messages.each { |msg| e.error(msg) }          ❾
      end
    end
...
  end
end
```

The to_xml method does a bunch of stuff with something called Builder::Xml-
Markup ❽ and then calls ❾ a method called full_messages ❷. Let's look at
how that method is implemented—it may give us some clues for how we could
build our to_xml_full method. We see that it uses a variable called @errors,
which is a Hash ❶ inside the Errors class. It calls the block for each key in the
Hash by calling the each_key ❸ method (http://www.ruby-doc.org/core/
classes/Hash.html#M000673) with an associated block. The keys are passed in as
the attr parameter ❹ and used to look up the Array of error messages for that
attr by saying @errors[attr]. This Array has its each method called with an
associated block, meaning that each element in the array is passed to the block
as the msg parameter. If the message is nil ❺, it's skipped. If not, the attr is
checked. If it's "base" ❻, then the message doesn't belong to a specific field, so
it's appended. If it isn't "base", then it belongs to a field. That field name is formatted nicely by calling @base.class.human_attribute_ name ❼ on the attr
and then appending a space and the message.

Now that we understand better how full_messages works, we have a better
idea of how we can implement our method. Without further ado, let's modify the
application.rb file to add the to_xml_full method to the ActiveRecord::Errors
class; see listing 7.7. This is the trickiest Ruby code we've seen so far; it will all be
explained afterward.

Listing 7.7   app\controllers\application.rb

```
...
module ActiveRecord #:nodoc:
  module Serialization
    # We force :dasherize to be false, since we never want it to
    # be true.
    unless method_defined? :old_to_xml
      alias_method :old_to_xml, :to_xml
      def to_xml(options = {})
        options.merge!(:dasherize => false)
        old_to_xml(options)
      end
    end
  end
end
module ActiveRecord #:nodoc:                       ❶
  class Errors #:nodoc:                            ❷
    def to_xml_full(options={})                    ❸
      options[:root] ||= "errors"
      options[:indent] ||= 2
      options[:builder] ||=                        ❹
        Builder::XmlMarkup.new(:indent => options[:indent])
      options[:builder].instruct! unless           ❺
        options.delete(:skip_instruct)
      options[:builder].errors do |e|              ❻
        # The @errors instance variable is a Hash inside the
        # Errors class
        @errors.each_key do |attr|                 ❼
          @errors[attr].each do |msg|              ❽
            next if msg.nil?                        ❾
            if attr == "base"                       ❿
              options[:builder].error("message"=>msg)        ⓫
            else                                    ⓬
              fullmsg = @base.class.human_attribute_name(attr) +    ⓭
                " " + msg
              options[:builder].error(             ⓮
                "field"=>attr, "message"=>fullmsg)
            end
          end
        end
      end
    end
  end
end

# Filters added to this controller apply to all controllers in
# the application. Likewise, all the methods added will be
# available for all controllers.
...
```

What we're doing here is opening up the definition of the `Errors` class ❷ inside the `ActiveRecord` module ❶ and adding the `to_xml_full` method ❸ we wish it came with.

Note how similar this method is to the `full_messages` method we examined earlier. In this method, we create a new `Builder::XmlMarkup` object ❹ with the indentation option passed in.

We add the XML processing instruction `<?xml version="1.0" encoding="UTF-8"?>` unless the `:skip_instruct` option was passed in ❺. We then create the root element `<errors>` by calling a method (errors) that *does not exist* ❻. We pass this nonexistent method a block ❻ (do |e| ... end), and inside the block we append each of the error messages by calling *another* nonexistent method (error) ⓫.

We use the `@errors` Hash ❼ `each_key` method to pass each key to a block that gets the `Array` of error messages for that key ❽ and passes each of them to another block. Inside the block, we skip empty messages ❾. If the `attr` is `"base"` ❿ we add an error element for the message with no field ⓫, otherwise ⓬ we build a full message called `fullmsg` ⓭ and create an `error` element ⓮ with a field attribute of `attr` and a message attribute of `fullmsg`.

If you read all that without flinching, congratulations: You've already taken the red pill. Furthermore, understanding this is the key to understanding Builder. From the Builder documentation on XmlMarkup:

> *All (well, almost all) methods sent to an XmlMarkup object will be translated to the equivalent XML markup. Any method with a block will be treated as an XML markup tag with nested markup in the block.*

> —http://api.rubyonrails.org/classes/Builder/XmlMarkup.html

Essentially, we're calling methods that *don't exist* (like `errors`), and the `Builder::XmlMarkup` class is smart enough to handle this and produce an XML structure as a result.

Whoa.

If you're a Java programmer, the "duck typing" of Ruby may have been liberating, scary, or both—but the idea of calling methods that *aren't there* probably seems like total voodoo. How could it possibly work?

The answer is that in Ruby, a method call is implemented as message passing to an object. (See *Programming Ruby* for the details.) If you try to call a method on an object and it isn't there, Ruby invokes that object's `method_missing` method. An inspection of the Builder documentation[1] shows that this is how Builder

---

[1] For more information about Builder, see http://builder.rubyforge.org/, http://www.myersds.com/notebook/2006/05/11/how_to_generate_rss_feeds_with_rails, and http://clarkware.com/cgi/blosxom/2005/07/12.

works: See the description and source code of `method_missing` at http://builder.rubyforge.org/classes/Builder/XmlBase.html#M000007 for the details. The `method_missing` method takes the block it's passed and uses it to create child XML elements. We can build an entire XML structure by calling a bunch of nonexistent methods.

If you're new to Ruby, understanding the power of blocks will put a smile on your face—if not now, then when you read a better explanation of them. If it hasn't yet, read *Programming Ruby*.

Enough chit-chat—let's test. Go back to the `UsersController`, and add a `logger.info` statement (listing 7.8 **❶**) that calls the new `to_xml_full` method.

Listing 7.8 app\controllers\users_controller.rb

```
class UsersController < ApplicationController
...
  def create
...
  rescue ActiveRecord::RecordInvalid
    logger.info "user errors: #{@user.errors.to_xml}"
    logger.info "user errors full: #{@user.errors.to_xml_full}"      ❶
    respond_to do |format|
      format.html { render :action => 'new' }
      format.xml { render :text => "error" }
    end
  end
end
```

Save the file, and stop and start our server (because we modified application.rb). Go back to the browser window, which should still be at http://localhost:3000/bin/Pomodo.html, and click Create Account again to try to create a user with Username `ludwig`, Email `blah`, Password `foo`, and Confirm Password `bar`. We get the same error dialog as before; let's see what's in development.log (listing 7.9).

Listing 7.9 log\development.log

```
Processing UsersController#create (for 127.0.0.1 at
  ➥2007-10-24 06:58:38) [POST]
...
user errors: <?xml version="1.0" encoding="UTF-8"?>
<errors>        ❶
  <error>Login has already been taken</error>
  <error>Password is too short (minimum is 4 characters)</error>/
  <error>Password doesn't match confirmation</error>
</errors>
```

```
user errors full: <?xml version="1.0" encoding="UTF-8"?>    ❷
<errors>
  <error message="Login has already been taken" field="login"/>    ❸
  <error                                                            ❹
    message="Password is too short (minimum is 4 characters)"
    field="password"/>
  <error message="Password doesn't match confirmation"             ❺
    field="password"/>
</errors>
...
```

After the not-so-useful to_xml output ❶, we have the to_xml_full output ❷. Each error ❸❹❺ has the field it belongs to as an attribute.

Hooray, it worked!

Now it's time to send these errors to Flex and display them on the fields. Before we do that, however, we need to take a basic look at Flex 3 validation.

7.4   *A Quick look at validation in Flex 3*

We've been discussing Flex 3 validation without showing any examples of it. To fix this, we'll add a Validator for the email address in the form. Modify the AccountCreateBox as shown in listing 7.10.

> **Listing 7.10   app\flex\com\pomodo\components\AccountCreateBox.mxml**

```
...
    </mx:HTTPService>
    <mx:EmailValidator id="emailValidator" source="{emailTI}"    ❶
        property="text"/>
    <mx:Form labelWidth="150">
        <mx:FormItem required="true" label="Username">
            <mx:TextInput id="loginTI"/>
        </mx:FormItem>
        <mx:FormItem required="true" label="Email Address">
            <mx:TextInput id="emailTI"/>    ❷
        </mx:FormItem>
...
```

We're creating an EmailValidator called, inventively, emailValidator ❶, whose source is the emailTI TextInput ❷. The property we'll validate is the text property. Rebuild and reload. The Create Account form will look unchanged. Next, click inside the newAccountEmailTI, and then press the Tab key to transfer focus to the next TextInput (newAccountFirstNameTI). We see the first change, a red highlight (see figure 7.3, but note that red won't show up in the book very well).

If we mouse over the Email Address field, we see that it's highlighted in red with an error tooltip (see figure 7.4).

By default, `Validators` such as `EmailValidator` have `required= "true"`.

Next, enter the name `ludwig` in the Email Address, Tab out, and mouse over the field again (see figure 7.5).

Now *that's* cool: The `EmailValidator` checked that we had an @ sign in our email address, and it complained that we didn't. Flex was also smart enough to realize that there wasn't enough room in my browser to fit the full tooltip, so it moved it above the field.

Let's go back in the field, enter an @ sign, and Tab out (see figure 7.6).

Cool. Now, enter `ludwig@pomodo. com` (see figure 7.7).

The validation error is cleared, and the field looks normal again.

We'll use more standard Flex validators soon, as well as building a custom validator for the password confirmation. For a detailed tour of Flex validators, read chapter 46, "Validating Data," of the *Flex 3 Developer's Guide.*

Figure 7.3   Red validation highlight

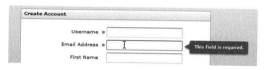

Figure 7.4   Red validation error callout

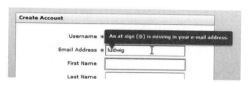

Figure 7.5   Validation error for incorrect email address

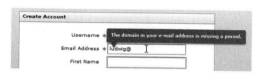

Figure 7.6   More email validation

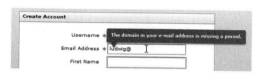

Figure 7.7   Validation error cleared

NOTE   All this work was done without talking to the server once! The more work we do on the client, the easier it is on our poor servers.

Now, it's time to have some fun: We'll integrate the errors from Rails with Flex 3.

7.5 *Integrating Rails validation with Flex 3 validation*

Rather than retrace my steps in how this was developed, I'll present the end result and explain the code. We'll start by modifying the create_xml method of Users-Controller; see listing 7.11.

Listing 7.11   app\controllers\users_controller.rb

```
...
  # POST /users
  # POST /users.xml
  def create
    @user = User.new(params[:user])
    @user.save!
...
  rescue ActiveRecord::RecordInvalid
    logger.info "user errors: #{@user.errors.to_xml}"             ❶
    logger.info "user errors full: #{@user.errors.to_xml_full}"
    respond_to do |format|
      format.html { render :action => 'new' }
      format.xml { render :text => "error" }
      format.xml do           ❷
        unless @user.errors.empty?           ❸
          render :xml => @user.errors.to_xml_full       ❹
        else
          render :text => "error"           ❺
        end
      end
    end
  end
end
```

If the @user.save! fails, we end up rescuing ActiveRecord::RecordInvalid. First, we delete the old logging code ❶. Then, we modify the format.xml block ❷—we'll leave the format.html unmodified. We change the syntax from the single-line convention of { ... } to the multiline convention of do ... end. Inside the block, we check whether the @user.errors (which is an ActiveRecord::Errors) is empty ❸. If it's non-empty, we render as XML the result of calling the new to_xml_full method that we added to ActiveRecord::Errors ❹. If it's empty, something truly bizarre has happened (an error with no errors), so we render "error" ❺ and ignore it. (If this was a real application, we would, of course, log the error.)

Next, we'll create two new files on the Flex side: ServerErrors (to store the errors from Rails in) and ServerErrorValidator (a custom validator that displays the errors from Rails). First, ServerErrors; see listing 7.12.

Listing 7.12   app\flex\com\pomodo\validators\ServerErrors.as

```
package com.pomodo.validators {
    import mx.validators.Validator;
    import mx.validators.ValidationResult;

    public class ServerErrors {
        public static const BASE:String = ":base";          ❶

        /**
         * The errors on specific fields (base errors are on the
         * BASE). The keys are the field Strings; the values are
         * Arrays of errors.
         */
        private var _allErrors:Object;          ❷

        public function ServerErrors(errorsXML:XML) {
            _allErrors = {};
            for each (var error:XML in errorsXML.error) {          ❸
                var field:String = error.@field;          ❹
                if (field == null || field == "") {
                    field = BASE;          ❺
                }
                if (_allErrors[field] == null) {
                    _allErrors[field] =          ❻
                      [ createValidationResult(error.@message) ];
                } else {
                    var fieldErrors:Array = _allErrors[field];          ❼
                    fieldErrors.push(
                        createValidationResult(error.@message));
                }
            }
        }

        /**
         * Return an Array of the errors (just Strings) for the
         * field, an empty Array if none.
         */
        public function getErrorsForField(field:String):Array {
            return _allErrors[field] == null ?          ❽
                [] : _allErrors[field];
        }

        private function createValidationResult(message:String):          ❾
        ValidationResult {
            return new ValidationResult(          ❿
                true,
                "",
                "SERVER_VALIDATION_ERROR",
```

```
            message);       ⑪
      }
   }
}
```

The `ServerErrors` class encapsulates the task of converting the errors we get from Rails into something we want to use in Flex. We anticipate doing this all over the place, so it's certainly functionality that should not be tied to a specific visual component.

Essentially, we want to provide a `String` name of a field and get back all the errors for that field. This is what the `getErrorsForField` function ❽ does. It checks the `_allErrors` map ❷ for the field in question and returns the `Array` that is stored for that field (an empty `Array` if none).

> **NOTE** Returning an empty `Array` or a "null object" instead of `null` is often a good thing to do in Flex, because otherwise we're putting the null-checking burden on whomever uses your class. This is true in many languages, but it's more true in Flex because so much is event-driven and asynchronous: In many cases, the data may not be there yet.

In the `ServerErrors` constructor, we iterate over the `errorsXML` XML with a for each loop ❸. For each error in the `errorsXML`, we get its `field` attribute ❹ with the slightly weird `errors.@field` syntax (@ is for attribute). If the `field` attribute is missing, we set it to the `BASE` field ❺, which is a `const String` key ❶ we're using to store errors that aren't for a specific field in the map. (We could use a separate variable if we were being super-paranoid about a name collision.)

Next, we check the `_allErrors[field]`. If it's `null`, then this the first error for that field, so we create a new `Array` containing a `ValidationResult` that has this `error.@message` (the message attribute) as its `message` property ❻. If it's non-null, then we already have one or more messages in an `Array`, so we push a new `ValidationResult` with the message property set to the `error.@message` onto it ❼. Both these functions use a new utility function called `createValidationResult` ❾, which returns a new `ValidationResult` ❿ containing the message ⑪. We create this array of `ValidationResults` instead of `Strings`, because the `ServerErrorValidator` that we'll create next needs to return an `Array` of `ValidationResults` from its `doValidation` method.

Next, we'll create the `ServerErrorValidator`. Its job is to show these `ServerErrors` on a field; see listing 7.13.

```
package com.pomodo.validators {
    import com.pomodo.validators.ServerErrors;
    import mx.validators.Validator;
    import mx.validators.ValidationResult;

    public class ServerErrorValidator extends Validator {          ❶
        /**
         * These are the ServerErrors that apply specifically to
         * this ServerErrorValidator.
         */
        private var _serverErrors:ServerErrors;          ❷

        /**
         * The field of the ServerErrors we are interested in.
         */
        public var field:String;          ❸

        /**
         * The ServerErrors we are interested in.
         */
        public function set serverErrors(          ❹
        pServerErrors:ServerErrors):void {
            _serverErrors = pServerErrors;
            validate();          ❺
        }

        public function ServerErrorValidator() {
            field = ServerErrors.BASE;//default to being on BASE          ❻
            _serverErrors = null;
            super();
        }

        override protected function doValidation(value:Object):          ❼
        Array {
            return _serverErrors.getErrorsForField(field);          ❽
        }
    }
}
```

The ServerErrorValidator extends Validator ❶. It stores a given ServerErrors object in a private variable _serverErrors ❷, and it stores the name of the field in the ServerErrors that it's interested in in a public variable called field ❸. The field defaults to the ServerErrors.BASE ❻. When the serverErrors are set ❹, the inherited validate function ❺ is called. This triggers the doValidation function ❼, which returns the result of calling the getErrorsForField function ❽ in the _serverErrors. (Note that this currently has the limitation of showing only one error message at a time in the callout.)

Next, we'll make some modifications to the AccountCreateBox to integrate the ServerErrors and ServerErrorValidator; see listing 7.14.

Listing 7.14   app\flex\com\pomodo\components\AccountCreateBox.mxml

```
<?xml version="1.0" encoding="utf-8"?>
<mx:VBox xmlns:mx="http://www.adobe.com/2006/mxml"
    xmlns:cpv="com.pomodo.validators.*"                         ❶
    width="100%" height="100%" label="Create Account">          ❷
<mx:Metadata>
    [Event(name="accountCreate",
           type="com.pomodo.events.AccountCreateEvent")]
</mx:Metadata>
<mx:Script>
<![CDATA[
    import mx.controls.Alert;
    import mx.events.ValidationResultEvent;                      ❸
    import mx.rpc.events.ResultEvent;
    import com.pomodo.events.AccountCreateEvent;
    import com.pomodo.validators.ServerErrors;

    [Bindable]
    private var _serverErrors:ServerErrors;                      ❹

    private function createAccount():void {
        svcAccountCreate.send();
    }

    private function handleAccountCreateResult(
    event:ResultEvent):void {
        Pomodo.debug(
            "AccountCreateBox#handleAccountCreateResult");        ❺
        var result:Object = event.result;
        if (result == "error") {
            Alert.show("Your account was not created.",
                "Error");
        } else {
            dispatchEvent(new AccountCreateEvent(XML(result)));   ❻
            var resultXML:XML = XML(result);                      ❼
            Pomodo.debug(resultXML.toXMLString());                ❽
            if (resultXML.name().localName == "errors") {         ❾
                Alert.show(
                    "Please correct the validation errors " +     ❿
                    "highlighted on the form.",
                    "Account Not Created");
                _serverErrors = new ServerErrors(resultXML);      ⓫
            } else {
                dispatchEvent(
```

```
                      new AccountCreateEvent(XML(result)));
                }
            }
        }
    ]]>
    </mx:Script>
        <mx:HTTPService
            id="svcAccountCreate"
...
        </mx:HTTPService>
        <mx:EmailValidator id="emailValidator" source="{emailTI}"
            property="text"/>
        <cpv:ServerErrorValidator        ⑫
            id="loginSV"
            field="login"
            listener="{loginTI}"
            serverErrors="{_serverErrors}"/>
        <cpv:ServerErrorValidator        ⑬
            id="emailSV"
            field="email"
            listener="{emailTI}"
            serverErrors="{_serverErrors}"/>
        <cpv:ServerErrorValidator        ⑭
            id="passwordSV"
            field="password"
            listener="{passwordTI}"
            serverErrors="{_serverErrors}"/>
        <cpv:ServerErrorValidator        ⑮
            id="passwordConfirmationSV"
            field="password_confirmation"
            listener="{confirmPasswordTI}"
            serverErrors="{_serverErrors}"/>
        <mx:Form labelWidth="150">
...
        </mx:Form>
    </mx:VBox>
```

We add an XML namespace cpv for our com.pomodo.validators ❶. I like to keep all my xmlns declarations together, so I moved the width attribute ❷. We also add some imports ❸ and create a _serverErrors variable for ServerErrors ❹.

Next, we modify the handleAccountCreateResult function. We output a debug message ❺ and then delete the old code ❻. Then, we cast the result to XML (it will always be XML since we're using a resultFormat of e4x) and store it in a resultXML variable ❼ and debug that variable ❽. The resultXML could either be the XML for the new user or the XML for the errors. To distinguish between them, we check the resultXML.name().localname ❾. It's a good idea to use the `localname` (assuming we're calling our own service) to avoid having to check and compare namespaces. If the `localName` is `"errors"`, the XML is for errors, so we pop up an `Alert` dialog ❿ and then create a new `ServerErrors` object out of the `resultXML` and assign it to the `_serverErrors` ⓫. This triggers all the bindings in the various `ServerErrorValidators` ⓬–⓯, which all have their `serverErrors` property bound to the `_serverErrors` variable. Each `Server-ErrorValidator` is for a different `TextInput` and specifies a different field (of the errors from Rails) that it's interested in and a different listener (Flex component) that cares about the validation errors.

That's it. It's fairly straightforward, given how impressive and usable the end result is.

Save, rebuild, reload, and try to create an account with Username `ludwig`, Email `lvb@pomodo.com`, Password `foo`, and Confirm Password `bar` (see figure 7.8).

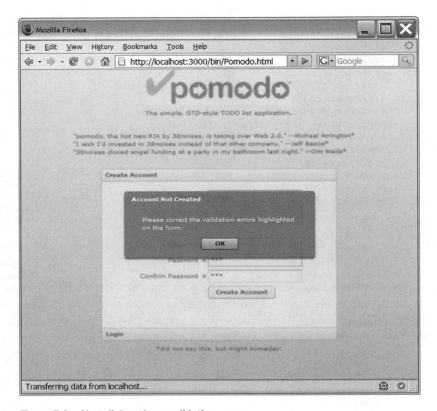

Figure 7.8 Alert dialog above validation errors

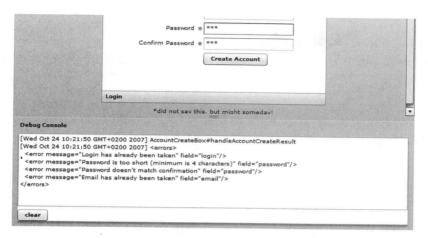

Figure 7.9 Debug console showing error messages as XML

Click OK, and drag the Debug Console up to see the error messages as XML (see figure 7.9).

Mouse over the different fields on the Create Account panel to see the various error messages returned from Rails correctly associated with their fields. For example, the login error is shown in figure 7.10.

Figure 7.10
Debug console showing error messages as XML

> **NOTE** Validating the uniqueness of an email address is probably a privacy violation of the person owning that email address: It confirms to a random stranger that this email address uses your site. Think before you do this. (I'd never thought of this until I saw an article online, but I can't remember or find where. If you're the originator of this idea: thank you.)

Note that the Password field will show only one error in the callout, not both of them.

Clearing server errors

Currently, validation errors in the various `ServerErrorsValidators` will only clear the next time the `_serverErrors` variable is set (because the `Server-ErrorValidator` class displays the `_serverErrors`). In our case, this is the next time the `handleAccountCreateResult` function gets called.

> **Clearing server errors** *(continued)*
>
> The `TextInput`s remain highlighted in red with the error callouts on mouse-over even after you've modified their contents, and they remain this way until we submit the form again.
>
> It's debatable whether this should be considered a bug or feature; if you think it's a bug, you can explicitly handle change events on the various `Text-Input`s that have `ServerErrorsValidator`s associated with them.

7.6 *Flex validators revisited*

Now that we have the Rails errors displaying in Flex, let's add more validators to the Flex side so we can prevent these errors from happening. This way, there's less load on the server and a more responsive UI.

While we're at it, we'll add a Terms of Service button that shows an alert displaying the terms of service. We'll also add an "I agree to the terms of service" check box and logic to ensure that it's checked before the Create Account button can be clicked.

We'll start by creating a `PasswordConfirmationValidator` that will ensure that the password confirmation matches the password (see listing 7.15).

Listing 7.15   app\flex\com\pomodo\validators\PasswordConfirmationValidator.as

```
package com.pomodo.validators {
    import mx.validators.Validator;
    import mx.validators.ValidationResult;

    public class PasswordConfirmationValidator
    extends Validator {
        /**
         * The password being compared to the confirmation.
         */
        public var password:String;       ❶

        public function PasswordConfirmationValidator() {
            super();
        }

        override protected function doValidation(       ❷
            passwordConfirmation:Object):Array
        {
            //We call base class doValidation() to get the
            //required logic.
            var results:Array =       ❸
```

```
            super.doValidation(passwordConfirmation);

        // Compare password and passwordConfirmation fields.
        if (password != passwordConfirmation) {          ❹
            results.push(
                new ValidationResult(          ❺
                    true,
                    "password_confirmation",
                    "passwordDoesNotMatchConfirmation",
          "The password does not match the confirmation."));
        }
        return results;          ❻
    }
  }
}
```

This `Validator` is straightforward. Its `doValidation` function ❷ takes a `password-Confirmation Object` (a `String`, we hope). It calls `super.doValidation(password-Confirmation)` ❸ to trigger the logic that adds a validation error if the field is required and the `passwordConfirmation` is empty. Because we want to compare the `passwordConfirmation` to a password, we create a public variable called `password` ❶ that we can compare this password to. (It doesn't need to be `[Bindable]`, because we're checking it explicitly in a function, not in response to it changing.) Then, in `doValidation`, we do a comparison ❹; if the `passwordConfirmation` isn't equal to the password, we push an error (`ValidationResult`) ❺ onto the `results` array. Finally, we return the `results` ❻.

Next, we'll modify the `AccountCreateBox` to take advantage of our new client-side validation functionality; see listing 7.16.

Listing 7.16   app\flex\com\pomodo\components\AccountCreateBox.mxml

```
...
    import mx.controls.Alert;
    import mx.events.ValidationResultEvent;
    import mx.rpc.events.ResultEvent;
    import mx.validators.Validator;          ❶
    import com.pomodo.events.AccountCreateEvent;
    import com.pomodo.validators.ServerErrors;

    [Bindable]
    private var _serverErrors:ServerErrors;

    private function createAccount():void {          ❷
      svcAccountCreate.send();
    }
```

```
        private function handleAccountCreateResult(
        event:ResultEvent):void {
...
        }

    private function validateAndSubmit():void {          ❸
        var results:Array = Validator.validateAll([        ❹
            usernameValidator,
            emailValidator,
            passwordValidator,
            passwordConfirmationValidator]);
        if (results.length > 0) {          ❺
            Alert.show("Please correct the validation errors " +    ❻
                "highlighted on the form.",
                "Account Not Created");
            return;          ❼
        }
        svcAccountCreate.send();          ❽
    }

    private function showTOS():void {          ❾
        Alert.show(
            "The first rule of pomodo is: Don't talk about " +
            "pomodo. The second rule of pomodo is: Don't " +
            "talk about pomodo.", "Terms of Service");
    }
]]>
</mx:Script>
    <mx:HTTPService
        id="svcAccountCreate"
...
    </mx:HTTPService>
    <mx:EmailValidator id="emailValidator" source="{emailTI}"
        property="text"/>
    <mx:StringValidator
        id="usernameValidator"          ❿
        source="{loginTI}"
        property="text"
        required="true"
        maxLength="80"/>
    <mx:StringValidator
        id="passwordValidator"          ⓫
        source="{passwordTI}"
        property="text"
        required="true"
        minLength="4"
        maxLength="40"/>
    <cpv:PasswordConfirmationValidator
        id="passwordConfirmationValidator"          ⓬
        password="{passwordTI.text}"
        source="{confirmPasswordTI}"
```

```
            property="text"
            required="true"/>
      <cpv:ServerErrorValidator
          id="loginSV"
          field="login"
          listener="{loginTI}"
          serverErrors="{_serverErrors}"/>
...
      <mx:Form labelWidth="150">
...

          <mx:FormItem required="true" label="Confirm Password">
              <mx:TextInput id="confirmPasswordTI"
                  displayAsPassword="true"/>
          </mx:FormItem>
          <mx:FormItem>
              <mx:LinkButton label="Terms of Service"        ⓭
                  click="showTOS()"/>
          </mx:FormItem>
          <mx:FormItem>
              <mx:CheckBox id="tosCB"          ⓮
                  label="I agree to the terms of service"/>
          </mx:FormItem>
          <mx:FormItem>
              <mx:Button id="createAccountButton"
                  label="Create Account"
                  toolTip="{tosCB.selected ? '' :          ⓯
    ➨ 'You must accept the terms of service.'}"
                  enabled="{tosCB.selected}"          ⓰
                  click="validateAndSubmit()"/>          ⓱
          </mx:FormItem>
      </mx:Form>
  </mx:VBox>
```

We start by adding an import ❶. Next, we delete the createAccount function ❷, because it's being replaced by the validateAndSubmit ❸ function. Inside validateAndSubmit, we call Validator.validateAll ❹ with an Array of the different client-side validators we have (we don't include the ServerErrorValidators, because those are only used to display errors from Rails). If any of these validators returns an error, it will be included in the results Array returned by validateAll, so we can test whether that Array's length ❺ is greater than 0 to see if there was an error. If so, we pop up an alert dialog ❻ telling the user to fix the errors, and we return ❼ *without* doing the service call; if it's false, we do the service call, which attempts to create the new account ❽. At this point, the Rails validations run and come back to the client with errors if there were any errors on the Rails side. If there were Rails validation errors, they're shown by the ServerErrorValidators for the fields they are associated with.

NOTE The really neat thing is this: In both cases, an alert dialog is popped up with the same title and error message. There is no distinction to the user whether it's a client error or a server error—it's all just validation. And the error highlighting and callouts make finding and fixing the errors so easy that users will be less inclined to give up and leave.

Next, we create the showTOS function ❾, which shows a cheesy alert box.

Next, we create three new Validators: a standard mx:StringValidator for the username ❿, another mx:StringValidator for the password ⓫, and our custom cpv:PasswordConfirmationValidator ⓬ for the password confirmation. Note that the String validator can enforce minimum length, maximum length, and so on. We bind the password property of our PasswordConfirmationValidator to the text property of the newAccountPasswordTI. (Hooray for Flex 3! We can't do this in Flex 1.5.)

Now, we create a LinkButton to show the terms of service ⓭ by calling showTOS on click. We then create a CheckBox that asks the user to accept the terms of service ⓮. We modify the createAccountButton definition, binding its enabled property ⓰ to the tosCB.selected value, in order to disable the Create Account button if the tosCB isn't selected. We also bind the toolTip property ⓯ to an expression that evaluates to the empty string if the tosCB is selected and to a stern order to accept the terms of service if the tosCB isn't selected. This will make our lawyers happy. We also modify the button to call ⓱ our new validateAndSubmit function.

Q. Why did we include code to enable/disable the Create Account button as part of an iteration on validation?

A. This is subtle: Flex validation is so good that many programmers fall into the trap of thinking it should be used to do everything. For example, we want to show a validation error on the terms of service check box if it isn't checked and the user clicks the Create Account button.
That sounds like a fine idea—but it's not.

Validation errors are an unfortunate occurrence, regardless of how good they look. If our legal department tells us that a user isn't allowed to create an account until they check a check box saying they've "read" some terms of service, then rather than telling the user "Bad user! No cookie!" if they don't check the check box before clicking the button, it would presumably be much better to *prevent them from clicking the button in the first place* until they've checked the check box. To prevent them from getting confused about why the button is disabled, we add the helpful tooltip.

Note also that if our legal department told us to, we could prevent the "I agree" check box from being clickable until the Terms of Service link was clicked. It would just be another flag and another tooltip.

Listing 7.17 app\flex\com\pomodo\components\SplashBox.mxml

```
. . .
        <mx:Spacer height="10"/>
        <mx:Accordion width="440" height="330">
            <pom:AccountCreateBox/>
. . .
```

One more thing: We need to modify the `SplashBox` to accommodate our bigger `AccountCreateBox`; see listing 7.17.

That's it.

Enough talk; let's run the app. Save, rebuild, and reload; see figure 7.11.

Note that the Create Account button is disabled.

Try to create an account with Username `ludwig`, Password `foo`, Confirm Password `bar`. We have to check the "I agree" check box (see figure 7.12).

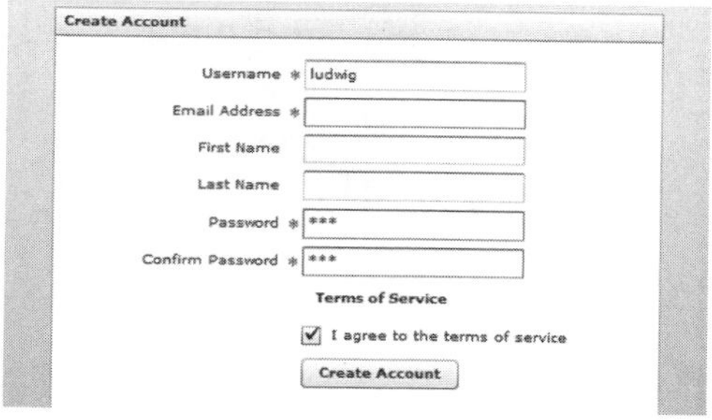

Note that the Username field isn't highlighted in error, because we haven't yet made a service call. If we mouse over the Password field, we see a validation error that was added by the `StringValidator` (see figure 7.13).

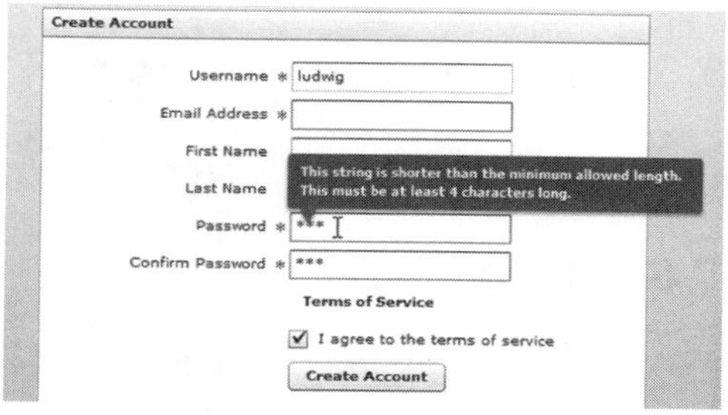

If we mouse over the Confirm Password field, we see the validation error added by our custom `PasswordConfirmationValidator` (see figure 7.14).

Play with the form a bit. Note how the Create Account button disables itself and shows the tooltip if we uncheck the check box (see figure 7.15).

That's it!

Figure 7.11   A TOS and a Disabled Create Account Button

Figure 7.12   Client-side validation galore

Figure 7.13   StringValidator in action

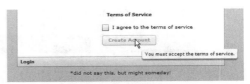

Figure 7.14 `PasswordConfirmation-`
`Validator` **in action**

Figure 7.15   Happy lawyers!

7.7   *Keeping our tests passing*

Finally, let's run the tests again; see listing 7.18.

Listing 7.18   Output

```
c:\peter\flexiblerails\current\pomodo>rake
...
Started
...............
Finished in 1.109 seconds.

16 tests, 29 assertions, 0 failures, 0 errors
...
Started
................................
Finished in 2.234 seconds.

35 tests, 65 assertions, 0 failures, 0 errors
...

c:\peter\flexiblerails\current\pomodo>
```

Everything still works. Hooray!

> The code at this point is saved as the iteration07 folder.

7.8   *Summary*

Both Flex and Rails feature validation support as an integral part of the framework. This is good, because doing something wrong is an *integral* part of how users
will use your application. The great thing is that integrating this validation support is easy. With little effort, you can use the built-in validation support in Flex
and Rails to create user-friendly applications that deal with error conditions in a
much better way than is the norm today.

Note too that Flex has formatters that can massage user input into a form that is acceptable. Read the "Formatting Data" chapter in the *Flex 3 Developer's Guide* for details. The interactions between formatters, validators, bindings, and so on can be complex if we're not careful. For now, I'd just like to warn you to think carefully about how much you should modify and validate user input—don't make your users frustrated and angry while ostensibly trying to help them.

The "where should validation live" question is interesting. Rails puts all its validation in the model, which is a good choice. However, it leads to some things that are odd. For example, there is no password_confirmation field in the users table, so what is password_confirmation doing in the model? And what are some of the special-case helper methods like validates_confirmation_of doing in the User model? Is this polluting the User model with constructs that don't belong there, merely to make HTML form validation easier? Because Flex has its own validation framework and can validate that a password confirmation field matches the password field before Rails is even involved, should we remove the password-confirmation stuff from the Rails side entirely? And if we're going to do this, why wouldn't we do the equivalent thing with JavaScript when we're using standard Rails? Oh, but the user might have disabled JavaScript, and so forth. This is a good argument to have—preferably with beer involved.

We could go on and on about validation, but we're rapidly hitting the point of diminishing returns. We've come a long way in this iteration, and the experience we've gained from it should be applicable however we want to use validation in the future. There won't be any more validation in the book.

7.9 Exercises for the reader

1 Hook up the Create Account button to be disabled when any validator has failed. When would you need to re-enable it?

2 Note how the PasswordConfirmationValidator is smart enough to update itself when the password confirmation changes, but not smart enough to update itself if we change the password field and click somewhere other than in the Confirm Password field. How would you fix this? (Hint: public function set.)

3 Build a custom validator that validates the username against usernames in the database by calling a method on the Rails side that returns whether a given username exists. How should that validator be triggered: whenever the user types, or only when the username field loses focus? Is this validator infallible?

4 Implement support for multiple server errors in validation error callouts.

5 (This is also an exercise for the author!) Should we make a standard Flexible Rails plugin instead of "monkeypatching" application.rb, which provides the following extensions to Rails for better interoperability with Flex (and other rich clients):

- A `to_xml_full` method (or a parameter to the `to_xml` method instead) for `ActiveRecord::Errors` to include the field attribute
- A way to turn off `dasherize` in `Hash`, `Array`, and `Serialization`

Part 3

Refactoring

Now that we've made substantial progress in our application, we've added enough code that the design issues are starting to become apparent. First, we notice that we have lots of data and behavior, but we aren't following a centralized approach—everything feels a little scattered. We'll address this by refactoring the code to use the Cairngorm framework, which is an application framework for Flex.

Next, we'll address the issue that there is no object model on the client, just a bunch of XML. We'll address this by doing a refactoring in which we add an object model.

This part includes two iterations:

- *Iteration 8*—"Refactoring to Cairngorm"
- *Iteration 9*—"Holding state on the client properly"

At the end of it, we'll have a much better understanding of design in Flex and of the options available to us for data exchange between Flex and Rails. Doing the refactoring to decouple the object model from its method of transport (currently XML) will enable us to consider using an alternate method of transport. Two more efficient choices we could use are JSON and RubyAMF.

In the next and final part, we'll first finish the application and then refactor again (to RubyAMF) because it uses the binary AMF protocol and thus has the most promise of efficiency improvements. Then, as an encore, we'll convert the application to being an AIR application.

Refactoring to Cairngorm

First, resist the opportunity to scatter state all over your application as strings, numbers, Booleans, and all manner of other primitive objects.

—Steven Webster[1]

---

[1]http://www.adobe.com/devnet/flex/articles/cairngorm_pt2_print.html.

In this iteration, we'll refactor the Flex code to use Cairngorm with `HTTPService`. We'll use Cairngorm in a slightly nonstandard way, to be slightly less verbose and more aligned with the design preferences of Rails. (This book won't attempt to explain "How to Use Cairngorm in the Standard Way." (Of course, there's not really a "standard way" any more, now that Cairngorm has been split into Cairngorm and Cairngorm Enterprise.) To learn the standard way of using Cairngorm, see the Cairngorm documentation.)

Note that Cairngorm is tough to explain in both an iterative and enjoyable fashion, because it has so many moving parts that work together. Furthermore, we're going to use some utility classes to make our use of Cairngorm less verbose. Rather than do the refactoring in this iteration iteratively, I'll present the finished result of the refactoring and explain the code all at once. As you see more and more of the code, you'll see how it all fits together—so don't worry if *why* we're doing something isn't 100% apparent at the time: By the end of the iteration, it will be.

Above all, keep in mind that Cairngorm is a Model-View-Controller (MVC) framework. As we create the various files, think about where they fit in the MVC pattern.

8.1   *Background and setup*

One of the biggest problems with Flex is that it makes writing code almost too easy.[2] How can this be a problem?

Well, it's possible to get a *lot* done without giving any thought to your application's design (earlier versions of this book demonstrated this by building a lot of functionality in one file: Pomodo.mxml. However, the process of refactoring it was tedious reading, so I dropped it). This can be dangerous: If other people (such as your client or marketing department) see a prototype running, they may get confused into thinking you have a fully functional app instead of an elaborate mock-up.

NOTE   There is a fairly famous "Napkin Look & Feel" (http://napkin-laf.sourceforge.net/) for Java Swing, which is a pluggable look and feel that replaces the default (ugly) Metal, ahem, Java look and feel with a look and feel that makes the UI look like it was drawn on the back of a

---

[2] I forget where I first saw this argument made about programming in general. A Google search turned up the following articles, which are good reads: http://butunclebob.com/ArticleS.MichaelFeathers. IsProgrammingTooEasy and http://www.joelonsoftware.com/articles/ThePerilsofJavaSchools.html.

napkin. The idea is to make the UI look like the mock-up that it is, so no one gets the wrong impression. There is a recent project to create a Napkin Skin in Flex (http://onreflexion.blogspot.com/2007/01/napkin-skins-in-flex_24.html) to achieve the same effect.

Another problem is that if we develop iteratively without any refactoring *(or thinking)*, we can end up with Rube Goldberg-like contraptions in our MXML:

> *...this variable gets set, which triggers this binding, which updates this model element, which in turn updates this model element, which triggers this function, which dispatches this event, which...*

Because, once again, Flex is so easy, it's possible to have somewhat working code even with a terrible muddle like this. Then one morning we go to add a small feature, get bogged down, and upon taking a fresh look at the code, realize it's *just a mess!*

There are many solutions to this problem. One fairly popular solution is Cairngorm.

8.1.1 Cairngorm history

Cairngorm was created by Steven Webster and Alistair McLeod, the two cofounders of a consulting firm called iteration::two, which was based in Scotland. They were acquired by Macromedia, which was then acquired by Adobe. (Steven and Alistair are famous in Flex circles for having written the definitive book on Flex 1.0, *Developing Rich Clients with Macromedia Flex.*)

Cairngorm is described by its authors as a *microarchitecture*: an architectural framework, or collection of design patterns. Essentially, just as Rails embodies many of DHH's opinions about how to write Ruby web applications (convention over configuration, DRY, and so on), Cairngorm embodies many of Steven Webster's and Alistair McLeod's opinions about how to write Flex applications. Because their book helped many developers (myself included) to learn Flex, these opinions have a lot of clout. And because Steven and Alistair are now at Adobe (and Cairngorm is at Adobe Labs), Cairngorm has gained even more mindshare[3] among Flex developers because of its somewhat "official" status.

---

[3] See http://jessewarden.com/2007/01/cairngorm-vs-joe-berkovitzs-mvcs.html for a comparison of Cairngorm and MVCS. Another alternative framework to consider is PureMVC: http://puremvc.org/.

8.1.2   *Do you need to use Cairngorm?*

No.

Steven Webster wrote a blog post entitled "Why I think you shouldn't use Cairngorm,"[4] which lists some prerequisites for using Cairngorm. Essentially, Cairngorm can be overkill for small, single-developer applications, and it can be confusing if you've never built a complete Flex application before. (We're up for the challenge, though.)

If, at the end of this iteration, you decide that you don't like Cairngorm—perhaps, as a Rails developer, it feels too much like Java for your tastes—don't worry: You can develop complete, innovative Flex applications without using Cairngorm.

That said, Cairngorm can make it easier to build larger Flex applications in a consistent way. Although you can roll your own framework, any developer new to your team will have to learn that framework—whereas there is a decent chance that they will already have been exposed to Cairngorm. Even if they don't know Cairngorm, they can learn it from *its* documentation—so this is less documentation for *you* to write and fewer emails and instant messages for you to answer. (This is good.)

Unfortunately, the Cairngorm documentation is sparse and outdated. The site http://www.cairngormdocs.org/ is devoted to collecting links to Cairngorm documentation and examples. In terms of tutorial documentation, the best starting place is the six-part article series that Steven Webster wrote for the Flex Developer Center. Part 1 is at http://www.adobe.com/devnet/flex/articles/cairngorm_pt1_print.html, and each part links to the next one. The articles develop an application called CairngormStore, which is a simple online store. These articles are rather outdated: At the time of this writing, Cairngorm is at version 2.2.1; the articles refer to version 0.99. However, they are a good way to learn the theory of Cairngorm, even if many of the details have changed.

I'm going to assume that if you're interested in using Cairngorm, you've read these articles or will read them, as well as other good[5] articles you find. As such, I won't duplicate their content. This book won't include a 5–10 page "theory of Cairngorm" section. Instead, in this iteration we'll learn Cairngorm by doing, refactoring pomodo to using Cairngorm 2.2.1 with Rails via `HTTPService`.

Let's dive in and learn Cairngorm.

---

4 http://weblogs.macromedia.com/swebster/archives/2006/08/why_i_think_you.cfm.

5 http://weblogs.macromedia.com/auhlmann/archives/2006/06/cairngorm_sampl.cfm and http://weblogs.macromedia.com/auhlmann/archives/2007/02/creating_a_popu.cfm.

8.1.3 Downloading Cairngorm 2.2.1

We'll start by downloading Cairngorm 2.2.1. It's currently found at the following URL: http://labs.adobe.com/wiki/index.php/Cairngorm:Cairngorm2.2.1:Download. Download the binary, source, and documentation zip files from the three separate links.

> **NOTE** Download Cairngorm 2.2.1, not Cairngorm Enterprise 2.2.1. (Cairngorm Enterprise is for LiveCycle Data Services.)

Unzip these files into their own folders. It doesn't matter where we put them, but the book assumes that we put them in the parent directory of the current directory (I use c:\peter\flexiblerails\current\pomodo for my development, so I downloaded the files to c:\peter\flexiblerails and unzipped them there).

8.1.4 Importing the Cairngorm sources into Flex Builder

Next, we'll import the Cairngorm project into Flex Builder so that we can easily browse it. (The zip file includes a Flex Builder .project file.) In Flex Builder, choose File > Import > Other. We see the dialog shown in figure 8.1.

Choose Existing Projects into Workspace, and click Next. In the Import dialog, browse to the Cairngorm2_2_1-src directory that was created when we unzipped the Cairngorm 2.2.1 sources. We know we found it when we see the Cairngorm project show up selected in the Projects list (see figure 8.2).

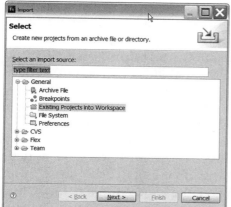

Figure 8.1 **Import dialog**

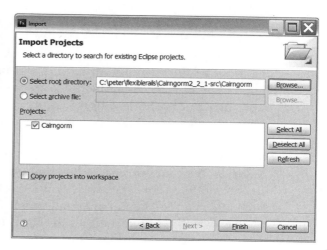

Figure 8.2 **Importing Cairngorm sources**

Click Finish to import the project. We're warned that an old version of Flex Builder was used to create this project. Leave Use Default SDK selected, and click OK. We see the dialog shown in figure 8.3.

Once the project is imported, we can expand it and open the ReleaseNotes.txt file. We can also browse the source code, starting by expanding the com folder.

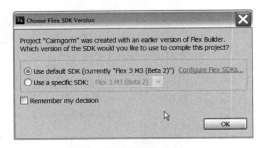

Figure 8.3   Choosing SDK for Cairngorm

There isn't much code, so you should read it all at some point.

8.1.5   Getting and running the ModifiedCairngormStore

NOTE   This subsection is optional. It's here because the ModifiedCairngorm-Store is a really good resource to start learning about Cairngorm.

Next, we'll download the ModifiedCairngormStore from Chen Bekor's blog at http://ntier.wordpress.com/2006/12/02/modified-cairngorm-store-uploaded/. Click on The File link (http://ntier.wordpress.com/files/2006/12/modified-cairngormstore.doc). After downloading, change the file extension to .zip from .doc, and unzip the zip file. Inside the ModifiedCairngormStore directory is a readme.txt file that contains simple instructions for getting the ModifiedCairngormStore running.

Because we're using Flex 3, we need to replace the Cairngorm.swc the ModifiedCairngormStore uses with the Cairngorm 2.2.1 swc. For me, this meant copying C:\peter\flexiblerails\Cairngorm2_2_1-bin\bin\Cairngorm.swc and pasting it into C:\peter\flexiblerails\modifiedcairngormstore\ModifiedCairngormStore\lib, replacing the 300+K file with this approximately 11K file. (The smaller file size is due to the fact that there is no longer a dependency on Flex Data Services (now LiveCycle Data Services) in the non-Enterprise version of Cairngorm.

Next, import the ModifiedCairngormStore into Flex Builder, using the same dialogs as the Cairngorm sources (the root directory I selected was C:\peter\flexiblerails\modifiedcairngormstore\ModifiedCairngormStore). Then, do a clean build and run the Main.mxml application. We see the screen shown in figure 8.4.

Play with the application a bit, selecting products, adding them to the cart, switching views, and checking out.

The ModifiedCairngormStore is the CairngormStore application that Steven Webster developed in his six-part article series, with a couple changes: It's

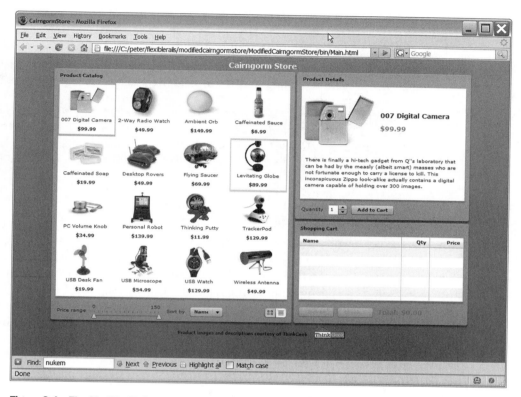

Figure 8.4   The ModifiedCairngormStore

updated to Flex 2 (and works in Flex 3) and Cairngorm 2.1 (and works with Cairngorm 2.2.1, as we just showed), and the LiveCycle Data Services calls are stubbed out with mocks. This way, we don't need to install LiveCycle Data Services and compile Java code to play with the CairngormStore. This fits our needs perfectly—we're using Rails instead of LiveCycle Data Services and Java, after all. This still lets us read and play with the code in conjunction with reading the articles. And because the code is current and the articles are outdated, this lets us see how Cairngorm has changed from version 0.99 to version 2.1.

Over the course of this iteration, pomodo will somewhat resemble the ModifiedCairngormStore, because they will both be Cairngorm applications—so if you want a sneak preview of where we're going, look at the ModifiedCairngormStore now. Also, note that ModifiedCairngormStore adheres closer to the standard way of using Cairngorm than we will.

> **Exercise for the ambitious reader**
>
> Modify the ModifiedCairngormStore to talk to a Rails backend instead of the mocks.
>   Start by copying and pasting the ModifiedCairngormStore directory, renaming it RailsCairngormStore.
>   Next, modify the .project file to rename the `<name>` element inside the `<projectDescription>` to be RailsCairngormStore instead of ModifiedCairngormStore. Then, import the RailsCairngormStore project into Flex Builder and go from there. You'll need to create a new Rails application with the `rails` command, and so on.

8.1.6 Adding Cairngorm to pomodo

Now that we've downloaded Cairngorm and played with an application that uses it, let's add Cairngorm to pomodo. We'll start by adding the Cairngorm SWC into the pomodo project. Create a directory called lib inside pomodo\app\flex, and paste the approximately 11K Cairngorm.swc file from the Cairngorm bin directory (for me, this was C:\peter\flexiblerails\Cairngorm2_2_1-bin\bin) into it. (We can also build Cairngorm from source, if we downloaded it ourselves. If you're doing this, you don't need my help: Do that, and then either paste the SWC or make the pomodo project depend on the Cairngorm one.)

   Next, right-click the pomodo project in the Navigator, and choose Properties. Choose the Flex Build Path and the Library Path tab. Click the Add SWC button to add the Cairngorm SWC to our library path. (We'll browse to the location of the Cairngorm.swc file inside our pomodo\app\flex\lib directory in our filesystem.) Once we do this, the dialog should look like figure 8.5.

   Click OK. We see the dialog shown in figure 8.6, which shows the Cairngorm SWC added to the Library path.

   Click OK. The Cairngorm classes now show up in Flex Builder. For example, open Pomodo.mxml, and type the following: `import com.adobe.cairngorm`. When we type the last period, we see a tooltip showing the Cairngorm classes. This convinces us that Flex Builder knows about them, so we have a reasonable expectation

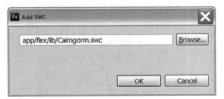

Figure 8.5 The Cairngorm.swc path (using UNIX path, even on Windows)

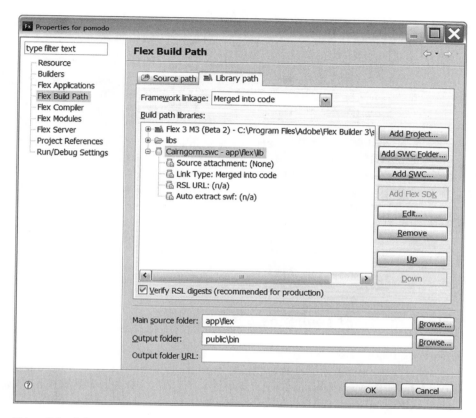

Figure 8.6 Cairngorm added to Flex Builder 3

of being able to compile and run once we start depending on Cairngorm. Now, close Pomodo.mxml without saving.

8.1.7   *Creating the standard directories*

The last setup task we'll do is to create *most* of the standard directories that are used in Cairngorm applications inside pomodo. Inside the app\flex\com\pomodo directory, create the following directories: business, command, control, and model.

Q. Didn't you forgot the `event` and `vo` packages?

A. No, I didn't forget them—I'm omitting them. We aren't going to create custom event subclasses of `CairngormEvent`—instead, we'll go against the officially recommended Cairngorm convention and dispatch plain `CairngormEvents` every time.

Q. Didn't you forgot the event and vo packages? *(continued)*

A. We'll set the data property to an anonymous object containing whatever we need. To me, the reduction in the amount of code is preferable to more type safety (especially on a smaller project such as this). On a larger project with lots of developers, the balance may be different.

Regarding creating a vo package for Value Objects,[6] we'll be using a proper object model in the next iteration—but as you'll see, we'll store those classes in the model folder. Adding an object model is something that should be done separately, especially if we want to do it properly. (We'll do this in the next iteration. Earlier versions of this book did this right away, but in a half-baked kind of way: The tasks had project_id and location_id instead of project and location references, and the projects and locations had no references to their tasks. I think it's more instructive and more in the spirit of refactoring to use XML in the first pass, because that's what we were using beforehand. We can—and do—refactor again afterward.)

8.2   *Cairngorm event sequence overview*

Before we begin, I'll present a brief overview of the typical sequence of events in how we'll use Cairngorm. It refers to a bunch of classes we haven't created yet but should help you understand what follows. (If it doesn't make sense now, don't worry—the goal isn't for it to completely make sense, but for it to make future sections make more sense when you read them):

1 A component (for example, TaskCreateBox) calls CairngormUtils.dispatchEvent with an event type specified in EventNames (which is a bunch of String constants).

2 Because of the PomodoController having called addCommand with that event type from EventNames, a command (for example, com.pomodo.command.CreateTaskCommand) has its execute method called.

3 This command creates a new *business delegate* (for example, com.pomodo.business.TaskDelegate), which contains functions related to a given Rails controller. It passes itself in as the IResponder so that when the

---

[6] Cairngorm uses the term *Value Object* instead of the term *Data Transfer Object (DTO)* or *Transfer Object (TO)* because it was conceived before those terms became popular. See http://www.adobe.com/devnet/flex/articles/cairngorm_pt2_print.html for details.

business delegate is done, the command's result or fault function will be invoked. Note that each `Delegate` corresponds to a Rails controller.

4 In typical Cairngorm applications, the business delegate retrieves services from a Services.mxml file and uses them. We don't do this. Instead, our business delegates themselves delegate all their work (a very businesslike thing to do) to the `ServiceUtils.send()` public static method. This method invokes a RESTful URL (with a _method of "PUT" or "DELETE" if necessary) that invokes the appropriate Rails controller action. It also attaches the responder to the service call, so that its result or fault handler will be triggered accordingly.

5 When the service call returns, the result or fault handler of the command is invoked accordingly. It does what it needs to do, such as making a state change in the `PomodoModelLocator`, dispatching another `CairngormEvent` with `CairngormUtils.dispatchEvent`, and so on.

That's about as much explanation up front as is useful. Let's see some code.

8.3 Creating com.pomodo.model.PomodoModelLocator

Let's start by creating the `PomodoModelLocator`, shown in listing 8.1. A standard Cairngorm application has one `ModelLocator`, which is a "single place where the application state is held."[7] This listing contains a lot of code; but much of it is cut and pasted from MainBox.mxml, so we can be selective in our explanation. Keep in mind that we're grabbing the state from all over the app and putting it here. The app will then bind to the variables in this file directly. This will save us from passing around a bunch of variables.

Listing 8.1 app\flex\com\pomodo\model\PomodoModelLocator.as

```
package com.pomodo.model {
    import com.adobe.cairngorm.model.IModelLocator;
    import com.pomodo.control.EventNames;
    import com.pomodo.util.CairngormUtils;
    import com.pomodo.util.XMLUtils;
    import com.pomodo.validators.ServerErrors;

    import mx.collections.ArrayCollection;
    import mx.collections.ICollectionView;
    import mx.collections.IViewCursor;
```

---

[7] http://www.adobe.com/devnet/flex/articles/cairngorm_pt2_print.html.

```
import mx.collections.XMLListCollection;

[Bindable]          ❶
public class PomodoModelLocator implements IModelLocator {          ❷
    public static const NO_PROJECT_XML:XML =
        <project>
            <name>- None -</name>
            <id type="integer">0</id>
        </project>;

    public static const NO_LOCATION_XML:XML =
        <location>
            <name>- None -</name>
            <id type="integer">0</id>
        </location>;

    public static const VIEWING_SPLASH_SCREEN:int = 0;          ❸
    public static const VIEWING_MAIN_APP:int = 1;

    public var user:XML;

    public var tasksXLC:XMLListCollection;

    public var projectIdMap:Object;

    public var locationIdMap:Object;

    public var projectsAndNoneXLC:XMLListCollection;

    public var locationsAndNoneXLC:XMLListCollection;

    public var accountCreateErrors:ServerErrors;

    public var workflowState:int = VIEWING_SPLASH_SCREEN;          ❹

    public var reviews:String =
    '"pomodo, the hot new RIA by 38noises, is taking ' +
    'over Web 2.0." --Michael Arrington*\n"I wish I\'d ' +
    'invested in 38noises instead of that other company."' +
    ' --Jeff Bezos*\n"38noises closed angel funding at a ' +
    'party in my bathroom last night." --Om Malik*';

    public function get projectsXLC():XMLListCollection {
        return _projectsXLC;
    }

    public function set projectsXLC(setValue:          ❺
    XMLListCollection):void {
        _projectsXLC = setValue;
        projectsAndNoneXLC =
            getProjectsAndNone(_projectsXLC.source);
```

```
        _gotProjects = true;
        projectIdMap = {};
        projectIdMap[0] = NO_PROJECT_XML;
        var projectsCursor:IViewCursor =
            projectsXLC.createCursor();
        while (!projectsCursor.afterLast) {
            var project:XML = XML(projectsCursor.current);
            projectIdMap[project.id] = project;
            projectsCursor.moveNext();
        }
        listTasksIfMapsPresent();          ❻
}

public function get locationsXLC():XMLListCollection {
    return _locationsXLC;
}

public function set locationsXLC(          ❼
    setValue:XMLListCollection):void
{
    _locationsXLC = setValue;
    locationsAndNoneXLC =
        getLocationsAndNone(locationsXLC.source);
    _gotLocations = true;
    locationIdMap = {};
    locationIdMap[0] = NO_LOCATION_XML;
    var locationsCursor:IViewCursor =
        locationsXLC.createCursor();
    while (!locationsCursor.afterLast) {
        var location:XML = XML(locationsCursor.current);
        locationIdMap[location.id] = location;
        locationsCursor.moveNext();
    }
    listTasksIfMapsPresent();          ❽
}

public function getProject(project_id:int):XML {          ❾
    if (projectIdMap == null) return null;
    return projectIdMap[project_id];
}

public function getLocation(location_id:int):XML {          ❿
    if (locationIdMap == null) return null;
    return locationIdMap[location_id];
}

private var _gotProjects:Boolean;

private var _gotLocations:Boolean;

private var _projectsAndNoneXLC:XMLListCollection;
```

```
private var _locationsAndNoneXLC:XMLListCollection;

private var _projectsXLC:XMLListCollection;

private var _locationsXLC:XMLListCollection;

private function getProjectsAndNone(projectsXL:XMLList):
XMLListCollection {
    var retval:XMLListCollection =
        new XMLListCollection(projectsXL.copy());
    retval.addItemAt(NO_PROJECT_XML, 0);
    return retval;
}

private function getLocationsAndNone(
locationsXL:XMLList):XMLListCollection {
    var retval:XMLListCollection =
        new XMLListCollection(locationsXL.copy());
    retval.addItemAt(NO_LOCATION_XML, 0);
    return retval;
}

private function listTasksIfMapsPresent():void {          ⑪
    if (_gotProjects && _gotLocations) {                 ⑫
        CairngormUtils.dispatchEvent(
            EventNames.LIST_TASKS);                      ⑬
    }
}

private static var modelLocator:PomodoModelLocator;      ⑭

public static function getInstance():PomodoModelLocator{  ⑮
    if (modelLocator == null) {
        modelLocator = new PomodoModelLocator();
    }
    return modelLocator;
}

public function PomodoModelLocator() {                   ⑯
    if (modelLocator != null) {
        throw new Error(
"Only one PomodoModelLocator instance may be instantiated.");
    }
    _gotProjects = false;
    _gotLocations = false;
    _projectsXLC = null;
    _locationsXLC = null;
    }
  }
}
```

The [Bindable] annotation ❶ on the class means that every public variable is bindable. Note that PomodoModelLocator implements com.adobe.cairn-gorm.model.IModelLocator ❷. IModelLocator is a marker interface: It has no methods. (It does, however, have a comment explaining that classes implementing it should be Singletons.) The PomodoModelLocator is a Singleton, so it creates a static modelLocator ❶ that is retrieved with the getInstance function ❶. Note that the Singleton pattern in ActionScript 3 is implemented in a cheesy way ❶, because constructors can't be private.

We create a new variable called workflowState, which is an int ❹. The work-flowState stores the state that the app is in. (Hazy memories of learning about Discrete Finite Automata float around the author's head.) For now, there are two states ❸: VIEWING_SPLASH_SCREEN (the initial state) and VIEWING_MAIN_APP (the state the app is in when a user logs in or a new user is created).

We create setters for projectsXLC ❺ and locationsXLC ❼. Both of these create their respective map between project/location ids and the projects/locations and then call ❻❽ listTasksIfMapsPresent ❶, which checks two flags ❶ to see if both the projects and locations have been retrieved, and if so dispatches an event ❶ to trigger the listing of tasks. (We'll look at CairngormUtils later, along with the classes that do the commands and service calls.)

> **NOTE** If working with XML and maps instead of an object model makes you cringe, note that you can build an object model instead—and we'll do so in the next iteration.

We also move the getProject ❾ and getLocation ❿ utility functions.

8.4 Creating com.pomodo.control.*

Next, we create the control package. It will contain two files: EventNames and PomodoController.

8.4.1 EventNames.as

First, we create EventNames.as; see listing 8.2. This isn't a standard Cairngorm class; instead, it's particular to our "no CairngormEvent subclasses" approach.

Listing 8.2 app\flex\com\pomodo\control\EventNames.as

```
package com.pomodo.control {
    public final class EventNames {
        public static const CREATE_LOCATION:String =
            "createLocation";
        public static const CREATE_PROJECT:String =
```

```
            "createProject";
        public static const CREATE_SESSION:String =
            "createSession";
        public static const CREATE_TASK:String = "createTask";
        public static const CREATE_USER:String = "createUser";

        public static const DESTROY_LOCATION:String =
            "destroyLocation";
        public static const DESTROY_PROJECT:String =
            "destroyProject";
        public static const DESTROY_TASK:String = "destroyTask";

        public static const LIST_LOCATIONS:String =
            "listLocations";
        public static const LIST_PROJECTS:String =
            "listProjects";
        public static const LIST_TASKS:String = "listTasks";

        public static const UPDATE_LOCATION:String =
            "updateLocation";
        public static const UPDATE_PROJECT:String =
            "updateProject";
        public static const UPDATE_TASK:String = "updateTask";
    }
}
```

This class lists all the event names, defining constants for each name. This ensures that we won't let a typo give us strange runtime behavior. I prefer this to using `Strings` everywhere for another reason, too: It makes it easier to check that we aren't using an event name that is already being used.

NOTE   We can pass `Strings` around without using constants—it's a question of "how much do you hate verbosity" versus "how much do you value safety". If we're totally concerned about safety, we create custom events for each event; if we totally hate verbosity, we skip this file. This approach is my compromise.

These event names will be associated with commands, as we'll see later.

8.4.2   *PomodoController.as*

Next, we create `PomodoController`, which extends `FrontController`; see listing 8.3. A standard Cairngorm application has one `FrontController` subclass, whose responsibility is to hook up the event names with the commands (which we'll see later). Typically, these event names come from the custom event subclasses; in our case, they come from `EventNames`.

Listing 8.3 app\flex\com\pomodo\control\PomodoController.as

```
package com.pomodo.control {
    import com.adobe.cairngorm.control.FrontController;
    import com.pomodo.control.EventNames;         ❶
    import com.pomodo.command.*;         ❷

    public class PomodoController extends FrontController {
        public function PomodoController() {
            initializeCommands();
        }

        private function initializeCommands():void {
            addCommand(EventNames.CREATE_LOCATION,         ❸
                CreateLocationCommand);
            addCommand(EventNames.CREATE_PROJECT,
                CreateProjectCommand);
            addCommand(EventNames.CREATE_SESSION,
                CreateSessionCommand);
            addCommand(EventNames.CREATE_TASK,
                CreateTaskCommand);
            addCommand(EventNames.CREATE_USER,
                CreateUserCommand);

            addCommand(EventNames.DESTROY_LOCATION,
                DestroyLocationCommand);
            addCommand(EventNames.DESTROY_PROJECT,
                DestroyProjectCommand);
            addCommand(EventNames.DESTROY_TASK,
                DestroyTaskCommand);

            addCommand(EventNames.LIST_LOCATIONS,
                ListLocationsCommand);
            addCommand(EventNames.LIST_PROJECTS,
                ListProjectsCommand);
            addCommand(EventNames.LIST_TASKS,
                ListTasksCommand);

            addCommand(EventNames.UPDATE_LOCATION,
                UpdateLocationCommand);
            addCommand(EventNames.UPDATE_PROJECT,
                UpdateProjectCommand);
            addCommand(EventNames.UPDATE_TASK,
                UpdateTaskCommand);
        }
    }
}
```

We import `EventNames` ❶ and all the commands ❷. (This is one case where the
`.*` import syntax is appropriate: We'll always need all the commands.) Finally, we
call the inherited `addCommand` method ❸ for each name + command combination. We'll see the commands soon.

8.5   Adding CairngormUtils and ServiceUtils
to com.pomodo.util.*

Next, we'll add two nonstandard classes that will simplify (without oversimplifying) how we use Cairngorm: `CairngormUtils` and `ServiceUtils`.

8.5.1   CairngormUtils.as

First, we'll create the `CairngormUtils` class; see listing 8.4. It isn't as necessary
now as it used to be (because `CairngormEvent` now has a `dispatch()` method, but
it still saves some typing, so we'll do it).

Listing 8.4   app\flex\com\pomodo\util\CairngormUtils.as

```
package com.pomodo.util {
    import com.adobe.cairngorm.control.CairngormEvent;
    import com.adobe.cairngorm.control.CairngormEventDispatcher;

    public class CairngormUtils {
        public static function dispatchEvent(          ❶
            eventName:String, data:Object = null):void    ❷
        {
            var event : CairngormEvent =
                new CairngormEvent(eventName);           ❸
            event.data = data;              ❹
            event.dispatch();             ❺
        }
    }
}
```

This class defines one public static function, `dispatchEvent` ❶. It takes ❷ a
required `eventName` parameter and an optional `data` parameter that defaults to
`null` if omitted. It creates a new `CairngormEvent` ❸ with the `type` set to the
`eventName`. It then sets ❹ the untyped `data` property to the `data` provided (or
`null` if omitted). Finally, it calls the event's `dispatch` method ❺, a relatively new
addition to Cairngorm that does the work of getting the shared instance of the
`CairngormEventDispatcher` for us.

We're going to use this method a *lot*.

8.5.2 *ServiceUtils.as*

Next, we create a nonstandard file called `ServiceUtils`, which contains one public static method called `send`. This method takes a bunch of parameters, all of which (except the URL) have sensible default values. (This is in line with the "convention over configuration" principle of Rails.) It then creates a disposable `HTTPService`, for use by this one call, properly configured with the URL and the various defaults.

> **NOTE**   This method lets us avoid using the standard Cairngorm approach of using a Services.mxml file that defines all the services. That approach is problematic when we use `HTTPService` with Rails, because hardly any properties of a given `HTTPService` remain constant between service invocations. Worse, if we don't explicitly set the properties to the values we want (even those where we want the default value), we can have unexpected behavior because the properties that a *previous* use of the `HTTP-Service` set will remain set that way. For example, we can have the wrong `contentType`, `resultFormat`, and so on if we (or some maintenance programmer) are careless. The disposable `HTTPService` approach we use here is a lot less bug-prone.

Without further ado, let's look at the code; see listing 8.5.

Listing 8.5   app\flex\com\pomodo\util\ServiceUtils.as

```
package com.pomodo.util {
    import mx.rpc.IResponder;
    import mx.rpc.AsyncToken;
    import mx.rpc.http.HTTPService;

    public class ServiceUtils {
        public static function send(
            url:String,            ❶
            responder:IResponder = null,        ❷
            request:Object = null,       ❸
            sendXML:Boolean = false,        ❹
            resultFormat:String = "e4x",      ❺
            method:String = null,      ❻
            useProxy:Boolean = false):void      ❼
        {
            var service:HTTPService = new HTTPService();      ❽
            service.url = url;
            service.request = request;
            service.contentType = sendXML ? "application/xml" :
                "application/x-www-form-urlencoded";
            service.resultFormat = resultFormat;
            if (method == null) {
```

```
                service.method = (request == null) ?
                    "GET" : "POST";          ⑨
            } else {
                service.method = method;      ⑩
            }
            service.useProxy = useProxy;
            var call:AsyncToken = service.send();   ⑪
            if (responder != null) {
                call.addResponder(responder);   ⑫
            }
        }
    }
}
```

The send method is currently hard-coded to use HTTPService, but this could be
refactored later if necessary. The parameters are as shown in table 8.1.

Table 8.1   Parameters to the ServiceUtils.send function

#	Parameter	Type	Default	Description
❶	url	String	N/A	This is the URL of the HTTPService. The url specifies the controller and action, regardless of whether RESTful controllers are being used.
❷	responder	IResponder	null	The delegate (such as the TaskDelegate) stores a reference to a responder, and the commands (such as the CreateTaskCommand) pass themselves to the delegate when creating it. The delegates call this method and pass it the_responder. If, for some strange reason, a responder isn't needed for a service call, this parameter can be omitted and no responder will be added.
❸	request	Object	null	This is the HTTPService request object. It's typed as Object so it can be anything (XML, an anonymous object created using { } syntax, and so on).
❹	sendXML	Boolean	false	This is a flag that sets the contentType to application/xml if true or to application/x-www-form-urlencoded if false.
❺	resultFormat	String	"e4x"	The result format is usually e4x, a nice way to handle XML.

Table 8.1 Parameters to the ServiceUtils.send function *(continued)*

#	Parameter	Type	Default	Description
6	method	String	null	This is the HTTP method of the `HTTPService`. If no method is specified, then it defaults to a `GET` if the request is null **9** or to a POST if the request is non-null **10**. Convention over configuration!
7	useProxy	Boolean	false	This is always false in this book.

Because most of the parameters have sensible default values, the typical call is short. (Hooray for convention over configuration!)

In the method, a new `HTTPService` called `service` is created **8** every time the method is called. The parameter values are set on the service, and then the `service.send()` call is made **11**. The responder is added to the `AsyncToken` returned by the `send()` call **12** so the responder methods can be invoked.

8.6   Creating com.pomodo.command.*

Next, we'll create all the commands.

8.6.1   CreateTaskCommand.as

First, the `CreateTaskCommand`; see listing 8.6.

Listing 8.6   app\flex\com\pomodo\command\CreateTaskCommand.as

```
package com.pomodo.command {
    import com.adobe.cairngorm.commands.ICommand;
    import com.adobe.cairngorm.control.CairngormEvent;
    import com.pomodo.business.TaskDelegate;
    import com.pomodo.control.EventNames;
    import com.pomodo.util.CairngormUtils;

    import mx.rpc.IResponder;
    import mx.rpc.events.FaultEvent;
    import mx.rpc.events.ResultEvent;

    public class CreateTaskCommand implements ICommand,
    IResponder {                    ❶
        public function CreateTaskCommand() {
        }

        public function execute(event:CairngormEvent):void {    ❷
            var delegate:TaskDelegate = new TaskDelegate(this);   ❸
```

```
                    delegate.createTask(event.data);        ❹
            }

            public function result(event:Object):void {      ❺
                CairngormUtils.dispatchEvent(EventNames.LIST_TASKS);      ❻
            }

            public function fault(event:Object):void {      ❼
                Pomodo.debug("CreateTaskCommand#fault: " + event);      ❽
            }
        }
    }
```

The `CreateTaskCommand`, like all the commands, implements the `com.adobe.cairngorm.commands.ICommand` and `mx.rpc.IResponder` interfaces ❶. The `ICommand` interface specifies exactly one function:

```
function execute( event : CairngormEvent ) : void;
```

As its comment states, the `execute` function is called by the `FrontController` (the `PomodoController` in our case) to execute the command.

Whereas the `ICommand` interface is Cairngorm-specific, the `IResponder` interface is part of standard Flex. It specifies two methods: `fault` (for error return) and `result` (for successful return).

Back to the `CreateTaskCommand`. In its `execute` method ❷, it creates a new `TaskDelegate` ❸, passing itself as the responder in the `this` parameter to the constructor. Next, it calls its `createTask` method ❹ with the `event.data`, which is the task XML.

NOTE The commands pass themselves to the `Delegates` as the `IResponders`, so that the `Delegates` can then call the result or fault functions accordingly.

Upon a successful return ❺ that is invoked by the `Delegate`, it uses our `CairngormUtils` class to dispatch ❻ a `CairngormEvent` whose type is `EventNames.LIST_TASKS`. This causes the `ListTasksCommand` to be executed, because we associated it with `addCommand` earlier.

If a fault happens ❼, we write a debug message ❽. Proper error handling makes for boring reading.

8.6.2   *CreateProjectCommand.as*

Next, we create the `CreateProjectCommand` as a copy-paste-modify of `CreateTaskCommand`; see listing 8.7.

Listing 8.7 app\flex\com\pomodo\command\CreateProjectCommand.as

```
package com.pomodo.command {
    import com.adobe.cairngorm.commands.ICommand;
    import com.adobe.cairngorm.control.CairngormEvent;
    import com.pomodo.business.ProjectDelegate;
    import com.pomodo.model.PomodoModelLocator;
    import com.pomodo.control.EventNames;
    import com.pomodo.util.CairngormUtils;

    import mx.rpc.IResponder;
    import mx.rpc.events.FaultEvent;
    import mx.rpc.events.ResultEvent;

    public class CreateProjectCommand implements ICommand,  ❶
    IResponder {
        public function CreateProjectCommand() {
        }

        public function execute(event:CairngormEvent):void {  ❷
            var delegate:ProjectDelegate =     ❸
                new ProjectDelegate(this);
            delegate.createProject(event.data);   ❹
        }

        public function result(event:Object):void {   ❺
            CairngormUtils.dispatchEvent(
                EventNames.LIST_PROJECTS);    ❻
        }

        public function fault(event:Object):void {   ❼
            Pomodo.debug("CreateProjectCommand#fault: " +
                event);    ❽
        }
    }
}
```

The `CreateProjectCommand` is, like all the commands, an `ICommand` and an `IResponder` ❶. In its `execute` method ❷, it creates a new `ProjectDelegate` ❸ and calls its `createProject` method ❹ with the `event.data`, which is the project XML.

Upon a successful return ❺, it uses our `CairngormUtils` class to dispatch ❻ a `CairngormEvent` whose type is `EventNames.LIST_PROJECTS`. This will cause the `ListProjectsCommand` to be executed, because we associated them with `addCommand` in the `PomodoController` section earlier.

If a fault happens ❼, we write a debug message ❽.

(Just as the code is a copy-paste-modify, so is the explanation.)

8.6.3 *CreateLocationCommand.as*

Next, we create the `CreateLocationCommand` as a copy-paste-modify of `Create-TaskCommand`; see listing 8.8.

```
package com.pomodo.command {
    import com.adobe.cairngorm.commands.ICommand;
    import com.adobe.cairngorm.control.CairngormEvent;
    import com.pomodo.business.LocationDelegate;
    import com.pomodo.control.EventNames;
    import com.pomodo.util.CairngormUtils;

    import mx.rpc.IResponder;
    import mx.rpc.events.FaultEvent;
    import mx.rpc.events.ResultEvent;

    public class CreateLocationCommand implements ICommand,
    IResponder {
        public function CreateLocationCommand() {
        }

        public function execute(event:CairngormEvent):void {
            var delegate:LocationDelegate =
                new LocationDelegate(this);
            delegate.createLocation(event.data);
        }

        public function result(event:Object):void {
            CairngormUtils.dispatchEvent(
                EventNames.LIST_LOCATIONS);
        }

        public function fault(event:Object):void {
            Pomodo.debug("CreateLocationCommand#fault: " +
                event);
        }
    }
}
```

8.6.4 *CreateSessionCommand.as*

The `CreateSessionCommand` is used to log in. I called it `CreateSessionCommand` instead of `LoginCommand` so that the Flex side uses the same terminology as the Rails side; see listing 8.9.

Listing 8.9 app\flex\com\pomodo\command\CreateSessionCommand.as

```
package com.pomodo.command {
    import com.adobe.cairngorm.commands.ICommand;
    import com.adobe.cairngorm.control.CairngormEvent;
    import com.pomodo.business.SessionDelegate;
    import com.pomodo.business.TaskDelegate;
    import com.pomodo.model.PomodoModelLocator;

    import mx.controls.Alert;
    import mx.rpc.IResponder;
    import mx.rpc.events.FaultEvent;
    import mx.rpc.events.ResultEvent;

    public class CreateSessionCommand implements ICommand,
    IResponder {
        public function CreateSessionCommand() {
        }

        public function execute(event:CairngormEvent):void {      ❶
            var delegate:SessionDelegate =                        ❷
                new SessionDelegate(this);
            delegate.createSession(event.data.login,              ❸
                event.data.password);
        }

        public function result(event:Object):void {              ❹
            var result:Object = event.result;
            if (event.result == "badlogin") {                     ❺
                Alert.show("Login failed.");
            } else {
                var model:PomodoModelLocator =                    ❻
                    PomodoModelLocator.getInstance();
                model.user = XML(event.result);                   ❼
                model.workflowState =              ❽
                    PomodoModelLocator.VIEWING_MAIN_APP;
            }
        }

        public function fault(event:Object):void {               ❾
            Pomodo.debug("CreateSessionCommand#fault: " +
                event);
            Alert.show("Login Failed", "Error");
        }
    }
}
```

The execute ❶ method creates a new `SessionDelegate` ❷ and calls its `create-Session` method ❸ with the login and password stored in the event data property (which is an anonymous `Object` that functions as a hash).

Upon a successful (by successful, I mean "non-fault") result ❹, the `Create-SessionCommand` shows an alert if a `badlogin` happened ❺. If a good login happened (or at least a non-badlogin), the shared `PomodoModelLocator` instance is retrieved ❻ and stored in the `model` variable. The `event.result` is then cast to XML and stored in the `model.user` variable ❼. Next, the `workflowState` is set ❽, which triggers the `MainBox` to show (as we'll see later).

Finally, we show an alert if a fault ❾ happens.

8.6.5 *CreateUserCommand.as*

The `CreateUserCommand` creates a new user account; see listing 8.10.

Listing 8.10 app\flex\com\pomodo\command\CreateUserCommand.as

```
package com.pomodo.command {
    import com.adobe.cairngorm.commands.ICommand;
    import com.adobe.cairngorm.control.CairngormEvent;
    import com.pomodo.business.UserDelegate;
    import com.pomodo.model.PomodoModelLocator;
    import com.pomodo.validators.ServerErrors;

    import mx.controls.Alert;
    import mx.rpc.IResponder;
    import mx.rpc.events.FaultEvent;
    import mx.rpc.events.ResultEvent;

    public class CreateUserCommand implements ICommand,
    IResponder {
        public function CreateUserCommand() {
        }

        public function execute(event:CairngormEvent):void {        ❶
            var delegate:UserDelegate = new UserDelegate(this);      ❷
            delegate.createUser(event.data);                ❸
        }

        public function result(event:Object):void {        ❹
            var result:Object = event.result;
            var model:PomodoModelLocator =
                PomodoModelLocator.getInstance();
            if (result == "error") {        ❺
                Alert.show(
"There was an error creating your account. Please try again later.",
"Account Not Created");
            } else {
```

```
                    var resultXML:XML = XML(result);        ❻
                    if (resultXML.name().localName == "errors") {        ❼
                        Alert.show(
"Please correct the validation errors highlighted on the form.",
"Account Not Created");
                        model.accountCreateErrors =
                            new ServerErrors(resultXML);
                    } else {        ❽
                        model.user = resultXML;        ❾
                        model.workflowState =        ❿
                            PomodoModelLocator.VIEWING_MAIN_APP;
                    }
                }
            }

            public function fault(event:Object):void {
                Pomodo.debug("CreateUserCommand#fault: " + event);
                Alert.show("Account Not Created", "Error");
            }
        }
    }
```

The `CreateUserCommand` execute method ❶ starts typically, creating a new `User-Delegate` ❷ and calling its `createUser` method ❸.

Upon successful return ❹, it checks whether the result is "error" ❺ and, if so, it shows an Alert. If it's not "error", the result is cast to XML (since we're using e4x this is safe) ❻. If this XML is a bunch of errors ❼, we show an Alert and do the tedious error handling; if it's not a bunch of errors ❽ we assume it's a new user ❾, assign it to the `model.user` property ❾, and set the `workflow-State` ❿, which triggers the `MainBox` to show (as we'll see later).

8.6.6   *UpdateTaskCommand.as*

Now that we're done with creation, it's on to update. First, `UpdateTaskCommand`; see listing 8.11.

Listing 8.11   app\flex\com\pomodo\command\UpdateTaskCommand.as

```
package com.pomodo.command {
    import com.adobe.cairngorm.commands.ICommand;
    import com.adobe.cairngorm.control.CairngormEvent;
    import com.pomodo.business.TaskDelegate;
    import com.pomodo.model.PomodoModelLocator;

    import mx.rpc.IResponder;
    import mx.rpc.events.FaultEvent;
    import mx.rpc.events.ResultEvent;
```

```
public class UpdateTaskCommand implements ICommand,
IResponder {
    public function UpdateTaskCommand() {
    }

    public function execute(event:CairngormEvent):void {
        var delegate:TaskDelegate = new TaskDelegate(this);     ❶
        delegate.updateTask(        ❷
            event.data.taskID,
            event.data.keys,
            event.data.values);
    }

    public function result(event:Object):void {        ❸
        var resultEvent:ResultEvent = ResultEvent(event);
        var model:PomodoModelLocator =       ❹
            PomodoModelLocator.getInstance();
        var newTask:XML = XML(event.result);      ❺
        for (var i:int = 0; i < model.tasksXLC.length; i++)      ❻
        {
            var ithTask:XML =
                XML(model.tasksXLC.getItemAt(i));      ❼
            if (ithTask.id == newTask.id) {
                model.tasksXLC.setItemAt(newTask, i);
                break;
            }
        }
    }

    public function fault(event:Object):void {
        Pomodo.debug("UpdateTaskCommand#fault: " + event);
    }
}
```

The execute function creates a new TaskDelegate ❶ and calls its updateTask ❷ function. (The source of the taskID, keys, and values will be explained more later.) The result ❸ handler gets the shared PomodoModelLocator ❹ and casts the event.result to XML and stores it in a local newTask variable ❺. It then searches through the tasksXLC XMLListCollection ❻ in the model, looking for the task with the same id we updated. When it finds the task (I say *when*, not *if*, because we're being lax about error-handling here too), it replaces that item in the tasksXLC with the updated item ❼.

8.6.7 *UpdateProjectCommand.as*

Next, the UpdateProjectCommand; see listing 8.12.

Listing 8.12 app\flex\com\pomodo\command\UpdateProjectCommand.as

```
package com.pomodo.command {
    import com.adobe.cairngorm.commands.ICommand;
    import com.adobe.cairngorm.control.CairngormEvent;
    import com.pomodo.business.ProjectDelegate;
    import com.pomodo.control.EventNames;
    import com.pomodo.model.PomodoModelLocator;
    import com.pomodo.util.CairngormUtils;

    import mx.rpc.IResponder;
    import mx.rpc.events.FaultEvent;
    import mx.rpc.events.ResultEvent;

    public class UpdateProjectCommand implements ICommand,
    IResponder {
        public function UpdateProjectCommand() {
        }

        public function execute(event:CairngormEvent):void {
            var delegate:ProjectDelegate =              ❶
                new ProjectDelegate(this);
            delegate.updateProject(                     ❷
                event.data.projectID,
                event.data.keys,
                event.data.values);
        }

        public function result(event:Object):void {
            CairngormUtils.dispatchEvent(
                EventNames.LIST_PROJECTS);              ❸
        }

        public function fault(event:Object):void {
            Pomodo.debug("UpdateProjectCommand#fault: " +
                event);
        }
    }
}
```

The execute function creates a new ProjectDelegate ❶ and calls its updateProject ❷ function. (The source of the projectID, keys, and values will be explained more later.) The result ❸ handler dispatches an event using our handy CairngormUtils class that causes projects to be listed. This is simpler but lower performance than what we did for tasks.

8.6.8 *UpdateLocationCommand.as*

Next, the UpdateLocationCommand; see listing 8.13.

Listing 8.13 app\flex\com\pomodo\command\UpdateLocationCommand.as

```
package com.pomodo.command {
    import com.adobe.cairngorm.commands.ICommand;
    import com.adobe.cairngorm.control.CairngormEvent;
    import com.pomodo.business.LocationDelegate;
    import com.pomodo.control.EventNames;
    import com.pomodo.model.PomodoModelLocator;
    import com.pomodo.util.CairngormUtils;

    import mx.rpc.IResponder;
    import mx.rpc.events.FaultEvent;
    import mx.rpc.events.ResultEvent;

    public class UpdateLocationCommand implements ICommand,
    IResponder {
        public function UpdateLocationCommand() {
        }

        public function execute(event:CairngormEvent):void {      ❶
            var delegate:LocationDelegate =           ❷
                new LocationDelegate(this);
            delegate.updateLocation(
                event.data.locationID,
                event.data.keys,
                event.data.values);
        }

        public function result(event:Object):void {
            CairngormUtils.dispatchEvent(
                EventNames.LIST_LOCATIONS);           ❸
        }

        public function fault(event:Object):void {
            Pomodo.debug("UpdateLocationCommand#fault: " +
                event);
        }
    }
}
```

(This code is obviously a copy-paste-modify of UpdateProjectCommand.) The execute function creates a new LocationDelegate ❶ and calls its updateLocation ❷ function. (The source of the locationID, keys, and values will be explained more later.) The result ❸ handler dispatches an event using our handy CairngormUtils class that causes locations to be listed.

8.6.9 *DestroyTaskCommand.as*

Now that update is done, on to destroy; see listing 8.14.

```
package com.pomodo.command {
    import com.adobe.cairngorm.commands.ICommand;
    import com.adobe.cairngorm.control.CairngormEvent;
    import com.pomodo.business.TaskDelegate;
    import com.pomodo.control.EventNames;
    import com.pomodo.model.PomodoModelLocator;
    import com.pomodo.util.CairngormUtils;

    import mx.controls.Alert;
    import mx.rpc.IResponder;
    import mx.rpc.events.FaultEvent;
    import mx.rpc.events.ResultEvent;

    public class DestroyTaskCommand implements ICommand,
    IResponder {
        public function DestroyTaskCommand() {
        }

        public function execute(event:CairngormEvent):void {      ❶
            var delegate:TaskDelegate = new TaskDelegate(this);   ❷
            delegate.destroyTask(event.data);       ❸
        }

        public function result(event:Object):void {
            var resultEvent:ResultEvent = ResultEvent(event);
            var model:PomodoModelLocator =
                PomodoModelLocator.getInstance();
            if (event.result == "error") {
                Alert.show(
                    "The task was not successfully deleted.",
                    "Error");
            } else {
                var deletedTask:XML = XML(event.result);      ❹
                var deletedTaskId:int = deletedTask.id;
                for (var i:int = 0; i < model.tasksXLC.length;
                    i++)
                {
                    var ithTask:XML =
                        XML(model.tasksXLC.getItemAt(i));
                    if (ithTask.id == deletedTaskId) {
                        model.tasksXLC.removeItemAt(i);
                        break;
                    }
                }
            }
        }
```

```
        }

        public function fault(event:Object):void {
            Pomodo.debug("DestroyTaskCommand#fault: " + event);
            Alert.show("The task was not successfully deleted.",
                "Error");
        }
    }
}
```

The `DestroyTaskCommand` execute method ❶ creates a new `TaskDelegate` ❷ and calls its `destroyTask` method ❸. Upon successful return ❹, it loops through the `tasksXLC` in the model until it finds the task XML with the matching id and removes it.

8.6.10 *DestroyProjectCommand.as*

Next, we destroy a project; see listing 8.15.

Listing 8.15   app\flex\com\pomodo\command\DestroyProjectCommand.as

```
package com.pomodo.command {
    import com.adobe.cairngorm.commands.ICommand;
    import com.adobe.cairngorm.control.CairngormEvent;
    import com.pomodo.business.ProjectDelegate;
    import com.pomodo.model.PomodoModelLocator;
    import com.pomodo.control.EventNames;
    import com.pomodo.util.CairngormUtils;

    import mx.rpc.IResponder;
    import mx.rpc.events.FaultEvent;
    import mx.rpc.events.ResultEvent;

    public class DestroyProjectCommand implements ICommand,
    IResponder {
        public function DestroyProjectCommand() {
        }

        public function execute(event:CairngormEvent):void {    ❶
            var delegate:ProjectDelegate =            ❷
                new ProjectDelegate(this);
            delegate.destroyProject(event.data);        ❸
        }

        public function result(event:Object):void {
            CairngormUtils.dispatchEvent(
                EventNames.LIST_PROJECTS);        ❹
        }
```

```
        public function fault(event:Object):void {
            Pomodo.debug("DestroyProjectCommand#fault: " +
                event);
        }
    }
}
```

The `DestroyProjectCommand` execute method ❶ creates a new `ProjectDelegate` ❷ and calls its `destroyProject` method ❸. Upon successful return ❹, it dispatches an event ❹ using our handy `CairngormUtils` class that causes projects to be listed. This is simpler but lower performance than what we did for tasks.

8.6.11 *DestroyLocationCommand.as*

Next, we destroy a location the same way as a project; see listing 8.16.

Listing 8.16 app\flex\com\pomodo\command\DestroyLocationCommand.as

```
package com.pomodo.command {
    import com.adobe.cairngorm.commands.ICommand;
    import com.adobe.cairngorm.control.CairngormEvent;
    import com.pomodo.business.LocationDelegate;
    import com.pomodo.model.PomodoModelLocator;
    import com.pomodo.control.EventNames;
    import com.pomodo.util.CairngormUtils;

    import mx.rpc.IResponder;
    import mx.rpc.events.FaultEvent;
    import mx.rpc.events.ResultEvent;

    public class DestroyLocationCommand implements ICommand,
    IResponder {
        public function DestroyLocationCommand() {
        }

        public function execute(event:CairngormEvent):void {
            var delegate:LocationDelegate =
                new LocationDelegate(this);
            delegate.destroyLocation(event.data);
        }

        public function result(event:Object):void {
            CairngormUtils.dispatchEvent(
                EventNames.LIST_LOCATIONS);
        }

        public function fault(event:Object):void {
            Pomodo.debug("DestroyLocationCommand#fault: " +
```

```
                                   event);
                     }
              }
       }
```

8.6.12 ListTasksCommand.as

Now, on to listing tasks; see listing 8.17.

Listing 8.17   app\flex\com\pomodo\command\ListTasksCommand.as

```
package com.pomodo.command {
    import com.adobe.cairngorm.commands.ICommand;
    import com.adobe.cairngorm.control.CairngormEvent;
    import com.pomodo.business.TaskDelegate;
    import com.pomodo.model.PomodoModelLocator;

    import mx.controls.Alert;
    import mx.rpc.IResponder;
    import mx.rpc.events.FaultEvent;
    import mx.rpc.events.ResultEvent;
    import mx.collections.XMLListCollection;

    public class ListTasksCommand implements ICommand,
    IResponder {
        public function ListTasksCommand() {
        }

        public function execute(event:CairngormEvent):void {      ❶
            var delegate:TaskDelegate = new TaskDelegate(this);
            delegate.listTasks();
        }

        public function result(event:Object):void {
            var model:PomodoModelLocator =
                PomodoModelLocator.getInstance();
            model.tasksXLC = new XMLListCollection(          ❷
                XMLList(event.result.children()));
        }

        public function fault(event:Object):void {
            Pomodo.debug("ListTasksCommand#fault: " + event);
            Alert.show("Tasks could not be retrieved!");
        }
    }
}
```

The execute function ❶ constructs a new TaskDelegate and calls its listTasks function. The successful result handler extracts the XMLList we get, builds an XMLListCollection out of it, and assigns it to model.tasksXLC ❷.

8.6.13 *ListProjectsCommand.as*

Next, we list projects in essentially the same way as tasks, calling the listProjects function of a ProjectDelegate ❶ and assigning the projectsXLC ❷ in the model as a result; see listing 8.18.

Listing 8.18   app\flex\com\pomodo\command\ListProjectsCommand.as

```
package com.pomodo.command {
    import com.adobe.cairngorm.commands.ICommand;
    import com.adobe.cairngorm.control.CairngormEvent;
    import com.pomodo.business.ProjectDelegate;
    import com.pomodo.model.PomodoModelLocator;

    import mx.controls.Alert;
    import mx.rpc.IResponder;
    import mx.rpc.events.FaultEvent;
    import mx.rpc.events.ResultEvent;
    import mx.collections.XMLListCollection;

    public class ListProjectsCommand implements ICommand,
    IResponder {
        public function ListProjectsCommand() {
        }

        public function execute(event:CairngormEvent):void {
            var delegate:ProjectDelegate =
                new ProjectDelegate(this);
            delegate.listProjects();          ❶
        }

        public function result(event:Object):void {
            var model:PomodoModelLocator =
                PomodoModelLocator.getInstance();
            model.projectsXLC = new XMLListCollection(     ❷
                XMLList(event.result.children()));
        }

        public function fault(event:Object):void {
            Pomodo.debug("ListProjectsCommand#fault: " + event);
            Alert.show("Projects could not be retrieved!");
        }
    }
}
```

8.6.14 ListLocationsCommand.as

The `ListLocationsCommand` is a copy-paste-modify as well; see listing 8.18.

Listing 8.19   app\flex\com\pomodo\command\ListLocationsCommand.as

```
package com.pomodo.command {
    import com.adobe.cairngorm.commands.ICommand;
    import com.adobe.cairngorm.control.CairngormEvent;
    import com.pomodo.business.LocationDelegate;
    import com.pomodo.model.PomodoModelLocator;

    import mx.controls.Alert;
    import mx.rpc.IResponder;
    import mx.rpc.events.FaultEvent;
    import mx.rpc.events.ResultEvent;
    import mx.collections.XMLListCollection;

    public class ListLocationsCommand implements ICommand,
    IResponder {
        public function ListLocationsCommand() {
        }

        public function execute(event:CairngormEvent):void {
            var delegate:LocationDelegate =
                new LocationDelegate(this);
            delegate.listLocations();
        }

        public function result(event:Object):void {
            var model:PomodoModelLocator =
                PomodoModelLocator.getInstance();
            model.locationsXLC = new XMLListCollection(
                XMLList(event.result.children()));
        }

        public function fault(event:Object):void {
            Pomodo.debug("ListLocationsCommand#fault: " + event);
            Alert.show("Locations could not be retrieved!");
        }
    }
}
```

Phew.

8.7 Creating com.pomodo.business.*

In this section, we'll create the business delegates that we've been using in the commands. (It's possible to use services in the commands, but standard Cairngorm practice is to create business delegates—and we've been defying enough conventions that we may as well stick with this one because [theoretically, anyway] it promotes code reuse.)

This is the section that will start to tie together the work done in the previous sections. If the previous sections have left you wondering why we're doing all this, it should start to become clear momentarily (and should fully become clear when we modify the components).

8.7.1 TaskDelegate.as

The TaskDelegate contains the functions that do the real work for tasks; see listing 8.20. They do this by invoking ServiceUtils.send, which is the real workhorse of our modified Cairngorm design.

Listing 8.20   app\flex\com\pomodo\business\TaskDelegate.as

```
package com.pomodo.business {
    import mx.rpc.IResponder;
    import com.pomodo.util.ServiceUtils;

    public class TaskDelegate {
        private var _responder:IResponder;            ❶

        public function TaskDelegate(responder:IResponder) {     ❷
            _responder = responder;        ❸
        }

        public function listTasks():void {        ❹
            ServiceUtils.send("/tasks.xml", _responder);      ❺
        }

        public function createTask(task:XML):void {      ❻
            ServiceUtils.send("/tasks.xml", _responder, task,
                true);      ❼
        }

        public function updateTask(taskID:int, keys:Array,      ❽
            values:Array):void
        {
            var params:Object = new Object();      ❾
            for (var i:int = 0; i < keys.length; i++) {     ❿
                params['task[' + keys[i] +']'] = values[i];     ⓫
            }
```

```
              params['_method'] = "PUT"; ⑫
              ServiceUtils.send( ⑬
                  "/tasks/" + taskID + ".xml", ⑭
                  _responder, ⑮
                  params); ⑯
          }

          public function destroyTask(taskID:int):void { ⑰
              ServiceUtils.send( ⑱
                  "/tasks/" + taskID + ".xml", ⑲
                  _responder, ⑳
                  {_method: "DELETE"}); ㉑
          }
       }
   }
```

The `TaskDelegate` contains an `IResponder` ❶ called _responder, which is a parameter to its constructor ❷ and is stored there ❸. This _responder is whatever `Command` is using the `Delegate`. Specifically, it's the following:

- The `CreateTaskCommand` that constructs a `TaskDelegate` and calls its createTask function ❻
- The `UpdateTaskCommand` that constructs a `TaskDelegate` and calls its updateTask function ❽
- The `DestroyTaskCommand` that constructs a `TaskDelegate` and calls its destroyTask function ⑰
- The `ListTasksCommand` that constructs a `TaskDelegate` and calls its listTasks function ❹

Note that the _responder is passed to all these calls ⑮⑳, so that `ServiceUtils` can add it as a responder to the service call. Also, note the use of an anonymous `Object` ❾, which will serve as an update object by having specially constructed keys ⑪ created for each key ⑩.

Note that all four of these functions specify ❺❼⑭⑲) RESTful URLs as parameters to the `ServiceUtils.send()` ⑬⑱ method. Also note that the _method parameter can be set to PUT ⑫ or DELETE ㉑ in the params ⑯.

> **TIP** Now might be a good time to re-read the `ServiceUtils` class, if its purpose wasn't totally clear the first time.

8.7.2 *ProjectDelegate.as*

The `ProjectDelegate`, a copy-paste-modify of `TaskDelegate`, contains the functions that do the real work for projects; see listing 8.21.

Listing 8.21   app\flex\com\pomodo\business\ProjectDelegate.as

```
package com.pomodo.business {
    import mx.rpc.IResponder;
    import com.pomodo.util.ServiceUtils;

    public class ProjectDelegate {
        private var _responder:IResponder;          ❶

        public function ProjectDelegate(responder:IResponder) {
            _responder = responder;          ❷
        }

        public function listProjects():void {          ❸
            ServiceUtils.send("/projects.xml", _responder);
        }

        public function createProject(project:XML):void {          ❹
            ServiceUtils.send("/projects.xml", _responder,
                project, true);
        }

        public function updateProject(          ❺
            projectID:int,
            keys: Array,
            values: Array):void
        {
            var params:Object = new Object();
            for (var i:int = 0; i < keys.length; i++) {
                params['project[' + keys[i] +']'] = values[i];
            }
            params['_method'] = "PUT";
            ServiceUtils.send(
                "/projects/" + projectID + ".xml",
                _responder,
                params);
        }

        public function destroyProject(projectID:int):void {          ❻
            ServiceUtils.send(
                "/projects/" + projectID + ".xml",
                _responder,
                {_method: "DELETE"});
        }
    }
}
```

It sets ❷ the _responder ❶ (which is the command that invoked it), and uses
ServiceUtils to list ❸, create ❹, update ❺, and destroy ❻ projects. Note

that the _responder is passed to all these calls, so that ServiceUtils can add it as a responder to the service call. This _responder is whatever Command is using the Delegate. Specifically, it's the following:

- The CreateProjectCommand that constructs a ProjectDelegate and calls its createProject function ❹
- The UpdateProjectCommand that constructs a ProjectDelegate and calls its updateProject function ❺
- The DestroyProjectCommand that constructs a ProjectDelegate and calls its destroyProject function ❻
- The ListProjectsCommand that constructs a ProjectDelegate and calls its listProjects function ❹

8.7.3 *LocationDelegate.as*

Next, we create the LocationDelegate, also a copy-paste-modify of TaskDelegate; see listing 8.22. It contains the functions that do the real work for locations.

> **Listing 8.22   app\flex\com\pomodo\business\LocationDelegate.as**

```
package com.pomodo.business {
    import mx.rpc.IResponder;
    import com.pomodo.util.ServiceUtils;

    public class LocationDelegate {
        private var _responder:IResponder;

        public function LocationDelegate(responder:IResponder) {
            _responder = responder;
        }

        public function listLocations():void {
            ServiceUtils.send("/locations.xml", _responder);
        }

        public function createLocation(location:XML):void {
            ServiceUtils.send("/locations.xml", _responder,
                location, true);
        }

        public function updateLocation(
            locationID: int,
            keys: Array,
            values: Array):void
        {
            var params:Object = new Object();
```

```
            for (var i:int = 0; i < keys.length; i++) {
                params['location[' + keys[i] +']'] = values[i];
            }
            params['_method'] = "PUT";
            ServiceUtils.send(
                "/locations/" + locationID + ".xml",
                _responder,
                params);
        }

        public function destroyLocation(locationID:int):void {
            ServiceUtils.send(
                "/locations/" + locationID + ".xml",
                _responder,
                {_method: "DELETE"});
        }
    }
}
```

You can look up the equivalent sections to see how it's used.

8.7.4 *UserDelegate.as*

Next, we create the UserDelegate, which contains the function that creates a new user; see listing 8.23.

Listing 8.23   app\flex\com\pomodo\business\UserDelegate.as

```
package com.pomodo.business {
    import mx.rpc.IResponder;
    import com.pomodo.util.ServiceUtils;

    public class UserDelegate {
        private var _responder:IResponder;

        public function UserDelegate(responder:IResponder) {
            _responder = responder;
        }

        public function createUser(user:XML):void {        ❶
            ServiceUtils.send("/users.xml", _responder, user,
                true);        ❷
        }
    }
}
```

The `createUser` function ❶ calls `ServiceUtils.send` ❷ with the RESTful / users.xml URL, the `_responder` we stored, the user XML passed in, and `true` for the value of `sendXML`.

8.7.5   *SessionDelegate.as*

Next, we create the `SessionDelegate`, which contains the function that creates a new session (logs the user in); see listing 8.24.

Listing 8.24   app\flex\com\pomodo\business\SessionDelegate.as

```
package com.pomodo.business {
    import mx.rpc.IResponder;
    import com.pomodo.util.ServiceUtils;

    public class SessionDelegate {
        private var _responder:IResponder;

        public function SessionDelegate(responder:IResponder) {
            _responder = responder;
        }

        public function createSession(login:String,        ❶
        password:String):void {
            ServiceUtils.send(              ❷
                "/session.xml",            ❸
                _responder,               ❹
                {login: login, password: password});   ❺
        }
    }
}
```

The `createSession` function ❶ calls `ServiceUtils.send` ❷ with the RESTful / session.xml URL ❸, the `_responder` ❹ we stored, and an anonymous `Object` containing the login and password ❺. It doesn't specify `sendXML`, so it defaults to `false`.

8.8   *Deleting the com.pomodo.events package*

Delete the `com.pomodo.events` package. Components will no longer dispatch these events, instead using Cairngorm. If we have Project > Build Automatically selected, we'll get a lot of errors. So, we may want to deselect it. (Or, leave it selected, and see the errors slowly disappear as we proceed through the rest of this iteration.)

8.9   *Modifying the com.pomodo.components.* *

Next, we'll modify the components to *use* all this infrastructure we just created. Essentially, we're doing the following with all the components:

- Deleting all the state, because this has been moved to the `PomodoModel-Locator`

- Deleting the `mx:Metadata`, because we no longer broadcast events from the components that way (instead using Cairngorm)

- Deleting all the `mx:HTTPServices`, because we use the `Cairngorm-Utils.dispatchEvent` function instead to trigger `ServiceUtils` (see section 8.2 for how this all fits together)

8.9.1   *TaskCreateBox.mxml*

We start with the `TaskCreateBox`; see listing 8.25.

```
Listing 8.25   app\flex\com\pomodo\components\TaskCreateBox.mxml

<?xml version="1.0" encoding="utf-8"?>
<mx:VBox xmlns:mx="http://www.adobe.com/2006/mxml"
     width="100%" height="100%" label="New Task">
<mx:Metadata>                                                        ❶
  [Event(name="taskCreate", type="com.pomodo.events.TaskEvent")]
</mx:Metadata>
<mx:Script>
<![CDATA[
    import mx.collections.XMLListCollection;                          ❷
    import mx.rpc.events.ResultEvent;
    import com.pomodo.events.TaskEvent;
    import com.pomodo.control.EventNames;                             ❸
    import com.pomodo.model.PomodoModelLocator;
    import com.pomodo.util.CairngormUtils;

    [Bindable]
    private var _model:PomodoModelLocator =                           ❹
        PomodoModelLocator.getInstance();
    [Bindable]
    public var projectsXLC:XMLListCollection;                         ❺
...
    private function handleTaskCreateResult(event:ResultEvent):
    void {
        var resultXML: XML = XML(event.result);
        Pomodo.debug("TaskCreateBox#handleTaskCreateResult:\n" +
           resultXML.toString());
        dispatchEvent(new TaskEvent(TaskEvent.TASK_CREATE,
           resultXML));
    }

    private function doTaskCreate():void {
```

```
        ~~_selectedProjectId = XML(projectsCB.selectedItem).id;~~         ⑥
        ~~_selectedLocationId = XML(locationsCB.selectedItem).id;~~
        ~~svcTasksCreate.send();~~
        var projectID: int = XML(projectsCB.selectedItem).id;            ⑦
        var locationID: int = XML(locationsCB.selectedItem).id;          ⑧
        var task : XML =                    ⑨
            <task>                          ⑩
                <name>{nameTI.text}</name>          ⑪
                <notes>{notesTI.text}</notes>       ⑫
                <project_id>{projectID}</project_id>        ⑬
                <location_id>{locationID}</location_id>     ⑭
            </task>;
        CairngormUtils.dispatchEvent(EventNames.CREATE_TASK,    ⑮
            task);
    }
]]>
</mx:Script>
    ~~<mx:HTTPService~~         ⑯
        ~~id="svcTasksCreate"~~
        ~~url="/tasks.xml"~~
...
        ~~</mx:request>~~
    ~~</mx:HTTPService>~~
    <mx:Form width="100%" height="100%">
        <mx:FormItem label="Task">
            <mx:TextInput id="nameTI" width="200"/>
        </mx:FormItem>
        <mx:FormItem label="Notes">
            <mx:TextArea id="notesTI" width="200" height="100"/>
        </mx:FormItem>
        <mx:FormItem label="Project">
            <mx:ComboBox id="projectsCB" width="200"
                labelField="name"
                dataProvider="{_model.projectsAndNoneXLC}"/>     ⑰
        </mx:FormItem>
        <mx:FormItem label="">
            <mx:CheckBox id="nextActionCheckbox"
                label="This is the Next Action"/>
        </mx:FormItem>
        <mx:FormItem label="Location">
            <mx:ComboBox id="locationsCB" width="200"
                labelField="name"
                dataProvider="{_model.locationsAndNoneXLC}"/>    ⑱
        </mx:FormItem>
        <mx:FormItem>
            <mx:Button label="Submit" width="160" height="30"
                click="doTaskCreate()"/>
        </mx:FormItem>
    </mx:Form>
</mx:VBox>
```

This is fairly straightforward. Because we no longer dispatch the `taskCreate`
`TaskEvent`, we delete the `Metadata` ❶. We then delete ❷ and add ❸ imports.
Next, we get a reference to our shared instance of the `PomodoModelLocator` ❹
and store it in a `_model` instance variable.

We then delete a bunch ❺ of instance variables that have been moved to
the `PomodoModelLocator` or that have become local variables inside `doTask-`
`Create` ❼❽. Inside `doTaskCreate`, we delete the old code ❻, set the local variables, and then build a `task` XML variable ❾ using the incredibly sexy XML syntax (❿–⓮) that includes bindings inside inline XML inside ActionScript. We
then call `CairngormUtils.dispatchEvent` ⓯ with `EventNames.CREATE_TASK`
and the new task XML.

Next, we delete the old `svcTasksCreate` `HTTPService` ⓰. Finally, we modify
the `dataProviders` ⓱⓲ to use the `_model`.

8.9.2 *ProjectCreateBox.mxml*

As is one of the themes of the book, once we figure out what to do with tasks, the
projects and locations are easy; see listing 8.26.

Listing 8.26   app\flex\com\pomodo\components\ProjectCreateBox.mxml

```
<?xml version="1.0" encoding="utf-8"?>
<mx:VBox xmlns:mx="http://www.adobe.com/2006/mxml"
    width="100%" height="100%" label="New Project">
<mx:Metadata>                                              ❶
    [Event(name="projectCreate",
           type="com.pomodo.events.ProjectEvent")]
</mx:Metadata>
<mx:Script>
<![CDATA[
    import mx.rpc.events.ResultEvent;                       ❷
    import com.pomodo.events.ProjectEvent;
    import com.pomodo.control.EventNames;                   ❸
    import com.pomodo.util.CairngormUtils;

    private function handleProjectCreateResult(             ❹
    event:ResultEvent):void {
        var resultXML: XML = XML(event.result);
        Pomodo.debug(
            "ProjectCreateBox#handleProjectCreateResult:\n" +
            resultXML.toString());
        dispatchEvent(new ProjectEvent(
            ProjectEvent.PROJECT_CREATE, resultXML));
    }
    private function doProjectCreate():void {
        svcProjectsCreate.send();                           ❺
        var project:XML =                                   ❻
```

```
                <project>        ⑦
                    <name>{nameTI.text}</name>      ⑧
                    <notes>{notesTI.text}</notes>      ⑨
                </project>;
            CairngormUtils.dispatchEvent(
                EventNames.CREATE_PROJECT, project);      ⑩
        }
    ]]>
    </mx:Script>
        <mx:HTTPService      ⑪
            id="svcProjectsCreate"
    ...
            </mx:request>
        </mx:HTTPService>
        <mx:Form width="100%" height="100%">
            <mx:FormItem label="Name">
                <mx:TextInput id="nameTI" width="200"/>
            </mx:FormItem>
            <mx:FormItem label="Notes">
                <mx:TextArea id="notesTI" width="200" height="100"/>
            </mx:FormItem>
            <mx:FormItem>
                <mx:Button label="Submit" width="160" height="30"
                    click="doProjectCreate()"/>
            </mx:FormItem>
        </mx:Form>
    </mx:VBox>
```

Because we no longer dispatch the projectCreate ProjectEvent, we delete the Metadata ❶. We then delete ❷ and add ❸ imports. We delete the handle-ProjectCreateResult handler ❹. Inside doProjectCreate, we delete the call to svcProjectsCreate.send ❺ and instead build a project XML variable ❻ using the new XML syntax ❼-❾. We then call CairngormUtils.dispatchEvent ❿ with EventNames.CREATE_PROJECT and the new project XML. Finally, we delete the old svcProjectsCreate HTTPService ⑪.

8.9.3 *LocationCreateBox.mxml*

Next, we do essentially the same thing to the LocationCreateBox; see listing 8.27.

Listing 8.27   app\flex\com\pomodo\components\LocationCreateBox.mxml

```
<?xml version="1.0" encoding="utf-8"?>
<mx:VBox xmlns:mx="http://www.adobe.com/2006/mxml"
    width="100%" height="100%" label="New Location">
<mx:Metadata>
    [Event(name="locationCreate",
```

```
                      type="com.pomodo.events.LocationEvent")]
    </mx:Metadata>
    <mx:Script>
    <![CDATA[
        import mx.rpc.events.ResultEvent;
        import com.pomodo.events.LocationEvent;
        import com.pomodo.control.EventNames;
        import com.pomodo.util.CairngormUtils;

        private function handleLocationCreateResult(
        event:ResultEvent):void {
            var resultXML: XML = XML(event.result);
            Pomodo.debug(
                "LocationCreateBox#handleLocationCreateResult:\n" +
                resultXML.toString());
            dispatchEvent(new LocationEvent(
                LocationEvent.LOCATION_CREATE, resultXML));
        }
        private function doLocationCreate():void {
            svcLocationsCreate.send();
            var location:XML =
                <location>
                    <name>{nameTI.text}</name>
                    <notes>{notesTI.text}</notes>
                </location>;
            CairngormUtils.dispatchEvent(
                EventNames.CREATE_LOCATION, location);
        }
    ]]>
    </mx:Script>
        <mx:HTTPService
            id="svcLocationsCreate"
            url="/locations.xml"
    ...
            </mx:request>
        </mx:HTTPService>
        <mx:Form width="100%" height="100%">
            <mx:FormItem label="Name">
                <mx:TextInput id="nameTI" width="200"/>
            </mx:FormItem>
            <mx:FormItem label="Notes">
                <mx:TextInput id="notesTI" width="200"/>
            </mx:FormItem>
            <mx:FormItem>
                <mx:Button label="Submit" width="160" height="30"
                    click="doLocationCreate()"/>
            </mx:FormItem>
        </mx:Form>
    </mx:VBox>
```

Having finished with the creation boxes, let's move on to the list boxes.

8.9.4 *TasksListBox.mxml*

Next, the `TasksListBox`. This code is really long but also really straightforward (so it can all be explained inline); see listing 8.28.

Listing 8.28 `app\flex\com\pomodo\components\TasksListBox.mxml`

```
<?xml version="1.0" encoding="utf-8"?>
<mx:VDividedBox xmlns:mx="http://www.adobe.com/2006/mxml"
    width="100%" height="100%" label="Tasks">
<mx:Script>
<![CDATA[
    import mx.collections.XMLListCollection;
    import mx.controls.Alert;
    import mx.rpc.events.ResultEvent;                    ◁──┐  Delete import
    import com.pomodo.components.MainBox;
    import com.pomodo.events.TaskEvent;                  ◁──┘
    import com.pomodo.control.EventNames;         ◁──┐  Add
    import com.pomodo.model.PomodoModelLocator;        │  imports
    import com.pomodo.util.CairngormUtils;        ◁──┘
    import com.pomodo.util.XMLUtils;

    public const NEXT_ACTIONS:int = 0;
    public const ALL_TASKS:int = 1;
    public const TASKS_IN_PROJECT:int = 2;
    public const TASKS_AT_LOCATION:int = 3;

    [Bindable]                                    ┌ Reference to shared
    public var model:PomodoModelLocator =    ◁──┘  PomodoModelLocator
        PomodoModelLocator.getInstance();

    private const SHOW_CHOICES:Array = [
        {label:"Next Actions", data:NEXT_ACTIONS,
            hasSubChoice:false},
        {label:"All Tasks", data:ALL_TASKS,
            hasSubChoice:false},
        {label:"Tasks in Project:", data:TASKS_IN_PROJECT,
            hasSubChoice:true},
        {label:"Tasks at Location:", data:TASKS_AT_LOCATION,
            hasSubChoice:true}];

    [Bindable]
    private var _subChoices:Array;

    [Bindable]                              ┌ Delete state and functions
    public var tasksXLC:XMLListCollection;   │ moved to PomodoModelLocator
  ...                                  ◁──┘
    public function getLocation(location_id:int):XML {
```

```
     if (locationIdMap == null) {
         return MainBox.NO_LOCATION_XML;
     }
     return locationIdMap[location_id];
}
public function updateSelectedTaskFromSummaryPanel():void {
    var selectedTask:XML = XML(tasksGrid.selectedItem);
    var params:Object = new Object();
    params['task[name]'] = nameTI.text;                    ◁──── Remove old code
...

    svcTasksUpdate.url = "/tasks/"+ selectedTask.id +".xml";
    svcTasksUpdate.send(params);
    CairngormUtils.dispatchEvent(          ◁──      Call new CairngormUtils.
        EventNames.UPDATE_TASK,                     dispatchEvent function
        { taskID: selectedTask.id,     ◁────────────────        taskID
          keys: ["name", "project_id", "location_id",    ◁──     with id of
                 "completed", "notes"],                          selectedTask
          values: [nameTI.text,        ◁──       keys Array
                  projectCB.selectedItem.id,       containing
                  locationCB.selectedItem.id,      names of
                  completedCB.selected,            properties
                  notesTI.text]                    to update
        }
    );                                     values Array containing
}                                          values to update

public function updateTaskCompleted(task:XML,
completed:Boolean):void {
    var params:Object = new Object();
    params['task[completed]'] = completed;
    params['_method'] = "PUT";
    svcTasksUpdate.url = "/tasks/" + task.id + ".xml";      Use new
    svcTasksUpdate.send(params);                            utility function
    updateTaskProperty(task, "completed", completed);  ◁──┘
}

public function updateTaskProject(task:XML, project:XML):
void {
    if (task.project_id != project.id) {
        var params:Object = new Object();
        params['task[project_id]'] = project.id;
        params['_method'] = "PUT";
        svcTasksUpdate.url = "/tasks/" + task.id + ".xml";
        svcTasksUpdate.send(params);
        updateTaskProperty(task, "project_id", project.id);   ◁──
    }                                                   Use new
}                                                       utility

public function updateTaskLocation(task:XML, location:XML):
void {
    if (task.location_id != location.id) {
```

```
            var params:Object = new Object();
            params['task[location_id]'] = location.id;
            params['_method'] = "PUT";
            svcTasksUpdate.url = "/tasks/" + task.id + ".xml";
            svcTasksUpdate.send(params);
            updateTaskProperty(task, "location_id",        ◁——  Use new utility
                location.id);                                    function
        }
    }

    private function handleTasksUpdateResult(event:ResultEvent):
    void {
...
    }
                                        Utility function to encapsulate
                                        approach for key/value pairfunction

    private function updateTaskProperty(task:XML, key:String,   ◁——
    value:Object):void {
        CairngormUtils.dispatchEvent(
            EventNames.UPDATE_TASK,
            { taskID: task.id, keys: [key], values: [value] }
        );
    }

    public function deleteTask(task:XML):void {
        svcTasksDestroy.url = "/tasks/" + task.id + ".xml";
        svcTasksDestroy.send({_method:"DELETE"});
        CairngormUtils.dispatchEvent(EventNames.DESTROY_TASK,   ◁——
            task.id);
    }                                                            Use
    private function handleTasksDestroyResult(              CairngormUtils
    event:ResultEvent):void {
...
    }
]]>
</mx:Script>                        Delete
    <mx:HTTPService   ◁——          services
        id="svcTasksUpdate"
        resultFormat="e4x"
        method="POST"
        result="handleTasksUpdateResult(event)"/>
    <mx:HTTPService
        id="svcTasksDestroy"
        resultFormat="e4x"
        method="POST"
        result="handleTasksDestroyResult(event)"/>
    <mx:VBox width="100%" height="60%">
        <mx:HBox width="100%" paddingLeft="5" paddingRight="5">
            <mx:Label text="Show:"/>
            <mx:ComboBox id="mainChoiceCB"
                dataProvider="{SHOW_CHOICES}"/>
            <mx:ComboBox id="subChoiceCB" width="100%"
```

```
                    dataProvider="{_subChoices}"
                visible="{mainChoiceCB.selectedItem.hasSubChoice}"/>
            </mx:HBox>
            <mx:DataGrid id="tasksGrid" width="100%" height="100%"
                dataProvider="{tasksXLC}">
                dataProvider="{model.tasksXLC}">
                <mx:columns>
...

                    <mx:DataGridColumn
                        headerText="Project"
                        dataField="project_id"
                        width="150"
                        editable="false"
                        sortable="false">
                        <mx:itemRenderer>
                            <mx:Component>
<mx:ComboBox
    width="150"
    labelField="name"
    dataProvider="{outerDocument.projectsAndNone}"
    selectedItem="{outerDocument.getProject(data.project_id)}"
    dataProvider="{outerDocument.model.projectsAndNoneXLC}"
    selectedItem="{outerDocument.model.getProject(data.project_id)}"
    dataChange="handleDataChange(XML(data))"
    change="outerDocument.updateTaskProject(XML(data), XML(selectedItem))">
    <mx:Script>
    <![CDATA[
        import com.pomodo.model.PomodoModelLocator;

        private function handleDataChange(data:XML):void {
            if (data != null) {
                selectedItem =
                    outerDocument.getProject(data.project_id);
                    outerDocument.model.getProject(
                        data.project_id);
            } else {
                selectedItem = MainBox.NO_PROJECT_XML;
                selectedItem =
                    PomodoModelLocator.NO_PROJECT_XML;
            }
        }
    ]]>
    </mx:Script>
</mx:ComboBox>
                            </mx:Component>
                        </mx:itemRenderer>
                    </mx:DataGridColumn>
                    <mx:DataGridColumn
                        headerText="Location"
                        dataField="location_id"
                        width="150"
```

Modify dataProvider of tasksGrid to be tasksXLC from shared PomodoModelLocator

Reference shared PomodoModelLocator

Reference shared PomodoModelLocator

```
                    editable="false"
                    sortable="false">
                    <mx:itemRenderer>
                        <mx:Component>
<mx:ComboBox
    width="150"
    labelField="name"
    dataProvider="{outerDocument.locationsAndNone}"
    selectedItem="{outerDocument.getLocation(data.location_id)}"
    dataProvider="{outerDocument.model.locationsAndNoneXLC}"      ◁
    selectedItem="{outerDocument.model.getLocation(data.location_id)}"
    dataChange="handleDataChange(XML(data))"
    change="outerDocument.updateTaskLocation(XML(data),
XML(selectedItem))">
    <mx:Script>
    <![CDATA[
        import com.pomodo.model.PomodoModelLocator;

        private function handleDataChange(data:XML):void {
            if (data != null) {
                selectedItem =
                    outerDocument.getLocation(data.location_id);
                selectedItem = outerDocument.model.getLocation(      ◁
                    data.location_id);
            } else {
                selectedItem = MainBox.NO_LOCATION_XML;
                selectedItem =
                    PomodoModelLocator.NO_LOCATION_XML;
            }
        }
    ]]>
    </mx:Script>
</mx:ComboBox>
                        </mx:Component>
                    </mx:itemRenderer>
                </mx:DataGridColumn>
...
            </mx:columns>
        </mx:DataGrid>
    </mx:VBox>
    <mx:Panel id="summaryPanel" title="Task" width="100%"
        height="40%" paddingLeft="5" paddingRight="5"
        paddingTop="5" paddingBottom="5">
        <mx:HBox width="100%">
...
        <mx:HBox width="100%" verticalAlign="middle">
            <mx:Label text="Project" width="50"/>
            <mx:ComboBox id="projectCB" width="200"
                labelField="name"
                dataProvider="{projectsAndNone}"
selectedItem="{getProject(tasksGrid.selectedItem.project_id)}"
```

**Reference shared
PomodoModelLocator**

```
                    dataProvider="{model.projectsAndNoneXLC}"
      selectedItem="{model.getProject(tasksGrid.selectedItem.project_id)}"
                />
            <mx:CheckBox label="This is the Next Action"/>
            <mx:Spacer width="100%"/>
            <mx:Label text="Location"/>
            <mx:ComboBox id="locationCB" width="200"
                labelField="name"
                dataProvider="{locationsAndNone}"
      selectedItem="{getLocation(tasksGrid.selectedItem.location_id)}"
                    dataProvider="{model.locationsAndNoneXLC}"
      selectedItem="{model.getLocation(tasksGrid.selectedItem.location_id)}"
                />
        </mx:HBox>
        <mx:HBox width="100%" height="100%">
            <mx:Label text="Notes" width="50"/>
            <mx:TextArea id="notesTI" width="100%" height="100%"
                text="{tasksGrid.selectedItem.notes}"/>
        </mx:HBox>
...
    </mx:Panel>
</mx:VDividedBox>
```

Reference shared PomodoModelLocator

Next, we make similar—but, fortunately, fewer—changes to `ProjectsListBox`
and `LocationsListBox`.

8.9.5 *ProjectsListBox.mxml*

We start with the `ProjectsListBox`; see listing 8.29.

Listing 8.29   app\flex\com\pomodo\components\ProjectsListBox.mxml

```
<?xml version="1.0" encoding="utf-8"?>
<mx:VDividedBox xmlns:mx="http://www.adobe.com/2006/mxml"
    width="100%" height="100%" label="Projects">
<mx:Metadata>                       <---- Delete Metadata
    [Event(name="projectUpdate",
        type="com.pomodo.events.ProjectEvent")]
    [Event(name="projectDelete",
        type="com.pomodo.events.ProjectEvent")]
</mx:Metadata>
<mx:Script>
<![CDATA[
    import mx.controls.Alert;
    import mx.collections.XMLListCollection;      <---- Delete imports
    import mx.rpc.events.ResultEvent;
    import com.pomodo.events.ProjectEvent;
    import com.pomodo.control.EventNames;          <---- Add imports
    import com.pomodo.model.PomodoModelLocator;
    import com.pomodo.util.CairngormUtils;
```

```
import com.pomodo.util.XMLUtils;

[Bindable]
public var projectsXLC:XMLListCollection;        ⟵──── Remove state
[Bindable]
private var _model:PomodoModelLocator =          ⟵    Reference to shared
    PomodoModelLocator.getInstance();                 PomodoModelLocator

public function updateSelectedProjectFromSummaryPanel():
void {
    var selectedProject:XML =
        XML(projectsGrid.selectedItem);
    var params:Object = new Object();
    params['project[name]'] = nameTI.text;
    params['project[completed]'] = completedCB.selected;
    params['project[notes]'] = notesTI.text;
    params['_method'] = "PUT";
    svcProjectsUpdate.url =
        "/projects/" + selectedProject.id + ".xml";
    svcProjectsUpdate.send(params);
    CairngormUtils.dispatchEvent(                      ⟵
        EventNames.UPDATE_PROJECT,
        {   projectID: selectedProject.id,
            keys: ["name", "completed", "notes"],
            values: [nameTI.text, completedCB.selected,
                     notesTI.text]
        }                                          Use CairngormUtils
    );                                          instead of local HTTPService
}

public function updateProjectCompleted(project:XML,
completed:Boolean):void {
    var params:Object = new Object();
    params['project[completed]'] = completed;
    params['_method'] = "PUT";
    svcProjectsUpdate.url =
        "/projects/" + project.id + ".xml";
    svcProjectsUpdate.send(params);
    CairngormUtils.dispatchEvent(                      ⟵
        EventNames.UPDATE_PROJECT,
        {   projectID: project.id,
            keys: ["completed"],
            values: [completedCB.selected]
        }
    );
}

public function deleteProject(data:Object):void {
    svcProjectsDestroy.url =
        "/projects/" + data.id + ".xml";
    svcProjectsDestroy.send({_method:"DELETE"});
    CairngormUtils.dispatchEvent(EventNames.DESTROY_PROJECT,  ⟵
```

```
            data.id);
    }
                                                            ┐ Delete
                                                            │ HTTPService result
    private function handleProjectsUpdateResult(      ◁──┘ handler functions
    event:ResultEvent):void {
        dispatchEvent(new ProjectEvent(
            ProjectEvent.PROJECT_UPDATE, XML(event.result)));
    }

    private function handleProjectsDestroyResult(
    event:ResultEvent):void {
        if (event.result == "error") {
            Alert.show(
                "The project was not successfully deleted.",
                "Error");
        } else {
            dispatchEvent(new ProjectEvent(
                ProjectEvent.PROJECT_DELETE,
                XML(event.result)));
        }
    }
    }
]]>
</mx:Script>
    <mx:HTTPService               ┐ Delete
                              ◁──┘ HTTPServices
        id="svcProjectsUpdate"
        resultFormat="e4x"
        method="POST"
        result="handleProjectsUpdateResult(event)"/>
    <mx:HTTPService
        id="svcProjectsDestroy"
        resultFormat="e4x"
        method="POST"
        result="handleProjectsDestroyResult(event)"/>
    <mx:DataGrid id="projectsGrid" width="100%" height="60%"
        dataProvider="{projectsXLC}">
        dataProvider="{_model.projectsXLC}">      ◁── ┐ Use shared
        <mx:columns>                                 │ PomodoModelLocator
...
        </mx:columns>
    </mx:DataGrid>
...
</mx:VDividedBox>
```

Note that throughout this example, we're passing complex anonymous `Objects` containing `Arrays` of keys and values to `CairngormUtils`. If this makes you uncomfortable, you can create a hierarchy of typed events.

8.9.6 *LocationsListBox.mxml*

We now make essentially the same changes to the `LocationsListBox`; see listing 8.30.

Listing 8.30   app\flex\com\pomodo\components\LocationsListBox.mxml

```
<?xml version="1.0" encoding="utf-8"?>
<mx:VDividedBox xmlns:mx="http://www.adobe.com/2006/mxml"
    width="100%" height="100%" label="Locations">
<mx:Metadata>                          <──── Delete Metadata
    [Event(name="locationUpdate",
          type="com.pomodo.events.LocationEvent")]
    [Event(name="locationDelete",
          type="com.pomodo.events.LocationEvent")]
</mx:Metadata>
<mx:Script>
<![CDATA[
    import mx.controls.Alert;
    import mx.collections.XMLListCollection;
    import mx.rpc.events.ResultEvent;         <──── Delete imports
    import com.pomodo.events.LocationEvent;
    import com.pomodo.control.EventNames;      <──── Add imports
    import com.pomodo.model.PomodoModelLocator;
    import com.pomodo.util.CairngormUtils;
    import com.pomodo.util.XMLUtils;

    [Bindable]
    public var locationsXLC:XMLListCollection;   <──── Remove state
    [Bindable]
    private var _model : PomodoModelLocator =   <─┐ Reference to shared
        PomodoModelLocator.getInstance();        │ PomodoModelLocator

    public function updateSelectedLocationFromSummaryPanel():
    void {
        var selectedLocation:XML =
            XML(locationsGrid.selectedItem);
        var params:Object = new Object();
        params['location[name]'] = nameTI.text;
        params['location[notes]'] = notesTI.text;
        params['_method'] = "PUT";
        svcLocationsUpdate.url =
            "/locations/" + selectedLocation.id + ".xml";
        svcLocationsUpdate.send(params);
        CairngormUtils.dispatchEvent(      <─┐ Use CairngormUtils instead
            EventNames.UPDATE_LOCATION,     │ of local HTTPService
            {
                locationID: selectedLocation.id,
                keys: ["name", "notes"],
                values: [nameTI.text, notesTI.text]
            }
```

```
            );
        }

        public function deleteLocation(data:Object):void {
            svcLocationsDestroy.url =                              ⊲──  Use
                "/locations/" + data.id + ".xml";                       CairngormUtils
            svcLocationsDestroy.send({_method:"DELETE"});               instead of local
            CairngormUtils.dispatchEvent(              ⊲───────────     HTTPService
                EventNames.DESTROY_LOCATION, data.id);
        }

        private function handleLocationsUpdateResult(   ⊲──  Delete HTTPService
        event:ResultEvent):void {                            result handler functions
            dispatchEvent(new LocationEvent(
                LocationEvent.LOCATION_UPDATE, XML(event.result)));
        }

        private function handleLocationsDestroyResult(
        event:ResultEvent):void {
            if (event.result == "error") {
                Alert.show(
                    "The location was not successfully deleted.",
                    "Error");
            } else {
                dispatchEvent(new LocationEvent(
                    LocationEvent.LOCATION_DELETE,
                    XML(event.result)));
            }
        }
    }
]]>
</mx:Script>                           Delete
    <mx:HTTPService           ⊲──┘     HTTPServices
        id="svcLocationsUpdate"
        resultFormat="e4x"
        method="POST"
        result="handleLocationsUpdateResult(event)"/>
    <mx:HTTPService
        id="svcLocationsDestroy"
        resultFormat="e4x"
        method="POST"
        result="handleLocationsDestroyResult(event)"/>
    <mx:DataGrid id="locationsGrid" width="100%" height="60%"
        dataProvider="{locationsXLC}">
        dataProvider="{_model.locationsXLC}">       ⊲──  Use shared
        <mx:columns>                                     PomodoModelLocator
...
        </mx:columns>
    </mx:DataGrid>
...
</mx:VDividedBox>
```

8.9.7 *AccountCreateBox.mxml*

Not much longer now! Next, we modify the `AccountCreateBox`; see listing 8.31.

Listing 8.31 `app\flex\com\pomodo\components\AccountCreateBox.mxml`

```
<?xml version="1.0" encoding="utf-8"?>
<mx:VBox xmlns:mx="http://www.adobe.com/2006/mxml"
    xmlns:cpv="com.pomodo.validators.*"
    width="100%" height="100%" label="Create Account">
<mx:Metadata>
    [Event(name="accountCreate",
        type="com.pomodo.events.AccountCreateEvent")]
</mx:Metadata>
<mx:Script>
<![CDATA[
    import mx.controls.Alert;
    import mx.events.ValidationResultEvent;
    import mx.rpc.events.ResultEvent;
    import mx.validators.Validator;
    import com.pomodo.events.AccountCreateEvent;
    import com.pomodo.control.EventNames;
    import com.pomodo.model.PomodoModelLocator;
    import com.pomodo.util.CairngormUtils;
    import com.pomodo.validators.ServerErrors;

    [Bindable]
    private var _model:PomodoModelLocator =
        PomodoModelLocator.getInstance();
    [Bindable]
    private var _serverErrors:ServerErrors;

    private function handleAccountCreateResult(
    event:ResultEvent):void {
...
    }

    private function validateAndSubmit():void {
        var results:Array = Validator.validateAll([
            usernameValidator,
            emailValidator,
            passwordValidator,
            passwordConfirmationValidator]);
        if (results.length > 0) {
            Alert.show("Please correct the validation errors " +
                "highlighted on the form.",
                "Account Not Created");
            return;
        }
        svcAccountCreate.send();
        var user: XML =       ◁
```

❶ **Build local XML variable and pass to CairngormUtils.send() call**

```
            <user>
                <login>{loginTI.text}</login>
                <email>{emailTI.text}</email>
                <first_name>{firstNameTI.text}</first_name>
                <last_name>{lastNameTI.text}</last_name>
                <password>{passwordTI.text}</password>
<password_confirmation>{confirmPasswordTI.text}
    ➥</password_confirmation>
            </user>
        CairngormUtils.dispatchEvent(
            EventNames.CREATE_USER, user);
    }

    private function showTOS():void {
        Alert.show(
            "The first rule of pomodo is: Don't talk about " +
            "pomodo. The second rule of pomodo is: Don't " +
            "talk about pomodo.", "Terms of Service");
    }
]]>
</mx:Script>
    <mx:HTTPService
        id="svcAccountCreate"
...
    </mx:HTTPService>
    <mx:EmailValidator id="emailValidator" source="{emailTI}"
        property="text"/>
...
    <cpv:ServerErrorValidator
        id="loginSV"
        field="login"
        listener="{loginTI}"
        serverErrors="{_serverErrors}"/>
        serverErrors="{_model.accountCreateErrors}"/>          ❷
    <cpv:ServerErrorValidator
        id="emailSV"
        field="email"
        listener="{emailTI}"
        serverErrors="{_serverErrors}"/>
        serverErrors="{_model.accountCreateErrors}"/>
    <cpv:ServerErrorValidator
        id="passwordSV"
        field="password"
        listener="{passwordTI}"
        serverErrors="{_serverErrors}"/>
        serverErrors="{_model.accountCreateErrors}"/>
    <cpv:ServerErrorValidator
        id="passwordConfirmationSV"
        field="password_confirmation"
        listener="{confirmPasswordTI}"
        serverErrors="{_serverErrors}"/>
```

```
        serverErrors="{_model.accountCreateErrors}"/>
    <mx:Form labelWidth="150">
...
    </mx:Form>
</mx:VBox>
```

Note that we're once again using an XML variable inside ActionScript ❶ populated with bindings before calling `CairngormUtils.send()`. Also note that the
`ServerErrorValidators` now use the `accountCreateErrors` from the `Pomodo-`
`ModelLocator` ❷.

8.9.8 *LoginBox.mxml*

Next, the `LoginBox`; see listing 8.32.

Listing 8.32   app\flex\com\pomodo\components\LoginBox.mxml

```
<?xml version="1.0" encoding="utf-8"?>
  <mx:Metadata>
    [Event(name="login", type="com.pomodo.events.LoginEvent")]
</mx:Metadata>
<mx:VBox xmlns:mx="http://www.adobe.com/2006/mxml" width="100%"
    height="100%" label="Login">
<mx:Script>
<![CDATA[
    import mx.controls.Alert;
    import mx.rpc.events.ResultEvent;
    import com.pomodo.events.LoginEvent;
    import com.pomodo.control.EventNames;
    import com.pomodo.util.CairngormUtils;

    private function login():void {
        svcAccountLogin.send(
        CairngormUtils.dispatchEvent(        ❶
            EventNames.CREATE_SESSION,
            {login: loginTI.text, password: passwordTI.text});
    }

    private function handleAccountLoginResult(
    event:ResultEvent):void {
        var result:Object = event.result;
        if (result == "badlogin") {
            Alert.show("The username or password is wrong.",
                "Login Error");
        } else {
            dispatchEvent(new LoginEvent(XML(result)));
        }
    }
}
```

```
    ]]>
  </mx:Script>
    <mx:HTTPService
        id="svcAccountLogin"
        url="/session.xml"
        resultFormat="e4x"
        method="POST"
        result="handleAccountLoginResult(event)"/>
      <mx:Form labelWidth="150">
        <mx:FormItem required="true" label="Username">
          <mx:TextInput id="loginTI"/>
        </mx:FormItem>
        <mx:FormItem required="true" label="Password">
          <mx:TextInput id="passwordTI"
              displayAsPassword="true"/>
        </mx:FormItem>
        <mx:FormItem>
          <mx:Button id="loginButton" label="Login"
              click="login()"/>
        </mx:FormItem>
      </mx:Form>
  </mx:VBox>
```

By now this is downright tedious. Again, we convert to using CairngormUtils ❶— note that we pass it the identical anonymous object.

8.9.9 *MainBox.mxml*

Next, the MainBox; see listing 8.33.

Listing 8.33   app\flex\com\pomodo\components\MainBox.mxml

```
<?xml version="1.0" encoding="utf-8"?>
<mx:HBox xmlns:mx="http://www.adobe.com/2006/mxml"
    xmlns:pom="com.pomodo.components.*"
    minWidth="1000"
    minHeight="680"
    paddingLeft="5"
    paddingRight="5"
    paddingTop="5"
    paddingBottom="5"
    width="100%"
    height="100%"
    backgroundColor="#FFFFFF"
    creationComplete="handleCreationComplete()">
<mx:Script>
<![CDATA[
    import mx.rpc.events.ResultEvent;
    import mx.collections.ArrayCollection;
```

```
~~import mx.collections.IViewCursor;~~                    Add/remove
~~import mx.collections.XMLListCollection;~~             imports
import com.pomodo.control.EventNames;          ◁─┘
import com.pomodo.util.CairngormUtils;
import com.pomodo.model.PomodoModelLocator;

~~[Bindable]~~                        State stored here moved
~~public var user : XML;~~     ◁─┘   to PomodoModelLocator

[Bindable]
private var _gotProjects : Boolean;
...
~~private function handleLocationsListResult(~~
~~event:ResultEvent):void {~~
~~    _gotLocations = true;~~
~~    var resultXML: XML = XML(event.result);~~
~~    Pomodo.debug("MainBox#handleLocationsListResult:\n" +~~
~~        resultXML.toString());~~
~~    updateLocationIdMap();~~
~~}~~

    [Bindable]                                 Reference to shared
    private var _model:PomodoModelLocator =  ◁─┘ PomodoModelLocator
        PomodoModelLocator.getInstance();

    private function handleCreationComplete():void {
        ~~_gotProjects = false;~~                  No longer set flags
        ~~_gotLocations = false;~~                 and call local methods;
        ~~listProjects();~~                        dispatch Cairngorm events
        ~~listLocations();~~
        CairngormUtils.dispatchEvent(EventNames.LIST_PROJECTS);   ◁─┘
        CairngormUtils.dispatchEvent(EventNames.LIST_LOCATIONS);
    }

    ~~private function getProjectsAndNone(projectsXL:XMLList):~~
    ~~XMLListCollection {~~
    ~~    var retval:XMLListCollection =~~
    ~~        new XMLListCollection(projectsXL.copy());~~
    ~~    retval.addItemAt(NO_PROJECT_XML, 0);~~
    ~~    return retval;~~
    ~~}~~
    ...
    ~~private function listTasksIfMapsPresent():void {~~
    ~~    if (_gotProjects && _gotLocations) {~~
    ~~        listTasks();~~
    ~~    }~~
    ~~}~~
]]>
</mx:Script>
    ~~<mx:HTTPService~~     ◁─┘  Delete HTTPServices
                               and XMLListCollections
```

```
        ~~id="svcTasksList"~~
        ~~url="/tasks.xml"~~
        ~~resultFormat="e4x"~~
        ~~result="handleTasksListResult(event)"/>~~

...

    ~~<mx:Binding~~
        ~~source="{getLocationsAndNone(locationsXLC.source)}"~~
        ~~destination="_locationsAndNoneXLC"/>~~

<mx:HBox width="100%" height="100%">
    <mx:VBox width="300" height="100%">
        <mx:Image source="com/pomodo/assets/logo_md.png"/>
        ~~<mx:Label text="{'Logged in as: ' + user.login +~~
            ~~' (' + user.email + ')'}"/>~~
        ~~<mx:Label text="{'Welcome back ' + user.first_name +~~
            ~~'!'}"/>~~
        <mx:Label text="{'Logged in as: ' +
            _model.user.login +
            ' (' + _model.user.email + ')'}"/>                 Use state stored in
                                                               PomodoModelLocator
        <mx:Label text="{'Welcome back ' +
            _model.user.first_name + '!'}"/>
        <mx:Accordion width="100%" height="350">
            ~~<pom:TaskCreateBox id="taskCreateBox"~~
                ~~taskCreate="listTasks()"~~
                ~~projectsXLC="{_projectsAndNoneXLC}"~~
                ~~locationsXLC="{_locationsAndNoneXLC}"/>~~        No need
            ~~<pom:ProjectCreateBox id="projectCreateBox"~~        to handle
                ~~projectCreate="listProjects()"/>~~               custom
            ~~<pom:LocationCreateBox id="locationCreateBox"~~      events
                ~~locationCreate="listLocations()"/>~~            and call
            <pom:TaskCreateBox id="taskCreateBox"/>               functions
            <pom:ProjectCreateBox id="projectCreateBox"/>
            <pom:LocationCreateBox id="locationCreateBox"/>
        </mx:Accordion>
        <mx:DateChooser id="dateChooser" width="100%"/>
    </mx:VBox>
    <mx:VBox width="100%" height="100%">
        <pom:CommandShell/>
        <mx:TabNavigator width="100%" height="100%">
            ~~<pom:TasksListBox id="tasksTab"~~
                ~~tasksXLC="{tasksXLC}"~~
                ~~projectIdMap="{_projectIdMap}"~~
                ~~locationIdMap="{_locationIdMap}"~~
                ~~projectsAndNone="{_projectsAndNoneXLC}"~~
                ~~locationsAndNone="{_locationsAndNoneXLC}"/>~~
            ~~<pom:ProjectsListBox id="projectsTab"~~
                ~~projectsXLC="{projectsXLC}"~~
                ~~projectUpdate="listProjects()"~~
                ~~projectDelete="listProjects()"/>~~
            ~~<pom:LocationsListBox id="locationsTab"~~
                ~~locationsXLC="{locationsXLC}"~~
```

```
            locationUpdate="listLocations()"
            locationDelete="listLocations()"/>
        <pom:TasksListBox id="tasksTab"/>          ◁─┐
        <pom:ProjectsListBox id="projectsTab"/>       │   No need to pass
        <pom:LocationsListBox id="locationsTab"/>      │   in local state to
        <pom:Notely id="notelyTab"/>                   │   be copied via
    </mx:TabNavigator>                                 │   bindings
  </mx:VBox>
 </mx:HBox>
</mx:HBox>
```

~~Hooray for strikethrough!~~ Note that we don't need to dispatch Event-
Names.LIST_TASKS in handleCreationComplete(). In the PomodoModelLocator,
we create setters for projectsXLC and locationsXLC that create their respective
map between project/location ids and the projects/locations and then call list-
TasksIfMapsPresent, which checks two flags to see if both the projects and locations have been retrieved, and if so dispatches an event to trigger the listing of
tasks. Also note how much simpler the use of the custom pom: components is,
without the need to handle custom events and call custom functions. This is one
of the key benefits of Cairngorm: We don't need to pass state around everywhere
via bindings.

8.9.10 SplashBox.mxml

Next, the SplashBox; see listing 8.34.

Listing 8.34   app\flex\com\pomodo\components\SplashBox.mxml

```
<?xml version="1.0" encoding="utf-8"?>
<mx:VBox xmlns:mx="http://www.adobe.com/2006/mxml"
    xmlns:pom="com.pomodo.components.*"
    horizontalAlign="center" verticalAlign="top"
    width="100%" height="100%">
<mx:Metadata>                        ◁── Remove custom Metadata
    [Event(name="accountCreate",
        type="com.pomodo.events.AccountCreateEvent")]
    [Event(name="login", type="com.pomodo.events.LoginEvent")]
</mx:Metadata>
<mx:Script>
<![CDATA[
    import com.pomodo.events.AccountCreateEvent;
    import com.pomodo.events.LoginEvent;
    import com.pomodo.model.PomodoModelLocator;        ◁── Change imports

    [Bindable]
    private var _reviews:String =
```

```
┊"pomodo, the hot new RIA by 38noises, is taking ┊ +
┊over Web 2.0." --Michael Arrington*\n"I wish I\'d ┊ +
┊invested in 38noises instead of that other company."┊ +
┊ --Jeff Bezos*\n"38noises closed angel funding at a ┊ +
┊party in my bathroom last night." --Om Malik*┊;
[Bindable]
private var _model:PomodoModelLocator =
    PomodoModelLocator.getInstance();
]]>
</mx:Script>
    <mx:VBox width="500" horizontalAlign="center">
        <mx:Image source="com/pomodo/assets/logo_md.png" />
        <mx:Label
            text="The simple, GTD-style TODO list application."/>
        <mx:Spacer height="10"/>
        <mx:Text width="100%" text="{_reviews}"/>
        <mx:Text width="100%" text="{_model.reviews}"/>
        <mx:Spacer height="10"/>
        <mx:Accordion width="440" height="330">
            <pom:AccountCreateBox/>
            <pom:LoginBox/>
        </mx:Accordion>
        <mx:Label text="*did not say this, but might someday!"/>
    </mx:VBox>
</mx:VBox>
```

Use shared PomodoModelLocator that includes stubbed-out reviews

Bind to reviews in shared PomodoModelLocator (no local var needed)

8.10 Modifying Pomodo.mxml

Finally (I mean it!), we modify Pomodo.mxml; see listing 8.35.

Listing 8.35   app\flex\Pomodo.mxml

```
<?xml version="1.0" encoding="utf-8"?>
<mx:Application
    xmlns:mx="http://www.adobe.com/2006/mxml"
    xmlns:pom="com.pomodo.components.*"
    xmlns:control="com.pomodo.control.*"
    layout="vertical"
    backgroundGradientColors="[#ffffff, #c0c0c0]"
    horizontalAlign="center"
    verticalAlign="top"
    paddingLeft="0"
    paddingRight="0"
    paddingTop="0"
    paddingBottom="0"
    width="100%"
    height="100%">
<mx:Script>
```

Import control package containing PomodoController

```
<![CDATA[
    import mx.core.Container;              <---- Add/remove imports
    import com.pomodo.components.DebugPanel;
    import com.pomodo.events.AccountCreateEvent;
    import com.pomodo.events.LoginEvent;
    import com.pomodo.util.DebugMessage;
    import com.pomodo.model.PomodoModelLocator;

    [Bindable]                            ┌─ Remove local state (_user
    private var _user : XML;        <─────┘  is now_model.user)

    [Bindable]                                      ┌─ Reference to shared
    private var _model : PomodoModelLocator =   <───┘  PomodoModelLocator
        PomodoModelLocator.getInstance();

    public static function debug(str:String):void {
        application.debugPanel.addMessage(        ┌─ Return what should  ❶
            new DebugMessage(str));               │  be selectedChild of
    }                                             │  mainStack based on
                                                  │  workflowState
    private function controlViewToShow(workflowState:int):  <─┘
    Container {
        if (workflowState ==
            PomodoModelLocator.VIEWING_SPLASH_SCREEN) {   ❷
            return splashBox;
        } else if (workflowState ==
            PomodoModelLocator.VIEWING_MAIN_APP) {   ❸
            return mainBox;
        } else {        ❹
            return splashBox;
        }                                       ┌─ Remove local
    }                                           │  functions and handlers
    private function handleAccountCreate(e:AccountCreateEvent):  <─┘
    void {
        login(e.user);
    }

    private function handleLogin(e:LoginEvent):void {
        login(e.user);
    }

    private function login(user:XML):void {
        _user = user;
        debug("user = " + user);
        mainStack.selectedChild = mainBox;
    }
]]>
</mx:Script>
    <!--
    the FrontController, containing Commands specific to this app
    -->
```

```
<control:PomodoController id="controller" />        <--- FrontController

<mx:VDividedBox width="100%" height="100%">
    <mx:ViewStack id="mainStack" width="100%" height="100%">
        <pom:SplashBox id="splashBox"
            accountCreate="handleAccountCreate(event)"
            login="handleLogin(event)"/>
        <pom:MainBox id="mainBox" user="{_user}"/>
    <mx:ViewStack id="mainStack" width="100%" height="100%"
selectedChild="{controlViewToShow(_model.workflowState)}">     ❺
        <pom:SplashBox id="splashBox"/>      ❻
        <pom:MainBox id="mainBox"/>          ❼
    </mx:ViewStack>
    <pom:DebugPanel id="debugPanel" width="100%"
        height="0%"/>
</mx:VDividedBox>
</mx:Application>
```

The `controlViewToShow` function ❶ is automatically invoked as part of a binding ❺ that controls the `selectedChild` of the `mainStack`. This function checks the `workflowState` in the `_model`. If it's `PomodoModelLocator.VIEWING_SPLASH_SCREEN` ❷ or an error ❹, we return the `splashBox` ❻; otherwise, if it's `PomodoModelLocator.VIEWING_MAIN_APP` ❸, we return `mainBox` ❼.

Note how much simpler the code for the `SplashBox` and `MainBox` is, compared to the old code.

And that's it—really!

8.11 *Running pomodo*

Rebuild, reload, and log in as ludwig. Our login was done via Cairngorm! Because everything works exactly as before (as it should when refactoring), no screenshot is required. Finally, run the tests again and confirm that everything still works.

> The code at this point is saved as the iteration08 folder.

That's it for this iteration!

Well, almost. As a bonus, we'll consider some `HTTPService` gotchas. These aren't Cairngorm-specific, but I didn't put this in iteration 5 because I didn't want to make iteration 5 overwhelming. (Furthermore, it's easier to test them now because of our utility methods.)

8.12 *HTTPService Gotchas*

We've seen that the HTTPService class has a method parameter. Some idiosyncrasies surround this parameter, and they vary based on the contentType of the HTTPService. These are summarized in table 8.2.

Table 8.2 HTTPService: WYSINAWYG (What You Send Is Not Always What You Get)

#	service.method	service.contentType	service.request	Rails sees	match?
1	GET	application/xml	some non-null XML	POST	N
2	POST	application/xml	some non-null XML	POST	Y
3	GET	application/xml	not set	GET	Y
4	POST	application/xml	not set	GET	N
5	GET	application/x-www-form-urlencoded	{foo:"bar"}	GET	Y
6	POST	application/x-www-form-urlencoded	{foo:"bar"}	POST	Y
7	GET	application/x-www-form-urlencoded	not set	GET	Y
8	POST	application/x-www-form-urlencoded	not set	GET	N

The interesting rows in the table are the mismatches (rows 1, 4, and 8). Basically, if we POST nothing, Rails sees a GET. This is true whether we have a contentType of application/xml (row 4) or application/x-www-form-urlencoded (row 8). If we send a GET with a contentType of application/xml and actual content in the service.request (row 1), Rails sees a POST. The rest of the table is pretty much what we'd expect.

If you want to verify this for yourself, or to at least see this shown with code, you're in luck. You don't need to follow along with any of the code next (and if you do follow along, you need to reset your code back to this point when you're done). The code is shown so you can follow along, if you're not sick of this iteration yet.

Table 8.2 is illustrated in more detail in the following tables, which show the Rails development.log after sending a request to /tasks.xml with various modified forms of the createTask method in TaskDelegate. The createTask method is being modified to explicitly set all parameters of a new HTTPService so the detail of what is being done isn't obscured (as it would be somewhat if we used Service-Utils.send()).

In all the following code listings, you need to add the imports ❶ ❷ and delete the previous `ServiceUtils.send()` call ❸ as shown in listing 8.36.

Listing 8.36   app\flex\com\pomodo\business\TaskDelegate.as

```
package com.pomodo.business {
    import mx.rpc.IResponder;
    import com.pomodo.util.ServiceUtils;
    import mx.rpc.AsyncToken;          ❶
    import mx.rpc.http.HTTPService;    ❷

    public class TaskDelegate {
...
        public function createTask(task : XML) : void {
            ServiceUtils.send("/tasks.xml", _responder, task, true);   ❸
...
```

These diffs aren't shown in the following two tables, because seeing them eight times would be repetitive. Note that each row in the table is a different version of the `createTask` function, with the diffs against the original code. The rest of the `TaskDelegate` class is unchanged, except for the modifications in table 8.3.

We start by showing the code that demonstrates the first four rows (with a contentType of `application/xml`) see table 8.3.

Table 8.3   Example code that uses a `contentType` of `application/xml`

app\flex\com\pomodo\business\TaskDelegate.as	log\development.log
```public function createTask(task : XML) : void { var service:HTTPService = new HTTPService(); ❶ service.url = "/tasks.xml"; service.contentType = "application/xml"; service.resultFormat = "e4x"; service.method = "GET"; service.request = task; ❷ var call:AsyncToken = service.send(); ❸ call.addResponder(_responder);}```	Processing TasksController#create (for 127.0.0.1 at 2007-08-18 15:31:50) [POST] Session ID: 25291760fadb8215775f44774e1bb868 Parameters: {"format"=>"xml", "action"=>"create", "task"=>{"name"=>"foo", "project_id"=>"0", "notes"=>"using a GET method and a task of foo", "location_id"=>"0"}, "controller"=>"tasks"} ...

Table 8.3 Example code that uses a `contentType` of `application/xml` *(continued)*

app\flex\com\pomodo\business\TaskDelegate.as	log\development.log

``
public function createTask(task : XML) : void {
  var service:HTTPService = new HTTPService();   ④
  service.url = "/tasks.xml";
  service.contentType = "application/xml";
  service.resultFormat = "e4x";
  service.method = "POST";
  service.request = task;   ⑤
  var call:AsyncToken = service.send();   ⑥
  call.addResponder(_responder);
}
``
	Processing TasksController#create (for 127.0.0.1 at 2007-08-18 15:45:43) [POST]
	  Session ID: 25291760fadb8215775f44774e1bb868
	  Parameters: {"format"=>"xml", "action"=>"create", "task"=>{"name"=>"foo", "project_id"=>"0", "notes"=>"using a POST method and a task of foo", "location_id"=>"0"}, "controller"=>"tasks"}
	...

``
public function createTask(task : XML) : void {
  var service:HTTPService = new HTTPService();   ⑦
 	
  service.url = "/tasks.xml";
  service.contentType = "application/xml";
  service.resultFormat = "e4x";
  service.method = "GET";
  var call:AsyncToken = service.send();   ⑧
 	
  call.addResponder(_responder);
}
``
	Processing TasksController#index (for 127.0.0.1 at 2007-08-18 15:50:36) [GET]
	  Session ID: 25291760fadb8215775f44774e1bb868
	  Parameters: {"format"=>"xml", "action"=>"index", "controller"=>"tasks"}
	...

``
public function createTask(task : XML) : void {
  var service:HTTPService = new HTTPService();   ⑨
  service.url = "/tasks.xml";
  service.contentType = "application/xml";
  service.resultFormat = "e4x";
  service.method = "POST";
  var call:AsyncToken = service.send();   ⑩
  call.addResponder(_responder);
}
``
	Processing TasksController#index (for 127.0.0.1 at 2007-08-18 15:49:01) [GET]
	  Session ID: 25291760fadb8215775f44774e1bb868
	  Parameters: {"format"=>"xml", "action"=>"index", "controller"=>"tasks"}
	...

We see that when using a contentType of application/xml, if we set the service.request to the task ❸ ❻, it doesn't matter whether the service.method is set to a GET ❷ or a POST ❺: In both cases, Rails sees a POST ❶❹. (The request it's processing is logged in square brackets: [POST].) Similarly, when using a contentType of application/xml, if we leave the service.request unset, it doesn't matter whether the service.method is set to a GET ❽ or a POST ❿: In both cases, Rails sees a GET ❼❾.

Next, we show the code that demonstrates the last four rows (with a contentType of application/x-www-form-urlencoded); see table 8.4.

Table 8.4 Example code that uses a contentType of application/x-www-form-urlencoded

app\flex\com\pomodo\business\TaskDelegate.as)	
```public function createTask(task : XML) : void { var service:HTTPService = new HTTPService(); ❶ service.url = "/tasks.xml"; service.contentType = "application/x-www-form-urlencoded"; service.resultFormat = "e4x"; service.method = "GET"; ❷ service.request = {foo:"bar"}; var call:AsyncToken = service.send(); call.addResponder(_responder); }```	Processing TasksController#index (for 127.0.0.1 at 2007-08-18 16:40:34) [GET] Session ID: 25291760fadb8215775f44774e1bb868 Parameters: {"format"=>"xml", "action"=>"index", "foo"=>"bar", "controller"=>"tasks"} ... Completed in 0.09400 (10 reqs/sec) | Rendering: 0.00000 (0%) | DB: 0.01600 (17%) | 200 OK [http://localhost/tasks.xml?foo=bar] ...

Table 8.4 Example code that uses a `contentType` of `application/x-www-form-urlencoded` *(continued)*

app\flex\com\pomodo\business\TaskDelegate.as)	

``
public function createTask(task : XML) : void {
    var service:HTTPService = new HTTPService();   ③
    service.url = "/tasks.xml";
    service.contentType = "application/x-www-form-
urlencoded";
    service.resultFormat = "e4x";
    service.method = "POST";   ④
    service.request = {foo:"bar"};
    var call:AsyncToken = service.send();
    call.addResponder(_responder);
}
``
	``
	Processing TasksCon-
	troller#create (for
	127.0.0.1 at 2007-08-
	18 16:32:13) [POST]
	Session ID:
	25291760fadb8215775f4477
	4e1bb868
	  Parameters: {"for-
	mat"=>"xml",
	"action"=>"create",
	"foo"=>"bar", "control-
	ler"=>"tasks"}
	...
	Completed in 0.23400 (4
	reqs/sec)
		Rendering:
		0.00000 (0%)
			DB:
			0.07800 (33%)
				200 OK
				[http://localhost/
				tasks.xml]
				...
				``

``
public function createTask(task : XML) : void {
    var service:HTTPService = new HTTPService();   ⑤
    service.url = "/tasks.xml";
    service.contentType = "application/x-www-form-
urlencoded";
    service.resultFormat = "e4x";   ⑥
    service.method = "GET";
    var call:AsyncToken = service.send();
    call.addResponder(_responder);
}
``
	``
	Processing TasksCon-
	troller#index (for
	127.0.0.1 at 2007-08-
	18 16:44:55) [GET]
	  Session ID:
	25291760fadb8215775f44
	774e1bb868
	  Parameters: {"for-
	mat"=>"xml",
	"action"=>"index",
	"controller"=>"tasks"}
	...
	Completed in 0.07800
	(12 reqs/sec)
		Ren-
		dering: 0.00000 (0%)
			
			DB: 0.03100 (39%)
				
				200 OK [http://local-
				host/tasks.xml]
				...
				``

Table 8.4   Example code that uses a `contentType` **of** `application/x-www-form-urlencoded` *(continued)*

app\flex\com\pomodo\business\TaskDelegate.as)	
```public function createTask(task : XML) : void { var service:HTTPService = new HTTPService(); ❼ service.url = "/tasks.xml"; service.contentType = "application/x-www-form- urlencoded"; service.resultFormat = "e4x"; ❽ service.method = "POST"; var call:AsyncToken = service.send(); call.addResponder(_responder); }```	```Processing TasksCon- troller#index (for 127.0.0.1 at 2007-08- 18 16:46:09) [GET] Session ID: 25291760fadb8215775f44 774e1bb868 Parameters: {"for- mat"=>"xml", "action"=>"index", "controller"=>"tasks"} ... Completed in 0.07800 (12 reqs/sec)	Rendering: 0.00000 (0%)	DB: 0.01500 (19%)	200 OK [http://localhost/ tasks.xml]```

We see that if we set the `service.request` to `{foo:"bar"}` ❷ ❹, the service.`method` is what Rails sees ❶ ❸. However, if we leave the `service.request` unset, it doesn't matter whether the `service.method` is set to a GET ❻ or a POST ❽: In both cases, Rails sees a GET ❺❼.

Now that we understand this, restore the `TaskDelegate` class to its state before we did all this (❶ in listing 8.37).

Listing 8.37   app\flex\com\pomodo\business\TaskDelegate.as

```
package com.pomodo.business {
    import mx.rpc.IResponder;
    import com.pomodo.util.ServiceUtils;
    import mx.rpc.AsyncToken;       ❶
    import mx.rpc.http.HTTPService;

    public class TaskDelegate {
...
        public function createTask(task : XML) : void {
            ServiceUtils.send("/tasks.xml", _responder, task,
                true);
        }
...
```

8.13 Summary

In refactoring the Flex code to use Cairngorm with `HTTPService` (albeit in a slightly nonstandard way), we've seen one way to structure large Flex applications. If Cairngorm doesn't appeal to you, you don't have to use it: You can create large Flex applications without it.

If you're a seasoned Rails developer, you may dislike Cairngorm because it reminds you too much of enterprise Java development. I understand this: I did a presentation about using Flex with Rails at Rails to Italy 2007, and afterward one experienced developer told me I was convincing until I started showing Cairngorm code! If this describes you, feel free to ignore Cairngorm and use either a different framework or none at all.

8.14 Exercise for the reader

- *[Advanced]* Extend the command mechanism to have the notion of undoable commands to function as edits (both simple and compound). Would creating an `IUndoableCommand` interface be a good idea? Look at the Java Swing API docs for ideas. How would this integrate with Rails?

Holding state
on the client properly

One key shift in mindset when you move from the development of web applications to rich Internet applications is that the client is stateful....

If you have been building desktop or rich-client applications with technologies such as Swing or AWT, for instance, you'll shrug your shoulders right now because all of this will sound all too familiar— it is.

—Steven Webster[1]

[1] http://www.adobe.com/devnet/flex/articles/cairngorm_pt2_print.html.

If you've spent any time building Flex applications with Cairngorm, or with any desktop UI framework such as Java Swing or Windows Forms, the thought of storing the data on the client as just XML (regardless of how cool the E4X way of dealing with XML is) is unsettling. Surely we should be creating and using a proper object model on the Flex side.

Furthermore, right now all the Flex code is tightly coupled to the fact that we're sending and receiving XML. However, what if we wanted to use JSON or YAML to send data to and from Rails—or even AMF (using RubyAMF or WebORB)? This should be a straightforward change, but as the code stands currently we would essentially need to do a massive refactoring of most of the Flex code. Obviously this is unacceptable.

Yes, we should probably be creating and using a proper object model on the Flex side. Not only will this result in better code, it will also decouple us from using XML.

NOTE For extremely small applications, an object model may be overkill: using XML may be just fine. As this iteration shows, you can always refactor to an object model later.

This is what we'll do in this iteration.

9.1 *Refactoring, samurai coder style*

We'll do this refactoring all at once. I called this approach "refactoring, fast-forwarded" earlier in the book. Whereas that implies a normal refactoring—albeit speeded up—it's more fitting to describe the type of refactoring we're doing as *samurai coder* style, because it brings to mind a "Kill Bill sequence of large-scale dismemberment"[2]. This refactoring wasn't done in neat, unit-tested pieces: I figured out what the object model should be, created the model objects, modified the `PomodoModelLocator`, and then dealt with the consequences in the rest of the codebase. Once the code compiled, I tested the features. No, I'm not claiming that this is a "best practice." It's not. However, I'm not selling a methodology, I'm selling a book that retraces my steps, however imperfect.

---

[2] http://www.opencurly.com/dev/confessions-of-a-samurai-coder. (I used to enjoy this style of refactoring a *lot* more when I was younger, more foolish and energetic, and not a parent.) If you have experience with this kind of refactoring, either successful or failed (presumably both), you'll probably find the article amusing.

9.2 Creating the model classes

We'll start by creating classes on the Flex side for `User`, `Task`, `Project`, and `Location`. Where should these classes go? We have the `com.pomodo.model` package; this holds the `PomodoModelLocator`, so it seems like a good spot. This corresponds to the *business objects*[3] in Cairngorm. However, Cairngorm also has the notion of *value object* (and an `IValueObject` marker interface) for the objects that are used to transfer data back and forth between Flex and the server. These value objects go in a vo package, which for us would be `com.pomodo.vo`. Should they go there?

> **NOTE** As discussed in the previous iteration, Cairngorm uses the term *value object* instead of *data transfer object* (DTO) or *transfer object* (TO) because it was conceived before those terms became popular.

It's tough to say. We're sending XML, not value objects, back and forth. We don't have any true value objects. And we'll add stuff to the model objects that doesn't belong in a value object.

It doesn't seem correct to call these objects value objects—they're model objects. As such, they will go in the `com.pomodo.model` package.

9.2.1 Task.as

We'll start by creating the `Task` model; see listing 9.1.

Listing 9.1   app\flex\com\pomodo\model\Task.as

```
package com.pomodo.model {
    import com.pomodo.util.XMLUtils;

    public class Task {
        public static const UNSAVED_ID:int = 0;        ❶

        [Bindable]
        public var id:int;        ❷

        [Bindable]
        public var name:String;

        [Bindable]
        public var notes:String;

        [Bindable]
```

---

[3] See http://weblogs.macromedia.com/auhlmann/archives/2006/06/cairngorm_sampl.cfm for a good discussion of business objects in Cairngorm.

```
public var project:Project;

[Bindable]
public var location:Location;

[Bindable]
public var nextAction:Boolean;

[Bindable]
public var completed:Boolean;

public function Task(            ❸
    name:String = "",
    notes:String = "",
    project:Project = null,
    location:Location = null,
    nextAction:Boolean = false,
    completed:Boolean = false,
    id:int = UNSAVED_ID)         ❹
{
    this.name = name;
    this.notes = notes;
    if (project == null) {
        project = Project.NONE;      ❺
    }
    project.addTask(this);
    if (location == null) {
        location = Location.NONE;    ❻
    }
    location.addTask(this);
    this.nextAction = nextAction;
    this.completed = completed;
    this.id = id;
}

public function toUpdateObject():Object {    ❼
    var obj:Object = new Object();
    obj["task[name]"] = name;
    obj["task[project_id]"] = project.id;    ❽
    obj["task[location_id]"] = location.id;  ❾
    obj["task[next_action]"] = nextAction;
    obj["task[completed]"] = completed;
    obj["task[notes]"] = notes;
    return obj;
}

public function toXML():XML {       ❿
    var retval:XML =
        <task>
            <name>{name}</name>
            <notes>{notes}</notes>
```

```
                    <project_id>{project.id}</project_id>        ⑪
                    <location_id>{location.id}</location_id>       ⑫
                    <next_action>{nextAction}</next_action>
                    <completed>{completed}</completed>
                </task>;
            return retval;
        }

        public static function fromXML(taskXML:XML):Task {        ⑬
            var model:PomodoModelLocator =        ⑭
                PomodoModelLocator.getInstance();
            return new Task(
                taskXML.name,
                taskXML.notes,
                model.getProject(taskXML.project_id),        ⑮
                model.getLocation(taskXML.location_id),        ⑯
                XMLUtils.xmlListToBoolean(taskXML.next_action),        ⑰
                XMLUtils.xmlListToBoolean(taskXML.completed),        ⑱
                taskXML.id);        ⑲
        }
    }
}
```

We begin by creating a static constant for an unsaved Task ❶ id. We then create a bunch ❷ of Bindable public vars for the various properties of a Task. Next, we define a constructor ❸ that takes all the properties of a Task as parameters, but which has default values for all of them. This is the most flexible way of doing things (and this book is all about being flexible). Note that the default value for the id is the UNSAVED_ID ❹.

A few things are subtle about how we'll use the model objects. First, Rails will never care about the id in a task, project, or location XML we send it. (For Rails to use that id would be inviting security holes. Also, we'll use the id of the task, project, or location as part of the RESTful update URL.) However, on the Flex side, it's nice to have ids in the Task, Project, and Location, as we'll see.

Next, if the project ❺ or location ❻ is null, we default it to Project.NONE or Location.NONE. This is a good use of the Null Object pattern:[4] We want to use Tasks on the Flex side without adding a lot of annoying special-case code to check if (task.project == null) all the time. This accomplishes that goal. Now, we create a method called toUpdateObject ❼. This is subtle: Recall that we can't send PUT or DELETE requests. So, we fake them using a _method parameter that we set to PUT or DELETE. But this only works in a normal application/x-www-form-urlencoded POST—that is, if we send XML, we can't use this hack. We can't do a PUT or DELETE

---

[4] If you haven't read Martin Fowler's *Refactoring*, read it.

with XML data. As such, we need a way to send an object's values as form parameters. That's what this cheesy method does. The nice thing is that all this hacking is encapsulated now, instead of sprinkled throughout the code. Also, note that we can use the project.id ❽ and location.id ❾ without worrying about them being null—hooray for the Null Object pattern.

One obvious refactoring would be to not use public vars for the project and location, but instead to use set functions that checked whether a project or location was being set to null and used the null object instead.

Next, we create a toXML function ❿ that can marshal a Task into XML. We're including the project_id ⓫ and location_id ⓬ in the XML, because this is how Rails stores the Task. (Note again that we can use project.id and location.id with impunity.)

We create a static fromXML function ⓭ that unmarshals XML into a Task. (It's static so we can say Task.fromXML to produce a new Task: We don't have a Task instance when calling it; we're trying to create one.) It uses the shared PomodoModelLocator instance ⓮ to set the project ⓯ and location ⓰.

NOTE   We're going to rely on the fact that we'll get the lists of Projects and Locations first, and only get the list of Tasks once the Projects and Locations have come back. We could have also used a mechanism that stores the project_id and location_id in the Task and used the shared PomodoModelLocator to look up the Project or Location in a get method (and that stored the id of the Project or Location in a set method). I chose the approach I did because it seemed simpler to have objects refer to other objects via proper references, rather than needing to use hashes for everything.

Next, we use the XMLUtils.xmlListToBoolean method to get proper Boolean values for the next_action ⓱ and completed ⓲ parameters. (We're not using the next_action yet, but we'll add support for it where it's straightforward to do so, so that when we do hook it up we're halfway there.) Finally, we pass in the id from the XML ⓳.

9.2.2   Project.as

Next, we'll create the Project model; see listing 9.2. This is similar to what we did for the Task model.

Listing 9.2   app\flex\com\pomodo\model\Project.as

```
package com.pomodo.model {
    import mx.collections.ArrayCollection;
    import com.pomodo.util.XMLUtils;
```

```
public class Project {
    public static const UNSAVED_ID:int = 0;
    public static const NONE_ID:int = 0;        ❶

    public static const NONE: Project =         ❷
        new Project("- None - ", "", false, NONE_ID);

    public function Project(
        name:String = "",
        notes:String = "",
        completed:Boolean = false,
        id:int = UNSAVED_ID)
    {
        this.name = name;
        this.notes = notes;
        this.completed = completed;
        this.id = id;
        tasks = new ArrayCollection([]);         ❸
    }

    [Bindable]
    public var id: int;

    [Bindable]
    public var name:String;

    [Bindable]
    public var notes:String;

    [Bindable]
    public var completed: Boolean;

    [Bindable]
    public var tasks: ArrayCollection;           ❹

    public function addTask(task:Task):void {    ❺
        task.project = this;                     ❻
        tasks.addItem(task);                     ❼
    }

    public function removeTask(task:Task):void {         ❽
        if (task.project == this) {                      ❾
            for (var i:int = 0; i < tasks.length; i++) {      ❿
                if (tasks[i].id == task.id) {                 ⓫
                    tasks.removeItemAt(i);                    ⓬
                    task.project = null;                      ⓭
                    break;
                }
            }
        }
    }
```

```
public function toUpdateObject():Object {        ⑭
    var obj:Object = new Object();
    obj["project[name]"] = name;
    obj["project[notes]"] = notes;
    obj["project[completed]"] = completed;
    return obj;
}

public function toXML():XML {        ⑮
    var retval:XML =
        <project>
            <name>{name}</name>
            <notes>{notes}</notes>
            <completed>{completed}</completed>
        </project>;
    return retval;
}

public static function fromXML(proj:XML):Project {        ⑯
    return new Project(
        proj.name,
        proj.notes,
        XMLUtils.xmlListToBoolean(proj.completed),
        proj.id);
}
}
}
```

We're creating a null object for "no project," so we create a NONE_ID const of 0 ❶ and then a NONE Project ❷ with "- None -" as its name and NONE_ID for its id.

Inside the Project constructor, we create ❸ a new ArrayCollection ❹ for the Tasks this Project will contain. We then add an addTask ❺ method that sets the Project of the Task ❻ to this and adds the Task to the tasks ArrayCollection ❼. Similarly, the removeTask ❽ method takes a Task as a parameter and checks that the Task's Project is the current Project ❾; if so, the method iterates ❿, looking for the task with the matching id ⓫, and, when it finds it, removes it from the tasks ArrayCollection ⓬ and sets its project to null ⓭.

Finally, we create toUpdateObject ⑭, toXML ⑮, and fromXML ⑯ methods, which are extremely similar to those of the Task class. Note that we don't marshal the tasks ArrayCollection—this isn't about sending an object graph to Rails, it's about sending exactly what Rails was already expecting. (This is a refactoring on the Flex side only: The Rails code is unchanged.)

9.2.3 *Location.as*

Next, we'll create the Location model; see listing 9.3. There is nothing new here; it's a copy-paste-modify of the Task or Project class.

Listing 9.3   app\flex\com\pomodo\model\Location.as

```
package com.pomodo.model {
    import mx.collections.ArrayCollection;

    public class Location {
        public static const UNSAVED_ID:int = 0;
        public static const NONE_ID:int = 0;

        public static const NONE: Location =
            new Location("- None - ", "", NONE_ID);

        public function Location(
            name:String = "",
            notes:String = "",
            id:int = UNSAVED_ID)
        {
            this.name = name;
            this.notes = notes;
            this.id = id;
            tasks = new ArrayCollection([]);
        }

        [Bindable]
        public var id: int;

        [Bindable]
        public var name:String;

        [Bindable]
        public var notes:String;

        [Bindable]
        public var tasks: ArrayCollection;

        public function addTask(task:Task):void {
            task.location = this;
            tasks.addItem(task);
        }

        public function removeTask(task:Task):void {
            if (task.location == this) {
                for (var i:int = 0; i < tasks.length; i++) {
                    if (tasks[i].id == task.id) {
                        tasks.removeItemAt(i);
                        task.location = null;
                        break;
                    }
                }
            }
        }
    }
}
```

```
public function toUpdateObject():Object {
    var obj:Object = new Object();
    obj["location[name]"] = name;
    obj["location[notes]"] = notes;
    return obj;
}

public function toXML():XML {
    var retval:XML =
        <location>
            <name>{name}</name>
            <notes>{notes}</notes>
        </location>;
    return retval;
}

public static function fromXML(loc:XML):Location {
    return new Location(loc.name, loc.notes, loc.id);
}
    }
}
```

NOTE Because we're further along in the book and your knowledge of Flex and Rails has grown, I'll be skipping redundant explanations that will probably only bore you. I'll only number the lines I'll explain.

9.2.4 *User.as*

Finally, we'll create the User model; see listing 9.4.

> **Listing 9.4   app\flex\com\pomodo\model\User.as**

```
package com.pomodo.model {
    public class User {
        [Bindable]
        public var login:String;

        [Bindable]
        public var email:String;

        [Bindable]
        public var firstName:String;

        [Bindable]
        public var lastName:String;

        [Bindable]
        public var notes:String;

        [Bindable]
```

```
    public var password:String;              ❶

    public function User(
        login:String = "",
        email:String = "",
        firstName:String = "",
        lastName:String = "",
        notes:String = "",
        password:String = "")
    {
        this.login = login;
        this.email = email;
        this.firstName = firstName;
        this.lastName = lastName;
        this.notes = notes;
        this.password = password;
    }

    public function toXML():XML {
        var retval:XML =
            <user>
                <login>{login}</login>
                <email>{email}</email>
                <first_name>{firstName}</first_name>
                <last_name>{lastName}</last_name>
                <notes>{notes}</notes>
                <password>{password}</password>              ❷
<password_confirmation>{password}</password_confirmation>            ❸
            </user>;
        return retval;
    }

    public static function fromXML(userXML:XML):User {
        var user:User = new User();
        user.login = userXML.login;
        user.email = userXML.email;
        user.firstName = userXML.first_name;
        user.lastName = userXML.last_name;
        user.notes = userXML.notes;                  ❹

        return user;
    }
  }
}
```

The one thing to note here is that the User model has a password property ❶ that is essentially one-way: It's used to create the User by setting the password ❷ and password_confirmation ❸ in the toXML method. Because no password comes back from Rails ❹, we don't set it in fromXML.

9.3 *Modifying the PomodoModelLocator*

Next, we'll modify the PomodoModelLocator. This is all straightforward; there's a lot of it, as shown in listing 9.5.

Listing 9.5   app\flex\com\pomodo\model\PomodoModelLocator.as

```
package com.pomodo.model {
    import com.adobe.cairngorm.model.IModelLocator;
    import com.pomodo.control.EventNames;
    import com.pomodo.util.CairngormUtils;
    import com.pomodo.util.XMLUtils;          ⟵── Remove import
    import com.pomodo.validators.ServerErrors;

    import mx.collections.ArrayCollection;
    import mx.collections.ICollectionView;     ⟵── Remove imports
    import mx.collections.IViewCursor;
    import mx.collections.XMLListCollection;
    import mx.collections.ListCollectionView;  ⟵── Add import
    import mx.formatters.CurrencyFormatter;

    [Bindable]
    public class PomodoModelLocator implements IModelLocator {
        public static const NO_PROJECT_XML:XML =    ⟵
            <project>                                     NO_PROJECT_XML and
                <name>  None  </name>                     NO_LOCATION_XML
                <id type="integer">0</id>                 replaced by
            </project>;                                   Project.NONE and
                                                          Location.NONE
        public static const NO_LOCATION_XML:XML =
            <location>
                <name>  None  </name>
                <id type="integer">0</id>
            </location>;

        public static const VIEWING_SPLASH_SCREEN:int = 0;
        public static const VIEWING_MAIN_APP:int = 1;

        public var user:User;        ⟵   Make user variable
        public var user:XML;             User, not XML           ❶ Replace tasksXLC
                                                                    XMLListCollection
                                                                    with tasks
        public var tasks:ListCollectionView;     ⟵                 ListCollectionView
        public var tasksXLC:XMLListCollection;

                                                              Store
                                                              Projects
        public var projects:ListCollectionView;     ⟵

                                                              Store Locations
        public var locations:ListCollectionView;    ⟵

                                                              Store Projects
                                                              and Project.NONE
        public var projectsAndNone:ListCollectionView;  ⟵
```

```
public var locationsAndNone:ListCollectionView;

public var projectIDMap:Object;

public var locationIDMap:Object;

public var projectsAndNoneXLC:XMLListCollection;

public var locationsAndNoneXLC:XMLListCollection;

public var accountCreateErrors:ServerErrors;

public var workflowState:int = VIEWING_SPLASH_SCREEN;

public var reviews:String =
'"pomodo, the hot new RIA by 38noises, is taking ' +
'over Web 2.0." --Michael Arrington*\n"I wish I\'d ' +
'invested in 38noises instead of that other company."' +
' --Jeff Bezos*\n"38noises closed angel funding at a ' +
'party in my bathroom last night." --Om Malik*';

public function updateTask(task:Task):void {
    for (var i:int = 0; i < tasks.length; i++) {
        var ithTask:Task = Task(tasks.getItemAt(i));
        if (ithTask.id == task.id) {
            tasks.setItemAt(task, i);
            break;
        }
    }
}

public function removeTask(task:Task):void {
    for (var i:int = 0; i < tasks.length; i++) {
        var ithTask:Task = Task(tasks.getItemAt(i));
        if (ithTask.id == task.id) {
            ithTask.project.removeTask(ithTask);
            ithTask.location.removeTask(ithTask);
            tasks.removeItemAt(i);
            break;
        }
    }
}

public function setTasks(list:XMLList):void {
    var tasksArray:Array = [];
    var item:XML;
    for each (item in list) {
        var task:Task = Task.fromXML(item);
        tasksArray.push(task);
    }
    tasks = new ArrayCollection(tasksArray);
}
```

Store Locations and Location.NONE

Rename for better style

Delete old XMLList-Collections

Find and replace task with matching id

Find and remove task with matching id

New Task for each XML item in XMLList

static Task.fromXML method, used to unmarshal XML into Task

```
public function setProjects(list:XMLList):void {          Construct
    projectIDMap = {};                                    based on
    projectIDMap[0] = Project.NONE;         Add           temporary
    var projectsArray:Array = [];           Project.NONE to  projectsAnd-
    var item:XML;                           projectIDMap   NoneArray
    for each (item in list) {
        var project:Project = Project.fromXML(item);
        projectsArray.push(project);
        projectIDMap[project.id] = project;
    }
    projects = new ArrayCollection(projectsArray);       ❷ Copy Array
    var projectsAndNoneArray:Array =                        with slice(0)
        projectsArray.slice(0);                             call
    projectsAndNoneArray.splice(0, 0, Project.NONE);
    projectsAndNone =                                        Add
        new ArrayCollection(projectsAndNoneArray);      Project.NONE
    _gotProjects = true;            Similar to          to beginning of
    listTasksIfMapsPresent();       projectsXLC         projectsAndNone
}                                   set method          Array

public function setLocations(list:XMLList):void {        Operates like
    locationIDMap = {};                                  setProjects
    locationIDMap[0] = Location.NONE;                    method
    var locationsArray:Array = [];
    var item:XML;
    for each (item in list) {
        var location:Location = Location.fromXML(item);
        locationsArray.push(location);
        locationIDMap[location.id] = location;
    }
    locations = new ArrayCollection(locationsArray);
    var locationsAndNoneArray:Array =
        locationsArray.slice(0);
    locationsAndNoneArray.splice(0, 0, Location.NONE);
    locationsAndNone =
        new ArrayCollection(locationsAndNoneArray);
    _gotLocations = true;
    listTasksIfMapsPresent();
}

public function get projectsXLC():XMLListCollection {
    return _projectsXLC;
}

public function set projectsXLC(setValue:
XMLListCollection):void {
...
}

public function get locationsXLC():XMLListCollection {
```

```
          return _locationsXLC;
    }

    public function set locationsXLC(
        setValue:XMLListCollection):void
    {

    }
```

**Return Project
instead of XML**

```
    public function getProject(projectID:int):Project {
        if (projectIDMap == null) return null;
        return projectIDMap[projectID];
    }
    public function getProject(project_id:int):XML {
        if (projectIdMap == null) return null;
        return projectIdMap[project_id];
    }
```

**Return Location
instead of XML**

```
    public function getLocation(locationID:int):Location {
        if (locationIDMap == null) return null;
        return locationIDMap[locationID];
    }
    public function getLocation(location_id:int):XML {
        if (locationIdMap == null) return null;
        return locationIdMap[location_id];
    }

    private var _gotProjects:Boolean;

    private var _gotLocations:Boolean;
```

**Delete
obsolete
code**

```
    private var _projectsAndNoneXLC:XMLListCollection;

    private var _locationsAndNoneXLC:XMLListCollection;

    private var _projectsXLC:XMLListCollection;

    private var _locationsXLC:XMLListCollection;

    private function getProjectsAndNone(projectsXL:XMLList):
    XMLListCollection {

    }

    private function getLocationsAndNone(
    locationsXL:XMLList):XMLListCollection {

    }

    private function listTasksIfMapsPresent():void {
        if (_gotProjects && _gotLocations) {
```

```
                CairngormUtils.dispatchEvent(
                    EventNames.LIST_TASKS);
            }
        }

        private static var modelLocator:PomodoModelLocator;

        public static function getInstance():PomodoModelLocator{
            if (modelLocator == null) {
                modelLocator = new PomodoModelLocator();
            }
            return modelLocator;
        }

        public function PomodoModelLocator() {
            if (modelLocator != null) {
                throw new Error(
    "Only one PomodoModelLocator instance may be instantiated.");
            }
            _gotProjects = false;          Delete
            _gotLocations = false;         obsolete
            _projectsXLC = null;      ◁──┘ code
            _locationsXLC = null;
        }
    }
}
```

We replace the `tasksXLC XMLListCollection` with a `tasks ListCollection-
View` ❶. `ListCollectionView` is the base class of `ArrayCollection`, which is
what the tasks will be. `ListCollectionView` implements `ICollectionView`
and `IList`.

Q. Shouldn't you make the tasks thing be an interface instead of a class? Isn't
programming to interfaces more flexible than programming to classes? Did you
fail Polymorphism 101?

A. In an ideal world, yes, I would make the tasks thing be an interface type. However, `ListCollectionView` implements two interfaces (`ICollectionView` and
`IList`). If I made it an `ICollectionView`, I couldn't pass it to something that
took an `IList`, and vice versa. Also, there are `IList` and `ICollectionView` methods I want to call. Given the way the Flex 3 class hierarchy is, using `List-
CollectionView` is more flexible. (If there was an `IListCollectionView`
interface, I would have used that.)

Note also that I've learned my lesson and removed the type suffix from my collections. If I had called the `tasksXLC` `XMLListCollection` tasks, I would have had less work to do. I'm calling the tasks `ListCollectionView` tasks instead of `tasksLCV`, so that if I change its type again I'll potentially have less work to do.

The `slice(0)` call ❷ is the way we copy an `Array`. The slightly convoluted way that the `projectsAndNone` `ArrayCollection` is initialized (all at once, as opposed to basing it on a copy of the `projectsArray` and then using `addItem` to add the `Project.NONE` to the beginning) is done for an obscure reason: This `ArrayCollection` is being used as the `dataProvider` to the `Project ComboBox` in the `TaskCreateBox`. If we create the `ArrayCollection` based on an `Array` and then do `addItem` to add an element to the beginning, that item is added correctly. However, it isn't the default selected item in the `ComboBox`—that item is the item that was the first element in the `Array` that we used to do the initial population of the `ArrayCollection`, which is now at index 1. We want the default project to be `"- None -"`, so we do this to do it all at once. (If that didn't make any sense, run the app at the end of this iteration and experiment using `addItem` instead.)

Now that we have a proper object model, we'll make the supporting changes to take advantage of this improved infrastructure. We'll start by modifying the `ServiceUtils` class, then the business delegates that use it, then the commands that use the business delegates, and finally the components that use the commands.

9.4 *Modifying ServiceUtils*

The `ServiceUtils` class has served us well, but it's time to make it even more useful. Having to explicitly do stuff like `params['_method'] = "PUT";` in the delegate classes is lame. Surely this should be wrapped in `ServiceUtils`.

We'll do that here, plus a little more. We'll also reorder the parameters, so the HTTP method (real or hacked) comes sooner; see listing 9.6.

Listing 9.6   app\flex\com\pomodo\util\ServiceUtils.as

```
package com.pomodo.util {
    import mx.rpc.IResponder;
    import mx.rpc.AsyncToken;
    import mx.rpc.http.HTTPService;

    public class ServiceUtils {
        public static function send(
            url:String,
            responder:IResponder = null,
            method:String = null,          ❶
            request:Object = null,
            sendXML:Boolean = false,
```

```
                    resultFormat:String = "e4x",
                    useProxy:Boolean = false):void
            {

                var service:HTTPService = new HTTPService();
                service.url = url;
                service.request = request;            ❷
                service.contentType = sendXML ? "application/xml" :
                    "application/x-www-form-urlencoded";
                service.resultFormat = resultFormat;
                if (method == null) {
                    service.method = (request == null) ?
                        "GET" : "POST";
                } else if ((method == "PUT") ||
                        (method == "DELETE")) {          ❸
                    service.method = "POST";             ❹
                    if (request == null) {               ❺
                        request = new Object();          ❻
                    }
                    request["_method"] = method;         ❼
                } else {
                    service.method = method;
                }
                service.request = request;            ❽
                service.useProxy = useProxy;
                var call:AsyncToken = service.send();
                if (responder != null) {
                    call.addResponder(responder);
                }
            }
        }
    }
```

We start by reordering the parameters ❶. Next, we move the `service.request` assignment lower ❷❽ because we're potentially constructing the request dynamically ❻. We adding a check to see whether the method is PUT or DELETE ❸; and if so, we set the service method to "POST" ❹ and construct a new request ❻ if the request was null ❺. We then set the request _method field ❼ to the "PUT" or "DELETE" that the user specified.

Note that we don't currently prevent ourselves from mistakenly trying to send XML with a PUT or DELETE. This would be a useful enhancement.

9.5   *Modifying the business delegates*

Now that we've finished with the model and the ServiceUtils, let's move one step up the food chain to the classes that use ServiceUtils: the business delegates. These changes are easy: All we're doing is modifying the business delegates to take our new model classes as parameters (instead of XML) and to call the modified `ServiceUtils.send` method.

9.5.1 *TaskDelegate.as*

We'll start with `TaskDelegate`; see listing 9.7.

Listing 9.7   app\flex\com\pomodo\business\TaskDelegate.as

```
package com.pomodo.business {
    import mx.rpc.IResponder;
    import com.pomodo.model.Task;          ⊲———┐ Add
    import com.pomodo.util.ServiceUtils;         │ import

    public class TaskDelegate {
        private var _responder:IResponder;

        public function TaskDelegate(responder:IResponder) {
            _responder = responder;
        }

        public function listTasks():void {
            ServiceUtils.send("/tasks.xml", _responder);
        }

        public function createTask(task:XML):void {
            ServiceUtils.send("/tasks.xml", _responder, task,
                true);
        public function createTask(task:Task):void {        ⊲———┐
            ServiceUtils.send("/tasks.xml", _responder, "POST",
                task.toXML(), true);                              │
        }                                                    Modify
                                                             createTask ❶

        public function updateTask(taskID:int, keys:Array,
            values:Array):void
        {
            var params:Object = new Object();
            for (var i:int = 0; i < keys.length; i++) {
                params['task[' + keys[i] +']'] = values[i];
            }
            params['_method'] = "PUT";
            ServiceUtils.send(
                "/tasks/" + taskID + ".xml",
                _responder,
                params);                                ❷ Modify
        public function updateTask(task:Task):void {  ⊲——┘ updateTask
            ServiceUtils.send(
                "/tasks/" + task.id + ".xml", _responder, "PUT",
                task.toUpdateObject(), false);
        }
```

```
public function destroyTask(taskID:int):void {
    ServiceUtils.send(
        "/tasks/" + taskID + ".xml",
        _responder,
        {_method: "DELETE"});
public function destroyTask(task:Task):void {          ← ❸ Modify
    ServiceUtils.send(                                        destroyTask
        "/tasks/" + task.id + ".xml",
        _responder,
        "DELETE");
    }
}
}
```

We modify the TaskDelegate createTask method ❶ to call ServiceUtils.send with the same URL and _responder, but with the method explicitly set to "POST", which is a consequence of having moved it earlier: We need to specify it more often. We also pass task.toXML() instead of just the task, which had been XML beforehand. Then, we specify true for the sendXML parameter.

Next, we modify the updateTask ❷ method to only take one parameter, the Task, instead of three ugly parameters. This is better, even if it means that we'll sometimes be doing redundant updates of some Task attributes—the code is much cleaner. We call ServiceUtils.send with the same URL, but this time the id comes from the task that was passed in. We use the same _responder, but we then do different things: We specify the method of "PUT" and call task.toUpdate-Object to generate the somewhat cheesy form parameters we need (recall that we can't send XML with the hacked PUT _method). Finally, we specify false for the sendXML parameter.

Finally, we modify the destroyTask ❸, calling ServiceUtils.send with a URL formed from the Task id, the same _responder, and a "DELETE" method instead of a hacked-up object to post as parameters. It's nice to keep the hacking inside ServiceUtils.

Next, we'll modify the ProjectDelegate.

9.5.2 *ProjectDelegate.as*

We make changes to the ProjectDelegate that are similar to those we made to the TaskDelegate; see listing 9.8.

Listing 9.8   app\flex\com\pomodo\business\ProjectDelegate.as

```
package com.pomodo.business {
    import mx.rpc.IResponder;
    import com.pomodo.model.Project;          ❶
```

```
import com.pomodo.util.ServiceUtils;

public class ProjectDelegate {
    private var _responder:IResponder;

    public function ProjectDelegate(responder:IResponder) {
        _responder = responder;
    }

    public function listProjects():void {
        ServiceUtils.send("/projects.xml", _responder);
    }

    public function createProject(project:XML):void {
        ServiceUtils.send("/projects.xml", _responder,
            project, true);
    public function createProject(project:Project):void {       ❷
        ServiceUtils.send("/projects.xml", _responder,
            "POST", project.toXML(), true);
    }

    public function updateProject(
        projectID:int,
        keys: Array,
        values: Array):void
    {
        var params:Object = new Object();
        for (var i:int = 0; i < keys.length; i++) {
            params['project[' + keys[i] +']'] = values[i];
        }
        params['_method'] = "PUT";
        ServiceUtils.send(
            "/projects/" + projectID + ".xml",
            _responder,
            params);
    public function updateProject(project:Project):void {       ❸
        ServiceUtils.send(
            "/projects/" + project.id + ".xml",
            _responder, "PUT", project.toUpdateObject(),
            false);
    }

    public function destroyProject(projectID:int):void {
        ServiceUtils.send(
            "/projects/" + projectID + ".xml",
            _responder,
            {_method: "DELETE"});
    public function destroyProject(project:Project):void {      ❹
        ServiceUtils.send(
            "/projects/" + project.id + ".xml",
```

```
                      _responder, "DELETE");
        }
    }
}
```

This is more of the same. We add an import ❶ and modify the createProject ❷, updateProject ❸, and destroyProject ❹ to use the new ServiceUtils.send method and the Project class that is now passed in.

Next, we'll modify the LocationDelegate.

9.5.3 *LocationDelegate.as*

The changes we make to the LocationDelegate are similar to those we made to the ProjectDelegate; see listing 9.9.

Listing 9.9   app\flex\com\pomodo\business\LocationDelegate.as

```
package com.pomodo.business {
    import mx.rpc.IResponder;
    import com.pomodo.model.Location;          <──── Add import
    import com.pomodo.util.ServiceUtils;

    public class LocationDelegate {
        private var _responder:IResponder;

        public function LocationDelegate(responder:IResponder) {
            _responder = responder;
        }

        public function listLocations():void {
            ServiceUtils.send("/locations.xml", _responder);
        }

        public function createLocation(location:XML):void {
            ServiceUtils.send("/locations.xml", _responder,
                location, true);
        public function createLocation(location:Location):void {   <──┐
            ServiceUtils.send("/locations.xml", _responder,
                "POST", location.toXML(), true);                       │
        }                                                     Modify
                                                         createLocation │
        public function updateLocation(
            locationID: int,
            keys: Array,
            values: Array):void
        {
```

```
var params:Object = new Object();
for (var i:int = 0; i < keys.length; i++) {
    params['location[' + keys[i] +']'] = values[i];
}
params['_method'] = "PUT";
ServiceUtils.send(
    "/locations/" + locationID + ".xml",
    _responder,
    params);
                                                          Modify
                                                          updateLocation
public function updateLocation(location:Location):void {  ◁———
    ServiceUtils.send(
        "/locations/" + location.id + ".xml",
        _responder, "PUT", location.toUpdateObject(),
        false);
}


public function destroyLocation(locationID:int):void {
    ServiceUtils.send(
        "/locations/" + locationID + ".xml",
        _responder,
        {_method: "DELETE"});               Modify destroyLocation
public function destroyLocation(location:Location):void {  ◁———
    ServiceUtils.send(
        "/locations/" + location.id + ".xml",
        _responder, "DELETE");
    }
  }
}
```

9.5.4 SessionDelegate.as

Next, we modify the `SessionDelegate` to specify a method of `POST`; see listing 9.10.

Listing 9.10   app\flex\com\pomodo\business\SessionDelegate.as

```
. . .
        public function createSession(login:String,
        password:String):void {
            ServiceUtils.send(
                "/session.xml",
                _responder,
                "POST",
                {login: login, password: password});
        }
. . .
```

9.5.5 UserDelegate.as

Finally, we modify the `UserDelegate`; see listing 9.11.

Listing 9.11 app\flex\com\pomodo\business\UserDelegate.as

```
package com.pomodo.business {
    import mx.rpc.IResponder;
    import com.pomodo.model.User;        ❶
    import com.pomodo.util.ServiceUtils;

    public class UserDelegate {
        private var _responder:IResponder;

        public function UserDelegate(responder:IResponder) {
            _responder = responder;
        }

        public function createUser(user:XML):void {
            ServiceUtils.send("/users.xml", _responder, user,
                true);
        public function createUser(user:User):void {    ❷
            ServiceUtils.send("/users.xml", _responder, "POST",
                user.toXML(), true);
        }
    }
}
```

We add an import ❶ and modify the createUser ❷ function to take a User as the parameter (again, a big improvement) and to call the new ServiceUtils.send method with a method of "POST" and the toXML() of the User passed in.

That's it for the business delegates. If you thought that was easy, it gets easier.

9.6 *Modifying the commands*

Next, we'll modify the commands that use the business delegates. This will be trivial.

9.6.1 *CreateSessionCommand.as*

First, we modify the CreateSessionCommand; see listing 9.12.

Listing 9.12 app\flex\com\pomodo\command\CreateSessionCommand.as

```
package com.pomodo.command {
...
    import com.pomodo.model.PomodoModelLocator;
    import com.pomodo.model.User;        ❶

    import mx.controls.Alert;
...
    public class CreateSessionCommand implements ICommand,
    IResponder {
```

```
...
        public function result(event:Object):void {
            var result:Object = event.result;
            if (event.result == "badlogin") {
                Alert.show("Login failed.");
            } else {
                var model:PomodoModelLocator =
                    PomodoModelLocator.getInstance();
                model.user = XML(event.result);
                model.user = User.fromXML(XML(event.result));      ❷
                model.workflowState =
                    PomodoModelLocator.VIEWING_MAIN_APP;
            }
        }
    ...
    }
```

All we're doing here is adding an import ❶ and setting the model.user (which is now a User) with the result of calling User.fromXML ❷.

9.6.2 *CreateUserCommand.as*

Next, we modify the CreateUserCommand; see listing 9.13.

Listing 9.13   app\flex\com\pomodo\command\CreateUserCommand.as

```
package com.pomodo.command {
    import com.adobe.cairngorm.commands.ICommand;
    import com.adobe.cairngorm.control.CairngormEvent;
    import com.pomodo.business.UserDelegate;
    import com.pomodo.model.PomodoModelLocator;
    import com.pomodo.model.User;                      ❶
    import com.pomodo.validators.ServerErrors;
...
    public class CreateUserCommand implements ICommand,
    IResponder {
...
        public function result(event:Object):void {
            var result:Object = event.result;
            var model:PomodoModelLocator =
                PomodoModelLocator.getInstance();
            if (result is XML) {
                var resultXML:XML = XML(result);
                if (resultXML.name().localName == "errors") {
...
                } else {
                    model.user = resultXML;
                    model.user = User.fromXML(resultXML);      ❷
                    model.workflowState =
```

```
                        PomodoModelLocator.VIEWING_MAIN_APP;
            }
        } else {
    ...
```

We add an import ❶ and set the model.user with the result of calling User.fromXML ❷ instead of using the XML.

9.6.3   *DestroyTaskCommand.as*

Next, we modify DestroyTaskCommand; see listing 9.14.

Listing 9.14   app\flex\com\pomodo\command\DestroyTaskCommand.as

```
package com.pomodo.command {
    import com.adobe.cairngorm.commands.ICommand;
    import com.adobe.cairngorm.control.CairngormEvent;
    import com.pomodo.business.TaskDelegate;
    import com.pomodo.control.EventNames;
    import com.pomodo.model.PomodoModelLocator;
    import com.pomodo.model.Task;                    ❶
    import com.pomodo.util.CairngormUtils;
    ...
    public class DestroyTaskCommand implements ICommand,
    IResponder {
    ...
        public function result(event:Object):void {
            var resultEvent:ResultEvent = ResultEvent(event);
            var model:PomodoModelLocator =
                PomodoModelLocator.getInstance();
            if (event.result == "error") {
                Alert.show(
                    "The task was not successfully deleted.",
                    "Error");
            } else {
                var deletedTask:XML = XML(event.result);        ❷
                var deletedTaskId:int = deletedTask.id;
                for (var i:int = 0; i < model.tasksXLC.length;
                    i++)
                {
                    var ithTask:XML =
                        XML(model.tasksXLC.getItemAt(i));
                    if (ithTask.id == deletedTaskId) {
                        model.tasksXLC.removeItemAt(i);
                        break;
                    }
                }
                model.removeTask(            ❸
                    Task.fromXML(XML(event.result)));
```

```
            }
        }
    ...
    }
```

Here we add an import ❶, delete a bunch of code ❷, and instead call the removeTask ❸ method that we created to do this for us in PomodoModelLocator with a new Task that we construct from the XML we received. Yes, it's wasteful to construct a new Task just to delete it—however, I prefer working with Tasks to passing ids or XML around.

Note that we don't need to modify the DestroyLocationCommand or the DestroyProjectCommand—those commands pass their event.data to delegate methods. Even though we'll change the delegates, the commands themselves are unchanged.

9.6.4   *ListLocationsCommand.as*

Next, we modify ListLocationsCommand; see listing 9.15.

Listing 9.15   app\flex\com\pomodo\command\ListLocationsCommand.as

```
package com.pomodo.command {
...
    import mx.rpc.events.ResultEvent;
    import mx.collections.XMLListCollection;

    public class ListLocationsCommand implements ICommand,
    IResponder {
        public function ListLocationsCommand() {
        }

        public function execute(event:CairngormEvent):void {
            var delegate:LocationDelegate =
                new LocationDelegate(this);
            delegate.listLocations();
        }

        public function result(event:Object):void {
            var model:PomodoModelLocator =
                PomodoModelLocator.getInstance();
            model.locationsXLC = new XMLListCollection(
            model.setLocations(           ❶
                XMLList(event.result.children()));
        }
    ...
    }
```

All we're doing here is calling `model.setLocations()` ❶ in the `result` handler instead of setting the `model.locationsXLC`.

9.6.5 ListProjectsCommand.as

Next, we modify the `ListProjectsCommand`; see listing 9.16.

Listing 9.16 app\flex\com\pomodo\command\ListProjectsCommand.as

```
package com.pomodo.command {
...
    import mx.rpc.events.ResultEvent;
    import mx.collections.XMLListCollection;

    public class ListProjectsCommand implements ICommand,
    IResponder {
...
        public function result(event:Object):void {
            var model:PomodoModelLocator =
                PomodoModelLocator.getInstance();
            model.projectsXLC = new XMLListCollection(
            model.setProjects(          ❶
                XMLList(event.result.children()));
        }
...
    }
}
```

Similarly, we're just calling `model.setProjects()` ❶ instead of assigning `model.projectsXLC`.

9.6.6 ListTasksCommand.as

Next, we modify the `ListTasksCommand`; see listing 9.17.

Listing 9.17 app\flex\com\pomodo\command\ListTasksCommand.as

```
package com.pomodo.command {
...
    import mx.rpc.events.ResultEvent;
    import mx.collections.XMLListCollection;

    public class ListTasksCommand implements ICommand,
    IResponder {
...
        public function result(event:Object):void {
            var model:PomodoModelLocator =
                PomodoModelLocator.getInstance();
            model.tasksXLC = new XMLListCollection(
```

```
            model.setTasks(        ❶
                XMLList(event.result.children()));
        }
    . . .
```

We call `model.setTasks()` ❶ instead of assigning `model.tasksXLC`.

9.6.7 *UpdateLocationCommand.as*

Now, we modify the `UpdateLocationCommand`; see listing 9.18.

Listing 9.18 app\flex\com\pomodo\command\UpdateLocationCommand.as

```
    . . .
        public function execute(event:CairngormEvent):void {
            var delegate:LocationDelegate =
                new LocationDelegate(this);
            delegate.updateLocation(
                event.data.locationID,
                event.data.keys,
                event.data.values);
            delegate.updateLocation(event.data);        ❶
        }
    . . .
```

We call `delegate.updateLocation()` with the `event.data` ❶ (which is now a `Location`) instead of with the `locationID`, `keys`, and `values` we had been using. This is much cleaner.

9.6.8 *UpdateProjectCommand.as*

Next, we modify `UpdateProjectCommand`; see listing 9.19.

Listing 9.19 app\flex\com\pomodo\command\UpdateProjectCommand.as

```
    . . .
        public function execute(event:CairngormEvent):void {
            var delegate:ProjectDelegate =
                new ProjectDelegate(this);
            delegate.updateProject(
                event.data.projectID,
                event.data.keys,
                event.data.values);
            delegate.updateProject(event.data);        ❶
        }
    . . .
```

We call `delegate.updateProject()`with the `event.data` ❶ (which is now a `Project`) instead of with the `projectID`, `keys`, and `values` we had been using.

9.6.9   *UpdateTaskCommand.as*

Finally, we modify the `UpdateTaskCommand`; see listing 9.20.

Listing 9.20   app\flex\com\pomodo\command\UpdateTaskCommand.as

```
package com.pomodo.command {
    import com.adobe.cairngorm.commands.ICommand;
    import com.adobe.cairngorm.control.CairngormEvent;
    import com.pomodo.business.TaskDelegate;
    import com.pomodo.model.PomodoModelLocator;
    import com.pomodo.model.Task;

    import mx.rpc.IResponder;
    import mx.rpc.events.FaultEvent;
    import mx.rpc.events.ResultEvent;

    public class UpdateTaskCommand implements ICommand,
    IResponder {
        public function UpdateTaskCommand() {
        }

        public function execute(event:CairngormEvent):void {
            var delegate:TaskDelegate = new TaskDelegate(this);
            delegate.updateTask(
                event.data.taskID,
                event.data.keys,
                event.data.values);
            delegate.updateTask(event.data);            ❶
        }

        public function result(event:Object):void {
            var resultEvent:ResultEvent = ResultEvent(event);
            var model:PomodoModelLocator =
                PomodoModelLocator.getInstance();
            var newTask:XML = XML(event.result);
            for (var i:int = 0; i < model.tasksXLC.length; i++)
            {
                var ithTask:XML =
                    XML(model.tasksXLC.getItemAt(i));
                if (ithTask.id == newTask.id) {
                    model.tasksXLC.setItemAt(newTask, i);
                    break;
                }
            }
            model.updateTask(Task.fromXML(XML(event.result)));     ❷
        }
```

```
    public function fault(event:Object):void {
        Pomodo.debug("UpdateTaskCommand#fault: " + event);
    }
  }
}
```

We modify the `execute` method to call `updateTask` ❶ with the `event.data` (which is now a `Task`) instead of the `id`, `keys`, and `values` we had been using. We then modify the `result` handler to call the `model.updateTask` function ❷ with a new `Task` that is constructed by calling `Task.fromXML()` on the `result` XML, instead of doing a bunch of code in this handler.

> **NOTE** How much code should go in the commands versus in model objects or the `ModelLocator` is a design decision I struggled with. I came to the conclusion that because code in commands can't be shared with other commands (other than copy-paste), code that looks general should be put somewhere else. Don't get carried away with this, though.

9.7 Modifying the components

Finally, we'll modify the components. Some of these changes are easy; others are tedious. The dominant theme is that we're abstracting ourselves from the messy details of XML, keys, values, and so on and dealing with `Tasks`, `Projects`, and `Locations`. This is much better.

9.7.1 MainBox.mxml

We'll start with a simple change, by modifying the `MainBox`; see listing 9.21.

Listing 9.21   app\flex\com\pomodo\components\MainBox.mxml

```
. . .
        <mx:Label text="{'Logged in as: ' +
            _model.user.login +
            ' (' + _model.user.email + ')'}"/>
        <mx:Label text="{'Welcome back ' +
            _model.user.first_name + '!'}"/>
            _model.user.firstName + '!'}"/>          ❶
        <mx:Accordion width="100%" height="350">
. . .
```

The `_model.user` is now a `User`, not XML. So, we refer to the Flex-style `first-Name` ❶ variable, instead of the `first_name` element in XML.

9.7.2   *TaskCreateBox.mxml*

Next, we modify the `TaskCreateBox`; see listing 9.22.

Listing 9.22   app\flex\com\pomodo\components\TaskCreateBox.mxml

```
<?xml version="1.0" encoding="utf-8"?>
<mx:VBox xmlns:mx="http://www.adobe.com/2006/mxml"
    width="100%" height="100%" label="New Task">
<mx:Script>
<![CDATA[
    import com.pomodo.control.EventNames;
    import com.pomodo.model.Task;              ❶
    import com.pomodo.model.Project;
    import com.pomodo.model.Location;
    import com.pomodo.model.PomodoModelLocator;
    import com.pomodo.util.CairngormUtils;

    [Bindable]
    private var _model:PomodoModelLocator =
        PomodoModelLocator.getInstance();

    private function doTaskCreate():void {
        var projectID: int = XML(projectsCB.selectedItem).id;
        var locationID: int = XML(locationsCB.selectedItem).id;
        var task : XML =
            <task>
                <name>{nameTI.text}</name>
                <notes>{notesTI.text}</notes>
                <project_id>{projectID}</project_id>
                <location_id>{locationID}</location_id>
            </task>;
        var task:Task = new Task(           ❷
            nameTI.text,
            notesTI.text,
            Project(projectsCB.selectedItem),
            Location(locationsCB.selectedItem));
        CairngormUtils.dispatchEvent(EventNames.CREATE_TASK,
            task);
    }
]]>
</mx:Script>
    <mx:Form width="100%" height="100%">
        <mx:FormItem label="Task">
            <mx:TextInput id="nameTI" width="200"/>
        </mx:FormItem>
        <mx:FormItem label="Notes">
            <mx:TextArea id="notesTI" width="200" height="100"/>
        </mx:FormItem>
        <mx:FormItem label="Project">
            <mx:ComboBox id="projectsCB" width="200"
```

```
                    labelField="name"
                    dataProvider="{_model.projectsAndNoneXLC}"/>
                    dataProvider="{_model.projectsAndNone}"/>        ❸
            </mx:FormItem>
            <mx:FormItem label="">
                <mx:CheckBox id="nextActionCheckbox"
                    label="This is the Next Action"/>
            </mx:FormItem>
            <mx:FormItem label="Location">
                <mx:ComboBox id="locationsCB" width="200"
                    labelField="name"
                    dataProvider="{_model.locationsAndNoneXLC}"/>
                    dataProvider="{_model.locationsAndNone}"/>       ❹
            </mx:FormItem>
            <mx:FormItem>
                <mx:Button label="Submit" width="160" height="30"
                    click="doTaskCreate()"/>
            </mx:FormItem>
        </mx:Form>
    </mx:VBox>
```

We add imports ❶ and then modify the doTaskCreate ❷ method to create a new Task, which has a Project and Location set. Note once again that using null objects lets us avoid special-case code. Next, we modify the dataProvider of the ComboBoxes for the Project ❸ and Location ❹ to use the new ListCollection-Views that contain Projects and Locations.

9.7.3 *ProjectCreateBox.mxml*

Next, we modify the ProjectCreateBox; see listing 9.23.

Listing 9.23   app\flex\com\pomodo\components\ProjectCreateBox.mxml

```
<?xml version="1.0" encoding="utf-8"?>
<mx:VBox xmlns:mx="http://www.adobe.com/2006/mxml"
    width="100%" height="100%" label="New Project">
<mx:Script>
<![CDATA[
    import com.pomodo.model.Project;
    import com.pomodo.control.EventNames;
    import com.pomodo.util.CairngormUtils;

    private function doProjectCreate():void {
        var project : XML =
            <project>
                <name>{nameTI.text}</name>
                <notes>{notesTI.text}</notes>
            </project>;
```

```
              var project:Project =        ❶
                  new Project(nameTI.text, notesTI.text);
              CairngormUtils.dispatchEvent(
                  EventNames.CREATE_PROJECT, project);
          }
      ]]>
      </mx:Script>
      ...
```

All we're doing here is creating a new `Project` object ❶ instead of XML that is sent in the `dispatchEvent` call.

9.7.4 *LocationCreateBox.mxml*

Next, we modify the `LocationCreateBox`; see listing 9.24.

Listing 9.24 app\flex\com\pomodo\components\LocationCreateBox.mxml

```
<?xml version="1.0" encoding="utf-8"?>
<mx:VBox xmlns:mx="http://www.adobe.com/2006/mxml"
    width="100%" height="100%" label="New Location">
<mx:Script>
<![CDATA[
    import com.pomodo.control.EventNames;
    import com.pomodo.model.Location;
    import com.pomodo.util.CairngormUtils;

    private function doLocationCreate():void {
        var location : XML =
            <location>
                <name>{nameTI.text}</name>
                <notes>{notesTI.text}</notes>
            </location>;
        var location:Location =        ❶
            new Location(nameTI.text, notesTI.text);
        CairngormUtils.dispatchEvent(
            EventNames.CREATE_LOCATION, location);
    }
]]>
</mx:Script>
...
```

We construct and send a `Location` ❶ instead of XML.

9.7.5 *AccountCreateBox.mxml*

Now, we modify the `AccountCreateBox`; see listing 9.25.

Listing 9.25 app\flex\com\pomodo\components\AccountCreateBox.mxml

```
<?xml version="1.0" encoding="utf-8"?>
<mx:VBox xmlns:mx="http://www.adobe.com/2006/mxml"
    xmlns:cpv="com.pomodo.validators.*"
    width="100%" height="100%" label="Create Account">
<mx:Script>
<![CDATA[
    import mx.controls.Alert;
    import mx.events.ValidationResultEvent;
    import mx.validators.Validator;
    import com.pomodo.control.EventNames;
    import com.pomodo.model.User;
    import com.pomodo.model.PomodoModelLocator;
    import com.pomodo.util.CairngormUtils;
    import com.pomodo.validators.ServerErrors;

    [Bindable]
    private var _model:PomodoModelLocator =
        PomodoModelLocator.getInstance();

    private function validateAndSubmit():void {
        var results:Array = Validator.validateAll([
            usernameValidator,
            emailValidator,
            passwordValidator,
            passwordConfirmationValidator]);
        if (results.length > 0) {
            Alert.show("Please correct the validation errors " +
                "highlighted on the form.",
                "Account Not Created");
            return;
        }
        var user: XML =
            <user>
                <login>{loginTI.text}</login>
                <email>{emailTI.text}</email>
                <first_name>{firstNameTI.text}</first_name>
                <last_name>{lastNameTI.text}</last_name>
                <password>{passwordTI.text}</password>
<password_confirmation>{confirmPasswordTI.text}
    </password_confirmation>
            </user>
        var user:User = new User(          ❶
            loginTI.text,
            emailTI.text,
            firstNameTI.text,
            lastNameTI.text,
            "",
            passwordTI.text);
        CairngormUtils.dispatchEvent(
```

```
                            EventNames.CREATE_USER, user);
    }
...
```

We construct and send a User ❶ instead of XML.

9.7.6 *TasksListBox.mxml*

Now, we'll make a ton of changes to the TasksListBox; see listing 9.26. This is the largest change left in this iteration, so grab a coffee if you need one.

Listing 9.26   app\flex\com\pomodo\components\TasksListBox.mxml

```
<?xml version="1.0" encoding="utf-8"?>
<mx:VDividedBox xmlns:mx="http://www.adobe.com/2006/mxml"
    width="100%" height="100%" label="Tasks">
<mx:Script>
<![CDATA[
    import mx.collections.XMLListCollection;
    import mx.controls.Alert;
    import com.pomodo.components.MainBox;
    import com.pomodo.util.XMLUtils;                    ❶ Remove/add
    import com.pomodo.control.EventNames;                  imports
    import com.pomodo.model.Location;              ⟵
    import com.pomodo.model.PomodoModelLocator;
    import com.pomodo.model.Project;
    import com.pomodo.model.Task;
    import com.pomodo.util.CairngormUtils;

    public const NEXT_ACTIONS:int = 0;
    public const ALL_TASKS:int = 1;
    public const TASKS_IN_PROJECT:int = 2;
    public const TASKS_AT_LOCATION:int = 3;

    [Bindable]
    public var model:PomodoModelLocator =
        PomodoModelLocator.getInstance();

    private const SHOW_CHOICES:Array = [
        {label:"Next Actions", data:NEXT_ACTIONS,
            hasSubChoice:false},
        {label:"All Tasks", data:ALL_TASKS,
            hasSubChoice:false},
        {label:"Tasks in Project:", data:TASKS_IN_PROJECT,
            hasSubChoice:true},
        {label:"Tasks at Location:", data:TASKS_AT_LOCATION,
            hasSubChoice:true}];
```

```
    [Bindable]
    private var _subChoices:Array;                          Remove      ❷
                                                            obsolete code

    public function updateSelectedTaskFromSummaryPanel():void {
        var selectedTask:XML = XML(tasksGrid.selectedItem);  ◁
        CairngormUtils.dispatchEvent(
            EventNames.UPDATE_TASK,
            { taskID: selectedTask.id,
              keys: ["name", "project_id", "location_id",
                    "completed", "notes"],
              values: [nameTI.text,
                        projectCB.selectedItem.id,
                        locationCB.selectedItem.id,
                        completedCB.selected,
                        notesTI.text]
            }                                               ❸ Get Task, set its
        );                                                     properties, call
        var task:Task = Task(tasksGrid.selectedItem);    ◁     updateTask
        task.name = nameTI.text;
        task.completed = completedCheckBox.selected;
        task.project = Project(projectComboBox.selectedItem);
        task.location = Location(locationComboBox.selectedItem);
        task.notes = notesTI.text;
        updateTask(task);
    }
                                                        ❹ Remove obsolete
    public function updateTaskCompleted(task:XML,    ◁      methods
    completed:Boolean):void {
        updateTaskProperty(task, "completed", completed);
    }
...
    private function updateTaskProperty(task:XML, key:String,
    value:Object):void {
        CairngormUtils.dispatchEvent(
            EventNames.UPDATE_TASK,
            { taskID: task.id, keys: [key], values: [value] }
        );
    }
    public function updateTask(task:Task):void {    ◁
        CairngormUtils.dispatchEvent(                      Replaces 4
            EventNames.UPDATE_TASK, task);              ❺ separate update
    }                                                      methods

    public function deleteTask(task:XML):void {
        CairngormUtils.dispatchEvent(EventNames.DESTROY_TASK,
            task.id);
    }                                                  ❻ Take/dispatch Task
    public function deleteTask(task:Task):void {    ◁    as event data
        CairngormUtils.dispatchEvent(EventNames.DESTROY_TASK,
```

Holding state on the client properly

```
                task);
        }
    ]]>
</mx:Script>
    <mx:VBox width="100%" height="60%">
        <mx:HBox width="100%" paddingLeft="5" paddingRight="5">
            <mx:Label text="Show:"/>
            <mx:ComboBox id="mainChoiceCB"
            <mx:ComboBox id="mainChoiceComboBox"
                dataProvider="{SHOW_CHOICES}"/>
            <mx:ComboBox id="subChoiceCB" width="100%"
            <mx:ComboBox id="subChoiceComboBox" width="100%"
                dataProvider="{_subChoices}"
                visible="{mainChoiceCB.selectedItem.hasSubChoice}"/>
        visible="{mainChoiceComboBox.selectedItem.hasSubChoice}"/>
        </mx:HBox>
        <mx:DataGrid id="tasksGrid" width="100%" height="100%"
            dataProvider="{model.tasksXLC}">
            dataProvider="{model.tasks}">

            <mx:columns>
                    <mx:DataGridColumn
                        headerText=""
                        width="25"
                        dataField="completed"
                        editable="false">
                        <mx:itemRenderer>
                            <mx:Component>
<mx:HBox width="25" paddingLeft="5">
    <mx:Script>
        <![CDATA[
            import com.pomodo.util.XMLUtils;
            import com.pomodo.model.Task;

            private function updateCompleted():void {
                outerDocument.updateTaskCompleted(
                    XML(data),
                    !XMLUtils.xmlListToBoolean(data.completed));
                var task:Task = Task(data);
                task.completed = !task.completed;
                outerDocument.updateTask(task);
            }
        ]]>
    </mx:Script>
    <mx:CheckBox
        selected="{XMLUtils.xmlListToBoolean(data.completed)}"
    <mx:CheckBox selected="{data.completed}"
        click="updateCompleted()"/>
</mx:HBox>
                            </mx:Component>
                        </mx:itemRenderer>
```

7 Renamed because CB suffix was ambiguous between CheckBox and ComboBox

8 Renamed because CB suffix was ambiguous

9 Use renamed ComboBox

10 Use model.tasks ListCollectionView

11 Modify import

12 Call updateTask instead of updateTaskCompleted

13 Bind to data.completed because data now Task

```
                    </mx:DataGridColumn>
                    <mx:DataGridColumn headerText="Name" width="300"
                        dataField="name"/>
                    <mx:DataGridColumn
                        headerText="Project"
                        dataField="project_id"
                        dataField="project"
                        width="150"
                        editable="false"
                        sortable="false">
                        <mx:itemRenderer>
                            <mx:Component>
<mx:ComboBox
    width="150"
    labelField="name"
    dataProvider="{outerDocument.model.projectsAndNoneXLC}"
    selectedItem="{outerDocument.model.getProject(
        data.project_id)}"
    dataChange="handleDataChange(XML(data))"
    change="outerDocument.updateTaskProject(XML(data),
        XML(selectedItem))">
    dataProvider="{outerDocument.model.projectsAndNone}"
    selectedItem="{data.project}"
    dataChange="handleDataChange(Task(data))"
    change="updateProject()">
    <mx:Script>
    <![CDATA[
        import com.pomodo.model.PomodoModelLocator;
        import com.pomodo.model.Task;
        import com.pomodo.model.Project;

        private function updateProject():void {
            var task:Task = Task(data);
            var project:Project = Project(selectedItem);
            if (task.project != project) {
                task.project = project;
                outerDocument.updateTask(task);
            }
        }

        private function handleDataChange(data:XML):void {
            if (data != null) {
                selectedItem =
                    outerDocument.model.getProject(
                        data.project_id);
            } else {
                selectedItem =
                    PomodoModelLocator.NO_PROJECT_XML;
            }
        }
        private function handleDataChange(task:Task):void {
```

- **14** dataField now project (Project)
- **15** Use new Task data
- **16** Modify imports
- **17** Update Task's project if different
- **18** Use new Task data

```
                    if (task != null) {
                        selectedItem = task.project;
                    } else {
                        selectedItem = Project.NONE;
                    }
                }
            ]]>
        </mx:Script>
    </mx:ComboBox>
                            </mx:Component>
                        </mx:itemRenderer>
                    </mx:DataGridColumn>
                    <mx:DataGridColumn
                        headerText="Location"
                        dataField="location_id"
                        dataField="location"          ⟵  ❶❾ dataField now
                        width="150"                              Location
                        editable="false"
                        sortable="false">
                        <mx:itemRenderer>
                            <mx:Component>
<mx:ComboBox
    width="150"
    labelField="name"
    dataProvider="{outerDocument.model.locationsAndNoneXLC}"
    selectedItem="{outerDocument.model.getLocation(
    data.location_id)}"
    dataChange="handleDataChange(XML(data))"
    change="outerDocument.updateTaskLocation(XML(data),
    XML(selectedItem))">                           ❷⓿ Use new
    dataProvider="{outerDocument.model.locationsAndNone}"  ⟵  Task data
    selectedItem="{data.location}"
    dataChange="handleDataChange(Task(data))"
    change="updateLocation()">
    <mx:Script>
    <![CDATA[
        import com.pomodo.model.PomodoModelLocator;   ❷❶ Modify
        import com.pomodo.model.Task;          ⟵          imports
        import com.pomodo.model.Location;
                                               ❷❷ Update Tasks's
        private function updateLocation():void {  ⟵  location if different
            var task:Task = Task(data);
            var location:Location = Location(selectedItem);
            if (task.location != location) {
                task.location = location;
                outerDocument.updateTask(task);
            }
        }

        private function handleDataChange(data:XML):void {
            if (data != null) {
```

```
                    selectedItem = outerDocument.model.getLocation(
                        data.location_id);
                } else {
                    selectedItem =
                        PomodoModelLocator.NO_LOCATION_XML;
                }
            }
        }
        private function handleDataChange(task:Task):void {
            if (task != null) {
                selectedItem = task.location;
            } else {
                selectedItem = Location.NONE;
            }
        }
      ]]>
    </mx:Script>
</mx:ComboBox>
                    </mx:Component>
                </mx:itemRenderer>
            </mx:DataGridColumn>
            <mx:DataGridColumn headerText="Notes"
                dataField="notes"/>
            <mx:DataGridColumn headerText="" width="70"
                editable="false">
                editable="false" dataField="name">
                <!-- arbitrary dataField -->
                <mx:itemRenderer>
                    <mx:Component>
                        <mx:Button label="delete"
            click="outerDocument.deleteTask(XML(data))"/>
            click="outerDocument.deleteTask(Task(data))">
                            <mx:Script>
                            <![CDATA[
                                import com.pomodo.model.Task;
                            ]]>
                            </mx:Script>
                        </mx:Button>
                    </mx:Component>
                </mx:itemRenderer>
            </mx:DataGridColumn>
        </mx:columns>
    </mx:DataGrid>
</mx:VBox>
<mx:Panel id="summaryPanel" title="Task" width="100%"
    height="40%" paddingLeft="5" paddingRight="5"
    paddingTop="5" paddingBottom="5">
    <mx:HBox width="100%">
        <mx:Label text="Name" width="50"/>
        <mx:TextInput id="nameTI" width="100%"
            text="{tasksGrid.selectedItem.name}"/>
```

㉓ Use new Task data

㉔ Need arbitrary dataField with Task objects

㉕ Modify Delete button to call deleteTask with Task data

㉖ Import Task so we can cast

```
            <mx:CheckBox id="completedCB" label="Completed"
    selected="{XMLUtils.xmlListToBoolean(tasksGrid.selectedItem.completed)}"
            />
            <mx:CheckBox id="completedCheckBox"        ⟵  Renamed because CB      (27)
                label="Completed"                          suffix ambiguous
                selected="{tasksGrid.selectedItem.completed}"/>   ⟵
        </mx:HBox>
        <mx:HBox width="100%" verticalAlign="middle">          completed        (29) Renamed
            <mx:Label text="Project" width="50"/>              now                  because
            <mx:ComboBox id="projectCB" width="200"            Boolean  (28)        CB suffix
            <mx:ComboBox id="projectComboBox" width="200"    ⟵                     ambiguous
                labelField="name"
                dataProvider="{model.projectsAndNoneXLC}"
    selectedItem="{model.getProject(tasksGrid.selectedItem.project_id)}"
                dataProvider="{model.projectsAndNone}"        ⟵
                selectedItem="{tasksGrid.selectedItem.project}"     ⟵
            />                                               project now       (30)
            <mx:CheckBox label="This is the Next Action"/>   Project
            <mx:Spacer width="100%"/>
            <mx:Label text="Location"/>                    Renamed because CB  (31)
            <mx:ComboBox id="locationCB" width="200"        suffix ambiguous
            <mx:ComboBox id="locationComboBox" width="200"   ⟵
                labelField="name"
                dataProvider="{model.locationsAndNoneXLC}"
    selectedItem="{model.getLocation(tasksGrid.selectedItem.location_id)}"
                dataProvider="{model.locationsAndNone}"
                selectedItem="{tasksGrid.selectedItem.location}"   ⟵
            />                                               location now      (32)
        </mx:HBox>                                           Location
        <mx:HBox width="100%" height="100%">
            <mx:Label text="Notes" width="50"/>
            <mx:TextArea id="notesTI" width="100%" height="100%"
                text="{tasksGrid.selectedItem.notes}"/>
        </mx:HBox>
        <mx:ControlBar width="100%" horizontalAlign="center">
            <mx:Button id="updateButton" label="Update"
                height="30"
                click="updateSelectedTaskFromSummaryPanel()"
                enabled="{tasksGrid.selectedItem != null}"/>
            <mx:Button id="deleteButton" label="Delete"
                height="30"
                click="deleteTask(XML(tasksGrid.selectedItem))"
                click="deleteTask(Task(tasksGrid.selectedItem))"   ⟵
                enabled="{tasksGrid.selectedItem != null}"/>
        </mx:ControlBar>
    </mx:Panel>                                             selectedItem
</mx:VDividedBox>                                           now Task     (33)
```

We start by modifying `imports` ❶. Next, we modify the `updateSelectedTaskfrom-SummaryPanel` method to not dispatch an event with a `taskID` and `Arrays` of keys and values ❷. Instead, we get the `Task` from the `tasksGrid` ❸ and set its `name`, `completed`, `project`, `location`, and `notes` properties. We then call `updateTask` with the task. The `updateTask` method ❺ calls `CairngormUtils.dispatchEvent` with the `Task`. This method is much simpler than the methods it replaces: `updateTaskCompleted`, `updateTaskProject`, `updateTaskLocation`, and `update-TaskProperty` can all be deleted ❹. (This is because we're updating all the properties of the `Task`.) Next, we modify the `deleteTask` ❻ method to take a `Task` instead of `XML` as its parameter and to dispatch the task instead of the task id as the event data.

We rename the `ComboBoxes` ❼–❾ because the CB suffix was ambiguous between `CheckBox` and `ComboBox`. Next, we modify the `tasksGrid dataProvider` ❿ to be the `model.tasks ListCollectionView` instead of the old `XMLListCollection`. This means the individual row data is no longer XML—it's a `Task`. This makes for much better code (most of the time).

Next, we modify the various `itemRenderers` for the `DataGridColumns`. This is still a bit messy.

We start by modifying the completed renderer, modifying the `update-Completed` method to get the `Task` ⓫ data, toggle its `completed` value ⓬, and call the `updateTask` method instead of the `updateTaskCompleted` method.

Next, we modify the `CheckBox` to bind to `data.completed` ⓭ instead of `XMLUtils.xmlListToBoolean(data.completed)`. We can do this because the data is now a `Task`, not XML.

Now, we modify the `dataField` of the `Project` column to be the `project` ⓮ (which is a `Project`), as opposed to the old `project_id`.

Next, we modify the `ComboBox itemRenderer` for the `Project`. We delete a bunch of code that was XML-heavy and replace it with code that uses our new `Task` data ⓯. We modify `imports` ⓰ and create an `updateProject` method ⓱ that is called whenever a change happens in the `ComboBox`. This method gets the `Task` data and the newly selected `Project`. If this `Project` is different than the task's `Project`, the task's project is updated and `outerDocument.updateTask` is called.

We also modify the `handleDataChange` method ⓲ to use the new task data, setting its `selectedItem` to the `task.project` if there is a task, or to the `Project.NONE` Null Object if there isn't one.

We make similar changes to `Location` ⓳–㉓.

We then update the Delete button column to have a `dataField` ㉔, because we need one when using `Task` objects (this worked with XML without one). We modify the Delete button to call `deleteTask` with the `Task` data ㉕. The fact that `delete-Task` takes a `Task` means we need to cast the data to a `Task`, which means we need to import the Task class ❷⑥ into our component. Yes, this is unfortunate. If we didn't like this, we could make deleteTask take an Object and cast it to a Task inside it.

Next, we update the summaryPanel. The big change here is that the tasks-Grid.selectedItem is now a Task, not XML. We rename the completedCB to completedCheckBox ❷⑦, and we don't need to use XMLUtils.xmlListToBoolean any more ❷⑧ because we're dealing with a Task. Similarly, we change the projectCB ❷⑨ to projectComboBox and make it use the tasksGrid.selectedItem.project ❸⓪. We then make a similar change for the task location ❸①❸②. Finally, we update the Delete button ❸③ to deal with a Task, not XML.

Phew.

9.7.7 *ProjectsListBox*

Next, we modify the ProjectsListBox; see listing 9.27.

```
Listing 9.27   app\flex\com\pomodo\components\ProjectsListBox.mxml
```

```
<?xml version="1.0" encoding="utf-8"?>
<mx:VDividedBox xmlns:mx="http://www.adobe.com/2006/mxml"
    width="100%" height="100%" label="Projects">
<mx:Script>
<![CDATA[
    import mx.controls.Alert;
    import com.pomodo.util.XMLUtils;                     ┐ Remove/add
    import com.pomodo.control.EventNames;                │ imports
    import com.pomodo.model.Project;           ◁─────────┘
    import com.pomodo.model.PomodoModelLocator;
    import com.pomodo.util.CairngormUtils;

    [Bindable]
    private var _model:PomodoModelLocator =
        PomodoModelLocator.getInstance();

    public function updateSelectedProjectFromSummaryPanel():
    void {
        var selectedProject:XML =
            XML(projectsGrid.selectedItem);
        CairngormUtils.dispatchEvent(
            EventNames.UPDATE_PROJECT,
            {   projectID: selectedProject.id,
                keys: ["name", "completed", "notes"],
                values: [nameTI.text, completedCB.selected,
                        notesTI.text]
            }
        );
        var project:Project =          ◁─────┐ Get project from
            Project(projectsGrid.selectedItem);│ projectsGrid
        project.name = nameTI.text;
```

```
            project.completed = completedCB.selected;
            project.notes = notesTI.text;
            updateProject(project);
        }

        public function updateProjectCompleted(project:XML,
        completed:Boolean):void {
            CairngormUtils.dispatchEvent(
                EventNames.UPDATE_PROJECT,
                {   projectID: project.id,
                    keys: ["completed"],
                    values: [completedCB.selected]
                }
            );
        }
        public function updateProject(project:Project):void {
            CairngormUtils.dispatchEvent(
                EventNames.UPDATE_PROJECT, project);
        }

        public function deleteProject(data:Object):void {
            CairngormUtils.dispatchEvent(EventNames.DESTROY_PROJECT,
                data.id);
        }
        public function deleteProject(project:Project):void {
            CairngormUtils.dispatchEvent(
                EventNames.DESTROY_PROJECT, project);
        }
    ]]>
</mx:Script>
    <mx:DataGrid id="projectsGrid" width="100%" height="60%"
        dataProvider="{_model.projectsXLC}">
        dataProvider="{_model.projects}">
        <mx:columns>
            <mx:DataGridColumn
                headerText=""
                width="25"
                dataField="completed"
                editable="false">
                <mx:itemRenderer>
                    <mx:Component>
<mx:HBox width="25" paddingLeft="5">
    <mx:Script>
        <![CDATA[
            import com.pomodo.util.XMLUtils;
            import com.pomodo.model.Project;

            private function updateCompleted():void {
                outerDocument.updateProjectCompleted(
                    XML(data),
                    !XMLUtils.xmlListToBoolean(data.completed));
```

Remove obsolete methods

Use simpler approach of updating all properties

Take Project instead of XML

Use model.projects ListCollectionView

Modify import

```
                        var project:Project = Project(data);
                        project.completed = !project.completed;
                        outerDocument.updateProject(project);
                    }
                ]]>
            </mx:Script>
            <mx:CheckBox
                selected="{XMLUtils.xmlListToBoolean(data.completed)}"
            <mx:CheckBox selected="{data.completed}"
                click="updateCompleted()"/>
        </mx:HBox>
                        </mx:Component>
                    </mx:itemRenderer>
                </mx:DataGridColumn>
                <mx:DataGridColumn headerText="Name" width="400"
                    dataField="name"/>
                <mx:DataGridColumn headerText="Notes"
                    dataField="notes"/>
                <mx:DataGridColumn headerText="" width="70"
                    editable="false">
                    editable="false" dataField="name">
                    <!-- arbitrary dataField -->
                    <mx:itemRenderer>
                        <mx:Component>
                            <mx:Button label="delete"
                    click="outerDocument.deleteProject(XML(data))"/>
                    click="outerDocument.deleteProject(Project(data))">
                                <mx:Script>
                                <![CDATA[
                                    import com.pomodo.model.Project;
                                ]]>
                                </mx:Script>
                            </mx:Button>
                        </mx:Component>
                    </mx:itemRenderer>
                </mx:DataGridColumn>
            </mx:columns>
        </mx:DataGrid>
        <mx:Panel id="summaryPanel"
            title="Project" width="100%" height="40%"
            paddingLeft="5" paddingRight="5" paddingTop="5"
            paddingBottom="5">
            <mx:HBox width="100%">
                <mx:Label text="Name" width="50"/>
                <mx:TextInput id="nameTI" width="100%"
                    text="{projectsGrid.selectedItem.name}"/>
                <mx:CheckBox id="completedCB" label="Completed"
        selected="{XMLUtils.xmlListToBoolean(
            projectsGrid.selectedItem.completed)}"/>
                    selected="{projectsGrid.selectedItem.completed}"/>
            </mx:HBox>
```

Get Project data, toggle completed, call updateProject

Modify CheckBox to bind to data.completed

Update Delete button column to have dataField

Call deleteProject and import Project

Bind selected property

```
            <mx:HBox width="100%" height="100%">
                <mx:Label text="Notes" width="50"/>
                <mx:TextArea id="notesTI" width="100%" height="100%"
                    text="{projectsGrid.selectedItem.notes}"/>
            </mx:HBox>
            <mx:ControlBar width="100%" horizontalAlign="center">
                <mx:Button id="updateButton" label="Update"
                    width="100%" height="30"
                    click="updateSelectedProjectFromSummaryPanel()"
                    enabled="{projectsGrid.selectedItem != null}"/>
                <mx:Button id="deleteButton" label="Delete"
                    height="30"
            click="deleteProject(XML(projectsGrid.selectedItem))"
            enabled="{projectsGrid.selectedItem != null}"/>
        click="deleteProject(Project(projectsGrid.selectedItem))"
                enabled="{projectsGrid.selectedItem != null}"/>        ◁──┐
            </mx:ControlBar>                                               │
        </mx:Panel>                                                        │
    </mx:VDividedBox>                                                      │
```

                                                                        Call
                                                             deleteProject

9.7.8 *LocationsListBox.mxml*

Finally (!), we modify the LocationsListBox; see listing 9.28.

Listing 9.28   app\flex\com\pomodo\components\LocationsListBox.mxml

```
<?xml version="1.0" encoding="utf-8"?>
<mx:VDividedBox xmlns:mx="http://www.adobe.com/2006/mxml"
    width="100%" height="100%" label="Locations">
<mx:Script>
<![CDATA[
    import mx.controls.Alert;
    import mx.collections.XMLListCollection;
    import com.pomodo.control.EventNames;
    import com.pomodo.model.Location;
    import com.pomodo.model.PomodoModelLocator;
    import com.pomodo.util.CairngormUtils;
    import com.pomodo.util.XMLUtils;

    [Bindable]
    private var _model : PomodoModelLocator =
        PomodoModelLocator.getInstance();

    public function updateSelectedLocationFromSummaryPanel():
    void {
        var selectedLocation:XML =
            XML(locationsGrid.selectedItem);
        CairngormUtils.dispatchEvent(
            EventNames.UPDATE_LOCATION,
```

```
                {
                    locationID: selectedLocation.id,
                    keys: ["name", "notes"],
                    values: [nameTI.text, notesTI.text]
                }
            );
            var location:Location =
                Location(locationsGrid.selectedItem);
            location.name = nameTI.text;
            location.notes = notesTI.text;
            CairngormUtils.dispatchEvent(
                EventNames.UPDATE_LOCATION, location);
        }

    public function deleteLocation(data:Object):void {
        CairngormUtils.dispatchEvent(
            EventNames.DESTROY_LOCATION, data.id);
    public function deleteLocation(location:Location):void {
        CairngormUtils.dispatchEvent(
            EventNames.DESTROY_LOCATION, location);
    }
    ]]>
</mx:Script>
    <mx:DataGrid id="locationsGrid" width="100%" height="60%"
        dataProvider="{_model.locationsXLC}">
        dataProvider="{_model.locations}">
        <mx:columns>
            <mx:DataGridColumn headerText="Name" width="400"
                dataField="name"/>
            <mx:DataGridColumn headerText="Notes"
                dataField="notes"/>
            <mx:DataGridColumn headerText="" width="70"
                editable="false">
                editable="false" dataField="name">
                <!-- arbitrary dataField -->
                <mx:itemRenderer>
                    <mx:Component>
                        <mx:Button label="delete"
                click="outerDocument.deleteLocation(XML(data))"/>
                click="outerDocument.deleteLocation(Location(data))">
                            <mx:Script>
                            <![CDATA[
                                import com.pomodo.model.Location;
                            ]]>
                            </mx:Script>
                        </mx:Button>
                    </mx:Component>
                </mx:itemRenderer>
            </mx:DataGridColumn>
        </mx:columns>
    </mx:DataGrid>
```

```
<mx:Panel id="summaryPanel" title="Location" width="100%"
    height="40%" paddingLeft="5" paddingRight="5"
    paddingTop="5" paddingBottom="5">
...

    <mx:ControlBar width="100%" horizontalAlign="center">
        <mx:Button id="updateButton" label="Update"
            width="100%" height="30"
            click="updateSelectedLocationFromSummaryPanel()"
            enabled="{locationsGrid.selectedItem != null}"/>
        <mx:Button id="deleteButton" label="Delete"
            height="30"
        click="deleteLocation(XML(locationsGrid.selectedItem))"
    click="deleteLocation(Location(locationsGrid.selectedItem))"
            enabled="{locationsGrid.selectedItem != null}"/>
    </mx:ControlBar>
</mx:Panel>
</mx:VDividedBox>
```

There's nothing new here that isn't equivalent to something we've done with the
ProjectsListBox.

That's it! Rebuild, reload, and log in as ludwig or create a new user. Everything
works as before. Finally, run the tests again and confirm that everything still
works.

9.8   *Summary*

Now that we have a proper object model on the client side, we're no longer tightly
coupled to the transport mechanism. Currently we're using XML, but this will
change in the next part of the book when we refactor to using RubyAMF. First,
however, we need to finish the application.

Hooray for samurai-coder refactoring!

The code at this point is saved as the iteration09 folder.

Part 4

Finishing up

In this final part of the book, we'll finish the application, refactor it to use RubyAMF, and extend it to running on the Adobe Integrated Runtime (AIR).

First, in iteration 10, we'll build the remaining features in pomodo. After we finish iteration 10, we'll have a reasonably complete application. It will be more realistic than the applications in most books, anyway.

In iteration 11, we'll refactor pomodo to use RubyAMF instead of XML for sending data between Flex and Rails. Because AMF is a binary protocol and XML is text (and verbose text at that), this has the potential to lead to substantial performance improvements.

In iteration 12, the last iteration of the book, we'll convert the code to run on AIR and modify the Notely feature that we'll build in this iteration to take advantage of AIR-specific features. This obviously won't be a complete tutorial introduction to AIR; instead, it will give you a taste of one of the exciting ways to take your Flex + Rails applications beyond the traditional web application model.

Finishing the application

The kids all dream of making it, whatever that means

—Arctic Monkeys

In this iteration, we'll build the remaining features in Pomodo. After we finish this iteration, we'll have a reasonably complete application.

10.1 Notely

One thing we've left totally stubbed out so far is Notely. Let's fix that now. Essentially, we'll implement Notepad in Flex. We'll be extremely simplistic and store one note, instead of having multiple versions and undo/redo support. Additionally, we'll add Notely using nested resources, using the new simplified RESTful routing[1] for nested resources in Rails 2.

> **NOTE**   For the "first real word processor for the web" in Flex, check out Buzzword. The company that built it was recently acquired by Adobe (they liked it so much, they bought the company).

All disclaimers aside, here we go. We won't use `scaffold_resource` this time; instead, we'll do things manually for variety.

We start by creating a new migration:

```
c:\peter\flexiblerails\current\pomodo>
ruby script\generate migration create_notes
      exists  db/migrate
      create  db/migrate/005_create_notes.rb

c:\peter\flexiblerails\current\pomodo>
```

Next, we edit the migration to create user_id, version, and content columns; see listing 10.1.

Listing 10.1   db\migrate\005_create_notes.rb

```
class CreateNotes < ActiveRecord::Migration
  def self.up
    create_table :notes do |t|          ❶
      t.integer :user_id, :default => 0, :null => false    ❷
      t.text :content        ❸
      t.timestamps      ❹
    end
  end

  def self.down
    drop_table :notes
  end
end
```

---

[1] Thanks to Ryan Daigle for explaining them well and concisely at http://ryandaigle.com/articles/2007/5/6/what-s-new-in-edge-rails-restful-routing-updates.

We modify create a new notes table ❶ that has user_id ❷, content ❸, and the created_at and updated_at columns created by timestamps ❹. The user_id defaults to 0 and is non-NULL.

Now, let's run the migration:

```
c:\peter\flexiblerails\current\pomodo>rake db:migrate
c:0:Warning: require_gem is obsolete.  Use gem instead.
(in c:/peter/flexiblerails/current/pomodo)
== 5 CreateNotes: migrating
  =====================================================
-- create_table(:notes)
   -> 0.2970s
== 5 CreateNotes: migrated (0.2970s)
   =================================================

c:\peter\flexiblerails\current\pomodo>
```

Open a mysql prompt, and confirm that the migration had the desired effect; see listing 10.2 (as always, the Extra column in the description is omitted for space concerns, but it shows that the id table column is set to auto_increment).

Listing 10.2   Commands

```
mysql> describe notes;
+------------+----------+------+-----+---------+
| Field      | Type     | Null | Key | Default |
+------------+----------+------+-----+---------+
| id         | int(11)  | NO   | PRI | NULL    |
| user_id    | int(11)  | NO   |     | 0       |
| content    | text     | YES  |     | NULL    |
| created_at | datetime | YES  |     | NULL    |
| updated_at | datetime | YES  |     | NULL    |
+------------+----------+------+-----+---------+
5 rows in set (0.01 sec)
```

The notes table has an id column as its primary key and the other columns we specified in the migration.

Next, let's create the Note model; see listing 10.3.

Listing 10.3   app\models\note.rb

```
class Note < ActiveRecord::Base
  belongs_to :user
end
```

We add the `belongs_to :user` line to associate the `Note` with the `User` it references.

Now, we modify the `User` model; see listing 10.4.

Listing 10.4   app\models\user.rb

```
require 'digest/sha1'
class User < ActiveRecord::Base
  has_many :tasks
  has_many :projects
  has_many :locations
  has_one :note
  . . .
```

A `User` has one `Note`.

Next, we need to modify the routes; see listing 10.5.

Listing 10.5   config\routes.rb

```
ActionController::Routing::Routes.draw do |map|
  . . .
  map.resources :tasks
  map.resources :projects
  map.resources :locations
  map.resources :users
  map.resources :users, :has_one => :note
  map.resource  :session
  . . .
end
```

We modify the `map.resources :users` call to specify that the `:users :has_one :note`. This sets up the routing so the note is a *nested resource,* which lets us use URLs like /users/3/note to refer to the note of the user with the `id` of 3.

Shouldn't everything be nested under the User?

As explained at http://ryandaigle.com/articles/2007/5/6/what-s-new-in-edge-rails-restful-routing-updates, we can also add a :has_many in the map.resources. We could have done the following:

```
map.resources :users, :has_one => :note, :has_many => [:tasks, :projects,
  :locations]
```

> **Shouldn't everything be nested under the User?** *(continued)*
>
> We didn't do this, because in my limited understanding the best practices around nested resources aren't fully agreed on and/or widely disseminated. There is still some art in this; see http://weblog.jamisbuck.org/2007/2/5/nesting-resources for details, and see David Black's *Rails Routing (Digital Shortcut) if you want to read a mini-book about routing. (I found it valuable.)* The bottom line is that I may be doing something in a less-than-ideal way—*but at least by being inconsistent, I'm not claiming to be presenting the optimal approach!*

Having modified the routes, we can look at them in the console with the new `rake routes` command. If we scroll through its output (which is too wide to fit in a book nicely), we can see the pretend HTTP method + URL combinations like `POST /users/:user_id/note.:format` and `PUT /users/:user_id/note.:format` for the new nested `Note` resource.

Now that we've set up our routes, we need to create the `NotesController` and `NotesHelper`. Note that these are plural names, not the singular `NoteController` and `NoteHelper`—using plural names for all controllers regardless of nested resources is the standard[2] in Rails 2.

We start with the `NotesController`; see listing 10.6.

Listing 10.6   app\controllers\notes_controller.rb

```
class NotesController < ApplicationController
  # GET /users/1/note
  # GET /users/1/note.xml
  def show                                    ❶
    if current_user.id != params[:user_id].to_i      ❷
      prevent_access                          ❸
    else
      @note = current_user.note               ❹
      respond_to do |format|                  ❺
        format.xml  { render :xml => @note.to_xml }    ❻
      end
    end
  end


  # PUT /users/1/note
  # PUT /users/1/note.xml
  def update     ❼
    if current_user.id != params[:user_id].to_i       ❽
```

---

[2] See http://weblog.rubyonrails.org/2007/9/30/rails-2-0-0-preview-release for details.

```
        prevent_access      ❾
    else
      @note = current_user.note      ❿
      respond_to do |format|      ⓫
        if @note.update_attributes(params[:note])      ⓬
          format.xml { render :xml => @note.to_xml }      ⓭
        else
          format.xml { render :xml => @note.errors.to_xml_full }      ⓮
        end
      end
    end
  end

  private
    def prevent_access      ⓯
      respond_to do |format|
        format.xml { render :text => "error" }
      end
    end
end
```

Note that because we're creating this manually, we create only the methods we need. (Yes, this means some of the routes for the nested note resource won't match anything.) Also, note that we support format.xml, because I'm too lazy to create an HTML UI for Notely.

We start by creating a show method ❶ that handles a GET request to the nested routes /users/:user_id/note and /users/:user_id/note.xml. We could have created an edit method instead (because we're showing for editing), but I prefer the show method because the URL for it is more straightforward and because it doesn't make sense to have edit without show. In the show method, we check whether the id passed in as the :user_id in the URL (which the note is nested in) belongs to the current_user ❷, and we prevent_access ❸⓯ if not. Note that we need to use to_i ❷ on the params[:user_id], because it is a String. If the id is that of the current_user, we get the current_user.note and store it in @note ❹ and have a respond_to block ❺ that renders the @note.to_xml ❻ for format.xml. (Yes, having @note is unnecessary right now, but this is a force of habit for me because presumably it would be used by an HTML view.)

Similarly, we create an update ❼ method that handles a PUT request (including a faked PUT request with the _method parameter) to the nested routes /users/:user_id/note and /users/:user_id/note.xml. This is the same URL as for show; only the HTTP method is different. Again, we check whether the id passed in as the :user_id in the URL (which the note is nested in) belongs to the current_user ❽, and we prevent_access ❾ if not. If the id is that of the current_user, we get the current_user.note and store it in @note ❿ and have a respond_to block ⓫ that does update_attributes ⓬. This is the same generic mechanism used for tasks, projects, and locations. We know that we're updating the content attribute, but there's no reason to hardcode it. We then render the @note.to_xml ⓭ for format.xml or the to_xml_full on the errors ⓮.

Next, some easy stuff. We need to create the NotesHelper so Rails doesn't complain; see listing 10.7.

Listing 10.7   app\helpers\notes_helper.rb

```
module NotesHelper
end
```

Now, we'll add a notes.yml fixture to load some sample data for us; see listing 10.8. Because we're being so lazy that we're not going to support a "new note" action, a User will always have a Note. Users that are created in the fixtures need notes, too.

Listing 10.8   test\fixtures\notes.yml

```
quentin:
  id: 1
  user_id: 1
  content: Quentin's notes

aaron:
  id: 2
  user_id: 2
  content: Aaron's notes

ludwig:
  id: 3
  user_id: 3
  content: Ludwig's notes

wolfgang:
  id: 4
  user_id: 4
  content: Wolfgang's notes
```

Finally (on the Rails side), we need to add a before_create method (❶ in listing 10.9) to the User class, to ensure that newly created Users have an empty Note. (This lets us make save always be an update, rather than a create or an update.)

Listing 10.9   app\models\user.rb

```
require 'digest/sha1'
class User < ActiveRecord::Base
  has_many :tasks
  has_many :projects
  has_many :locations
  has_one :note

  def before_create          ❶
    self.note = Note.new
  end

  # Virtual attribute for the unencrypted password
  attr_accessor :password
...
```

Now, we need to make the modifications to the Flex side. This is all fairly straight-forward.

We start by creating a Note class; see listing 10.10.

Listing 10.10   app\flex\com\pomodo\model\Note.as

```
package com.pomodo.model {
    public class Note {
        public function Note(content:String = "") {
            this.content = content;
        }

        [Bindable]
        public var content:String;          ❶

        public function toUpdateObject():Object {          ❷
            var obj:Object = new Object();
            obj["note[content]"] = content;
            return obj;
        }

        public static function fromXML(note:XML):Note {          ❸
            return new Note(note.content);
        }
    }
}
```

The Note class stores content ❶ and has toUpdateObject ❷ and fromXML ❸ methods. Note that we don't have a toXML method because we don't need it yet.

Also, we don't use `created_at` or `updated_at` in the UI at the moment, so we don't include them.

Next, we need to modify the `PomodoModelLocator` to add `Note` to it (❶ in listing 10.11).

Listing 10.11   app\flex\com\pomodo\model\PomodoModelLocator.as

```
public var user:User;

public var note:Note;          ❶

public var tasks:ListCollectionView;
```

We also need to modify the `User` class. I had added a notes field to it, which was speculative and thus, unsurprisingly, wrong. We need to remove it, and add a field for the id (which we now need, for the purposes of the nested route for the note); see listing 10.12.

Listing 10.12   app\flex\com\pomodo\User.as

```
package com.pomodo.model {
    public class User {
        [Bindable]
        public var login:String;

        [Bindable]
        public var email:String;

        [Bindable]
        public var firstName:String;

        [Bindable]
        public var lastName:String;

        [Bindable]
        public var notes:String;          ❶
        [Bindable]
        public var password:String;

        [Bindable]
        public var id:int;          ❷

        public function User(
            login:String = "",
            email:String = "",
            firstName:String = "",
            lastName:String = "",
```

```
        notes:String = "",        ❸
        password:String = "",
        id:int = 0)               ❹
    {
        this.login = login;
        this.email = email;
        this.firstName = firstName;
        this.lastName = lastName;
        this.notes = notes;       ❺
        this.password = password;
        this.id = id;             ❻
    }

    public function toXML():XML {
        var retval:XML =
            <user>
                <login>{login}</login>
                <email>{email}</email>
                <first_name>{firstName}</first_name>
                <notes>{notes}</notes>        ❼
                <last_name>{lastName}</last_name>
                <password>{password}</password>
<password_confirmation>{password}</password_confirmation>
            </user>;
        return retval;
    }

    public static function fromXML(userXML:XML):User {
        var user:User = new User();        ❽
        user.login = userXML.login;
        user.email = userXML.email;
        user.firstName = userXML.first_name;
        user.lastName = userXML.last_name;
        user.notes = userXML.notes;
        return user;
        return new User(              ❾
            userXML.login,
            userXML.email,
            userXML.first_name,
            userXML.last_name,
            "",
            userXML.id);
    }
}
}
```

We remove the notes field ❶ and add the id ❷. Next we modify the constructor ❸–❻, the `toXML` ❼, and the `fromXML` ❽❾ methods accordingly. Note that we're changing the `fromXML` method to use the `User` constructor better ❾ as well as removing the `notes` and adding the `id`, instead of letting the arguments all default and then setting the properties.

Next, we create the business delegate and the commands. This is tedious by now. We start with the `NoteDelegate`; see listing 10.13.

> **TIP** If you do a lot of Cairngorm work, you may want to use the Cairngorm generator: http://code.google.com/p/cairngorm-rails-generator/. For some documentation, see http://onrails.org/articles/2007/02/21/cairngorm-generators.

Listing 10.13 app\flex\com\pomodo\business\NoteDelegate.as

```
package com.pomodo.business {
    import mx.rpc.IResponder;
    import com.pomodo.model.Note;
    import com.pomodo.model.User;
    import com.pomodo.model.PomodoModelLocator;
    import com.pomodo.util.ServiceUtils;

    public class NoteDelegate {
        private var _responder:IResponder;

        public function NoteDelegate(responder:IResponder) {
            _responder = responder;
        }

        public function showNote():void {
            var model:PomodoModelLocator =
                PomodoModelLocator.getInstance();
            ServiceUtils.send(
                "/users/" + model.user.id + "/note.xml",      ❶
                _responder);
        }

        public function updateNote():void {
            var model:PomodoModelLocator =
                PomodoModelLocator.getInstance();
            ServiceUtils.send(
                "/users/" + model.user.id + "/note.xml",      ❷
                _responder,
                "PUT",
                model.note.toUpdateObject(),
                false);
        }
    }
}
```

The only thing worth noting is that the relative URLs ❶❷ use the nested route, so it is the id of the user that is needed, not the id of the Note.

Now for the commands, starting with the ShowNoteCommand; see listing 10.14.

Listing 10.14   app\flex\com\pomodo\command\ShowNoteCommand.as

```
package com.pomodo.command {
    import com.adobe.cairngorm.commands.ICommand;
    import com.adobe.cairngorm.control.CairngormEvent;
    import com.pomodo.business.NoteDelegate;
    import com.pomodo.control.EventNames;
    import com.pomodo.model.PomodoModelLocator;
    import com.pomodo.model.Note;
    import com.pomodo.util.CairngormUtils;

    import mx.rpc.IResponder;
    import mx.rpc.events.FaultEvent;
    import mx.rpc.events.ResultEvent;

    public class ShowNoteCommand implements ICommand,
    IResponder {
        public function ShowNoteCommand() {
        }

        public function execute(event:CairngormEvent):void {
            var delegate:NoteDelegate = new NoteDelegate(this);   ❶
            delegate.showNote();            ❷
        }

        public function result(event:Object):void {
            var model:PomodoModelLocator =
                PomodoModelLocator.getInstance();
            model.note = Note.fromXML(event.result);    ❸
        }

        public function fault(event:Object):void {
        }
    }
}
```

The execute function creates a new NoteDelegate ❶ and calls its showNote method ❷. The result function builds a new Note from the event.result ❸ and assigns it to the model.note.

Next, the UpdateNoteCommand; see listing 10.15.

Listing 10.15 `app\flex\com\pomodo\command\UpdateNoteCommand.as`

```
package com.pomodo.command {
    import com.adobe.cairngorm.commands.ICommand;
    import com.adobe.cairngorm.control.CairngormEvent;
    import com.pomodo.business.NoteDelegate;
    import com.pomodo.control.EventNames;
    import com.pomodo.model.PomodoModelLocator;
    import com.pomodo.util.CairngormUtils;

    import mx.rpc.IResponder;
    import mx.rpc.events.FaultEvent;
    import mx.rpc.events.ResultEvent;

    public class UpdateNoteCommand implements ICommand,
    IResponder {
        public function UpdateNoteCommand() {
        }

        public function execute(event:CairngormEvent):void {
            var delegate:NoteDelegate = new NoteDelegate(this);    ❶
            delegate.updateNote();        ❷
        }

        public function result(event:Object):void {
        }

        public function fault(event:Object):void {
        }
    }
}
```

The execute method creates a new `NoteDelegate` ❶ and calls its `updateNote` method ❷.

Next, we need to hook up our two new commands. We start by adding the constants (❶❷ in listing 10.16) to `EventNames`.

Listing 10.16 `app\flex\com\pomodo\control\EventNames.as`

```
package com.pomodo.control {
    public final class EventNames {
...
        public static const LIST_TASKS:String = "listTasks";

        public static const SHOW_NOTE:String = "showNote";        ❶

        public static const UPDATE_LOCATION:String =
            "updateLocation";
```

```
        public static const UPDATE_PROJECT:String =
            "updateProject";
        public static const UPDATE_TASK:String = "updateTask";
        public static const UPDATE_NOTE:String = "updateNote";      ❷
    }
}
```

Next, we add the commands (❶❷ in listing 10.17) to the `PomodoController`.

Listing 10.17   app\flex\com\pomodo\control\PomodoController.as

```
...
        addCommand(EventNames.UPDATE_TASK,
            UpdateTaskCommand);
        addCommand(EventNames.UPDATE_NOTE,          ❶
            UpdateNoteCommand);

        addCommand(EventNames.SHOW_NOTE, ShowNoteCommand);      ❷
    }
  }
}
```

Finally, we can modify the components.

First, we need to modify the `AccountCreateBox` to use the updated `User` constructor; see listing 10.18.

Listing 10.18   app\flex\com\pomodo\components\AccountCreateBox.mxml

```
...
    private function validateAndSubmit():void {
...
        var user:User = new User(
            loginTI.text,
            emailTI.text,
            firstNameTI.text,
            lastNameTI.text,
            "",          ❶
            passwordTI.text);
        CairngormUtils.dispatchEvent(
            EventNames.CREATE_USER, user);
    }
...
```

We delete the empty `String` ❶ for notes.

Next, we modify the `MainBox`; see listing 10.19.

Listing 10.19   app\flex\com\pomodo\components\MainBox.mxml

```
...
    private function handleCreationComplete():void {
        CairngormUtils.dispatchEvent(EventNames.SHOW_NOTE);
        CairngormUtils.dispatchEvent(EventNames.LIST_PROJECTS);
        CairngormUtils.dispatchEvent(EventNames.LIST_LOCATIONS);
    }
...
```

We need to also dispatch an event with the `SHOW_NOTE` name on `creation-Complete`, in order to populate the Notely tab.

Finally, we modify the Notely tab. After all the work we've done, it's trivial; see listing 10.20.

Listing 10.20   app\flex\com\pomodo\components\Notely.mxml

```
<?xml version="1.0" encoding="utf-8"?>
<mx:VBox xmlns:mx="http://www.adobe.com/2006/mxml"
    width="100%" height="100%" label="Notely" paddingLeft="5"
    paddingRight="5" paddingTop="5" paddingBottom="5">
<mx:Script>
<![CDATA[
    import com.pomodo.control.EventNames;
    import com.pomodo.model.PomodoModelLocator;
    import com.pomodo.util.CairngormUtils;

    [Bindable]
    private var _model:PomodoModelLocator =              ❶
        PomodoModelLocator.getInstance();

    private function doSave():void {
        _model.note.content = notelyTA.text;             ❷
        CairngormUtils.dispatchEvent(EventNames.UPDATE_NOTE);  ❸
    }

    private function doRevert():void {
        notelyTA.text = _model.note.content;             ❹
    }
]]>
</mx:Script>
    <mx:TextArea width="100%" height="100%"/>
    <mx:TextArea id="notelyTA" width="100%" height="100%"    ❺
        text="{_model.note.content}"/>                   ❻
    <mx:ControlBar width="100%" horizontalAlign="center">
        <mx:Button id="saveButton" label="Save" width="100%"
```

```
        height="30"/>
        height="30" click="doSave()"/>            ❼
    <mx:Button id="revertButton" label="Revert"
        height="30"/>
        height="30" click="doRevert()"/>          ❽
  </mx:ControlBar>
</mx:VBox>
```

We start by getting the shared PomodoModelLocator ❶ and storing it in _model. In the doSave method, we assign the shared _model.note.content ❷ and then call CairngormUtils.dispatchEvent for EventNames.UPDATE_NOTE ❸. The doRevert function assigns the notelyTA.text with whatever the _model.note.content ❹ is—it doesn't need to talk to the server. Next, we give the TextArea an id ❺ and bind its text to the _model.note.content ❻. Finally, we modify the saveButton ❼ and revertButton ❽ to call the doSave() and doRevert() functions.

With all this done, stop the server and run newdb.bat. (We need to load the fixtures for the notes.) Start the server, and then rebuild, reload, and log in as ludwig. Switch to the Notely tab. We see the screen shown in figure 10.1.

Figure 10.1
Notely, working
at last!

Play with adding notes, saving, and reverting.

Now where's our funding round? Should we add file upload support and start reselling Amazon S3 storage at a markup? Nah—some teenager in England (specifically, Alex MacCaw: see http://www.eribium.org/aireo/) would probably end up doing a better job than us. (See appendix B for links to various resources on file upload.) Instead, we'll add more mundane features such as the Next Action concept, filtering tasks, the command prompt, and—because we can—a couple of effects. The end result will be to give our app some polish and make it demoable.

10.2   *Better security with attr_accessible*

If we're going to even think about deploying this, we need to tighten up the security. One of the ways we'll do this is with attr_accessible.

Rails has many methods, such as update_attributes, that conveniently allow mass-assignment of attributes of models from hashes like the params hash. We've been using this happily in our TasksController without worrying about it:

```
...
def update
    @task = current_user.tasks.find(params[:id])

    respond_to do |format|
      if @task.update_attributes(params[:task])
...
```

However, there is no checking what is in the params[:task]. A user could, without much effort, send a POST (with a _method of PUT) with parameters in the task that shouldn't be there. This could let a user create a task and then reassign it to another user by setting the user_id (thus spamming other users), and so forth.

This won't do. We need to protect certain attributes from being assigned. In Rails, there are two ways to do this: the "I'm perfect and don't make mistakes, let's juggle knives" way, and the "I'm human and make mistakes (or the person maintaining this will), let's be paranoid" way. This could also be described as the "almost definitely false sense of security" way and the "better chance of being secure" way. (Note that I'm not saying *insecure* or *secure*. We can implement *either* approach incorrectly.) Table 10.1 shows this in more detail.

Table 10.1 The two different approaches to preventing mass assignment

Approach	Preventing mass assignment
Knife juggling	`attr_protected :attr_to_omit_1, :attr_to_omit_2`
Paranoia	`attr_accessible :attr_to_include_1, :attr_to_include_2`

For comparison, table 10.2 shows how restricting access to methods works.

Table 10.2 The two different approaches to restricting access to methods

Approach	Restricting access to methods
Knife juggling	`before_filter :authmethod, :only [:auth_method_1, :auth_method_2]`
Paranoia	`before_filter :authmethod, :except [:no_auth_method_1, ...]`

Rails lets you choose either, and many examples unfortunately seem to advocate the knife-juggling approach. In this section, we'll use attr_accessible to advocate the paranoid approach.

NOTE   See http://somethinglearned.com/articles/2006/05/24/best-practices-a-strong-case-for-attr_accessible-part-2 for an in-depth discussion of the problems with attr_protected.

With all this said, we'll basically add four lines of code—one to each of the model classes (except the `User` model, which we'll ignore). First, the `Task`; see listing 10.21.

Listing 10.21   app\models\task.rb

```
class Task < ActiveRecord::Base
  attr_accessible :name, :notes, :next_action, :completed,     ❶
    :project_id, :location_id, :created_at, :updated_at

  belongs_to :user
  belongs_to :location
  belongs_to :project

  def before_save
    self.project_id = nil if self.project_id == 0
    self.location_id = nil if self.location_id == 0
  end
end
```

We allow all but the `user_id` and `id` attributes to be mass-assigned ❶.

Next, the `Project`; see listing 10.22.

Listing 10.22   app\models\project.rb

```
class Project < ActiveRecord::Base
  attr_accessible :name, :notes, :completed, :created_at,     ❶
    :updated_at

  belongs_to :user
  has_many :tasks
end
```

Again, we allow all but the `user_id` and `id` attributes to be mass-assigned ❶.

Now, the `Location`; see listing 22.3.

Listing 10.23   app\models\location.rb

```
class Location < ActiveRecord::Base
  attr_accessible :name, :notes, :created_at, :updated_at     ❶

  belongs_to :user
  has_many :tasks
end
```

Once again, we allow all but the `user_id` and `id` attributes to be mass-assigned ❶. Finally, the `Note`; see listing 10.24.

Listing 10.24   app\models\note.rb

```
class Note < ActiveRecord::Base
  attr_accessible :content, :created_at, :updated_at

  belongs_to :user
end
```

10.3   GTD semantics, including the
Next Action concept and :dependent

At the beginning of the book, we said that pomodo was going to be a *Getting Things Done (GTD)* todo list application. Well, *we've* gotten a lot of things done, but we've left the fundamental idea from GTD stubbed out in pomodo: the concept of the *Next Action*. This is the task that must be done next in a given project, and it's the feature of our pomodo that we need to get done now.

We also need to enforce GTD semantics regarding the relationship between `Tasks` and `Projects` that we've omitted up to now. For example, setting a `Project` to complete should set all of its `Tasks` to complete. Setting a `Task` to incomplete should set its `Project` to incomplete. We'll add these features along with the Next Action features.

While we're editing the models, we also need to specify what happens with dependent `Tasks` when we delete `Projects` and `Locations`, and what happens with dependent `Tasks`, `Projects`, and `Locations` when we delete a `User`. Thinking about this, we decide that deleting a `Project` should delete all of its `Tasks`, but that deleting a `Location` should null out the `location_id` in a `Task`. Obviously, deleting a `User` should delete all of their `Tasks`, `Projects`, and `Locations`.

Let's do all this now. We'll start by modifying the `Project` model; see listing 10.25.

Listing 10.25   app\models\project.rb

```
class Project < ActiveRecord::Base
  attr_accessible :name, :notes, :completed, :created_at,
    :updated_at

  belongs_to :user
  has_many :tasks                                      ❶
  has_many :tasks, :dependent => :delete_all           ❷
  has_one :next_action,                                ❸
```

```
              :class_name => "Task",        ④
              :conditions => "next_action='1'"      ⑤

      def save_with_gtd_rules!        ⑥
        if self.completed        ⑦
          transaction do        ⑧
            self.tasks.update_all(:completed => true)      ⑨
            if self.next_action        ⑩
              self.next_action.next_action = false      ⑪
              self.next_action.save!      ⑫
            end
            self.save!      ⑬
          end      ⑭
        else
          self.save!      ⑮
        end
      end
end
```

We start by specifying that deleting a `Project` should delete all of its `Tasks` by adding `:dependent => :delete_all` to the `has_many :tasks` declaration ❶❷. The next action of a `Project` is a `Task` that has its `next_action` `true` in Rails, which in MySQL is `'1'`; we add a `has_one` call ❸, which specifies that the `next_action` is a `Task` ❹ with these conditions ❺.

Next, we add a `save_with_gtd_rules!` method ❻. (We use the `!` at the end, to indicate that we're using the "throw exceptions if things don't work!" `save!` methods, instead of the "return false if save didn't work" `save` methods.) In this method, we check whether the `Project` is completed ❼. If so, we open a transaction ❽ and set all the `tasks` in the `Project` to completed ❾. Inside the transaction, we also check whether the `Project` has a `next_action` `Task` ❿. If so, we set its `next_action` flag to `false` ⓫ and save it ⓬. Finally, we save the `Project` ⓭ and close the `transaction` ⓮. If the `Project` isn't completed, we save it ⓯. Note that this isn't optimal: We'll do the `transaction` even if the `Project`'s completed status isn't changing. (Exercise for the reader: Optimize this to do the `transaction` only if the `Project` wasn't previously completed—that is, if it's being set as `completed`.)

> **NOTE**   If you don't like relying on remembering to call `save_with_gtd_rules!`, you can consider overriding `save!` using the `alias_method` technique shown in iteration 5 for `to_xml`. Alternatively, you could use a `before_save` filter to enforce the various rules. (Thanks to Chris Bailey.)

Next, we'll modify the `Location`; see listing 10.26.

Listing 10.26   app\models\location.rb

```
class Location < ActiveRecord::Base
  attr_accessible :name, :notes, :created_at, :updated_at

  belongs_to :user
  has_many :tasks
  has_many :tasks, :dependent => :nullify
end
```

We specify that deleting a `Location` should nullify the `location_id` in its `Tasks` by adding `:dependent => :nullify` to the `has_many :tasks` declaration.

Now, we'll modify the `User` model; see listing 10.27.

Listing 10.27   app\models\user.rb

```
require 'digest/sha1'
class User < ActiveRecord::Base
  has_many :tasks
  has_many :projects
  has_many :locations
  has_one :note
  has_many :tasks, :dependent => :delete_all          ❶
  has_many :projects, :dependent => :delete_all       ❷
  has_many :locations, :dependent => :delete_all      ❸
  has_one :note, :dependent => :destroy               ❹
  has_many :next_actions,                             ❺
           :class_name => "Task",                     ❻
           :conditions => "next_action='1'"           ❼

  def before_create
    self.note = Note.new
  end

  # Virtual attribute for the unencrypted password
  attr_accessor :password
...
```

We specify that deleting a `User` should delete all its `tasks` ❶, projects ❷, and locations ❸ with the `:dependent => :delete_all` option. We then specify that deleting a `User` should delete the `note` with `:dependent => :destroy` ❹. For `has_many`, `:delete_all` is faster than `:destroy` because the delete is done with one SQL statement, and we can use it because we're deleting everything owned by the `User` and not relying on any of the callbacks that are triggered when an ActiveRecord is deleted with `:destroy`. (If we needed to delete all the `locations`

of a User and have their :dependent => :nullify take effect, we would use
:destroy instead of :delete_all.) Now, we add the Next Action concept to the
User. We say that a User has_many :next_actions ❺. Each of them is a Task ❻
that has its next_action true (in Rails), which in MySQL is '1' ❼.

Finally (as far as the model changes go), we need to add GTD semantics to the
Task model; see listing 10.28.

Listing 10.28   app\models\task.rb

```
class Task < ActiveRecord::Base
  attr_accessible :name, :notes, :next_action, :completed,
    :project_id, :location_id, :created_at, :updated_at

  belongs_to :user
  belongs_to :location
  belongs_to :project

  def before_save
    self.project_id = nil if self.project_id == 0
    self.location_id = nil if self.location_id == 0
  end

  def save_with_gtd_rules!                            ❶
    if self.completed                                 ❷
      # A completed task cannot be the next_action, so one of
      # these flags has to win. Arbitrarily, we decide that the
      # completed flag takes precedence over the next_action
      # flag.
      self.next_action = false                        ❸
    end
    if self.project                                   ❹
      prev_next_action = self.project.next_action     ❺
      next_action_changing =                          ❻
        prev_next_action && (self != prev_next_action)
      project_completed_changing =                    ❼
        !self.completed && self.project.completed
      if next_action_changing || project_completed_changing    ❽
        # If either of these are also changing, we need an
        # explicit transaction.
        transaction do                                ❾
          if next_action_changing                     ❿
            prev_next_action.next_action = false       ⓫
            prev_next_action.save!                      ⓬
          end
          if project_completed_changing                ⓭
            self.project.completed = false             ⓮
            self.project.save!                          ⓯
          end
          self.save!                                    ⓰
```

```
      end      ⑰
    else
      self.save! # We just need to save the task.      ⑱
    end
  else
    # No project, so if we're not completed we force the
    # next_action to true.
    if !self.completed      ⑲
      self.next_action = true      ⑳
    end
    self.save!      ㉑
  end
end
end
```

Again, we add a `save_with_gtd_rules!` method **❶**, with the `!` present because of the use of `save!` rather than `save`. In this method, we check whether the `Task` is completed **❷**. If so, we force its `next_action` flag to `false` **❸**. (One of the flags needs to "win," unless we're going to have whiny validation. You may prefer to use validation here.)

NOTE   Unlike the scaffolding, I'm using the `save!` `normal_case` `rescue` `error_handling` not `if save normal_case else error_handling` style because Jamis Buck prefers it[3] and I agree with his reasoning. (I'm sure he's thrilled.)

Next, we check whether the `Task` has a project **❹**. If so, we get the `next_action` of the project **❺** and store it in a variable called `prev_next_action` to preserve our sanity. We set a `next_action_changing` flag to whether this `prev_next_action` `Task` exists and isn't the same `Task` as this `Task` **❻**. We also set a `project_completed_changing` flag **❼** to whether the `Task` isn't `completed` and the project is `completed` (to `true` if we need to force the `project` to be not `completed` because the `Task` isn't `completed`).

If either of these flags are `true` **❽**, we need to begin a `transaction` **❾** to update everything at once. Inside that `transaction`, if the `next_action_changing` flag is `true` **❿**, we set the `next_action` flag of the `prev_next_action` **⓫** to `false` and save it **⓬**. Still inside the `transaction`, if the `project_completed_changing` flag is `true` **⓭**, we set the `completed` flag of the `project` **⓮** to `false` and save it **⓯**. Finally, we save the `Task` **⓰** and close the `transaction` **⓱**.

Otherwise, if both flags are `false`, we save the `Task` **⓲**.

---

[3] http://mtnwestrubyconf2007.confreaks.com/session10.html (around minute 28).

If there is no `project`, then none of this flag-setting and -checking happened: We check whether the `Task` isn't `completed` ⑲ and, if so, set its `next_action` flag to true ⑳ because all tasks with no `project` are the Next Action. We then save the `Task` ㉑.

Phew.

NOTE   The good thing about doing all this work in the model is that our controllers can be a lot smaller. Business logic like this belongs in the model, not the controller. See Jamis Buck's "Skinny Controller, Fat Model" article[4] for details.

Next, we need to update the `TasksController` and `ProjectsController` to call these new `save_with_gtd_rules!` methods. First, the `TasksController`; see listing 10.29.

Listing 10.29   app\controllers\tasks_controller.rb

```
...
  # PUT /tasks/1
  # PUT /tasks/1.xml
  def update
    @task = current_user.tasks.find(params[:id])
    @task.attributes = params[:task]           ❶
    @task.save_with_gtd_rules!                 ❷

    respond_to do |format|
      if @task.update_attributes(params[:task])          ❸
        flash[:notice] = 'Task was successfully updated.'
        format.html { redirect_to(@task) }
        format.xml  { render :xml => @task }
      else
        format.html { render :action => "edit" }
        format.xml  { render :xml => @task.errors,
          :status => :unprocessable_entity }
      end
      format.html do
        flash[:notice] = 'Task was successfully updated.'
        redirect_to(@task)
      end
      format.xml  { render :xml => @task }      ❹
    end
  rescue ActiveRecord::RecordInvalid            ❺
    respond_to do |format|
      format.html { render :action => "edit" }
```

---

[4] http://weblog.jamisbuck.org/2006/10/18/skinny-controller-fat-model.

```
      format.xml  { render :xml => @task.errors.to_xml_full }     ➏
    end
  rescue ActiveRecord::RecordNotFound => e
    prevent_access(e)
  end
...
```

We delete the old code inside the respond_to block, including the call to
@task.update_attributes(params[:task]) ➌. It's instructive to look at the
source for the update_attributes method in ActiveRecord::Base that is in ven-
dor\rails; see listing 10.30.

Listing 10.30   vendor\rails\activerecord\lib\active_record\base.rb

```
...
    def update_attributes(attributes)
      self.attributes = attributes
      save
    end
...
```

We see that update_attributes sets self.attributes and calls save. We want to
set the attributes of the @task with the same params[:task] that was passed to
update_attributes before calling save_with_gtd_rules!, so that's what we do
(➊ and ➋ in listing 10.29). Note that our use of attr_accessible in the Task
model ensures the user can't try anything sneaky with the user_id. If no exceptions were raised, we send @task to Flex ➍ as before (the to_xml method is automatically called). If a RecordInvalid is raised ➎, we send the @task.errors.
to_xml_full ➏. Note that besides using exception control flow instead of return-
code checking, we also send the to_xml_full now and don't bother with the
HTTP status code that we're ignoring. (Also note that the errors aren't used in our
Flex code; using them is an exercise for the reader.)

Next, we need to do something similar for projects. Modify the Projects-
Controller as shown in listing 10.31.

Listing 10.31   app\controllers\projects_controller.rb

```
...
  # PUT /projects/1
  # PUT /projects/1.xml
  def update
    @project = current_user.projects.find(params[:id])
```

```
    @project.attributes = params[:project]          ❶
    @project.save_with_gtd_rules!          ❷

  respond_to do |format|
    if @project.update_attributes(params[:project])          ❸
      flash[:notice] = 'Project was successfully updated.'
      format.html { redirect_to(@project) }
      format.xml  { render :xml => @project }
    else
      format.html { render :action => "edit" }
      format.xml  { render :xml => @project.errors,
        :status => :unprocessable_entity }
    end
    format.html do
      flash[:notice] = 'Project was successfully updated.'
      redirect_to(@project)
    end
    format.xml  { render :xml => @project }          ❹
  end
  rescue ActiveRecord::RecordInvalid
    respond_to do |format|
      format.html { render :action => "edit" }
      format.xml  { render :xml => @project.errors.to_xml_full }          ❺
    end
  rescue ActiveRecord::RecordNotFound => e
    prevent_access(e)
  end
...
```

Again, we set the attributes ❶ and call the save_with_gtd_rules! ❷ method, but this time it's of a Project (@project). Next, we delete the old code ❸ and then render :xml either the @project (the to_xml method is automatically called) on success ❹ or the @project.errors.to_xml_full ❺ on error.

Before we finish this section, we need to make two small changes on the Flex side: modifying the UpdateTaskCommand to list Projects and UpdateProject-Command to list Tasks. We start with the UpdateTaskCommand; see listing 10.32.

Listing 10.32   app\flex\com\pomodo\command\UpdateTaskCommand.as

```
package com.pomodo.command {
    import com.adobe.cairngorm.commands.ICommand;
    import com.adobe.cairngorm.control.CairngormEvent;
    import com.pomodo.business.TaskDelegate;
    import com.pomodo.control.EventNames;          <─┐
    import com.pomodo.model.PomodoModelLocator;      ├ Add import
    import com.pomodo.model.Task;                    │
    import com.pomodo.util.CairngormUtils;          <─┘
```

```
...
    public class UpdateTaskCommand implements ICommand,
    IResponder {
...
        public function result(event:Object):void {
            var resultEvent:ResultEvent = ResultEvent(event);
            var model:PomodoModelLocator =
                PomodoModelLocator.getInstance();
            model.updateTask(Task.fromXML(XML(event.result)));
            CairngormUtils.dispatchEvent(
                EventNames.LIST_PROJECTS);          ❶
        }
...
```

We call `CairngormUtils.dispatchEvent(EventNames.LIST_PROJECTS)` ❶ from the `result` handler of the `UpdateTaskCommand`. This is a simple way of getting any changes to the `Task`'s `Project` caused by the change to the `Task`—it's by no means the most efficient way this could be done.

Next, we make a similar change to the `UpdateProjectCommand`; see listing 10.33.

Listing 10.33   app\flex\com\pomodo\command\UpdateProjectCommand.as

```
package com.pomodo.command {
...
    public class UpdateProjectCommand implements ICommand,
    IResponder {
...
        public function result(event:Object):void {
            CairngormUtils.dispatchEvent(EventNames.LIST_TASKS);      ❶
            CairngormUtils.dispatchEvent(
                EventNames.LIST_PROJECTS);
        }
...
```

We already had the `imports`, so all we need to do is to call `CairngormUtils.dispatchEvent(EventNames.LIST_TASKS)` ❶ from the `result` handler of the `UpdateProjectCommand`.

That's it. We won't bother testing now, because we have more UI work to do.

10.4   *Filtering tasks*

Now that we've implemented the Next Action concept, let's implement the task filtering in the task list. This is also something we've left stubbed out for a long time.

The cool thing is that the `ListCollectionView` already supports the notion of filtering with a `filterFunction` (see the `ListCollectionView` API docs), so this is easy to do: We filter the tasks according to what is selected in the combo boxes. We also decide to add another option to show only the incomplete tasks, because this is probably one of the most useful filters—and we're surprised we forgot it.

One more thing: Because the `summaryPanel` requires the user to click Update before updating the data on the server, it will be helpful for us to keep the client-side data in a legal state if we can. By this, I mean that a completed `Task` can't be the Next Action of its project. We'll also add logic to the `completedCheckBox` and `nextActionCheckBox` to ensure that when the user clicks one of them, the other one is unchecked. Although we handle bogus input on the Rails side, if we can prevent it on the client it's a good thing to do because the UI is more intuitive.

Modify the `TasksListBox` as shown in listing 10.34.

Listing 10.34   app\flex\com\pomodo\components\TasksListBox.mxml

```
<?xml version="1.0" encoding="utf-8"?>
<mx:VDividedBox xmlns:mx="http://www.adobe.com/2006/mxml"
    width="100%" height="100%" label="Tasks">
<mx:Script>
<![CDATA[
    import mx.collections.ListCollectionView;        ❶ Add
    import mx.controls.Alert;                           import
    import com.pomodo.components.MainBox;
    import com.pomodo.control.EventNames;
    import com.pomodo.model.Location;
    import com.pomodo.model.PomodoModelLocator;
    import com.pomodo.model.Project;
    import com.pomodo.model.Task;
    import com.pomodo.util.CairngormUtils;

    public const NEXT_ACTIONS:int = 0;
    public const ALL_TASKS:int = 1;
    public const TASKS_IN_PROJECT:int = 2;
    public const TASKS_AT_LOCATION:int = 3;        ❷ Modify constants
    public static const ALL_TASKS:int = 0;              to be static
    public static const INCOMPLETE_TASKS:int = 1;     ❸ Add constant for
    public static const NEXT_ACTIONS:int = 2;            INCOMPLETE_TASKS
    public static const TASKS_IN_PROJECT:int = 3;
    public static const TASKS_AT_LOCATION:int = 4;

    [Bindable]
    public var model:PomodoModelLocator =
        PomodoModelLocator.getInstance();

    private const SHOW_CHOICES:Array = [           ❹ Rearrange
        {label:"All Tasks", data:ALL_TASKS,             SHOW_CHOICES
```

```
             hasSubChoice:false},
        {label:"Incomplete Tasks", data:INCOMPLETE_TASKS,
             hasSubChoice: false},
        {label:"Next Actions", data:NEXT_ACTIONS,
             hasSubChoice:false},
        {label:"All Tasks", data:ALL_TASKS,
             hasSubChoice:false},
        {label:"Tasks in Project:", data:TASKS_IN_PROJECT,
             hasSubChoice:true},
        {label:"Tasks at Location:", data:TASKS_AT_LOCATION,
             hasSubChoice:true}];

[Bindable]
private var _subChoices:Array;
private var _subChoices:ListCollectionView;    ⟵ 5 Change type to
                                                     ListCollectionView

public function updateSelectedTaskFromSummaryPanel():void {
    var task:Task = Task(tasksGrid.selectedItem);
    task.name = nameTI.text;
    task.completed = completedCheckBox.selected;

    task.project = Project(projectComboBox.selectedItem);
    task.location = Location(locationComboBox.selectedItem);
    task.notes = notesTI.text;
    task.nextAction = nextActionCheckBox.selected;   ⟵ 6 Set
    updateTask(task);                                      task.nextAction
}

public function updateTask(task:Task):void {
    CairngormUtils.dispatchEvent(
        EventNames.UPDATE_TASK, task);
}

public function deleteTask(task:Task):void {
    CairngormUtils.dispatchEvent(EventNames.DESTROY_TASK,
        task);
}                                                  7 Add 4
                                                     filter
public function incompleteTasksFilterFunc(item:Object):  ⟵ functions
Boolean {
    return !item.completed;
}

public function nextActionsFilterFunc(item:Object):Boolean {
    return item.nextAction;
}                                          Use state of  8
                                         subChoiceComboBox
public function tasksAtLocationFilterFunc(item:Object):
Boolean {
    return item.location == subChoiceComboBox.selectedItem;  ⟵
}
```

```
public function tasksInProjectFilterFunc(item:Object):
Boolean {
    return item.project == subChoiceComboBox.selectedItem;
}

private function updateMainChoice():void {
    switch (mainChoiceComboBox.selectedItem.data) {
        case TasksListBox.TASKS_AT_LOCATION:
            _subChoices = model.locationsAndNone;
            break;
        case TasksListBox.TASKS_IN_PROJECT:
            _subChoices = model.projectsAndNone;
            break;
        default:
            break;
    }
    updateTasksFilter();
}

private function updateTasksFilter():void {
    switch (mainChoiceComboBox.selectedItem.data) {
        case TasksListBox.ALL_TASKS:
            model.tasks.filterFunction = null;
            break;
        case TasksListBox.INCOMPLETE_TASKS:
            model.tasks.filterFunction =
                incompleteTasksFilterFunc;
            break;
        case TasksListBox.NEXT_ACTIONS:
            model.tasks.filterFunction =
                nextActionsFilterFunc;
            break;
        case TasksListBox.TASKS_AT_LOCATION:
            model.tasks.filterFunction =
                tasksAtLocationFilterFunc;
            break;
        case TasksListBox.TASKS_IN_PROJECT:
            model.tasks.filterFunction =
                tasksInProjectFilterFunc;
            break;
        default:
            Pomodo.debug("Unrecognized choice:" +
                mainChoiceComboBox.selectedItem.data);
            break;
    }
    model.tasks.refresh();
}

private function handleNextActionCheckBoxClicked():void {
    if (nextActionCheckBox.selected) {
```

**Update _subChoices based on
mainChoiceComboBox.selectedItem.data** **9**

**Switch on 10
mainChoiceComboBox.selectedItem.data**

**When one is checked, 11
other is unchecked**

```
            completedCheckBox.selected = false;
        }
    }

    private function handleCompletedCheckBoxClicked():void {
        if (completedCheckBox.selected) {
            nextActionCheckBox.selected = false;
        }
    }
]]>
</mx:Script>
    <mx:VBox width="100%" height="60%">
        <mx:HBox width="100%" paddingLeft="5" paddingRight="5">
            <mx:Label text="Show:"/>
            <mx:ComboBox id="mainChoiceComboBox"
                dataProvider="{SHOW_CHOICES}"
                change="updateMainChoice()"/>
            <mx:ComboBox id="subChoiceComboBox" width="100%"
            <mx:ComboBox id="subChoiceComboBox" width="200"
                dataProvider="{_subChoices}"
        visible="{mainChoiceComboBox.selectedItem.hasSubChoice}"
                change="updateTasksFilter()"
                labelField="name"/>
        </mx:HBox>
...
    </mx:VBox>
    <mx:Panel id="summaryPanel" title="Task" width="100%"
        height="40%" paddingLeft="5" paddingRight="5"
        paddingTop="5" paddingBottom="5">
        <mx:HBox width="100%">
            <mx:Label text="Name" width="50"/>
            <mx:TextInput id="nameTI" width="100%"
                text="{tasksGrid.selectedItem.name}"/>
            <mx:CheckBox id="completedCheckBox"
                label="Completed"
                selected="{tasksGrid.selectedItem.completed}"
                click="handleCompletedCheckBoxClicked()"/>
        </mx:HBox>
        <mx:HBox width="100%" verticalAlign="middle">
            <mx:Label text="Project" width="50"/>
            <mx:ComboBox id="projectComboBox" width="200"
                labelField="name"
                dataProvider="{model.projectsAndNone}"
                selectedItem="{tasksGrid.selectedItem.project}"
            />
            <mx:CheckBox label="This is the Next Action"/>
            <mx:CheckBox id="nextActionCheckBox"
                label="This is the Next Action"
                selected="{tasksGrid.selectedItem.nextAction}"
```

12 Handle change event to call updateMainChoice

13 Adjust width of subChoiceComboBox

14 Handle change event to call updateTasksFilter

15 Handle click event to sync CheckBoxes

16 Bind selected property to tasksGrid.selectedItem.nextAction

```
        click="handleNextActionCheckBoxClicked()"/>
    <mx:Spacer width="100%"/>
    <mx:Label text="Location"/>
    <mx:ComboBox id="locationComboBox" width="200"
        labelField="name"
        dataProvider="{model.locationsAndNone}"
        selectedItem="{tasksGrid.selectedItem.location}"
    />
  </mx:HBox>
...
  </mx:Panel>
</mx:VDividedBox>
```

**Handle click event to
sync CheckBoxes** ⓱

We start by adding an import ❶ and modifying the constants to be static ❷. We also add a constant for INCOMPLETE_TASKS ❸. Next, we rearrange the SHOW_CHOICES and add INCOMPLETE_TASKS to them ❹. We then modify ❺ the _subChoices to be a ListCollectionView, because that's what it will be assigned to from the model. We set the task.nextAction to the value of the selected property of the nextActionCheckBox ❻.

Next, we add the various filter functions ❼. These all check the item (which is typed as Object but which is a Task) and return Boolean if it matches the filter and should be shown. Note that the tasksAtLocationFilterFunc and tasksIn-ProjectFilterFunc use the state of the subChoiceComboBox ❽. (Flex 1.5 developers: You don't need to use Delegate.create any more to correct this reference.) Now, we add an updateMainChoice ❾ function that updates _subChoices to be either model.locationsAndNone or model.projectsAndNone based on the mainChoiceComboBox.selectedItem.data. (We don't have to handle the other cases, because the subChoiceComboBox will be hidden.) After the _subChoices are updated in updateMainChoice, we call updateTasksFilter ❿. This function switches on mainChoiceComboBox.selectedItem.data and updates model.tasks.filterFunction accordingly (or to null in the case of TasksList-Box.ALL_TASKS) and then calls model.tasks.refresh() to update the model.tasks ListCollectionView.

Next, we add the handleNextActionCheckBoxClicked ⓫ and handleComplet-edCheckBoxClicked functions, which ensure that when either the completed-CheckBox or nextActionCheckBox is selected by the user, the other one is deselected. We add these functions as click event handlers ⓯⓱ in order for them to be invoked after the selected property is set on user click only.

Now, we modify the two ComboBoxes to handle their change events and to adjust the width of the subChoiceComboBox ⓬–⓮. Finally, we give the This Is the Next Action CheckBox an id of nextActionCheckBox and bind its selected property to tasksGrid.selectedItem.nextAction ⓰.

Rebuild, reload, and—nah, we're so close, let's keep going and finish this iteration before testing.

10.5 *The CommandShell*

Another thing we've left stubbed out for now is the CommandShell; see listing 10.35. Let's implement that too. We'll keep it simple and use it to create tasks for now. A full command shell will be left as an exercise for the reader.

Listing 10.35   app\flex\com\pomodo\components\CommandShell.mxml

```
<?xml version="1.0" encoding="utf-8"?>
<mx:HBox xmlns:mx="http://www.adobe.com/2006/mxml" width="100%">
<mx:Script>
<![CDATA[
    import com.pomodo.control.EventNames;
    import com.pomodo.model.Task;
    import com.pomodo.util.CairngormUtils;

    private function parseCommand():void {          ❶
        var cmdArray:Array = cmdTI.text.split(":");     ❷
        if (cmdArray.length < 1) return;            ❸
        var newTask:Task = new Task(            ❹
            cmdArray[0],                    ❺
            (cmdArray.length > 1 ? cmdArray[1] : ""));      ❻
        CairngormUtils.dispatchEvent(EventNames.CREATE_TASK,    ❼
            newTask);
    }
]]>
</mx:Script>
    <mx:Label text="pomodo:"/>
    <mx:TextInput id="cmdTI" width="100%"
        enter="parseCommand()"/>         ❽
</mx:HBox>
```

This is easy: We modify cmdTI to call ❽ the parseCommand function ❶ when the enter event is broadcast. In parseCommand, we split the text ❷ of the cmdTI by the : character, because we're going to support a syntax of name:notes—"finish this iteration:write the rest of the content"—to create a new Task whose name is "finish this iteration" and whose notes are "write the rest of the content". We ensure that we have a task name: that is, that the cmdArray has at least one element in it ❸. If so, we create a new Task ❹ with the name ❺ and optional notes ❻. Finally, we dispatch an event whose name is EventNames.CREATE_TASK ❼ and whose data is the newTask.

That's it! Everything else is handled for us. One of the great things about Cairngorm is it doesn't matter where commands originated—we can easily expand our application in new and unexpected ways.

10.6 Logging out

Another thing we missed was the ability to log out. Oops! Let's add support for that.

What do we want to do when we log out? Because I want to promote this book, I decided to do a bit of marketing and send the user to http://www.flexible-rails.com when they log out. It will be instructive, too, because it will show techniques we haven't seen before.

This will be more work than the CommandShell, because we'll need to create a new event name, command, and so on.

We'll start by creating a LoadURLCommand; see listing 10.36.

Listing 10.36   app\flex\com\pomodo\command\LoadURLCommand.as

```
package com.pomodo.command {
    import com.adobe.cairngorm.commands.ICommand;
    import com.adobe.cairngorm.control.CairngormEvent;
    import flash.net.navigateToURL;              ❶
    import flash.net.URLRequest;

    public class LoadURLCommand implements ICommand {
        public function LoadURLCommand() {
        }

        public function execute(event:CairngormEvent):void {   ❷
            var request:URLRequest = new URLRequest(event.data);   ❸
            try {
                navigateToURL(request, "_top");       ❹
            }
            catch (e:Error) {
            }
        }
    }
}
```

This is simple. The LoadURLCommand imports the navigateToURL function ❶. In its execute function ❷, it constructs a new URLRequest ❸ for the event.data as the URL. It then calls navigateToURL ❹ inside a try block that catches and ignores any Errors. We specify "_top" ❹ to replace the current browser window in which the Flex application is running.

Next, we'll hook up this command, starting with adding a LOAD_URL constant in EventNames; see listing 10.37.

Listing 10.37 app\flex\com\pomodo\control\EventNames.as

```
package com.pomodo.control {
    public final class EventNames {
...
        public static const SHOW_NOTE:String = "showNote";

        public static const LOAD_URL:String = "loadURL";
...
    }
}
```

Now, we'll make an addCommand call in PomodoController; see listing 10.38.

Listing 10.38 app\flex\com\pomodo\control\PomodoController.as

```
...
        private function initializeCommands() : void {
...
            addCommand(EventNames.SHOW_NOTE, ShowNoteCommand);
            addCommand(EventNames.LOAD_URL, LoadURLCommand);
        }
    }
}
```

We'll also modify the MainBox to add the UI to trigger logout; see listing 10.39.

Listing 10.39 app\flex\com\pomodo\components\MainBox.mxml

```
...
<mx:Script>
<![CDATA[
    import com.pomodo.control.EventNames;
    import com.pomodo.util.CairngormUtils;
    import com.pomodo.model.PomodoModelLocator;

    [Bindable]
    private var _model:PomodoModelLocator =
        PomodoModelLocator.getInstance();

    private function logout():void {          ❶
        CairngormUtils.dispatchEvent(EventNames.LOAD_URL,     ❷
            "/logout");
    }
```

```
    private function handleCreationComplete():void {
        CairngormUtils.dispatchEvent(EventNames.SHOW_NOTE);
        CairngormUtils.dispatchEvent(EventNames.LIST_PROJECTS);
        CairngormUtils.dispatchEvent(EventNames.LIST_LOCATIONS);
    }
]]>
</mx:Script>
    <mx:HBox width="100%" height="100%">
        <mx:VBox width="300" height="100%">
...

            <mx:DateChooser id="dateChooser" width="100%"/>
            <mx:Button label="logout" width="100%"       ❸
                click="logout()"/>
        </mx:VBox>
...
```

We add a `logout` function ❶ that calls `CairngormUtils.dispatchEvent` with a `LOAD_URL` name and a `"/logout"` URL ❷. We then call this function from the click handler of a logout button ❸.

Finally, we modify the `SessionsController`; see listing 10.40.

Listing 10.40   app\controllers\sessions_controller.rb

```
# This controller handles the login/logout function of the site.
class SessionsController < ApplicationController
...
  # DELETE /session
  # DELETE /session.xml
  def destroy
    self.current_user.forget_me if logged_in?
    cookies.delete :auth_token
    reset_session
    flash[:notice] = "You have been logged out."           ❶
    redirect_back_or_default('/')           ❷
    redirect_to "http://www.flexiblerails.com"           ❸
  end
end
```

We remove the flash notice ❶ and the redirect to the site root ❷ and instead redirect_to http://www.flexiblerails.com ❸.

Cheesy redirects? The urge to do some marketing is upon us!

10.7 *Marketing!*

If we're building a fake Web 2.0 app, we need to improve our marketing. Also, if we want to theoretically deploy pomodo as a demo app for *Flexible Rails*, we need to make it as persuasive as possible. Besides redirecting the users when they log out, how else can we convince them to buy the book? Well, we could try adding a link at the top of the app. While we're at it, we'll add a copyright notice at the bottom and add a couple effects to make things look cool. Finally, we'll modify the compiler settings to output into public instead of public\bin. This way, all we have to do is rename Pomodo.html to index.html (and delete the default route), and we'll be able to test the app at http://localhost:3000 instead of http://localhost:3000/bin/Pomodo.html. Then we could deploy it at, say, http://www.pomodo.com instead of http://www.pomodo.com/bin/Pomodo.html.

First, we'll modify Pomodo.mxml; see listing 10.41.

Listing 10.41   app\flex\Pomodo.mxml

```
<?xml version="1.0" encoding="utf-8"?>
<mx:Application
    xmlns:mx="http://www.adobe.com/2006/mxml"
    xmlns:pom="com.pomodo.components.*"
    xmlns:control="com.pomodo.control.*"
    layout="vertical"
    backgroundGradientColors="[#ffffff, #c0c0c0]"
    horizontalAlign="center"
    verticalAlign="top"
    paddingLeft="0"
    paddingRight="0"
    paddingTop="0"
    paddingBottom="0"
    width="100%"
    height="100%"
    creationCompleteEffect="fadeIn">           ❶
<mx:Script>
<![CDATA[
    import mx.core.Container;
    import com.pomodo.components.DebugPanel;
    import com.pomodo.control.EventNames;            ❷
    import com.pomodo.util.CairngormUtils;
    import com.pomodo.util.DebugMessage;
    import com.pomodo.model.PomodoModelLocator;

    private static const COPYRIGHT:String =          ❸
        "Copyright (c) 2007, Peter Armstrong.";

    private static const MARKETING:String =          ❹
        "To learn how this app was built, click here to go " +
        "to http://www.flexiblerails.com.";
```

```
    [Bindable]
    private var _model : PomodoModelLocator =
        PomodoModelLocator.getInstance();

    public static function debug(str:String):void {
        application.debugPanel.addMessage(
            new DebugMessage(str));
    }

    private function controlViewToShow(workflowState:int):
    Container {
...
    }

    private function loadFlexibleRails():void {            ⑤
        CairngormUtils.dispatchEvent(EventNames.LOAD_URL,
            "http://www.flexiblerails.com");
    }
]]>
</mx:Script>
    <mx:Fade id="fadeIn" duration="500"/>            ⑥
    <mx:WipeUp id="wipeUp" duration="500"/>

    <!--
    the FrontController, containing Commands specific to this app
    -->
    <control:PomodoController id="controller" />

    <mx:HBox backgroundColor="#000000" width="100%" height="30"
        horizontalAlign="center" verticalAlign="middle">
        <mx:LinkButton color="#FFFFFF"
            click="loadFlexibleRails()" label="{MARKETING}"/>            ⑦
    </mx:HBox>
    <mx:Spacer height="10"/>

    <mx:VDividedBox width="100%" height="100%">
        <mx:ViewStack id="mainStack" width="100%" height="100%"
selectedChild="{controlViewToShow(_model.workflowState)}">
            <pom:SplashBox id="splashBox"/>
            <pom:MainBox id="mainBox" showEffect="wipeUp"/>            ⑧
        </mx:ViewStack>
        <pom:DebugPanel id="debugPanel" width="100%"
            height="0%"/>
    </mx:VDividedBox>
    <mx:HBox backgroundColor="#000000" width="100%" height="30"
        horizontalAlign="center" verticalAlign="middle">
        <mx:Label color="#FFFFFF" text="{COPYRIGHT}"/>            ⑨
    </mx:HBox>
</mx:Application>
```

We create two effects **6**, an mx:Fade called fadeIn and an mx:WipeUp, both of which last 500 milliseconds. We set the creationCompleteEffect **1** of the mx:Application to be the fadeIn. We then add some imports **2** and constants for the copyright **3** and marketing **4** Strings. Next, we create a loadFlexibleRails function **5** that dispatches the same LOAD_URL event we used to log out, but it doesn't log out—it goes to http://www.flexiblerails.com. (This would be useful if we supported automatically showing the MainBox if the user was logged in, which is straightforward to do—and is an exercise for the reader.) Next, we make some UI changes to show our new copyright notice **9** and marketing link **7**. Note that the mainBox now has the wipeUp effect as its showEffect **8**. Also note that the mx:LinkButton **9** is a control we haven't seen before in the book. It is what it says it is: a button that looks like a link. (Of course, I'm modifying its color, so it looks less so.)

Next, right-click the pomodo project in the Navigator, and choose Properties to modify the compiler settings. Change the output folder from public\bin to public; see figure 10.2.

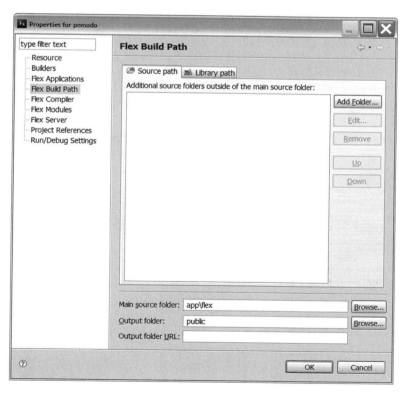

**Figure 10.2
Updating the
output folder in
the build path**

Click OK.

Before we test, we suddenly realize that we've been so focused on creating things (tasks, projects, locations) in the course of building the application that we haven't paid attention to what we should do when we delete them. Furthermore, to our horror, we realize that there is no way to delete a user at the moment—we have no support for it in the UserController or in the UI. *Oops!* Clearly, we should address these issues before declaring that we're finished! Otherwise, we won't be able to demo the app on the Internet without getting angry "I can't delete my account" emails. This won't do.

10.8 Deleting users

We'll start by creating a destroy action in the UsersController; see listing 10.42.

Listing 10.42   app\controllers\users_controller.rb

```
class UsersController < ApplicationController
  skip_before_filter :login_required, :only => [ :new, :create ]      ❶

  # GET /users/new
  # GET /users/new.xml
  def new
    # render new.rhtml
  end

  # POST /users
  # POST /users.xml
  def create
...
  end

  # DELETE /users/1
  # DELETE /users/1.xml
  def destroy           ❷
    if current_user.id == params[:id].to_i &&      ❸
      current_user.destroy
      cookies.delete :auth_token       ❹
      reset_session       ❺
      render :text => "success"       ❻
    else
      render :text => "error"       ❼
    end
  end
end
```

We start by modifying the `skip_before_filter` ❶ to only skip `new` and `create`, because we want to ensure that the user is logged in before we attempt to destroy a user. We then create a `destroy` method ❷. We then also check ❸ that the `current_user.id` is the `params[:id]` (converted from a `String` to a `Fixnum` with `to_i`). If the `id` matches, we call `current_user.destroy` ❹ to delete the `current_user`. We clear out the cookies and session ❹❺ using code copied from the `SessionsController` and then render the text `"success"` ❻. If anything goes wrong (for example, the ids don't match or the destroy failed), we render the text `"error"` ❼.

Now, to the Flex side. We'll create an Account tab, which will hold a Delete Account button and nothing else. In a real application we would allow the user to update all their details; doing this in pomodo is left as an exercise for the reader. We'll also add a new command (`DestroyUserCommand`) to do the work, modifying the `UserDelegate`, and so on. By now, this should be routine.

We'll start with `EventNames`; see listing 10.43.

Listing 10.43   app\flex\com\pomodo\control\EventNames.as

```
package com.pomodo.control {
    public final class EventNames {
...
        public static const DESTROY_TASK:String = "destroyTask";
        public static const DESTROY_USER:String = "destroyUser";
...
```

We add a `DESTROY_USER` const for `"destroyUser"`.

Next, we'll modify the `PomodoController` to hook this `DESTROY_USER` event name up to a new `DestroyUserCommand`; see listing 10.44.

Listing 10.44   app\flex\com\pomodo\control\PomodoController.as

```
package com.pomodo.control {
...
    public class PomodoController extends FrontController {
...
        private function initializeCommands():void {
...
            addCommand(EventNames.DESTROY_TASK,
                DestroyTaskCommand);
            addCommand(EventNames.DESTROY_USER,
                DestroyUserCommand);
...
```

Now, we'll create the new `DestroyUserCommand`; see listing 10.45.

Listing 10.45   app\flex\com\pomodo\command\DestroyUserCommand.as

```
package com.pomodo.command {
    import com.adobe.cairngorm.commands.ICommand;
    import com.adobe.cairngorm.control.CairngormEvent;
    import com.pomodo.business.UserDelegate;
    import com.pomodo.control.EventNames;
    import com.pomodo.model.User;
    import com.pomodo.model.PomodoModelLocator;
    import com.pomodo.util.CairngormUtils;

    import mx.controls.Alert;
    import mx.core.Application;
    import mx.events.CloseEvent;
    import mx.rpc.IResponder;
    import mx.rpc.events.FaultEvent;
    import mx.rpc.events.ResultEvent;

    public class DestroyUserCommand implements ICommand,
    IResponder {
        public function DestroyUserCommand() {
        }

        public function execute(event:CairngormEvent):void {        ❶
            var delegate:UserDelegate = new UserDelegate(this);      ❷
            delegate.destroyUser(event.data);        ❸
        }

        public function result(event:Object):void {        ❹
            var resultEvent:ResultEvent = ResultEvent(event);
            var model:PomodoModelLocator =
                PomodoModelLocator.getInstance();
            if (event.result == "success") {        ❺
              · Alert.show(        ❻
                    "Your account was deleted.",
                    "Delete Successful",
                    Alert.OK,
                    Application(Application.application),
                    alertClickHandler);
            } else {
                Alert.show(        ❼
                    "Your account was not successfully deleted.",
                    "Error");
            }
        }

        private function alertClickHandler(event:CloseEvent):        ❽
```

```
        void {
            CairngormUtils.dispatchEvent(EventNames.LOAD_URL,      ❾
                "http://www.flexiblerails.com");
        }

        public function fault(event:Object):void {
            var faultEvent:FaultEvent = FaultEvent(event);
            Alert.show("The user was not successfully deleted.",
                "Error");
        }
    }
}
```

In the execute ❶ method, we create a new `UserDelegate` ❷ and call its
`destroyUser` method ❸, which we'll add momentarily. In the `result` handler ❹,
we check whether the result is a `"success"` ❺ and show an `Alert` ❻ saying
the delete was successful if it was, or an `Alert` saying it wasn't successful if it
wasn't ❼. In the `alertClickHandler` ❽ for the successful deletion Alert box
(which is triggered when the OK button of the Alert dialog is clicked, since we
attached it above ❻), we send the user to http://www.flexiblerails.com by dispatching a Cairngorm `LOAD_URL` ❾ event. This has the effect of getting rid of any
application state, too.

Next, we'll add the `destroyUser` method to the `UserDelegate`; see listing 10.46.

Listing 10.46   app\flex\com\pomodo\business\UserDelegate.as

```
package com.pomodo.business {
    import mx.rpc.IResponder;
    import com.pomodo.model.User;
    import com.pomodo.util.ServiceUtils;

    public class UserDelegate {
        private var _responder:IResponder;

        public function UserDelegate(responder:IResponder) {
            _responder = responder;
        }

        public function createUser(user:User):void {
            ServiceUtils.send("/users.xml", _responder, "POST",
                user.toXML(), true);
        }

        public function destroyUser(user:User):void {       ❶
            ServiceUtils.send("/users/" + user.id + ".xml",  ❷
                _responder, "DELETE");
```

```
        }
     }
  }
```

In the `destroyUser` function ❶, we call `ServiceUtils.send` ❷ with a URL that contains the `user.id` and a method of `"DELETE"`.

Now, we'll create the `AccountBox`; see listing 10.47.

Listing 10.47   app\flex\com\pomodo\components\AccountBox.mxml

```
<?xml version="1.0" encoding="utf-8"?>
<mx:VBox xmlns:mx="http://www.adobe.com/2006/mxml"
    width="100%" height="100%" label="Account"
    paddingLeft="5" paddingRight="5" paddingTop="5"
    paddingBottom="5">
<mx:Script>
<![CDATA[
    import com.pomodo.control.EventNames;
    import com.pomodo.model.PomodoModelLocator;
    import com.pomodo.util.CairngormUtils;
    import mx.controls.Alert;
    import mx.events.CloseEvent;

    [Bindable]
    private var _model:PomodoModelLocator =
        PomodoModelLocator.getInstance();

    private function handleDeleteAccount(event:Event):void {
        Alert.show(         ❶
    "Do you want to delete your account? This is irreversible.",
            "Delete Account",
            Alert.YES | Alert.NO,
            this,
            handleAlertClick);         ❷
    }

    private function handleAlertClick(event:CloseEvent):void {
        if (event.detail == Alert.YES) {
            CairngormUtils.dispatchEvent(         ❸
                EventNames.DESTROY_USER, _model.user);
        }
    }
]]>
</mx:Script>
    <mx:Button label="Delete Account"         ❹
        click="handleDeleteAccount(event)"/>
</mx:VBox>
```

We create a Delete Account button ❹ whose click handler, `handleDeleteAc-count`, shows an `Alert` ❶ asking for confirmation. This `Alert` has a `closeHandler` of `handleAlertClick` ❷ specified in the constructor, which dispatches a `DESTROY_USER` ❸ named event if the user clicks Yes.

Finally, we need to modify `MainBox` to add the `AccountBox` to it. This is trivial; see listing 10.48.

Listing 10.48 app\flex\com\pomodo\components\MainBox.mxml

```
...
                <pom:Notely id="notelyTab"/>
                <pom:AccountBox id="accountTab"/>
            </mx:TabNavigator>
        </mx:VBox>
    </mx:HBox>
</mx:HBox>
```

That's it! Rebuild, and rename (or copy-paste) public\Pomodo.html to public\index.html. (As far as I can tell, you'll have to do this after every clean build, or automate the process with a script.)

Q. What about the default route? Shouldn't we delete it?

A. The index.html file wins, so it doesn't matter. You can delete it if you wish.

Next, reload and (all together now) log in as ludwig—but this time using http://localhost:3000.

We see the screen shown in figure 10.3 on the following page.

Play with selecting the different Tasks view filters, entering new tasks in the pomodo command shell, and so on. Mouse over the `LinkButton` at the top to see its highlight. Try clicking Logout or the `LinkButton` to be taken to http://www.flexiblerails.com. Hooray!

We see that deleting a project deletes its tasks, whereas deleting a location sets the location of tasks that had that location to None (which is how the UI shows a null location).

Finally, switch to the Account tab. We see the Delete Account button (see figure 10.4).

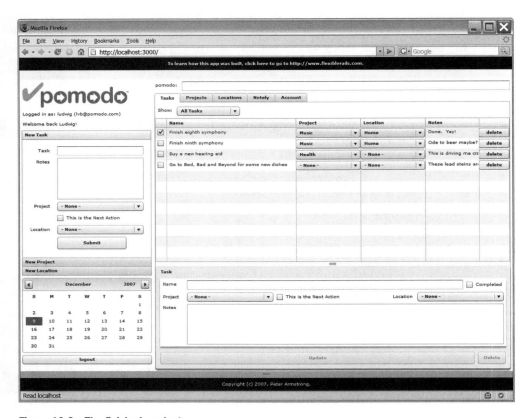

Figure 10.3 The finished product

Figure 10.4 37signals doesn't have a monopoly on simplicity.

Figure 10.5   Deleting Ludwig

Click the Delete Account button. The app is grayed out, and we see the alert shown in figure 10.5.

Click Yes to delete ludwig. *(Sniff.)* The delete is processed, and we're notified that the delete was successful (see figure 10.6).

When we click OK, we're whisked off to http://www.flexiblerails.com/.

Finally, run the tests again with `rake` and confirm that everything still works. We're done!

Well, almost. In the next iteration, we'll refactor pomodo to use RubyAMF for the data exchange between Flex and Rails. Then, in the final iteration, we'll convert pomodo to be an AIR application and add support for online/offline detection.

Figure 10.6   Goodbye, Ludwig.

The code at this point is saved as the iteration10 folder.

10.9 *Exercises for the Reader*

1 Fully implement the pomodo command prompt. Is support for deleting tasks usable? How would you make it more usable?

2 Add code to automatically show the `MainStack` if there is already a session.

3 Add support for updating the user first name, last name, email, and so on.

Refactoring to RubyAMF

11

RubyAMF is an Open Source, MIT-licensed (with one exception, as explained in a moment) Flash Remoting gateway for Ruby on Rails. It focuses on speed, and it integrates directly with RESTful Rails controllers via `render :amf`. Because of this, RubyAMF can be used as a more efficient wire format for sending information between Flex and Rails. (Of course, any time you see a claim that something is more efficient, you should do your own benchmarks or profiling. As such, I'm not going to do it for you here.)

RubyAMF also features a standalone implementation that doesn't depend on Rails—it's called *RubyAMF* and not *RailsAMF*. But because this book is about Rails in particular and not just Ruby—it's called *Flexible Rails*, not *Flexible Ruby*—the standalone RubyAMF is beyond the scope of the iteration.

In this iteration, we'll start by installing RubyAMF and doing a quick "Hello World" test. We'll then refactor the tasks, projects, locations, and note to be sent between Flex and Rails via `RemoteObject` to RubyAMF instead of using `HTTPService` and XML. (We won't touch the login code: There's no reason to do so, and I want to keep this iteration as small as possible.)

Doing the refactoring will show how RubyAMF integrates with our RESTful controllers and how we can modify our Flex application to use RubyAMF via `RemoteObject` instead of XML via `HTTPService`. We'll also replace the `ServiceUtils.as` class with the standard Cairngorm `Services.mxml` class: Doing this will bring our code more in line with standard Cairngorm, which will be instructive. (Also, because we're focusing on performance, it means we won't create numerous disposable `RemoteObjects`.)

Before we begin, I'll disclose my conflicts of interest up front. In so doing, I also get to stealthily establish the claim that I'm qualified to write about RubyAMF.

11.1 Warning: biased author

In this book, I like to play the role of unbiased (but opinionated) obsever of the technologies I'm writing about. In this iteration, however, I'm not impartial. There are currently two AMF technologies for Ruby: RubyAMF and WebORB for Rails. I'm not going to write about WebORB for Rails at all in this book, because I may be biased in favor of RubyAMF. Here's why:

- I've advocated RubyAMF as the most promising AMF implementation for Ruby in various presentations.
- I have commit access on RubyAMF, http://code.google.com/p/rubyamf/ —*although as of 2007-11-10 I've committed nothing.*

- There is a `flexiblerails` branch of RubyAMF (which as of 2007-11-10 was identical to the 1.5 release) so that readers of this book can follow along with something which is stable.

- A few months ago, Aaron Smith, the creator of RubyAMF, was kind enough to write some code that refactored an older version of pomodo to talk to an older version of RubyAMF (the standalone version, not the Rails version). Although this codebase isn't used in this iteration—RubyAMF has changed *a lot* since then—I've learned from it.

- Most important, I've had a number of productive email exchanges with Aaron Smith over the past months, including two email exchanges that constitute contributions to the RubyAMF project:

  - On June 20, 2007, I helped to convince Aaron to change the RubyAMF license from the GPL back to the MIT license (which RubyAMF had previously been licensed under). (Rails is also MIT-licensed, and Ruby uses a license which is similar to the MIT license.)

  - On June 29, 2007, I proposed the `format.amf { render :amf => @task.to_amf }` approach for integration with RESTful controllers and helped to convince Aaron that integration with RESTful controllers was a worthwhile feature. (Aaron subsequently implemented this, and it works well (as you'll soon see.) Note that we don't need to say `to_amf` with Rails 2; we can say `format.amf { render :amf => @task }` instead.)

In my opinion, the use of the MIT license alone will ensure that RubyAMF becomes the dominant AMF implementation for Ruby—especially since Rails also uses the MIT license, which means that RubyAMF and Rails are completely compatible. (As of 2007-11-10, WebORB for Rails was available under two licenses: the GPL and a commercial license.) Furthermore, the RESTful controller integration will help persuade Rails users that RubyAMF can be used as a more efficient wire format for Rails.

> **Note about the RubyAMF 1.5 license**
>
> RubyAMF 1.5 (and the `flexiblerails` branch) is released under a slightly modified MIT license, with one clause added: "There is one exception to the above MIT license. WebORB may not use this code base in any of their releases of WebORB for RoR."
>
> Nobody ever said Open Source isn't competitive!

> ## Note about the RubyAMF 1.5 license *(continued)*
>
> The interesting thing about this clause is that it counteracts the license inequality of the GPL and the MIT license: Under the terms of the GPL, MIT + GPL code = GPL code. (The GPL is the most viral of the Open Source licenses—GPL'd code can incorporate MIT-licensed code and stay GPL'd, but MIT-licensed code can't incorporate GPL'd code without becoming GPL'd itself. Throughout human history, this type of approach has been an easy way for an idea to spread itself.) Under the GPL, WebORB [GPL] could have copied from RubyAMF [MIT], but RubyAMF could not have copied from WebORB. This clause means that neither project can copy from the other.

I've made contributions (however minor) to RubyAMF, and as such I'm biased in its favor. Although I'll strive to be impartial in this iteration, you can assume that because of my closeness to the project, I'm biased, and adjust your expectations accordingly.

11.2 Hello RubyAMF

We'll start by getting the `flexiblerails` branch of RubyAMF, as shown in listing 11.1.

Listing 11.1 Installing the flexiblerails RubyAMF branch

```
c:\peter\flexiblerails\current\pomodo>ruby script\plugin install
   ➥http://rubyamf.googlecode.com/svn/branches/flexiblerails/rubyamf
+ ./CHANGELOG
+ ./LICENSE
+ ./README
+ ./app/actions.rb
+ ./app/amf.rb
+ ./app/configuration.rb
+ ./app/fault_object.rb
+ ./app/filters.rb
+ ./app/rails_gateway.rb
+ ./app/request_store.rb
+ ./exception/exception_handler.rb
+ ./exception/rubyamf_exception.rb
+ ./init.rb
+ ./install.rb
+ ./io/amf_deserializer.rb
+ ./io/amf_serializer.rb
+ ./io/read_write.rb
+ ./rails_installer_files/crossdomain.xml
```

```
+ ./rails_installer_files/rubyamf_config.rb
+ ./rails_installer_files/rubyamf_controller.rb
+ ./rails_installer_files/rubyamf_helper.rb
+ ./util/action_controller.rb
+ ./util/active_record.rb
+ ./util/string.rb
+ ./util/vo_helper.rb

c:\peter\flexiblerails\current\pomodo>
```

Next, because we're new to RubyAMF, we'll do a quick "Hello World" example. After that, I'll show the result of refactoring to RubyAMF all at once, without dwelling on the basics of RubyAMF. These basics are explained extremely well at the following tutorial[1], written by Bryan Carlson of Trailtracer (http://trailtracer.com/): http://panscendo.com/beginners-tutorial-to-rubyamf-with-restful-rails/. As such, I'll keep my "Hello World" example extremely brief and explain RubyAMF as I present the result of the refactoring.

We don't need to do any configuration of RubyAMF at this point—the defaults in config\rubyamf_config.rb are good enough for "Hello World."

We'll start by creating a new `HelloController` with a `hello` action; see listing 11.2.

Listing 11.2   app\controllers\hello_controller.rb

```
class HelloController < ApplicationController
  skip_before_filter :login_required      ❶
  def sayhello
    render :amf => "hello world"      ❷
  end
end
```

It doesn't get much simpler than this: We create a `HelloController` that doesn't require login ❶ and which has a `sayhello` action which renders the `String` `"hello world"` via AMF ❷.

The trick is that this doesn't work from a normal HTTP request—try it in the browser or on the command line with `curl`: You get nothing. We need to call it using AMF—specifically, using `RemoteObject`, which uses AMF. From the *Flex 3*

---

[1] This tutorial used to live at http://natureandtech.blogspot.com/2007/10/beginners-tutorial-to-rubyamf-with.html. Since it was the first really good RubyAMF tutorial, you'll see various links to that URL online.

Developer's Guide: "RemoteObject components let you access the methods of server-side objects, such as ColdFusion components (CFCs), Java objects, PHP objects, and .NET objects, without configuring the objects as web services. You can use RemoteObject components in MXML or ActionScript."[2] (Of course, it didn't mention Ruby—maybe the next version will.)

NOTE Flex 3 includes two `RemoteObject` classes: `mx.rpc.remoting.Remote-Object` and `mx.rpc.remoting.mxml.RemoteObject`. The latter is intended for use in MXML; what makes it confusing is that `mx.rpc.remoting.mxml.RemoteObject` extends `mx.rpc.remoting.RemoteObject`.

We'll need to create and use a `RemoteObject` that uses AMF to talk to RubyAMF. The problem is, we haven't configured AMF on the Flex side yet. Let's fix that now; see listing 11.3.

NOTE This file is taken directly (with permission) from Bryan Carlson's tutorial.

Listing 11.3   app\flex\services-config.xml

```
<?xml version="1.0" encoding="UTF-8"?>
<services-config>
 <services>
  <service id="rubyamf-flashremoting-service"         ❶
   class="flex.messaging.services.RemotingService"
   messageTypes="flex.messaging.messages.RemotingMessage">
   <destination id="rubyamf">         ❷
    <channels>
     <channel ref="rubyamf"/>
    </channels>
    <properties>
     <source>*</source>
    </properties>
   </destination>
  </service>
 </services>
 <channels>
  <channel-definition id="rubyamf"         ❸
    class="mx.messaging.channels.AMFChannel">
   <endpoint uri="http://localhost:3000/rubyamf/gateway"         ❹
       class="flex.messaging.endpoints.AMFEndpoint"/>
  </channel-definition>
 </channels>
</services-config>
```

---

[2] *Flex 3 Developer's Guide, Beta 2, p. 85.*

Explaining this type of file in depth is best left to reference documentation; all we need to note is that we're creating a service whose id is `"rubyamf-flashremoting-service"` ❶ and whose destination has an id of `"rubyamf"` ❷. We're also creating a channel whose id is `"rubyamf"` ❸ and whose endpoint URI (the cool-kid way of saying what amounts to a URL) points at the URL of the rubyamf gateway on our local server ❹: http://localhost:3000/rubyamf/gateway.

All we need to do now is write the Flex code to test this. To keep things simple, we'll modify Pomodo.mxml to include our "Hello World" code; see listing 11.4.

Listing 11.4   app\flex\Pomodo.mxml

```
<?xml version="1.0" encoding="utf-8"?>
<mx:Application
    xmlns:mx="http://www.adobe.com/2006/mxml"
...
    creationCompleteEffect="fadeIn">
<mx:Script>
<![CDATA[
    import mx.core.Container;
    import mx.rpc.events.ResultEvent;        ⟵── Add imports
    import mx.rpc.events.FaultEvent;
    import com.pomodo.components.DebugPanel;
    import com.pomodo.control.EventNames;
    import com.pomodo.util.CairngormUtils;
    import com.pomodo.util.DebugMessage;
    import com.pomodo.model.PomodoModelLocator;
...
    private function loadFlexibleRails():void {
        CairngormUtils.dispatchEvent(EventNames.LOAD_URL,
            "http://www.flexiblerails.com");
    }

    private function handleHelloResult(e:ResultEvent):void {    ❶
        Pomodo.debug("hello result:\n" + e.message);
    }

    private function handleFault(e:FaultEvent):void {    ❷
        Pomodo.debug("FAULT:\n" + e.fault.faultString);
    }
]]>
</mx:Script>
    <mx:RemoteObject id="helloRO"              ❸
        source="HelloController"               ❹
        destination="rubyamf"                  ❺
        fault="handleFault(event)">
        <mx:method name="sayhello"             ❻
            result="handleHelloResult(event)"/>
    </mx:RemoteObject>
```

```
        <mx:Fade id="fadeIn" duration="500"/>
    ...
        <mx:HBox backgroundColor="#000000" width="100%" height="30"
            horizontalAlign="center" verticalAlign="middle">
            <mx:LinkButton color="#FFFFFF"
                click="loadFlexibleRails()" label="{MARKETING}"/>
        </mx:HBox>
        <mx:Button label="hello" click="helloRO.sayhello.send()"/>      ❼
        <mx:Spacer height="10"/>
    ...
    </mx:Application>
```

We add a `RemoteObject` called `helloRO` ❸, which has one `mx:method` whose name is `sayhello` ❻. This method is invoked by clicking the button ❼ whose label is hello. We add a `fault` handler method called `handleFault` ❷ for the entire `Remote-Object` and a `handleHelloResult` ❶ method for the result of the `sayhello` method. Both the `fault` handler and the `result` handler call `Pomodo.debug()`.

Note that the `source` of the `helloRO` `RemoteObject` is `HelloController` ❹; this is the name of the controller we created in Rails. We also see that the destination is `rubyamf` ❺: This refers to the `id` of the `destination` we defined in `services-config.xml` earlier.

Before we run, we need to add the argument `-services "services-config.xml"` to the compiler arguments so the compiler knows to use our services; see figure 11.1.

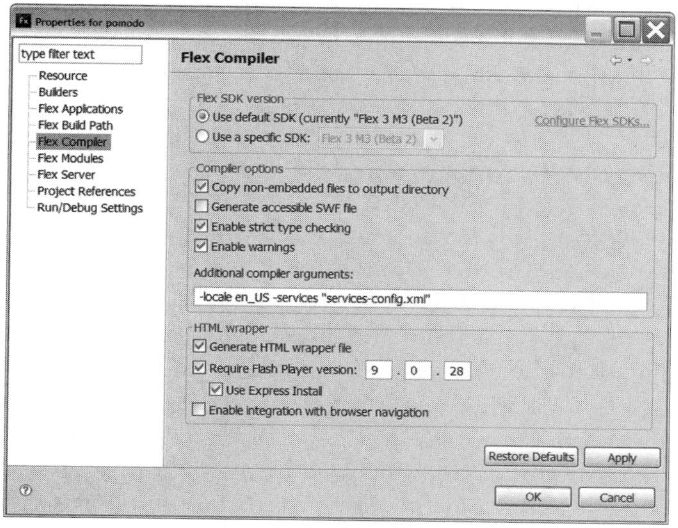

Figure 11.1
Adding the services-config.xml to the compiler arguments

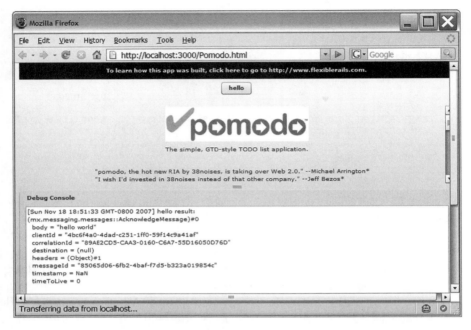

Figure 11.2 "Hello World" from RubyAMF

With this done, we restart our server (to pick up the RubyAMF configuration), rebuild the Flex project, and load http://localhost:3000/Pomodo.html. We see the pomodo application with a Hello button on it. Drag the debug console into view, and click the Hello button; we see something like figure 11.2.

Note that the body of the AcknowledgeMessage is "hello world", which is what we rendered with render :amf => "hello world".

11.3 *Refactoring to RubyAMF, fast-forwarded*

The result of this refactoring will be presented all at once. I got it working for tasks with a standalone tester inside pomodo and then ported the changes to projects and locations. However, because tasks, projects, and locations are so similar, it makes sense to present them together. I'll start by showing the rubyamf_config.rb file, then the changes to the controllers, and then the various changes to the Flex code. This will include replacing the ServiceUtils.as class with the standard Cairngorm Services.mxml class: Doing this will bring our code more in line with standard Cairngorm, which will be instructive. We'll also violate the Don't Repeat Yourself (DRY) principle (I'm sorry, Dave) and create a layer of value object (VO) classes to marshal and unmarshal. This turns out to be simpler, because we don't need to worry about the logic we've built into our model constructors conflicting with the unmarshaling.

NOTE   Joking aside, principles such as DRY are meant to be applied pragmatically, not absolutely. Dave Thomas would be the first person to agree with this, being a Pragmatic Programmer after all. If you find yourself twisting into contortions to stay true to DRY, ask yourself if the contortions are worth it. (This was one of Zed Shaw's many points in his Rails to Italy keynote.)

Enough talk. Let's get coding!

11.3.1 Modifying rubyamf_config.rb

We'll start by modifying the rubyamf_config.rb file, as shown in listing 11.5. Note that I made a *lot* of changes to make it fit the page width without showing those changes as diffs.

Listing 11.5   config\rubyamf_config.rb

```
require 'app/configuration'
module RubyAMF
  module Configuration
    #set the service path used in all requests
    # RubyAMF::App::RequestStore.service_path =
    #   File.expand_path(RAILS_ROOT) + '/app/controllers'

    # => CLASS MAPPING CONFIGURATION

    # => Global Property Ignoring
    # By putting attribute names into this array, you opt in to
    # globally ignore these properties on incoming objects.
    # If you want to ignore specific properties on certain
    # objects, use the :ignore_fields property in a
    # Class Mapping definition (see CLASS MAPPING DEFINITIONS)
    ClassMappings.ignore_fields =
      ['created_at', 'created_on', 'updated_at', 'updated_on']    ◁┘

    # => Case Translations
    # Most actionscript uses camelCase instead of snake_case.
    # Set ClassMappings.translate_case to true if want
    # translations to occur.
    # The translations only occur on object properties
    # An incoming property like myProperty gets turned into
    # my_property.  An outgoing property like my_property gets
    # turned into myProperty.
```

Ignore
because
auto-set
by Rails

```
ClassMappings.translate_case = true    ⊲┐ Change case to use proper
                                         │ coding conventions
# => Force Active Record Ids
# includes the id field for activerecord objects even if you
# don't specify it when using custom attributes. This is
# important for deserialization where ids are needed to keep
# active record association integrity.
ClassMappings.force_active_record_ids = true    ⊲┐ True because using
                                                  │ ActiveRecord
# => Assume Class Types
# This tells RubyAMF to assume class type transfers. So when
# you register a class Alias from Flash or Flex like this:
# Flash::    fl.net.registerClassAlias('User',User)
# Flex::     [RemoteClass(alias='User')]
# RubyAMF will automagically convert it to a User active
# record without you having to create a class mapping.
# This also works with non active record class mappings. See
# the wiki on the google code page for a downloadable
# example.
ClassMappings.assume_types = false    ⊲┐ Doing ClassMappings
                                        │ manually, so false
# => Class Mapping Definitions
# A Class Mapping definition conists of at least these two
# properties:
# :actionscript  # The incoming ActionScript class to watch
#                # for
# :ruby          # The Ruby class to turn it into
#
# => Optional value object properties:
# :type          # Used to specify the type of VO; valid
#                # options are 'active_record', 'custom',
#                #(or don't specify at all)
# :associations  # Specify which associations to read on
#                # the active record (only applies to
#                # active records)
# :attributes    # Specifically which attributes to include
#                # in the serialization
# :ignore_fields # An array of field names you want to
#                # ignore on incoming classes
#
# If you are using ActiveRecord VO's you do not need to
# specify a fully qualified class path to the model, you can
# just define the class name; for example:
# ClassMappings.register(:actionscript => 'vo.Person',
#   :ruby => 'Person', :type => 'active_record')
#
# If you are using custom VO's you would need to specify the
# fully qualified class path to the file, for example:
# ClassMappings.register(:actionscript => 'vo.Person',
#   :ruby => 'org.mypackage.Person')
...
```

```
ClassMappings.register(
  :actionscript => 'com.pomodo.vo.TaskVO',
  :ruby => 'Task',
  :type => 'active_record',
  :attributes => ["id", "name", "notes", "next_action",
    "completed", "project_id", "location_id"])
ClassMappings.register(
  :actionscript => 'com.pomodo.vo.ProjectVO',
  :ruby => 'Project',
  :type => 'active_record',
  :attributes => ["id", "name", "notes", "completed"])
ClassMappings.register(
  :actionscript => 'com.pomodo.vo.LocationVO',
  :ruby => 'Location',
  :type => 'active_record',
  :attributes => ["id", "name", "notes"])
ClassMappings.register(
  :actionscript => 'com.pomodo.vo.NoteVO',
  :ruby => 'Note',
  :type => 'active_record',
  :attributes => ["content"])
```
⊲⎤ **Map TaskVO**
 ⎦ **to/from Task**

⊲⎤ **Map ProjectVO**
 ⎦ **to/from Project**

⊲⎤ **Map LocationVO**
 ⎦ **to/from Location**

⊲⎤ **Map NoteVO**
 ⎦ **to/from Note**

```
# => Class Mapping Scope (Advanced Usage)
...
# => Check for Associations
# Enabling this will automagically pick up eager loaded
# association data on objects returned through RubyAMF.
# If this is disabled, you will need to specify any
# associations you DO want picked up in the ClassMapping
ClassMappings.check_for_associations = false
```
⊲⎤ **Don't want**
❶ **associations**

```
# => NAMED PARAMETER MAPPING CONFIGURATION

#=> Always Put Remoting Parameters into the "params" hash
# If set to true, arguments from Flash/Flex will come in to
# the controllers as params[0], params[1], etc.. This is
# especially useful if you are sending huge objects
# from Flex into Ruby so it doesnt eat up all your output
# window with outputting the params in the controller/action
# header information while in dev mode.
# Even if its set to false, if you specify specific
# ParameterMappings, those will still get entered as the
# param keys you specify. Likewise, you always have access
# to the parameters from rubyamf in your controller by
# calling rubyamf_params[0], rubyamf_params[1], etc
# regardless of if it this is set or not.
ParameterMappings.always_add_to_params = true
```
⊲⎤ **Want parameters**
 ⎦ **in params**

```
# => Return Top Level Hash
# For those scaffolding users out there, who want the
# top-level object to come as a hash so scaffolding works
```

```
    # out of the box.
    ParameterMappings.scaffolding = false
    ...
      end
  end
```

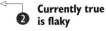
2 Currently true is flaky

Basically, this file is the result of a lot of ~~hacking~~experimentation. By the time you read this, some of the more automatic ways of using this configuration file may work better—this is the way that worked for me. The most important setting is `ParameterMappings.scaffolding = false` **2**, which didn't work when `true` (using Rails 1.99.0 and the `flexiblerails` RubyAMF branch). Also, note that we set check_for_associations to false **1**, since we're just transferring objects, not object graphs.

All this talk of parameter mapping is making me hungry—for some tables of type conversions. The type conversions that are done by RubyAMF when converting between Flash and Ruby are found at http://code.google.com/p/rubyamf/wiki/AMFTypeConversions and are shown in table 11.1.

Table 11.1 ActionScript 3 to Ruby and Ruby to ActionScript 3 conversions done by RubyAMF

ActionScript 3	...converted to Ruby	...converted to ActionScript 3
undefined	nil	null
null	nil	null
false	false	false
true	true	false
Number	Fixnum	Number
int	Integer	Number
String	String	String
XML	String (cast in your service)	-
-	BeautifulSoup	XML
-	REXML::Doc	XML
Array	Array	Array
MixexArray	Hash	Object
Object	Hash	Object
Custom Class	Ruby Class	Custom Class

See the RubyAMF wiki for details.

11.3.2 *Modifying the Rails controllers*

Next, we need to modify the Rails controllers. We start by deleting app\controllers\hello_controller.rb.

Next, we'll modify the `TasksController`; see listing 11.6.

Listing 11.6 app\controllers\tasks_controller.rb

```
class TasksController < ApplicationController
  # GET /tasks
  # GET /tasks.xml
  def index
    @tasks = current_user.tasks

    respond_to do |format|
      format.html # index.html.erb
      format.xml  { render :xml => @tasks }
      format.amf  { render :amf => @tasks }          ◁─┐ Render tasks as
                                                        AMF—it's that easy
    end
  end

  # GET /tasks/1
  # GET /tasks/1.xml
  def show
    @task = current_user.tasks.find(params[:id])
    @task = current_user.tasks.find(                ◁─┐ params[0] instead
      is_amf ? params[0] : params[:id])                of in params[:id]

    respond_to do |format|
      format.html # show.html.erb
      format.xml  { render :xml => @task }
      format.amf  { render :amf => @task }           ◁─┐ Render task
    end                                                 as AMF
  rescue ActiveRecord::RecordNotFound => e
    prevent_access(e)
  end

  # GET /tasks/new
  # GET /tasks/new.xml
  def new
    @task = Task.new

    respond_to do |format|
      format.html # new.html.erb
      format.xml  { render :xml => @task }
    end
  end
```

```
# GET /tasks/1/edit
def edit
  @task = current_user.tasks.find(params[:id])
rescue ActiveRecord::RecordNotFound => e
  prevent_access(e)
end

# POST /tasks
# POST /tasks.xml
def create
  @task = current_user.tasks.build(params[:task])
  if is_amf                           ◁──────────  Task in params[0], not
    @task = params[0]                              Hash in params[:task]
    @task.user_id = current_user.id
    @task.created_at = @task.updated_at = Time.now
  else
    @task = current_user.tasks.build(params[:task])
  end
  respond_to do |format|
    if @task.save
      format.html do
        flash[:notice] = 'Task was successfully created.'
        redirect_to(@task)
      end
      format.xml  { render :xml => @task, :status => :created,
        :location => @task }
      format.amf  { render :amf => @task }           ◁── Render task
    else                                                  as AMF
      format.html { render :action => "new" }
      format.xml  { render :xml => @task.errors,
        :status => :unprocessable_entity }
      format.amf  { render :amf => @task.errors }    ◁── Render task
    end                                                   errors as AMF
  end
end

# PUT /tasks/1
# PUT /tasks/1.xml
def update
  @task = current_user.tasks.find(params[:id])
  @task.attributes = params[:task]
  @task = current_user.tasks.find(        ◁────── Task in params[0],
    is_amf ? params[0].id : params[:id])          not id in params[:id]
  if is_amf
    @task.name = params[0].name
    @task.notes = params[0].notes
    @task.project_id = params[0].project_id       ❶
    @task.location_id = params[0].location_id
    @task.next_action = params[0].next_action
    @task.completed = params[0].completed
  else
```

```
      @task.attributes = params[:task]        ❷
    end
    @task.save_with_gtd_rules!

    respond_to do |format|
      format.html do
        flash[:notice] = 'Task was successfully updated.'
        redirect_to(@task)
      end
      format.xml  { render :xml => @task }
      format.amf  { render :amf => @task }         ◁── Render task
    end                                                 as AMF
  rescue ActiveRecord::RecordInvalid
    respond_to do |format|
      format.html { render :action => "edit" }
      format.xml  { render :xml => @task.errors.to_xml_full }
      format.amf  { render :amf => @task.errors }  ◁── Render task
    end                                                 errors as AMF
  rescue ActiveRecord::RecordNotFound => e
    prevent_access(e)
  end

  # DELETE /tasks/1
  # DELETE /tasks/1.xml
  def destroy
    @task = current_user.tasks.find(params[:id])
    @task = current_user.tasks.find(          ◁── params[0] instead
      is_amf ? params[0] : params[:id])            of in params[:id]
    @task.destroy

    respond_to do |format|
      format.html { redirect_to(tasks_url) }
      format.xml  { render :xml => @task }
      format.amf  { render :amf => @task }         ◁── Render task
    end                                                 as AMF
  rescue ActiveRecord::RecordNotFound => e
    prevent_access(e)
  end

  private
    def prevent_access(e)
      logger.info "TasksController#prevent_access: #{e}"
      respond_to do |format|
        format.html { redirect_to(tasks_url) }
        format.xml  { render :text => "error" }
        format.amf  { render :amf => "error" }     ◁── Render String
      end                                               "error" as AMF
    end
end
```

This code has only a couple of changes. First, there is a new format: `format.amf`. This is set for us by RubyAMF so we can `respond_to` it. Next, note that the parameters we receive from `RemoteObject` method invocations come in as `params[0]`, `params[1]`, and so on. These parameters are converted from ActionScript to Ruby following the rules shown in table 11.1. Also note that when responding to Flex, we now `render :amf` instead of `render :xml`.

> **NOTE** Yes, the params[0], params[1] stuff is unfortunate. I hope a better way will work in the future.

No logic anywhere ensures that the `project_id` and `location_id` refer to projects and locations that belong to the user, so a user who wanted to hack them could cause mischief. This needs to be prevented for both the AMF case where they are assigned explicitly ❶ and the XML over HTTP case where a mass assignment is done ❷. (Exercise for the reader: Fix this.)

Next, we make extremely similar changes to the `ProjectsController`; see listing 11.7.

Listing 11.7 app\controllers\projects_controller.rb

```
class ProjectsController < ApplicationController
  # GET /projects
  # GET /projects.xml
  def index
    @projects = current_user.projects

    respond_to do |format|
      format.html # index.html.erb
      format.xml  { render :xml => @projects }
      format.amf  { render :amf => @projects }      ◁──┐ Render
    end                                                  projects as AMF
  end

  # GET /projects/1
  # GET /projects/1.xml
  def show
    @project = current_user.projects.find(params[:id])
    @project = current_user.projects.find(          ◁──┐ params[0] instead
      is_amf ? params[0] : params[:id])                  of in params[:id]

    respond_to do |format|
      format.html # show.html.erb
      format.xml  { render :xml => @project }
      format.amf  { render :amf => @project }        ◁──┐ Render project
    end                                                  as AMF
  rescue ActiveRecord::RecordNotFound => e
    prevent_access(e)
```

```
end

# GET /projects/new
# GET /projects/new.xml
def new
  @project = Project.new

  respond_to do |format|
    format.html # new.html.erb
    format.xml  { render :xml => @project }
  end
end

# GET /projects/1/edit
def edit
  @project = current_user.projects.find(params[:id])
rescue ActiveRecord::RecordNotFound => e
  prevent_access(e)
end

# POST /projects
# POST /projects.xml
def create
  @project = current_user.projects.build(params[:project])
  if is_amf
    @project = params[0]
    @project.user_id = current_user.id
    @project.created_at = @project.updated_at = Time.now
  else
    @project = current_user.projects.build(params[:project])
  end

  respond_to do |format|
    if @project.save
      format.html do
        flash[:notice] = 'Project was successfully created.'
        redirect_to(@project)
      end
      format.xml  { render :xml => @project,
        :status => :created, :location => @project }
      format.amf  { render :amf => @project }
    else
      format.html { render :action => "new" }
      format.xml  { render :xml => @project.errors,
        :status => :unprocessable_entity }
      format.amf  { render :amf => @project.errors }
    end
  end
end

# PUT /projects/1
```

Project in params[0], not Hash in params[:project]

Render project as AMF

Render project errors as AMF

```
# PUT /projects/1.xml
def update
  @project = current_user.projects.find(params[:id])
  @project.attributes = params[:project]
  @project = current_user.projects.find(          ← Project in params[0],
    is_amf ? params[0].id : params[:id])             not id in params[:id]
  if is_amf
    @project.name = params[0].name
    @project.notes = params[0].notes
    @project.completed = params[0].completed
  else
    @project.attributes = params[:project]
  end
  @project.save_with_gtd_rules!

  respond_to do |format|
    format.html do
      flash[:notice] = 'Project was successfully updated.'
      redirect_to(@project)
    end
    format.xml  { render :xml => @project }
    format.amf  { render :amf => @project }          ← Render project
  end                                                   as AMF
rescue ActiveRecord::RecordInvalid
  respond_to do |format|
    format.html { render :action => "edit" }
    format.xml  { render :xml => @project.errors.to_xml_full }
    format.amf  { render :amf => @project.errors }   ← Render project
  end                                                   errors as AMF
rescue ActiveRecord::RecordNotFound => e
  prevent_access(e)
end

# DELETE /projects/1
# DELETE /projects/1.xml
def destroy
  @project = current_user.projects.find(params[:id])
  @project = current_user.projects.find(          ← params[0] instead
    is_amf ? params[0] : params[:id])                of params[:id]
  @project.destroy

  respond_to do |format|
    format.html { redirect_to(projects_url) }
    format.xml  { render :xml => @project }
    format.amf  { render :amf => @project }          ← Render project
  end                                                   as AMF
rescue ActiveRecord::RecordNotFound => e
  prevent_access(e)
end

private
```

```
    def prevent_access(e)
      logger.info "ProjectsController#prevent_access: #{e}"
      respond_to do |format|
        format.html { redirect_to(projects_url) }
        format.xml  { render :text => "error" }
        format.amf  { render :amf => "error" }          ⟵  Render String
      end                                                    "error" as AMF
    end
end
```

We also make similar changes to the `LocationsController`; see listing 11.8.

Listing 11.8   app\controllers\locations_controller.rb

```
class LocationsController < ApplicationController
  # GET /locations
  # GET /locations.xml
  def index
    @locations = current_user.locations

    respond_to do |format|
      format.html # index.html.erb
      format.xml  { render :xml => @locations }       Render locations
      format.amf  { render :amf => @locations }   ⟵   as AMF
    end
  end

  # GET /locations/1
  # GET /locations/1.xml
  def show
    @location = current_user.locations.find(params[:id])
    @location = current_user.locations.find(       ⟵   params[0] instead
      is_amf ? params[0] : params[:id])                 of params[:id]

    respond_to do |format|
      format.html # show.html.erb
      format.xml  { render :xml => @location }
      format.amf  { render :amf => @location }    ⟵   Render location
    end                                                as AMF
  rescue ActiveRecord::RecordNotFound => e
    prevent_access(e)
  end

  # GET /locations/new
  # GET /locations/new.xml
  def new
    @location = Location.new

    respond_to do |format|
```

```
      format.html # new.html.erb
      format.xml  { render :xml => @location }
    end
  end

  # GET /locations/1/edit
  def edit
    @location = current_user.locations.find(params[:id])
  rescue ActiveRecord::RecordNotFound => e
    prevent_access(e)
  end

  # POST /locations
  # POST /locations.xml
  def create
    @location = current_user.locations.build(params[:location])
    if is_amf                          ◁          Location in params[0], not
      @location = params[0]                       Hash in params[:location]
      @location.user_id = current_user.id
      @location.created_at = @location.updated_at = Time.now
    else
      @location = current_user.locations.build(
        params[:location])
    end

    respond_to do |format|
      if @location.save
        format.html do
          flash[:notice] = 'Location was successfully created.'
          redirect_to(@location)
        end
        format.xml  { render :xml => @location,
          :status => :created, :location => @location }
        format.amf  { render :amf => @location }      ◁   Render location
      else                                                as AMF
        format.html { render :action => "new" }
        format.xml  { render :xml => @location.errors,
          :status => :unprocessable_entity }
        format.amf  { render :amf => @location.errors }   ◁   Render location
      end                                                    errors as AMF
    end
  end

  # PUT /locations/1
  # PUT /locations/1.xml
  def update
    @location = current_user.locations.find(params[:id])
    @location = current_user.locations.find(        ◁
      is_amf ? params[0].id : params[:id])               Location in params[0],
    if is_amf                                            not id in params[:id]
      @project.name = params[0].name
```

```
      @project.notes = params[0].notes
      @project.completed = params[0].completed
    else
      @location.attributes = params[:location]
    end
    @location.save!            ❶

    respond_to do |format|
      if @location.update_attributes(params[:location])
        flash[:notice] = 'Location was successfully updated.'
        format.html { redirect_to(@location) }
        format.xml  { render :xml => @location }
      else
        format.html { render :action => "edit" }
        format.xml  { render :xml => @location.errors,
          :status => :unprocessable_entity }
      end
      format.html do
        flash[:notice] = 'Location was successfully updated.'   ❷
        redirect_to(@location)
      end
      format.xml  { render :xml => @location }
      format.amf  { render :amf => @location }      ◁─ Render location
    end                                                as AMF
  rescue ActiveRecord::RecordInvalid
    respond_to do |format|
      format.html { render :action => "edit" }
      format.xml  { render :xml => @location.errors.to_xml_full}
      format.amf  { render :amf => @project.errors }  ◁─ Render location
    end                                                  errors as AMF
  rescue ActiveRecord::RecordNotFound => e
    prevent_access(e)
  end

  # DELETE /locations/1
  # DELETE /locations/1.xml
  def destroy
    @location = current_user.locations.find(params[:id])
    @location = current_user.locations.find(     ◁─ params[0] instead
      is_amf ? params[0] : params[:id])             of params[:id]
    @location.destroy

    respond_to do |format|
      format.html { redirect_to(locations_url) }
      format.xml  { render :xml => @location }
      format.amf  { render :amf => @location }    ◁─ Render location
    end                                               as AMF
  rescue ActiveRecord::RecordNotFound => e
    prevent_access(e)
  end
end
```

```
private
  def prevent_access(e)
    logger.info "LocationsController#prevent_access: #{e}"
    respond_to do |format|
      format.html { redirect_to(locations_url) }
      format.xml  { render :text => "error" }
      format.amf  { render :amf  => "error" }      ◁──  Render String
    end                                                  "error" as AMF
  end
end
```

This is more of the same, except that we're now using @location.save! ❶ and only building the flash[:notice] in the case of rendering HTML ❷.

Next, the NotesController; see listing 11.9.

Listing 11.9   app\controllers\notes_controller.rb

```
class NotesController < ApplicationController
  # GET /users/1/note
  # GET /users/1/note.xml
  def show
    if current_user.id != params[:user_id].to_i        ❶
      prevent_access
    else
      @note = current_user.note
      respond_to do |format|
        format.xml { render :xml => @note.to_xml }
      end
    end
    if is_amf        ❷
      render :amf => current_user.note
    else
      if current_user.id != params[:user_id].to_i
        prevent_access
      else
        @note = current_user.note
        respond_to do |format|
          format.xml { render :xml => @note }
        end
      end
    end
  end

  # PUT /users/1/note
  # PUT /users/1/note.xml
  def update
    if current_user.id != params[:user_id].to_i        ❸
      prevent_access
```

```
    else
      @note = current_user.note
      respond_to do |format|
        if @note.update_attributes(params[:note])
          format.xml { render :xml => @note.to_xml }
        else
          format.xml { render :xml => @note.errors.to_xml_full }
        end
      end
    end
    if is_amf                    ❹
      @note = current_user.note
      @note.content = params[0].content
    else
      if current_user.id != params[:user_id].to_i
        prevent_access
      else
        @note = current_user.note
        @note.attributes = params[:note]
      end
    end
    @note.save!          ❺

    respond_to do |format|
      format.xml { render :xml => @note }
      format.amf { render :amf => @note }
    end
  rescue ActiveRecord::RecordInvalid
    respond_to do |format|
      format.xml  { render :xml => @note.errors.to_xml_full }
      format.amf  { render :amf => @note.errors }
    end
  end

  private
    def prevent_access
      respond_to do |format|
        format.xml { render :text => "error" }
        format.amf { render :amf  => "error" }          ❻
      end
    end
end
```

This is fairly simple: We start by moving the old code ❶ of the show method inside
the else case of an is_amf test ❷. If the request is_amf, we render the current
user's note. In the update method, we refactor the code ❸ to set the properties of
the @note, doing the right thing depending on whether the request is_amf ❹.

We then call the `save!` method ❺ and respond appropriately. Finally, we add support for AMF to the `prevent_access` method ❻.

11.3.3 Creating Services.mxml and modifying Pomodo.mxml

Next, we'll create a new file called Services.mxml. (If this approach reminds you too much of Java, you'll understand why I created `ServiceUtils` earlier when we were using HTTPService.) We'll use this file to define our `RemoteObjects`, one for each Rails controller we want to talk to; see listing 11.10.

Listing 11.10   **app\flex\com\pomodo\business\Services.mxml**

```
<?xml version="1.0" encoding="utf-8"?>
<cairngorm:ServiceLocator                          ❶
        xmlns:mx="http://www.adobe.com/2006/mxml"
        xmlns:cairngorm="http://www.adobe.com/2006/cairngorm">
    <mx:RemoteObject id="taskRO"                   ❷
        source="TasksController"                   ❸
        destination="rubyamf">                     ❹
        <mx:method name="index"/>                  ❺
        <mx:method name="create"/>
        <mx:method name="update"/>
        <mx:method name="destroy"/>
    </mx:RemoteObject>
    <mx:RemoteObject id="projectRO"                ❻
        source="ProjectsController"
        destination="rubyamf">
        <mx:method name="index"/>
        <mx:method name="create"/>
        <mx:method name="update"/>
        <mx:method name="destroy"/>
    </mx:RemoteObject>
    <mx:RemoteObject id="locationRO"               ❼
        source="LocationsController"
        destination="rubyamf">
        <mx:method name="index"/>
        <mx:method name="create"/>
        <mx:method name="update"/>
        <mx:method name="destroy"/>
    </mx:RemoteObject>
    <mx:RemoteObject id="noteRO"                    ❽
        source="NotesController"
        destination="rubyamf">
        <mx:method name="show"/>
        <mx:method name="update"/>
    </mx:RemoteObject>
</cairngorm:ServiceLocator>
```

Services.mxml is a Cairngorm `ServiceLocator` ❶. If you've created a project for the Cairngorm source code, the source file is `com.adobe.cairngorm.business.` `ServiceLocator`. The `ServiceLocator` is a `Singleton` that manages `HTTPServices`, `WebServices`, and `RemoteObjects` for you. The code is fairly simple, so you should read it if you plan to use it.

We create four `RemoteObjects`: a taskRO ❷ whose source is the Tasks-Controller ❸, a projectRO ❻, a locationRO ❼, and a noteRO ❽. All of them have a destination of "rubyamf" (for example, ❹), which is the destination id we defined in services-config.xml earlier. Finally, each `RemoteObject` defines each of its methods. Note that the taskRO has no `show` method ❺, and neither do the projectRO and locationRO. We're not creating one because we don't use it. (I did use it when I was doing my standalone experiments with RubyAMF and tasks, so I'm still showing the code in the controllers because I hope it's useful. Strictly speaking, I should delete that code too because I'm not using it.)

Next, we modify Pomodo.mxml; see listing 11.11.

Listing 11.11   app\flex\Pomodo.mxml

```
<?xml version="1.0" encoding="utf-8"?>
<mx:Application
    xmlns:mx="http://www.adobe.com/2006/mxml"
    xmlns:pom="com.pomodo.components.*"
    xmlns:business="com.pomodo.business.*"          Create new XML namespace
    xmlns:control="com.pomodo.control.*"            for business services
    layout="vertical"
    backgroundGradientColors="[#ffffff, #c0c0c0]"
    horizontalAlign="center"
    verticalAlign="top"
    paddingLeft="0"
    paddingRight="0"
    paddingTop="0"
    paddingBottom="0"
    width="100%"
    height="100%"
    creationCompleteEffect="fadeIn">
<mx:Script>
<![CDATA[
    import mx.core.Container;                        Remove obsolete
    import mx.rpc.events.ResultEvent;               imports
    import mx.rpc.events.FaultEvent;
    import com.pomodo.components.DebugPanel;
    import com.pomodo.control.EventNames;
    import com.pomodo.util.CairngormUtils;
    import com.pomodo.util.DebugMessage;
    import com.pomodo.model.PomodoModelLocator;
...
```

```
        private function loadFlexibleRails():void {
            CairngormUtils.dispatchEvent(EventNames.LOAD_URL,
                "http://www.flexiblerails.com");
        }
```

Remove "hello world" code

```
        private function handleHelloResult(e:ResultEvent):void {
            Pomodo.debug("hello result:\n" + e.message);
        }

        private function handleFault(e:FaultEvent):void {
            Pomodo.debug("FAULT:\n" + e.fault.faultString);
        }
    ]]>
    </mx:Script>
```

Remove "hello world" code

```
        <mx:RemoteObject id="helloRO"
            source="HelloController"
            destination="rubyamf"
            fault="handleFault(event)">
            <mx:method name="sayhello"
                result="handleHelloResult(event)"/>
        </mx:RemoteObject>
        <mx:Fade id="fadeIn" duration="500"/>
        <mx:WipeUp id="wipeUp" duration="500"/>

        <business:Services id="services" />            ❶

        <control:PomodoController id="controller" />

        <mx:HBox backgroundColor="#000000" width="100%" height="30"
            horizontalAlign="center" verticalAlign="middle">
            <mx:LinkButton color="#FFFFFF"
                click="loadFlexibleRails()" label="{MARKETING}"/>
        </mx:HBox>
        <mx:Button label="hello" click="helloRO.sayhello.send()"/>
        <mx:Spacer height="10"/>
    ...
    </mx:Application>
```

Remove "hello world" code

Because we created a new XML namespace called business, we get to create our business services by saying business:Services ❶ to create the ServiceLocator. This is kind of cute, so it's the Cairngorm convention.

11.3.4 *Creating the value objects*

Next, we need to create the value objects (VOs), which are extremely boring classes with a bunch of public bindable variables. Note that we're not going to send object graphs: A ProjectVO won't contain its TaskVOs. I'm doing this to keep things simple and as close as possible to how I was using XML over `HTTPService`. (This provides the most direct comparison and lets us reuse the most code.)

First, we'll create the `TaskVO`; see listing 11.12.

```
package com.pomodo.vo {
    [RemoteClass(alias='com.pomodo.vo.TaskVO')]        ❶
    [Bindable]          ❷
    public class TaskVO {
        public var id:int;
        public var name:String;
        public var notes:String;
        public var projectId:int;
        public var locationId:int;
        public var nextAction:Boolean;
        public var completed:Boolean;
    }
}
```

The `RemoteClass` annotation ❶ defines the name that this class is known to RubyAMF by (as specified in the config\rubyamf_config.rb file earlier. Note also that we annotate the entire class ❷ as `[Bindable]`, to spare ourselves from annotating every field.

Next, we create the `ProjectVO`, `LocationVO`, and `NoteVO` classes; see listings 11.13, 11.14, and 11.15.

```
package com.pomodo.vo {
    [RemoteClass(alias='com.pomodo.vo.ProjectVO')]
    [Bindable]
    public class ProjectVO {
        public var id:int;
        public var name:String;
        public var notes:String;
        public var completed:Boolean;
    }
}
```

```
package com.pomodo.vo {
    [RemoteClass(alias='com.pomodo.vo.LocationVO')]
    [Bindable]
```

```
        public class LocationVO {
            public var id:int;
            public var name:String;
            public var notes:String;
        }
    }
```

Listing 11.15   app\flex\com\pomodo\vo\NoteVO.as

```
package com.pomodo.vo {
    [RemoteClass(alias='com.pomodo.vo.NoteVO')]
    [Bindable]
    public class NoteVO {
        public var content:String;
    }
}
```

That was easy.

11.3.5 *Modifying the model objects to produce value objects*

Now, we need to modify the model objects so they have the ability to convert themselves to and from the value objects. We start with the Task class; see listing 11.16.

Listing 11.16   app\flex\com\pomodo\model\Task.as

```
package com.pomodo.model {
    import com.pomodo.util.XMLUtils;        Add
    import com.pomodo.vo.TaskVO;      ◁───┘ import
    public class Task {
...
        public function Task(
            name:String = "",
            notes:String = "",
            project:Project = null,
            location:Location = null,
            nextAction:Boolean = false,
            completed:Boolean = false,
            id:int = UNSAVED_ID)
        {
            this.name = name;
            this.notes = notes;
            if (project == null) {        ◁────   Use separate VO class
                project = Project.NONE;          approach to avoid issues here
            }
            project.addTask(this);
            if (location == null) {
```

```
            location = Location.NONE;
        }
        location.addTask(this);
        this.nextAction = nextAction;
        this.completed = completed;
        this.id = id;
    }

    public function toVO():TaskVO {          ◁──┐ Convert Task
        var taskVO:TaskVO = new TaskVO();         to TaskVO
        taskVO.id = id;
        taskVO.name = name;
        taskVO.projectId = project.id;
        taskVO.locationId = location.id;
        taskVO.nextAction = nextAction;
        taskVO.completed = completed;
        taskVO.notes = notes;                         Create new
        return taskVO;                                Task from
    }                                                 TaskVO
                                                      (method is
    public static function fromVO(taskVO:TaskVO):Task {  ◁── static)
        var model:PomodoModelLocator =
            PomodoModelLocator.getInstance();
        return new Task(
            taskVO.name,
            taskVO.notes,
            model.getProject(taskVO.projectId),
            model.getLocation(taskVO.locationId),
            taskVO.nextAction,
            taskVO.completed,
            taskVO.id);
    }

    public function toUpdateObject():Object {
...
```

Next, the Project class; see listing 11.17.

Listing 11.17   app\flex\com\pomodo\model\Project.as

```
package com.pomodo.model {
    import mx.collections.ArrayCollection;
    import com.pomodo.util.XMLUtils;           Add
    import com.pomodo.vo.ProjectVO;   ◁──────┘ import

    public class Project {
...
        public function removeTask(task:Task):void {
...
```

```
        }
        public function toVO():ProjectVO {          ◁─┐  Convert Project
            var projectVO:ProjectVO = new ProjectVO();    to ProjectVO
            projectVO.id = id;
            projectVO.name = name;
            projectVO.notes = notes;
            projectVO.completed = completed;              Create new Project
            return projectVO;                               from ProjectVO
        }                                                   (method is static)

        public static function fromVO(projectVO:ProjectVO):  ◁─┐
        Project {
            return new Project(
                projectVO.name,
                projectVO.notes,
                projectVO.completed,
                projectVO.id);
        }

        public function toUpdateObject():Object {
    ...
```

Now the Location class; see listing 11.18.

```
package com.pomodo.model {
    import mx.collections.ArrayCollection;
    import com.pomodo.vo.LocationVO;        ◁─┐  Add
                                                 import
    public class Location {
    ...
        public function removeTask(task:Task):void {
    ...
        }
                                                    Convert Location
        public function toVO():LocationVO {   ◁─┐    to LocationVO
            var locationVO:LocationVO = new LocationVO();
            locationVO.id = id;
            locationVO.name = name;
            locationVO.notes = notes;
            return locationVO;
        }

        public static function fromVO(locationVO:LocationVO):  ◁─┐
        Location {                              Create new Location
            return new Location(                   from LocationVO
                locationVO.name,                    (method is static)
```

```
            locationVO.notes,
            locationVO.id);
    }

    public function toUpdateObject():Object {
...
```

Finally, the Note class; see listing 11.19.

Listing 11.19   app\flex\com\pomodo\model\Note.as

```
package com.pomodo.model {
    import com.pomodo.vo.NoteVO;          ⟵——  Add
                                                import
    public class Note {
        public function Note(content:String = "") {
            this.content = content;
        }

        [Bindable]
        public var content:String;

        public function toVO():NoteVO {     ⟵——  Convert Note
            var noteVO:NoteVO = new NoteVO();      to NoteVO
            noteVO.content = content;
            return noteVO;
        }

        public static function fromVO(noteVO:NoteVO):Note {   ⟵
            return new Note(noteVO.content);
        }                                            Create new Note
                                                     from Note VO
        public function toUpdateObject():Object {    (method is static)
            var obj:Object = new Object();
            obj["note[content]"] = content;
            return obj;
        }

        public static function fromXML(note:XML):Note {
            return new Note(note.content);
        }
    }
}
```

Now that we've created VO classes and our model classes know how to convert themselves to and from these VO classes, we're almost done. All we need to do is modify the business delegates to send the new VOs over the new RemoteObjects, make a small change to the `PomodoModelLocator`, and then modify the commands that use the business delegates.

First, we'll modify the business delegates.

11.3.6 *Modifying the business delegates*

This is where all the setup work we did starts paying off. We start with the `TaskDelegate`; see listing 11.20.

Listing 11.20   app\flex\com\pomodo\business\TaskDelegate.as

```
package com.pomodo.business {
    import com.adobe.cairngorm.business.ServiceLocator;
    import com.pomodo.model.Task;

    import mx.rpc.IResponder;
    import com.pomodo.model.Task;
    import com.pomodo.util.ServiceUtils;
    import mx.rpc.remoting.RemoteObject;

    public class TaskDelegate {
        private var _responder:IResponder;

        private var _taskRO:RemoteObject;              ❶

        public function TaskDelegate(responder:IResponder) {
            _responder = responder;
            _taskRO =
                ServiceLocator.getInstance().getRemoteObject(    ❷
                    "taskRO");
        }

        public function listTasks():void {
            ServiceUtils.send("/tasks.xml", _responder);
            var call:Object = _taskRO.index.send();        ❸
            call.addResponder(_responder);
        }

        public function createTask(task:Task):void {
            ServiceUtils.send("/tasks.xml", _responder, "POST",
                task.toXML(), true);
            var call:Object = _taskRO.create.send(task.toVO());   ❹
            call.addResponder(_responder);
        }

        public function updateTask(task:Task):void {
            ServiceUtils.send(
                "/tasks/" + task.id + ".xml", _responder, "PUT",
                task.toUpdateObject(), false);
            var call:Object = _taskRO.update.send(task.toVO());   ❺
```

Add import

```
        call.addResponder(_responder);
    }

    public function destroyTask(task:Task):void {
        ServiceUtils.send(
            "/tasks/" + task.id + ".xml",
            _responder,
            "DELETE");
        var call:Object = _taskRO.destroy.send(task.id);      ❻
        call.addResponder(_responder);
    }
  }
}
```

We create a _taskRO RemoteObject variable ❶ to store a reference to the shared
"taskRO" RemoteObject gotten from the ServiceLocator ❷. We then do remote
method calls on its index ❸, create ❹, update ❺, and destroy ❻ methods,
passing either nothing ❸, the task.toVO() ❹❺, or the task.id ❻. Because our
Task class can make a TaskVO, we can keep this class fairly thin.

    Next, we make essentially the same changes to the other business delegates.
First, the ProjectDelegate; see listing 11.21.

Listing 11.21 app\flex\com\pomodo\business\ProjectDelegate.as

```
package com.pomodo.business {
    import com.adobe.cairngorm.business.ServiceLocator;      ◁
    import com.pomodo.model.Project;
    import mx.rpc.IResponder;                                      Add
    import com.pomodo.model.Project;                               import
    import com.pomodo.util.ServiceUtils;
    import mx.rpc.remoting.RemoteObject;                     ◁

    public class ProjectDelegate {
        private var _responder:IResponder;

        private var _projectRO:RemoteObject;          ❶

        public function ProjectDelegate(responder:IResponder) {
            _responder = responder;
            _projectRO =
                ServiceLocator.getInstance().getRemoteObject(       ❷
                    "projectRO");
        }

        public function listProjects():void {
            ServiceUtils.send("/projects.xml", _responder);
            var call:Object = _projectRO.index.send();          ❸
```

```
                        call.addResponder(_responder);
                }

                public function createProject(project:Project):void {
                    ServiceUtils.send("/projects.xml", _responder,
                        "POST", project.toXML(), true);
                    var call:Object = _projectRO.create.send(        ❹
                        project.toVO());
                    call.addResponder(_responder);
                }

                public function updateProject(project:Project):void {
                    ServiceUtils.send(
                        "/projects/" + project.id + ".xml",
                        _responder, "PUT", project.toUpdateObject(),
                        false);
                    var call:Object = _projectRO.update.send(        ❺
                        project.toVO());
                    call.addResponder(_responder);
                }

                public function destroyProject(project:Project):void {
                    ServiceUtils.send(
                        "/projects/" + project.id + ".xml",
                        _responder, "DELETE");
                    var call:Object =
                        _projectRO.destroy.send(project.id);          ❻
                    call.addResponder(_responder);
                }
            }
        }
```

We create a _projectRO RemoteObject variable ❶ to store a reference to the shared
"projectRO" RemoteObject gotten from the ServiceLocator ❷. We then do
remote method calls on its index ❸, create ❹, update ❺, and destroy ❻ methods, passing either nothing ❸, the project.toVO() ❹❺, or the project.id ❻.
Again, because our Project class can make a ProjectVO, we can keep this class
fairly lightweight.

Next, LocationDelegate, which is more of the same; see listing 11.22.

Listing 11.22   app\flex\com\pomodo\business\LocationDelegate.as

```
package com.pomodo.business {
    import com.adobe.cairngorm.business.ServiceLocator;
    import com.pomodo.model.Location;
    import mx.rpc.IResponder;
    import com.pomodo.model.Location;
    import com.pomodo.util.ServiceUtils;
```

```
import mx.rpc.remoting.RemoteObject;

public class LocationDelegate {
    private var _responder:IResponder;

    private var _locationRO:RemoteObject;

    public function LocationDelegate(responder:IResponder) {
        _responder = responder;
        _locationRO =
            ServiceLocator.getInstance().getRemoteObject(
                "locationRO");
    }

    public function listLocations():void {
        ServiceUtils.send("/locations.xml", _responder);
        var call:Object = _locationRO.index.send();
        call.addResponder(_responder);
    }

    public function createLocation(location:Location):void {
        ServiceUtils.send("/locations.xml", _responder,
            "POST", location.toXML(), true);
        var call:Object = _locationRO.create.send(
            location.toVO());
        call.addResponder(_responder);
    }

    public function updateLocation(location:Location):void {
        ServiceUtils.send(
            "/locations/" + location.id + ".xml",
            _responder, "PUT", location.toUpdateObject(),
            false);
        var call:Object = _locationRO.update.send(
            location.toVO());
        call.addResponder(_responder);
    }

    public function destroyLocation(location:Location):
    void {
        ServiceUtils.send(
            "/locations/" + location.id + ".xml",
            _responder, "DELETE");
        var call:Object =
            _locationRO.destroy.send(location.id);
        call.addResponder(_responder);
    }
}
}
```

Finally, `NoteDelegate`, which is also more of the same; see listing 11.23.

Listing 11.23   app\flex\com\pomodo\business\NoteDelegate.as

```
package com.pomodo.business {
    import com.adobe.cairngorm.business.ServiceLocator;
    import com.pomodo.model.Note;
    import com.pomodo.model.PomodoModelLocator;
    import mx.rpc.IResponder;
    import com.pomodo.model.Note;
    import com.pomodo.model.User;
    import com.pomodo.model.PomodoModelLocator;
    import com.pomodo.util.ServiceUtils;
    import mx.rpc.remoting.RemoteObject;

    public class NoteDelegate {
        private var _responder:IResponder;

        private var _noteRO:RemoteObject;

        public function NoteDelegate(responder:IResponder) {
            _responder = responder;
            _noteRO =
                ServiceLocator.getInstance().getRemoteObject(
                    "noteRO");
        }

        public function showNote():void {
            var model:PomodoModelLocator =
                PomodoModelLocator.getInstance();
            ServiceUtils.send(
                "/users/" + model.user.id + "/note.xml",
                _responder);
            var call:Object = _noteRO.show.send();
            call.addResponder(_responder);
        }

        public function updateNote():void {
            var model:PomodoModelLocator =
                PomodoModelLocator.getInstance();
            ServiceUtils.send(
                "/users/" + model.user.id + "/note.xml",
                _responder,
                "PUT",
                model.note.toUpdateObject(),
                false);
            var call:Object = _noteRO.update.send(
                model.note.toVO());
            call.addResponder(_responder);
        }
    }
}
```

That was easy.

At this point, we'd expect to go modify the commands that use these business delegates. We'll do this, but first we need to modify the PomodoModelLocator.

11.3.7 Modifying the PomodoModelLocator

The PomodoModelLocator has methods called setTasks, setProjects, and set-Locations that take an XMLList. But we're getting an Array of VOs back from RubyAMF, so we need similar methods to handle these. We don't want a lot of duplication, so we'll refactor out the common functionality as we go. (I don't want to delete the XMLList-using code, because it's nice to have both approaches at our disposal, and because I'm trying to provide as much working code as will fit in a book.)

This is what we'll do. There is a fair bit of new code, but it's all straightforward; see listing 11.24.

Listing 11.24   app\flex\com\pomodo\model\PomodoModelLocator.as

```
package com.pomodo.model {
    import com.adobe.cairngorm.model.IModelLocator;
    import com.pomodo.control.EventNames;
    import com.pomodo.util.CairngormUtils;
    import com.pomodo.validators.ServerErrors;
    import com.pomodo.vo.TaskVO;        ◁──┐ Add
    import com.pomodo.vo.ProjectVO;         │ imports
    import com.pomodo.vo.LocationVO;     ──┘

    import mx.collections.ArrayCollection;
    import mx.collections.ListCollectionView;

    [Bindable]
    public class PomodoModelLocator implements IModelLocator {
...
        public function removeTask(task:Task):void {
            for (var i:int = 0; i < tasks.length; i++) {
                var ithTask:Task = Task(tasks.getItemAt(i));
                if (ithTask.id == task.id) {
                    ithTask.project.removeTask(ithTask);
                    ithTask.location.removeTask(ithTask);
                    tasks.removeItemAt(i);
                    break;
                }
            }
        }

        public function setTasks(list:XMLList):void {   ◁── Rename old setTasks method to setTasksFromList
```

```
...
    }
    public function setTasksFromVOs(taskVOs:Array):void {        ⟵
        var tasksArray:Array = [];                                      Create new
        for each (var item:TaskVO in taskVOs) {                       setTasksFromVOs
            tasksArray.push(Task.fromVO(item));                       method for AMF
        }
        tasks = new ArrayCollection(tasksArray);                       Rename setTasks
    }                                                                    method to
                                                                       setTasksFromList
    public function setTasksFromList(list:XMLList):void {        ⟵
        var tasksArray:Array = [];
        for each (var item:XML in list) {
            tasksArray.push(Task.fromXML(item));
        }                                                            Rename old
        tasks = new ArrayCollection(tasksArray);                     setProjects
    }                                                                method to
                                                                     setProjects-
    public function setProjects(list:XMLList):void {        ⟵       FromList
...
    }
    public function setProjectsFromVOs(projectVOs:Array):        ⟵
    void {                                                         Create new
        var projectsArray:Array = [];                            setProjectsFromVOs
        for each (var item:ProjectVO in projectVOs) {            method for AMF
            projectsArray.push(Project.fromVO(item));
        }                                                            Rename
        setProjects(projectsArray);                              setProjects method to
    }                                                            setProjectsFromList

    public function setProjectsFromList(list:XMLList):void {        ⟵
        var projectsArray:Array = [];
        for each (var item:XML in list) {
            projectsArray.push(Project.fromXML(item));
        }                                                            Common
        setProjects(projectsArray);                              functionality factored
    }                                                            out into method

    public function setProjects(projectsArray:Array):void {        ⟵
        projectIDMap = {};
        projectIDMap[0] = Project.NONE;
        for each (var project:Project in projectsArray) {
            projectIDMap[project.id] = project;
        }
        projects = new ArrayCollection(projectsArray);
        var projectsAndNoneArray:Array =
            projectsArray.slice(0);
        projectsAndNoneArray.splice(0, 0, Project.NONE);
        projectsAndNone =
            new ArrayCollection(projectsAndNoneArray);
```

```
        _gotProjects = true;
        listTasksIfMapsPresent();
    }
```

Rename old
setLocations method to
setLocationsFromList

```
...

    public function setLocations(list:XMLList):void {

    }
    public function setLocationsFromVOs(locationVOs:Array):
    void {
        var locationsArray:Array = [];
        for each (var item:LocationVO in locationVOs) {
            locationsArray.push(Location.fromVO(item));
        }
        setLocations(locationsArray);
    }
```

Create new
setLocationsFromVOs
method for AMF

Rename setLocations
method to
setLocationsFromList

```
    public function setLocationsFromList(list:XMLList):
    void {
        var locationsArray:Array = [];
        for each (var item:XML in list) {
            locationsArray.push(Location.fromXML(item));
        }
        setLocations(locationsArray);
    }
```

Common
functionality factored
out into method

```
    public function setLocations(locationsArray:Array):
    void {
        locationIDMap = {};
        locationIDMap[0] = Location.NONE;
        for each (var location:Location in locationsArray) {
            locationIDMap[location.id] = location;
        }
        locations = new ArrayCollection(locationsArray);
        var locationsAndNoneArray:Array =
            locationsArray.slice(0);
        locationsAndNoneArray.splice(0, 0, Location.NONE);
        locationsAndNone =
            new ArrayCollection(locationsAndNoneArray);
        _gotLocations = true;
        listTasksIfMapsPresent();
    }

    public function getProject(projectID:int):Project {
        if (projectIDMap == null) return null;
        return projectIDMap[projectID];
    }
...
```

All that is left is modifying the commands!

11.3.8 Modifying the commands

Again, this is straightforward. We'll start with the `DestroyTaskCommand`; see listing 11.25.

Listing 11.25   app\flex\com\pomodo\command\DestroyTaskCommand.as

```
package com.pomodo.command {
...
    import com.pomodo.model.Task;              Add
    import com.pomodo.vo.TaskVO;       ◁───    import
    import com.pomodo.util.CairngormUtils;
...
    public class DestroyTaskCommand implements ICommand,
    IResponder {
...
        public function result(event:Object):void {
            var resultEvent:ResultEvent = ResultEvent(event);
            var model:PomodoModelLocator =
                PomodoModelLocator.getInstance();
            if (event.result == "error") {
                Alert.show(
                    "The task was not successfully deleted.",
                    "Error");
            } else {
                model.removeTask(
                    Task.fromXML(XML(event.result)));          Create new Task
                    Task.fromVO(TaskVO(event.result)));   ◁──  from TaskVO, not
            }                                                  XML
        }
...
}
```

Next, the `ListTasksCommand`; see listing 11.26.

Listing 11.26   app\flex\com\pomodo\command\ListTasksCommand.as

```
package com.pomodo.command {
...
    public class ListTasksCommand implements ICommand,
    IResponder {
...
        public function result(event:Object):void {
            var model:PomodoModelLocator =
                PomodoModelLocator.getInstance();
            model.setTasks(
                XMLList(event.result.children()));         Set Tasks from
            model.setTasksFromVOs(event.result);    ◁───   VOs, not XML
```

```
        }
    ...
    }
```

Now, the `ListProjectsCommand`; see listing 11.27.

Listing 11.27 app\flex\com\pomodo\command\ListProjectsCommand.as

```
package com.pomodo.command {
...
    public class ListProjectsCommand implements ICommand,
    IResponder {
...
        public function result(event:Object):void {
            var model:PomodoModelLocator =
                PomodoModelLocator.getInstance();
            model.setProjects(
                XMLList(event.result.children()));
            model.setProjectsFromVOs(event.result);           ◁┐ Set Projects from
        }                                                       ┘ VOs, not XML
...
    }
```

Next, the `ListLocationsCommand`; see listing 11.28.

Listing 11.28 app\flex\com\pomodo\command\ListLocationsCommand.as

```
package com.pomodo.command {
...
    public class ListLocationsCommand implements ICommand,
    IResponder {
...
        public function result(event:Object):void {
            var model:PomodoModelLocator =
                PomodoModelLocator.getInstance();
            model.setLocations(
                XMLList(event.result.children()));
            model.setLocationsFromVOs(event.result);           ◁┐ Set Locations from
        }                                                        ┘ VOs, not XML
...
    }
```

Now, the `ShowNoteCommand`; see listing 11.29.

Listing 11.29   app\flex\com\pomodo\command\ShowNoteCommand.as

```
package com.pomodo.command {
...
    public class ShowNoteCommand implements ICommand,
    IResponder {
...
        public function result(event:Object):void {
            var model:PomodoModelLocator =
                PomodoModelLocator.getInstance();
            model.note = Note.fromXML(event.result);          Set Note from the
            model.note = Note.fromVO(event.result);    ◁─┘    VO, not XML
        }
...
```

Finally, the UpdateTaskCommand; see listing 11.30.

Listing 11.30   app\flex\com\pomodo\command\UpdateTaskCommand.as

```
package com.pomodo.command {
    import com.adobe.cairngorm.commands.ICommand;
    import com.adobe.cairngorm.control.CairngormEvent;
    import com.pomodo.business.TaskDelegate;
    import com.pomodo.control.EventNames;
    import com.pomodo.model.PomodoModelLocator;
    import com.pomodo.model.Task;
    import com.pomodo.util.CairngormUtils;           Add
    import com.pomodo.vo.TaskVO;         ◁─────────┘  import
...
    public class UpdateTaskCommand implements ICommand,
    IResponder {
...
        public function result(event:Object):void {
            var resultEvent:ResultEvent = ResultEvent(event);
            var model:PomodoModelLocator =
                PomodoModelLocator.getInstance();
            model.updateTask(Task.fromXML(XML(event.result)));
            model.updateTask(Task.fromVO(TaskVO(event.result)));   ◁─┐
            CairngormUtils.dispatchEvent(
                EventNames.LIST_PROJECTS);            Update Task by
        }                                              creating Task
...                                                   from VO, not XML
```

Did I forget UpdateProjectCommand, UpdateLocationCommand, and UpdateNote-
Command? No—they're unchanged.

That's it! Run newdb.bat to recreate the ludwig user that we deleted at the end of iteration 10, then restart your server, rebuild, reload, and log in as ludwig. Everything works as before. Finally, run the tests again and confirm that everything still works.

> The code at this point is saved as the iteration11 folder.

11.4 Summary

Now that we have a proper object model on the client side, we're no longer tightly coupled to the transport mechanism. This let us refactor the code to using RubyAMF and keep the object model essentially unchanged (except for adding the ability to convert to/from value objects).

RubyAMF is a promising and fast-moving project. The fact that it's essentially MIT-licensed and that it plays so nicely with Rails means that I expect it to become the dominant AMF implementation for Ruby. It has a lot of momentum behind it at the moment.

Using RubyAMF isn't an all-or-nothing proposition: You can use it in performance-critical parts of your application, if you want to minimize the amount of code you're writing. For example, in this iteration I didn't feel like revisiting the login code, so I left it using XML and HTTPService. Besides demonstrating how lazy I'm getting, this also demonstrated that RubyAMF and HTTPService can be used side by side.

In the next and final iteration, we'll revisit the pomodo application one last time, extending it to becoming an Adobe AIR application.

Rails on AIR
(Adobe Integrated Runtime)

12

> *And Adobe is leaning hard on Flash, Adobe Integrated Runtime or*
> *AIR (formerly code-named Apollo), and Flex. My money is on Adobe*
> *simply because of those two invisible weapons, PDF and Flash.*
>
> —"Robert X. Cringely";
> I, Cringely; The Pulpit, June 29, 2007[1]

---

[1] http://www.pbs.org/cringely/pulpit/2007/pulpit_20070629_002360.html.

In this iteration, we'll have a bit of fun. We'll make pomodo be a Flex 3 AIR application, and we'll add online/offline network detection (and change the UI accordingly). We won't solve any hard problems (synchronizing local and remote data, and so on). The primary purpose of this iteration is to get you up and running with AIR and to get pomodo built and running as an AIR application in case you want to use it as a starting point for your own AIR projects. This isn't an attempt to provide any kind of comprehensive AIR tutorial.

12.1 Converting pomodo to an AIR application

Flex Builder 3 already has support for AIR. In this iteration, I'll assume you're using Flex Builder 3. If you've already been using Flex Builder 3 for the rest of the book, you'll create a new project out of the same files. The first thing we'll do is delete our existing project (but keep the files) and then create a new AIR project in the same spot.

12.1.1 Deleting the old project

First, copy the current folder to current_flex3 if you want to play with it later (in Flex 3, but not with AIR). Next, delete the pomodo project. Right-click the pomodo project folder in the Navigator, and choose Delete. Leave Do Not Delete Contents selected, and click Yes (see figure 12.1).

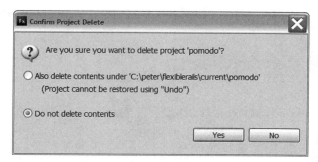

Figure 12.1
Deleting the pomodo project

12.1.2 Creating the new project

Choose File > New > Flex Project. Enter the Project Name pomodo, browse to the correct location, choose Desktop Application (Runs in Adobe AIR), and leave Application Server Type set to None. We see something like figure 12.2.

Click Next. We're taken to the wizard pane, where we specify the location of the compiled Flex application. Choose public\bin as the folder. Note that if you did a clean build in iteration 11 after setting the output folder to be public, you'll

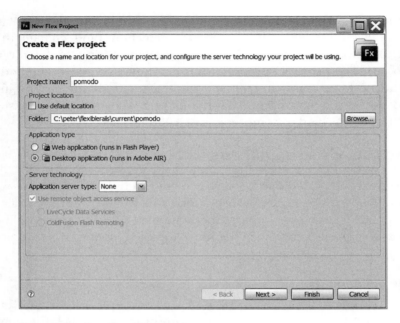

Figure 12.2   New Flex AIR project

probably need to create the bin directory inside public; switch to Windows Explorer or a command prompt and do this first. Then browse to public\bin; we see figure 12.3.

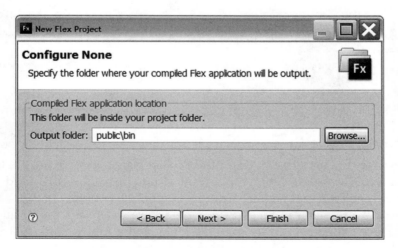

Figure 12.3   Configuring the compiled Flex application location

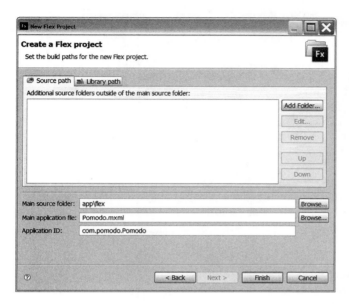

Figure 12.4
Configuring the build paths

Click Next. We're taken to the build path dialog. Browse to app\flex for the Main source folder. Next, rename the Main application file to Pomodo.mxml (or click Browse to select it). Finally, enter an Application ID of `com.pomodo. Pomodo`. When finished, the dialog should look like figure 12.4.

Next, switch to the Library Path tab. Click the Add SWC button, and browse to app/flex/lib/Cairngorm.swc (see figure 12.5).

Click OK. The Library Path tab looks like figure 12.6.

Click Finish. The AIR project is created, and the Flex Navigator shows a folder icon with a red AIR icon on it.

Next, just as in iteration 11, we also need to add the argument `-services "services-config.xml"` to the compiler arguments so that the compiler knows to use our services. (We are creating a new project, after all, so these arguments won't have been set for us.) Right-click on the pomodo project

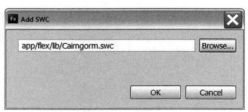

Figure 12.5 Adding Cairngorm to the library path

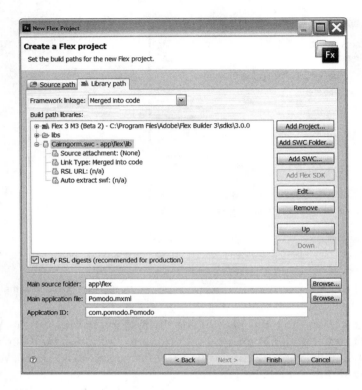

Figure 12.6
Adding Cairngorm
to the library path

in the Navigator, choose the Properties menu item, switch to the Flex compiler view, and do that now; see figure 12.7.

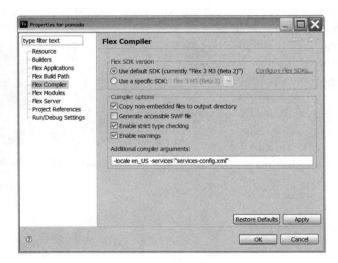

Figure 12.7
Don't forget to specify
your services-config.xml!

You may think this is a superfluous figure, and you're right. However, it's my way of trying to ensure that you don't just skim these instructions and miss this step—that's what happened to me when I updated this iteration from being based on iteration 10 to being based on iteration 11!

12.1.3 Getting it running

We'll make a couple of small changes before trying to run the application. First, we'll edit the Pomodo-app.xml file, which was generated for us when we created the new AIR project; see listing 12.1. Yes, Rails programmers, we're about to edit an XML configuration file; hold your nose and follow along—in TextMate, if it makes you feel better. (Note that this file is based on Flex 3 Beta 2; it has been reformatted slightly in Flex 3 Beta 3. Regardless, the attributes are still there and need to be set.)

Listing 12.1 app\flex\Pomodo-app.xml

```
<?xml version="1.0" encoding="UTF-8"?>
<application xmlns="http://ns.adobe.com/air/application/1.0.M5"
  appId="com.pomodo.Pomodo" version="1.0 Beta">
<!--
    AIR Application Descriptor File:
    Specifies parameters for identifying, installing, and
    launching AIR applications.
...
-->

  <!--
      The application name displayed by the operating system.
      (Required.)
  -->
  <name>com.pomodo.Pomodo</name>            ❶
...
    <!--
        Other settings for the initial window.
    -->
    <!--  <minimizable>true</minimizable> -->
    <!--  <maximizable>true</maximizable> -->
    <!--  <resizable>true</resizable> -->
    <width>1200</width>            ❷
    <height>900</height>            ❸
    <x>50</x>            ❹
    <y>50</y>            ❺
    <!--  <minSize>300 300</minSize> -->
    <!--  <maxSize>800 800</maxSize> -->
  </initialWindow>
...
```

Note that the name for the application that we specified in the wizard is present ❶ here. Next, we set the default width ❷ and height ❸ in pixels, as well as the default x ❹ and y ❺ coordinates of the app. (If you have a smaller monitor, change the values accordingly.)

Next, we'll make a couple of changes to Pomodo; see listing 12.2.

Listing 12.2   app\flex\Pomodo.mxml

```
<?xml version="1.0" encoding="utf-8"?>
<mx:Application          ❶
<mx:WindowedApplication         ❷
    xmlns:mx="http://www.adobe.com/2006/mxml"
    xmlns:pom="com.pomodo.components.*"
    xmlns:control="com.pomodo.control.*"
    layout="vertical"
    backgroundGradientColors="[#ffffff, #c0c0c0]"
    horizontalAlign="center"
    verticalAlign="top"
    paddingLeft="0"
    paddingRight="0"
    paddingTop="0"
    paddingBottom="0"
    title="Pomodo"          ❸
    width="100%"
    height="100%"
    creationCompleteEffect="fadeIn">
...
</mx:Application>          ❹
</mx:WindowedApplication>          ❺
```

We start by converting the mx:Application ❶❹ to the new mx:Windowed-Application ❷❺ component, which is what we're supposed to use for AIR applications. Next, we add a title ❸ for the application.

Run newdb.bat, and start the server. Click the Run button on the toolbar. We see the screen shown in figure 12.8.

That's hot!

Switch to the Login panel, and try to log in as ludwig (see figure 12.9).

That's not!

Thinking about this, we realize that we're in a desktop application *(duh)*, not a web browser. So, we need to allow the user to specify the root URL of the server they're talking to. All the URLs that Rails uses will be relative to this root. Modify the PomodoModelLocator as shown in listing 12.3.

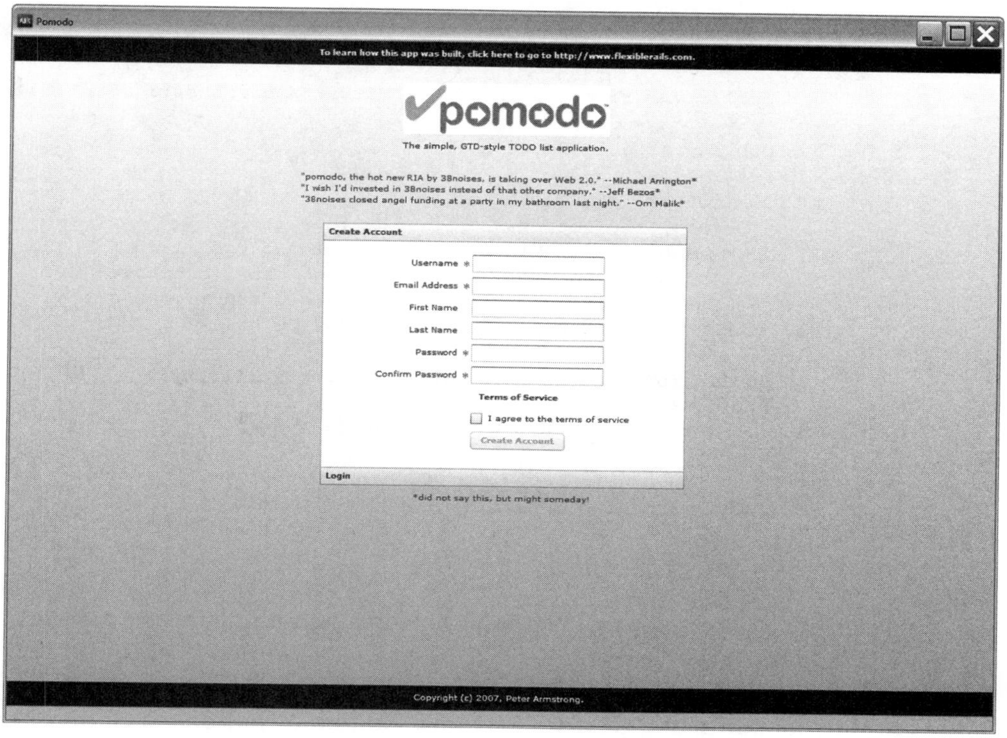

Figure 12.8   Our first AIR application

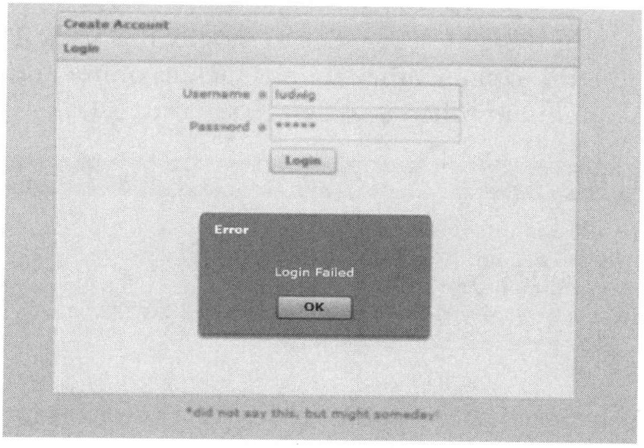

Figure 12.9
Failed login

Listing 12.3   app\flex\com\pomodo\model\PomodoModelLocator.as

```
. . .
        public var remoteURL:String = "http://localhost:3000";      ❶

        public var user:User;
. . .
        public var reviews:String =
        '"pomodo, the hot new RIA by 38noises, is taking ' +
        'over Web 2.0." --Michael Arrington*\n"I wish I\'d ' +
        'invested in 38noises instead of that other company."' +
        ' --Jeff Bezos*\n"38noises closed angel funding at a ' +
        'party in my bathroom last night." --Om Malik*';

        public function getRemoteURL(relativeURL:String):      ❷
        String {
            return remoteURL + relativeURL;      ❸
        }

        public function updateTask(task:Task):void {
. . .
```

We create a `remoteURL` variable ❶, which, like everything in `PomodoModelLocator`, is `Bindable`. For development purposes, we'll hardcode this URL to http://localhost:3000 in the code. When we're closer to production we can change this to our domain name or leave it empty. Note that we don't include a trailing /, because all the Rails URLs have been using a leading / already. Next, we create a `getRemoteURL()` utility function ❷, which returns the result of concatenating the `remoteURL` base and the `relativeURL` ❸ passed in.

Now, we need some place in the UI for the user to modify this URL. Thinking ahead a bit, we realize we'll want to show other things, such as online/offline status. To do so, we create a component called `StatusBox`; see listing 12.4.

Listing 12.4   app\flex\com\pomodo\components\StatusBox.mxml

```
<?xml version="1.0" encoding="utf-8"?>
<mx:HBox xmlns:mx="http://www.adobe.com/2006/mxml"
    xmlns:pom="com.pomodo.components.*"
    paddingLeft="5" paddingRight="5" backgroundColor="#FFFFFF"
    horizontalAlign="left" verticalAlign="middle"
    width="100%" height="40">
<mx:Script>
<![CDATA[
    import com.pomodo.model.PomodoModelLocator;

    [Bindable]
```

```
        private var _model:PomodoModelLocator =        ❶
            PomodoModelLocator.getInstance();
]]>
</mx:Script>
    <mx:Label text="URL:"/>
    <mx:TextInput id="remoteURLTI" width="100%"
        text="{_model.remoteURL}"        ❷
        change="_model.remoteURL = remoteURLTI.text"/>        ❸
</mx:HBox>
```

This component gets the shared PomodoModelLocator ❶ and stores it in a variable called _model. Then, it binds the text property ❷ of a TextInput called remoteURLTI to the _model.remoteURL. Finally, it handles the change event of the remoteURLTI ❸ and assigns the _model.remoteURL with the remoteURLTI.text. *(No, I'm not doing this via Cairngorm. I won't tell our architect if you don't.)*

Now that we have a StatusBox, we need to add it to Pomodo (❶ in listing 12.5).

Listing 12.5   app\flex\Pomodo.mxml

```
. . .
    <control:PomodoController id="controller" />

    <pom:StatusBox id="statusBox"/>        ❶
    <mx:HBox backgroundColor="#000000" width="100%" height="30"
        horizontalAlign="center" verticalAlign="middle">
. . .
```

Now, we need to change all the URLs we use in our entire application, throughout all the Cairngorm commands. This is going to be a ton of work, because—oh, wait, because we used ServiceUtils it's trivial; see listing 12.6.

Listing 12.6   app\flex\com\pomodo\util\ServiceUtils.as

```
package com.pomodo.util {
    import mx.rpc.IResponder;
    import mx.rpc.AsyncToken;
    import mx.rpc.http.HTTPService;
    import com.pomodo.model.PomodoModelLocator;        ❶

    public class ServiceUtils {
        /**
         * Note: PUT and DELETE don't work with XML since the
         * _method hack workaround doesn't work.
         */
```

```
public static function send(
    url:String,                            ❷
    relativeURL:String,          ❸
    responder:IResponder = null,
    method:String = null,
    request:Object = null,
    sendXML:Boolean = false,
    resultFormat:String = "e4x",
    useProxy:Boolean = false):void
{
    var service:HTTPService = new HTTPService();
    service.url = url;                     ❹
    var model:PomodoModelLocator =         ❺
        PomodoModelLocator.getInstance();
    service.url = model.getRemoteURL(relativeURL);      ❻
    service.contentType = sendXML ? "application/xml" :
        "application/x-www-form-urlencoded";
    ...
}
    }
}
```

We start by importing PomodoModelLocator ❶. Next, we rename the url ❷ parameter to relativeURL ❸, to be more self-documenting. We delete the straight assignment ❹ and instead get the shared PomodoModelLocator ❺ and call its getRemoteURL method ❻ to get the remote URL to use. We then assign this URL to the service.url ❻ property.

NOTE   This approach also would have worked even if we hadn't refactored to RubyAMF in iteration 11—that is, you could have started this iteration with the iteration 10 code and just made these changes to get the application to work.

Rebuild, run the app, and log in as ludwig. We see the screen shown in figure 12.10.

NOTE   If this didn't work for you (for example, if you get an Adobe Flash Player 9 dialog with an exception trace starting with "TypeError: Error #1009: Cannot access a property or method of a null object reference"), fear not: This issue will be addressed in the next section.

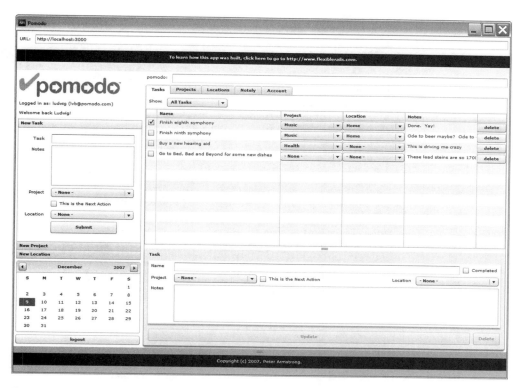

Figure 12.10   Pomodo on AIR!

12.2 *Refactoring event triggering*

When I was coding this iteration, I hit a mysterious bug: When the application loaded, I got a "TypeError: Error #1009: Cannot access a property or method of a null object reference" exception. I figured this out and fixed it, but then when it was time to write this iteration up, the TypeError turned out to be hard to reproduce. (For example, we didn't hit it just now.) So, we will make a small modification to ensure the bug occurs, and then we will fix it.

> **NOTE** When I was originally coding this iteration, I had based it on the iteration 10 code, not the iteration 11 code. Under these circumstances, the bug we're about to see also caused Windows to pop up a password dialog—three times! (If you skipped iteration 11, this may happen to you.) In either case, the fixes that we will make will solve this problem too, so this iteration will work regardless of whether you followed along with iteration 11.

We'll start by making a seemingly innocuous change; see listing 12.7.

Listing 12.7   app\flex\Pomodo.mxml

```
...
        <mx:ViewStack id="mainStack" width="100%" height="100%"
            creationPolicy="all"
    selectedChild="{controlViewToShow(_model.workflowState)}">
            <pom:SplashBox id="splashBox"/>
...
```

Figure 12.11   TypeError in Pomodo

All we're doing is changing the `creationPolicy` of the `mainStack` to create all of its components when it's created. No big deal, right?

Let's check: Rebuild, run the app and login as ludwig. We see the dialog shown in figure 12.11.

So, if the `mainStack` creates all its children right away, our application is wrecked. But why? (Exercise for the reader: close the book, switch to Flex Builder, figure out the problem and implement a solution that works when the `creationPolicy="all"` for the `mainStack`. If you need a hint, look at the title of this section.)

If the `mainStack` creationPolicy is "all", this means that all its children—including the `mainBox`—are created right away. Looking at the code in the `MainBox`, we see listing 12.8.

Listing 12.8   app\flex\com\pomodo\components\MainBox.mxml

```
<?xml version="1.0" encoding="utf-8"?>
<mx:HBox xmlns:mx="http://www.adobe.com/2006/mxml"
```

```
      xmlns:pom="com.pomodo.components.*"
      minWidth="1000"
      minHeight="680"
      paddingLeft="5"
      paddingRight="5"
      paddingTop="5"
      paddingBottom="5"
      width="100%"
      height="100%"
      backgroundColor="#FFFFFF"
      creationComplete="handleCreationComplete()">          ❶
  ...
      private function handleCreationComplete():void {      ❷
          CairngormUtils.dispatchEvent(EventNames.SHOW_NOTE);       ❸
          CairngormUtils.dispatchEvent(EventNames.LIST_PROJECTS);       ❹
          CairngormUtils.dispatchEvent(EventNames.LIST_LOCATIONS);      ❺
      }
  ...
```

When the `MainBox` is created, it broadcasts the `creationComplete` event. This is handled ❶ by the `handleCreationComplete()` ❷ function, which dispatches Cairngorm events ❸❹❺ that trigger the retrieving of the note (with the `Show-NoteCommand`), projects (with the `ListProjectsCommand`) and locations (with the `ListLocationsCommand`). (Look in the `PomodoController` to see which commands are triggered by which `EventNames` constants.) Then, when the projects and locations come back, the tasks are retrieved as well (with the `ListTasksCommand`). Doing a bit of experimenting, we quickly determine that the `ShowNoteCommand` causes the `TypeError` exception, and the three `List___Command` commands, and the three `List___Command` commands triggered the three password dialogs that occured when I originally created this iteration based on the iteration 10 code.

We realize that what these all have in common is that things go wrong because the user variable in the `PomodoModelLocator` isn't set. So, rather than dispatching the events in the `handleCreationComplete()` function in `MainBox`, we decide to make the user variable a property with set/get methods, and fire off the events in the set method. We could take other approaches, but this is the one we'll take because it's fairly simple.

We'll start by modifying `MainBox`; see listing 12.9.

Listing 12.9 app\flex\com\pomodo\components\MainBox.mxml

```
<?xml version="1.0" encoding="utf-8"?>
<mx:HBox xmlns:mx="http://www.adobe.com/2006/mxml"
    xmlns:pom="com.pomodo.components.*"
    minWidth="1000"
    minHeight="680"
```

```
    paddingLeft="5"
    paddingRight="5"
    paddingTop="5"
    paddingBottom="5"
    width="100%"
    height="100%"
    backgroundColor="#FFFFFF">
    creationComplete="handleCreationComplete()">      ①
<mx:Script>
...
    private function logout():void {
        CairngormUtils.dispatchEvent(EventNames.LOAD_URL,
            "/logout");
    }

    private function handleCreationComplete():void {    ②
        CairngormUtils.dispatchEvent(EventNames.SHOW_NOTE);
        CairngormUtils.dispatchEvent(EventNames.LIST_PROJECTS);
        CairngormUtils.dispatchEvent(EventNames.LIST_LOCATIONS);
    }
]]>
</mx:Script>
```

All we're doing is removing the creationComplete handler ①②.
Next, we modify the PomodoModelLocator; see listing 12.10.

Listing 12.10   app\flex\com\pomodo\model\PomodoModelLocator.as

```
...
        public var remoteURL:String = "http://localhost:3000";
        //for development

        public var user:User;                        ①
        private var _user:User;                      ②

        public function set user(newUser:User):void {        ③
            if (_user != newUser) {              ④
                _user = newUser;                 ⑤
                workflowState =                  ⑥
                    PomodoModelLocator.VIEWING_MAIN_APP;
                CairngormUtils.dispatchEvent(           ⑦
                    EventNames.SHOW_NOTE);
                CairngormUtils.dispatchEvent(           ⑧
                    EventNames.LIST_PROJECTS);
                CairngormUtils.dispatchEvent(           ⑨
                    EventNames.LIST_LOCATIONS);
            }
        }
```

```
public function get user():User {
    return _user;
}

public var note:Note;
```

...

We're changing the public user variable ❶ into a private _user variable ❷ and then creating a set function ❸. This function checks whether the newUser is different ❹ and if so assigns the _user ❺, sets the workflowState ❻, and dispatches the three events ❼❽❾ that used to be dispatched in the creationComplete handler in MainBox.

Having done this, we need to modify the CreateSessionCommand and CreateUserCommand to get rid of the model.workflowState assignment; see listings 12.11 and 12.12.

Listing 12.11 app\flex\com\pomodo\command\CreateSessionCommand.as

```
...
        public function result(event:Object):void {
            var result:Object = event.result;
            if (event.result == "badlogin") {
                Alert.show("Login failed.");
            } else {
                var model:PomodoModelLocator =
                    PomodoModelLocator.getInstance();
                model.user = User.fromXML(XML(event.result));
                model.workflowState =
                    PomodoModelLocator.VIEWING_MAIN_APP;
            }
        }
...
```

Listing 12.12 app\flex\com\pomodo\ command\CreateUserCommand.as

```
...
        public function result(event:Object):void {
            var result:Object = event.result;
            var model:PomodoModelLocator =
                PomodoModelLocator.getInstance();
            if (result is XML) {
                var resultXML:XML = XML(result);
                if (resultXML.name().localName == "errors") {
...
                } else {
```

```
                    model.user = User.fromXML(resultXML);
                    model.workflowState =
                        PomodoModelLocator.VIEWING_MAIN_APP;
                }
            } else {
    ...
            }
        }
    ...
```

That's it. Rebuild, reload, and log in as ludwig. Everything works: We see the screenshot shown in figure 12.10 again (or for the first time).

12.3   Online/Offline support

An in-depth discussion of the features of AIR and how AIR relates to Rails is beyond the scope of this book—it's a full book-length topic of its own. *(Hmm, someone should write such a book...)* In *Flexible Rails*, we'll content ourselves with implementing the beginnings of online/offline support. Specifically, when we're offline, we'll show Notely, so we can type notes that we can save the next time we're online.

We'll add support for detecting when the application is online or offline and updating the look of the application accordingly, using an approach largely based on an excellent article[2] on Adobe Labs by John C. Bland II. Adapting the approach in John's article to implement saving to the local filesystem and synchronizing with the server's database will be left as an exercise for the reader.

We'll begin by adding the UI code to update pomodo when the online/offline status changes. If we were attempting to provide full online/synchronization of tasks, projects, locations, and so on, this would be a very tricky problem—luckily I'm in control of my own requirements here, and that's not one of them.

We'll begin by creating an OfflineMainBox, based on the current MainBox; see listing 12.13.

> **Listing 12.13   app\flex\com\pomodo\components\OfflineMainBox.mxml**

```xml
<?xml version="1.0" encoding="utf-8"?>
<mx:HBox xmlns:mx="http://www.adobe.com/2006/mxml"
    xmlns:pom="com.pomodo.components.*"
    minWidth="1000" minHeight="680"
    paddingLeft="5" paddingRight="5" paddingTop="5"
```

---

[2] http://labs.adobe.com/wiki/index.php/AIR:Articles:Taking_Apollo_Applications_Offline.

```
            paddingBottom="5" width="100%" height="100%"
            backgroundColor="#FFFFFF">
<mx:Script>
<![CDATA[
    import com.pomodo.control.EventNames;
    import com.pomodo.util.CairngormUtils;
    import com.pomodo.model.PomodoModelLocator;

    [Bindable]
    private var _model:PomodoModelLocator =
        PomodoModelLocator.getInstance();
]]>
</mx:Script>
    <mx:HBox width="100%" height="100%">
        <mx:VBox width="300" height="100%">
            <mx:Image source="com/pomodo/assets/logo_md.png"/>
            <mx:Label text="{'Logged in as: ' +
                _model.user.login +
                ' (' + _model.user.email + ')'}"/>
            <mx:Label text="{'Welcome back ' +
                _model.user.firstName + '!'}"/>
            <mx:Label text="Working Offline"/>           ❶
            <mx:DateChooser id="dateChooser" width="100%"/>
        </mx:VBox>
        <mx:VBox width="100%" height="100%">
            <mx:TabNavigator width="100%" height="100%">
                <pom:Notely id="notelyTab"/>           ❷
            </mx:TabNavigator>
        </mx:VBox>
    </mx:HBox>
</mx:HBox>
```

All we do is remove most of the components, add a Working Offline label ❶, and leave only the Notely tab ❷ in the TabNavigator. (Note, however, that using this approach gives us more flexibility than adding a bunch of flags to the MainBox— this way, we can totally change the layout, and so on.)

Next, we add more shared state to the PomodoModelLocator; see listing 12.14.

Listing 12.14   app\flex\com\pomodo\model\PomodoModelLocator.as

```
...
        public var online:Boolean;           ❶

        public var onlineCheckURL:String =
            "http://www.google.com";           ❷

        public var unsavedNoteContent:String;           ❸
```

```
public var remoteURL:String = "http://localhost:3000";

private var _user:User;
```

...

We add a flag for whether we're online ❶, an onlineCheckURL ❷, and an unsavedNoteContent variable for the unsaved content of Notely ❸. The unsaved-NoteContent variable is necessary because there will be two Notely instances, and we want them to share the same state. The onlineCheckURL is necessary because the remoteURL is referring to a URL on our machine—even if we're offline, this URL will work (and thus be a useful demo—we don't want to have to also stop our Rails server for it to work). In reality, all that matters is that we can talk to our remoteURL, so this is book code/demo code.

Next, we modify Pomodo to show a different view when it's online or offline; see listing 12.15.

Listing 12.15   app\flex\Pomodo.mxml

```
    ...
    public static function debug(str:String):void {
        //application.debugPanel.addMessage(
        //    new DebugMessage(str));
    }

    private function controlViewToShow(workflowState:int,
    online:Boolean):Container {              ❶
        if (workflowState ==
            PomodoModelLocator.VIEWING_SPLASH_SCREEN) {
            return splashBox;
        } else if (workflowState ==
            PomodoModelLocator.VIEWING_MAIN_APP) {
            return online ? mainBox : offlineMainBox;   ❷
        } else {
            return splashBox;
        }
    }

    private function loadFlexibleRails():void {
        CairngormUtils.dispatchEvent(EventNames.LOAD_URL,
            "http://www.flexiblerails.com");
    }
]]>
</mx:Script>
    <mx:Fade id="fadeIn" duration="500"/>
    <mx:WipeUp id="wipeUp" duration="500"/>
    <mx:WipeDown id="wipeDown" duration="500"/>      ❸
```

```
<!--
the FrontController, containing Commands specific to this app
-->
<control:PomodoController id="controller" />

<pom:StatusBox id="statusBox"/>
<mx:HBox backgroundColor="#000000" width="100%" height="30"
    horizontalAlign="center" verticalAlign="middle">
    <mx:LinkButton color="#FFFFFF"
        click="loadFlexibleRails()" label="{MARKETING}"/>
</mx:HBox>
<mx:Spacer height="10"/>

<mx:VDividedBox width="100%" height="100%">
    <mx:ViewStack id="mainStack" width="100%" height="100%"
        creationPolicy="all"
selectedChild="{controlViewToShow(_model.workflowState,      ❹
    _model.online)}">
            <pom:SplashBox id="splashBox"/>
            <pom:MainBox id="mainBox" showEffect="wipeUp"/>
            <pom:OfflineMainBox id="offlineMainBox"        ❺
                showEffect="wipeDown"/>
    </mx:ViewStack>
    <pom:DebugPanel id="debugPanel" width="100%"
        height="0%"/>
</mx:VDividedBox>
<mx:HBox backgroundColor="#000000" width="100%" height="30"
    horizontalAlign="center" verticalAlign="middle">
    <mx:Label color="#FFFFFF" text="{COPYRIGHT}"/>
</mx:HBox>
</mx:WindowedApplication>
```

We modify the `controlViewToShow` function ❶ to take two parameters:
`_model.workflowState` and `_model.online` ❹, instead of `_model.workflowState`.
This causes the binding for the `selectedChild` of the `mainStack` to execute when
either the `workflowState` or the `online` status changes. Inside `controlViewToShow`,
we return `mainBox` if online and `offlineMainBox` if offline ❷. We also add a `Wipe-`
`Down` effect ❸ and make the `offlineMainBox` trigger it as its `showEffect` ❺.

Next, we modify `Notely` to take use the `unsavedNoteContent` that we're now
storing in the `PomodoModelLocator`; see listing 12.16.

Listing 12.16   app\flex\com\pomodo\components\Notely.mxml

```
<?xml version="1.0" encoding="utf-8"?>
<mx:VBox xmlns:mx="http://www.adobe.com/2006/mxml"
    width="100%" height="100%" label="Notely" paddingLeft="5"
```

```
            paddingRight="5" paddingTop="5" paddingBottom="5">
    <mx:Script>
    <![CDATA[
        import com.pomodo.control.EventNames;
        import com.pomodo.model.PomodoModelLocator;
        import com.pomodo.util.CairngormUtils;

        [Bindable]
        private var _model:PomodoModelLocator =
            PomodoModelLocator.getInstance();

        private function doSave():void {
            _model.note.content = notelyTA.text;          ❶
            _model.note.content = _model.unsavedNoteContent;    ❷
            CairngormUtils.dispatchEvent(EventNames.UPDATE_NOTE);
        }

        private function doRevert():void {
            notelyTA.text = _model.note.content;          ❸
            _model.unsavedNoteContent = _model.note.content;    ❹
        }
    ]]>
    </mx:Script>
        <mx:TextArea id="notelyTA" width="100%" height="100%"
            text="{_model.note.content}"/>          ❺
            text="{_model.unsavedNoteContent}"          ❻
            change="_model.unsavedNoteContent = notelyTA.text"/>    ❼
        <mx:ControlBar width="100%" horizontalAlign="center">
            <mx:Button id="saveButton" label="Save" width="100%"
                height="30" click="doSave()"
                enabled="{_model.online}"/>          ❽
            <mx:Button id="revertButton" label="Revert"
                height="30" click="doRevert()"/>
        </mx:ControlBar>
    </mx:VBox>
```

We modify notelyTA to now have its text bound to _model.unsavedNote-
Content ❻ instead of _model.note.content ❺ and to update this _model.
unsavedNoteContent on change ❼. This simplifies the synchronization (it's
completely trivial). Having done this, we modify the doSave function to update
_model.note.content based on _model.unsavedNoteContent ❶❷, and we
modify the doRevert function to assign _model.unsavedNoteContent from
_model.note.content ❸❹. We don't need to assign notelyTA.text explicitly,
because it's bound to _model.unsavedNoteContent. Finally, note that we now
enable the Save button only when online ❽.

Next, we make a trivial change to the ShowNoteCommand; see listing 12.17.

Listing 12.17   app\flex\com\pomodo\command\ShowNoteCommand.as

```
. . .
        public function result(event:Object):void {
            var model:PomodoModelLocator =
                PomodoModelLocator.getInstance();
            model.note = Note.fromVO(event.result);
            model.unsavedNoteContent = model.note.content;
        }
. . .
```

We modify the command to assign model.unsavedNoteContent as well. This is necessary for the initial loading of the content into Notely.

Finally, we need to modify the StatusBox to tie this all together; see listing 12.18.

Listing 12.18   app\flex\com\pomodo\components\StatusBox.mxml

```
<?xml version="1.0" encoding="utf-8"?>
<mx:HBox xmlns:mx="http://www.adobe.com/2006/mxml"
    xmlns:pom="com.pomodo.components.*"
    paddingLeft="5" paddingRight="5" backgroundColor="#FFFFFF"
    horizontalAlign="left" verticalAlign="middle"
    width="100%" height="40"
    creationComplete="handleCreationComplete()">       ❶
<mx:Script>
<![CDATA[
    import com.pomodo.model.PomodoModelLocator;

    [Bindable]
    private var _model:PomodoModelLocator =
        PomodoModelLocator.getInstance();

    private function handleCreationComplete():void {       ❷
        NativeApplication.nativeApplication.addEventListener   ❸
            (Event.NETWORK_CHANGE,onNetworkChange);
        checkIsOnline();       ❹
    }

    private function onNetworkChange(event:Event):void {       ❺
        checkIsOnline();       ❻
    }

    private function checkIsOnline():void {       ❼
        var request:URLRequest =
            new URLRequest(_model.onlineCheckURL);       ❽
        var requestLoader:URLLoader = new URLLoader();
```

```
            requestLoader.addEventListener(Event.COMPLETE,
                requestCompleteHandler);
            requestLoader.addEventListener(IOErrorEvent.IO_ERROR,
                requestErrorHandler);
            requestLoader.load(request);
        }

        private function requestErrorHandler(event:IOErrorEvent):    ❾
        void {
            _model.online = false;        ❿
            statusLabel.text = "Offline";  ⓫
            statusLabel.setStyle("color", "#FF0000");  ⓬
        }

        private function requestCompleteHandler(event:Event):void {  ⓭
            _model.online = true;  ⓮
            statusLabel.text = "Online";  ⓯
            statusLabel.setStyle("color", "#00FF00");  ⓰
        }
    ]]>
</mx:Script>
    <mx:Label text="URL:"/>
    <mx:TextInput id="remoteURLTI" width="100%"
        text="{_model.remoteURL}"
        change="_model.remoteURL = remoteURLTI.text"/>
    <mx:Label id="statusLabel"/>  ⓱
</mx:HBox>
```

We start by attaching a `creationComplete` handler ❶ `handleCreation-Complete` ❷, which first adds the `onNetworkChange` function ❺ as an `Event-Listener` for the `Event.NETWORK_CHANGE` event ❸. (Note that `Native-Application.nativeApplication` ❸ used to be called `Shell.shell` in Flex 3 Beta 2 and below; it was renamed in Flex 3 Beta 3.) The `handleCreationComplete` function then calls ❹ `checkIsOnline` to do the initial online/offline check. The `onNetworkChange` function ❺ also calls ❻ `checkIsOnline` to do the online/offline check. (I've seen an approach that toggled, but this seems to me to be too unreliable: If the state gets out of sync *once*, it's wrong *forever*.) The `checkIsOnline` function ❼ essentially pings the `_model.onlineCheckURL`, which is http://www.google.com ❽—Google can handle the load. On a successful request, the `requestCompleteHandler` ⓭ is called, which sets `_model.online` to true ⓮, the `statusLabel` ⓱ text to "Online" ⓯, and the `statusLabel` color to green ⓰. On an unsuccessful request, the `requestErrorHandler` ❾ is called, which sets `_model.online` to false ❿, the `statusLabel` text to "Offline" ⓫, and the `statusLabel` color to red ⓬.

Figure 12.12
`StatusBox`
showing online

Ensure we're connected to the internet, and then rebuild and reload. We see the screen shown in figure 12.12.

Log in as ludwig. We see the screen shown in figure 12.13.

Next, disconnect from the Internet (unplug your ethernet cable). After a few seconds, we see the screen shown in figure 12.14.

Figure 12.13   Logged in as ludwig, online

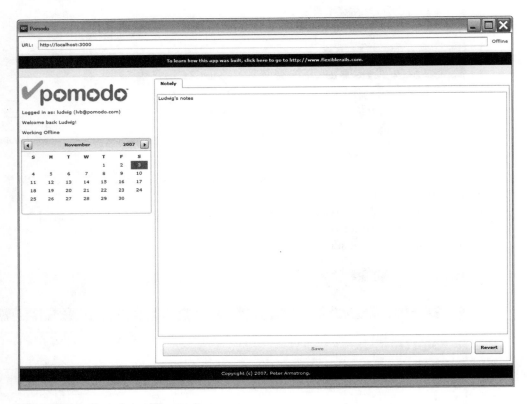

Figure 12.14   Pomodo in offline mode

Note how the StatusBox shows the Offline status. Also, note how the UI is swapped out (with a funky visual transition) and the OfflineMainBox (containing just Notely) is shown. Furthermore, the Save button in Notely is disabled because we don't support offline saving and synchronizing.

Enter some text in Notely, and reconnect to the Internet. After a few seconds' delay, AIR will detect that the online status has changed, the request to Google will be done, and pomodo will switch back to online mode, complete with all the tabs, the ability to save, and so forth.

Run the tests again with rake, and confirm that everything still works.

The code at this point is saved as the iteration12 folder.

12.4 Summary

We've seen that it's *extremely* easy to get up and running with AIR, getting pomodo built and running as an AIR application and adding new features with hardly any code.

12.5 Exercises for the reader

1 Add support for saving to the local filesystem (in a file or in the local SQLite database) when offline, and synchronizing with Rails when online again. See http://labs.adobe.com/wiki/index.php/AIR:Articles:Taking_Apollo_Applications_Offline#Managing_data for a great place to start. The easy thing to do in terms of synchronizing is to adopt a rule such as "local changes clobber remote ones" or "newer changes win." You can use the fact that the time that the record is saved is stored in the updated_at column of the notes table to implement whatever policy you want. (If you're really bored, implement a nice GUI merge tool to merge the content of the local and remote Notely.)

2 Add support for an initially offline state (that is, there is no logged-in user, but you want to use Notely and have it synchronize the next time you're online).

12.6 Conclusion

Wow. We've come a long way from `rails pomodo`. We've seen how Flex and Rails can be integrated to build a next-generation rich Internet application, through what was (I hope!) an interesting and complex enough example to show what developing using Flex and Rails together is like. Although pomodo isn't perfect, it's more realistic than the code examples in most books.

Whether that was good or bad is left as an exercise for the reader: Please email any thoughts—good or bad—about the book to me at peter@ruboss.com. If you don't mind being quoted in print and online, please say so in the email, and include your name and, optionally, your job title and/or blog URL. Don't worry, I won't print or share your email address.

Because the code for Pomodo is all MIT-licensed, please feel free to use it as a starting point for your own applications. Although I've made fun of Web 2.0 occasionally throughout the book, I admire anyone who creates their own Web 2.0 startup and takes a shot at changing the world, or at least achieving fame and fortune. Like everyone else here, I have a few Web 2.0 startup ideas up my own sleeve. I hope the combination of Flex and Rails is something you can use to develop a product, get to market quickly, figure out how to scale, and either get acquired or IPO. (This too is left as an exercise for the reader!) If it works out for you, I won't say no to unsolicited gifts and/or stock grants...

It has been over a year since I started writing *Flexible Rails* and more than 18 months since I first had the idea. Now it's done and has become a Manning book. (This is fitting and satisfying to me personally, because Manning's *Swing* book—one of the best technical books I have read—was the inspiration for the numbering format in the extended code examples. However, when I was reading *Swing* I was a young and eager developer in Silicon Valley at a BPM startup—not the ~~old and bitter~~ seasoned developer I am today.)

Furthermore, I'm going to write a book entitled *Rails on AIR* that takes the Pomodo example in *Flexible Rails* in some interesting new directions as a full-blown Adobe AIR application. Check http://www.railsonair.com sometime in early 2008 for more information—I have some secret things planned...

I can't believe this book is actually over!

> *Every journey has an end;*
> *When at the worst affairs will mend;*
> *Dark the dawn when day is nigh;*
> *Hustle your horse and don't say die.*
>
> —W. S. Gilbert, *Iolanthe*

How to use Subversion with Flex + Rails

In this appendix, we'll install Subversion, create a new repository, import our project into it, and configure Subversion to ignore the appropriate files. A full discussion of Subversion is far beyond the scope of this book—see http://svnbook.red-bean.com/ if you're interested.

> **NOTE**   If you aren't afraid of the command line, consider Git instead of Subversion. To learn why, see Linus Torvalds' (creator of Git and Linux) Tech Talk at Google: http://www.youtube.com/watch?v=4XpnKHJAok8.

First, we need to have Subversion installed. Run the following commands:

```
c:\peter\flexiblerails\current\pomodo>svn --version
svn, version 1.4.2 (r22196)
   compiled Nov  3 2006, 16:53:07
...

c:\peter\flexiblerails\current\pomodo>svnadmin --version
svnadmin, version 1.4.2 (r22196)
   compiled Nov  3 2006, 16:53:07
...

c:\peter\flexiblerails\current\pomodo>
```

If you don't get something telling you which svn version you have, go to http://subversion.tigris.org/project_packages.html#binary-packages and download and install the appropriate version of Subversion.

Next, create a Subversion repository. I'll create mine in c:\peter; you should pick a good spot to use:

```
C:\peter>mkdir svnrepo

C:\peter>svnadmin create c:\peter\svnrepo

C:\peter>
```

Next, we import the pomodo app into subversion. The approach we'll take is based on the approach used to set up a new Subversion repository using the approach in the "quick start" (http://svnbook.red-bean.com/nightly/en/svn.intro.quickstart.html) of the book *Version Control with Subversion* (http://svnbook.red-bean.com/nightly/en/index.html).

First, stop the WEBrick server. Next, we'll set up the standard branches, tags, and trunk directories. We rename the pomodo directory to trunk and then create directories for branches and tags:

```
C:\peter\flexiblerails\current>move pomodo trunk

C:\peter\flexiblerails\current>mkdir branches

C:\peter\flexiblerails\current>mkdir tags
```

Now, we import our structure into our new repository:

```
C:\peter\flexiblerails\current>
svn import . file:///c:/peter/svnrepo -m "new"
Adding          trunk
...
Adding          branches
Adding          tags

Committed revision 1.

C:\peter\flexiblerails\current>
```

> **NOTE** On OS X, the file:///c:/peter URL would be file:///Users/peter.

Next, we check out our new project from Subversion. Close Flex Builder before continuing:

```
C:\peter\flexiblerails\current>cd ..

C:\peter\flexiblerails>move current currentbak
        1 file(s) moved.

C:\peter\flexiblerails>mkdir current

C:\peter\flexiblerails>cd current

C:\peter\flexiblerails\current>
svn co file:///c:/peter/svnrepo/trunk pomodo
A    pomodo\test
A    pomodo\test\unit
...
A    pomodo\public\stylesheets
A    pomodo\public\favicon.ico
Checked out revision 1.

C:\peter\flexiblerails\current>
```

Now that we have the project checked out, we'll configure Subversion to ignore the public\bin directory, because that is all generated code and compiled SWF files. We'll also configure Subversion to ignore the files that should be ignored in all Rails applications.

To do this, go to http://wiki.rubyonrails.org/rails/pages/HowtoUseRailsWith-Subversion and follow along with the instructions to remove the log files and temp files. You may also wish to ignore database.yml, as explained at that wiki page.

Finally, we'll install Subclipse. This is an optional step, because we can use Subversion entirely from the command line. Subclipse is an Eclipse plugin, and because Flex Builder is built on top of Eclipse, it will work in Flex Builder.

Go to http://subclipse.tigris.org/ for more general information on Subclipse. To install Subclipse, start Flex Builder, and follow the instructions at http://subclipse.tigris.org/install.html. (The instructions are for Eclipse, but they work with Flex Builder.) After installing Subclipse, we see in the Navigator that the pomodo project displays as pomodo [trunk] and the files show their version numbers.

To use Subclipse, right-click a file or folder in the Navigator window, and mouse down to the Team submenu. We see a bunch of useful Subversion commands. We can also choose Window > Perspective > Other and choose SVN Repository Exploring or Team Synchronizing to use other handy perspectives.

Before we end this Appendix, helpful reader Cédric Deltheil gave the following advice via email:

> *Just another thing, related to the configuration files, and more specifically to* `.actionScriptProperties`. *It is trivial, but, if you decide to add resources to your Flex project via the library path, this has an impact on* `.actionScriptProperties`. *So, if you do not take care, you can promote to the repos a version of this file that contains references to local path:*

```
<libraryPathEntry kind="3" linkType="1" path="/Users/
Cedric/myComponent.swc"/>
```

> *I think the best way is to define a new path variable in Preferences -> General -> Workspace -> Link resources, so as to avoid such a problem:*

```
<libraryPathEntry kind="3" linkType="1" path=
"${MYCOMPONENT}"/>
```

If you're in a team environment, this is indeed good advice.

That's it. You should be set up to use Subversion with Flex and Rails.

Handwaving at omitted topics

This appendix is my version of handwaving at important topics that aren't covered in the book. There are varied reasons for their omission. For example:

- I don't have infinite time.
- A really good tutorial has been written, and I wouldn't be adding much value.
- The topic is important but too far outside the scope of the book.
- The topic is primarily a Flex or Rails topic, and the interaction isn't particularly interesting.
- I don't have anything interesting or original to say about the topic.

Regardless of the reason, important topics have been omitted from the book. However, I would feel guilty if I didn't at least mention them. So, here goes.

Testing

Testing is very important. How dare I relegate it to a section of an appendix? The simple reason is this: There isn't that much for me to say about how to test Flex and Rails together. On the Flex side, there is FlexUnit (http://code.google.com/p/as3flexunitlib/), a JUnit-esque testing framework. I've personally used it to test public static methods, and not much else. On the Rails side, there is an extensive focus on testing, as described in *AWDwR*. Specifically, look at test/unit, test/spec, and RSpec for how to test Rails applications.

In terms of testing the interaction between Flex and Rails, the best thing to do is to provide inputs that mimic what Flex will provide to Rails, and then test the output. We can use `assert_match`, `assert_no_match`, and `assert_select`. (Thanks to the readers in the flexiblerails Google Group for the thoughtful discussion of testing.) `assert_select` is cool, and its creator Assaf Arkin (a former coworker of mine, when I was young and stupid) is extremely smart and prolific: buildr, scrAPI, co.mments, and so on. See Assaf's blog at http://labnotes.org/. Finally, Assaf is also co-authoring a Manning book; see http://www.manning.com/mcanally/ for details. (I would read and promote this book regardless of who was publishing it.)

Multiple-file upload with Flash, Flex, AIR, and Rails or Merb

Another important topic, another few paragraphs. (Next: world peace.) File upload is very tricky with Flex and Rails and also inefficient as far as Rails is concerned. Lots of the new (in December 2007), cool, rich Internet applications are adding file upload, typically backed by Amazon S3. For one of the most promising examples that doesn't rhyme with *bounce*, see Alex MacCaw's Aireo (http://www.eribium.org/blog/?p=83). For pure Rails file upload, Rick Olson (of `restful_authentication`, `acts_as_authenticated`, Lighthouse, Mephisto, and Beast fame) has done most of the work for us—this time with a plugin called attachment_fu. (Yes, even the name is cool.) For the Rails side of it, read Mike Clark's excellent tutorial: http://clarkware.com/cgi/blosxom/2007/02/24. The attachment_fu plugin supports `:storage` of `:file_system`, `:db_file`, and `:s3`. Note that `attachment_fu` has all kinds of special support for uploading images, generating thumbnails, and so on—see Mike Clark's tutorial and the tutorial messages printed by installing `attachment_fu` for more details. (If we were going to be completely stereotypical in this book, we'd find an excuse to add support for uploading images and resizing them into a 40x40 pixel avatar.)

Note that the filesystem storage defaults to using the public directory, which essentially provides no security: Anyone who knew the secret URL would be able to get at the file. There are solutions to store the file somewhere outside of the Rails public directory. Be careful that you don't trust the user input and accidentally open up your entire filesystem, though! See one of Ben Curtis' blog posts (http://www.bencurtis.com/archives/2006/11/how-to-handle-uploaded-files-with-rails/) for more information. Note that an issue with Rails file upload is that it doesn't handle multiple-file upload well—which is part of what led Ezra Zygmuntowicz to create Merb (http://brainspl.at/articles/tag/merb):

> *This is one of the things that Merb was written for. Rails doesn't allow multiple concurrent file uploads at once without blocking an entire rails backend for each file upload. Merb allows multiple file uploads at once.*
>
> —http://blog.vixiom.com/2007/06/29/merb-on-air-drag-and-drop-multiple-file-upload/

Alastair Dawson at Vixiom Axioms, the blog of Vixiom Communications, wrote two *absolutely excellent tutorials* (http://blog.vixiom.com/2006/09/08/multiple-file-upload-with-flash-and-ruby-on-rails/ and http://blog.vixiom.com/2007/06/29/merb-on-air-drag-and-drop-multiple-file-upload/) showing how to do multiple-file upload with Flash and Rails and how to do multiple-file upload with Merb and AIR.

File upload is also one of the examples in *Programming ActionScript 3.0* (one of the PDF documents referred to in iteration 3, section 3.5.4, "Flex 3 documentation? Where?"), specifically the "Example: Uploading and downloading files" (p. 408) section of the Networking and Communication chapter. If you want to get the code for this example, go to http://www.adobe.com/go/as3examples, download and unzip the zip file, and look in the ProgrammingAS3_Examples\FileIO folder.

WebORB

WebORB for Rails is an implementation of Flash and Flex Remoting for Ruby. The best place to learn about WebORB for Rails is Derek Wischusen's four-part tutorial on using Flex with WebORB; see http://flexonrails.net/?p=31 for details. Frankly, Derek knows WebORB better than I do, and thus his tutorial is highly recommended.

For another good starting point, go to http://www.themidnightcoders.com/weborb/rubyonrails/faq.htm and browse from there.

index

MORE TITLES FROM MANNING

Ruby for Rails

by David A. Black
ISBN: 1-932394-69-9
532 pages
$44.95
May 2006

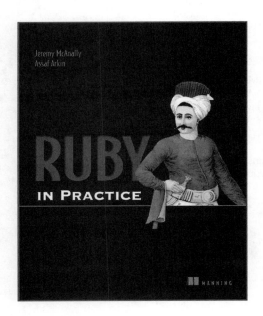

Ruby in Practice

by Jeremy McAnally and Assaf Arkin
ISBN: 1-933988-47-9
375 pages
$39.99
June 2008

For ordering information go to www.manning.com

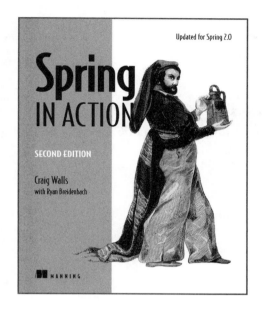

Spring in Action, Second Edition
by Craig Walls,
with Ryan Breidenbach
ISBN: 1-933988-13-4
768 pages
$44.99
August 2007

Test Driven
Practical TDD and Acceptance TDD
for Java Developers
by Lasse Koskela
ISBN: 1-932394-85-0
544 pages
$44.99
October 2007

For ordering information go to www.manning.com

MORE TITLES FROM MANNING

Laszlo in Action
   by Norman Klein and Max Carlson
      with Glen MacEwen
   ISBN: 1-932394-83-4
   552 pages
   $44.99
   January 2008

Adobe AIR in Action
   by Joseph Lott, Kathryn Rotondo,
      Samuel Ahn, Ashley Atkins
      and Max Jackson
   ISBN: 1-933988-48-7
   300 pages
   $39.99
   July 2008

For ordering information go to www.manning.com